J.G. Schottelius's *Ausführliche Arbeit von der Teutschen HaubtSprache* (1663) and its place in early modern European vernacular language study

Publications of the Philological Society, 44

**WILEY-
BLACKWELL**

J.G. Schottelius's *Ausführliche Arbeit von der
Teutschen HaubtSprache* (1663) and its place in early
modern European vernacular language study

Publications of the Philological Society, 44

WILEY
BLACKWELL

J.G. Schottelius's *Ausführliche Arbeit von der Teutschen HaubtSprache* (1663) and its place in early modern European vernacular language study

Nicola McLelland

Publications of the Philological Society, 44

WILEY-BLACKWELL

This edition first published 2011

©2011 The Philological Society

Blackwell Publishing was acquired by John Wiley & Sons in February 2007. Blackwell's publishing program has been merged with Wiley's global Scientific, Technical, and Medical business to form Wiley-Blackwell.

Registered Office

John Wiley & Sons Ltd, The Atrium, Southern Gate, Chichester, West Sussex, PO19 8SQ, United Kingdom

Editorial Offices

350 Main Street, Malden, MA 02148-5020, U

9600 Garsington Road, Oxford, OX4 2DQ, UK

The Atrium, Southern Gate, Chichester, West Sussex, PO19 8SQ, UK

For details of our global editorial offices, for customer services, and for information about how to apply for permission to reuse the copyright material in this book please see our website at www.wiley.com/wiley-blackwell.

The right of Nicola McLelland to be identified as the author of this work has been asserted in accordance with the UK Copyright, Designs and Patents Act 1988.

Library of Congress Cataloging-in-Publication Data

Library of Congress Cataloging-in-Publication Data is available for this work.

A catalogue record for this book is available from the British Library.

Set in Times by SPS (P) Ltd., Chennai, India

Printed in Singapore

1 2011

CONTENTS

ACKNOWLEDGEMENTS

This book has been several years in the making. I would like to thank several cohorts of final-year students at Trinity College, Dublin, for their spirit in reading Schottelius's orations in the original, for it was only after plunging into teaching the *Ausführliche Arbeit* that I began to research it too. I am grateful to Lisa Lambert and Kathleen Mallett, whose transcriptions of the orations of Book I of the *Ausführliche Arbeit* (funded by a Trinity College Arts Faculty grant) proved invaluable. I undertook much of the research for the book in 2003–2004 whilst on a sabbatical from Trinity College, Dublin, funded by a fellowship awarded by the Irish Humanities and Social Sciences Research Council. Generous support from the German Academic Exchange Service and the Humboldt Foundation allowed me to spend periods in 2003 and 2004 at the Herzog August Bibliothek in Wolfenbüttel, and I should like to thank Dr Gillian Bepler and all the library staff there for their patient help. The draft of the book was written while on sabbatical from the University of Nottingham in 2008, and I am very grateful to the Arts Faculty Dean's Fund and to the School of Modern Languages and Cultures at the University of Nottingham for making possible those two semesters of sabbatical.

Those who have provided moral, practical and intellectual support to me in writing this book are too numerous to mention. I would especially like to thank David Cram for excellent suggestions on the first draft, but above all Bill Jones, who read the entire draft manuscript with great care (most of it twice), gave me invaluable assistance on many points of detail, and also allowed me to use his electronic texts for Jones (1995), on which much of Chapter 8 is based. Wini Davies, Martin Durrell and Ingrid Tieken all commented on a draft of that chapter, on Schottelius's influence on language use, for which Tom Reader helped with the statistical analysis. It was John Trim who provided the inspiration for that chapter, and who also made countless other useful suggestions and corrections, as too did John Flood. John Considine's expertise made light work of identifying some of the sources whose identity had eluded me. Tom Reader picked up many stylistic infelicities. Any remaining weaknesses are of course my own.

In the long course of working on this book, I have had the great good fortune to gain a husband and two children. They have heard more about Schottelius than anyone could imagine possible or desirable, so I dedicate this book to them.

Nicola McLelland, Nottingham 2010

ABBREVIATIONS

AA	Justus Georg Schottelius, *Ausführliche Arbeit der Teutschen HaubtSprache* (1663)
FG	*Fruchtbringende Gesellschaft*
FZG	Georg Philipp Harsdörffer, *FrauenzimmerGesprächsspiele* (1644–49)
SPG	Georg Philipp Harsdörffer, *Specimen Philologiae Germanicae* (1646)

1

AN INTRODUCTION TO THE *AUSFÜHRLICHE ARBEIT VON DER TEUTSCHEN HAUBTSPRACHE* (1663) AND ITS PLACE IN EUROPEAN LINGUISTIC THOUGHT

1.1. INTRODUCTION

This book pursues three aims. The first is to demonstrate the lasting contribution of the German scholar Justus Georg[ius] Schottelius (1612–1676) to European linguistic thought; the second, in the light of his importance for the history of linguistic ideas, is to provide a comprehensive analysis of Schottelius's *Ausführliche Arbeit von der Teutschen HaubtSprache* (1663, henceforth *AA*), located at the intersection of a number of different discourses about language; my third aim is to attempt an evaluation of Schottelius's contribution to the standardization of the German language.

The first of these aims may seem an assertion of the obvious, but in fact Schottelius's position in Europe has been rather misrepresented. Like Claude Lancelot (1616–1695) and Antoine Arnauld (1612–1694), the authors of the Port-Royal grammar (1660), Schottelius took a 'rationalist' view of language. That is, he stood in the same tradition of Latinate rationalism, expressed in the important grammars of J.C. Scaliger (1484–1558), Franciscus Sanctius (1523–1601) and Johann Gerhard Vossius (1577–1649) that also influenced the Port-Royal grammarians. But while the Port-Royal grammarians associated *ratio* with the universal processes of the human mind in formulating language and thought, Schottelius was merely interested in the *ratio* inherent in language as an organism in its own right (without much interest in its speakers). He believed (with the likes of Theodor Bibliander (1504–1564) in his programmatically titled 'commentary on the rational basis [*ratio*] […] of all languages', 1548) that all languages shared a common *ratio*. For this reason Padley (1985: 224–31), in his study of European vernacular grammar, treated Schottelius as an early exponent of universal grammar, and in this narrative, Schottelius's *AA* amounts to a cul-de-sac in the history of linguistic reflection in Europe.[1] Robins, in his admittedly concise but nonetheless magisterial *Short History of Linguistics*

---

[1] Padley was also misled by Schottelius's parroting of Vossius's (1635) distinction between natural [i.e. universal] and artificial grammar (*AA* 180), a distinction which in fact had no effect on the details of his own grammar (cf. 5.3).

(Robins 1997), accordingly makes no mention of Schottelius at all; nor does the third volume, on Renaissance and Early Modern Linguistics, of Lepschy's *History of Linguistics* (Lepschy 1992, English transl. 1998). Seuren (1998: 46), who admittedly concentrates on the modern period, sums up the mid-seventeenth century onwards as 'Port-Royal and after', and, perhaps not surprisingly, the most recent survey of the history of linguistics in English (Allan 2007) does not deviate from the tradition of overlooking Schottelius.

Schottelius is certainly given due recognition in *German* linguistic historiography, where interest in him began in the modern era with Koldewey (1899), Jellinek (1913–14) and Gundolf (1930). He has been called one of the fathers of German studies (Berns 1976: 14), and a plaque on the house where he lived in Wolfenbüttel calls him the 'father of German grammar'. He is prominently discussed in key surveys, such as those by Gardt (1999), Kaltz (2005), Polenz (1994), and Jungen & Lohnstein (2007), and is a central figure in two important monographs on German linguistic awareness in the seventeenth century (Gardt 1994, Hundt 2000).[2] That his wider importance for the history of linguistics in Europe has not been so readily acknowledged is, I believe, symptomatic of a skewed reading of the history of linguistic ideas in Europe of the seventeenth and eighteenth centuries. Schottelius has been seen (since Bornemann 1976, Huber 1984) too much within the specific tradition of German cultural patriotism. It is symptomatic that when Cherubim (1996, 2009[2]) notes the legacy of Schottelius, he limits himself to the German context. Yet Schottelius participated in several—to some extent even competing—European discourse traditions, including those of practical German grammar and cultural patriotism, but also theoretical Latin grammar and legal discourse (cf. Seiffert 1990a) (and his debt to the doctrine of natural law offers an interesting comparison to discussions about customary law amongst the French *remarqueurs*; see 3.4). The way in which Schottelius combined ideas from these disparate discourse traditions in turn had a wider impact in Europe than just on German grammar and lexicography. I certainly do not wish to claim that Schottelius's *Ausführliche Arbeit* is more important than the Port-Royal grammar of 1660, but I will argue that it *is* important in its own right, and that it left its own important legacy in currents running through European grammatography and wider reflection on language: in the grammatographical traditions of separate languages, in lexicography, in debates on the origin of language, and in comparative linguistics. This is the substance of Chapter 7.

Given the importance of Schottelius for European linguistic historiography, my second aim in this book is to provide a comprehensive reading of Schottelius's *magnum opus* as a coherent work, by situating it at the

---

[2] Aspects of Schottelius's work have also received detailed examination in several dissertations, including Plattner (1967), Gützlaff (1989a, b), Barbarić (1981), Neuhaus (1991), and Schneider (1995). See 1.3.

intersection of several discourses about language. Such a comprehensive reading will enable readers to recognize the overlaps and differences compared to the discourses of other European linguistic traditions: in such matters as the choices of grammatical categories, the typical metaphorical fields of linguistic purism, the recourse to legal notions of customary and natural law like that of the French *remarqueurs* to conceptualize correctness, the organic conception of language, the importance of the *ars combinatoria* (cf. universal language schemes), the importance of amassing and collating data about the language, and the close relationship between grammatical codification and the codification of poetry. That is the concern of the earlier chapters. For readers' convenience, all citations from primary literature are given both in the original and in English translation; secondary literature is cited in English translation only.[3]

Finally, historical sociolinguists have recently begun to investigate to what extent grammars influence the actual language of speech communities. Evaluating the relationship between Schottelius's grammar and language practice is, therefore, the task of Chapter 8, although, as will become clear there, that relationship is by no means straightforward to assess.

The present chapter provides an introduction to the life and work of Schottelius (1612–1676) and his social and intellectual context (1.2), as well as a first introduction to the *Ausführliche Arbeit* (1.3); an interpretation of the iconography and emblematics of the frontispiece and other visual material in the *AA* will reveal the pious, cultural-patriotic ideology which infuses the work (1.4). Chapter 2 outlines Schottelius's theory of language. The points raised in that chapter are re-visited in later chapters, but it serves as a first introduction. Chapter 3 identifies six distinct discourse traditions in linguistic thought that Schottelius drew on and combined in the *AA*. Identifying these streams of influence helps both to assess Schottelius's contribution to linguistic theory and to clarify his position in the European intellectual context, as well as to explain some of the complexities and contradictions in the *AA*. The next three chapters present, in essence, a *transtextual* close reading of the work (in the sense of Genette 1982).[4]

---

[3] The availability of a facsimile reprint (ed. Hecht 1967, rpt. 1995) does not change the fact that Schottelius's *AA* is long, dense, and complex, and that its highly rhetorical style makes it hard for non-experts to read. Blume (1983) calculated that Schottelius's average sentence-length was 74.48 words, which he contrasted with an average of 34.76 for the near-contemporary Swede Olaf Rudbeck (1630–1702) in his *Atlantica* (1679), whose writing was also less complex syntactically.

[4] My inspiration for the transtextual approach is the application of the framework to a similarly voluminous and complex (albeit literary) work, the late medieval Prose Lancelot (Merveldt 2007). To aficionados of Genette's notion of transtextuality, it may seem odd to apply it to an academic text like Schottelius's *AA*, but after all, the *AA* is highly rhetorical, indeed actually literary in aspiration in places. Furthermore, Schottelius's *AA* is the very model of a complex network of relations, both within the text and with other texts. Beginning with the orations of Book I, reading it 'plunges us into a network of textual relations', to cite Allen's text-book definition of intertextuality (Allen 2000: 1).

Chapters 4 and 5 offer a comprehensive reading of the entire *AA*, reading all of its many text-types against the 'architexts' of their respective discourse traditions. Chapter 6, together with the Appendix, provides the first detailed account of the sources on which Schottelius drew. Chapter 7 considers the important legacy of the *AA*, not just in Germany, but elsewhere in Europe, including the Netherlands, Sweden and Russia. Chapter 8, finally, assesses the extent of Schottelius's influence on the subsequent development of German and on its standardization.

1.2. SCHOTTELIUS IN THE SOCIAL AND INTELLECTUAL CONTEXT OF SEVENTEETH-CENTURY EUROPE

The axiom that historians of linguistics, like any historians, need 'a grasp of the main historical and cultural developments in the period under study' (Law 2003: 4) is never more true than when studying seventeenth-century Germany, with its pious and war-torn society and with beliefs about language—whether on matters of style or on the assumed 'facts' of history—that can seem very alien today. This section therefore provides some first points of orientation, beginning with a brief biographical sketch, followed by an outline of what was going on in Germany—politically, culturally and intellectually—during Schottelius's lifetime, as well as of the key developments in linguistic ideas in other countries of Europe around the same time.

1.2.1 *Schottelius's life and works*

Schottelius's biography is in essence that of an intelligent, pious, and ambitious man with sufficient determination to overcome some difficult circumstances in his early life, and so to enjoy a successful academic career.[5] Schottelius was born in 1612 in Einbeck, in today's Lower Saxony, a Low German speaking area. In sixteenth-century Germany, it had been common under the influence of Humanism to adopt a Latin form of one's surname, and it appears that one of Schottelius's ancestors did just this—*Schottelius* comes from the Low German surname *Schotteler* (i.e. the Low German equivalent of *Schüßler* 'maker of bowls', Berns 1974: 7). It is still common to hear German scholars use the name *Schottel*, but Schottelius himself never used any other form than *Schottelius*. He also always used the hyphenated form of his first name in the title pages of his works, *Justus-Georgius* (Seiffert 1990a: 257 n.1). However, both Kaspar von Stieler

---

[5] The following account is based on Berns (1974, 1976, 1984); cf. also Waldberg (1891) and Hundt (2007). A brief and very readable survey of the importance of Schottelius's life and work is given by Cherubim (2001).

(1632–1707), who based his dictionary, *Der Teutschen Sprache Stammbaum und Fortwachs* (1691), on principles outlined by Schottelius, and Daniel Morhof (1639–1691) already used the form *Schottel* (Stieler 1691, vol.1: *Vorrede* [p.15]; Morhof 1682: 457), within a few years of Schottelius's death, and in the nineteenth century the form *Schottel* became more widely used.

Schottelius grew up as the son of a Protestant pastor, while his mother came from a family of merchants. As the son of a pastor, he belonged to a class with access to education and with aspirations to higher education, but without the certainty of wealth and noble title to back him. He was in this regard typical of many of the more active members of the German language societies in the seventeenth century (Berns 1974: 8). He attended the local town-school, of which his father had earlier been assistant director (Berns 1974: 10). In 1625, the Thirty Years' War (1618–1648) reached Einbeck. Einbeck itself was not taken, but the inhabitants of the surrounding countryside took refuge within its walls, and plague broke out in the cramped conditions. Schottelius's father died of the plague in 1626, when Schottelius was fourteen. Schottelius left school and began an apprenticeship, but soon abandoned it and left home to pursue his education. From 1627 to 1630, he attended the *Gymnasium* in nearby Hildesheim, paying his way by private tutoring. Aged eighteen, he moved to Hamburg and, again financing himself by tutoring, he attended from 1631 to 1634 the so-called Academic Gymnasium, which provided education up to the standard of first or second year university. The principal of the school, Joachim Jungius (1587–1657), who had known both the philologist Christoph Helwig (1581–1617) and the educational reformer Wolfgang Ratke (Ratichius, 1571–1635) in Gießen, may be partly responsible for awakening Schottelius's interest in the German language, and for shaping his view of language as both natural and divinely inspired (Berns 1974: 13; Padley 1985: 313). Also a pupil at the school was the later poet, pastor, *Pfalzgraf*, and linguistic purist Johann Rist (1607–1667), with whom Schottelius remained friends all his life. Schottelius, like many of his compatriots, then went to the Netherlands to study at university proper. After a brief stint in Groningen, he enrolled in 1635 at Leiden University, which, founded in 1575, was the most important university in seventeenth-century northern Europe. Amongst the scholars who had been drawn to Leiden were several whom Schottelius later cited in his own work. They include Justus Lipsius (1547–1606), whose glossed edition of the psalms Schottelius would later cite; Vossius, on whose *De Arte Grammatica* (1635) Schottelius drew for his notion of analogy in language; and Daniel Heinsius (1580–1655), whose pioneering poetry in the vernacular Martin Opitz (1597–1639) had already begun to translate into German in 1619 (cf. 3.4, 6.2).

Returning to Germany in 1636, Schottelius rapidly abandoned an attempt to settle back into Einbeck, and went instead to Leipzig, and then—when Leipzig proved too expensive—to Wittenberg to continue his studies, where he seems also to have achieved the rank of a junior university teacher (Berns 1974: 18). However, the Thirty Years' War once again caught up with him. Wittenberg University closed in 1638, as Swedish troops had taken Meißen and were threatening Wittenberg. Schottelius headed for home, but was offered a private tutorship on the way, and soon afterwards became tutor to Prince Anton Ulrich (1633–1714), son of Duke August the Younger (1579–1666) of Braunschweig (still sometimes called in English Brunswick) and Lüneburg. In 1644, Schottelius moved with the Duke's family back to their residence in Wolfenbüttel, which the family (allied with the Protestant side against the Emperor and the Catholic League) had been forced to yield to the Emperor in 1627. Here Schottelius had access to the Duke's library, the largest library in Europe (Berns 1976: 9). In 1646, he obtained a doctorate in laws from the University of Helmstedt, and also married.

Schottelius made his first foray into print in 1640 with an allegorical poem *LAMENTATIO Germaniae exspirantis. Der numehr hinsterbenden Nymphen GERMANIAE elendeste Todesklage* ('lamentation of Germania dying', 1640), in which he already gave vent to cultural patriotic concerns. The poem portrayed Germany as a queen reduced to beggary as the result of war. In 1643, he published his *Der Teutschen Sprach Einleitung* 'introduction of the German language', a verse work which canvassed many cultural-patriotic arguments in defence of German. Schottelius's first theoretical work was his German grammar titled *Teutsche Sprachkunst,* published in 1641, when he was 29. Berns (1974: 19) argues that Schottelius must have already been working on it before he joined the Duke's service. Upon its publication, the Duke saw to it that Schottelius became a member of the most important language society of the time, the *Fruchtbringende Gesellschaft* (founded in 1617, henceforth FG). Schottelius had already contributed to the society's discussions with a scathing review of the German grammar prepared by Christian Gueintz (1592–1650) (also published in 1641). Gueintz's grammar was admittedly pretty poor (cf. 5.2), but Gueintz was nevertheless the protégé of none other than the founder of the society himself, Prince Ludwig of Anhalt-Köthen (1579–1650). Clearly Schottelius did not lack confidence.

One of Schottelius's duties as household tutor from 1638 to the mid-1640s was to write and produce plays to be performed by his young charges; six plays survive (Berns 1984). Performing plays had been a plank of Protestant education ideals ever since Luther had advocated it, but Schottelius's plays were also representational theatre, to be performed at court (Smart 1989). Schottelius also published occasional verse—a collection with the title *Fruchtbringender Lustgarte* ('fruitful pleasure-garden') appeared in 1647. His poetics—first printed in 1645, but re-printed in 1656 and again as part of his *Ausführliche Arbeit* of 1663—was dedicated to the wife of his employer, Sophie Elisabeth, Duchess of Braunschweig.

In 1651, Schottelius's *Teutsche Sprachkunst* was re-printed, with some revisions and with the addition of a tenth oration missing from the first, 1641 edition. In 1663, the *Teutsche Sprachkunst* was published (again with revisions) as books I to III of the *AA*, along with the poetics of 1645, and a number of other works. The *AA* thus marked the culmination of Schottelius's work as a champion of the German language. It was followed in 1673 by Schottelius's 'grammatical war' (*Horrendum Bellum Grammaticale. Der schreckliche Sprachkrieg*), a sort of dramatization of how the elements of the German language interact, which sought to popularize the ideas of the *AA* by providing many page references to it at relevant points (Schottelius 1673a; cf. Czucka 1997; Hundt 2000: 329–35, 2006: 121–33; Fonsén 2006, 2007). Finally, in the year of Schottelius's death, 1676, an extract from Schottelius's grammar was published for use in schools under the title *Brevis & fundamentalis Manuductio ad ORTHOGRAPHIAM & ETYMOLOGIAM in Lingua Germanica. Kurtze und gründliche Anleitung Zu der RechtSchreibung Und zu der WortForschung In der Teutschen Sprache. Für die Jugend in den Schulen | und sonst überall nützlich und dienlich* 'A short and thorough introduction to the spelling and etymology of the German language. Useful and helpful for young people in schools, and everywhere else'. Otherwise, the publications of Schottelius's later years are largely devotional,[6] besides a German ethics, published in 1669 but of no influence (cf. Berns 1980). Another late work bears testimony to Schottelius's expertise in law, his *Kurtzer Tractat Von Unterschiedlichen Rechten in Teutschland* or 'short treatise on various laws in Germany' (1671). An overview of Schottelius's works can be found in Berns (1984: 429–32), and Neuhaus (1991: 235–41), besides in Dünnhaupt's comprehensive bibliography (Dünnhaupt 1990–93); see also Cherubim (1996, 2009[2]).

We know from Schottelius's surviving letters (Berns 1978) that his correspondents included Georg Philipp Harsdörffer (1607–1658), who was a close friend and ally within the FG, as well as two other poets of the Nuremberg circle, Johann Klaj (1616–1656) and Sigmund von Birken (1626–1681), his former school-companion Johann Rist, another purist and writer Philipp von Zesen (1619–1689), the unfortunate grammarian Gueintz, the Helmstedt professor Hermann Conring (1606–1681), whose model for structuring a text Schottelius explicitly followed in the first oration of the *AA* (cf. 1.5.2), the theologian Johann Valentin Andreae (1586–1654), and the satirist Johann Michael Moscherosch (1606–1669). However, the records of Schottelius's correspondence are too incomplete to allow a full reconstruction of his network of contacts. Some of Schottelius's

---

[6] They include a depiction of the last judgement (Schottelius 1668); a depiction of eternal life and a treatise on the art of dying (Schottelius 1673b); a depiction of the state of the body and soul before, during and after death (Schottelius 1674); a verse gospel harmony (Schottelius 1675); and a depiction of hell (Schottelius 1676b); see also Schottelius (1666) and (1676c).

correspondence within the FG is published in Krause (1873 [1955]). A project led by Klaus Conermann in Wolfenbüttel to publish all the correspondence of the FG may bring more to light (Conermann 1992– 2006).

1.2.2 *The social, political and intellectual context in Germany*

Schottelius was a pious man—most of his works after 1663 are devotional – and, in tune with mainstream Protestant thought of the period he was a believer in witches (Berns 1984: 423). After all, Schottelius lived in the same century in which Galilei Galileo (1564–1642) was judged guilty of heresy for advocating the Copernican claim that the earth revolved around the sun. Yet Schottelius's career also ran contemporary with the foundation of the Royal Society in Britain, founded in 1660 to promote experimental science, building on less formal meetings since the 1640s. In short, Europe was on the cusp of a new way of thinking about the world, but was in many ways still rooted in the Middle Ages. Schottelius himself occupies a similar borderline zone in the area of linguistic thought. The belief – shared by all his contemporaries – that the languages of his day had their beginnings in the confusion of tongues at the Tower of Babel, as related in the Bible, was still essentially unchanged from the medieval era. Despite this, the structure Schottelius imposed on the German language and his periodization of it laid the foundations for establishing German as a subject for serious academic study from the eighteenth century onwards—and provided a model for similar progress in other languages too.

Since Saussure, it is usual to say that language is a system made up of arbitrary signs. But Schottelius lived in a society that believed that *all* signs in the world (and not just signs in language) carried, or at least could carry, a meaning which pointed to the purpose of God in the world. As an extreme example, Jakob Böhme (1575–1624) believed he had been granted enlightenment to interpret the traces of the original God-inspired language, the *Natursprache,* preserved in German, where the very manner of articulation of sounds expressed metaphysical truths about God's creation (cf. Gardt 1994). A more mainstream manifestation of the fascination with reading signs was the genre of emblem-books. The genre combined an image with mottoes and/or verses to yield a meaning, and was a veritable craze that developed throughout Europe of the Renaissance and flourished into the seventeenth and eighteenth centuries. That pansemiotic, emblematic view of the world suffuses Schottelius's work.

The Thirty Years' War (1618–1648) marks a low point in German history. Its devastation accompanied Schottelius's early life, and had a lasting effect on him and on the society in which he lived. The symbolism of the title page of the *AA* and the 'Acclamation for Peace' at the end, which jointly bracket the whole of the *AA* (see 1.4 below), and the allegorical

'Grammatical War' (1673) together stand as testimony to Schottelius's lasting awareness of the stark alternatives of war and peace. It is said that the Thirty Years' War reduced the German population by about a fifth (Parker et al. 1997: 211). Thus traumatized, impoverished, and politically fragmented into multiple small states under a weak Empire, German society developed a sort of inferiority complex in the face of the political, military and cultural dominance of France in particular, which was flourishing under the 'Sun King' Louis XIV (1638–1715), who was twenty years into his reign when Schottelius published his *AA* in 1663. In reaction to these decades of misery, Schottelius's heartfelt 'Acclamation of Peace' is symptomatic of the hopes and expectations awakened in the growing middle classes by the signing of the Westphalian Treaty and the end of the Thirty Years' War in 1648. Schottelius was also one of several scholars who wrote *Friedensspiele* 'peace plays' to celebrate the peace; his own was performed at the court in Wolfenbüttel (Berns 1981, Smart 1989).

Linguistically, too, Germany was undergoing massive upheaval. Low German (the German of the northern lowlands) was being abandoned by administrations and Protestant populations,[7] a result both of the influence of Martin Luther's (1483–1546) translation of the Bible (1534), and of the fact that the low/high distinction was increasingly becoming one of status rather than of geography: High German now meant the prestige variety, the correct form of the language to be used in writing, the sense in which it is still used today. So Schottelius (1663: 174, § 7) stipulated that the focus (*Ziel*, lit. 'goal') of his comprehensive grammar of German was *die Hochteutsche Sprache [...] welche die Teutschen | sonderlich aber das Teutsche Reich selbst | in den Abschieden | in den Cantzleyen Gerichten und Trückereyen [...] gebraucht hat* ('the High German language [...] which the Germans [...] have used in decrees, in chancelleries, courts and printing-houses'. At the same time, both the monopoly of Latin in the universities and its dominance at school level, and the adoption of French in more elevated social life, were socially divisive and increasingly resented. The educational reformer Ratke pleaded in his *Memorial* of 1612 for the use of the mother tongue in schools; later in the century, the philosopher Christian Thomasius (1655–1728) planned a course in practical German style for his university students (Weithase 1961: 268–272; Leweling 2005: 99). Numerous 'language societies' sprang up with the aim of cultivating German as a language equal to all others, to develop it as a literary language, and to defend it from foreign influences (Otto 1972, Ingen 1986). The first of these, and the largest, was the FG already mentioned. German cultural

---

[7] For example, the Rostock chancellery had started using High German alongside Low German for both internal and external correspondence in 1598; Low German disappeared entirely from correspondence after 1640. In Magdeburg and in Schottelius's own Braunschweig, closer to the High/Low German boundary, the shift to High German occurred earlier (Gabrielsson 1983).

patriots—including Schottelius, Rist, and the many other members of the FG and other such societies—strove to resist the influence of French culture, morals and language on German. Satirists like Andreas Gryphius (1616–1664) in his *Horribilicribrifax* (1648, but first printed in 1663) lampooned the pretentious mixing of words and phrases from French, Italian and Latin (and even Greek and Hebrew) in the German of the socially or intellectually ambitious (see Jones 1995 for many examples, including an extract from the *Horribilicribrifax, pp.* 462–465). German linguistic purism – rejecting modish foreign borrowed words and seeking to replace them with native alternatives, as Schottelius very deliberately did for his grammatical terminology – was another important expression of this cultural patriotism (Polenz 1994: 107–34, Jones 1999).

While Germany had to endure and then slowly recover from the Thirty Years' War, the Netherlands—although involved in the war—was experiencing its Golden Age, a period of material and cultural wealth fuelled by successful trade and a policy of religious tolerance. This, the age of the artist Rembrandt (1606–1669), made possible the publication of the *Statenbijbel* (the 'authorized' Dutch translation of the Bible) in 1637, an important symbolic cultural, political and linguistic landmark, the result of several years of collaboration amongst translators from various dialect areas to produce an authorized version. In the face of the flourishing literary culture in France (where, for example, the playwright Molière (1622–1673) was a contemporary of Schottelius), the so-called Dutch Movement in Germany looked to the thriving Netherlands for models in poetics and literary translation in particular (Bornemann 1976). Schottelius was no exception, as the influence of Netherlands-based scholars on his linguistic ideas shows, especially his debt to the Dutch mathematician Simon Stevin (1548–1620) (cf. 3.4). Such specifically *linguistic* patriotism was in fact a long-standing pan-Germanic affair, for German, Dutch and Scandinavian scholars had in effect been pooling arguments about the worth of the Germanic languages since the sixteenth century.

1.2.3 *Linguistic thought in Western Europe*

Schottelius came to prominence with his German grammar at around the same time as the mathematician John Wallis (1616–1703) published the first edition of his radically straightforward English grammar, *Grammatica linguae Anglicanae* (1653). With its separate treatise on the pronunciation of the sounds, Wallis's grammar typifies the close link between the natural sciences and linguistics in seventeenth-century England, quite unlike Germany, where Schottelius instead placed his grammar alongside his endeavours in poetry and poetics in the *AA*. Schottelius did value the sound of language, which should *wollauten* 'sound well' (e.g. *AA* 51, 4: 2), but in marked contrast to Wallis's empiricist approach to the sounds of English he was not interested in the spoken word as the basis for developing a standard, and concentrated virtually entirely on the written language as his object of study (cf. 2.2.1).[8] In France, Lancelot and Arnauld published their highly influential *Grammaire générale et raisonnée* (1660), a universal grammar of language (which had no impact on Schottelius, it must be said). In the Netherlands, Vossius had published the most important Latin theoretical grammar of the century, *De Arte Grammatica*, in 1635, a work which did have a significant influence on Schottelius (cf. 3.6). In Germany the auto-didact mystic Böhme had published between 1612 and 1623 his meandering reflections on the traces of the God-inspired *Natursprache* in German that seemed to him to be guarantors of the true and reliable bond between language and metaphysical truth (Gardt 1994: 469). Yet elsewhere in Europe, philosophers like Francis Bacon (1561–1626), Thomas Hobbes (1588–1679) and John Locke (1632–1704) were beginning to express serious doubts about the reliability of language for talking about the world (Padley 1976: 132–53; Salmon 1972). Projects for artificial, universal languages in the face of the imperfections of natural languages appeared even as Schottelius was completing his *AA*. Johann Joachim Becher (1635–1682) and Athanasius Kircher (1602–1680) published their efforts in 1661 and 1663 respectively (Strasser 1988: 155–95). The most elaborate and best-known project for a universal language, by Bishop Wilkins, was published just five years after the *AA*, in 1668 (Subbiondo 1992; Cram & Maat 2000; Lewis 2007). Although contemporary with many of these scholars, Schottelius ploughed a different furrow.[9] He might have agreed with the philosophers that the words of *some* languages had but a poor link to reality and truth, but would have argued that German was fortunately superior. The reasons for such an assertion will become clear in Chapter 2.

On the practical side of linguistic reflection, language teaching, Wolfgang Ratke's pleas for use of the mother tongue in education, and for careful progression through the material, were having an influence in Germany. So too, on the international stage, were the ideas of the Bohemian Jan Amos Komenský (Comenius, 1592–1670; Caravolas 1994, 2000: 1016–21; Hüllen 2002: 137ff.). Comenius shared with Ratke a belief in the importance of systematic instruction in the mother tongue. He also emphasized the importance of progression from the easy to the more difficult, and the need for instruction to have a clear link to everyday reality. Comenius apparently visited Lüneburg in 1646—it is possible, though unfortunately pure speculation, that he and Schottelius might have met (Kusova 1986: 53).

---

[8] The suggestion by Weithase (1961: 115) that Schottelius 'advocated the view of unity of pronunciation and writing' is thus somewhat misleading.

[9] Only twenty years later, however, Morhof, though still standing very much in the shadow of Schottelius in his *Unterricht Von der Teutschen Sprache und Poesie* (1682), noted these schemes for a universal language with great interest.

1.3 The *Ausführliche Arbeit* (1663) for readers new to the work

Schottelius's oeuvre is a substantial one, and even the *AA* alone—the subject of this study—is over 1500 pages in length,[10] a compendium of over twenty years' work. Schottelius had already produced a grammar of German, the *Teutsche Sprachkunst*, in 1641 (reprinted in 1651), in which the first book contained a number of orations in praise of the German language (*Lobreden*). His 'Comprehensive Work' of 1663 includes the same grammar and orations, along with a guide to verse-writing in German (first published 1645), and the allegorical poem *Einleitung zur Teutschen Sprache* (first published in 1643), extensive lists of German rootwords, proper names and proverbs, a treatise on translation into German, and a short acclamation of peace in Latin, dating from 1648. While the combination of such disparate types of texts might strike us as strange today, it was not unusual in the seventeenth century to publish loosely related texts in a single volume, in part as a means of maximizing sales. To take another example from the domain of language cultivation, Johann Rudolf Sattler (1577–1628) published a rhetoric, a guide to letter-writing and a punctuation guide in a single volume (Sattler 1604; cf. Moulin-Fankhänel 1997b: 264–73). Schottelius's unifying title (*Ausführliche Arbeit* ... 'comprehensive work') suggests something more than mere opportunism, however. For Schottelius, each of the texts contributed to a 'comprehensive' study of German, and the *AA* is a demonstration of the overlapping and interdependence of the genres and discourses used for the transmission of knowledge in the seventeenth century. It is a truism about the Baroque period, but a useful one, that poetry and the academic pursuit of knowledge were inextricably linked (thus, e.g., Berns 1976: 18). Each attempted to give an adequate account of the world (Westerhoff 2000: 121–22), and each relied on the other to do so. As Conrad Celtis (1459–1508) had already put it in his *Ars versificandi* (c. 1486), the purpose of poetry was to give *Ein wahres Bild der Dinge* ('a true picture of things', Entner 1972: 354), and the Baroque was the age of the *poeta doctus*, the 'learned poet' (Westerhoff 2000), who must use all his knowledge and skill to provide the most metaphysically complete description of the world. At the same time, poetry was viewed as a suitable medium to express any kind of knowledge, giving rise to didactic verse as an important means of conveying knowledge. Entner (1972: 363) summed up the view of Andreas Corvinus (1589–1648), who was writing at the same time as Celtis, 'that poetry is nothing other than a particularly effective linguistic form for the contents of the actual sciences'. In turn, in

---

[10] The work consists of 1494 pages, but the numbering begins after 36 pages of introductory material, and stops at p.1466. The index and *acclamatio pro pace* have no page numbers, but occupy a further 28 pages. The total is thus 1558 pages.

the sixteenth century and well beyond, following in the tradition of Horace, poetics could border on rhetoric. Mastery of poetics in this guise meant mastery of the techniques of *descriptio* and *amplificatio*. To express reality as closely as possible meant to be as convincing—like a rhetorician—in the presentation of the subject as possible. The *AA* exemplifies this interweaving of scientific knowledge, rhetoric and poetry. Even at the most superficial glance, we can see that the *AA* contains orations, poetry, and academic treatises, and closer study reveals that all these genres present overlapping knowledge, in part using overlapping rhetorical techniques. In a period for which we still know too little about the full range of written text-types (as opposed to the narrowly literary genres) (Hundt 2000: 29), the *AA* is representative of the variety of genres in which knowledge could be presented in the seventeenth century. Chapters 4 and 5 are therefore devoted to looking closely at the range of genres in which knowledge (or assertion) is presented in the *AA*.

Most studies of the *AA* to date have concentrated their attention on certain parts of the work only—usually the orations or the grammar (depending on whether the researcher's concern is on the history of linguistic theory or on the history of grammars), occasionally on the poetics of Book 4 (for instance, Huber 1984: 197–201; scattered discussion in Hundt 2000). Alternatively, scholars have examined particular aspects of Schottelius's work, such as his morphological theory (Gützlaff 1989a; 1989b; Neuhaus 1991), his contribution to lexicography (Schneider 1995; Henne 2001a), or his grammatical terminology (Barbarić 1981). Blackall (1959:10–11) acknowledged Schottelius's efforts towards developing a language fit for the expression of all intellectual ideas. In the history of grammatography, Padley (1985, 1988) recognized Schottelius's place within the emerging vernacular grammatical traditions of Europe, calling the *AA* 'epoch-making' and 'of central importance for the history of German grammar' (Padley 1988: 259)—it marked the start of a trend towards theoretical grammars of German, works no longer aimed principally at foreign learners. Jellinek (1913–14) and Barbarić (1981) remain useful references for the details of Schottelius's grammar and its debts to earlier works; Moulin (2000) and Glück (2002) also situate Schottelius within German vernacular grammar-writing.

There have been several studies of Schottelius's debt to Dutch and Flemish sources and in particular to Simon Stevin (Kiedrón 1985a; 1985b; 1987; Gützlaff 1988; Klijnsmit 1993), and there is general acknowledgement of his extensive use of learned works with a bearing on language from all over Europe, so that Hankamer (1927: 124) aptly described the *AA* as a 'Baroque *summa philologica*'. Yet to the average reader today the sources are inaccessible and unfamiliar, the references in any case often incomplete, and the language of the sources (usually Latin) a barrier to understanding, a problem which Chapter 6 and the Appendix address.

Two studies of Schottelius are more wide-ranging than those discussed so far. Gardt (1994) includes an extremely valuable study of Schottelius's ideas about language within the wider context of seventeenth-century reflections on language, with particular emphasis on what Gardt calls *ontologizing linguistic patriotism*. (By *ontologizing*, Gardt means conceiving of the German language as Something, some essence, that has continuity over time, and which can thus provide a source of cultural identity.) Hundt (2000) traces in detail how Schottelius and his close ally Harsdörffer translated their linguistic-patriotic ambitions into concrete *Spracharbeit* 'work on language' at every level of the language: spelling, letters and sounds, lexicography, phraseology, semantics, etymology, morphology. Hundt emphasizes the wide range of text-types in which *Spracharbeit* is carried out—not just in grammars *per se*, but in riddles, word-lists, plays, and in other popularizing works. These two studies examine Schottelius within the German context, however, and do not situate Schottelius within the wider European linguistic landscape.

In the context of European linguistic thought, Schottelius's *AA* has been seen as a forerunner of linguistic universalism (e.g. Padley 1985: 224–31), sometimes equated with 'linguistic rationalism' (e.g. Allan 2007: 175), though the latter is a potentially misleading term. After all, virtually no grammatical text has ever disputed the rational foundation of language; merely the grounds for justifying the assertion and the means for describing the rationalism have varied, and Schottelius has rather little in common with the specific linguistic rationalism of Lancelot & Arnauld or of Leibniz, as already noted and as Padley (1985: 232) ultimately conceded (cf. 7.4.1). In any case, German scholarship has long since overcome an earlier tendency to see the seventeenth century as a mere transition period between the sixteenth century (Luther, Reformation, Humanism, and championing of the vernacular) and the eighteenth century (the emergence of rationalist linguistic philosophy, represented in Germany by Leibniz, and the emergence of New High German as a fully fledged literary language). Consequently, both Gardt (1994) and Hundt (2000) examine Schottelius as part of a movement of cultural and linguistic patriotism, which they rightly see as the defining feature of seventeenth-century linguistic reflection in Germany. But in the orations of the *AA* especially, Schottelius engaged with ideas that had been circulating widely in Europe on the nature and origins of languages, and his influence reached across a number of European countries. This study therefore emphasizes Schottelius's place in the European history of ideas—not just as a German patriot, but also as a voice participating in wider European reflections on language.

1.4 SCHOTTELIUS'S IDEOLOGY AND ASPIRATIONS REVEALED IN THE PARATEX-
TUAL MATERIAL OF THE *AUSFÜHRLICHE ARBEIT*

As a first step to overcoming the 'foreignness' of the *AA* to a modern
reader, I shall conclude this introduction by showing how the 'paratextual'
or external features of the *AA*—visual material and visual effects that
accompany the text proper—would have guided the contemporary reader
in approaching Schottelius's *magnum opus*. I interpret the category of
paratextuality loosely, to include also *textual* material that does not belong
to the work proper, but that nevertheless helped shape the reader's
expectations of the work. The features to consider fall into two categories:

I. Visual features of the work that structure our reading of it: that is, the
   macro-structure evident in visible divisions into books, chapters,
   paragraphs, etc., as well as typographical features.
II. Accompanying material that is not part of the work proper, whether
    primarily visual *or* textual, such as dedications, engravings, and title
    pages.

Such paratextual material affected how the work would be read, received
and disseminated. As will become clear, it emphatically asserted the
authority of the work and the standing of its author as *the* leading scholar
of the German language, a significant factor in its later reception. It
explicitly recognized and invited two different readerships: a local German
public and an international, Latin-reading one. Finally, it made the entire
project of cultivating German appear part of a patriotic endeavour, which
was in turn part of a wider Christian ideology.

1.4.1 *Visual features that structure the AA*

In the *AA*, Schottelius was chiefly re-publishing previously published and at
first glance quite disparate material. Books I to III consist of ten orations in
praise of German (Book I), followed by two books of grammar (Book II
contains the etymology, Book III the syntax). These three books had
already appeared together twice before, under the title of *Teutsche
Sprachkunst* in 1641 and 1651. Their three-book structure was unchanged
in 1663 from these earlier editions, but they were no longer presented as a
complete work in themselves. Book IV of the *AA* contains the *Verskunst* or
poetics, first published in 1645. More than the other books, its presentation
reveals its independent history: on the title page, the 1644 dedication to
Sophie Elizabeth, Duchess of Braunschweig, has not been updated, and the
book is divided itself into three books.[11] Book V is the most heterogeneous

---

[11] Confusingly, the numbering of these three books determines the running header, so that the
header indicates Book I, II, or III, while we are, overall, in Book IV.

of the five in the *AA*. It contains poetry, plain prose, dialogue, word-lists, and a summary of contents. The disparate nature of the texts is glossed over by listing them at the start of the book as seven *Traktate*, or treatises. The first of these treatises, like the poetics, repeats an original dedication from 1643 to Prince Ludwig. Despite the disparate publishing history of these different works over some twenty years, the structure of five books imposed on the whole gives the impression of a unified and coherent project. Readers are invited to accept that this one volume (for the original, unlike the 1967 reprint edition, *was* a single volume) contains all we need to know about the German language, even though there is, for instance, no treatment of rhetoric.

Within each book, there are further divisions, whether into orations (Book I), chapters (Books II–IV), or treatises (Book V). Chapters and orations are further sub-divided into numbered paragraphs, rules or remarks. New to the 1663 edition of the previously published material, there are Latin outlines (often numbered by paragraph) at the head of each chapter,[12] each numbered paragraph being summed up in a sentence or phrase. For example, *Quid sit Grammatica* 'what grammar may be', is the summary for Chapter 2, paragraph 1 of the grammar. These smaller divisions and the outlines accommodated an international and scholarly audience who could readily orient themselves by such Latin signposts.

At the front of the book, the scholarly credentials of the work are underlined by a list of sources (*AA* c2^r to [c4^r]),[13] in part duplicated by the more detailed list of writers on or in German presented in Book V (cf. 4.4.3 and Chapter 6). The structure of the material at the back of the book also accommodates non-German scholars consulting the work. Working inwards from the back, the reader finds (preceding the Acclamation of Peace, discussed below, and the customary list of typographical errors and emendations) an index (*AA* [1467]–[1482] = Bbbbbbbbb ij^v] [*sic*]), a list of key German grammatical terminology with Latin equivalents (*AA* 1462–1466), and an outline table of contents. These are in turn appended to a Latin treatise (the seventh and last of the *Traktate* in Book V) which gives an overview of the contents of the work (*AA* 1452–1459), including book, chapter and page numbers. Indices and tables of contents in Latin like this were customary for scholarly works in Latin, but they were unusual for grammars in the vernacular, and the various apparatus of this sort (index; table; discursive overview) demonstrate Schottelius's determination by 1663 to be read by an international scholarly audience. The *Latin* overview of contents in fact replaced a brief outline given in *German* (pp. [C7^r] to [C8^v]

---

[12] An exception is the fifth treatise of Book V, a dialogue about translating into German, arguably of lesser interest to non-German readers; the summary of the fourth treatise appears at the end rather than at its start (cf. 5.4.3). The seventh treatise is in Latin.

[13] The square brackets [ ] indicate that the page is not numbered.

in the 1651 edition of the *Sprachkunst*)—the switch in language is clearly a programmatic decision.

It is worth looking a little more closely at the outline table of contents (*AA* 1460–61). A double-page spread in the seventh treatise is given over to this hierarchically arranged outline table (Figure 1.1), one half devoted to *Sprachkunst*, 'grammar', the other to *Verskunst* 'poetics'. It fulfilled three functions:

1. to present German key terms with their Latin equivalents,
2. to serve as a ready reference index, and
3. to make plain the place of key topics in Schottelius's concept of language.

For instance, finding the term *Zuwörter*, we see at a glance that it means in Latin *Adverbia*, is dealt with in Book II, chapter 17, and is seventh of nine numbered parts of speech. The parts of speech are in turn a sub-topic of the study of whole words, viewed either by their category, or by their formation (eleven topics covering inflection, derivation and compounding). The study of whole words is, in turn, one of three branches of *etymology*, alongside the study of the letters and the syllables. Etymology and Syntax together make up the *Sprachkunst*.

As Figure 1.2 illustrates, any page of the *AA* is likely to exhibit a great many different typefaces which are striking to a modern reader, though usual in seventeenth-century Germany. Potentially, at least, the typeface was a patriotic or political statement. The fact that German had its own (gothic) typeface implicitly elevated German to a place alongside the sacred languages of Hebrew, Greek and Latin, each with their own distinctive scripts (Flood 1993). In practice, however, by the seventeenth century, gothic typeface was the norm for German language printing,[14] while it was usual too to use *antiqua* when citing other languages. Particularly in the early books of the *AA*, where, over the course of three editions, Schottelius steadily increased the amount of Latin, this mixture of typefaces certainly does not make the work any more accessible for today's readers. But it is an obvious visual marker of his increasing participation in the learned Latin tradition of international scholarship, compared to the 1641 edition of the grammar, where Latin running text appeared on only 17 pages, and even then was usually limited to only a few lines (cf. 5.3).

1.4.2 *Accompanying material*

The visual and textual material preceding the *AA* proper established the social standing and scholarly authority of Schottelius. A dedication to

---

[14] When Martin Aedler (1643–1724) decided to print his German grammar for English learners in antiqua (*High Dutch Minerva*, 1690), this was criticized by Heinrich Offelen (fl. 1686–1687), whose *Double Grammar* sought to improve on Aedler's and who reverted to black letter for the German. See Van der Lubbe (2007: 201).

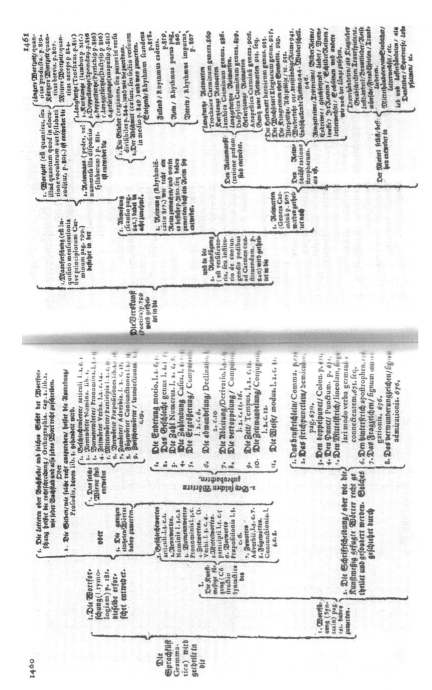

Figure 1.1: The outline table of contents (*AA* 1460–61)

124   Die achte Lobrede

Sprache nicht allein was viele Wörter/sondern auch den Grund und die Arten zureden belan-
get/guten teihls aus dem Teutschen sey: Welches auch nach der länge und ausführlich bewei-
sen/Besoldus, Lazius, Goropius, Aventinus.

4. *Besoldus cap. 17. de nat. pop.* sagt: Galli quamplurimas voces Latinas addidice-
runt, sed ad formam, & constructionem Germanicæ linguæ connexuerunt & pronuncia-
runt, Latinamque dialectum continuis Germanismis deformatam condiderunt. Frustra-
que *Stephanus Pasquierus lib. 7. de rechrr. cap. 1.* mirmtus, unde verba auxiliaria in Gallicam, Italicam, & Hispanicam linguam irrepserint, &c. *Henricus Stephanus* hat in einem
eignen Büchlein Græcismos linguæ Gallicæ aufgeschrieben/aber Besoldus cap. 9. sagt darauf
omnes esse merè germanismos. Und Cap. 18. sagt er: Ipsi Galli unde suas dictiones habent,
nesciunt; Ideoque in lexicis suis & in etymis indagandis vano nisu mirè se torquent.
Und machen wunderseltzame Derivationcs, damit sie eine adsonantiam des Frantzösischt Wortes
finden: Marschalk (unser Teutsches Wort Marschalck) sagt Bovillus, *Vient de Mars, Dieu des
batailles, & de Schalk, qui signifie fin, entendu & rusé, quasi pour dire fin & entendu
pour aux affaire de Mars.* Quiâ verò. I nune, sagt Glareanus (der dieses auch berührt)
& pete, citra linguæ Germanicæ peritiam, vocum Gallicarum Etymologiam, quàm belli
scribuntur elenchi? Anzgezogener Wolfgangus Hungerus spricht: Nunquam Gallus tàm
ineptè rimaturus hæc erat, si vel mediocrem linguæ Germanicæ haberet cognitionem. Jn
dem Silvio und Bovillo, zweyen Frantzösischen Grammaticis ist zuersehen/wie erbärmlich sie
misrahten und sich quälen/ die Teutschen Stammwörter (derer Deutung sie nicht wissen) aus
Lateinischer oder Griechischer Sprache abzuzwingen. Zum Exempel/ das Frantzösische Riche
(dives) muß ihnen herkommen vom Lateinschen Risco, die rechte Teutsche Wurtzel riF oder
reich wissen sie nicht. Garder, derivirt *Bovillus* von videre, syFisw aber ἀπὸ τῆς καρδίας, qua-
re? quia cor viræ principium & caloris nativi fons est. Die Teutsche Wurtzel Warthen ist ihnen unbekant (Vid. infra lib. 2. cap. 3. in lit P. Crier, clamare (schreyen/schreyen) derivirt Bovillus) von καλέω.

Marefchus somniat Bovillus *à Martello* vel *Malleo* deducendum esse: (vid. infra Mar-
schall in indice) *Esuté* (Stuve) hypocaustum, muß herkommen von στῦφο, quod Græci di-
cunt στύφω, quod ea loca ob calorem stipentur: Nam u. in y, & p, in b, ut mutetur, non adeo
infrequens esse. Bone Deus! nimirum Germani autochtones misûs legatis in Asiam hy-
bernaculis suis septentrionalibus nomen (si Diis placet) petiverunt, qui pro sui cœli clemen-
tia, id habitationis genus atque opus haberent, neque vidissent unquam, ita ait *Iacobus Spi-
gelius in Lexico juris.*

Mehr Exempla mag ich nicht anführen/weil zum Uberfluß aus angezogenen erhellet/
wie die Unkundigkeit Teutscher Sprache so viel vornehme Leute/ so den Grund ausser Teut-
schem Grunde suchen/in lauter Absurditeten verleite; gleichwol finden sich noch wol grosse
Teutsche Hansen/die Gebührungsweis ihren eigenen Senf haben/und immer was abgauckeln/
und die Sprösslinge an stat der Wurtzel liebhaben wollen.

5. Eines annoch/so das Vermögen etlicher Teutscher/von anderen unwissend misbrauch-
ter Wörter betrifft/und bisher unberührt geblieben/will ich annoch erinnern.

Die Frantzosen sagen *mespriser, fastidire, despicere,* ist unlaugbarlich das Teutsche Wort
Misspreisen: Item/ sie sagen *Bouleverd propugnaculum,* ist unser Teutsches Wort Bolwerk/
                Item

Figure 1.2: *AA* 124 (from the eighth oration of Book 1)

Herzog August, Schottelius's patron, and a similar preface to him repeated
from the earlier edition of the *Sprachkunst*, emphasized the prestige of the
author by identifying his powerful patron.[15] The printing of the official
imperial privilege (a warrant of imperial protection, a sort of copyright) was
also a mark of distinction reserved for serious works (Metcalf 1978,
Koppitz 2008). The title page (Figure 1.3) further emphasized that the *AA*
was published not just with an imperial privilege, but with particular
imperial approval *als einer gemeinnutzigen und der Teutschen Nation zum*

---

[15] On the role of dedications in the period, see Maché (1991).

Figure 1.3: The title page of the *AA*

besten angesehene[n] Arbeit 'as a useful work likely to benefit the German nation'. Schottelius clearly set store by this, for he made special mention of it when he noted the success of the *AA* on p. 2 of his 1673 *Sprachkrieg* (Hecht 1967: 6–7*).

Further indications of the author's stature are the good wishes of other prominent scholars, expressed in six occasional poems (six of a total of at least thirty-three such poems we know were composed in Schottelius's honour: Berns 1978: 100), and two letters.[16] Schottelius mobilized his

---

[16] The poetics of Book IV is also prefaced by an assessment by Harsdörffer of the 1645 edition (*AA* 794–798).

friends to help him promote his work, and correspondence between him and at least four of the seven well-wishers survives: Birken, Harsdörffer, Rist and Conring. The poem of the Nuremberg theologian and poet Johann Michael Dilherr (1604–1669), a member of the literary society *Pegnesischer Blumenorden*, likened Schottelius to Cicero and suggested he had increased the honour of the German people; the theologian and writer Andreas Heinrich Buch(h)oltz (1607–1671) called Schottelius a great man and the glory of the Teutonic language; Johann Rist contributed a letter calling Schottelius a *vir excellentissime* 'a most excellent man'; Sigmund von Birken—a writer and poet, a member of both the FG and Harsdörffer's *Blumenorden*, and a regular correspondent with Schottelius (Berns 1978: 96)—offered a poem dubbing Schottelius the *patrem Patriae Linguae* 'the father of the language of the fatherland', and called him a German Varro, a title also accorded him by Jacob Sturm (fl. 1662) in his poem. M. Joachimus Scriverius (?-?) opted for a different analogy in his laudatory epigram: Schottelius, true to his name as *Der Suchende* 'the seeker', had explored the hidden recesses of the German Pallas's treasure trove.

The last of the poems printed was based on a letter-puzzle, and was composed by Schottelius's close associate Harsdörffer (who had died in 1658). The puzzle equated *Justus Georgius Schottelius* with *Varro Teutonicus, vindex linguae* ('Teutonic Varro, defender of the language'). By letter substitution, where each letter is replaced with a number in sequence such that a = 1, z = 23 (I and J and U and V are not distinguished; Y is not included), both phrases 'add up' to 345. (Sometimes the total arrived at in such puzzles could be significant too, but in this case I see no significance in the value 345; the important point is the equation of the two expressions.) This fitting equivalence is then developed in Harsdörffer's short poem, beginning *Tu vindex Linguae, Tu Varro Teutonicus*. This language game—typical of those with which Harsdörffer filled his conversation books, *Frauenzimmer Gesprächsspiele* 'conversation games for women' (Harsdörffer 1644–1649, henceforth *FZG*)—is an example of pansemioticism in action: new meanings are constructed by combining signs in new ways, often combining playful combination with a serious underlying message (Hundt 2000: 174ff., Hundt 2006).

A recurrent theme in the dedicatory material is the notion of Schottelius as the German equivalent of Roman scholars famous for their promotion of Latin: either as Cicero, or repeatedly, as a German Varro—a reference to M. Terentius Varro (116–27 B.C.), whose *De lingua latina* (47–45B.C.) was a landmark work attempting to give a fundamental account of Latin and of language in general (Cherubim 1995; cf. Law 2003: 43–49). Schottelius dwelt at some length on Varro's achievement (*AA* 40, 3: 32–33),[17] crediting him with 'fixing' the Latin language, above all in its *Gründe | Stämme | und*

---

[17] References to the orations of Book I are in the form *AA page number, oration: paragraph.*

Redarten 'in its foundations, stems and idioms.' A comparison with Varro was thus a proud claim indeed to be able to set at the head of a study of German. Schottelius may well have hinted at this theme when soliciting poems—three of the congratulatory poems at the front of the 1651 edition of the *Sprachkunst* had likewise shared a theme, in that case of Schottelius as a miner, using a lamp to explore and light up the hidden roots of the language (by Dominus Stubendorf, Harsdörffer and Rist, in Schottelius 1651: b3^r, b4^v, b6^v). The choice of Varro in particular is telling, too. While Quintilian often typified the views of anomalists about language, Varro stood for the analogist camp (Jensen 1990: 180), and it was the latter camp with which Schottelius firmly identified himself in contemporary discussions about German (cf. 3.6.1, 3.8.1).

The last of the promotional material is a lengthy letter to Schottelius from the Helmstedt professor Hermann Conring, although it is missing from some copies. Dated 1663, it was presumably composed specially for publication in the *AA*, and was evidently added late in the printing process. At the foot of fol. D4^v, the catchword *Die* originally anticipated the title of the first Lobrede on fol. A^r; the small gathering signed *e* (Conring's *Epistola*) was added later.[18] Conring's letter rehearses well-known ideas about the history of language since the confusion of tongues at Babel, but begins and ends with praise of Schottelius's achievements in the *AA*:

> Tu demum nos omnes rectè scribere, (quae laus [...] me quidem judice, fuit huc usque unius Hollandiae) rectè prima vocum rudimenta ex originibus suis eruere, aptè omnia connectere, concinne pedum mensuram ac numeros observare, docuisti

> 'You it is who have taught us all to write correctly, to determine correctly the origins of words from their first beginnings (which was thus far the merit [...] of Holland alone) [this is a reference to the dominance of Dutch and Flemish scholars in this field; cf. 3.4], to join all together appropriately, to observe fittingly the length and number of metrical feet'

Schottelius has, says Conring, contained the whole sphere of the language in fixed laws (both in grammar and poetics, given equal weight by Conring). Perhaps in return for this specially composed letter, Schottelius cited Conring's principles for good writing prominently in the first oration of the 1663 edition (*AA* 3, 1:8), principles which he used to structure his outline of the contents of his work in the paragraphs that follow.

One final visual effect to note is the sheer size, weight and thickness of the *AA*. The book is seven centimetres thick, and over 1500 pages of quarto. An inscription in one of the copies held at the Institute for Germanic and

---

[18]   I am grateful to Bill Jones for alerting me to this fact.

Romance Studies, London, indicates that in 1674 it cost two *Taler* and four *Groschen* unbound, plus eight *Groschen* for the binding (Jones 2000: 620). In the mid-eighteenth century, the *AA* still cost two *Taler*. Just six or seven times that amount would have bought a good horse; other grammars of German were at most a sixth of the price (costing between three and ten *Groschen*; there were 30 *Groschen* to a *Taler*).[19] All of this points to a prestigious piece of work whose author was not afraid to proclaim his standing as the leading authority on the German language.

1.4.3 *Engravings, title pages, and the acclamation of peace*

From the written material, let us turn now to the images that appear at the very front of the *AA* and that precondition the reader to what is to follow. There are two engravings—one a portrait of the author himself (Figure 1.4), the other, facing it, a frontispiece (Figure 1.5).

The mere inclusion of the portrait of Schottelius set this work on the German language apart from any previously published grammars of German, and emphasized Schottelius's status. It followed the example of, for instance, the 'arch-humanist' Conrad Celtis (Schade 1991: 179), and of Adriaan van Schrieck (1560–1621) in his ambitious work on the history and origins of the Flemish, Celtic, and Hebrew languages. The portrait announces not just the presence, but also the authority of Schottelius in his work, for it is deliberately self-representational. The oval frame rests on a quadrilateral base which bears the name and professional titles of the sitter, as if displayed in a gallery. The pose has a deliberately intellectual focus. With the body hidden under a robe, our attention is drawn to the scholar's head, the seat of the intellect. Schade (1991, whose analysis of this engraving I largely follow) interprets the construction of the portrait—which approximates to a sphere resting on a cube—as *Quies* ('calm') or *sapientia constans* ('steadfast wisdom') personified.

The second engraving serves as a frontispiece and an additional title page (Figure 1.5). It is another example of pansemioticism in action; every aspect of the picture can and should be interpreted. As in an emblem-book, there is a verse explanation of the engraving, located on the reverse of the title page proper. The engraving shows a banner bearing the title of the work, against the background of a cultivated landscape. The banner is suspended between two ornate pillars, which bear (left) the device of the FG (the palm-tree, with its motto *Alles zu nutzen* ('all is useful' or 'to use all'), for it was believed that every part of the palm-tree had its use) and (right) the alpine ox-eye which was Schottelius's own emblem in the society, together with his nickname, *Der*

---

[19] These prices are taken from the *Europäisches Bücher-Lexikon* of Theophil Georgi (1742), a kind of catalogue of books in print of the time. For comparison, Johann(es) Clajus's (1535–1592) grammar of German (first published in 1578 but available in 1742 in a 1689 edition) cost just three *Groschen*.

Figure 1.4: Engraved portrait of Justus-Georgius Schottelius

Suchende (cf. 3.7). Their presence here means that the work is explicitly published in accord with the cultural-patriotic aims of the 'fruit-bearing' language society (cf. 3.5.5). The *lingua germanica* of the title banner forms the portal to a land of apparent peace, prosperity and *conversatio* behind it—Germany as she could be. It is immediately striking that the engraving presents us with a key pair of notions—art and nature. First, there is the visual pairing of a natural landscape and elaborate Baroque columns, products of human art. Second, the neat cultivated fields and towns in the landscape show signs of the application of human skill, while the columns are adorned with natural motifs—not just the palm-tree and ox-eye, but decorative tendrils of leaves and flowers. Art and nature overlap and flow into each other. This combination of the organic and the imagery of artful construction characterizes the *AA* as a whole, especially the orations.[20]

---

[20] Here and elsewhere in this book I have used the word 'artful'—translating Schottelius's *kunstvoll, kunstmessig,* etc.—in its literal sense: 'in accord with art, expressing mastery of an art', rather than in the sense of 'sly', as in Dickens' 'artful dodger'. Another alternative in English is 'skilful', though this lacks the transparent link to the 'art'.

Figure 1.5: The title engraving of the *Ausführliche Arbeit*

The intermingling of nature and art in the engraving of 1663 becomes all the more significant when contrasted with the engraving of the 1651 *Teutsche Sprachkunst*, reproduced in Figure 1.6. (The 1641 edition had no engraving). In 1651, two allegorical figures, *Consuetudo* (Custom) and *Ratio* (Reason), hold a banner bearing the title of the work, together forming an archway through which a landscape can be seen. In the centre of the landscape is a garden. With its geometrically shaped beds (in the French style, ironically!) grouped around a fountain, the garden is the place where art, with the help of reason, improves on nature (cf. Cottone 2000). On the right stands an obelisk, a perfect pyramid in shape, part of Schottelius's personal 'coat of arms'.[21] It is aligned with the straight staff held by *Ratio*, with which she is describing in the earth at her feet a perfect, regular circle,

---

[21] The obelisk featured in the 'coat of arms' used on the seals for Schottelius's letters. It appears too in the frontispiece of the first edition of the *Verskunst* (1645), and of the *Fruchtbringende Lustgarte* (1647), and would appear again in his *Anleitung Zu der Rechtschreibung* (1676) (Berns 1980: 7). In the *Lustgarte* it appears with the motto *Labore surgit* 'It [the obelisk] rises up through labour'. Schottelius's complete motto runs: *Surgit labore bene ordinato* 'He/it rises through well-ordered labour' (Berns 1984: 419).

Figure 1.6: The title engraving of the *Teutsche Sprachkunst* (1651)

suggesting Schottelius's allegiance to *Ratio* over *Consuetudo*. Although the two figures are of equal size and height, *Ratio* looks straight ahead. *Consuetudo*, by contrast, has a weaker look, eyes downcast, and holds a drooping branch rather than a staff. The *Sprachkunst* is here already presented as a delicate balance between *Consuetudo* and *Ratio*, but *Ratio* is more reliable, for it is she who gives geometrical shapes their unchanging perfection, and who imposes regularity on nature to cultivate the beautiful garden of the background.[22] So too, we infer, must language be cultivated. The tension between *Consuetudo* and *Ratio* in cultivating a language runs through Schottelius's work and is one of its lasting influences too, as we

---

[22] Lange (2005: 81) interprets the frontispiece as 'conciliatory', with no suggestion that the one figure is stronger than the other.

shall see (3.8.1; 7.6–7.8). For now, let us note the shift in emphasis by 1663, where the frontispiece suggests a happier combining of nature and art, and places the work in a less narrowly linguistic, more widely cultural patriotic context.

Less immediately obvious than the imagery of nature and art in the 1663 frontispiece, but more explicit, are the two ribbons by which the central banner is fixed. They read (left) *Ad destinata fastigia tendet lingua germanica* ('The German language reaches for its destined pinnacles', where *fastigium* is literally the apex or gable of a building) and (right) *Tandem efflorescit in artes lingua germanica* ('Finally the German language blossoms into the arts'). These are ongoing processes, as yet incomplete, and to which it is implied that Schottelius's work contributes.

The engraving is more than just a collection of images. First, it is clear that Schottelius takes credit for helping in the elevation and blossoming of the German language proclaimed in the banners. Second, the scene depicted also contains a clear moral message, and here the verse *Erklärung des Kupfertitels* ('explanation of the title engraving', on the verso of the engraving) helps us interpret it:

> Was der Gothe / Cimber / Sachs / Däne / Wahle / Franke / Schwabe/ Vormals / nach Mundarten köhr / mit geknall geredet habe / Suchstu das? Such Teutschen grund. Teutsche Sprache / Teutsches Land Ist der Thon und ist der Ort wo zur Kunst helt grund und stand Die Weltweite Celtisch Sprache. Hochteutsch muß die Kunst hochziehen; Unsers höchsten Käisers Throne durchs Geschikk dis ist verliehen. Sprachverwante Nordenleute / rahmt den Kunstweg recht mit ein: Teutschgesinte greift mit zu / Teutsch kan wol vollkommen sein.

> 'Do you seek what the Goth, the Cimbrian, Saxon, Dane, Welsh [presumably in the sense of 'European Celt'], Frank, Swabian used to speak, with force according to the manner [*lit.* choice] of their dialect? Then seek German ground. German language and German land is the sound and is the place where the worldwide Celtic language holds its ground and its standing for art. Art must raise up High German. Fate has granted this to the throne of our most high emperor. Language-related Northern people, join us on the path of art. German-minded people, lend a hand: German can surely attain perfection.'

This rather compressed verse—not improved in my rather literal translation—is far from a mere explanation of the engraving, for it makes additional points of its own. The first half proclaims that fate has decreed that the German language and its Emperor should keep alive the ancestral 'Celtic' language formerly spoken by Goths, Gauls, Danes, Franks. A duty rests on the emperor, then. Two distinct potential audiences are then addressed in the second half of the verse. German patriots are called to help perfect German, but first, and strikingly, those speakers of other peoples of the north (*Sprachverwante Nordenleute*) are called to join German on its path to artful perfection, making explicit what we must otherwise infer from Schottelius's increased use of Latin in 1663 compared to the earlier editions of 1641, 1651: he seeks an international readership, and intends his work to serve as a model for other nations in their cultivation of the ancestral German(ic) language.

Meanwhile, the reminder of the emperor's duty to the language (*Unsers höchsten Käisers Throne durchs Geschikk dis ist verliehen* 'Fate has granted this to the throne of our most high emperor'), and the call on *Teutschgesinte Leute* ('German-minded people') reflects the cultural patriotic ideology which informs Schottelius's thinking about the German language. There is an urgency in the call, for a closer inspection of the engraving's landscape suggests that the fate of both German and Germany hangs in the balance. The left of the landscape (traditionally the favoured side in iconography) is sunlit, and a broad path leads into the gateway of a town whose tall towers suggest its prosperity. In the foreground a smartly dressed pikeman looks up attentively to the ribbon which is holding the title banner *Lingua Germanica* in place, furled around his slender halberd. But on the right, the shadows of war loom. Dark clouds roll in from the edge of the picture, and the town on the hillside has rounded fortification turrets, with no visible means of access; an armed, menacing-looking soldier seems to use his heavy mace to tug at the *Lingua Germanica* ribbon, perhaps threatening to pull it down. The message is clear. War could be the ruin of Germany and its language; with peace comes both a strong German language and a prosperous land.

The analogy Schottelius draws between the state of the language and the state of war or peace is reminiscent of the educational reformer Wolfgang Ratke's *Memorial* of 1612 (the year of Schottelius's birth), in which Ratke had called for education in a unified German language to secure national unity and harmony (*einen Weg zu zeigen, wie im ganzen Reich eine Sprache, eine einträchtige Religion und Regierung einzuführen und zu erhalten sei* 'to show a way how one language, one unified religion and government in the whole empire is to be achieved'; Ising 1959: 101–10). But in Schottelius's frontispiece, the relationship between language and peace is different. Peace appears here as a prerequisite for a strong language, and not the other way round as in Ratke's vision. Still, it is clear from elsewhere in the *AA,* as well as from some of his other works, that Schottelius also believed that the language could in turn influence the moral development of its speakers and hence the wellbeing of the land. In his drama *FriedensSieg* (performed in 1642 to celebrate the Peace of Goslar between the Emperor and the Welfs, the house of Schottelius's patron, even as the Thirty Years' War raged on elsewhere; cf. Berns 1981, Smart 1989), Schottelius explored the theme of the purity of the German language, contrasting the pure German of two ancient German figures, Arminius and Henricus Auceps (Henry the Fowler, 876–936)[23] with that of a contemporary peasant whose language is sprinkled with foreign military terms and the 'alamode' style of the cavalier Bolderian. In 1673, ten years after the publication of the *AA*, Schottelius's *Schrecklicher Sprachkrieg* 'Terrible Grammatical War' developed the analogy, only implicit here, between the state of the nation and the state of the language, presenting a variant on the well-established genre of the grammatical war (cf. Czucka 1997; Hundt 2000: 329–35, 2006: 121–33; Fonsén, 2006, 2007). The first 'grammatical war' had been written by Andrea Guarna in 1511 as a way of presenting a number of irregularities in Latin. It was immensely popular, especially in Germany, where no fewer than 60 editions were printed, and it also spawned a number of imitations (Bolte 1908: 18). Harsdörffer was the first to apply the genre to encourage readers of his conversation books to reflect on the rules, irregularities, and changes in German (Harsdörffer 1644–1649 [1968–1969], vol. 5: 75–84). At the end of Harsdörffer's war, the words have undergone various injuries but are better off for the experience. The derivational suffix *–schafft* has lost an *f*, but feels the better for it, for example. Peace is rapidly restored. Schottelius's war of 1673 does not end optimistically, in contrast, but with devastation and ruin, as a result of which many German words and endings have become misshapen, unrecognizable or even lost altogether. The concluding verses warn:

> Teutschland / dein uneinig = sein Theilet dir Mark und Gebein: Teutschland / einig und vertraut / Sich in Glück und Segen schaut.'
> (Schottelius 1673a: 151)

> 'Germany, your disunity divides you in marrow and bone. Germany united and trusting sees itself in happiness and blessing.'

German disunity is again linked to the state of the language, just as in the *FriedenSieg* play, and foreign (linguistic) influence proves divisive. The entire grammatical war makes it clear that an important part of Germany's fortune is its language, and that the language too suffers under a state of war. The fates of the two—language and Germany itself—are inextricably linked.

The concern with war and peace expressed in these works and reflected in the frontispiece of the *AA* is made more explicit in the *Acclamatio Pro Pace* at the other end of the *AA*.[24] This nine-page celebration of peace, in Latin,

---

[23] Arminius (Hermann) (18/ 17B.C.–A.D. 21) was the leader of the Cherusci who defeated the Roman troops at the Battle of the Teutoburger Forest (9 A.D.); Henry the Fowler was King of the eastern Franks.

[24] The preoccupation with war and peace reflects the influence of Justus Lipsius (1547–1606) on thinkers of his time (cf. Leira 2007) and has parallels in the ideas not just of Schottelius's contemporary and direct influence Hugo Grotius (1583–1645), but also in the thinking of the philosopher Thomas Hobbes.

appears on the very last pages, after the index and a list of printing errors. It is found in all the surviving copies of the book inspected by the modern editor (Hecht 1967: 26*), and it must therefore be considered an integral part of the *AA*, but it seems to have been universally ignored to date. Yet the engravings and the *acclamatio* stand like bookends at either end of the work, together sending a strong message about its scope and purpose. The title page of the acclamation reads in full, *Acclamatio pro PACE Inter Christianos firmâ & fidâ SERENISSIMO PRINCIPI AC DOMINO Dno. AVGUSTO Duci Brunsvicensium ac Luneburgensium, &c. HEROI PIO PACIFICO Ad primum PACIS nuncium Oblata, Anno 1648. à JUSTO-GEORGIO SCHOTTELIO D.* 'An acclamation of the firm and faithful peace between Christians: presented to the most serene prince and lord August, Duke of Braunschweig and Lüneburg, etc., pious and peaceful hero, on the first announcement of peace in the year 1648, by Dr. Justus-Georgius Schottelius.' (1648 was the year of the Westphalian treaty which marked the end of the Thirty Years' War.) A motto at the bottom of the page reads *A solis armis, magna interdum, sed brevis est potentia: à pacis studio, si parvum, at fidum & duiturnum est imperium* 'the power of arms alone is great, but brief; but the might of the study of peace, if it be slight, is faithful and lasting.' The acclamation celebrates peace after many years of war in Europe, and praises the addressee Duke August for his enduring love of peace, earning him alone the epithet of *pacificus*. Furthermore, *obstinatum Tibi, pietatem accuratißimo studio promovere, […] patrio more, Patriâ virtute, Patriâ linguâ inclarescere* 'You are firmly resolved to promote piety by most accurate study […] to celebrate the custom of the Fatherland, the virtue of the Fatherland, the Language of the Fatherland (p. Cccccccc recto). 'PEACE AND PIETY,' continues Schottelius further down the same page in block capitals, 'is the centre from which all lines of human activity run.' After recalling the miseries of war and after further lengthy pious wishes for the preservation of peace, the acclamation concludes with a prayer for peace and happiness amongst all Christians, especially for the house of the Welfs, and finally for Prince August himself.

Once again, the language of the *patria* is tied here to the customs and virtue of the land. Their shared fate rests in turn on the preservation of peace, equated with Christian piety. Both the frontispiece at one end and the acclamation at the other, then, embed the *AA* in a clearly cultural-patriotic but also explicitly pious, Christian value system.

Besides the frontispiece itself, there is, as already noted, a further straightforward title page. To be precise, there are two title pages: the German one is followed on the next recto page by one in Latin (and this is also true of the title pages for each of the five books of the *AA*). Their contents are the same, except for one significant addition in the Latin, which notes that the book is *Germanicè quidem, ita tamen ut in toto Opere Lingua Latina sit simul explicatrix* 'in German, admittedly, but the Latin language is also used to give explanations throughout the work'. Once again, as in the explanatory verse of the engraving, two distinct audiences are addressed in these title pages: one, the local German readership; the other, an international one.

To conclude, the examination of the paratextual material of the *AA* has shown, first, that Schottelius's account of German is far from value-neutral. He subordinates the task of language cultivation to larger patriotic and Christian concerns for the wellbeing of his country and its people. Second, Schottelius presents the *AA* as the outstanding and complete study of German of his generation. Finally, he provides the means for non-Germans as well as Germans to study this landmark work, and, in the case of the other northern Europeans, to follow its example in cultivating their own languages. We shall see in the following chapters to what extent the *AA* and its reception lived up to these aspirations.

2

SCHOTTELIUS'S CONCEPT OF LANGUAGE

2.1 Introduction

As a prelude to examining the textual details of the *AA*, this chapter introduces Schottelius's concept of language in general, and of German in particular, in the context of German studies and more widely in the European context.[1]

Adapting Sonderegger's model (Sonderegger 1998, 1999), we can identify three key features of a growing linguistic consciousness in the later Early New High Geman era, of which Schottelius is the defining exemplar for the seventeenth century. First, Schottelius approached German as a *written* language. His grammatographical work is part of the European wave of (written) language standardization and prescriptivism (cf. Deumert & Vandenbussche 2003). He also sought like predecessors such as Georg Henisch (1549–1618) in his dictionary of 1616 to document the specialist vocabulary of the burgeoning vernacular technical literature, and reflected explicitly on the art of translation, drawing on a discourse tradition that goes straight back to Martin Luther. Second, Schottelius and his contemporaries were acutely aware of *regional* linguistic variation. As they strove to establish a prestige variety amongst competing linguistic varieties, they sought to present various models as authoritative: the model provided by an influential individual (often Luther), the usage of a particular social group, institution (such as the German chancelleries), or particular text-type (such as the imperial decrees) (Josten 1976). Schottelius himself made reference to all of these at one time or another in the *AA* (cf. 2.2), but rejected outright any model that gave preference to the variety of a particular region, especially that of East Central German. Not being a native speaker of that variety (unlike many other members of the FG), he argued for a supraregional variety in principle, the details of which were to be determined using the language-internal criterion of analogy.

Third, Schottelius shared with his contemporaries a *historical* awareness of German that had its roots largely in the preoccupation of sixteenth-century humanists with Tacitus's rediscovered *Germania*, their readings of it, and

---

[1] This is far from the first such introduction. Overviews of Schottelius's conception of language are given in Plattner (1967); Rössing-Hager (1984), particularly on language history and language change; Padley (1985, 1988); Gützlaff (1989a, 1989b) on the nature of the rootword; Seiffert (1990a); Gardt (1994); Cherubim (1996, 2009[2]); and Moulin–Fankhänel (2000), particularly on Schottelius as a grammarian.

their re-castings of it to yield a German national history (Mertens 2004; Krebs 2010), which increasingly led to speculations on the history of the German language too. A key notion was the rootword, which emerged in humanist discourse as a typically German phenomenon (cf. McLelland, *forthcoming a*), and which Schottelius greatly developed from its first simple assertion in Irenicus (1518) (Franz Friedlieb 1494 or 1495–1553) (Jellinek 1898 [1985 rpt.]: 60) to make it the basis both of his morphological theory and the cognitive metaphor which underlies his entire language concept (2.4). Also characteristic of German humanists' speculation on the history of German was the penchant for onomastics and etymologizing, which finds expression in Schottelius's list of rootwords (cf. 4.4.1).

Besides Schottelius's concept of German as a supraregional, written, historical language (2.2), and his rootword concept (both as a cognitive metaphor and as a key theoretical tenet) (2.4), this chapter also examines Schottelius's view of the *nature* of the German language, if only to underline how different is his linguistic rationalism to that of Port-Royal—contrary to Padley's (1985: 224–31) rather misleading categorization of Schottelius as an early universalist (2.3, 2.5.2). Revealing too are the criteria by which Schottelius believed language could be evaluated. The practical, language-external criteria by which he and his contemporaries argued for the superiority of one German language variety over another have been noted above (cf. Josten 1976), but in 2.5 the focus is on the language-internal criteria. What did Schottelius assume a good language 'ought' to be like? Here we encounter the notion of linguistic analogy from Latin theoretical grammar, applied by Schottelius to a vernacular language for the first time.

2.2 WHAT IS 'THE' GERMAN LANGUAGE?

We begin by considering what Schottelius believed about the nature and origin of language, and of 'the' German language, the object of his study.

2.2.1 *'The' German language as a supraregional written language variety*

In the sixteenth century, J. C. Scaliger had set a new course for theoretical grammar in Europe. For Scaliger, the raw material of language (the 'material cause' in his terminology, applying Aristotle's *four causes* to language) consisted in its elements, which were the *sounds* pronounced, regardless of whether the words were written down or not.[2]

---

[2] Elsewhere Scaliger used *elements* and *letters* interchangeably in his work (Jensen 1990: 115–116), but the distinction between sounds and letters had already been made in antiquity, even if it was not always observed by later grammarians (Law 2003: 61).

For Scaliger, grammar was concerned only secondarily, accidentally with the written language. In seventeenth-century England, Wallis (1653)—devoting a separate treatise in his grammar to the pronunciation of the sounds of language—was in accord with this shift. Schottelius, however, gave primacy to the written language. He stipulated that the focus (*Ziel*, lit. 'goal') of his study was *die Hochteutsche Sprache [...] welche die Teutschen [...] in den Abschieden | in den Canzeleyen | Gerichten und Trükkereyen [...] gebraucht hat* ('the High German language [...] which the Germans [...] have used in decrees, in chancelleries, courts and printing-houses', *AA* 174, §7). This language was the 'actual' German language itself, *Lingua ipsa Germanica: Die Hochteutsche Sprache aber | davon wir handelen und worauff dieses Buch zielet | ist nicht ein Dialectus eigentlich| sondern Lingua ipsa Germanica* ('but the High German language which we are discussing and at which this book aims is no one actual dialect, but the German[ic] language itself', *AA* 174, § 8). Measured against the linguistic theory of Scaliger and Wallis, equating written language with the language proper like this was a step backwards. Yet for the development of a prestige German language, it was a step forwards, part of a move since the sixteenth century to identify and promote a supraregional standard German variety, *Hochteutsch* (cf. Josten 1976). As Padley put it, 'Schottel[ius]'s work ushers in a completely new sense of the language. It is now [...] a matter for the eye, so that its users end up seeing it as something quite independent of speech, with a separate existence of its own' (Padley 1985: 315). In other words, it was only by looking at the written form of the language that the speaker could achieve the distance to view the language as a separate object of study at all. It is no accident that Schottelius's analyses of internal word-structures, his lengthy word-lists, his word-games—which all served him as important demonstrations of the clarity of the language, its richness, its flexibility—are all visual.

This distancing, reifying step also made it possible to study the history of the language. The continuity between Old High German texts as the oldest attestations of *Teutsch* and the contemporary language could be demonstrated visually, by comparing surviving writings with present-day German.[3] Privileging the visual—letters rather than sounds as the elements of language—also made admissible evidence for the authentic and pure origins of German. So the first of Schottelius's criteria for the *untadelhafte Vollkommenheit* ('irreproachable perfection') of 'rootwords' in a language is *Daß sie in ihren eigenen Natürlichen | und nicht in frömbden Letteren bestehen* 'that they consist in their own Natural letters and not in foreign letters' (*AA* 51, 4:2; cf. 3.8.2). Such a claim of authenticity was more easily made on the level of the written language, about letters rather than sounds, about whose origin in one language rather than another scholars could only speculate. In contrast, it was perfectly possible to demonstrate to

---

[3] For an example see Section 2.2.4 below.

Schottelius's satisfaction that the oldest German *letters*, identified by Schottelius with the Gothic alphabet, were native to the 'Celtic-Germanic' people (cf. 2.2.3). The authenticity of German could thus be demonstrated.

Finally, for a language standardizer, the evident variation in the spoken language was an insurmountable problem. In his poetical treatise, for instance, Schottelius came to the conclusion that it was impossible to determine how words might be pronounced by speakers from Silesia and Meißen, Upper Germany, and Lower Saxony. He therefore declared that rhyming should be determined by the spelling. Any attempt to impose a spoken standard according to one's own view of correct pronunciation was doomed to failure:

> Diese Meynung ist gar grundbrüchig und hinfällig / welche hievon etzliche also haben/ daß sie hoffen dürfen/ den Thon der Teutschen Wörter nach jhrer eingebildeten oder angemasseten Ausrede zurechtfertigen oder zuverdammen.

> 'This view that several hold is quite flawed and unsound, that they permit themselves to hope to justify or to condemn the sound of German words according to their conceited or arrogant pronunciation.'

(*AA* 862)

Schottelius had some justification for his scepticism, as it would be another three centuries before Siebs produced the first codification of a standard pronunciation (Siebs 1898). The primacy Schottelius gave the written language explains the emphasis given to lists of written sources in the *AA* as the evidence base for everything he asserted about the language.

2.2.2 The 'object language' of the Ausführliche Arbeit: Haubtsprache vs Hochteutsch

Despite Schottelius's tendency to refer to the object language in the orations as the *Teutsche Haubtsprache* 'German cardinal language', it was clear to him that High German specifically was the prestige variety of German to be elaborated, that it *die jenige eintzig seyn wird / kan / und muß / darin die Grundrichtigkeit gepflantzet / kunstmessige Ausübung gesetzet / und alle wahre Zier / Kunst / Lob / Pracht und Vollkommenheit gesuchet / gefunden / behalten /' und fortgepflantzet werden muß* 'will, can and must be the one in which the fundamental correctness must be implanted, artful exercise applied, and all true adornment, art, praise, splendour and perfection be sought, found, kept and propagated' (*AA* 175, § 9). High German is for

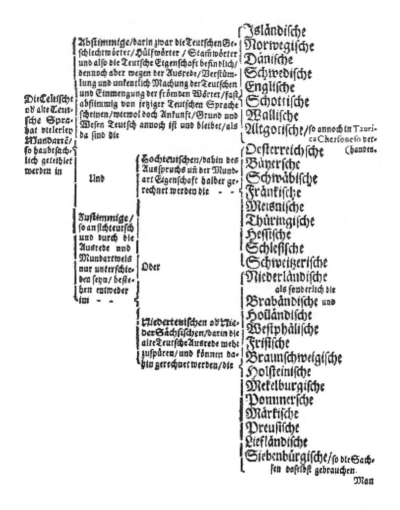

Figure 2.1a: Schottelius's sub-groupings of *Teutsch* (*AA* 154)

German what the Attic dialect was to Greek and the Roman dialect to Latin. In fact, Schottelius's term *Haubtsprache* (or *Hauptsprache* in modern spelling) is chiefly a rhetorical tool rather than a technical term.[4] The equivalent Latin terms would be *linguae matrices* 'mother or matrix

---

[4]   Jungen & Lohnstein (2007: 139–44) view the distinction *Hauptsprache* vs *Nebensprache* as a systematic distinction analogous to that of *Hauptendung* vs *Nebenendung* on the level of derivational and inflectional morphology, attributing to Schottelius a theoretical consistency across all levels of his linguistic theory. The parallel is attractive but not quite accurate.

The Celtic or old German language has many dialects, which are chiefly divided into:	More distant ones [Latin *remotiores*, German *abstimmig*, lit. deviating, non-according] languages. In these the German articles, auxiliaries, rootwords and thus the German characteristic (*Eigenschaft*) are to be found, but because of the pronunciation, because the German words have been distorted and rendered unrecognizable, and because of the mixing in of foreign words, these languages appear very deviant [*fast abstimmig [...] scheinen*] from today's German language, although the origin, foundation and essence [*Ankunft, Grund und Wesen*] is and remains German. They are:	Icelandic Norwegian Danish Swedish English Scottish Welsh Old Gothic (which still exists in the Crimea)
	and	
	Closer ones [Latin *propiores* 'closer', German *zustimmig* lit. 'conforming, agreeing'], which are German in themselves [*an sich teutsch*] and which are distinguished only by their pronunciation and dialectally [*mundartweis*]. They consist either of:	High German ones, to which are reckoned, because of their pronunciation and characteristic of the dialect: or	Austrian Bavarian Swabian Frankish Meissenish Thuringian Hessenish Silesian Swiss
		Low German or Low Saxon ones, in which the old German pronunciation is more detectable. To these can be reckoned:	Netherlandish, in particular Brabantish and Hollandish Westphalian Frisian Brunswickish Holsteinish Mecklenburgish Pommeranian Markish Prussian Lieflandish Transylvanian [in Romania], which the Saxons use there.

Figure 2.1b: Schottelius's sub-groupings of *Teutsch* (*AA* 154), in translation

languages' (which occurs three times (*AA* 52, 4: 6, 143, 9: 17 and 151, 10: 6), and *lingua cardinalis*, which originated with Dante Alighieri (1265–1321), but which does not occur in the orations at all. From the occurrences of *linguae matrices*, it is evident that they are only those languages which arose at Babel after the confusion of the *lingua primaeva*. This would include Latin but not, say, its later spin-offs French and Italian. Now, the German term *Haubtsprache* could carry the same sense. In the third oration (*AA* 30, 3: 5), Schottelius cited Philip Cluverius's (1580–1623) view that Hebrew's origins did not pre-date Babel, but that it arose there *neben allen andern jetz bekantlichen Haubtsprachen* 'alongside all other cardinal languages now known'. Yet in the vast majority of instances Schottelius did not use

Haubtsprache is this technical sense. Though very frequent (see Barbarić 1981: 28–31 for a list of occurrences), it is nearly always used *only* of German, and carries an ideology, as Barbarić (1981: 34) noted. On the very title page, the Latin simply refers to *lingua germanica*, but the German term *Teutsche Haubtsprache* makes a stronger assertion of its place amongst the languages of the world (and likewise in the titles of the orations in Book I). In the main text of the orations itself, *unsere Haubtsprache* is used not just in contexts emphasizing the age of the language (*AA* 4, 1: 10; 16, 2: 1; 21, 2: 23; 32, 3: 9; 123, 8: 2; 137, 9: 3; 166, 10: 19), but also the language's capacity and richness (*AA* 2, 1: 2; 11, 1: 33; 74, 6: 4; 94, 6: 39; 97, 6: 53; 117, 7: 34; 125, 8: 4; 146, 9: 25), its might (4, 1: 9; 97, 6: 52), artfulness (74, 5: 5; 94, 6: 40; 97, 6: 53; 112, 7: 20; 146, 9: 26), or naturalness (16, 2: 2) (other occurrences: 74, 6: 4; 112, 7: 20). We do well to remember that in the orations—rhetorical pieces—Schottelius uses language as a cultural patriot first, and as a tidy exponent of linguistic theory second.

2.2.3 *The ancestry of German*

Schottelius's view of the origin of linguistic diversity drew together two discourse traditions. The first was the learned, Latinate tradition of European scholarship that examined languages, assuming their starting point to be the confusion of tongues at Babel. The second discourse tradition, building on the first and developing over the century and a half or so before the date of the *AA*, was the pan-Germanic cultural patriotic tradition, concerned with the status of German alongside other languages. At the same time, the views that Schottelius and his contemporaries held of the origin of language at Babel really continued a more or less unbroken tradition from the Church Fathers, through the Middle Ages and onwards, which assumed the existence of 72 languages, the same as the number of peoples that arose after Noah's descendants spread out over the earth (Genesis 10). Schottelius himself opted for the variant tradition that arrived at a total of 69 languages (*AA* 34, 3: 13).[5] The cultural patriotic discourse of late humanist writers had simply built on the as yet unquestioned assumption that linguistic diversity had its origin at Babel. Scholars of

---

[5] The actual number of tribes listed in the Bible here does not add up to 72, and the total number of languages arrived at by various commentators varied: sometimes it was found to be 69, 75 or 76. The idea of a total of 72 languages in the world came under increasing pressure in the Renaissance, as Europeans came into contact with non-European languages. Conrad Gessner included information about over 120 languages in his *Mithridates* of 1555, but reconciled this multiplicity with the required total of 72 by considering the possibility of treating some languages as dialects of others. Indeed, the perceived need to limit the number of post-Babel languages to 72 was one of the factors that encouraged scholars to group languages into families descended from a common ancestor. See Borst (1995 [1960]) for exhaustive documentation of how successive generations of scholars interpreted the Babel story, or, for an overview, Jones (2001).

the Germanic languages were keen to show the ancient origins of their language, taking antiquity and originality as a measure of its worth, just as speakers of Romance languages could already claim their roots in the prestigious Latin. A favoured line of argument was to assert that one's own vernacular could be traced back to Babel, as Joannes Goropius Becanus (1519–1572) sought to do for Flemish, and Georg Stiernhielm (1598-1672) for Swedish (1671). Schottelius took the same view about the ancestral German language (which he called by various names: *T(h)eutisca* or *Germanica, Celtisch oder Teutsch*; others called it *Scythica* or *Cimbrica*).[6]

Like his contemporaries, Schottelius assumed that the spread of a language was tied to the movements of people, and so he traced the ancestry both of German and of its speakers in Europe back to Adam, through Noah and his descendants. Ascenas, Noah's great-grandson (through Japhet and Gomer) *hat mit sich die alte Celtische oder Teutsche Sprache von Babel gebracht* 'brought with him the ancient Celtic or German language' (*AA* 34, 3: 14). From the *alte Teutsche Sprache* were derived two groups of languages: those that were *an sich teutsch* 'actually German' (*AA* 154, 10: Table; Figure 2.1), and those more remote from present-day German. The latter were the North Germanic languages, Gothic, and English, Scottish and Welsh (!). The former, 'actually German', Schottelius further divided into High and Low German.[7] The list of Low German dialects included Dutch.[8]

If Books II to V of Schottelius's *AA*—despite the title referring to the *Teutsche[n] HaubtSprache* 'the German cardinal language'—really dealt with High German alone, much of Book I took a wider view. On the one hand, Schottelius emphasized the unchanging essence of German over time, talking of a *Teutsche[n] SprachNatur* (*AA* 16, 2: 2), and the titles of all ten

---

[6] For instance, in the same year that Schottelius published his *AA*, the Dane Peder Syv (1631–1702) published his treatise *Om det Cimbriske Sprog* 'About the Cimbric language' (1663 [1979]). (The name *Cimbri* had been used by classical sources to refer to a people of Northern Germania, in Holstein, Silesia and Jutland.) Comparing Syv's treatise with Schottelius's work is instructive. Without apparently having had access to Schottelius's works (but referencing Harsdörffer's *Specimen Philologiae Germanicae* (1646) instead, cf. 7.8.1), Syv cited the same battery of authorities as Schottelius, including Becanus, Stevin, Lazius, Lipsius, Wormius, etc., in order to advance very similar cultural-patriotic arguments. On Scythian, see van Hal (2010), Considine (2010).

[7] A similar list presented by Hieronymus Megiser (1553–1618) in his *Thesaurus Polyglottus* of 1603 (fol.)(8ʳ; cf. Jones 1999: 18–19) also implicitly recognized a Germanic language family. Headed *Germanica lingua, seu, Teutonica vel Alemannica*, it began with *Germanica vel Teutonica antiqua seu prisca*, followed by Swiss, then a number of other German dialects (both lower and upper German, not distinguished), *Saxonica seu Germaniae inferioris* (which subsumed the Dutch and Flemish dialects, as well as Frisian), followed by Danish, Swedish, Gothic, Norwegian, Icelandic, English, Scottish, and *Rotwelsch* or thieves' cant, and the dialect of the enclave Gotttschee / Kočevje.

[8] It was clear to Schottelius that a language variety might be both a dialect of some ancestral language, and a language in its own right.

orations include *von der Uhralten HaubtSprache der Teutschen* 'of the ancient cardinal language of the Germans', implying that the language he described was the best manifestation of that ancient language. On the other hand, Schottelius needed to acknowledge Dutch and others as descendants of the same ancestral language, which meant making the German of his era just one of many descendants too. The paradox is well-caught in *AA* 29–30, (cf. Gardt 1994: 36–39), where the German of Schottelius's current day is both the *same* as *die alte Teutsche*, and her *beliebteste natürliche Tochter* 'favourite natural daughter'. The reason for such double-thinking is simple. Scholars from the various Germanic-speaking countries borrowed from each other their evidence and lines of arguments about the primacy of 'their' language. Recognizing that their particular vernacular was one of a number of modern-day variants of the ancestral language meant that arguments presented on behalf of, say, Dutch or its ancestral language could apply equally to German, at times by dint of some sleight of hand. A telling case is Goropius Becanus's remark that it was right to have respect for the mother tongue *apud te*, and, later, that the *cimbrica lingua* 'Cimbric' should be valued for the elaboration which it had undergone to perfect it. Now, Becanus explicitly *excluded* the southern (High) German dialects from the *cimbrica lingua* (Dibbets 1992: 21–22). However, Schottelius disregarded these specifics. In his German rendering of Becanus's Latin, *apud te* became more narrowly *du Teutscher*, and the narrower *cimbrica lingua* became the all-embracing *Uhralte Teutsche Sprache* (*AA* 18, 2: 14). Later in the oration, Schottelius likewise silently altered Becanus's references to *lingua nostra* and *sermoni nostro vernaculo* ('our language', 'our vernacular tongue') into the more explicit *unsere[r] Teutsche[n] Sprache* 'our German language' (*AA* 26, 2: 41). Similarly, Schottelius had no qualms about taking the Dutchman Petrus Scriverius's (1576–1660) reference to the *Princes van alle talen* 'princess of all languages' as being 'von der Teutschen Sprache' (*AA* 22, 2: 26), even though the original context suggests Scriverius had the language of Holland specifically in mind (cf. McLelland 2003). In short, the precise details of 'the' German language presented by Schottelius the linguistic scholar are inseparable from the strategies of Schottelius the rhetorician.

Appealing to a common ancestral language for the likes of Dutch and High German was fair enough. Justifiable only as rhetorical strategy is the way Schottelius drew loose equivalences between the different, partly competing notions of the ancestral language in circulation at the time. His preferred term for the ancestor of German was the *alte Teutsche Sprache* which might alternatively be called *Celtisch* (*Germanica* or *Teutonica* in Latin; cf. Figure 2.1, *AA* 154; also 151, 10: 9). But he also embraced further equivalences made by other authors such as Adriaan van Schrieck, who saw Etruscan as *Japhetica sive Celtica* (cited *AA* 42, 3: 30), or referred to the *linguam ... Celticam, sive Teutonicam, sive Scythicam sive Belgicam (quae una est)* 'the Japhetic or Celtic language', or 'the Celtic, or Teutonic, or Scythian or Belgian language, which is all one' (cited *AA* 19, 2:17); and Becanus with his *Scytismum/ wie ers nennet/ oder die alte Teutsche oder Cymbrische Sprache* 'the Scythic, as he calls it, or the ancient German or Cimbrian language' (*AA* 30, 3: 5). Schottelius was thus able to situate *Teutsch* in a network of equivalences, over time and space: *Teutsch* = (can be traced back to) Japhetic = Scythian = Cimbrian = Celtic = Teutonic = ancient *Teutsch/ vetus germanica.*

Such equivalences drawn between these labels for language varieties allowed Schottelius to argue for the antiquity of German letters, which was important for setting German alongside the prestigious triumvirate of Latin, Greek and Hebrew, each with their own scripts, by appropriating the Gothic alphabet. (Conveniently, the Gothic alphabet had already been declared the oldest, God-given one by a certain Salicaeus, Bishop of Toledo, in a passage cited by Duret (1619: 890).[9]

Over the course of several paragraphs, Schottelius constructs a loose equivalence of Gothic–Celtic–German. It begins, *Daß aber die Gotische Sprache eben diese/ welche man die Teutsche nennet/ im Grunde gewesen sey/ ist gar gewiß* 'But it is quite certain that the Gothic language was basically the one which one calls German' (*AA* 54, 4: 11). That is, Gothic can be seen as *Teutsch.*

The second step was to equate Celtic and *Teutsch*, which was already not uncommon (see Jones 1999: 12ff.).[10] Schottelius himself later cited Adriaan van Schriek's mention of *Celtica seu Teutonica* (*AA* 126, 8: 6). Yet the equivalence was not as uncontroversial as Schottelius would have us believe. Schottelius cited Claude Duret's (1565–1611) observation that some considered Gothic to have been *du tout semblable à la langue des Celtes; Autres affirment, que c'estoit la mesme langue Theutonique* ('entirely similar to the language of the Celts; others affirm that it was the same Teutonic language' Duret 1613, as cited *AA* 54, 4: 11), where it is clear that Duret offered the Celtic or Teutonic origin as two *alternative* explanations—for

---

[9]   See Brough (1985: 65, 90). Note that the reference is to the Gothic alphabet proper, and not to the black type letters in which German was printed at this time, often called Gothic type. It is not clear to me whether Schottelius realized that the two were very different.

[10] Bonfante (1953: 689) credited Abraham Mylius (1563–1637) with the first systematic demonstration that Germanic and Celtic might belong to the same language family, in his *Lingua Belgica* (1612), though Becanus (1569) and others had suggested a kinship between Gallic and Germanic in the sixteenth century, while Guillaume Postel (1510–1581) and others again had likewise already made connections between Gallic and Greek. Metcalf (1974) considered the uncertainty over the status of Celtic which he found in Jäger (1686)—where Celtic is portrayed sometimes as an ancestor of all later European languages, especially of Germanic, and sometimes as a descendant of the ancestral language—as symptomatic of the era. See also Metcalf (1953b) and Schaeffer (1983) on Schottelius's perception of German in relation to other European languages.

him at least *Teutsch* and Celtic were distinct. Yet Schottelius wilfully interpreted them as two versions of the *same* claim. Similarly Schottelius downplayed Tacitus's report (in his *Germania*, 19) that the *Teutschen* were ignorant of writing, by instead foregrounding the oral learning of the (Celtic) druids, whose name *kommt von einem Teutschen uhralten Stammworte* 'comes from an ancient German rootword' (*AA* 56, 4: 16). Once claimed as *Teutsch*, these Celts' learning could compensate for the lack of written learning amongst the early *Teutsch* attested by Tacitus. The letters of Gothic—'basically German' for Schottelius, as we saw above— were then also equated with Celtic, in accordance with the view of the Icelander Arngrímur Jónsson (1569–1648), who referred to *[linguam] antiquam Gothicam seu Celticam* 'the ancient Gothic or Celtic language' cited (*AA* 57, 4: 20). Ultimately Schottelius drew this three-way equivalence together in the claim:

> Es sind aber die uhralten Teutische oder Celtische oder Gotische Buchstaben oder Letteren / was die itzige ausgeübte Teutsche Sprache antrift/ in dieselbe bekante / angenehme und schikliche Form/ darin sie überall gemein und bekand/ endlich gerahten.

> 'But the ancient German or Celtic or Gothic letters, as far as the German language practised today is concerned, finally ended up in the same familiar, pleasing and fitting form in which they are commonly known everywhere.'

> (*AA* 56, 4: 17)

Now, Schottelius had in fact presented evidence of early *Gothic* letters only (not of Celtic or of *Teutsch* in the narrower sense). He also had evidence of Celtic oral learning. He could only claim the prestige value of both of these for *Teutsch* by setting up the crucial 'Gothic = *Teutsch* = Celtic' equivalence. Yet Celtic is in fact for Schottelius the *ancestor* of *Teutsch*; the Germans are the *pars maxima* of the Celts (*AA* 151, 10: 9); *Teutsch* is the *vornehmste Dialectus von der alten Celtischen oder Japhetischen Sprache* ('the foremost dialect of the old Celtic or Japhetic language', *AA* 151, 10:10). Celtic is an ancient version of *Teutsch, welche vor ein/ zwei / dreitausend Jahren Celtisch geheissen hat* 'which was called Celtic one, two, three thousand years ago' (*AA* 42; 3: 38). That is, Celtic is the hypernym, *Teutsch* the hyponym; Gothic is in turn subordinate to *Teutsch*, just one manifestation of it, as indeed is *Hochteutsch* itself. Yet these vague equivalences—Celtic is a parent of *Teutsch*, Gothic is *im Grunde Teutsch* 'basically German'—are glossed over by the rhetorical sleight of hand in the words *die uhralten Teutische oder Celtische oder Gotische Buchstaben oder Letteren*, with the *oder* 'or' suggesting linked synonyms.

2.2.4 *How and why has German changed over time?*

When seeking to explain language change, Schottelius rehearsed the commonplace explanations of his era: the passage of time, the mixing of peoples, and neglect by the speakers (*AA* 166, 10: 20–21); but in practice, he was ambivalent about acknowledging evidence of language change in German. He maintained that German had remained the same 'in essence' since the time of the Greeks and Romans: its rootwords, inflectional and derivational endings remained, as did the processes for compounding, and *nach dem Grunde* ('in its fundament, basically', *AA* 42, 3: 38), the language was the same as it had been two to three thousand years ago. At the same time, Schottelius's remarks on Low German and High German dialect in the tenth oration show that Schottelius was certainly aware of High German *s, tz, zz* as a development from Low German *t* (*AA* 157, 690), although there is no sign that he was aware of the parallel $d > t$ development (Watts 2001, Francis 2003).[11] Rather, Schottelius seemed conscious only of loose variation between *d* and *t*, without assigning any specific geographical significance to it (*AA* 152, 10: 10; *AA* 155, 10: 13, see also *AA* Book II, 207, § 28, 217, § 41).

Perhaps inspired by Hesiod's (ca. 700 B.C.) well-known five ages of man (golden, silver, bronze, heroic and iron ages), Schottelius presented the first ever periodization of German language history, dividing it into five eras, a periodization largely adopted by Reimmann (1709) (Jones 2001: 1110): 1. the epoch before Charlemagne; 2. beginning with Charlemagne, 3. beginning with Rudolf I (ruled 1273–1291); 4. beginning with Luther. Finally, the fifth and final epoch should begin in the current era, *if* German were properly purified, cultivated and codified. Schottelius was able to illustrate changes in German by comparing passages from Old High German texts, made accessible thanks to the editors amongst sixteenth-century German humanist cultural patriots (Moulin-Fankhänel 1997a; cf. 6.2), with contemporary forms, comparing the *heutige völlige Ausrede* ('today's complete pronunciation') of words with *jhre rechte Wurtzel* ('their proper root') (*AA* 43–44, 3: 42–43). For instance, Schottelius compared an extract from Otfrid (9th C) with its modern-day translation:

Allo ziti thio tho sin	Allezeit die da sein
Kristus jo komo tha[z][12] muat sin/	Christus ja komme in den Muht sein
Bimide ouch alla pina /	Vermeide auch alle Pein
GOtt fruue Sela sina.	GOtt erfreu die Seele seyn/

---

[11] Both consonant changes are part of the same 'High German' sound shift which took place (very roughly indeed) around 500 A.D. See e.g. McMahon (1994: 227) for a basic summary.

[12] Schottelius's text reads *thag* here for *thaz*.

'All times that are/ Christ may come into his mind/ Avoid all pain/ May God fill your soul with joy'

Schottelius was, then, on the cusp of a change in thinking about language. On the one hand, his view of language (and of German) was basically ahistoric: linguistic diversity arose at Babel; German is and remains the same through the centuries ever since. At the same time, however, Schottelius was aware of changes in the language. He resolved this contradiction by allowing for some inner, unreachable linguistic essence which remained the same across time, despite superficial changes. It is this very essence that defines German. Schottelius's analogy of the language tree helps here (2.4). Even as new branches and twigs grow, and as old ones die off, the tree changes above ground, but its roots remain, and it is still the same tree. Schottelius did not, in fact, spell out this aspect of the tree analogy so explicitly, but the point is nonetheless valid.

2.3 LANGUAGE, MEANING, AND THE 'NATURE' OF THE GERMAN LANGUAGE

2.3.1 *The German* SprachNatur *'linguistic nature' (AA 16, 2: 2)*

What, then, was the unchanging, ahistoric essence that characterized German? In Schottelius's view, the special nature of German lay in the way that it permitted a particularly strong link between the linguistic signs—i.e. German letters and words—and the world. The mere existence of this specifically German quality helped make German and Germany what they were.[13] For the language was equated with the people, an equation already evident in the assumption that if certain people (Ascenas and his forefathers, as the ancestors of the Germans) could be shown to have come from Babel, then so did the language. By the same token, if the language was praiseworthy and in good health, so too, by extension were its speakers and their state.[14] As the Acclamation of peace made plain (1.4.3), a healthy language was equated with a strong and peaceful state. The influence worked in both directions, though. If the language was threatened and diseased (because of neglect, or because of too many foreign influences, the concern of the ninth oration), so too the strength of the state and the morality of the German people was at risk.

If the seventeenth century was a highpoint of such equations between language and other external values and entities for patriotic ends, there was also a tendency to mystify the inner essence of the language, a continuation of a current of Protestant thinking about language expressed authoritatively

---

[13] For Schottelius's place in the history of reflections about a specifically German linguistic spirit or *Sprachgeist*, cf. Schlaps (2000: 310–13; 2004) and see 7.4.2.

[14] Cf. Gardt (2000: 248), Stukenbrock (2005: 436–37) for such loose equivalences as a characteristic of linguistic patriotism.

by Martin Luther.[15] Schottelius cited Luther as an authority for the special capacity of German words to express meanings and feelings better than other languages:

> Lutherus sagt von dem Wort **Liebe** also: Jch weis nicht / ob man auch das Wort **Liebe** so hertzlich und gnugsam in Lateinischer / oder einiger anderen Sprache reden müchte / daß also dringe und klinge in das Hertze / und durch alle Sinne / wie es thut in Teutscher Sprache / Tom.5. pag.142. Und solche Kunst stekket durch und durch in den Teutschen Wörteren / welche aus denen / also von der innersten Natur und unseren Vorfahren geordneten Letteren / so lebhaftiglich geboren werden.

> 'Luther says of the word *Liebe* 'love': I do not know if one can express the word love as heartfelt and as adequately in Latin or in any other language, such that it penetrates and resonates in the heart and through all the senses as it does in German. Vol. 5 p. 142. And such art runs through and through in the German words that are born so full of life from the letters ordered by innermost nature and by our ancestors.'

> (*AA* 60, 4: 26)

Valentin Ickelsamer (1534), an early codifier of German spelling, had likewise written that every word in German had *seinen Namen von seinem Ambte / aus einer sonderlichen Geheimniß und Bedeutung* 'its name from its office, from a peculiar mystery and significance' (as cited by Schottelius *AA* 60, 4: 30, slightly deviating from the edition in Müller 1872 [1969]: 148–49). Such mystic tendencies found more extreme expression in the early decades of the seventeenth century in the writings of Jakob Böhme, but Schottelius's belief in the power of German was not esoteric like Böhme's. Nevertheless, he shared with the Nuremberg circle of poets (members of the *Pegnesischer Blumenorden* language society) a belief in the power of German sounds to achieve phonaesthetic effects, and so to convey meanings more fully than other languages could. The pronunciation and sound of German (*Ausrede* and *Geschall*, *AA* 60, 4: 28) were, he believed, formed *nach Geheiß der innersten Eigenschaft* 'according to the dictate of the innermost quality' [of the referent], and so German exceeded Latin and Greek in its *naturmessiger Vorstellung* 'natural representation'. The question of the essence of German was thus a re-statement of the perennial question of the relationship between language, meaning and reality.

---

[15] Despite the mystic tendency of such remarks, Luther and his followers themselves were careful to distance themselves from the outright mysticism of those they called the *Schwärmer*. Cf. Haas (1997).

2.3.2. *The problem of language and meaning*

> *Es ist eine alte Streit Frage | Ob die Wörter von Natur oder Kur | oder | ob sie wilkührlich oder natürlich weren | jhrem Uhrsprunge nach.*

'It is an ancient debate whether words are, in their origin, by nature or by choice, arbitrary or natural.' (*AA* 64, 4: 40)

Discussion amongst philosophers and language scholars about how and why words convey meaning in language (by nature, or by mere convention) can be traced back to Plato's Cratylos dialogue, where the question received thorough and nuanced discussion (cf. Joseph 2000; cf. also Gardt 1994: 44–51, and 51–68 for an overview of attitudes to the possible linguistic naturalness of words). Do words convey their meaning by their nature (*physei*) or merely by convention (*thesei*)? A common answer over the centuries has been a partial 'yes' to the *physei* view. Words originally conveyed meaning naturally, either because language was given by God, or by a first namegiver; or (to give a rationalist, eighteenth-century answer) because the first language began as a natural expression of emotion, or exertion; or because language (or a subset of language) began as the imitation of sounds found in nature. Nowadays, however, the argument would run, only a small portion of words still preserved this natural affinity to meaning, in onomatopoeia. However, Schottelius considered that German was a special case. Its natural affinity to meaning was founded on more than onomatopoeic effects, though he did cite them as examples of the perfect harmony between words and meanings (e.g. *Wasser fliessen | gesäusel | sanft | stille | zc. wie künstlich ist es | wie gleichsam wesentlich fleust das Wasser mit stillem Gesäusel von unser Zungen?* 'Wasser, fliessen, gesäusel, sanft, stille, zc [Water, flow, murmuring, soft, silent, etc.] how artful it is, how essentially, as it were, flows the water with the silent rushing from our tongue?' *AA* 59, 4: 26). German's natural affinity with reality was also dependent on more general synaesthetic effects which Schottelius found in words like *Blitz* 'lightning', but also *stille* 'silent', and *lieblich* 'charming'. Schottelius shared this view with the German seventeenth-century mainstream: Ratke, Zesen, Klaj, Harsdörffer and Johann Heinrich Schill (1615?–1645) all took a similar view, as examples given by Gardt (1994: 51–64) illustrate. Schottelius attributed the particular strength of these onomatopoeic and synaesthetic effects in German to the special character of the German 'letters' (here—as generally amongst German writers of this era—still conflated with sounds). This was why it was so important to Schottelius to establish that the German alphabet was German in origin, and not borrowed from elsewhere (cf. 2.2.1).

Beyond the level of the letter, German words were, Schottelius believed, also naturally linked to meaning, first thanks to the stock of monosyllabic rootwords, which express the basic concepts of thought concisely and swiftly, and second thanks to the ways in which these rootwords combined in compounding and derivation, yielding meanings which were transparently based on the rootwords of which they were composed. Schottelius gave a detailed demonstration of this advantage, in the capacity to form compounds and derivates to name not just the principal colours, but all the many shades in between, such as *Wachsgelb, Saffrangelb* 'wax yellow, saffron yellow' (*AA* 82–84, 6: 23; cf. Jones 2003).[16]

Where German could use a single compound word, Latin often required a whole phrase (*AA* 80–81, 6: 21), proof that German was best able to describe the world succinctly. For Schottelius the power of the rootword was therefore (on his terms) factual and scientific evidence for, and the incontrovertible explanation of, the superiority of German over other languages.

In sum, at three separate 'levels of the language' (though those are not the terms in which Schottelius discussed the matter), Schottelius found in German guarantees of the intimate link between language and nature (see Table 2.1): It is significant that Schottelius made no claim at all for the next level up of the language: there is no suggestion that the way that words combine in German *sentences* expressed thought more truly or more clearly, in the way that the contemporary Port-Royal grammarians (1660) imagined a relationship between thought-propositions and syntax. Nor was Schottelius troubled by whether words expressed reality, or (merely) our thoughts, our conception of reality. Later in the seventeenth century, John Locke's *Essay Concerning Human Understanding* (1690) made an important distinction

Table 2.1: Language and nature in German, according to Schottelius

Level of language	Guarantees natural expression of meaning because …	The advantage of German over other languages
Letters (and their sounds)	Letters express natural meaning by synaesthesia or onomatopoeia	The letters with this capacity are authentically German in origin
Rootwords	Plentiful monosyllabic rootwords are ideal to convey our thoughts, *kurz und schnell* 'concisely and swiftly' (*AA* 61, 4: 32)	The abundance of monosyllabic rootwords is unique to German
Word-formation: compounds and derivation	Combinations of rootwords make it easy to coin new words transparently	German can easily coin new words as needed, drawing on its own resources

[16] Hundsnurscher (1986: 313) is critical of the 'ultimately unsemantic thinking' behind Schottelius's assumption of transparency in all German compounds, still rehearsed today. Hundsnurscher argues that the meaning of a word like *Ungehörsamkeit* 'disobedience' can hardly be readily deduced from the sum of its parts as Schottelius claimed (*AA* 90–91), though Schottelius would arguably have disagreed. See his analysis of that example, cited in 7.7.

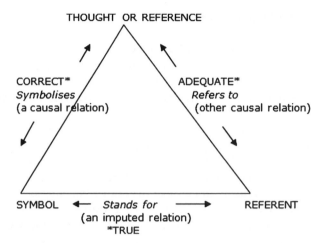

THOUGHT OR REFERENCE

CORRECT*
Symbolises
(a causal relation)

ADEQUATE*
Refers to
(other causal relation)

SYMBOL ◄— *Stands for* ——► REFERENT
(an imputed relation)
*TRUE

Figure 2.2: The Semiotic Triangle (or Semantic Triangle). Adapte from Ogden & Richards
(1923: 11)

between the real essences of things and the appearance of them in the mind,
their merely 'nominal', apparent essence. According to Locke, the two were
often at odds.[17] Schottelius, however, was a Neostoicist. He believed that
nature was rational; so too was the human mind. Since both nature and the
human mind had the same rational and natural basis, Schottelius could talk
in the same breath of *natürliche[r] Verstand* and *verständliche Natur*
('natural reason/understanding' and 'reasonable/comprehensible nature'
AA 16, 2: 2). There was no danger of a conflict between the two. In the
classic semiotic triangle of Ogden & Richards (1923; cf. Figure 2.2), the
relation between the 'thought' and the 'referent' remained entirely
unproblematic, for the two were equated with each other.

Schottelius's confidence in words put his theory of language at odds not
just with Locke, but also with universalists whose desire to develop an
artificial language was motivated by a concern that the categories and
symbols of natural languages did not accord perfectly (in an unambiguous
one-to-one way) with the world. Schottelius simply did not see any such
problems with meaning and language at all. Whilst assuming a considerable
degree of naturalness in the word-thing correspondences of German, he
also recognized the potential to ascribe meanings by pure convention, as in
the case of a white flag for surrender (*AA* 1105). Indeed, Schottelius
delighted in the scope offered by emblematics and language games for
creating new and additional links between linguistic signs and meanings: in
number and letter substitution riddles, in mottoes, symbols and analogies
(see 3.7). Schottelius was a practical linguist, rather than a philosopher.

---

[17] See Padley (1976: 132–53) for the problem of the relationship between words and things in
Locke and elsewhere in English philosophy.

2.4 Imagining language: banyans and buildings[18]

Die Wörter aber machen ja die Sprache

'But words make the language.' (*AA* 42, 3: 38)

We have just noted that the guarantees of natural and perfect expression of reality that Schottelius found in German stopped at the level of the word, and he made no claims at all about German word order. For him, *words* made the language, as the citation above states. More particularly, monosyllabic rootwords were the building blocks of language. While it was a matter of pride and of principle that these rootwords were themselves composed of authentically German letters, the rootwords, and not the letters, were Schottelius's basic unit of analysis (3.8.2). They formed the starting point for Schottelius's grammatical theory, and (less successfully) for his poetics and prosody (5.5.2–3; 4.5.3).

Before Schottelius could analyse language, however, he faced the considerable challenge—as the first major theorist of German grammar—of inventing a theoretical framework with which to talk about it. In essence, he had to find a way to imagine, to visualize 'the' German language. He did so with the help of two overlapping and even partially contradictory analogies: the tree and the building, images of nature and art that are already intertwined in the iconography of the title page (cf. 1.4.3). These metaphors affected how his theory developed.[19]

2.4.1 The language as a banyan tree

Schottelius had encountered the concept of *grondwoorden*, lit. 'foundation words'—monosyllabic original words from which new words could be formed—in Stevin's work (cf. 3.4, 3.8.2), but he re-cast the imagery into that of the rootword (*Wurzelwort* or *Stammwort*) as part of a wider language-tree analogy.[20]

Wurzelwort—which translates literally as 'rootword'—occurs only occasionally in the *AA,* while *Stammwort*, Schottelius's usual term, literally

---

[18] Parts of this section appeared in McLelland (2002).

[19] On the importance of such cognitive metaphors in shaping our thinking, see the seminal work of Lakoff & Johnson (1980). A recent study of metaphor in German linguistic discourse is Stukenbrock 2005; see also Marras (1999). On the metaphor of living things to conceptualize language, see Haas (1956–57).

[20] The term *Stammwort* was very possibly borrowed from Gueintz, who used it once (Barbarić 1981: 1208–9). Barbarić also notes the less frequent alternatives in Schottelius: *Wurtzel* and—least frequent of all—*Stamm. Wurtzel* had been used by Sebastian Helber in his *Teutsches Syllabierbüchlein* (1593) (Barbarić 1981: 1209). Stevin wrote of monosyllabic *grontwoorden, grontnamen.* The arts (*de consten*) need a firm foundation in the shape of those 'base-words', *een vasten gront* (Stevin 1608). For Schottelius, *Grundwort* was more narrowly the term for a base rootword to which affixes can be added.

means 'stem-word'. German *Stamm* 'stem' is far richer in connotations than *Wurzel* 'root': *Stamm* can mean not just a stem or trunk, but also a tribe, with connotations of a shared lineage; it also has connotations of sturdiness, strength and reliability that are reflected in the modern German *stämmig* 'sturdy, stocky'. Though we need to bear these connotations in mind, I have translated *Stammwort* throughout this book with 'rootword', as a more familiar term in English than 'stem-word'. In any case, Schottelius's imagery for the German language seems to blur the distinction between roots and stems or trunks, for he seems to visualize it as a banyan tree. The language tree, which must be cared for by careful pruning and grafting, was an image that already had a long tradition in Renaissance thinking about the vernaculars (going back to Speroni 1542; cf. Entner 1984: 52). The image of the banyan tree is Schottelius's innovation, however, and is most fully developed in the *AA* in two passages (*AA*: 50, 4: 1; 68–70, 5: 6–7), reproduced here:

> Also einer jeglichen Sprache Kunstgebäu bestehet gründlich in jhren uhrsprünglichen natürlichen **Stammwörteren**: welche als stets saftvolle Wurzelen den gantzen Sprachbaum durchfeuchten / dessen Spröslein / Ast= und Aderreiche Zweige in schönester Reinligkeit / steter Gewisheit und unergründender Mannigfaltigkeit / reumiglich und hoch ausbreiten lassen. Nach dem auch eine Sprache an solchen Stammwörteren kräftig und Wurtzelreich ist / kan sie auch schöne / herrliche und vielfältige Früchte geben; nicht anders wie ein Baum / nach dem saftigen Stande seiner ausgebreiteten Wurtzelen die Früchte reich= oder kärglich wachsen lässet.

> 'So the artful/skilful construction of every language consists in its original, natural rootwords, which, as ever sap-rich roots, give moisture to the whole tree, and allow its shoots, branch- and vein-rich boughs to spread out spaciously and high in most beautiful purity, in constant certainty and infinite multiplicity. When a language is strong in such stemwords [rootwords], and is root-rich, it can also bear beautiful, splendid and manifold fruits, just like a tree, which bears abundant or meagre fruit according to how the sap fills the outstretched roots.'

(*AA* 50, 4: 1)[21]

> Gleich wie aber unsere Teutsche Letteren und die Teutsche Stammwörter einsilbig / festes Grundes / reines Ursprunges / und

---

[21] This passage has marked similarities to a passage in Schottelius's 1640 critique of Gueintz's grammar (cited in 3.8.2).

eines lieblichen Geläutes sind: Also sind gleicher weise an diesem Sprachbaume die ausgewachsene Rieser und Nebenspröslein / die durch und durch in dem gantzen Baume von oben bis unten nebenwachsen / nebenstehen / und durch solchen jhren Neben = oder Beystand / eine absonderliche schöne Gestalt und Wirkung / dem / dabey sie stehen / geben / einsilbig oder einlautend. Solche Neben = Spröslein oder Neben = wörter sind entweder in Teutscher Sprache die zufälligen Endungen / als: e / em / en / es / et / er / est / ete / etest / etet / ere / erer / erest / erster / erstes / erstem / ersten / este / ester / estes / estem / esten / [...]

[§]7. Oder aber es sind die Hauptendungen der abgeleiteten: daheraus in der Teutschen Sprache entstehet die Ableitung. An der Zahl sind solcher Haubtendungen drey und zwanzig / als: Bar / e / ey / el / er / ern / en / haft / heit / icht / ig / inn / isch / keit / lich / ling / lein / niß / sal / sam / schaft / tuhm / ung.

'Just as our German letters and the German rootwords are monosyllabic, of a firm foundation, of pure origin and of a charming sound, so in the same way on this language tree are the grown twigs and side-shoots, which grow alongside in the whole tree [though *nebenwachsen* and *nebenstehen* might simply be intended to mean: 'are subsidiary to the trunk'], through and through, from above to below, standing alongside, and which, by this their standing or support alongside, monosyllabic, give a particular, beautiful form and effect to that which they support. Such off-shoots or affix-words [lit. 'alongside-words'] are in German either the inflectional [lit. the coincidental] endings, namely e / em / en / es / et / er / est / ete / etest / etet / ere / erer / erest / erster / erstes / erstem / ersten / este / ester / estes / estem / esten /. [...]

[§]7. Or they are the main endings of the derived [words]: out of these, derivation arises in German. Such main endings are twenty-three in number, as Bar / e / ey / el / er / ern/ en / haft / heit / icht / ig / inn / isch / keit / lich / ling / lein / niß / sal / sam / schaft / tuhm / ung.'

(*AA* 68–69, 5: 6–7)

The second passage strongly suggests that the imagined German language tree is a banyan tree, or Indian fig-tree, which spreads by means of aerial roots that descend from branches to stand alongside the trunk and ultimately become indistinguishable from trunks (as Barbarić 1981: 1181–

82 suggested, and despite Gützlaff's scepticism 1989a: 68 ff.).[22] Viswanathan (1968) suggested that Milton, who also described an Indian fig-tree with wonder in his 1667 *Paradise Lost* (IX, 1095, 1101–1111), might have read about it in East India Company sources published in the 1590s. Evidently the image of the tree, already described in Pliny's natural history (xi.5), enjoyed renewed currency in the seventeenth century, and perhaps (to judge by Milton and Schottelius) in particular as a sign of God's marvellous work in creation.[23] A representation of the German-language banyan tree graced the title page of Stieler's 1691 *Der Teutschen Sprache Stammbaum und Fortwachs,* reproduced in Figure 2.3. The analogy of this tree expressed key assumptions about the greatness of the German language: it is *natural*; it is *rich* in roots; it is *wide-ranging*, able to grow and spread across large geographical areas; it is *exceptional* among languages, just as the banyan is exceptional among trees. In Schottelius's visualization (summed up in Table 2.2), the German language grows, bears fruit, and renews itself, but remains in essence the same tree, the same German language. Each rootword is a *Stamm* 'trunk', or, less frequently, a *Wurzel* 'root'.[24] Derivational and inflectional endings are imagined as offshoots. The roots reach down into the ground, drawing up nature's sap of reason (*AA* 68, 5: 5). The ground is the raw material of language use, as recorded in written texts over the centuries.[25]

The banyan tree analogy, with its 'flat' structure, may help explain some limitations in Schottelius's morphological theory. Each trunk (or aerial root) stands alongside others, but their relationship with each other is

[22] This essentially organic view of language makes me wary of Jungen & Lohnstein's (2007:143) summary of Schottelius's linguistic theory as essentially one of mathematical combinations, 'a sort of computer programme'. While his inspiration, Stevin, was a mathematician, and his friend Harsdörffer also had a mathematical interest which he applied to language in the *Denckring* (cf. 3.7), Schottelius's fundamental conception of language is *not* mathematical.

[23] See McLelland (2002) for a fuller discussion. Schottelius does not mention aerial roots explicitly (hence Gützlaff's scepticism about whether a banyan tree is meant), but the inflectional and derivational endings are conceived of as branches which grow 'down from top to bottom' (*AA* 50, 4: 1). We can imagine these growing down until, fixed in the ground, they give the main trunk support (*Beystand*). It is worth noting too that in the 1640s, the image of the banyan tree with aerial roots also became current in the FG: it was allocated to Johann Georg, Herzog zu Sachsen-Weimar when he joined the society in 1645 as *der Trachtende* ('the Striver', cf. the description of the *Wurtzelbaum* 'root-tree' in his verse, Krause 1855 [1973]: 452); and in 1648 another unnamed member was keen to adopt the symbol. Prince Ludwig suggested the Hungarian balsam tree instead, since it similarly had aerial roots (Krause 1855 [1973]: 182–83). Alternatively, he suggested, the Indian fig-tree (or banyan) could be re-used, but with the name *Thronreiche*, as there was room for plenty of thrones in the shade of such a majestic tree—an image which perhaps inspired the title page of Stieler's dictionary of 1691 in Figure 2.2 (Stieler, 1691 [1968]).

[24] As already noted, the distinction between trunks and roots is scarcely valid for the banyan, as aerial roots grow down and become full stems or trunks (Barbarić 1981: 1208–09).

[25] Harsdörffer wrote that a dictionary must be compiled *aus den Gründen, nämlich aus allen Teutschen Büchern* 'from the foundations, namely from all German books' (Krause 1855 [1973]: 388).

Figure 2.3: The German language as a banyan tree (image from Stieler 1691)

purely one of adjacency rather than of hierarchy. Now, following Stevin, Schottelius did in fact recognize a hierarchical structure between the base and modifier in binary compounds (cf. 5.5.4). Indeed, he emphasized that *Braunschwartz* 'brown-black, i.e. brownish black' and *Schwartzbraun* 'black-brown, i.e. blackish brown' must refer to different shades because the roles of base and modifier were reversed (*AA* 80, 6: 20). But beyond that level of the binary compound, he failed to describe the internal hierarchical structures of word-formation, even though he knew that longer compounds and derivates could be formed by the successive addition of elements. Furthermore, while he generally treated derivation and compounding as distinct, he also presented derivation as a subcategory of *Verdoppelung*

Table 2.2: Schottelius's language banyan tree

Tree	Corresponding linguistic feature
Wurzel 'root' *Stamm* 'trunk or stem'	*Stammwörter* or *radices*. Root-words (*Wurzel* and *Stamm* are not cleanly distinguished, understandable if the image is a banyan tree)
Nebenspröslein 'sideshoots'	*Hauptendungen* (derivational endings) or *zufällige Endungen* (inflectional endings)
Grund	the raw material of the German language, as recorded in written texts?

'compounding' (*AA* 90–91, 6: 35). The distinction would be clarified by Kramer (1694; cf. 7.7), but Schottelius's slight confusion in the *AA* was perhaps encouraged by the fact that the banyan analogy offered no obvious way to visualize the different types of dependency in derivates like *Klarheit* 'clarity' and compounds like *sonnenklar* 'sun-clear, i.e. as clear as day'. Finally, the notion of the rootword itself was ambiguous. On the one hand, rootwords were the elements that combined to form new words. On the other hand, they were the roots in the sense of the *original* words, out of which the language grows. These twin notions of rootwords were not clearly distinguished until Adelung (cf. Section 7.3.1 and Rousseau 1984).

2.4.2 *The language as a building*

The tree, then, is one key analogy on which Schottelius's theory of language rested. It provided the language for talking about the elements of language, and for how they could combined, and indeed arguably accounts for some of the limitations in Schottelius's thinking. A second image of language is also important, however: the notion of the language as a building. Here the language is not the organic growth of language over centuries, ever-changing but still the same. Rather, the language must be built by human labour. The metaphor of the building resting on sure foundations is ancient—at least as old as the biblical parable of the two men who built their homes on rock and on sand respectively (Mathew 7: 24–27). Becanus had already called his mother tongue a *subtilis structura*, rendered by Schottelius as *Ein künstlich schönes Gebeu* 'an artfully beautiful edifice' (*AA* 19, 2: 14; cf. also *Kunstgebau AA* 6, 1: 15). Schottelius echoed the biblical imagery when he warned against following the usage of any one dialect, particularly in pronunciation or spelling, which might result in placing the language on *Triebsand* 'shifting sands' rather than on a firm foundation (*AA* 158, 10: 15). If in the image of the tree, the *Stammwörter*, *Hauptendungen* and *Nebenendungen* are equated with roots, stems and off-shoots, then in the building these essential elements of language are seen as the foundations:

> EIn jedes standfestes Gebäu beruhet auf seinen unbeweglichen wolbepfälten Gründen: Also einer jeglichen Sprache Kunstgebäu bestehet gründlich in jhren uhrsprünglichen natürlichen **Stammwörteren**

> 'Any firm edifice rests on its immovable, well driven foundations. So the artful edifice of any language consists fundamentally in its original, natural rootwords.'

(*AA* 50, 4: 1)[26]

But the details of the building's architecture are not developed any further in the *AA*. The focus is instead on how it can be safely maintained for its purpose:

> Sol man aber etwas taugliches aufbringen / muß man das untaugliche hinweg schaffen: Sol man den Grund recht und fest in Teutscher Sprache setzen / muß man das grundbrüchige ausfesten / das löcherichte vollstampfen / und dasselbe nicht gut heissen / wodurch das schöne Gebäu gerüttelt / und grundfellig gemacht werden wil. Viel und oft unrecht gehen / machet darum den Weg nicht recht.

> 'But in order to construct something useful, one must get rid of what is not useful. To set a right and firm basis in German, one must build support for what is crumbling, stop up the holes, and not approve that which will make the fine edifice shaky and prone to collapse. To go wrong much and often does not make it the right way.'

(*AA* 137, 9: 4; similarly *AA* 170, 10: 23)

Only when the language is used and developed on firm and right foundations, in accord with nature, does Schottelius consider it *grundrichtig*. Schottelius's notion of *Grundrichtigkeit*, usually equated with analogy, in fact goes further than analogy in its original sense, where it applied only to regular inflectional paradigms, to a deeper level of regularity and rightness (hence *Grund*– 'ground, basis') which runs through every aspect of

---

[26] This extract continues into the description of the language as a tree, cited above.

the language and includes the basic rightness of the rootwords. Schottelius did not oppose inherent *Grundrichtigkeit* with human usage in principle, any more than he saw the edifice of the German language and the natural German language tree in opposition. On the contrary, just as the key distinction is between giving the edifice sure or shaky foundations, so Schottelius differentiated between right and wrong usage.[27] Right usage accords with the nature of the language; wrong usage, on the other hand, will produce language which, built on uncertain and wrong foundations, is weak and in danger of crumbling. For this reason, to follow *blinde[n] wanckelende[n] Gewonheit* ('blind, unsteady custom') is to *ein ungewisses zerrüttetes Wesen in dieser Sprache aufbauen / die doch auff gewissen Gründen festiglich beruhet* (*AA* 10, 1: 29), 'build up an uncertain, shaky essence in this language, which after all rests solidly on firm foundations'.

How, though, do we know if the language edifice we construct is *grundrichtig*? Fortunately, human reasoning is natural, in accord with nature, and so will reflect nature and its natural law. Following Grotius and the Neostoicists (cf. 3.4, 3.8.1), natural law can be deduced

> aus einer gemeinen Gleichhaltung bey allen / oder doch bey den vornemsten Völkeren abnehmen: Den was bey allen verständigen Menschen gemein und beliebt ist / hat keine andere uhrsprüngliche Ursache / als den gemeinen Menschlichen Verstand

> 'from the common opinion of all, or at least of the most noble peoples: For what is common to and popular amongst all reasonable people / has no other original cause than common human reason'[28]

> (*AA* 16, 2: 2)

The image of an edifice which must be given sure foundations occurs almost exclusively when Schottelius argues that the *High* German language must be carefully looked after and protected, although his deliberately catholic use of the term *Teutsch* masks the distinction. The *Teutsch* that Schottelius had in mind here was, then, not the broad-ranging all-encompassing German of the magnificent language-tree, which suggested German's natural greatness, but more narrowly High German, to which human skill or art (*Kunst*) must be applied in order to uncover and describe the principles according to which it could be properly learnt and then further developed to fulfil new tasks. As a counterpoint to the natural image of the tree, this language edifice is explicitly 'artful', a *Kunstgebeu* 'artful construction'. That is made very clear, for instance, when the topos of

---

[27] On the development of Schottelius's thinking on analogy and anomaly, cf. 3.8.1, and the meticulous study of Takada (1985).

[28] Cf. Huber (1984: 58); Seiffert (1990a) discussed this passage with an emphasis on customary rather than 'natural' law.

art as an imitator of nature is applied specifically to the art of language. As the world changes, further development of the language is needed in order to express new ideas:

> Auch wie [...] / die Welt sich fast numehr umgekehret / und ein fast anderer Geist die Menschen eingenommen hat; Also muß auch die Kunst / die Nachäffinn der Natur / sich nach der itzigen Natur der Welt richten.

> 'And as the world has now changed much and a very different spirit has taken over people, so must art / the imitator of nature / follow the present nature of the world' (*AA* 109, 7: 13)

In such thinking, the application of human skill is paramount, and the dangers of not applying, or of misapplying, such language art are emphasized in the image of the edifice in danger of collapse. In the context of Schottelius's 'ethically inspired patriotism' (Seiffert 1989: 241), such an image is rather more powerful than the organic image of pruning or weeding. The inevitable biblical overtones reinforce a moral message as well as a statement of language theory.

2.5 EVALUATING LANGUAGE

I conclude this introduction to Schottelius's concept of language by outlining the criteria by which Schottelius judged German. In seeking not just to describe German, but also to demonstrate its equal worth, even its superiority, compared to other languages, he had in his arsenal both traditional criteria for assessing language, and his own trio of ultimate arbiters: analogy, *ratio*, and naturalness.

2.5.1 *Traditional criteria*

When Schottelius judged the relative worth of languages, it was a foregone conclusion that German triumphed, whatever criterion was applied, and the sole purpose of the second oration was to demonstrate as much (*AA* 16, 2: 1). Criteria where German scored well were viewed as immutable virtues of the language. Areas of weakness were viewed as contingent, as temporary blips that were the result of neglect, but on the way to being corrected. Other criticisms were the result of the critics' ignorance of German.

Most of Schottelius's yardsticks had a pedigree going back to antiquity, but had been applied in the past to distinguish good language *usage* from bad. Schottelius (like Henisch in his dictionary of 1616; cf. Polenz 1994: 183–84; Kämper 2001) now applied the same criteria to judge the quality of an *entire language*, German. The qualities he canvassed included clarity, brevity, copiousness, euphony, elegance, antiquity, and purity. German excelled in clarity thanks to the close affinity of its rootwords to their referents, and thanks to the way in which they could be transparently combined. (As noted earlier, clarity at the level of syntax was not explored). As for brevity, the capacity for combining rootwords in compounding and derivation guaranteed succinctness, for new words could be coined where other languages required a whole phrase. German's richness was not in doubt either, given its demonstrably large stock of rootwords compared to other languages. German was, therefore, a complete (*völlig*) language.[29] On euphony, German was more vulnerable, for it had been criticized by its neighbours for its execrable consonant clusters, but Schottelius simply met assertion with counter-assertion. Far from being ugly, the plentiful consonants yielded a *prächtige und doch klingende Ausrede | die reget und beweget* 'a splendid and yet ringing pronunciation, that stirs and moves' (*AA* 24, 2: 34). An apparent lack of elegance was not an immutable feature of the language, merely evidence of poor usage, for *kein Gold bleieren wird | ob schon ein giftiger | oder schmakloser Trank darin enthalten ist* 'no gold becomes lead, just because it contains a poisonous or tasteless drink' (*AA* 146, 9: 25). German possessed all that was necessary for good expression, even if some did not yet make the best of its qualities.

As for the antiquity of German, that is the subject of the third oration. Schottelius argued that German dated back through five eras in its history (via Luther, Emperor Rudolf I, and Charlemagne) to the arrival of the ancestor of today's Germans, Ascenas, descendant of Noah (*AA* 34, 3: 13–14). German was the oldest of all the European languages, and its apparent purity was taken as evidence of its antiquity. The result was that the ancient meanings of many of the proper names and topographical names of Europe were still discernible in German, and only in German (the claim of the eighth oration). German's purity was, however, under threat: Schottelius's ninth oration was devoted to how neglectful users of German had needlessly reduced the language to the state of a 'beggar' and 'mongrel' by thoughtless borrowing from other languages (cf. 3.5.2).

Clarity, brevity, copiousness, euphony, elegance, antiquity and purity all had a long history since the Roman era as traditional criteria for judging language, a history renewed by Latinate humanists, and enjoying lasting

---

[29] The concern for a 'complete' language has returned in current language policy in several Germanic languages that are under threat of domain loss to English, and so once again lacking terminology for some technical domains; cf. Linn & Oakes (2007), McLelland (2009). The concern of policy-makers to ensure a 'complete' language is parallel to Schottelius's view of the state of German in the seventeenth century: *Welche Sprache die nohtwendigen Sprachstükke hat | dieselbe ist völlig* 'Any language which has the necessary language components is complete'. German meets this criterion and so is *zu alle dem was zu reden | gnugsam* 'adequate for anything that needs to be said' (*AA* 146, 9: 25), as Schottelius's insistence on coining German technical terms was intended to demonstrate (*AA* 12).

popularity into the eighteenth century and beyond.[30] So far, so typical, we might say. However, overriding all these traditional criteria for evaluating language in Schottelius was a triumvirate of values: *ratio*, naturalness and analogy. The way in which Schottelius combined them and applied them to the vernacular was novel, and of lasting influence.

2.5.2 *Ratio, naturalness and linguistic analogy*

The central importance of *ratio* and nature as expressed in the title engravings of Schottelius's work was noted in 1.4, and Schottelius equated the two with each other in Neostoicist fashion (cf. his equation of *verständliche Natur* and *natürlicher Verstand*, 2.3.2). Analogy was the linguistic-theoretical proof of these twin qualities in language. Analogy, in its origins, is a mathematical relation that expresses similarity: 'As A is to B, so C is to D'. For example, 4 is to 20 as 7 is to 35, i.e. one-fifth. Analogy is sufficiently powerful that we can use it to solve problems where our information is incomplete. Given '4 is to 20 as 7 is to ?' we can supply the missing number by using our knowledge of the relationship 4/20. In the sixteenth and seventeenth centuries, a period of expanding horizons and a wealth of new data to be examined in order to understand the world, such analogical thinking was a way of making sense of the unfamiliar by recourse to the familiar, of expressing the relationship of the individual to the macrocosm. Indeed, analogical thinking was second nature to seventeenth-century educated society, whose emblems and poetry relied on drawing analogies. Small wonder that Schottelius—likened by the analogies of his friends in their dedicatory poems to a miner casting light into the unknown depths of the German language—depended on analogy to help understand the new realm he uncovered. The evolution of his view of analogy is discussed more fully in 3.8.1, but the following serves as a first orientation.

Analogy is central to the *AA* in two different guises: as a rhetorical, or indeed conceptual strategy, and as a technical concept. Schottelius's rhetorical tendency to analogy is evident in the frequency of the formulations *Gleich wie ...*, *gleicher Gestalt*, 'just as ...', 'in the same way', etc., often early on in an oration, where a likeness is established to determine the argument in favour of German over the ensuing para-graphs.[31] The language tree and the language building were powerful

---

[30] A century after Schottelius, Daniel Jenisch (1762–1804) adopted a subset of the same criteria, consisting of copiousness, energy (i.e. the capacity to move), clarity and euphony (Hüllen 1999: 223–230). Purity has once again become a prominent goal for the German language society *Verein Deutsche Sprache*, founded in 1997.

[31] *AA* 8, 1: 23; 9, 1: 27; 11, 1: 33; 14, 1: 43; 16, 2: 2; 16, 2: 3; 29, 3: 4; 40, 3: 31; 48, 3: 53; 61, 4: 31; 67, 5: 2, 68, 5: 6; 74, 6: 3; 76, 3: 11; 97, 6: 53; 105, 7: 5; 114, 7: 26; 136, 9: 1; 137, 9: 4; 146, 9: 26; 152, 10: 12.

analogies that encouraged readers to think of German as a living, organic whole, and as a structure that must be built on sure foundations. Music was another powerful analogy: a peasant lass may sing a melody, but is not qualified to write an artful *Capellenstück*, for she knows less than nothing about music (*AA* 10, 1: 30). Beware, therefore, of those who claim to know something about the German language, just because they speak it. This music analogy legitimized one of the strongest claims of Schottelius's work, that the German language was a subject for technical study. Schottelius repeated the claim early in the fifth oration:

> Gleich wie aber die edle Kunst der Music nicht aus ungewissen Gründen / oder dem Geläute des Pöbels / sonderen *ex certissimis numerorum musicalium proportionibus, earumque demonstrationibus* entstehet; Also erhebet sich absonderlich die Teutsche Sprache aus den gewissesten Gründen / welche GOtt und die Natur darin aus-gewirket haben / empor:

> 'Just as the noble art of music does not arise from uncertain foun-dations or from the sounds of the throng, but rather [here Schot-telius switches to the prestigious Latin to underline his point] from the most certain proportions of musical numbers and of their de-monstration; so the German language in particular rises up from the most certain foundations which God and nature have worked in it:'

(*AA* 67, 5: 2)

Music rests like mathematics on fixed and clear proportions—on analogies in the technical sense, in fact. So too, Schottelius's rhetorical analogy tells us, must language. Just as it is possible to produce a most unmusical and unpleasant noise with musical instruments, if one disregards the principles of music, so too a language can be rendered clumsy and ugly if its rules and principles are not followed.

This rhetorical analogy brings us back to the technical analogy which Schottelius employed. As a technical term in language study, analogy (*analogia*) already referred to the expectation of patterns of similarity (i.e. regularity) between parts of the language. To apply such analogy to German is to recognize, for instance, that *machen* is to *gemacht* as *spielen* is to *gespielt*. Verbs where we can indeed 'calculate' the past participle by following an established pattern in this way are defined as regular. Schottelius (*AA* 557) accordingly placed these verbs in the category of *Conjugatio Analoga seu inflectio verbi regularis* 'analagous conjugation or regular verb inflection'. All such regular verbs retain their *Stammletteren* (their root-letters) unchanged. Verbs that did not conform to this predictable pattern Schottelius called anomalous (*Conjugatio verborum Germanicorum Anomala*) or irregular verbs, like *singen, sang, gesungen* 'sing, sang, sung', where the vowel of the root is changed. This distinction between the regular and irregular verbs in German was not new, but was already present in Ritter (1616).[32] However, if the study of German was to have the same status as music, as a technical discipline, regular correspondences must govern the language as a whole, not just its regular verbs. And so, in a radical step, Schottelius applied the notion of analogy not just to inflectional paradigms, but to every aspect of the language—compounding and derivation too followed regular rules. New words *entstehen nicht schlumpsweis | sondern aus fleissiger Lesung guter Bücher | aus Beobachtung der künstlich zusammenstimmenden Grundsätzen und Haubtregulen der Teutschen Sprache | und sonderlich durch hülfreiche Zuneigung eines Teutschliebenden Geistes* 'do not emerge sloppily, but from diligent reading of good books, *from observing the artfully harmonious principles and chief rules of the German language*, and especially through the helpful application of a German-loving spirit' (*AA* 91, 6: 36, my emphasis).[33] Furthermore, one must be a *Sprachkündiger*, with knowledge of words that not just anyone possessed (*AA* 98, 6: 53). Leaving aside the x-factor mentioned here in the art of compounding—possessing a German-loving spirit—it is clear that Schottelius considered word-formation to be just as rule-governed as the inflectional paradigms. Schottelius also applied the principle of analogy to spelling, generating general principles from which the details of individual spelling rules followed logically. He even adhered to analogous patterns he had worked out where they flew in the face of established usage. This was most obvious in spelling (cf. 5.5.3, fifth spelling principle), but Matthias Kramer (fl. 1719–1746) famously accused Schottelius's disciple Stieler of doing the same in the area of word-formation in his dictionary (1691), listing words that were theoretically possible but unattested (cf. 7.5).

Schottelius was from a Low German area where High German had, over the preceding sixty years or so, ousted Low German as the language of institutions and administration in urban centres, and High German was increasingly becoming the language of urban populations of Northern Germany. His adherence to analogy through thick and thin has been seen by Jellinek (1913: 179) and Padley (1985: 227) as the response of a Low German speaking outsider to the expectation of an in-group of East Central German speakers that their own usage norm was right. Where Schottelius disagreed with them, very probably in part because of Low German influence (cf. Chapter 8), he needed a principled basis for his arguments. That principled basis was the assumption that order and regularity were the

---

[32] It was only in the early eighteenth century, however, that the patterns of Ablaut behind verbs like *sing, sang, gesungen* were grasped, by the Dutchman Lambertus ten Kate (1674–1731); cf. Noordegraf (2001: 1117), Jongeneelen (1992).

[33] Again, Schottelius saw the *written* language—*gute Bücher* 'good books'—as the basis from which the language must be further developed.

natural state of the language and were the expression of its rationality. But Schottelius's stubbornness on some points of detail (in spelling, for instance, in his insistence that nouns ending in *–er, –el* should carry an *–e* to mark the plural unambiguously, cf. 3.8.1) also seem consistent with the desire of an ambitious man to make his name.

Despite contemporaries' criticism of Schottelius's stubborn reliance on analogy in German, it did serve his purpose in two ways:

1. It helped Schottelius make a strong case for raising the status of studying of the German language. If the German language is a regular, analogy-governed system (only in syntax does the notion of an analogy not play a systematic and prominent role), then the study and use of the German language becomes an academic discipline. It is a perfect expression of the *ratio* inherent in nature. At the same time, its mastery is a *Kunst*, an art.
2. Schottelius laid important groundwork for the continuing task of standardizing the German language. By extending analogy beyond inflectional paradigms to spelling and lexicology, he made clear his belief that these areas too could and must be governed by generalized rules.

These are important and lasting achievements of principle, even if some details of the grammatical descriptions that Schottelius arrived at gradually became dated (cf. 7.6).

3

INTERSECTING DISCOURSE TRADITIONS IN THE *AUSFÜHRLICHE ARBEIT*

3.1. INTRODUCTION

Because the *AA* is an encyclopaedic landmark, is a mine of quotable linguistic patriotism, and contains important innovations in vernacular grammatical theory, one can forget to be surprised at just how different it is both from its predecessors in Germany and from the benchmark grammars written around the same time in England and France: John Wallis' *Grammatica linguae anglicanae* (Wallis 1653) and the (very different) universalist Port-Royal grammar of Lancelot & Arnauld, published in France in 1660. Despite their differences, these two are both slim volumes that one can read relatively readily from beginning to end, whether an expert in the language or not. The *AA*, in contrast, is very long, is full of cross-references, and is even, especially in the panegyrics of Book I, a jumble of German and Latin.[1] To help explain why Schottelius's work is as it is, then, this chapter will situate Schottelius in the intellectual current of his time by identifying six different discourse communities, or discourse traditions, on which he drew and in which he himself sought to participate:[2]

3.2 Legal discourse

---

[1] See McLelland (2004b) for an analysis of how Schottelius's efforts to write German *Lobreden* as showpieces for German are stymied by his own tendency to switch to Latin. About a quarter of the book of orations is in Latin. Although 89% of paragraphs begin in German, 35% of these codeswitch to Latin at some point within the paragraph. What may strike the reader today as a confusing mix of Latin and German was of course no more than the everyday language of the educated elite of the sixteenth and seventeenth centuries (cf. Seiffert 1990b: 318–19; on humanists' Latin and German, cf. Drux 1984, Knape 1984, Stolt 1964).

[2] A discourse community has broadly shared goals, and has established means of communication amongst its members. It is likely to make use of particular genres for which certain norms are accepted, such as specialized terminology. Discourse communities exist not just at a single point in time, but can persist over time, over several generations. I shall generally use the term 'discourse tradition' (already widely used in *Romanistik* and *Germanistik*) to emphasize this persistence of shared goals and norms over time. The term 'discourse community' was coined by Nystrand (1982), and developed by Swales (1990). On the notion of discourse and critical discourse analysis see also Fairclough (1992), Foucault (1977). Haapamäki usefully applied the notion of 'discourse community' to the history of linguistics in a paper on the history of Swedish grammars presented at the joint meeting of the Henry Sweet Society and the Studienkreis Geschichte der Sprachwissenschaft, Helsinki 2007. Linn (2008) also appealed to it in his study of Anglo-Scandinavian linguistic contacts. Watts (2008) distinguishes a discourse community from a "community of practice", a potentially useful differentiation, but one that I do not make here

3.3 Practical German grammatography

3.4 The Leiden University network, a group of loosely interconnected scholars whom—or whose works—Schottelius encountered during and after his studies in Leiden

3.5 German cultural patriotism, and especially the *Fruchtbringende Gesellschaft*, the cultural-patriotic language society of which Schottelius became the 397th member in 1642 (Krause 1855 [1973]: 279)

3.6 International linguistic reflection: Latin grammatography, but also scholarly Latinate discussions about the nature, origin and history of language(s)

3.7 Pansemioticism, the 'emblematic world-view' characteristic of the Dutch and German Baroque, according to which any object, whether natural or artificial, could signify one or several other objects, qualities, or events.

Section 3.8 illustrates how these discourses intersected in Schottelius's thinking, in two of his most central theoretical notions: *Grundrichtigkeit/* analogy (3.8.1) and the notion of the *Stammwort* (3.8.2).

That Schottelius's linguistic patriotism owed a heavy debt to a sort of Pan-Germanic patriotic discourse about the nature and history of German(ic) *(lingua germanica, Teutsch)*, particularly to that of Low Countries scholars, and most of all to Simon Stevin, has been noted repeatedly since Bornemann's important study of Dutch–German influences in the Baroque (Bornemann 1976, Kiedrón, 1985a, 1985b, Gützlaff 1988). Such Pan-Germanic scholarship in turn interacted with wider discussions across Europe in the sixteenth and seventeenth centuries both about the origin and history of language more generally, and about the nature of grammar. Increasingly (more so in 1663 than in the first edition of his *Sprachkunst* of 1641), Schottelius drew on and at the very least *tried* to contribute to this international scholarly debate too. Metcalf (1953a), Schaeffer (1983), Rössing-Hager (1985) and Moulin (1997) have looked at his contribution to historical linguistic reflections of the time. Schottelius's legal training provided further influences (Seiffert 1990a). Finally, Höpel (2000, 2002) has drawn attention to Schottelius's direct participation in the 'pansemiotic' world-view that pervaded the German Baroque (Westerhoff 2000, 2001), with his contribution to the publication in 1643 of an emblem-book, the *Dreiständige Sinnbilder*, together with fellow FG-member Julius von dem Knesebeck.

Such different ways of reflecting on language and on communicating meanings in the Early Modern period can usefully be treated as discrete. For each discourse historians of ideas can identify distinct series of typical texts, which could be considered 'canonical', and identify characteristic discourse features. And yet, while differing in their geographical spread, their membership, and their longevity, it is obvious that these discourses overlap in practice. For instance, with the exception of grammars aimed at young children, there is scarcely a grammar of German in the seventeenth century that does not also draw explicitly on cultural-patriotic arguments to assert the worth of the vernacular. Vossius, the author of the important and influential linguistic study of Latin *De arte grammatica* (1635), taught in Leiden for nearly two decades. Legal scholars like Goldast took a particular philological interest in older legal texts in German (cf. Section 6.2.2). The Latin grammar of the leading humanist Philipp Melanchthon (1497–1560) served as a funnel through which ideas from Latinate grammatography found their way into German grammar-writing too. And it is obvious that the emblematic world-view of pansemioticism suffused the practices of the FG, which assigned emblems, nicknames, and enigmatic verses to each of its members. Schottelius's *AA* is, however, quite an extreme case of overlap of—and to some extent even competition between—discourse traditions. Understanding their interactions provides a way to grasp Schottelius's complex text, complete with its occasional contradictions.

It would of course be possible to identify further lines of tradition. For instance, there is a Protestant religious and even mystical tendency in some of what Schottelius writes about German with a history of its own (which Luther, Ratke and Böhme all represent in their different ways). A small genre of poetic treatises could also be identified (a genre to be traced back to the Netherlands; cf. Bornemann 1976). But the six traditions listed above are those most clearly identifiable as separate discourses in the full sense in which Foucault (1977) views them in the history of ideas. Such discourses function for Foucault 'as discontinuous practices which intersect and sometimes come together' (Foucault 1977: 54–55). A given discipline (such as grammar) will have its own discourse which can be recognized 'as a domain of objects, a collection of methods, a corpus of propositions held to be true, an interplay of rules, definitions, techniques and instruments'. A society or group may also have its own discourse; the *Fruchtbringende Gesellschaft* (FG) is a case in point.

3.2 LEGAL DISCOURSE

The legal discourse tradition is a slightly different case from the others to be discussed below, because while Schottelius certainly drew on it, he did not seek to contribute to it in the *AA*, though he did elsewhere. Schottelius received his doctorate in law from the University of Helmstedt in 1646, he was a privy councillor in the Duke's secular and ecclesiastical councils (Berns 1976: 24–26), and his works include a major treatise on laws and

customs within the German Empire (Schottelius 1671). Despite its title of
Kurtzer Tractat [...] 'short treatise', the treatise was nearly 600 pages in
length and was reprinted after 1686 and again ca. 1725, as well as finding a
continuator in Johann Werner (Gericke 1718) (cf. Seiffert 1990a: 242).

Schottelius's familiarity with the world of law had three tangible effects
on the *AA*, at three different levels. First, at the level of the source material,
Schottelius drew on more than two dozen legal texts of various kinds (cf.
6.2.2). Older legal codes especially supplied useful attestations of rare
German rootwords, while more recent legal treatises were evidence of the
ability of German to supply the terminology for any technical domain.
Second, Schottelius's legal training encouraged a particular way of
thinking. Assertions must be backed by evidence. No wonder, then, that
so much of the *AA* is devoted to furnishing evidence for the claims
Schottelius made about language: lists of proper names, rootwords, and
German writers in the treatises of Book V, and plentiful exemplification in
the grammar and in the poetics (cf. Chapters 4 and 5). Where there are
conflicting interpretations of available evidence, one must present both
sides and judge between them by reasoned argument, and this is
characteristic of Schottelius's approach too. For instance, in the second
oration, Schottelius presents the 'testimonies' of various authorities on the
qualities of German (*Zeugnissen*, *AA* 14, title) and then discussion of how
these testimonies are to be understood: for example, as *inepte* or *cum
limitatione* 'inept; limited' (*AA* 15 §30, §14). Indeed, Schottelius's legalistic
approach to the topic is very explicit in the Latin summary of this oration
(*AA* 14–15), where the points made in the individual paragraphs are
summarized in legal terms: *probationes* ('proofs'), *testimonium* ('testimony',
4x), *testa(n)tur* ('bear witness', 2x), *attestata* ('attested'), *allegatur* ('is
alleged' 2x), and *iudicium* ('judgement', 5x). Whatever the topic, Schottelius
presented all the available testimonies, and formed his judgement
accordingly. An example of this method of argumentation, concerning
the relative antiquity of German and Hebrew, is discussed in 3.6.3 below.

Thirdly and finally, at the level of theory, Schottelius's view of correct
German was inspired by Grotius's doctrine of natural law, though the
Neostoicist view of natural law was also well-known outside the discipline
of law itself. It is also just one of several aspects of Schottelius's linguistic
theory that owe a debt to what I have called the Leiden network, to which I
return in 3.4 below.

3.3 PRACTICAL GERMAN GRAMMATOGRAPHY

The 1641 *Teutsche Sprachkunst*, out of which the *AA* ultimately grew, was
first and foremost a German grammar. Full discussion of Schottelius's
grammar is reserved till Chapter 5, but some brief remarks here will show

how Schottelius embedded himself in the existing tradition of grammatical works of German. Lest this be seen as stating the obvious, or indeed the inevitable, it is worth comparing again the near-contemporary grammars in England and France, Wallis (1653) and Lancelot &Arnauld (1660). Wallis (1653: 109–10) deliberately distanced himself from earlier grammarians of English—he mentioned Alexander Gil(l) (1567–1635), Ben Jonson (1572–1637), and Henry Hexham (c. 1585–1658)—who have

> all forced English too rigidly into the mould of Latin (a mistake which nearly everyone makes in descriptions of other modern languages too), giving many useless rules about the cases, genders and declensions of nouns, the tenses, moods and conjugations of verbs, the government of nouns and verbs, and other things of that kind, which have no bearing on our language, and which confuse and obscure matters instead of elucidating them.

Wallis emphasized that he had chosen 'to employ a completely new method, which had its basis not, as is customary, in the structure of the Latin language but in the characteristic structure of our own.' He emphasized too the newness of his method for pronouncing the letters.

Likewise, the authors of the Port-Royal grammar—while referring to Claude Favre Vaugelas's (1585–1650) *Remarques* (1647) a number of times—did not attempt to embed themselves in an existing vernacular grammatical tradition, but rather emphasized their new approach. Their preface states that the work was written *n'ayant rien veu* [sic] *dans les anciens Grammairiens, ny dans les nouveaux, qui fust plus curieux ou plus juste, sur cette matiere* ('having seen nothing in the ancient grammarians, nor in the new ones, which is more curious or more accurate on this subject matter', Kemp 1972: 4).

Schottelius, in contrast, presented his work not as a radical break with misguided predecessors, but as the first complete *fulfilment* of their mission. Despite the availablity of other grammars, 'a complete self-contained work has yet to be completed' (*ein völliges eigenes Werk aber* [...] *ist unverfertigt geblieben, AA* 4, 1: 9),[3] and so Schottelius sought to fulfil the task previous grammarians had set themselves. In this aim he arguably succeeded: he did indeed provide what became the definitive grammar of German for nearly a century. So Schottelius's grammar stands squarely in the existing tradition of German grammars that we can trace back to the 1570s or earlier, if we count Valentin Ickelsamer's (1500–1541) *Grammatica* of 1534, chiefly restricted to matters of spelling (Rössing-Hager 1984). Predecessors such as Ickelsamer, Laurentius Albertus (1573) (whom Schottelius more often refers to as Ostrofrank) and Johannes Clajus (1578) are all already

---

[3] Likewise, a key criticism Schottelius made of Gueintz's grammar was its incompleteness, that too many rules of German were missing (Krause 1855 [1973]: 247).

mentioned in the orations. The order of treating the parts of speech largely also followed the tradition of German grammars, inherited in turn from grammars of Latin (see Barbarić 1981: 500ff.; cf. 5.5.2).

Schottelius also owed a clear debt, chiefly in the area of terminology, to Christoph Gueintz—the FG member whose 1641 grammar of German Schottelius had read and reviewed very critically in draft form in 1640. Without acknowledging as much, as Gueintz protested in a letter to the society's head in March 1643 (Krause 1855 [1973]: 260), Schottelius was indebted to Gueintz for terms such as *Geschlechtswort* for article and *Endung* for case ending (Schottelius used *Zahlendung*).[4] *Zeitwort* and *Mittelwort* ('verb' and 'participle') are terms coined by Ratke but which Schottelius would also have encountered in Gueintz (1641) (Barbarić 1981: 527, 635; 808, 911). Schottelius's decision to treat number as a section in its own right was possibly also inspired by Gueintz (1641 [1978]: 31–33), who was the first to discuss it coherently (Barbarić 1981: 609ff.).

Within this practical grammatical tradition, Schottelius also made important innovations, most significantly in treating German word-formation thoroughly for the first time.[5] This was an important addition to German grammatical theory, and indeed to European grammatical theory (cf. 7.7–7.8). It reached its full natural conclusion in German only when Grimm treated word-formation as a separate aspect of grammar, between inflection and syntax (Barbarić 1981: 1180).

3.4 THE LEIDEN UNIVERSITY NETWORK—THE ROOTS OF SCHOTTELIUS'S LINGUISTIC THEORY IN DUTCH AND FLEMISH SCHOLARSHIP

Section 3.5 will consider the discourse tradition of cultural patriotism within Germany. This seventeenth-century German movement was auto-chthonous in its patriotic spirit, but nevertheless drew many of its basic tenets and practices from the already well-established cultural patriotism in the Low Countries, which was expressed both in the *Rederijkerkamers* (rhetoricians' societies) and in many scholars' writings on the nature and history of language, and which had a particular centre in Leiden. Indeed, the whole innovative thrust of Schottelius's grammatical enterprise (the importance of rootwords, and of analogy) is unthinkable without his exposure to Dutch and Flemish ideas. There is evidence enough of the

---

[4]   *Zahlendung* was in fact a misnomer, since Schottelius meant endings that marked case as well as number (Barbarić 1981: 635).

[5]   Although Schottelius did not yet use the term *Wortbildung* (still current in German for word-formation), the corresponding periphrastic phrasing *Bildung der Wörter* does occur (*AA* 113–14, 7: 24). However, the relationship between derivation and compounding as sub-types of a common phenomenon of word-formation was not yet clarified (cf. 2.4.1 and 7.6–7.7).

Leiden influence in the number of Dutch or Flemish scholars with whose works Schottelius shows familiarity. In 1641, it was Dutch names (Stevin, Becanus, Scrieckius, Heinsius) that Schottelius listed first of all as his authorities; only after them did German names follow, together with yet another Dutchman, Scriverius:

> auch vieler Hochgelahrter Leute Urtheile und Lobsprüche über unsere Muttersprache ich gelesen / als deß *Stevini, Goropii[,] Becani, Scrieckij Rodornij, Heinsii, Trithemii, Lutheri, Scriverij, Opitij, Hutteri & c.*[6]

> 'also I read the judgements and praises of many highly learned people about our mother tongue, such as Stevin, Goropius Becanus, Scrieckius Rodornius, Heinsius, Trithemius, Luther, Scriverius, Opitz, Hutter, etc.'

(Schottelius 1641: 9)

With the exception of Schottelius's contemporary Opitz, the German names in the list are prominent figures from the German reformation of the sixteenth century. All the more recent are figures from the Dutch scholarly world that Schottelius could have encountered either directly during his time studying in Leiden (1635–1636) (cf. Berns 1974: 15–18), or thereafter. Joannis Goropius Becanus (1519–1572) was long dead, but Heinsius (1580–1655) had been lecturing in Leiden since 1602, and Scriverius (1576–1660) studied at Leiden and was a close friend of Heinsius. Schrieckius (Adriaan van Schriek, 1560–1621) and Stevin (1548/9–1620) were only a generation or so older than Schottelius. Altogether, seventeen Dutch sources are listed by Schottelius,[7] a comparatively small number out of the hundreds of works he consulted, but they include members of what Van de Velde (1966: 66) called the 'Leiden philological school' like Vulcanius, and the influence on Schottelius of ten or so of these is out of all proportion to their number. In this respect, Schottelius is typical of German scholarship and cultural patriotism. It is well-known that the so-called 'Dutch movement' in Germany drew on Dutch models for German efforts to raise the status

---

[6] The first oration was substantially re-written for the publication of the *AA* in 1663, and this passage no longer appears. The comma after *Goropii* is an error: the scholar's name is Joannis Goropius Becanus.

[7] They are: Ogier de Busbecq, Johannes de Laet, Joannis Becanus Goropius, Hugo Grotius, Daniel Heinsius, Levinus Hulsius, Franciscus Junius, Bartholomaeus Keckermann, Justus Lipsius, Abraham Mylius, Josephus Justus Scaliger, considered the founder of the Leiden philological school (as well as his father Julius Caesar Scaliger, who himself spent most of his career in France), Petrus Scriverius, Adriaan van Schrieck, Simon Stevin, Richard Rowlands Verstegan, Gerhard Vossius, and Bonaventura Vulcanius. For further details on these figures, see Chapter 6 and the Appendix. On the Leiden philological school and on Junius, see Van de Velde (1966: 66–84, 130–65).

of German language, literature and culture. It is symptomatic, for example, that an anonymous poem programmatically placed at the front of Opitz's *Teutsche Poemata* (1624, inspired by Heinsius's *Nederduytsche poemata* of 1616) had in fact originally been composed by a Dutch scholar for a Dutch work: Hugo Grotius's *Ad Germanicam Linguam*, originally prefaced to Abraham Mylius's *Lingua Belgica* (1612) (Bornemann 1976: 95–96).

Leiden University had been founded in 1575 by William of Orange, and was Europe's leading Protestant university (its motto is still *Praesidium libertatis* 'bulwark of freedom'), and in the years 1575 to 1750, some 11000 Germans studied there; in the first half of the seventeenth century, they made up 27% of all students there (Bornemann 1976: 13). Amongst those Dutch scholars who most influenced Schottelius (in ways that we shall see below), some were near-contemporaries in Leiden: Vossius, Grotius, Heinsius, Scriverius, and Schrieckius. Others were a generation earlier: Lipsius, J. J. Scaliger, Becanus, Mylius, and Stevin. In all those aspects of linguistic scholarhip where Schottelius's contribution is recognized as significant—in grammatical theory, the notion of the rootword, conceptions of language, language history—the Dutch connection is of fundamental importance.

Amongst Schottelius's near-contemporaries in Leiden was Vossius, who taught first theology, then Greek and rhetoric at Leiden (1614–1632), and later history and philology at Amsterdam. Vossius's *De arte grammatica* (1635) was published in the year that Schottelius arrived in Leiden, and it had a lasting influence in Europe, and on Schottelius in particular. Hugo Grotius (Huig de Groot, 1583–1645), a friend of Vossius, had studied at Leiden from 1594 (aged 11!) to 1598. His father had studied at Leiden too, with Justus Lipsius. Justus Lipsius (Joost or Josse Lips, 1547–1606) was himself a Flemish philologist who was professor of history in Leiden 1579–1590. His Neostoicism sought to reconcile Stoicism—with its belief in the universal rationality to be found in nature—with Christianity, and was in turn an influence on Grotius.[8] Grotius advocated the concept of natural law, holding that the principles of natural law were binding on all peoples, even overriding local customs that might deviate from these natural principles. Schottelius referred to Grotius's *De jure belli ac pacis libri tres* ('On the laws of war and peace', 1625), but also to his historical studies, including *De antiquitate reipublicae Batavicae* ('On the Antiquity of the Batavian Republic'). Josephus Justus Scaliger (1540–1609), who replaced Lipsius as professor of history at Leiden in 1593, was the son of Julius Caesar Scaliger (1484–1558), who had written *De causis latinae linguae* in

---

[8] Neostoicism served as a sort of dominant 'popular philosophy' of the Baroque (Brockhaus Enzyklopädie, 17th ed. 1971, 13: 296; see also 19th ed. 1991, 15: 511).

1540, the earliest post-medieval Latin theoretical grammar (discussed more fully below in 3.6).[9]

We come now to a group of scholars whose writings on their language and on its history were to influence Schottelius profoundly. Petrus Scriverius (= Peter Schrijver or Schryver, 1576–1660) spent most of his life in Leiden, and was a friend of both Hugo Grotius and Daniel Heinsius, whose poems he published. Daniel Heinsius (= Heins; 1580–1655) was professor of poetics (from 1603) and then Greek (1605) at Leiden; from 1607 he was librarian of Leiden University. Besides the crucial influence on German poetry and poetics of his *Nederduytsche poemata* (1616) (for which Scriverius supplied the preface and poem in praise of Dutch),[10] noted above, Heinsius is significant too as the author of the first emblem-book published in Dutch (see Figure 3.1), which appeared in 1601 under the pseudonym of Theocritus from Ghent, *Quaeris quid sit Amor...?* ('Do you ask what love is?'), a model that the 1643 emblem-book to which Schottelius contributed sought to emulate.

Adriaan van Schriek published a number of works on Dutch and Belgian history, including *Adversariorum libri IIII. His argumentis: Linguam*

Figure 3.1: Title page of Heinsius's emblem book *Quaeris quid sit Amor...?* (1601)

---

9   In this chapter, I refer both to J. C. Scaliger (1484–1558), author of *De causis linguae latinae* (Lyon 1540; see 3.6.1 below) and his son, J. J. Scaliger (1540–1609), who is one of the participants in the discussion of the question of language origin. Where confusion is possible, I include their initials.

10   An extract of the poem is cited by Schottelius, *AA* 22, 2: 26

Hebraicam esse divinam & primogeniam [...] (1620). He argued for the primacy of the Flemish language, following in the footsteps of Goropius Becanus, a physician with linguistic interests whose works include nine *Origines Antwerpianæ* ('The origins of Antwerp', 1569) and *Hermathena* (1580, published posthumously). Becanus indulged in wild etymologies to 'prove'—to his own satisfaction at least—that Flemish was the original language spoken in paradise. He was much mocked by contemporaries (including J. J. Scaliger and Lipsius) and by later scholars (such as Grotius) in a controversy of which Schottelius was aware and to which we shall return below. Becanus argued that the most ancient language on earth would be the simplest language, and that the simplest language would contain the most monosyllabic rootwords. Since the number of short words was (he asserted) higher in Flemish than in Latin, Greek or Hebrew, Becanus reasoned that his was the oldest language, from which all others were derived. He attempted to demonstrate this by showing that words in other languages were originally composed of Flemish rootwords. For instance, he argued that the name of the Germanic tribe of Saxons has at its root *sagun*, a compound made up of the two roots *Sac* + *Gun*, where *Sac* = 'Sack' or 'causa':

> *Prima littera sibilo suo motionem ad aliquid, media littera quadrato suo sono stationem & moram, ultima spiritus in se retractione suum cuique commodum ad se trahendum docet*

> 'The first letter with its sibilance indicates a motion towards something; the second with its square sound, halt and pause; and the final, by the retraction of the breath, teaches that that which is suitable needs to be drawn to one'.

(Becanus 1569: 579)

Now, the first cause is of course God. Meanwhile, *–gun* is the rootword for 'favour, love', so that *Sagun* means 'God shows favour, God loves'. Self-evidently for Becanus the Saxons, the tribe founded by the descendants of Gomer, Japhet and Noah were God's favoured people.[11]

Abraham Mylius (vander Mijle, 1563–1637) had studied in Leiden in the early 1580s. He had heard Lipsius lecture, and later corresponded with him. In his *Lingua Belgica* (1612) he maintained, as Becanus had done, that Flemish was the original language, for only it had suffered no change over time. Other languages were more or less corrupted dialects of Belgian (Metcalf 1953b).

Last in the list of Dutch and Flemish scholars is Simon Stevin (1548–1620), the mathematician and polyhistor in Bruges, where the statue in

---

[11] This summary follows Metcalf (1974: 243–44), whose English translation from the Latin I also cite. Becanus himself took 70 folio pages to argue the case to his satisfaction.

Figure 3.2: Statue of Simon Stevin, Bruges (photo by the author)

Figure 3.2 can be found, and who moved to Leiden in 1593. He is a sufficiently important figure in the history of mathematics for his principal works to have been translated into English (Dijksterhuis 1955); his advances include introducing the regular use of decimal fractions in mathematics. In the history of linguistic reflection, Stevin is important for his *Vytspraeck vande Weerdicheyt der duytsche tael*, his 'oration on the worth of the *duytsch* language',[12] which occupied 24 sides at the front of his work *De Weeghdaet* ('On the art of weighing', 1586). This oration at the front of the book served the purpose of justifying the author's use of his Dutch vernacular in the work that followed. In it, Stevin argued that simple

---

[12] It is difficult here to translate *Duytsch*. It means for Stevin something that encompasses Dutch and German at least. Evidence of its wider sense is the anecdote Stevin relates of the Swiss humanist Henricus Glareanus (1488–1563) switching from Latin to German during an oration on Suetonius because he found the German words to have the greater emotional appeal (Stevin 1586, in Dijksterhuis 1955: 86–87; Schottelius paraphrases Stevin's account in the *AA* 64–65, 4: 42). Here, Stevin uses for German the same word, *Duytsch*, that he uses for his own vernacular.

things merit simple (i.e. monosyllabic) words, an idea that Stevin seems to have taken from Becanus, or at the very least shares with him. Such monosyllabic rootwords can then be combined together to form new, more complex terms, a facility especially useful for coining technical terms. Stevin did not indulge in Becanus's wild etymological speculations. However, he did share his partisan view of his own language compared to the prestige languages of the day, as the following extract shows:

> Want dit moet ghy weten, dat de sprakens goetheyt niet alleen voorderlick en is om de Consten bequaemlick daer duer te leeren, maer oock den Vinders in haer soucking [...] wy segghen van Stoffwaerheyt, [...] en dierghelijcke, daer t'volghende vol af is; welcke woorden de Griecken soo cort, ende by haren yderman soo verstaenlic, oock so eyghentlick haer grondt beteeckenende, noyt en hebben connen segghen, nu niet en connen, noch, dat kennelick ghenouch is, inder eewicheyt niet connen en sullen. want datter niet in en is en cander niet uytghetrocken worden.

> 'For you must know that the excellence of language is conducive not only to learning the arts well through it, but also to the search of the inventors [...] we talk of *Stoffwaerheyt* ['specific gravity'], [...] and the like, in which the following [text] abounds; which words the Greeks never were, are not now, and never to all eternity will be able to say so shortly and so universally intelligibly to everyone of them, and also describing its nature so aptly, as is sufficiently obvious. For what is not in it [sc. in a language], cannot be extracted from it'.

> (from *De Beghinselen des Waterwichts* (Stevin 1586: 5–6; Dijksterhuis 1955: 384–87)

Similarly, in a passage lifted wholesale by Schottelius (*AA* 14, 1: 42), Stevin took pride in the unique ability of *Duytsch* to form compounds:

> want waer wildy spraken halen daermen duer segghen sal, Eu-estaltwichtich, Rechthefwicht, Scheefdaellini, en dierghelijcke daer de Weeghconst vol af is? sy en sijn der niet, de Natuer heeft daer toe aldereyghentlicxt het Duytsch veroirdent.

> 'for where would you find any languages in which one can say *Eu-estaltwichtich, Rechthefwicht, Scheefdaellini* ['of equal apparent weight', 'vertical lifting weight', 'oblique lowering line'] and the like, in which the Art of Weighing abounds? They do not exist, Nature has specially designed *Duytsch* for it.'

> (Dijksterhuis 1955: 86–87)

Like Becanus (and presumably under his influence) Stevin took the view that monosyllabic rootwords were indicative of *d'uyterste volmaectheyt* 'the highest perfection' (Dijksterhuis 1955: 80–81) in language, although Stevin argued, with a somewhat different reasoning that reflected his mathematical background, that 'the elements in the arts should be the simplest of all' (see Dijksterhuis 1955: 80).

We have identified a network of scholars linked by friendships and teaching across two generations in the fifty years or so around 1600, and sharing in Leiden their intellectual home. There is no evidence that Schottelius knew personally or corresponded with any of these scholars (see Berns 1978 on the very incomplete record of Schottelius's correspondence), but he nevertheless attached himself intellectually to their discourse tradition, picking up many of their key ideas. First, from Stevin Schottelius took the idea of the monosyllabic *grondwoord* or rootword as guarantor of German linguistic superiority. Indeed, Schottelius 'plagiarized' Stevin extensively (to use an anachronistic term), paraphrasing or even simply translating his Dutch into German, and applying the claims made for *Duytsch* to German (cf. 6.2.3. and Table 6.5). Second, from Vossius (1635), Schottelius took the notion of privileging *analogy*—the regular patterns which language observes (or should observe)—over mere usage, so that analogy became the governing, structuring principle in his own grammar, and one that competed with the dominant view of language in the FG. Third, Schottelius drew on the Neostoicism of Lipsius to justify the primacy he accorded analogy and to determine what is *grundrichtig* in language. Analogy is rational, which is natural, and so in accord with the nature of the language. Non-analogical forms, being irrational and unnatural, whether sanctioned by usage or not, were by this reasoning inherently inferior, as noted in 2.4.2; Schottelius cited Grotius's (1626) view that general custom should be in accord with natural law, since both custom (based on human reasoning) and nature had their basis in reason.

> [...] man [muss] aber die Kraft des natürlichen **Rechts** / entweder aus der Kraft des natürlichen **Verstandes** beweisen / [...]: (aldieweil dasselbe / was uns die verständliche Natur befihlt / gewislich das natürliche **Recht** seyn muß/) Oder aber / man muß das natürliche Recht aus einer gemeinen Gleichhaltung bey allen / oder doch bey den vornemsten Völkeren abnehmen: Den was bey allen verständigen Menschen gemein und beliebt ist / hat keine andere uhrsprüngliche Ursache / als den gemeinen Menschlichen Verstand

> '[...] one must prove the strength of natural law either by force of natural reason (since that which reasonable nature commends to us must surely be the natural law), or from the common opinion of all, or at least of the most noble peoples. For what is common to and

popular amongst all reasonable people has no other original cause than common human reason'

(*AA* 16, 2: 2)[13]

The essence of German may thus be discovered in exactly the same way. *Die vornehmsten Gründe unserer HaubtSprache* spring *aus einem Gebot der Teutschen SprachNatur* ('the most noble foundations of our cardinal language [spring] from the dictate of the nature of the German language'). Failing that, though, we may rely on the *Ubereinstimmung und vereinbarte Meinung vieler gelahrten Männer* ('the common view and agreed opinion of many learned men'). It is this second method of discovering the essence of German that Schottelius pursued in the *AA* (being himself a learned man with a vested interest in the matter):[14] *Grundrichtigkeit* may be detected in the opinions of those well-versed in the art of language, such as himself. So the doctrine of natural law made relying on the learned grammarians' authority appear the only way to proceed (*vs*, for instance, adopting the usage of a prestigious individual, text-type or region). The doctrine was also a handy way of justifying the grammarians' authority in the face of opposing practices, which could be dismissed as perversions of the natural language. For, Schottelius warned (*AA* 16, 2: 3), natural law does not change one iota when people are deprived of their natural reason and so fail to discern the natural law. Though a madman may call honey bitter, it remains sweet, true to its nature. Thus in one fell swoop all who might disagree with Schottelius could be dismissed as either deprived of their natural reason or too ignorant to judge, an important rhetorical achievement on page 16 of a 1500-page work.

It is interesting to observe that the French *remarqueurs* contemporary with Schottelius also drew on arguments about the basis of laws, particularly the doctrine of customary law, in their own discussions of usage *vs* analogy in French (cf. Weinrich 1960, 1989). For instance, Vaugelas (1647) was criticized by Dupleix (1651) for his misrepresentation

---

[13]   Schottelius's references are to Book 1, Chapter 1, (X. and XII.1), pages 6 and 9 of Grotius's *De Ivre Belli ac Pacis* (Moeno-Francofvrti: Wechelius, 1626); cf. Grotius, *Vom Recht des Krieges und des Friedens*, ed. Schätzel (1950: 50, 52): *Das natürliche Recht ist ein Gebot der Vernunft* 'Natural law is a command of reason' and 'But one is accustomed to prove partly directly, partly indirectly, that there are certain requirements according to natural law; the direct proof is more incisive, the indirect more generally comprehensible. The first consists in showing that something is necessarily either in accord with reasonable nature and society, or is not. An indirect proof is when one, admittedly not with full certainty, but nevertheless with a very high probability, derives the natural legality of a requirement from the fact that it is held as such by all peoples, or by all civilized peoples. For a generally observed effect presupposes a general cause; but the reason for such a general opinion can surely only be found in what one calls good common sense' (my translation).

[14]   On the power of specialist knowledge in creating and preserving a social elite, see Huber (1984: 248 ff.).

of customary law in a pronouncement in favour of usage, *communis error facit ius*, 'common error makes the law'. Evidently notions of natural *vs* customary law were 'in the air' in Europe of the time.

Fourth and finally, Schottelius also eagerly added his voice to the controversies raging over the views of Becanus amongst Schrieckius, Grotius, Lipsius, and others about the origin of language (and of German and Dutch especially). Here, the Leiden connection overlaps with international Latinate discourse (for the Dutch and Flemish scholars were not the only voices in the debate) (cf. 3.6 below). We can safely conclude already, however, that Schottelius's theory of language, his linguistic philosophy, *and* his view of language history are all heavily indebted to discussions of Leiden-based Flemish and Dutch scholars of his own and of the previous generation. Ironically, as Bornemann (1976) long ago observed of the influence of the Dutch movement on German cultural patriotism, much that allowed Schottelius to give vent to his specifically German cultural and linguistic patriotism in fact had its roots abroad, in the Low Countries.

3.5 CULTURAL PATRIOTISM

Let us consider now the place of the *AA* in the discourse of cultural and linguistic patriotism, first in general terms (3.5.1), then with a focus the following aspects and their relevance for Schottelius's *AA*: the metaphors of linguistic purism; yardsticks for evaluating the language; key genres of cultural patriotism; and the role of language societies, especially the *Fruchtbringende Gesellschaft* ('Fruit-bearing Society').

3.5.1 *Introduction: cultural and linguistic patriotism*

Huber (1984:16) understands by *cultural patriotism* the 'demonstration of love to the culture of the fatherland, whether it [i.e. the national culture] already exists or whether it is yet to be created' [as was certainly the case in seventeenth-century Germany] (my translation). During and in the aftermath of the Thirty Years' War, when the German empire was politically weak and the regions politically and religiously divided, German cultural patriotism rested to a considerable extent on 'the' German language as a unifying factor transcending the everday linguistic reality of a mass of dialects. Across a range of language-related genres (grammars, poetics, dictionaries and rhetorics), a progression can be observed from the earliest arguments in defence of German based on its usefulness (early grammarians like Albertus and Ölinger emphasize the usefulness of their grammars to foreign learners, for instance), to asserting the *equal* worth of German alongside other vernaculars, to the ultimate assertion of the *superiority* of

German (Huber 1984: 230–33). Schottelius represents the third stage, and indeed Huber sees in Schottelius the apogee of German cultural patriotism *tout court*, for successors referred to him, and no new arguments were adduced.[15] Passionate assertions of the worth of the German vernacular, often adducing the achievements of respected vernacular authors in support, went hand in hand with laments over its decay, as in Martin Opitz's youthful lament *Aristarchus sive De Contemptu Linguae Teutonicae* ('On the contempt of the German language', 1617). In Schottelius's *AA*, the inherent qualities of German were contrasted with its current neglected state. The full title of Schottelius's ninth oration sums up this lamenting tendency:

> Die neundte Lobrede von der Uhralten HaubtSprache der Teut-schen / begreift Eine kurtze Entdekkung des unbegründeten Wesens / dadurch unsere HaubtSprache zum Sproslinge / Menglinge und Bettlerin wird gemacht: auch wie von denen sonst fleissigen und sinnreichen Teutschen die Teutschen Sprache sey verseumt und veracht worden. Samt angeführten Uhrsachen / wordurch die rechte Ausübung und Werthaltung deroselben / noch itzo guten theils verhindert werde.

> 'The ninth oration of the ancient cardinal language of the Germans consists of a brief discovery of the unfounded means by which our cardinal language is reduced to an offshoot, a mongrel and a beggar: also how the German language has been neglected and despised by the otherwise so industrious and intelligent Germans. Together with causes given, by which the correct exercise and valuing of the same [language] is still now largely prevented.'

> (*AA* 135, 9: title)

3.5.2 *The metaphors of linguistic purism*

Schottelius's ninth oration, with the title just cited, is typical of the branch of linguistic patriotism whose exponents were preoccupied with preserving or restoring the *purity* of the language. Purity might extend to the grammar of the language, as when Schottelius sought to elimate forms at odds with the 'nature' of the language (a sense in which *puritas* was already applied to Latin). But most commonly, linguistic purism took the form of foreign

---

[15]   Rather, the next step in linguistic reflection was the confidence to move away from chauvinist comparisons, permitting a return to reflecting on the usefuless of German, but now concentrating on its *Wirkung* (to use a key term from rhetoric of the seventeenth century), its *effect* on the listener or reader, for literary and rhetorical ends.

word purism.[16] Typical topoi of seventeenth-century foreign word purism include the creation of sharp dichotomies such as pure/impure, own/ foreign, *teutsch/unteutsch*, and the emotive deployment of metaphors: legal imagery (naturalization), clothing (rags, cobbled together), food and drink (mother's milk, pepper contaminated with mouse droppings), subjugation, disease, metallurgy and coins, language as a vulnerable female (reduced to poverty, ravaged, ill or dying), and language as a fruitful tree (cf. Jones 1999: 59–83 and Stukenbrock 2005: 80–155).[17] Virtually all of these metaphor types are found in Schottelius's *AA*, too (*AA* 8, 1: 23 coin; 18, 2: 14 and 141, 9: 12 milk; 29, 3: 3 gold; 110, 7: 13 yoke; 141, 9: 12 cooking; 144, 9: 18 rags; see also Schottelius 1640: Diij[r]; for the image of the language tree, cf. 2.4.1). The image of naturalization (Schottelius *AA* 1272–73) expresses Schottelius's relatively moderate purism, where he allowed for words which had become established in the language, and criticized overly radical purism. The following example—again from the ninth oration, where the language appears as a queen reduced to rags and poverty—illustrates the typically heavily metaphorical style of Schottelius's purism:

> Mehr als zuviel ist bekant / wie die Teutsche Sprache jhre eigene Wörter verlieren / deutlos und unbekant lassen / jhren herrlichen Reichtuhm verarmet sehen / und jhre eigene reinliche Gestalt verfrömdet und verschandflekket leiden muß / in dem nicht allein einem jeden nach Beliebung / durch gestatteten Misbrauch freygelassen wird allerley Wörter aus allerley Sprachen hinein zulappen / als ob keine zierliche Rede geschehen / noch einige Schrift abgefasset werden könte / Zier und Wolstand sey dañ von Frömden entlehnet / und unsere so herrliche / prächtige / Majestätische Sprache zur armen hungerigen Bettlerin gemacht

> 'It is only too well known how the German language is obliged to lose her own words, leave them meaningless and unknown, see her great wealth impoverished, and suffer her pure form to be corrupted and shamefully stained, not only in that everyone is free to plug his speech with all sorts of words from all sorts of languages, just as he likes, as if no fitting speech were possible, and no writing could be

---

[16] Thomas (1991:12) defines linguistic purism as 'the manifestation of a desire on the part of a speech community (or some section of it) to preserve a language from, or rid it of, putative foreign elements or other elements held to be undesirable (including those originating in dialects, sociolects and styles of the same language. [...] it may be directed at all linguistic levels, but primarily the lexicon. Above all, purism is an aspect of the codification, cultivation and planning of standard languages'. On purism in German see Jones (1999), and and for comparative approaches to purism in the Germanic languages, see the contributions in Langer &Davies (2005). Thomas (1991) remains the most comprehensive comparative study of purism in many vernacular language traditions.

[17] The texts in Jones (1995) furnish numerous examples, to which Jones (1999) provides page references.

composed, unless adornment and wealth be borrowed from for-
eigners, and our so glorious, splendid and majestic language be reduced to a hungry beggar-woman.'

(*AA* 137, 9: 6)

3.5.3 *Cultural-patriotic yardsticks for evaluating the language*

Linguistic patriots were also at pains to demonstrate in their language the
qualities of *Deutlichkeit* (*perspicuitas* 'clarity'), *Kürze* (*brevitas* 'brevity') and
Reichtum (*copia* 'richness, abundance'), all language yardsticks familiar
across Europe and with their origins in ancient Rome. We have already
seen how for Schottelius, the *Reichtum* of German was evident in its greater
number of rootwords compared to other languages, and its *Kürze* in the fact
that these rootwords are monosyllabic (and that such simplicity was
simultaneously also a guarantor for other key values: antiquity and
originality). Both *Reichtum* and *Kürze* were demonstrated by the limitless
capacity for forming succinct compounds, avoiding the need for wordy
circumlocutions. Clarity was guaranteed by the transparency of German
compounding and derivation, as well as by the fact that for many words
common in European languages 'what the word properly means' (*was aber
das Wort recht bedeute, AA* 125, 8: 4) is clear only in *die rechte Teutsche
Wurtzel* ('the proper German root' *AA* 124, 8: 4), an observation that
Schottelius interpreted as evidence that the German roots were truer than
other languages to the original language. Another traditional yardstick was
Zierlichkeit (*ornatus* 'adornment, embellishment'), and so Schottelius
emphasized the need to spend time and effort acquainting oneself properly
with German, in order to be able to 'clothe' (*einkleiden*) a new or unfamiliar
concept in *rechte natürliche Teutsche Zier* 'in proper natural German
adornment' (*AA* 10, 1: 31). The question of appropriate adornment
naturally led (as here, with the term *einkleiden*) back to a rejection of
foreign borrowings: German had no need of foreign cloth, offering
adornment enough of its own (*AA* 19, 2: 15).[18]

As is characteristic of any ideology, the German cultural patriotism of the
seventeenth century also tended to equate one concept or quality with
others, whether implicitly or explicitly, to encourage value judgements. The
German language was typically elevated by association with morality and
with religious faith. In the following passage, German is the language in
which we approach God, and knowledge of German can encourage virtue,
reverence, obedience (here a positive quality!), and 'much good' (Schottelius
AA 146–47, 9: 26):

---

[18] On the role of such yardsticks as clarity, richness and ornament in eighteenth-century
Germany, see Leweling (2005); cf. also Gardt (2008) on the changing interaction between
'clarity' and 'naturalness' as yardsticks.

Dan ja nicht zuleugnen / daß rechte Lust und Kündigkeit der so wortreichen Sprache / zu manchem guten Gedanken und Vornehmen jhren Liebhaber auffrischen / und das jenige / was also lieblich und wol darin alsdan geschrieben und getahn wird / den Leser nicht weniger aufmuntere / und zur Tugend / Gottesfurcht / Gehorsam / und vielen Guten / gleichsam unvermerket ungezwungen anlokke

For it cannot be denied that proper pleasure in and knowledge of the language, so rich in words, spur on the lover of it to many a good thought and undertaking, and what is written and done in it so charmingly and well [can] encourage the reader no less, and entice [one]—unremarked and without forcing, as it were—to virtue, fear of God, obedience and to many a good thing.

3.5.4 *Key genres of linguistic patriotism*

Every one of the genres included by Schottelius in the *AA* already had an established place in German cultural patriotism. The grammar showed the worth of German and provided a guide to good writing in German. Schottelius's poetical treatise (dating from 1645) likewise provided a guide to good writing, but in the form of verse, and was part of the impetus that drove works of the same type published by other members of the FG, including Martin Opitz's *Buch von der deutschen Poeterey* (Opitz 1624), August Buchner's *Kurzer Weg-Weiser zur deutschen Tichtkunst* (published posthumously in 1663, although Buchner's ideas were already highly influential in the 1640s), and Harsdörffer's *Poetischer Trichter* (1648–1653). The panegyrics were intended to inspire good literary and good technical writing, both by their content and by example, and had a direct precursor in the *Uytspraeck* of Stevin, and in earlier sixteenth-century defences of the vernacular in Italy and France (Speroni 1542; du Bellay 1549). The apparently disparate and unconnected treatises in the fifth and final book of the *AA* also make sense as part of the same cultural-patriotic impetus. The verse *Einleitung zur Teutschen Sprache* (reprinted from 1643) is at once a demonstration of the potential of German for literary purposes, an emotional appeal to cultivate the language as it deserved, and a vehicle for conveying a great deal of information about the language, in the copious footnotes which accompany the text. The second treatise, a listing of Germanic proper names, provided an opportunity to show the ancient origins of the German language, and to demonstrate how its elements conveyed meaning, as well as to showcase the abundance of its rootwords and their almost infinite combinability. The collection of proverbs in Treatise 3 must be seen in the same light: the sheer number of proverbs is a measure of the richness of the language, and Schottelius's collection was a reply to collections of proverbs for Latin. The list of *Stammwörter* in Treatise 4 made the same point, but was also intended to form the basis for a dictionary organized by root elements. Since for Schottelius, 'the' language was the language of writing (2.2.1), the list of German authors, past and present, in Treatise 5 was proof of the strength of German by association with the prestige of its writers. In the imagined language tree, these writers' works formed the very ground on which the German language was planted and must be nurtured. In his outline of a workplan for a dictionary (dating from 1647), Harsdörffer called for a *Vollständiges Wortbuch*, 'complete dictionary', to be compiled on the basis of these established writings—for lexicography, too, is a key cultural-patriotic 'heritage-building' genre of Early Modern Europe (cf. Considine 2008 and review by Jones 2009):

> aus den Gründen } nemlich aus allen Teutschen Büchern, und Zu solcher Durchlesung wird die gesammte hilff erfordert, dz nemlich einer aus den Reichsabschieden, der ander aus dem Goldast, der dritte aus D. Luther, der vierte aus den Poëten & c., alle besondere Stammwörter, Sprüche und redarten Ziehe, und muß hierinnen großer fleiß angewendet, und nach meiner meinung kein alter, noch neuer Scribent außgelassen werden, als in welchen der Grund der Sprache Zu untersuchen kommet.

> 'from the foundations } namely from all German books and for such a reading-through the help of everyone is called for, such that one must draw all particular rootwords, sayings and idioms from the imperial decrees, another from Goldast, another from Dr Luther, the fourth from the poets, etc., and great diligence must be applied here and, in my view, no older nor modern writer be omitted in which the foundation of the language is to be investigated.

> (Krause 1855 [1973]: 388–89).

The *Grund* of the language, its real basis, is the ground accumulated over the years of writing in German, ground which the members of the FG must work, in order to bring forth the fruit.

Finally, the guide to translating (Treatise 6) is a an instruction book for one of the key activities explicitly expected of members of the leading patriotic language society, the *Fruchtbringende Gesellschaft*, that they should, if not writing new works, publish edifying works from Greek, Latin and other peoples, *getreulich verhochdeutschet* 'faithfully translated' (constitution of the FG, §7).

3.5.5 *Language societies, the* Fruchtbringende Gesellschaft *('Fruit-bearing Society') and society members' impact on the* AA

As Harsdörffer's dictionary plan of 1647 shows, an important vehicle for debating and disseminating language-focussed cultural patriotism was provided by the numerous language societies in Germany in the seventeenth century, inspired in part by the Low Countries *rederijkerskamers* ('rhetorical societies' or guilds which had existed since the medieval period, and which in the sixteenth century increasingly became fora for promoting and discussing the vernacular) and the Italian Accademia della Crusca, founded in Florence in 1582. One such society was the *Pegnesischer Blumenorden* ('Pegnesian order of flowers'), founded in 1644 in Nuremberg by Harsdörffer and Johann Klaj, which pursued particularly poetic interests and which numbered Birken, Rist and Schottelius himself amongst its members, as well as Katharina von Greiffenberg, the only female poet whom Schottelius cites in the *AA*. Not all had this narrowly poetic focus—but all the societies shared the broad aim of 'cultivating' German and of promoting good writing in the vernacular, whether by literary production, literary translation from other languages, or seeking to minimize the use of lexical borrowings that were felt to contaminate German. In 1643, Schottelius became a member of the first and most important of these societies, the *Fruchtbringende Gesellschaft* or Fruit-bearing Society (established in 1617, and ultimately boasting 890 members).[19] The society's emblem (Figure 3.3) was reproduced alongside Schottelius's own emblem on the title page of the *AA*, indicating that it was published under the auspices of the society.

The most obvious impact of the *FG* and of the wider cultural-patriotic movement on Schottelius's writings was his decision to write his grammar in German. This might seem barely worthy of comment. His contemporary and rival Gueintz (1641) had done just that. A number of other grammars of German *in* German had also already appeared in the early years of the seventeenth century, though these were very elementary and incomplete, aimed at children or adult learners of little education (cf. for example McLelland, 2005; Moulin-Fankhänel 2000 is an overview of grammato-graphy of the period). Yet the best-selling grammar of the period, that of Clajus (1578), was in Latin, and Schottelius's tendency to codeswitch from German to Latin in the orations (see footnote 1 above) betrays the fact that to write in German on academic matters did not yet come naturally. Schottelius's use of German as the language of exposition for what aimed to be the most comprehensive grammar of German to date was thus programmatic, as Schottelius made clear in the first oration of the first (1641) edition of his grammar:

---

[19]   On the language societies of the seventeenth century, see Roelcke (2000), Ingen (1986), Otto (1972), Polenz (1994: 112–21). Other societies besides the FG and the *Pegnesischer Blumenorden* were the *Deutschgesinnte Genossenschaft* 'German-minded club' (founded 1642/43 in Hamburg by Philipp von Zesen) and—competing with the latter—the *Elbschwanenorden* 'order of [River] Elbe Swans', founded by Rist in Wedel near Hamburg in 1658, as well as the *Aufrichtige Tannengesellschaft* 'Sincere fir-tree society' (a deliberately small society, founded 1633 in Strasbourg).

Figure 3.3: The emblem of the *Fruchtbringende Gesellschaft*

Alldieweil ich aber in verfertigung dieser Sprachkunst mich gar
nichts gekehret / noch kehren sollen an das jenige / was etwa in
einer Griechischen und Lateinischen *Grammatic* zu finden ist / So
habe ich auch gar keine wichtige Uhrsache ersehen können /
warumb ich die Griechischen und Lateinischen *Terminos Gram-
maticales* behalten solte; denn man von Teutscher Sprache teutsch
und nicht Griechisch oder Lateinisch reden soll: [...]. Derowegen
habe ich es bey mir für einen Eckel und Schande gehalten / etwas
von Athen oder Rom zu erbetteln / welches in unserem Teuts-
chlande schöner / safftiger und dem Teutschen Verstande kräfftiger
verhanden ist.

'Since in preparing this grammar I have not bothered, nor should I
have bothered about, what is to be found in a Greek or Latin
grammar, so I have also seen no good reason why I should keep
the grammatical terms; for about the German language one should

write German and not Greek or Latin: [...] for which reason I have held it disgusting and a disgrace in myself to beg something from Greek or Latin which is present more beautifully and more juicily in Germany and more clearly and more powerfully in German reason.'

(Schottelius 1641: 15)

The emotive language here, with its appeal to morality (*Schande, Ekel*) and its use of metaphor (*erbetteln*) is typical of energetic linguistic patriotism, not just of the period, but indeed across the centuries (cf. Stukenbrock 2005; 3.5.2 above). It expressed the requirement of the FG that its members (or at least those members who were competent to do so) should *die allernützlichsten Bücher in allerhand Wissenschaften und Künsten [...] in Hochdeutscher Sprache rein und zierlich geschrieben [...] heraus[zu]geben* 'publish [...], written purely and with delicacy in High German, the most useful books in all branches of science and art [...]' (constitution of the FG, §7). Schottelius said as much in 1663 too: he explained that his use of German for all rules and terminology in the earlier editions of the grammar was *auch teihls der hochlöblichen Fruchtbringenden Gesellschafft halber* 'also in part for the sake of the very-praiseworthy Fruitbearing Society' (*AA* 2, 1:2). The fact that Schottelius deviated from this principle in the 1663 edition, to provide Latin summaries and (partial) translations of grammatical rules, is a mark of his ambition by then to be read internationally; he mentioned potential French and Dutch readers in particular (*AA* 169, 10: 23).

Members of the FG regularly commented on drafts of each other's work, and those comments in some cases had a very direct influence on Schottelius's *AA*. In some cases, Schottelius was faced with competing expectations from the cultural patriotism expressed by members of the FG and from the other discourse traditions in which he was participating. One such instance concerns the use of German for topics at the time more usually treated in Latin. Despite their own frequent practice of writing amongst themselves in Latin, the society's members took a lively and interventionist interest in individual members' efforts to develop appropriate technical terminology in German. Schottelius's German translation of the title of his *poetica germanica, Teutsche Verskunst oder Reimkunst* (1645), ran into criticism when first circulated among members of the FG, when Prince Ludwig, the head of the FG, commented:

Verskunst kan darumb die deutsche Poesi nicht heissen, weil der Vers nur in einer Zeile mit seinem gewissen masse bestehet. Alle deutschen Poesien aber sich reimen, und Zwey oder mehr Zeilen haben. Sind es also Rhytmi reime und nicht Verse, ob sie schon auch ihr gewis gesetztes mas haben, und ist so eigentlicher Reimkunst genant.

The German poesy cannot be called *Verskunst* ['art of *Vers*'], because the *Vers* ['line of poetry'] consists only in a line with a particular metre. But all German poesies rhyme, and have two or more lines. So they are *Rhytmi*, rhymes, and not *Verse* ['lines'] even if they also have a certain metre, and so it is more accurately called *Reimkunst* ['art of rhyme'].

(Krause 1855 [1973]: 293).

Schottelius pointed out that *Reimen* was just a small part of the art of poetry as a whole, and thus preferred the term *Verskunst* (explaining that the loanword *Vers* has become integrated into German vocabulary: Krause 1855 [1973]: 291; *AA* 800). But he was a pragmatist. In the face of the objection from this powerful FG member, he kept both German terms—*Verskunst* and *Reimkunst*—in the title of the published work.[20]

A similar dispute had arisen with the publication of Schottelius's grammar in 1641. His definition of grammar, here cited from the 1663 edition (*AA* 180), runs:

Die Sprachkunst ist eine Wissenschaft / oder kunstmessige Fertigkeit / recht und rein Teutsch zureden oder zuschreiben.

'Grammar is a science or an artful competence to speak or write German correctly and purely'

Here the particular German formulation of *recht und rein* is the result of discussion, in correspondence between August Buchner (1591–1661) and Prince Ludwig about Gueintz's (1641) grammar, of just what is meant by *recht* and *rein* (Krause 1855 [1973]: 234–235). This will be discussed more fully in 5.3. Here it is sufficient to note that Schottelius was again pragmatic and opted for both terms in his definition, adopting a wording advocated by influential members of the FG.

These examples concern mere nuances in nascent German terminology. A more fundamental discussion within the FG concerned the status of the rootword, as we shall see in 3.8.2 below, but first we shall consider Schottelius's place in *international* scholarly reflection on language.

---

[20] On the other hand, Schottelius appears to have taken no notice of suggestions for names of the metrical feet (Krause 1855 [1973]: 294); cf. *AA* 835.

3.6 INTERNATIONAL LATINATE LINGUISTIC REFLECTION

Despite the fact that Schottelius portrayed his grammar as the fulfilment of an existing practical German grammatical tradition, he also sought increasingly to contribute to the wider, international discussion of the important linguistic questions of his day—questions that had hitherto been and still were largely being discussed in Latin.[21] It is a measure of Schottelius's scholarly aspiration that he cited some three hundred sources in the first book of the *AA* alone, in order to discuss the history of German within the context of contemporary deliberations about the oldest language, the origins of writing, and the question of the relationships among the various languages. That particular discussion is considered in 3.6.3 below. But Schottelius also built his language theory on the state of the art in Latinate discussions of grammatical theory, to which we turn first.

3.6.1 Grammatical theory in the Latin tradition[22]

Schottelius's chief source for the cutting edge in questions of grammatical theory was Vossius's *De Arte Grammatica* (1635). Vossius in turn revisited key questions addressed by his predecessors in the important post-medieval Latin theoretical grammars, especially by J. C. Scaliger (1540), Ramus (1550s), and Sanctius (1587). Of particular importance here is the place of *ratio* in grammar, and the question of what was understood by *ratio*. Simplifying greatly, we can see a see-saw over the centuries between, on the one hand, relying on logic and *ratio* as the basis for determining correct language, and, on the other, turning to rhetorical criteria and usage, even if at each see-saw the two opposing positions changed somewhat. The very word 'elegance' in the title of Laurentius Valla's (1405-1457) work *De linguae Latinae elegantia* (1540) was indicative of the humanist shift in emphasis, away from the arid logical categories of the logic-based, universal speculative grammars of the medieval period, towards studying grammar by observing good usage. By 'good usage' the *elegant* Latin to be found in classical authors was meant, not the barbarous Latin of medieval scholars. But Valla's contemporary J. C. Scaliger swung the pendulum back the other way. The title of his *De causis linguae Latinae* (1540) proclaimed his allegiance to Aristotelian logic, applying to language the 'four causes' of Aristotle (a way of explaining the world by examining the factors that

---

[21] A notable exception, which Schottelius also cited, is Claude Duret's *Thrésor de l'histoire des langues de cest univers* (1613), in French.

[22] For the exposition of the ideas of J. C. Scaliger, Ramus, Sanctius and Vossius, I chiefly follow Padley (1976), as well as Jensen (1990), and Rademaker (1992).

contribute to making it the way it is).[23] Petrus Ramus (1515–1572) backed away again somewhat from Aristotle (albeit not nearly as much as the famous title of his 1536 thesis 'all Aristotle's doctrines are false' might suggest: Padley 1976: 78). Ramus aimed to keep logic and rhetoric properly distinct, each in their 'proper' domains. He favoured like Valla the teaching of Latin by literary rather than logical methods. Sanctius's *Minerva. De causis linguae Latinae* (1587), harked back in its title to J. C. Scaliger's Aristotelianism, though in practice it was a not always happy marriage of ideas from Scaliger and Ramus.

One obvious symptom of the tug-of-war between logic-based approaches and a more rhetorical approach to grammar was the way the parts of speech were defined. Schottelius's definitions are thus a handy measure by which to see where he stood in this tradition. Throughout the sixteenth century there had been a strong tendency to rely on purely semantic rather than formal criteria to define the parts of speech. The long-transmitted definition of the noun by Donatus ran: *Nomen est pars orationis cum casu corpus aut rem proprie communiterve significans* 'a noun is a part of speech with case, signifying a body or a thing, properly or commonly'. It combined both semasiological criteria ('signifying a body or thing') and formal criteria ('with case') (Padley 1976: 38). But the German humanist Melanchthon dispensed with the formal criteria, leaving only semasiological criteria in *Nomen significat rem, non actionem* 'a noun signifies a thing, not an action' (Melanchthon 1527: 26ʳ, cited Padley 1976: 46). Similarly, his definition of the verb was 'a part of speech signifying *actio* or *passio*'.[24] Such definitions were patently inadequate for rigorous distinctions between parts of speech, and they reflected a loss of faith in the need for adequate

---

[23] 'Cause' is the somewhat misleading, but traditional, translation of Aristotle's Greek term meaning something like 'factor responsible', or perhaps 'explanatory factor'. The 'four causes' of Aristotle provide answers to four types of question one might ask about something, for example, about a man: 1. 'What is it made from?' 'Flesh and so on' (material cause); 2. 'What is its form or essence?' 'A two-legged creature capable of reason' (formal cause); 3. 'What produced it?' 'The father (according to Aristotle's biology!)' (efficient cause); 4. 'For what purpose?' 'To fulfil the function of a man' (meaning something like 'to live a life in accordance with reason') (final cause). Applied to language, the 'material cause' was the *elements*, the sounds that are combined in language. The 'formal cause' was that by which form is imposed on these, the raw material of language—not, as we might assume today, formal *grammatical* structure, but rather the shaping of the raw material by the imposition of *meaning* on it. The 'efficient cause', whether artisan, artist or God, was that by which form was imposed on the substance. The 'final cause' was the end to which this form was imposed.

[24] Padley (1976: 38–39) overstates the significance of Melanchthon's scanty definition *Nomen significat rem* when he suggests that it makes Melanchthon a 'forerunner of seventeenth century attitudes', with the 'typically seventeenth-century preoccupation, the urge to undertake a conceptual classification of the universe with a one-to-one correspondence between names and things'. Roman grammarians already used very similar terms (e.g. Consentius: *pars orationis rem unam aliquam significans*, cited Jellinek 1914: 79), so such definitions do not really indicate a typically seventeenth-century obsession with one-to-one correspondences between words and things.

formal, scientific criteria. The emphasis was rather on mastering elegant style than on scientifically rigorous definition.[25] J. C. Scaliger was less extreme than Melanchthon, adding the formal criterion 'without tense' when he defined the noun as a *dictio declinabilis per casum, significans rem sine tempore* 'a word declinable according to case, signifying a thing without tense', whereas Vossius stated simply *Est igitur nomen vox ex instituto rem primo significans* 'A noun is therefore basically a word signifying a thing'.

Schottelius's own definition was a combination of the purely semasiological definition of Melanchthon with the formal criteria found in Scaliger (inflecting, and without tense), and runs *Nomen est vox variabilis, significans rem & non actionem, sed sine tempore* 'A noun is a variable [i.e. declinable] word, signifying a thing and not an action, but without tense' (cf. discussion in Barbarić 1981: 536–39). However, in the paragraph following his definition (*AA* 231, § 2) Schottelius adds the *signs* by which the part of speech can be recognized (in this case: one can add *der, die, das*), which had been a commonplace in the pedagogical Latin grammatical tradition since at least about 1500 and which had then also been applied to the vernacular (cf. Puff 1995: 228–43). His Latin explanation of the *signa* of the noun is identical to that of the German grammarian Clajus (1578), for instance. The example of the noun illustrates, then, how Schottelius drew *both* on the Latinate grammatical tradition (the likes of Melanchthon and J. C. Scaliger) *and* on earlier German grammars.

A further fundamental question in grammatical theory, to which the answer was regularly changing, was just what the province of grammar was. The question could be posed in at least two different ways: i. what was the object of study? and ii. what was the purpose of such study? In answer to the first question, J. C. Scaliger (1540) set a new course for theoretical grammar with his interest in the *material cause* of language: the elements or sounds of language, its basic substance. For Scaliger, grammar was concerned only secondarily, accidentally with the written language. We have seen, however, that Schottelius remained primarily interested in the written language—pronunciation was interesting only from an aesthetic perspective, *wollauten* 'sounding good' (cf. 2.2.1). The second question about grammar concerned its purpose: was grammar to be *methodica, enarrativa* or *critica*? J. C. Scaliger, privileging the spoken substance of language, naturally saw no place in grammar proper for *grammatica enarrativa*, grammar as the interpretation of authors, and Vossius (1635) followed Scaliger in this. For Vossius, the province of grammar was the specifying of grammatical rules, *grammatica methodica*. (*Grammatica critica* was concerned with textual criticism, requiring elelements of both of the

---

[25] Ramus is a prominent but fairly isolated exception to this sixteenth-century trend, restoring the formal definition of the parts of speech. For instance, the noun is for Ramus a *vox numeri cum genere et casu* 'a word with number, gender and case', while the verb is a *vox numeri cum tempore et persona* 'a word with number, tense and person'.

other two to form judgements and amend texts as necessary). Schottelius (in an addition to the grammar made only in the 1663 edition) cited the distinction between these three types of grammar, as in Vossius, but it suited him to embrace them all. It was obvious that he presented a *grammatica methodica*, giving rules. But he also noted that he included *was* [...] ad enarrativam, *auch ofters was* ad Criticam *gehörig seyn mag* 'what might belong to exegetical grammar, and quite often also to critical grammar', *AA* 177 § 13). This rather brief, superficial engagement with the fundamental question about the purpose of grammar reads like a post-hoc self-justification, and it may even be a belated response to the dispute in the 1640s between Schottelius and Gueintz about what does or does not belong in a grammar. Schottelius's review of Gueintz's grammar had noted that he had not covered 'even a thirtieth' of what there was to say about derivation and composition of adjectives, and that *Es müsten auch die stammworter in viel-größerer Zahl aufgesucht ... werden* ('the rootwords must be sought out in much greater numbers', Krause 1855 [1973]: 250); Gueintz had retorted *Da sollen auch nicht alle Wörter da sein, denn es gehöret in das Lexicon oder Wörterbuch* ('There shouldn't be all words there, for that belongs in a lexicon or dictionary', Krause 1855 [1973]: 257). Perhaps it was in response to such criticism that Schottelius justified scouring the writings of German authors of all periods in search of words, as *grammatica enarrativa*. He then appealed to the third division of grammar, *grammatica critica*, to justify the judgements that he made about what he found there. It was, he said, impossible to search the works of writers for such words *ohn beuhrtheilung* 'without judging'. Schottelius therefore made his own judgements as permitted by *grammatica critica*, noting that *der gute Gebrauch und grundrichtige Uhrsach | jedesmahl so viel möglich uhrtheilfasser gewesen* 'each time good usage and the fundamental cause were arbiters as much as possible' (*AA* 178 §13).

In 1663, then, Schottelius had recourse to the ancient distinctions between the *grammatica methodica, explicativa* and *critica,* distinctions still being made in learned Latinate discourse, to legitimize his listing of a great deal of lexical information in his grammar, something which had been criticized by Gueintz within the discourse of the FG. However, Schottelius's engagement with this theoretical discussion was very superficial. He simply embraced all three types (post-hoc, in 1663) to give himself licence for including in the grammar what he wanted. A more profound influence on his grammatical theory was the centrality of *ratio* to the study of language, a common thread running through the sixteenth and early seventeenth centuries in the works of Scaliger, Sanctius, and Vossius, as well as their lesser contemporaries. Scaliger, reacting against humanist enthusiasm for observing usage, did not deny the place of usage, but argued that usage must conform to reason. The true object of his study was, Scaliger wrote, the *communis ratio* of language (Padley 1976: 62, citing J. C. Scaliger 1540:

cap. lxxvi: 136). Scaliger uncovered this common *ratio* by applying the explanatory framework of the Aristotelian notion of the 'four causes' to language. Sanctius concentrated on revealing the *ratio* of language where it was not immediately apparent lay in examining syntax, especially on explicating the underlying sense of elliptical expressions.[26] Vossius also believed that *ratio* was the key to language, but he now sought its realization in *analogy*, in regular patterns underlying language. Vossius (1635) represented the cutting edge of linguistic theory in Schottelius's lifetime, and so it was in this version—in the primacy attributed to linguistic analogy—that Schottelius took from Vossius the basic, long-standing doctrine that language is fundamentally rational.

3.6.2 *Analogy*

Vossius picked up on a theoretical discussion already contained in J. C. Scaliger (1540), which was in turn a revival of an ancient debate and that had gained renewed relevance in the context of humanism, as Vossius well knew: the question of the criteria by which, in the face of competing variants, correct language could be determined: *usus* or reason?[27] This was the aspect of Latinate grammatical theory that had the most influence on Schottelius, that caused the most controversy amongst contemporaries, and that, through him, had a significant impact on other vernacular grammatical traditions too (Chapter 7). I will therefore trace its origins in the Latinate tradition in some detail.

The emphasis of humanists like Valla (1540) was firmly on practice rather than on theory, on (good) usage, so on rhetoric as a guide to mastering Latin, rather than on logic. Analogy tended to impose a rationality on language that clashed with custom, which might well be 'anomalous', i.e. not fitting the regular patterns demanded by analogy. *Consuetudo* 'custom' was an acceptable, indeed perhaps preferable way of getting to grips with Latin. It was against this prevailing view that J. C. Scaliger (1540) reacted when he presented *usus* as an irrational factor, an irritant that caused changes to a linguistic system that was originally rational. The conflict between *usus* and rationality could not be clearer: *usus* was presented by J. C. Scaliger as a 'tyrant, making us use some words without rationality, indeed often against rationality' (Jensen 1990: 157).

---

[26] For this reason, Sanctius is taken, e.g. by Allan (2007: 175), as the beginning of 'rationalist grammar', here used in the particular (and to my mind rather too teleological) sense of that particular type of mentalist grammar that differentiates underlying and surface structures, represented in the twentieth century by Chomsky and his followers. To me it is not clear that J. C. Scaliger's theory of language is any less 'rationalist' in the broad sense of 'based on *ratio*'.

[27] Whether directly or indirectly, Schottelius was also aware of the intellectual tradition in which Vossius stood, for he cited J. C. Scaliger on the question of usage *vs.* the *Grund der Sprachen*. See 3.8.1 below.

The analogy *vs* anomaly discussion ultimately had its origins in Greek grammar, where analogy (regularity) was equated with linguistic naturalness (*physis*), and anomaly (irregularity, aberration from the system) with the naming of things by convention (*nomos, thesis*). The analogist *vs. consuetudo* discussion was taken over by Roman grammarians too, and was often crystallized in humanist and subsequent reception in the supposedly opposing positions of the two Roman authorities, Varro (116–27 B.C.) and Quintilian (35–95 A.D.), where Varro stood for the analogist camp, and Quintilian for the anomalist. In fact, the two overlapped in their views to a considerable degree. Both Varro in his *De lingua Latina* (45–47 B.C.) and Quintilian (Chapter 6 of Book I of *Institutio oratoria*) saw *analogia* in (potential) opposition to the dictates of established authority, custom, and (in the case of Quintilian) of antiquity. Both equated *analogia* with *ratio*, which was in turn, in Stoicist fashion, equated with nature (for the Stoicists expected to detect in nature an inherent universal, God-given reason). Varro weighed arguments for and against the operation of analogy in language, and came to the conclusion that both analogy and anomaly had their place. Anomaly—irregular or even arbitrary language use—was acceptable in name-giving. Once such names were established, however (and this 'name-giving' might include deriving new names or words from existing names or words), they then submitted to the same regular patterns of inflection (i.e. analogy) as any other word. A century later, Quintilian discussed four principles for determining correctness of *sermo*, all in potential conflict: *ratio* (embracing both *analogia* [limited here to inflectional paradigms] and *etymologia* [here in the sense of the origins of words, particularly by derivation]), antiquity, authority and custom (Matthews 1994: 57–66; see also Law 2003: 43–49, 62). Quintilian certainly did not argue against analogy as a whole, but allowed for more instances where analogy might not operate; he did not restrict anomaly to the area of name-giving alone, as Varro had done.

Varro's *De lingua latina* (45–47 B.C.) survives in just one manuscript.[28] After the rediscovery of the work by Giovanni Boccaccio (1313–1375) in 1355, it was read with great excitement by humanists. No wonder that J. C. Scaliger seized on Varro as an answer to the humanist obsession with usage and with the authority of good authors. Just as Varro had pitted analogist arguments against anomalist ones in a lively debate in his *De lingua latina*, so J. C. Scaliger now took some of the same anomalist arguments presented by Varro and argued against them (Jensen 1990: 181–83). Scaliger began by attacking four such arguments:

---

[28] Of the original 25 books, six—Books 8 to 13—dealt with the role of analogy and anomaly in language and with examples of analogy, but of these, only books 8 to 10 survive (Law 2003: 43).

1. Speech was invented for utilitarian purposes so should be short and simple. Yet compound or derived words formed by analogy are not short and simple.
2. Things are there for their utility, not similarity, which is why women wear different clothes from men. Analogy, which rests on similarity, is not in the nature of things.
3. Variety (failure to conform to a pattern) is found in nature; limbs have different functions.
4. Stylishness is a purpose of speech, and this is achieved through variation, not through similarity.

All of these arguments tend in the direction that analogy is not natural. A further anomalist argument was to imply that because it was not always observed, analogy did not properly exist at all. To counter these arguments, Scaliger gave various examples to persuade us, rather than to prove, that deviations from the natural order do not mean the natural order does not exist. For instance, normally people have five digits on each hand, but there are exceptions. He also argued against anomalists' assertion that etymology (discovering the origins of words) could not be meaningfully studied because it dealt with change and corruption. Scaliger retorted that there is a place for the study of language change in grammar, so that we can then make scientific statements about it. In view of Schottelius's application of analogy to German, it is important to note that Scaliger concluded that analogy had a place not just in inflection, but also in derivation and composition (viewed as part of 'etymology'), allowing us to inquire into the origins of derived words. Only once we get down to the primary words is the analogical method of no use. This, in fact, is more or less the conclusion to which Varro had come.

This is the background against which Vossius (1635) turned to the analogy-anomaly question, landing like Scaliger firmly on the side of the analogists, in Books 3 to 6 of his work under the heading *De vocum analogia et anomalia* 'on the analogy and anomaly of words'.[29] It is significant that Vossius even gave the third part of grammar, traditionally called the *etymologia*, the programmatic title of *analogia*. The name-change reflected Vossius's belief that all the paradigms of the word-classes could be accounted for by appealing to *analogia* (the inherent patterns of regularity in the language), with exceptions described as anomalies. Vossius's work

---

[29]   Vossius mentioned in his preface that he had in mind to call his work *Aristarchus*, after the Greek analogist Aristarchus (ca. 216–144 B.C.), who, together with his master Aristophanes of Byzantium (ca. 257–180 B.C.), developed criteria by which analogies could be drawn (with the aim of ensuring that like really was being compared with like; cf. Law 2003: 54–55, Mathews 1994: 54–58). Vossius's work did indeed become known as *Aristarchus* from its second edition (Rademaker 1992: 115). Contemporary scholars were very aware of Vossius's debt to Sanctius and Scaliger, discussed for instance by Perizonius in his 1687 commentary on Sanctius's *Minerva*.

was highly influential, becoming in Padley's words 'the standard grammar for Germany and Holland', and it was last printed in Halle in 1833–34 (Padley 1976: 119; Rademaker 1992: 110).

Schottelius was quite of his time, then, in taking up Vossius's ideas. What was new was that he applied them authoritatively to a vernacular, to German. Vossius's new distinction between natural grammar (common to all languages) and artificial grammar (specific to individual idioms)—while of great interest to anyone today seeking precursors of universal grammar—was merely parroted by Schottelius (*AA* 180–81), and not developed in any meaningful way. Much more importantly, the anomaly *vs* analogy discussion became for Schottelius the theoretical tool by which to solve the pressing problem of choosing the correct form of language amongst competing variants—far more pressing for German than for Latin, already long standardized.

3.6.3 History and origin of language

A further fundamental question exercising the minds of scholars in Europe of the sixteenth and seventeenth centuries was the history and origin of language, and whether Hebrew or some other candidate could be shown to be the oldest language (Droixhe 2000). Theodor Bibliander (1548) was, like his contemporary J. C. Scaliger, in search of the *communis ratio* of languages, but he addressed this question by investigating their common origin at Babel and their subsequent diversification (Metcalf 1980; Tavoni 1998). What had happened at Babel and thereafter was of particular concern to cultural patriots, keen to demonstrate the antiquity (and therefore worth) of their own vernacular compared to other European languages. Schottelius continued to reflect on this issue, adding new references and nuances to his argument across the three editions of the orations (1641, 1651, 1663). In particular, many new additions made in 1663 were drawn from the works of the Flemish scholar Adriaan van Schriek, who defended the view of his fellow Fleming Goropius Becanus that Flemish was the oldest language, from which Hebrew was derived (cf. 2.2.3–4, 3.4 above). Besides these Dutch scholars, another key source for Schottelius was the Frenchman Claude Duret's *Thrésor* (1613). Schottelius's own discussion of language origin and language change adhered to the discursive methods and assumptions established in the discourse of the preceding decades and centuries, relying still on logical argument and refutation of established authorities, rather than on the observation and interpretation of empirical data (Rössing-Hager 1985: 1582; cf. also 7.3). Having read widely in this discourse tradition, he now sought to participate in it, re-creating in his third oration the atmosphere of debate, pitting well-known voices in the discussion against each other. A key passage, *AA* 31, 3: 7–8, illustrates his approach. In the passage, Schottelius addresses the question of whether Dutch–German could be the oldest or original language, something on which Schottelius had earlier agreed with Becanus. But he now ceded the position of oldest language to Hebrew, like most of his contemporaries.[30] Schottelius concedes that Becanus was admittedly guilty of eloquently praising what he loved (his own language), even where such praise contradicted the facts (as Plato had Socrates observe of his fellow diners in his Symposium). And yet Becanus's work was not without merit. Schottelius's defence of Becanus begins by using the very words of one of Becanus's fiercest critics, Hugo Grotius, to defend him. Grotius had written in quite another context that an attempt to exaggerate often harms one's cause, for the effort is so easily discovered that the worth of one's other pronouncements is called into question, even when they are true.[31] Now, Schottelius applies Grotius' own pronouncement to defend Becanus, whose etymologizing *gar zu frey um sich greifft* ('is far too free'), but whose basic premise—that the oldest language must be the one with the oldest words with the *eigentlichsten* ('most proper') meanings—remains valid. Against Becanus, Schottelius cites Duret (1613), as well as J. J. Scaliger (son of J. C. Scaliger), and Lipsius. Amongst those who supported Becanus, he cites Adriaan van Schriek and Laevinus Torrentius (1525–1595), who had published some of Becanus's writings after his death (Goropius Becanus 1580). Scaliger is then discredited because he did not know German; Lipsius said more against Becanus than he proved. Finally, in an addition only made in 1663 (perhaps when a copy of the relevant work became available to Schottelius, for there are many insertions drawing on it in this edition), Adriaan van Schriek's critique of Lipsius, which had merely been noted in the earlier editions, is advanced at some length. The conclusion Schottelius reaches is that Becanus is wrong to assert that German is older than Hebrew, but right that German is older than Greek or Latin. For good measure, Schottelius then cites Augustine (354–430) and Jerome (ca. 347–420), Church Fathers who remain heavy-hitting voices in the debate, and who likewise suggest Hebrew could be the oldest language. Still, Schottelius is able to conclude:

---

[30] In 1640 Schottelius had taken issue with Gueintz's suggestion that many German words are derived from Hebrew (Becanus argued the reverse); Gueintz countered testily that it is *aus Gotteswortt klar* ('clear from the word of God', Krause 1855 [1973]: 255) that German is derived from Hebrew. Gueintz was clearly aware that Becanus was an influence on Schottelius, for only a few lines later, defending his plural form *Meister* against Schottelius's preferred *Meister-e,* he commented acerbically in support of his preferred shorter form, *Je kurtzer, ie beßer sagt ia der Becanus, deßen Schüler dieser sein will* 'the shorter, the better, says Becanus, after all, whose pupil this man wants to be'.

[31] See the *Prolegomena* of Grotius's *De Ivre Belli ac Pacis* (1626), page b3ᵛ: 'Verum hic ipse nimium contra nitendi conatus sæpe adeo non proficit vt obsit etiam, quia deprehensum facile quod in his nimium est, etiam aliis dictis intra verum stantibus auctoritatem detrahit' (Grotius 1625, ed. Schätzel 1950: 37).

Dieses bleibet aber wahr / daß diese uhralte Hauptsprache der Teutschen in jhren Gründen jhr eygen / rein und Welträumig ist: davon Goropius Beca[n]us[32] (exceptis frivolis) wie auch Abrahamus Mylius in seinem Buche von der Niederteutschen Sprache / wie auch Scriekius Rodornius aufs weitläuftigste zu besehen;

'But this remains true, that the ancient cardinal language of the Germans is in her foundations unique, pure and widespread: as Goropius Becanus (excepting his frivolous examples) and Abraham Mylius in his book on Low German as well as Schriekius have shown at length.'

(*AA* 32, 3: 9)

This passage demonstrates how Schottelius positioned himself in the midst of international scholarly debate—or at least how he tried to. Although most of the voices in the discussion just summarized are Flemish, Dutch or German, Schottelius was careful to incorporate the Frenchman Duret's views too, though without giving room to his full criticism of Becanus. And he continued to add references from his reading through each edition, for instance adding work from the recent publications by the Dane Ole Worm (1588–1655) on 'runic' writings and by the Englishman Thomas Hayne (1582–1645), as well as many older works from the sixteenth century (cf. 6.2), and making other additions that increased the number of parallels between the cultivation of German and the cultivation of Latin and Greek. In fact, though, Schottelius's voice in the debate was some fifty years late, for the real period for international discussion of this topic was the early decades of the seventeenth century. The most recent contributions to the discourse tradition—Duret (1613), Schrieckius (1615, 1620) and Clüver (1616)—had all published their works in the first quarter of the seventeenth century. Over the next decades after Schottelius, the discussion would come to be framed in new terms (cf. Considine & Van Hal 2010), so that already Gottfried Leibniz (1646–1715) would pose the question about the history of German quite differently (see 7.3.1).

The passage just discussed is also an illustration of how the cultural patriotic precept that one should write in German (formalized in the exhortation to members of the FG, as we have seen) came under pressure from the need to cite and discuss scholarly sources in Latin, and the desire to participate in an international discourse tradition. As can be seen from a glance at Figure 3.4, Schottelius began in German, but Latin ended up dominating. Schottelius's friend Harsdörffer had already found it necessary to defend himself for writing his *Specimen Philologiae Germanicae* in Latin (1646). In a letter to Prince Ludwig in 1646, he

---

[32] The text reads *Becamus* for *Becanus*.

von der Teutschen HaubtSprache.   31

te/wiewol auf ein anders gerichtet/in proleg. ad lib. de Jure bell. & pac. lauten : In contrani-
tendi conatu, si facilè deprehendatur, quod est nimium, id etiam aliis dictis, intra verum stantibus authoritatem demit.

7. Deß Becani Grundsatz ist dieser : Daß dieselbige Sprache die allerältefte seyn
müffe/welche die allerälteften Wörter/ und die eigentlichften Bedeutungen der Dinge
habe. Denn was Duret p.811. dict. lib. vom Becano alfo fagt: Goropius pofe puer fondement
de fes difcours , que la langue Cimbrique n' a rien emprunte d' aucune autre, que d' elle l'
hebraïque eft iffue , & que mefmes l' hebraïque a emprunte de la Cimbrique : Solches ist
nicht Becani eigentlicher Haubtgrund gewefen/ fondern er hat ein folches fich bemühet zu bewei-
fen. Weil er aber im Beweisruhme deffen gar zu frey um fich greifft/ fonderlich in dem Buche
Indofcytica und in der Hermathena, und wider die Hebraïfche Sprache einen gefehrlichen miß-
lichen Beweisftuhm zu offt antrit/als haben daher vornehme Leute anlaß genommen/fein ganzes
Buch/und ganzes Vorhaben/ als einen Irrweg zuverwerffen. Denn er ift vom Scaligero und
Lipfio gar übel ausgeftrichen : Wiewol er doch hernachmals einen Vertreter den Lævinum Tor-
rentium bekommen/wider welchen fo wol/als wider den Becanum felbft Lipfius ferner aufgetre-
ten : Einer mit Rahmen Annius Verolonius ift noch vor Goropio, eben deß Goropii Meinunge
gewefen wider welchen weitläuftig deswegen gefchrieben Lybius Geraldus, wie deffen auch Duret gedenket. Es fol auch Lipfius in etlichen mehr wider Becanum gefagt/ als bewiefen haben :
Auch der hochberühmter Scaliger, weil er der Teutfchen Spracheunfündig gewefen / wider den
Becanum zureichenden Beweisstuhm nicht beygebracht haben. Dem Liebhaber diefer Händel zu-
gefallen(weil doch folche Bücher in weniger Händen befindlich)will des *Adriani Rodermi Sersekkei*
Worte ich anhero fetzen ex præfat. fecunda in monita : Scaliger, inquit, nihil contra Becanum
demonftravit, nec per linguæ noftræ imperitiam potuit. Optimè tamen acerrimo fuo judicio
Becani commenta non poffe conflare, intellexit. Lipfius demonftrationem aliquam fecit : fed
dum fundum rei quodammodo impugnat,& circa tempora Caroli M. hæret, nec ad antiqui-
tatem ullâ retro greditur, nec originem confiderat,in majores incidit errores, & fibi ipfi con-
tradicit. Certè fi Lipfius veram originem,Linguamq; Patriam iam infpexiffet, quàm exter-
nis fe mifcuit, antiqua illa Belgica,quæ profert,non aliter derivata potuiffet, quàm ex primo
illo Hebraifmo,& illam Dialecti diverfitatem , quàm in Pfalterio veteri vidit, ejusdem effe
fundi vidiffet,tàm cum Lingua primogenio proximâ, quàm cum hodierna noftra. Et in eo
peccarunt, errarunt Lipfius & cæteri, quod Linguam noftram Græcæ & Latinæ inferiorem, tàm
tempore, quàm qualitate exiftimaverint. Hebraicam Linguam effe primogeniam , Japheti-
cam verò fecundam, quam & Scythicam, Teutonicam, Belgicam , Danicam & Septentriona-
lem nunc vocamus; quodq; ea lingua Japhetica primis temporibus fuit univerfalis, & omni-
nò antiquior fit Græcâ & Latinâ, adeoq; populos illos Celticos & Romanis & Græeis funt an-
tiquiores,per omnes cafus & in *Originibus* & in *hoc monstrorum libris* probavimus.

8. Wir laffen es/was den Streit des uhralterruhmes anlanget / dabey bewenden was
Auguftinus lib. 16. c. 11. de civitate Dei fagt : Lingua omnium hominum communis, rema-
fit in Eberi gente, à cujus nomine, nomen accepit.   Und Hieronymus Ep ift. 144. Ebræam
Linguam, quâ vetus Teftamentum fcriptum eft, effe initium oris & communis eloquij, u-
niverfa credidit antiquitas.

9. Diefes

Figure 3.4: *AA* 31

had explained that he wrote in Latin *weil die darinnen angeregte
Strittigkeiten in andere Haubtsprachen einlauffen, und notwendig von den
Gelehrten verglichen werden müssen* 'because the debates concern other
languages too, and must necessarily be compared by scholars' (Krause
1855 [1973]: 354). Evidently Schottelius came to the same conclusion, for
in 1663, he in essence turned his work—including the grammar—into a
bilingual enterprise (cf. footnote 1 above). The orations remained in
German, in conception, but with very large amounts of Latin citation, not
translated, as Schottelius rather hastily observed at the end of the tenth
oration:

> Es hat auch durchgehendes nicht können alles Teutsch geschrieben
> werden / weil Grichische / Lateinische / Frantzösische und Nie-
> derländische Authores so oftmals angezogen / und deren Worte / wie
> sie lauten / sind behalten / und gar selten Teutsch gegeben oder
> verdolmetscht worden.

'Not everything could be written in German throughout because
Greek, Latin, French and Dutch authors have so often been referred
to, and their words kept as they are, and very rarely given in German
or translated.'

(*AA* 170, 10: 23)

Far and away the majority of non-German passages are in Latin, though
the other languages listed by Schottelius here do all occur too. Schottelius
seems to have tried in the first two orations to paraphrase or translate his
sources, but thereafter the attempt is abandoned.[33]

In 1641 the version of the orations, Schottelius had been laying the
foundations for his grammar, in part in response to Gueintz's effort; he had
been setting out the theoretical groundwork for a German dictionary; and
he had been advancing detailed cultural patriotic arguments in favour of
German. By 1663, though, he was also participating in—or wanting to
participate in—international linguistic debate.

3.7 PANSEMIOTICISM

The final discourse tradition in which Schottelius participated is what
Westerhoff calls the pansemioticism of the Baroque, according to which
'every object, whether natural or artificial, signifies one or several other
objects (which can in turn be abstract qualities, virtues or vices, or
particular states of affairs', Westerhoff 2000: 92).[34] Pansemioticism was a
sort of emblematic approach to the world, a popular philosophy of the
Baroque—Johann Gottfried von Herder (1744–1803) famously looked
back on the seventeenth century as the emblematic century (Herzog 1979:
92). Emblematics functioned like a second, image-based language that
could be learnt. It was evident in the FG's practice of assigning nicknames,
mottoes and plant emblems to members, whose significance—not
immediately obvious as a rule—was explained in occasional verses. (See
Krause 1855 [1973] for examples.) Schottelius was known in the society as
Der Suchende, the seeker, and his emblem was a *Gämseblümchen*
(*doronicum, arnica montana* or *arnica chamissonis*, alpine ox-eye, a hardy
mountain perennial with yellow, daisy-like flowers, said to protect against

---

[33] Schottelius contrasts here with the younger Germanic cultural patriot, the Swede Olaf
Rudbeck, who wrote in Swedish and faithfully translated all citations into Swedish in his
Atlantica (1679), and published the work with a parallel Latin translation (Blume 1983).

[34] Westerhoff took the term pansemioticism from Eco (1995: 25); cf. also Westerhoff (1998,
1999, 2001). Though Westerhoff talks of a pansemiotic 'world view', this world view was
associated with its own type of *discourse* in Foucault's terms, whose object was the
interpretation of signs according to recognized methods, to arrive at their true meaning.

giddiness); his motto was *Reine Dünste* 'pure mists'. His verse elucidates each of these signals (Krause 1855 [1973]: 279):

> Die Gemsenwurzel wird auch Schwindelkraut genant,
> Von Jägern die dem thier' in bergen hoch nachsteigen:
> Die reinen Dünst' ich such' und mache sie bekant,
> Die unsrer Deutschen sprach' in ihrer art seind eigen,
> Recht auf dem grunde geh', und drin bleib' unverwand:
> Heiß Suchend, auch wil fort, was ich drin finde zeigen,
> Zu bringen frucht, die wol dem Vaterlande nutzt,
> Und mit der Deutschen Zung' all' andre fremde trutzt.

> 'The chamois-wort is also called giddy-plant, by hunters who climb high in the mountains following their quarry: I seek and make known the pure mists, which are particular to our German language in her kind/nature. Right to the ground I go, and will not be deterred. Am called Seeking, and will show forth what I find there, to bring forth fruit that profits the fatherland, and that with the German tongue stands firm against all others.'

Only with the verse do the nickname, motto and emblem make sense. The three together combine to yield a meaning explained in the verse. The same principle lies behind the emblem-books that were a modish expression of this world-view, which also left its mark in virtually every aspect of everyday life (including architecture, furniture, music, portraiture, and pedagogy; cf. Strasser & Wade 2004; review McLelland 2006).[35] But the pansemiotic world-view was not limited to emblematics. It also influenced how people used the elements of language, as in language games like those devised by Harsdörffer for his conversation books (Harsdörffer 1644–49; cf. Hundt 2006, and Hundt 2000: 210–243). The familar notation of letters and numbers could be combined in novel ways and associated with new, different meanings, for more or less earnest purposes: in language games and riddles, but also in the phonaesthesia of the Nuremberg poets (see 4.5.4), in secret languages, or (increasingly, in the latter half of the seventeenth century) in artificial language schemes (Strasser 1988; Lewis 2007). Schottelius's own patron, Duke August, had written a *Cryptographia* (1624), a guide to writing in code, which included

---

[35] Emblematics were of course not a peculiarly Dutch and German phenomenon, but had many exponents throughout Europe, spreading later to the Low Countries and Germany. The Stirling Maxwell Collection in Glasgow University Library contains 26 sixteenth-century French emblem books (cf. the French Emblems project at http://www.emblems. arts.gla.ac.uk/french/); see also the University of Coruña project on Hispanic emblematic literature (http://rosalia.dc.fi.udc.es/emblematica/index.jsp). The Library of the University of Illinois at Urbana-Champaign hosts an Open Emblem portal with links to these and other projects.

a commentary on the *Polygraphia* (1518) of Johannes Trithemius (1462–1516).

One manifestation of pansemioticism was a fascination with the so-called *ars combinatoria*, the combining of elements in novel ways in order to generate new meanings. The *Fünfffacher Denckring* 'the five-fold thought-ring' of Harsdörffer (1651: 516-19) is a good example of how it could be applied to language to generate new words and ideas. Five concentric rings contained 48 prefixes and prefixoids, 60 initial letters or letter combinations, 12 'middle letters', 120 'end letters', and finally 24 suffixes. This device could generate something approaching 100 million combinations (though naturally not all combinations would yield valid words). Novel combinations might stimulate one's invention—hence 'thought-ring'.[36] Schottelius contributed the preface to the emblem-book of his fellow FG-member Franz Julius von dem Knesebeck,[37] *Dreiständige Sinnbilder* ('Threefold emblems', 1643), and later re-worked it to include in his treatise on proverbs in Book V of the *AA* (Höpel 2000, 2002; cf. 4.4.2; see Figure 3.5),[38] and we have already seen that the frontispiece of the *AA* was to be read emblematically, in conjunction with both the title page and the verse *Erklärung des Kupfertitels* given on the reverse of the title page. The all-pervasive influence of pansemioticism, also on ways of seeing and interpreting language, explains a number of peculiarities in Schottelius's *AA*, in particular of the grammar. For instance, where we might have expected Schottelius to be prescriptivist, favouring one usage over another, we find him delighting at times in the fact that the same thing could be said by combining different elements of the language in different ways (cf. 5.5.5).[39] But the fascination of applying the *ars combinatoria* to linguistic signs finds its most important expression in the *AA* in Schottelius's exhaustive analysis and exemplification of compounding and derivation in German, structurally a mere sub-section of the accidence of the noun, but which ended up dwarfing the rest of the grammar, as it ran to over two hundred pages (*AA* 317–533; cf. 5.5.4). Similarly the section on the *Vorwort* ('preposition, particle') is dominated by a listing and exemplification of verb prefixes, not distinguished here from the prepositions with identical forms, as in *vor, über, auf, an, ab* ... (*AA* 613–55). But beyond these

---

[36]   Discussion and illustrations of the *Fünfffacher Denckring* can be found in Gardt (1994: 208; 1999: 125), Hundt (2000: 283) and Faust (1981).

[37]   Knesebeck joined the FG in the same year as Schottelius, 1642, and was the highest official at Duke August's court where Schottelius worked (Berns 1984: 423). His life-dates are not known.

[38]   These tri-partite emblems consisted of a picture, a motto or proverb, and a verse (like the three elements assigned to FG members). The meaning of the emblem could only be fully understood by looking at all three elements together.

[39]   'Prescriptive' is not an unproblematic term. For discussion, see 8.1.

Figure 3.5: Frontispiece of the *Dreiständige Sinnbilder* ('Threefold Emblems', 1643)

sections, which are central to Schottelius's cultural-patriotic and theoretical agendas in any case, there are many other instances where the pansemiotic idea seduces Schottelius on a smaller scale. There are several pages (*AA* 253–60) devoted to the ability of the prefixoids *erz–, ur–, hoch–,* and *höchst–* to change the meaning of an adjective, just as the comparative or superlative adjective form can, as in *hochgelert, uhrplötzlich* 'highly learned, very suddenly', etc. In the section on syntax, Schottelius is fascinated by the variety of ways the same meaning can be expressed in different combinations of words, using either a genitive of a noun, or a preposition with the noun, as in *gühtliches Weges, in gühtlichen Wege, nach gütlichen Wege* ('by a good way' *AA* 717). Schottelius introduced in 1651 and expanded in 1663 a list of homonyms (some of which are only homophones today; *AA* 684–85) and a separate list of homonymous verbs (*AA* 760–61), as in *vergeben*: 'to forgive', and 'to give away'. Indeed, the grammar as a whole ended with an observation on how easy it was in German to achieve the same meaning in many different ways: for 'thanks', Schottelius supplied twenty-four examples (*AA* 789–90).[40]

---

[40] In such cases, the pansemiotic approach to language as a system of combinations overlaps with the still humanist appreciation of stylistic variation as an admirable quality.

The lure of the *ars combinatoria* even had an impact on the structure of Schottelius's grammar. Schottelius (*AA* 668), introducing his section on *Schriftscheidung*, pointed out from the 1651 edition onwards that punctuation is part of *Rechtschreibung*. Yet even in these later editions, where he had an opportunity to re-structure the grammar (for instance, between 1651 and 1663, he split the chapter on the conjunction and interjection into two separate chapters; cf. 5.5.2), he did not, as one might expect, move punctuation to the end of the chapter where the rest of *Rechtschreibung* is dealt with. The reason is probably that the contents of the end of the section on orthography, where the punctuation might logically have been inserted, had drifted away from rules for writing into a discussion of the combinatorial possibilities of the letters; punctuation rules would have sat oddly with these pansemiotic musings.[41] Schottelius instead ended with examples of number puzzles,[42] and also noted words which took on a different meaning, depending on whether they were read forwards of backwards. Thus *trew* 'faithful' become *wert* 'worthy' when read backwards. This, Schottelius's very first example, contravened a spelling rule given earlier (*AA* 200) that diphthongs were to be written with *−u* rather than *−w* (so *treu*, not *trew*). Schottelius's work has numerous such contradictions between his prescriptions and his practice, but the contradiction here betrays how he brought together, but did not perfectly synthesize, ideas from different discourses—here, the grammatical tradition and the pansemiotic fascination with combining signs to yield new meanings.

The treatises of Book V on translating and on German *Redarten* (idioms or proverbs) reflect the same pansemiotic preoccupation with the rich *combinatorial* possibilities of German to convey meanings. The treatise on the proverbs was no more than a revision of the preface that Schottelius had written to the *Dreiständige[n] Sinnbilder* (1643; Höpel, 2000: 1000). The poetical treatise of Book IV also dwelt on playful verse forms such as the *Bild der Reimen* (like concrete poetry, where the arrangement of the lines yields a meaningful shape such as a cross or chalice; cf. Figure 4.2 in

---

[41] A reference to Ickelsamer which concluded the chapter in the 1641 edition, and which did bring the discussion back to matters of principles for correct spelling, was deleted in the later editions.

[42] For examples, given the rules that w = 500, a = 10, e = 1, i = 5, o = 100 and u = 1000, then the following sentence, meaning 'God grant peace again now in your land', 'adds up' to the year 1641:

Gott	gib	itz	wieder	Glukke	in	deinem	Lande
100	+ 5	+ 5	+ 500 + 5 + 1 + 1	+ 1000 + 1	+ 5	+ 5 + 1 + 1	+ 10 + 1

Chapter 4), as well as on riddles, anagrams, and number puzzles, where the letters of a word or phrase stood for numbers, which when totalled produced a significant figure. All of these are the sort of thing with which Harsdörffer illustrated at length in his *FrauenzimmerGesprächsspiele* (1644–49)—they are language games for the parlour. But such games also reflected a serious and core theoretical belief about the rich combinability of language (Gardt 1994: 206–26, Hundt 2005), and crucially, the belief in the serious, moral purpose behind the search for meaning. It is no accident that in Schottelius's examples, the concrete poetry shapes are the religious symbols of the cross and the chalice, or that the number puzzles (*AA* 222; 989–90) are pious expressions of the desire for peace, or that the emblems and proverbs in *the emblem-book* to which he contributed with Knesebeck often emphasize a link between correct language use and godly peace in the land (Höpel 2002: 653). After all, the frontispiece—like the later grammatical war (1673; cf. Fonsén 2006)—suggested that language cultivation and peace go hand in hand. In Schottelius's particular brand of Protestant pansemioticism, seeking and expressing meanings in German in the right way was part both of cultural patriotism and of the greater task of seeking God's plan in the world.

3.8 INTERSECTING DISCOURSES IN THE *AA*

The six discourse traditions identified had a significant influence on the structure and content of the *AA*, and in particular they interacted to shape Schottelius's twin key ideas: 1. *Analogie vs Anomalie* 'analogy' *vs* 'anomaly' or *Regel / Grundrichtigkeit vs Gewohneit* 'rule / 'basic correctness' *vs* 'custom', and 2. the rootword (*Stammwort*).

3.8.1 *Analogy and Anomaly*—Regel, Grundrichtigkeit *and* Gewohnheit

Schottelius, supported by Harsdörffer, stood in the FG for the view that language should be regular, following patterns, and that the task of the grammarian was to record, but in some cases also to reconstruct, these regular patterns—for instance, if they had become obscured in usage. Other members of the FG, including Gueintz and Prince Ludwig, took a different view, arguing that where irregularities existed, established usage must take precedence over some notional rule. The debates around this point swirled through the correspondence of the FG. Schottelius's review of Gueintz's manuscript grammar of 1640 criticized usages that he called *misbrauch*. The *rechte pluralis* 'correct plural' of words like *Meister–e* 'master(s)' was to be preferred as *kreftig* 'strong', even if it was at odds with 'general usage', or rather 'abuse', *den algemeinen misbrauch*. Gueintz retorted *Der Gebrauch aber doch muß den Anschlag geben, unndt nicht die Regel dem gebrauch* 'but usage must be the guide, and the rule should not guide usage' (Krause 1973[1855]: 249, 253–54, 365, 371, 374; cf. Takada 1998: 22–24). Takada (1985, 1998: 24–48) has shown how Schottelius's own formulations of the competition between the two principles of analogy and custom developed over the course of his life, reaching the strongest analogist position in 1651 (reflected in the iconography of the frontispiece, cf. 1.5), but achieving a compromise between the two views by 1663. To situate Schottelius's linguistic theory in its European context, we must also consider how Schottelius's ideas in this debate—first expressed within the FG—interacted with and were affected by ideas from the other discourses in which he participated. We can indeed trace this development by examining the changes from the 'hypotexts' underlying the *AA*: the earlier versions of Schottelius's ideas expressed first in correspondence within the FG in 1640, then in the 1641 and 1651 editions of the *Teutsche Sprachkunst*, leading to their definitive version of 1663.

The Leiden influence is clear. Schottelius's fullest formulation of the primacy of rule over custom, at the start of the second oration, drew on the idea of natural law as outlined by the Dutch scholar Hugo Grotius, who reconciled the law with the custom of the good or of the majority: natural law is indeed natural, but is reflected in the custom of the majority anyway.[43] The same point is made in the first oration (*AA* 9, 1: 26), again in a legalistic framework, distinguishing crucially between *consuetudo* / *Gebrauch* 'usage' and *corruptela* / *Misbrauch* 'misuse', this time with reference to language:

> Eben also ist es mit dem Gebrauche und der Gewonheit in den Sprachen bewant / davon Scaliger lib.1. de Ling. lat. cap.11. also sagt: Derselbiger Gebrauch / dem ein Hauptgesetz / oder der Grund der Sprachen entgegen laufft / ist kein Gebrauch / sondern eine mißbräuchliche Verfälschung.

> So it is with usage and custom in languages, about which [J.C.] Scaliger says in Book I of *De causis Linguae latinae*, Chapter 11: Usage to which a chief rule or the fundament of the language runs counter is not usage, but rather an abusive falsification.

(*AA* 9, 1: 26, but already in Schottelius 1641)

---

[43] Reference here is to the 1663 edition, but the same key passage is in all three editions of Schottelius's work, from 1641 onwards. One must not overstate, therefore, the changes in position outlined by Takada (1998); they are changes of emphasis. After all, on one key point of debate—that nouns ending in *-er, -el* should be given an additional *e* to mark the plural, an issue debated within the FG since 1640—Schottelius remained immovable throughout all three editions. (On the other hand, for *slagen vs schlagen* etc. he accepted *schl-* reluctantly in 1641, rejected it in 1651 (Takada 1998: 84, 100), also in his own spelling in the work, but returned to it in 1663; cf. 5.5.3.

In 1640 and 1641, Schottelius couched the discussion in terms of *Regel* and *Gewonheit / Gebrauch* ('rule' and 'custom / usage'), and of being in accord with the *Grund* 'foundation' of the language. A similar notion of the *Grund* of the language had already been used in other grammatical works from the first half of the seventeenth century, equating the *Grund* of the German language with natural rationality. The title of Olearius's 1630 *Deutsche Sprachkunst Aus den allergewissesten / der Vernunfft und gemeinen brauch Deutsch zu reden gemässen / gründen* claimed to present German 'taken from the surest foundations of reason and common custom in speaking German'. Here, then, *Grund* is equated with both reason *and* usage. A few years later, Hager observed in the preface of his 1634 *Orthographia*:

> Als stähe ich in ohnzweifflichern Hoffnung / es werde etwan den Liebhabern der Teütschen Sprache dadurch weitere Anleytungen gäben werden / den Grund derselben mit mehrern nachzusetzen / und so viel möglichst / die übel begründete / lange und alte Geb-räuche / so nicht Natur gemäß / durch den Druck und täglich Schreiben abzuhelffen / sich angelegen seyn lassen.

> So I stand in confident hope that sometime the lovers of the German language will be given further guidance about the foundation [*Grund*] of the language and, as much as possible, will feel moved to help do away with the ill-founded [*übel begründet*], long and old usages that are not in accord with nature, in print and in their daily writing.

> (Hager 1634: Aiiii^r)

In the same vein, Hager (1634: Av^r) also wrote of *unserer MutterSprache [...] die warlich in der Natur so fäst gegründet ist* 'our language that is truly so firmly founded in nature'. That is, Hager argued that the German language must be based firmly in nature, which he equated with the *Grund* of the language.[44] Well before Schottelius, then, we already find the trio of equivalences in German grammatical thinking, as in the Latinate tradition too: *Grund der Sprache* = *Vernunft* (reason, rationality) = *Natur*. Whether or not *Vernunft* could in turn be equated with *Gebrauch* 'custom, usage', as Olearius's title assumed, would, of course, become with Schottelius and his contemporaries the source of controversy. Still, it was this belief in the universal natural rationality of language that had made it possible for early grammarians such as Clajus (1578) to venture a grammar of German at all. For if all languages had a common *ratio*, then that *ratio* could be found in the vernaculars just as much as in Latin, Greek and Hebrew. Indeed, Clajus

---

[44] The idea that Nature is rational—based on reason (*ratio*)—was, as noted earlier, a Neostoicist idea in common circulation, emanating from Justus Lipsius in Leiden (*De constantia* 1584) (Huber 1984: 55).

defined grammar at the start of his work as a *ratio* found *in omnibus linguis* 'in all languages'.

In 1640–41, then, the question of correct language was still couched by Schottelius in these familiar terms.[45] Only in 1651, in a new paragraph inserted then (*AA* 9–10, 1: 28), was the debate about the *Grund* of the German language given a more theoretical underpinning. The term *Grundrichtigkeit*, which had occurred only once in Schottelius's 1641 grammar, was now an established term for him, equated with the ancient notion of analogy.[46] Schottelius had evidently now read Vossius (see Takada 1998: 32; recall that Vossius's work had only been published in 1635), and now introduced the term *analogia,* citing both the Greek grammarian Aristarchus and the Roman Varro. Finally, in 1663, Schottelius made the same principle explicit, again citing Aristarchus and Varro, in the statement of grammatical theory with which the grammar proper of the *AA* began (*AA* 181)—now in Latin *only,* and drawing for the first time explicitly on Vossius's work on grammatical theory. The initial debate about *Regel vs Gewonheit* within the FG was thus first influenced by Low Countries Neostoicists, and then, having been re-cast in the terms of an ancient and ongoing European debate about correct language, ultimately found its way into the theoretical statement that 'headlined' the 1663 grammar.

The fact that the original dichotomy of *Regel / Grundrichtigkeit vs Gewonheit* was now equated with that of *analogia* and *anomalia*[47] should not make us blind to the original image behind the key German term, *Grund.* The *Grund* is the ground—the writings in German to date—from which the language tree grows, as we saw in Harsdörffer's words cited above (3.5.4).[48] The term *Grundrichtigkeit* inevitably resonated with the metaphorical field of a tree (or a construction) that needs a firm and authentic foundation, recalling the imagery that was already central to the

---

[45] See also Harsdörffer's defence of Schottelius's position in letters written in 1646 (Krause 1855 [1973]: 349–54).

[46] Cf. *eine gewisse und grund = richtige Kündigkeit unserer Teutschen Sprach beyzubringen* 'to inculcate a certain and fundamentally correct knowledge of our German language' (Schottelius 1641: 175–76). By the 1651 edition it had become an established term for Schottelius, occuring 21 times as a noun or adjective (Takada 1998: 40). The earliest known attestation of *grundrichtig* appears to be in Ratke's thinking (cf. Josten 1976: 174–75, citing Helwig & Jungius (1614), *Kurtzer Bericht Von der Didactica oder Lehrkunst Wolfgangi Ratichii,* contained in Stoetzner (1892: 71).

[47] In the index of technical terms (*AA* 1466), *Grundrichtigkeit* is rendered as *Analogia fundamentalis* (as indeed already in the list 1651: [903, not numbered]: *Grundrichtig* is *Analogicè consideratum, vel eâ certitudine quid habitum, quae respicit consonantiam fundamentalem* 'considered analogically, or from that certainty which is customary, which concerns the fundamental consonant'; *Gleichrichtigkeit* is reserved for the narrower *Analogia,* presumably 'analogical patterns in grammatical paradigms only'.

[48] To complicate matters further, in places the rootwords are themselves *equated* by Schottelius with the *Grund* of the language (*AA* 70, 3: 10; cf. 4.4.4), yielding a threefold ambiguity for *Grund* as 'good writings', 'rationality' and 'rootwords'.

FG and that was expanded upon in the second half of the verse attached to Schottelius as a member of the FG (cited above, 3.7):

> Recht auf dem grunde geh', und drin bleib' unverwand:
> Heiß Suchend, auch wil fort, was ich drin finde zeigen,
> Zu bringen frucht, die wol dem Vaterlande nutzt,
> Und mit der Deutschen Zung' all' andre fremde trutzt.

> 'Right to the ground I go, and will not be deterred. Am called Seeking, and will show forth what I find there, to bring forth fruit that profits the fatherland, and that with the German tongue stands firm against all others.'

Here, then, multiple discourses—German and Latin grammar, cultural patriotic imagery and emblematics, and international linguistic scholarship over centuries—all meet in the one theoretical tenet of *Grundrichtigkeit*—even if in practice it comes down to justifying whether one should write *Meister* or *Meistere*. The interaction of all these different discourses in Schottelius's *AA* helps make this work so multifaceted compared to the equivalent landmark grammars of the seventeenth century in England and France.

3.8.2 The Rootword (Stammwort)

The second important theoretical notion where several discourses interact in the *AA* is the *Stammwort*. We have already seen that like analogy/*Grundrichtigkeit*, the rootword was absolutely central to Schottelius's thinking. It provided the framework for discussing morphology, but was also Schottelius's principal unit of analysis for deciding between spelling variants in the orthography, for scanning different metres in the poetics, for supplying the basis of a dictionary, and for analysing the proper names that preserve the history of the language. It fulfilled the important linguistic patriotic task of allowing German to appear superior to other languages in its brevity, richness, antiquity and clarity.

Europeans had encountered the notion of the root—long a key notion in Arabic and Hebrew linguistics—through humanist Hebrew grammars such as Sebastian Münster's *Compendium hebraicae grammaticae* of 1525, but the history of the notion in the West since then is 'not altogether straightforward' (Law 2003: 249; cf. Rousseau 1984). Parallel with the sixteenth-century European encounter with the Semitic root, and presumably not unconnected with it, it is in the context of positive 'heritage-building' that the notion of the characteristically German rootword emerged. Tacitus's *Germania* had said almost nothing about the language of the Germanic peoples (though Tacitus cited two words, for spear and amber), but Franciscus Irenicus (Franz Friedlieb 1494 or 1495–1553), in his *Germaniae exegesis* (1518)—described by Mertens (2004: 78) as 'a sort of handbook about "Germany" that combines ethnography, history, geography and natural history in a factual outline' [49] —wrote of the German language that

> omnis imperatiuus, ac omnia pene germanica uocabula monosyllaba sunt ut brot, susz, disch, der, dem, lisz, morn etc. et pene quicquid monosyllabam excedit, peregrinum ac non germanicum est ...

> 'every imperative and almost every German word is monosyllabic, such as *brot, susz, disch, der, dem, lisz, morn*, etc. and almost everything that is longer than a monosyllable, is foreign and not German'.

> (Irenicus 1518, lib. II cap. 31 fo. 38ᵛ, cited Jellinek 1898 [1985]: 60).

In this short statement, three crucial features that characterized later discourse about rootwords are already present:

1. They are monosyllabic;
2. They are identical with the (second person singular) imperative form of the verb;
3. They are characteristically German.

The idea evidently spread rapidly. Schottelius cited both Beatus Rhenanus (1531: 112) and Johannes Cuspinianus (1528) in support of the claim that the rootwords of the *lingua germanica* are monosyllabic.[50] Perhaps Schottelius's discussion of *Stammletterern* (root-letters) within the root owes a separate debt to Hebrew grammar, but the features of the rootword Schottelius certainly took from this humanist patriotic tradition.[51] He then borrowed the idea of identifying and listing these monosyllabic rootwords wholesale from the Fleming Stevin, for whom the number of monosyllabic *grondwoorden* was a criterion for determining the richness of the language.

---

[49] On Irenicus's own sources in turn, see Cordes (1966).

[50] Rhenanus stated in his work *Rerum Germanicarum libri tres* ('Three books on Germanic matters', 1531: 112), the first major treatment of the origins and the cultural achievements of the Germanic peoples, that *[Germanica lingua] gaudet vocis primogeniis monosyllabis* '[the German language] rejoices in monosyllabic primitive words'. On the early history of the rootword see Jellinek (1898), who cites Rhenanus (1531: 61). Cf. the edition and translation of Rhenanus (1531) by Mundt (2008), pp. 268-89. On Rhenanus in the context of sixteenth-century humanist, cultural-patriotically motivated German(ic) philology, see Sonderegger (1998: 420–422).

[51] Ritter (1616) and Harsdörffer's *Specimen Philologiae Germanicae* (= *SPG*, 1646) both drew similarities between the German and Hebrew roots, something for which Harsdörffer had been castigated by Gueintz (Krause 1855 [1973]: 368; on Harsdörffer's *SPG*, cf. Hundt 2000: 78). Yet I can find no evidence that Schottelius himself did so, as has often been implied in studies of his grammatography (Takada 1998: 25, n. 98; Barbarić 1981: 1195, presumably misunderstanding Jellinek 1913: 138, who himself had already pointed out the notion of the monosyllabic rootword in Irenicus (1518); cf. Jellinek 1898). Indeed, insisting on monosyllabic rootwords, as Schottelius did, was completely at odds with the Semitic grammatical tradition, in which roots were triliteral and therefore bisyllabic, and where the root was not the imperative, but the third person perfect.

Stevin had demonstrated in a series of tables (1586: 67–79) that *Duytsch* had *742 eensilbighe woorden inden eersten persoon; daerder de Latinen alleenlick 5 hebben; de Griecken gheen eyghentlicke, maer langhe vercort tot 45* '742 monosyllabic words in the first person, while the Latins have only 5 and the Greeks have no monosyllables, but only 45 long words that have been contracted.' The demonstration was developed further in a reworking of the treatise that appeared in 1608 (Stevin 1608: 24–38), where Stevin listed the monosyllabic verb roots as in the 1586 *Uytspraeck*, but added 1428 monosyllabic nouns, adjectives, etc. for *Duytsch*, 158 for Latin, 220 for Greek, giving totals of 2170 for *Duytsch*, 163 for Latin, and 265 for Greek. Since *Duytsch* had by far the most rootwords, Stevin argued that *Duytsch* was a richer and more capable language than either of the classical languages, and particularly well-suited to coining new terms in mathematics (of which *wiskonde* 'mathematics' is a prime example; today Dutch is the only European language that does not use some variant of *mathematica*, from the Greek, via Latin). Recognizing the value of the rootword as a cultural-patriotic weapon, Schottelius went one better than Stevin in greatly increasing the number of rootwords to a list that extends to over 170 pages (*AA* 1271–1450). According to Schottelius's manifesto in the fourth oration (*AA* 51, 4: 2), rootwords must have (and in German do have) the following properties:

1. Rootwords are made up of natural, native letters (cf. 2.2).
2. They should *wollauten* ('sound well') and *ihr Ding eigentlich ausdrükken* ('express their thing [referent] properly'). Note that *Wollaut* is more than mere euphony, and means an accord between word and meaning, whether by onomatopoeia, synaesthesia, or some other more or less mystical affinity between German words and their *ding* (again, cf. 2.3.2).
3. They must be sufficiently numerous. Their number is finite, for it is not possible for new rootwords to be invented at will (*AA* 97–98, 6: 53).
4. They permit derivation of new words as needed (demonstrated in the fifth oration).
5. They permit compounding (the topic of the sixth oration).
6. They are monosyllabic (*AA* 4–5, 1: 11; 41, 3: 36; 68, 5: 6; 144, 9: 18; 1272).

These criteria were inspired by the four arguments with which Stevin supported his claim for the excellence of *Duytsch*: the greater number of monosyllabic rootwords compared to other languages (cf. Schottelius's third point); the ease of compounding, and hence its suitability for teaching the arts, through its capacity for concise formulation (cf. Schottelius's fourth and fifth points); and the faculty of *beweeghlicheyt*, the ability to appeal directly to the heart more than any other language (cf. Schottelius's second point, under which he asserted that German words *wollauten* and express what they represent *eigentlich*, i.e. most aptly and fittingly).[52] Schottelius's first point is also arguably implicit in Stevin's belief that the *Duytsch* letters, being monosyllabic names, must be original and that Latin borrowed them from the *Duytsch*. Despite the untestable claim of the second requirement, these criteria are chiefly formal rather than semantic. There is no requirement, for instance, that rootwords express semantic primes, or basic meanings, or that they not overlap in meaning, all of which were relevant factors to the designers of *artificial* languages at this time.

If Stevin stood in the foreground (borrowed, cited, translated, often unacknowledged, cf. 6.2.3), Becanus stood in the background, as an internationally known (albeit much criticized) proponent of identifying original monosyllabic rootwords to establish the value and antiquity of a language. Without doubt, then, the fundamental notion of the *Stammwort* rested firmly on Low Countries' linguistic patriotism and scholarship.[53] But the way that Schottelius applied the notion of the *Stammwort* to German orthography and grammar was, in turn, much discussed in correspondence among members of the FG, and the requirement that rootwords be monosyllabic came under attack at once—only Harsdörffer supported Schottelius (Barbarić 1981: 1192–93). Finally, just like the notion of *Grundrichtigkeit*, the *Stammwort* must be understood as part of a pansemiotic world. For it is once again a term which evokes an entire metaphorical field, that of a language tree, with all its associated connotations.

We can trace the interaction of all these discourse traditions in the *AA* quite precisely by examining Schottelius's 1663 formulation of his ideas in comparision with its hypotexts: the earlier versions of 1641 and 1651. Schottelius's earliest discussion of the *Stammwort* is found in his review of Gueintz in 1640, in a passage which was then re-worked and expanded for use in his fourth oration, first published in 1641 (*AA* 50, 4: 1, cited 2.4.2):

> die Teutsche Sprache ruhet fest und unbeweglich in ihren, von Gott eingepflanzten haubtgründen, welche lautere, reine, deütliche, meist-einsilbige Stammwörter sind, die ihre spröslein, ast- und aderreiche Zweige in schönster reinlikeit, steter gewisheit und unergründter mannigfältigkeit reümig und weit ausbreiten, das es gar nicht nötig mit frembden Leütteton darunter Zu werfen; und die reislein Zu Zerbrechen und Zu miswachs Zu machen.

> 'the German language rests firm and immoveable in its God-given, implanted main foundations, which are pure, clear, mostly mono-syllabic rootwords, which spread out their shoots, branch- and

---

[52] On the concept of *Eigentlichkeit*, see Gardt (1995).
[53] For fuller discussion of the history of the rootword-concept, see McLelland (*forthcoming a*).

vein-rich boughs in finest purity, constant certainty and limitless multiplicity, spaciously and wide, so that it is not necessary to add in foreign sounds and to make the twigs break and grow awry.'

(Krause 1855 [1973]: 247)

In its very first formulation, then, Schottelius's *Stammwort* was not a dry technical term on a par with noun, verb, case, number, and the like. It was already linked to the rich image of a language tree, long associated with the FG, whose name and symbol of the palm-tree relied on the same metaphorical field: language as a tree with shoots, twigs, and branches.

Furthermore, discussions in the FG may also have shaped Schottelius's view of the *Stammwort*. It is clear that a work by Stevin *über die deutsche Sprache in Niederländisch* ('about the German language in Dutch') was read by some members of the FG (presumably either the *Uytspraeck* or the later version in *Vande Vervnievwing des Wysentijts*of 1608); Schottelius appears to have lent a copy to Prince Ludwig in 1643, who invited Gueintz to come and read it. When Harsdörffer compiled a summary of the rootword's features in the outline he presented for a German dictionary in 1647 (Krause 1855 [1973]: 387–392), other members of the FG in turn responded with criticisms. These included the concern that Harsdörffer (and Schottelius) had adopted what Prince Ludwig misleadingly called 'the Dutch way, taken from Stevin' of declaring the *Stammwort* to be the monosyllabic, second person singular imperative form of the verb (*Nach der Niederländischen art, die von Stefino herkommet*, Krause 1973 [1855]: 395). Prince Ludwig in 1648 repeated the criticism already made by Gueintz in 1645, that the second person imperative singular is not monosyllabic, but ends in an –e (*weise*, and not *weis*) (Krause 1855 [1973]: 102, 300, 394–97). Ludwig conceded that second person imperatives were monosyllabic in Dutch, but they were not so in *Hochdeutsch*. The influence of such discussions in the FG correspondence can be traced in Schottelius's ongoing revisions to his discussion of monosyllabic rootwords in his fourth oration. Italics in the passages below (*AA* 61–62, 4: 35 and its equivalents from 1641 and 1651) highlight the small adjustments made to the 1641 original in the later versions. In 1641, before the controversy broke, Schottelius cheerfully allowed for the fact that some German rootwords nowadays had a second unstressed syllable, but noted that they might have been monosyllabic in the past, and that people were 'in the habit of' (*man pflegt*) omitting the –e anyway. Adding an –e goes against the nature of things and is abject copying from other languages.

Es haben aber etzliche wenige Stammwörter ein zweysilbiges Geläut / also daß die letztere Silb ein E allezeit in sich hat / welches doch die alten Teutschen vielleicht einsilbiger weise außgeredet haben; gestaltsam es annoch gebräuchlich / daß man so wol im reden / als im schreiben / solches E unterweilen zu übergehen pflegt. Derselbe aber redet wider den Lauff deß natürlichen Verstandes / welcher diese so treffliche Meisterstücke deß Menschlichen Verstandes / auß lauter Unverstande von Griechen / Lateinern oder anderen abbetelen wil

'Some few rootwords have a bisyllabic sound, as the last syllable has an E in it, which [words] the ancient Germans perhaps pronounced monosyllabically; bearing in mind that it is still usual that one is accustomed sometimes to pass over such an E, both in writing and in speaking. But whoever wants to beg these so excellent masterpieces of human reason, out of sheer ignorance, from Greeks, Latins and others, speaks against natural reason.'

Schottelius (1641: 89–90)

In 1651, after the discussions summarized above, Schottelius adjusted his stance. He now conceded that in High German, some rootwords definitely had a second syllable (though elsewhere he maintained that German rootwords were *fast überall* 'certainly always' or perhaps more likely 'almost always' monosyllabic, *AA* 144, 9: 18; the meaning of *fast* shifts around this time from an intensifier to its modern sense of 'almost'). Nonetheless, as we can see by reading the revised wording (with changes italicised by me), he was also now more definite (though wrong) that in older German, at least, such words *were* monosyllabic. So too in (Low) Saxon German one could still find the monosyllabic root:

Es haben aber etzliche *Teutsche* Stammwörter / *der Hochteutschen Mundart nach* / ein zweysilbiges Geläut / also daß die letztere Silb ein E in sich *hat* / welches doch die alten Teutschen *auch* einsilbiger weise ausgeredet haben; Gestaltsam es annoch gebräuchlich / daß man so wol im reden / als im schreiben / solches E unterweilen zu übergehen pflegt. *Als Adler / Vater / Mutter / Himmel / Leber / zc. Solche heissen aber nach alten Teutschen Arndt / Vaer / Moer / Himl / Lefr / zc. Und also in anderen / da man die einsilbige Sachsische Würzel wol finden kan.*

'Some *German* rootwords have a bisyllabic sound, *according to the High German dialect*, as the last syllable has an E in it, which [words] the ancient Germans *also* pronounced monosyllabically; bearing in mind that it is still common that one is accustomed sometimes to pass over such an E, both in writing and in speaking. *As in Adler / Vater / Mutter / Himmel / Leber / ['eagle, father, mother, heaven, liver']* etc. *But according to the ancient German manner, such words*

*have the form Arndt | Vaer | Moer | Himl | Lefr | etc. And thus in
others where one can find the monosyllabic Saxon root.'*

Schottelius (1651: 124)

By 1663, the argument implicit in the 1651 version was made explicit.
(Again the additions made in 1663 are highlighted by me in italics.) Yes,
some rootwords are not monosyllabic, but this is a peculiarity of High
German, and the peculiarity is viewed only as a tendency (*zu halten pflege,*
not *hat*). In any case, occasional rootwords that are not monosyllabic do
not change the basic argument that these words were originally
monosyllabic (*benimt der uhrankünftlichen einsilbigkeit nichts*), and that
the original monosyllabic forms can still be found in Low German and Low
Saxon. For good measure, Schottelius then threw in some authoritative
Latin, repeating the point that in the rootwords, the language's original
basis had been preserved.

> Es haben aber etzliche Teutsche Stammwörter / *sonderlich der
> Hochteutschen Mundart nach /* ein zweysilbiges Geläut / also daß die
> letztere Silb ein E in sich *zu halten pflege /* welches doch die alten
> Teutschen auch einsilbiger weise ausgeredet haben; Gestaltsam es
> annoch gebräuchlich / daß man so wol im reden / als im schreiben /
> solches E unterweilen zu übergehen pflegt. Als Adler / Vater /
> Mutter / Himmel / Leber / zc. Solche heissen aber nach alten
> Teutschen Arndt / Vaer / Moer / Himl / Lefr / & c. Und also in
> anderen / da man die einsilbige Sachsische Würtzel wol finden kan.
> *Wan man demnach alle itzige bekandte / und nach unserer Hoch-
> teutschen Mundart auszusprechende Stammwörter würde zusammen
> bringen / können viel darunter des angenommenen Ausspruchs halber /
> nicht einsilbig sein / ein solches aber benimt der uhrankünftlichen
> einsilbigkeit nichts / dan das Hochteutsche ist nur eine hochlautende
> wolgeschmükte Mundart der Sprache / das Niederteutsche und Nie-
> dersächsische aber erstrekt sich viel weiter / darin oftmals / ob ein
> Wort Echt und Recht / und was dessen eigentliche Bedeutung / zu-
> suchen und zufinden* & lingua ipsa avitam suam & Regiam & nun-
> quam destructam sedem ab omni ævo hic sibi servavit.

'Some German rootwords have a bisyllabic sound, *especially according to the High German dialect*, as the last syllable *is accustomed
to have* an E in it, which [words] the ancient Germans also pronounced monosyllabically; bearing in mind that it is still common
that one is accustomed sometimes to pass over such an E, both in
writing and in speaking. As in Adler / Vater / Mutter / Himmel /
Leber / ['eagle, father, mother, heaven, liver'] etc. But according to
the ancient German manner, such words have the form Arndt / Vaer

/ Moer / Himl / Lefr / etc. And thus in others one can find the monosyllabic Saxon root. *If one were, accordingly, to bring together all rootwords that were to be pronounced monosyllabically according to our High German dialect, many of them could not be monosyllabic from their accepted pronunciation. But this does not detract from their original monosyllabicity at all, for High German is merely a high-sounding, well-embellished dialect of the language. Low German and Low Saxon, however, stretches far further, and we have often to seek and find in it a word in its right and original form, and what its actual meaning is. And it is here that the language itself has preserved for itself its ancestral, royal and never-detroyed seat, through all time.*

(*AA* 61–62, 4: 35)

This rather detailed textual comparison across the hypotexts of three editions and the Gueintz review shows how we need to understand the *AA* as a point of intersection of ideas. In one dimension, the hypotextual, we have the layers of text added over the course of the various editions—three editions in the case of the grammar and the orations. By 1663, a whole new layer had been added to this partial palimpsest, as a great deal of material had been added, much in Latin. But these changes were the result of ebb and flow in another dimension, as ideas from the discourses of German grammars, cultural patriotism, and international scholarship all intersected. Permeating all of these, in turn, was the pansemiotic, emblematic way of thinking that made itself felt in imagery that is inseparable from theory.

4

THE GENRES OF THE *AUSFÜHRLICHE ARBEIT* AND THEIR ARCHITEXTS

4.1 ARCHITEXTUALITY IN THE *AUSFÜHRLICHE ARBEIT*: INHERITING AND EXPLORING GENRES

Schottelius called his 1663 work an *ausführlich* 'comprehensive' work on the German language. Such a book today, whatever topics it covered, would contain only one sort of text: discursive, expositional writing, albeit broken up by illustrative figures, diagrams and tables. The reader would probably encounter a number of formalisms, but there would be no place for exposition of ideas in verse or in dialogue; no rhetorical show-pieces in praise of the language; and no long lists of words, names or phrases. Yet all of these feature prominently in Schottelius's *AA*, and such different ways of presenting reflections on language in the Baroque are rather 'reception-hindering' (*rezeptionshindernd*) for the modern reader, as Hundt (2000: 2) remarked. Working with Genette's (1982) notion of architextuality, this chapter therefore makes clear the function of each of these texts-types in a 1663 comprehensive study of German.[1]

The full list of text-types in the *AA* is as follows (in the order in which they are first encountered in the *AA*):

- the *Lobrede* 'panegyric, discourse of praise' in honour of the language, ten of which make up Book I of the *AA*
- the grammar which makes up Books II and III
- the poetics of Book IV

and the various text-types all presented under the misleadingly uniform title of *Traktat* ('treatise') in Book V:

- a long poem, the *Einleitung zur Teutschen Sprache* (presented as the first 'treatise' of Book V, *AA* 1002–1028, including the accompanying explanatory notes)
- a treatise on the ancient German proper names (the second treatise, *AA* 1029–1098)
- a list of proverbs with accompanying discussion (the third treatise, *AA* 1099–1147)

---

[1] Architexts are the genres or text-types that serve as models (or anti–models) for the text to be examined. Architextuality refers to the awareness of such text-types, and of the unwritten rules and expectations that govern them.

- a treatise on authors who have written about Germany or in German (the fourth treatise, *AA* 1148–1215)
- a dialogue about how to translate into German (the fifth treatise, *AA* 1216–1268)
- a list of rootwords, with accompanying discussion (the sixth treatise, *AA* 1269–1450)

The seventh 'treatise', not listed here, serves as an overview of the work for Latin readers. Some of the shorter text-types in Book V have so far received almost no attention at all.[2]

4.2 The orations (Book I, *AA* 1–170)

> **Lobrede** / *vernimt man vermittelst getahner Anzeige* / *daß es eine solche Rede sey* / *darin etwas herausgestrichen und gelobet sey*

> 'Discourse of praise / one understands by this label that it is a discourse in which something is to be singled out and praised'

> (*AA* 75, 6: 9)

Book I of the *AA* consists of ten *Lobreden* 'discourses of praise, praise orations' (for convenience generally referred to, shorthand, as orations).[3] Only the first nine appeared in the 1641 *Sprachkunst*, for Schottelius was in a hurry to bring out his *Sprachkunst* to compete with that of Gueintz. The tenth was added in the 1651 edition. The orations are monologic discourses made up of numbered paragraphs, and include many citations from other sources, and lists of words and expressions; each oration is preceded by a Latin summary. Table 4.1 provides a summary of their contents, with English translations of their titles.[4] The genre of the *Lobrede* was both a *demonstration* of the art of rhetoric par excellence, and a *legitimation* of German by argument, using all the techniques of the art.

---

[2] The notable exception is Hundt (2000), where pp. 83–98 deal with the text-types of the orations and of Book V; lists are dealt with pp. 319–329.

[3] Neither the *elogium* nor the German *Lobrede* was necessarily intended for oral delivery, so that the term 'oration' in English is perhaps a little misleading, but I have preferred it both to 'eulogy' (with its connotations today of commemorating the dead—Schottelius certainly did not consider German dead) and to 'panegyric' which—meaning a laudatory discourse—is accurate, but rare in English, and which lacks the deliberate transparency of the German term *Lobrede*. The term 'oration' should therefore be understood throughout this book as shorthand for the rather clumsy 'praise oration' or 'discourse of praise'.

[4] Hundt (2000: 83–87) and Römer (1986) provide summaries of contents; cf. also Seiffert 1988; for an overview of additions made between editions, see 6.1.

Table 4.1: Ten orations in praise of the German language Book I (AA 1–170)*

Oration	German title (abbreviated)	English translation	Overview of contents
1 (*AA* 1–14)	*Die Veranlassung / den Inhalt und Ordnung dieses* Operis, *und was von allgemeinem guten Gebrauche in der Sprache / auch von den Kunstwörteren oder* terminis artium *anfangs zuerinneren*	'On the motivation, the content and structure of this work, and what to bear in mind at the start regarding general good usage in language and regarding terminology or *termini artium*'	Introduction to theoretical foundations (analogy / rootwords as the foundation of the language) and to the contents of the *AA*; technical terms, including grammatical terminology; and their formation from the monosyllabic rootwords of German.
2 (*AA* 14–27)	*Die Zeugnissen vieler hoher / vortreflicher und gelahrter Männer / die sie von ihrer Teutschen MutterSprache getahn / und dazu angemahnt haben / samt Widerlegung des irrigen Uhrteihls und Deuteley / so unterschiedliche vornehme Ausländer in ihren Schriften über die Teutsche Sprache hinterlassen*	'The testimonies of many prominent, excellent and learned men on their German mother tongue, and refutation of the erroneous judgement and misinterpretations about the German language which have been made by various distinguished foreigners in their writings'	The qualities of German: assertions of the prestige of German by citing authorities, and rebuttals of criticisms of the language made by other (non-German) authorities.
3 (*AA* 27–49)	*Deroselben [= German's] Uhrankunft und Uhraltertuhm / auch daß / und wie / die itzige Teutsche Sprache / eben annoch im Grunde die Uhralte Sprache sey: Auch von den Denkzeiten (*Epochis*) Teutscher Sprache*	'The origin and antiquity of the German language, also how the German language today is still basically the ancient language; also on the periods (epochs) of German'	The antiquity and originality of today's German; its descent from Babel and its relationship to Celtic, Latin, and Greek; the unchanging essence of German, i.e. its rootwords and capacity for derivation and compounding; teleological view of five eras in the history of German.
4 (*AA* 49–65)	*Den Natürlichen Uhrsprung und vortrefliche Eigenschaften der Teutschen S[t]ammwörter und Letteren ingemein*	'The natural origin and excellent characteristics of the German rootwords and letters'	The excellent essence of German already presented in the third oration, the rootwords: rootwords are present in sufficient number to allow derivation and compounding, are monosyllabic, and are composed of natural (i.e. orginal German) letters; an attempt, therefore, to prove the origin of the alphabet is Germanic / Celtic; naturalness of rootwords because they express their meaning *eigentlich* [i.e. the linguistic sign is not arbitrary in German].

Table 4.1: (Continued)

Oration	German title (abbreviated)	English translation	Overview of contents
5 (*AA* 66–71)	*Eine kurtze Anleitung und Anzeige zu der sonderlichen / und andern Sprachen gantz ungemeiner Ableitung der Wörter / welche in unserer MutterSprache so überreichlich zu finden*	'A short introduction and demonstration of the special derivation of words, so abundant in our mother tongue and very unusual in other languages'	Derivation and inflection in German: language, like music, must be composed by rules of the art; rootwords are the sure foundation from which new words are formed; lists of derivational and inflectional suffixes.
6 (*AA* 72–103)	*Eine richtige Eröfnung der Gründen und wunderreichen Eigenschaften / welche in Verdoppelung der Teutschen Wörter aufs allerglücklichste verhanden seyn*	'A correct explanation of the foundations and wonderful characteristics that are most happily found in the compounding of German words'	Compounding: compounding allows German to capture the multiplicity of nature concisely, e.g. all shades of colours, e.g. *Meergrün, Lilienweiß*; the types of compounding, with numerous examples: 1. noun + noun (incl. adjective), e.g. *Rahthaus, Saftgrün* 2. noun + verbal (agentive) noun e.g. *Rahtgeber* 3. particle (*Vorwort*) + noun or verb, e.g. *Weggleiten* 4. rootword(s) plus affix, i.e. derivation as in oration 5, e.g. *Sprachkunstlos*.
7 (*AA* 103–122)	*Eine kurtze Anregung in gemein von der Poesi / auch wie dahin in Teutscher Sprache zugelangen*	'A brief proposal on poetry in general and how to achieve it in German'	German poetics (written before the *Verskunst* of Book IV had been written): *Verskunst* must be learnt as an art in accordance with the nature of the language, though it relies too on inspiration from God; Germans have no shortage of suitable topics for poetry in their history, such as war and peace; German verse must respect the quality (*Wortklang*) and length (*Wortzeit*) of words; an Erasmus-like demonstration of *copia verborum*: over 150 synonymous expressions for *die, kill* (*AA* 117–122).

Table 4.1: (Continued)

Oration	German title (abbreviated)	English translation	Overview of contents
8 (*AA* 122–134)	*Einen kurtzen Beweistuhm / daß annoch bis auf diese Zeit / die Wurtzelen oder Stammwörter der Teutschen Sprache sich fast in allen üblichen Europeischen Sprachen finden lassen: Auch daß der alten Gallier Sprache sey Teutsch gewesen / samt mehren Anführungen von Reinlichkeit und Räumigkeit der Teutschen Sprache*	'A brief proof that the roots or rootwords of the German language are found in almost all the usual European languages; also that the language of the Gauls was German, together with more evidence of the purity and wide reach of the German language'	Pure ancestry of German: German is pure and unmixed, despite foolish efforts to derive its words from other languages; German is the source of much of the vocabulary in other European languages; these languages are derived from 'old' German, called Celtic or German; examples of the Lord's Prayer in Germanic languages, taken from Gessner's *Mithridates* (1555), plus a Gothic word-list.
9 (*AA* 135–148)	*Eine kurtze Entdekkung des unbegründeten Wesens / dadurch unsere HaubtSprache zum Sproslinge / Menglinge und Betlerin wird gemacht: auch wie von denen sonst fleissigen und sinnreichen Teutschen die Teutschen Sprache sey verseumt und veracht worden. Samt angeführten Uhrsachen / wordurch die rechte Ausübung und Werthaltung deroselben / noch itzo guten theils verhindert werde*	'A brief explanation of the unfounded factors by which our language is being turned into an off shoot, mongrel, and beggar; also how it has been neglected and disparaged by the otherwise diligent and sensible Germans. Together with causes by which the correct exercise and valuing of German has largely been hindered.	Lampooning of others' attempts to seek the origins of German words in other languages; lament over German's impoverishment and corruption because of foreign influence; need for care and proper study of German, not neglect; refutations of reasons given for not studying German, one's mother tongue; the *AA* is commended to the reader as offering *vielfältige Gründe / Exempla und Beweistühmer* 'many reasons, examples and proofs' (*AA* 148) that German lacks nothing, but must be studied properly.
10 (*AA* 148–170)	*Einen unmaasgeblichen Bericht von den Mundarten oder Dialectis, auch wie die Teutsche Sprache in Dialectos geteihlet sey; samt Anführung / wie ein völliges Lexicon in Teutscher Sprache / so annoch niemals verhanden gewesen / zuverfertigen / und warum die Muttersprache nicht in der alltäglichen ungewissen Gewonheit / sonderen in kunstmässigen Lehrsätzen und gründlicher Anleitung fest bestehen müsse*	'A preliminary account of the dialects, and how the German language is divided into dialects, together with a guide as to how to make a complete dictionary in German, which there has never been to date, and why the mother tongue must consist not in uncertain custom, but in artful principles and in thorough instruction'	Exhortation to further cultivation of and more general study of the language, as did the Greeks and Romans; the natural love for one's language; overview of the German dialects and German(ic) languages; the need for a dictionary of German, to be ordered by rootword; three reasons why languages change: 1. the passage of time, 2. mixing of peoples, 3. neglect and uncertainty in everyday speech.

In prefacing the grammar proper with these rhetorical pieces in praise of the language, Schottelius followed common practice, but greatly expanded on it. All earlier comparable grammars of the vernacular began with more or less lengthy learned discourses which dealt with the history and status of the language. The fourteen-side preface to Clajus's (1578) Latin grammar of German had precisely that aim; the dedication to Ritter's grammar written specifically for French learners of German (Ritter 1616) argued point by point that German deserved the fourth place after the three sacred languages Latin, Greek and Hebrew, on the basis of its antiquity, purity, gravity and amplitude; only in sweetness, or suavity, might others outdo it, but this was more than outweighed by German's superior energy, number of compounds, use of metaphors and abundance of phrases. Such a rhetorical defence of German was, then, part of established practice, at least in grammar-writing aimed at a learned, adult audience. (In elementary grammars such as those of Ratke (Anon. 1619), Brücker (1620) or Olearius (1630), such discussions had no place.) Gueintz, Schottelius's rival as a grammarian in the FG, had followed suit in his *Sprachlehre* of 1641. Gueintz's dedication stressed a line of continuity from antiquity: from the Roman Empire, to Charlemagne's efforts to promote German, down to the FG of his own day. In addition, Gueintz's grammar proper began with a treatment under subheadings of the origin of German, the beginnings of German writing, an overview of noteworthy writers in German, the usefulness of German, and its richness. It was Gueintz who for the first time in a grammar of German covered this cultural–patriotic material *in German*.

In Schottelius's later *Sprachkrieg* (1673), the kings of the two sides of the 'language war' were named *Lob* and *Kunst*. *Kunst* stood for *Sprachkunst*, the art of *recte dicendi*, correct language use or grammar, while *Lob* ('praise') personified *pars pro toto* the complementary branch of language study, rhetoric, the *ars bene dicendi*, the art of speaking well (see Czucka 1997: 76). Ideally, Praise and artful Rhetoric would complement each other, and the orations of the *AA* were an exemplification of this happy co–existence, as praise in and of the language and the codification of grammatical art were presented together. Furthermore, the *elogium* or *Lobrede*—as the *genus demonstrativum* in Aristotelian rhetoric, and unlike the other two Aristotelian genera, the *genus iudicale* or *genus deliberata-vum*—required no decision from the audience. It was, therefore, tradition-ally the rhetorician's exhibition piece, where the performance of the genre was as much to be admired, as attention paid to the contents (Lausberg 1988: 102–03, § 239). A model genre of rhetoric, it enjoyed a revival in the sixteenth and seventeenth centuries (cf. for instance the Latin *Orationes* of Daniel Heinsius, 1609), and could even take the form of a sort of academic test of skill, so Heinsius's collection concluded with an oration in praise of the unpraiseworthy, the louse. One of the earliest defences of German, Opitz's *Aristarchus* (1617)—a plea for purifying German of foreign borrowings—began life as just such a rhetorical exercise, completed while Opitz was still at school. As a demonstration piece aimed at a learned audience, the oration was, therefore, an obvious text-type to try out in the vernacular, especially when the object of its emphatic and persuasive praise was the language itself. For following the printing of Dante's Latin *De vulgari eloquentia* (written 1303–1307), in 1529, such praises of the vernacular *in* the vernacular had already become established as 'a Renaissance genre' elsewhere in Europe (Burke 2004: 65): the *Dialogo delle lingue*, a defence of Italian *in* Italian in 1542 by Sperone Speroni (1500–1588); the 1549 *Défense et illustration* of French by Joachim du Bellay (1522?–1560); and Simon Stevin's Dutch-language *Uytspraeck Vande Werdicheyt der Duytsche Tael* (1586) 'Oration in Praise of the Worth of the *Duytsch* Language', in 1586. Schottelius's ten *Lobreden* in German were directly inspired by Stevin's *Uytspraeck*, almost half of which Schottelius actually cited or paraphrased in his own orations (cf. Table 6.5).[5] It was also not unusual to preface poetical works with a verse eulogy in justification of using the vernacular (Bornemann 1976: 94). Scriverius's rhymed eulogy of Dutch printed at the front of Heinsius's *Nederduytsche Poemata* (1616, collected and published by Scriverius) was well-known and was indeed still cited by Schottelius (in the original Dutch) in the *AA* (*AA* 22, 2: 26).[6] Paragraphs 31 and 33 of Schottelius's second oration (*AA* 23–24, 2: 31, 33) are based on the oration *Contra Galliam* 'against France' of Thomas Lansius (1577–1657) (cf. Lansius's *Orationes aliquot*, 1616).

Schottelius's mid–seventeenth–century devotion to this model cultural–patriotic text–type illustrates how late Germans came to the notion of emphatic praise of their vernacular.[7] The contrast with the preface to Wallis's *Grammatica Linguae Anglicanae* (1653) is instructive. There Wallis outlined the origin of the English language, but his is a sober account, lacking the rhetorical energy which Schottelius devoted in his orations to

---

[5] Stevin glossed the word *Uytspraeck* as *elogium*: Stevin (1586) in Dijksterhuis (1955: 58).

[6] Similarly, as noted in 3.4, Opitz's own *Teutsche Poemata* (1624) were prefaced by an anonymous poem *Ad Linguam Germanicam* (actually written by Hugo Grotius for Abraham Mylius's *Lingua Belgica,* 1612) (Bornemann 1976: 95–96). The *Lobrede* is the prose pendant to such verse *Lobgesang*. Bornemann (1976: 202–210) discusses the reception of this genre in Germany from the Netherlands. The same general point would hold true for the *Lobrede*.

[7] The publication of Schottelius's *Lobreden* in 1641 spawned imitation, however, notably by two close friends. Johann Rist's *Rettung der Edlen Teutschen Hauptsprache* in 1642 (Mast 2001) and Harsdörffer's *Schutzschrift für die Teutsche Spracharbeit* (1644) (Hundt 2000: 58–71) both belong to the genre of 'praise of one's language', even if they are not orations. Harsdörffer also composed a *Lobrede des Geschmacks* ('oration in praise of taste') which appeared in 1651, in honour of the new head of the FG, Duke William IV of Sachsen–Weimar, whose society name was *Der Schmackhafte* 'the tasteful one'. Hundt's discussion of its rhetorical techniques (Hundt 2000: 413–20) is equally applicable—*mutatis mutandis*—to Schottelius's own orations. Strategies noted by Hundt include the use of proverbs, cumulation of terms, reliance on the idea that older = better, anticipation of counter-arguments, use of analogies, and reference to authorities (on the last point, cf. Chapter 6). On Harsdörffer's *Lobreden* see also Zeller (1974: 33–36).

raising the status of German. Schottelius's preoccupations are comparable with those of du Bellay in his 1549 *Défense et illustration de la language francaise* almost a whole century earlier. The first part of du Bellay's work, the *Défense* part, contained twelve chapters whose titles include matters such as the origins of languages; an assertion that the French language should not be called barbarous; why the French language is not as rich as Greek and Latin; that French is not so impoverished as many consider it; that translations alone are not sufficient to perfect French; on bad translators, and on not translating poetry;[8] and how the Romans enriched their language. Schottelius combined such universal concerns about the origin, worth and cultivation of the vernacular with the crucial notion that he found in Stevin (1586/1608), that of the monosyllabic rootwords. Schottelius's orations are thus a mix of the 'usual' arguments in defence of the language (antiquity, purity, richness, a reminder that even Latin and other languages needed cultivation, the importance of poetry in the vernacular) and the new idea about the basic structure of the language taken from Stevin. Three of the ten orations—orations four to six—are in fact wholly devoted to expounding the theory of the rootword, derivation and compounding.

The *Reden* 'discourses, orations' were never delivered as such, unlike Johann Klaj's *Lobrede der Teutschen Poeterey* (1645; cf. Ingen 1990), but were aimed rather at a learned readership comfortable with reading Latin citations in support of the points made. Nevertheless, the orations do also—especially in the opening paragraphs of each oration—contain rhetorical *tours de force* illustrating the resources available to the German rhetorician. Schottelius wrote no treatise on rhetoric, as he did a poetics (cf. 4.5), so we have in the *Lobreden* just the *demonstration* of the art of rhetoric in German, without a theoretical exposition with which to compare it.[9] Still, it is revealing to note briefly some of the rhetorical techniques displayed in the orations. Gardt (1994: 36–41) has already shown Schottelius's careful *dispositio* of his arguments. Examining the beginning of the third oration and drawing on Dyck (1969), Gardt provides a detailed analysis of the argumentational structures that Schottelius built up to be persuasive; Blume (1983) noted Schottelius's strategy of pre-empting arguments on the

---

[8]   On reflections on translation in Renaissance France, cf. Worth (1988).

[9]   The first German rhetoric (Meyfart 1634, [1977]), by Johann Meyfart (1590–1642), was apparently viewed by contemporaries as so definitive that many writers cited it as their reason for not producing a rhetoric themselves (Barner 1970: 160, fn.67). Certainly Schottelius's assessment of Meyfart's *Teutsche Redekunst* on p. 1177 of his treatise on writers is entirely positive. An alternative explanation for the lack of a separate rhetoric in the *AA* is almost contradictory: that the existence of rhetoric as a separate art was questionable at the time, for *inventio* and *dispositio* belonged since Ramus to the domain of logic (Padley 1976: 80–81); the remainder of rhetoric (in Ciceronian terms: style, memory and delivery) might be treated as mere stylistic adornment, under poetics.

opposing side. A passage from the ninth oration (*AA* 137–138, 9: 6) may serve as an example of Schottelius's skill in *inventio* and in style:

> Mehr als zuviel ist bekant / wie die Teutsche Sprache jhre eigene Wörter verlieren / deutlos und unbekant lassen / jhren herrlichen Reichtuhm verarmet sehen / und jhre eigene reinliche Gestalt verfrömdet und verschandflekket leiden muß / in dem nicht allein einem jeden nach Beliebung / durch gestatteten Misbrauch freygelassen wird allerley Wörter aus allerley Sprachen hinein zulappen / als ob keine zierliche Rede geschehen / noch einige Schrift abgefasset werden könte / Zier und Wolstand sey dann von Frömden entlehnet / und unsere so herrliche / prächtige / Majestätische Sprache zur armen hungerigen Bettlerin gemacht. Und müssen die verhandene reine / alte / klare / deutliche Teutsche Wörter den Teutschen unangenehm / und nicht so reputirlich lauten und vorkommen / und wird durch solche beliebt Frömdsucht / auch das sonst den Teutschen ins gemein angebohrne ehr= und redlich seyn und gutes einheimisches Wesen / in hochfahrenden Wankelsinn und in eine schädliche ausländische Wunschgier verendert;

> 'It is all too well known how the German language must endure seeing her own words lost, meaningless and unrecognized, her great wealth impoverished, and her own pure form contaminated and stained. Not only is it left to each and every person, by permitted abuse, to add in all sorts of words from all sorts of languages as they like, as if no elegant [*zierlich*] speech nor any writing could be composed, unless adornment/embellishment [*Zier*] and wealth are borrowed from foreigners, and our so glorious, splendid majestic language is made into a poor, hungry beggarwoman. And the existing pure, old, limpid, clear German words appear unpleasant to the Germans, and don't sound or seem so 'reputable', and by such widespread desire for what is foreign, the good, honest native essence that is otherwise innate in the Germans in general is changed into a haughty fickleness and a damaging foreign craving.'

The much–vaunted German capacity for creative compounding is demonstrated here in terms like the emphatic *Wunschgier* ('desire, covetousness') or the wonderfully expressive compound *Wankelsinn* ('inconstancy, fickleness', lit. 'wobble-sense'). Note too the emotive personification, the cumulation of attributive adjectives, the dramatic contrasts (wealth–poverty, majesty–beggar), and irony (*reputirlich* is an à-la-mode foreignism of the type deplored) (cf. also Gardt 1994: 146–151).

4.3 THE DIALOGUE ON TRANSLATING (*AA* 1216–1268)

The fifth treatise in Book V of the *AA*, on the art of translating, takes the form of a dialogue. Like the orations, it has demonstrative character, intended as a model for the genre in German (cf. Hundt 2000: 91–92, Czapla 1988). Plato's Socratic dialogues, which featured his teacher Socrates in debate with other characters, founded the tradition of the scholarly dialogue in the West,[10] and dialogues enjoyed renewed popularity as a means of expounding an argument or conveying knowledge from the Renaissance onwards in Europe (cf. Heitsch & Vallee 2004), particularly in the Protestant tradition of education of ordinary folk. In Reformation Germany, pamphlets on disputed points of theology were often presented in dialogue form (Campbell 2003, Schwitalla 1983, Schuster, 2001; on the textual composition of the Reformation dialogue, cf. especially Bentzinger 2003). The dialogue was also already established as a genre in which to defend the vernacular in the sixteenth century, as in Speroni's *Dialogo delle lingue* (1542) already noted, or in Hendrik Laurenszoon Spieghel's (1549–1612) *Twe-Spraack* of 1584 (Dibbets 1985).

The accessible format of the dialogue genre—a conversation that can be read aloud and discussed—is an effective way of dealing with complex ideas. In the *AA*, the dialogue on translating was a way of making accessible and piquing interest in the more theoretical sections of the *AA*, to which Schottelius was careful to make more or less explicit references throughout the dialogue. As in many such dialogues, questioning by an inquisitive pupil gives scope for the participants (and the readers or listeners) to test ideas and develop their argument step by step. The first participant is *Wolrahm*, a name interpreted in Schottelius's name-list (*AA* 1097) as *der wol zurahmen und recht zutreffen sich fleißiget*, roughly 'he who strives to order well and to do right'. True to his name, then, Wolrahm is the questioner here, keen to learn and to do right. He asks leading questions, such as 'Isn't it enough to translate such that one can understand the meaning of the foreign language, no matter how the German words sound?' Wolrahm's interocutor Siegeraht offers advice, meanwhile, for his name means *victoriae consilium*, interpreted as 'advising so as to achieve victory' (*AA* 1084).[11] In genre-typical form, the dialogue on translating is a hybrid between orality and written text. Ostensibly oral, its opening words fix it as a text found at a particular place in a book, as Wolrahm begins *Demnach aus vorhergehendem Tractat wol abzunehmen* … 'As we can gather from the previous

---

[10] Indeed one of them, the *Cratylos* dialogue on the 'rightness of names' is still much discussed in linguistics today. See Law (2003: 26) for accessible discussion of dialogue as a tool for reasoning; cf. also Joseph (2000) for detailed discussion of the *Cratylos* dialogue from a linguist's perspective.

[11] Schottelius used the same two figures again as the narrators in his *Horrendum Bellum Grammaticale* of 1673.

treatise ....' (*AA* 1218). What concerns the two participants is the question of why many texts translated into German appear less well-written than those simply written in German without reference to a foreign model. It is pointed out that one cannot write well in German without thorough knowledge of the language, obtained only by applying *Zeit / Fleiß und Arbeit* (*AA* 1221), 'time, diligence and labour'. In other words, we are indirectly advised to apply ourselves to the grammar. One must be *recht und gründlich kündig* ('properly and thoroughly knowledgeable') in the language, have a large *Vorraht Teutscher Wörter* ('store of German words', *AA* 1221, a remark that is a clear echo of Luther both in spirit and in phrasing),[12] including the *abegeleitete[n]* and *gedoppelte[n] Worte[n]* 'derived and compound words' (*AA* 1226), and one must use *der Teutschen Sprach zugehörigen Worten und Redarten* 'words and idioms that belong to the German language' (*AA* 1225). In other words, we should consult the list of German rootwords, and the list of proverbs in the other treatises. The sixth oration is also commended to the reader, in order to learn more about the formation and interpretation of German words (*AA* 1229). There is a reference to the verse *Einleitung* (cf. 4.6); and we are also encouraged to consult older German writings for examples of authentic German words, compounds and sayings in action.

The style of the dialogue is in accord with the text-type. We find straightforward language (the complex compounds favoured by Schottelius in his verse and in the orations are conspicuously absent); a reasoned tone; readily understood and plausible analogies (the German language is like good cloth or silver cutlery that does not lose its value just because it is put to poor use, *AA* 1219); and humour and satire, in the form of a Low German *Spottgedicht* on bad High German verse (*AA* 1260). We are also presented with models of idiomatic translation (from Opitz's translation of John Barclay (1582–1621), for example: *AA* 1222). Repetition is a typical feature, too, as the motif of the precious silver cutlery is repeated (*AA* 1219, 1233). The dialogue concludes in genre-typical fashion when Siegeraht simply announces that it is time to finish, and implicitly invites the reader or hearer to reflect on what has been said: *Nun es ist Zeit / daß wir vor dieses mahl unser Gesprech endigen / ein jeder kan es deuten wie er wil* 'Now it is time to finish our conversation for the time being. Each person can make of it what he wants' (*AA* 1268).

Despite these typical features, the dialogue form of the treatise competes with Schottelius's desire to include lengthy examples: ten pages of the *Kolbenrecht*, an older German 63-article set of laws (*AA* 1234–1242; cf. 6.2.2), lists of place-names (*AA* 1252–1254), a quotation from Luther in

---

[12]   Cf. Luther's *Sendbrief* (1530): *wer dolmetschen wil mus grosse vorrath von worten haben das er die wal könne haben wo eins an allen orten nicht lauten wil* 'whoever wants to translate must have a large store of words so that he can have the choice where one word does not suit all places [i.e. contexts].'

Latin (*AA* 1258), and lists of words in *Rotwelsch*, the language of thieves (*AA* 1262–1265). It also arguably wanders away from its core subject. A discussion of language games of the pig-Latin type used to serve as a secret language amongst thieves is a reflection of the dominance of pansemioticism (cf. 3.7), and would no doubt have fascinated the interested lay audience targeted by the popularizing text-type: Schottelius's example is *mapachepe dipich aupaus depem Staupaubepe* = *Mache dich aus dem Staube*, 'clear off!' (*AA* 1267). Notwithstanding such digressions into lengthier quotation and wordlists, the questions and comments by Wolrahm serve to structure the text and to raise the key issues about translating, including the extent to which foreign borrowed words should be permitted in German, and questions about how to write German poetry. Standing in the background as architexts here are not just the wider tradition of defence of the language as in du Bellay (1549), but more specifically the famous 'Open Letter on Translating' by Luther, already noted above (*Ein Sendbrieff vom Dolmetzschen*, 1530), where Luther had made the point about idiomatic translation that Schottelius emphasized here.[13] Siegeraht even quoted from Luther's letter at length (*AA* 1229). Recall that Schottelius declared that the fourth epoch in the history of German began with Luther's championing of the vernacular, and that the fifth and final epoch should begin in his own time, with renewed championing of the vernacular (third oration, *AA* 48–49, 3: 54–59). Schottelius, it seems, is an heir to Luther's mantle in this fifth era.

4.4 Lists: *Vielfaltige Gründe* / *Exempla und Beweistühmer* ('manifold grounds, examples and proofs', *AA* 148, 10: 30)

In accord with the seventeenth–century fascination with collecting and cataloguing the world, Schottelius's *AA* contains numerous lists. Already the dialogue just discussed contained word-lists, and there are others in the orations too, as well as in the grammar: lists of compounds of different types (sixth and tenth orations, *AA* 78–94, 161–65), synonyms for dying (seventh oration, *AA* 117–22, 7: 35), the Lord's Prayer in multiple Germanic languages (eighth oration, *AA* 130–31, 8: 10, based on Gessner's *Mithridates* (1555); cf. Moulin-Fankhänel 1997a), and compounds formed from the rootword *Mann* (chapter VII of the grammar, *AA* 286–90). Schottelius's list of colour terms in the sixth oration (*AA* 80–84, 6: 24) was still being cited by Ignaz Schiffermüller (1727–1809) in 1772 Vienna (Jones 2003: 892). Combining colour bases and modifiers (e.g. *blass, bleich, bunt, dunkel, fahl, finster*), Schottelius listed a sample of 126 colour compounds

---

[13] Excerpts from the Luther and du Bellay texts can be found in English translation in Robinson (2002).

that he considered current, although the bases and modifiers listed could generate over 500 possible permutations (Jones 2003: 887). The second, third and sixth treatises of Book V consist chiefly of such word-lists, with brief introductions: lists of German names (second treatise *AA* 1038–98), of German proverbs (third treatise, *AA* 1112–46), and of German rootwords (sixth treatise, *AA* 1277–1450). As Schottelius says at the end of the ninth oration:

> Jn diesem *opere* wird hierbey dismahl anders nichts getahn / als durch vielfaltige Gründe / *Exempla* und Beweistühmer vor Augen gestellet / daß es der Teutschen Haubtsprache an dem Vermögen und guter Bequämlichkeit dazu nicht ermangelen könne / jedoch erfodert dieses zureichenden fleiß und grundrichtige Kundigkeit / dessen vornehme gelahrte Leute / so an dieses Werk Gedanken wenden / nicht abredig seyn.

> 'In this work I do nothing other than show by manifold grounds, examples and proofs that the German language lacks nothing in capacity and good adaptability. However this requires sufficient diligence and fundamentally correct knowledge, which refined edu-cated people who turn their attention to this work will not deny.'

(*AA* 148)

The function of the various lists to be discussed here, then, was to furnish the necessary proofs of the good qualities of German. They provided an evidence–base for the arguments presented elsewhere in the *AA*, in order to demonstrate the richness of the German language (*copia verborum*) (Hundt 2000: 89, cf. also 319–329). The lists of proverbs and of proper names in particular each stood in their own text-type tradition, in whose context they must be seen; in these text-types, just as in the dialogue and the oration, Schottelius aligned himself with an existing tradition of scholarship with its roots in humanism, in particular by referencing both Luther, champion of the vernacular, and Desiderius Erasmus of Rotterdam (1466-1536), champion of *latinitas*.

4.4.1 *The list of proper names (AA 1029–1098):* die rechten Teutschen wolklingende Nahmen *('the proper German, good-sounding names', AA 1031, §1)*

Schottelius presented an analysis of the roots of personal proper names, listed alphabetically in Treatise 2 of Book V, in lieu of a complete study of the roots of *all* proper names, which would include geographical names, and to which Schottelius judged that a whole book would need to be devoted, but which he considered to be *eine schwere mühsame Arbeit*, 'a hard, laborious task' (*AA* 1273). An interest in German onomastics was characteristic of the developing German linguistic consciousness of the early modern era (Sonderegger 1999: 196–99), and Schottelius acknowledged several sources for his list, chiefly works by sixteenth- and early seventeenth-century late-humanist authors, on whom he drew to a greater or lesser extent, and whom he had already cited in the orations: Johannes Aventinus (1477–1534), Beatus Rhenanus, Wolfgang Lazius (1514–1565), Melchior Goldast (1576–1635), Christoph Besoldus (1577–1638), Philipp Cluverius (1580–1623), Hugo Grotius, and Franciscus Junius (1591–1677) (cf. 6.2). The Protestant humanist pedagogue Melanchthon had also included onomastic reflections in his editions of Tacitus's *Germania* for school use (Melanchthon 1538, 1557), just as Beatus Rhenanus had discussed German proper names at length in the commentary to his edition of *Germania* in 1519 (Mertens 2004: 92; cf. Sonderegger 1998: 422). For Melanchthon, the value in etymological study of German proper names lay on the one hand in the reminder of the inconstancy of all human concerns, but on the other in engendering a love for one's fatherland (*patriae amor*, cf. Mertens 2004: 94). So identifying rootwords in German names became the duty of any cultural patriot. Within this broad humanist tradition, though, Schottelius' treatise on proper names has, like the dialogue on translating, one particularly illustrious antecedent to which Schottelius again made explicit reference: the *Aliquot Nomina Propria Germanorum ad Priscam Etymologiam restituta* 'Some German proper names restored to their original etymology', which Schottelius attributed to Luther. (It was published anonymously in Wittenberg in 1537 but was attributed in editions from 1559 onwards to Luther; cf. Fiedler 1942; Sonderegger 1998: 425). As with the dialogue on translating, then, Schottelius took up in the fifth age of the German language where he believed that Luther had left off in the fourth.

Schottelius's elucidations of proper names, many of which seem to be identical to, or are slight re-wordings of, entries in the *Aliquot Nomina* text, indulged the pansemiotic fascination with seeking and combining meanings where they are not explicit. The name *Luther*, for instance, Schottelius interpreted as a variant of *Lotharius*, derived from *Leuther*, 'master of people'. More importantly, the interpretations allowed Schottelius to demonstrate at greater length what he had argued in the eighth oration: how many names common in Europe find their 'true' interpretation as compounds of German rootwords. (Here the topic is personal names; in the oration, the focus was on geographical names.) This in turn provided evidence for the assertion central to the *AA* that it was German that best preserved the ancestral Celto-Germanic language of Europe (cf. 2.2.3). Furthermore, the list had an explicit promotional aim: to remind people of *die rechten Teutschen wolklingende Namen* ('the proper German good-sounding names') which had been forgotten in favour of *die frömden Unteutschen Nahmen* ('the foreign un-German names' *AA* 1031 §1) since the time of Emperor Friedrich II (1194–1250).

4.4.2 *The list of proverbs (AA 1099–1147)*[14]

> Der Kern der Wissenschaft / der Schluß aus der Erfahrung / der Menschlichen Hendel kurtzer Ausspruch und gleichsam des weltlichen Wesens Spiegel
>
> 'the heart of science, the conclusion drawn from experience, the short expression of human actions, and, as it were, the mirror of the ways [lit. essence, being] of the world'
>
> (*AA* 1102, § 1)

Lists of proverbs were a more frequent and probably better known text-type than lists of proper names in Early Modern Europe, if only thanks to Erasmus's extremely influential *Adagia*, first published in 1500 with a collection of some eight hundred Greek and Latin proverbs. By the time of his death, Erasmus had expanded the collection to over four thousand. The *Adagia* collection was widely known across Europe, and Schottelius mentioned it first amongst the proverb collections he noted (*AA* 1110). In the face of such riches in the classical languages, it is not surprising that German humanists like Josua Maaler (1529–1599) sought to equal the achievement for their own language in the course of the sixteenth century. Maaler's German dictionary (1551) was an alphabetical list of *Alle wörter / namen / und arten zu reden* 'all words, names, and sayings' (my emphasis), as the title states. Similarly, the title of Georg Henisch's more systematic but unfinished dictionary (reaching only G) (1616) likewise reflects his compilation of German proverbs as well as words: his *Teütsche Sprach und Weißheit* 'German language and wisdom' is estimated to contain some 25,000 sayings and proverbs (Wiegand 1998: 652; cf. Considine 2008, chapter 4, section 3; see also Kämper 2001). It is against this tradition of proverb collections (on which cf. Weickert 1997, Mieder 2003 and further literature there) that Schottelius's own collection in the third treatise of Book V must be seen. The first such collection of the sixteenth century had been compiled by the German protestant humanist Johannes Agricola (1494–1566), the most complete edition of which, containing 750 proverbs, appeared posthumously in 1592. According to Mieder (1982, 2003), Schottelius's treatise contains some 1230 proverbs and another 560 proverbial expressions. The order of proverbs, which Schottelius himself stated he had listed *sine ordine* ('not in any order', *AA* 1101), was determined in part by the effect of compilation (which also accounts for some repetitions; cf. Schafferus 1932 and Mieder 1982).[15] For instance, the

---

[14] Some parts of this section appear in McLelland (2011).

[15] Much larger, and alphabetically ordered, lists of German phraseologisms had also already been published in the seventeenth century by Friedrich Petri (1604–05) and Christoph Lehmann (1630), each exceeding some 20,000 entries (Mieder 2003: 2652–53). Martin Luther too published a collection of 489 German proverbs, but in this instance Schottelius did not make explicit reference to it amongst his named sources (*AA* 1111).

entries on *AA* 1120–1128 correspond—though selectively, and with some
additions and alterations—to a collection of proverbs by Sebastian Franck
(1499–1539/1542/43) printed by Christian Egenolff (1502–1555) in 1548,
while those on *AA* 1128–1140 correspond to Agricola (1592).[16]

Schottelius considered proverbs the distillation of a people's wisdom
acquired over time. They were an expression of both nature and reason
(*die Natur und Vernunft*, *AA* 1102, §1), for their good sense had been
confirmed by long testing and experience over time, and only those
natural ideas that had been found useful by many people, and so were
evidently in accord with reason, survived. The proverb was thus a special
instance of the natural law that Schottelius made the basis of his entire
language theory at the start of the second oration: whatever all people of
good sense naturally approve is *both* natural and reasonable (cf. *AA* 16,
2:1; cf. 2.6.2). But the list of proverbs and idioms (not clearly
distinguished) also fulfilled a combination of other functions for
Schottelius (cf. Hundt 2000: 356–361):

- **Moral edification:** Historically, dating back to medieval collections,
  proverb collections had often served as sources of exempla, to which
  stories might be attached, for the edification of the listener.[17]
  Schottelius still recognized this traditional function of proverbs,
  particularly in the education of the young.

  > Wehre auch der Teutschen Jugend zu vielen guten ersprießlich / wan
  > die Teutschen Sprichwörter recht bey Zeiten beygebracht und erk-
  > läret würden: Solches könte oft viel böses hindern.

  > 'It would also be of benefit to German youth in many ways if
  > German proverbs were taught and explained to them at the right
  > time: such a thing could often prevent much evil.'

  > (*AA* 1111–12 §19; see also *AA* 1110, §16).

Schottelius annotated only a small percentage of the proverbs he listed, but
some of those annotations do indeed reflect his declared concern with
inculcating virtues. The two examples below (from *AA* 1122) are both
variants on *practice makes perfect*, and one can imagine their appeal to
someone like Schottelius, so preoccupied with the need to train young
people thoroughly in their own language:

---

[16] Schafferus (1932) believed Schottelius mistaken in thinking the Egenolff 1548 collection to
be by Sebastian Franck (1499–1539/1542/43), arguing that he had confused it with Franck's
1541 collection. However, it seems that the 1548 collection was indeed also by Franck,
though with additions made after his death by Kaspar Brusch (1518–1559): cf. the
bibliographical record in VD16 F 2125.

[17] For predecessors in the late medieval tradition see Gilman (1977: 78), Gilman (1971);
Eikelmann (1995).

Sing so lernestu singen. die übung bringt Erfahrung / die Erfahrung vermag alles

'Sing, and you will learn to sing'. Practice brings experience. Experience can do anything

Müde Ochsen treten hart. durch übung und erfahrung wird man verstendig

'Weary oxen have a solid tread'. One learns through practice and experience

Even more directly relevant to Schottelius's enterprise was the moral that he extracted from the saying *Es ist grundlos mit ihm* ('It is pointless [lit. baseless] with him', *AA* 1132):

> Was ohn Grund gebauet ist / kan nicht bestehen / wie der gantzen Natur und aller erschaffenen Ding Art anzeiget. Sol ein Baum vom Winde nicht umgestürtzet werden / so müssen seine Wurtzeln in der Erde gar fest haften / sol ein Bau stehen / so muß man jhn auf einen guten Grund setzen. Sol jemand dem Rechten folge thun / so muß er gründlich wissen / was Recht sey / und wer sich auf zweifelhaftige / irrige Sachen legt / ehe dan der rechte Grund erfahren wird / der betreugt *[sic]* und verführt sich selbst.

> What is built without foundation cannot last, as the way of all natural and all created things demonstrates. If a tree is not to be knocked over by the wind, then its roots must hold fast in the earth. If a building is to stand, then one must set it on a good foundation. If someone is to follow what is right, then he must know thoroughly (*gründlich*) what is right, and he who relies on doubtful erroneous things, before the right foundation is discovered, deceives himself and leads himself astray.

The interpretation Schottelius attached to this proverb is arguably only marginally present in the saying that prompted the discussion. It is significant that Schottelius expanded on it so much, applying the notion of *Grund* both to a building and to a tree, the twin metaphors that run through all his thinking about the German language, for which the *AA* was intended to demonstrate the *Grund*, the grounding (cf. 2.4).

- **Demonstration of copia:** *Es ist aber unsere Teutsche Sprache sonderlich reich / lieblich / und angefüllet von Sprichwörtern* ('But our German language is especially rich, charming and filled with proverbs', *AA* 1110 §16)

A second function of the proverb collection was to demonstrate the richness of German, implicitly compared to that of other languages. The sheer quantity of proverbs and proverbial expressions that Schottelius amassed (nearly 1800 all told) compared respectably with the first edition of Erasmus's *Adagia,* with its eight hundred entries. (In the same way, incidentally, the list of synonymous expressions for death in the seventh oration, on poetics (*AA* 117–122, 7: 35) matched the 150 or so for *delectare* in Erasmus (1512), which had become a standard school textbook throughout Europe.) Two contrived letters, printed at the end of the treatise on proverbs (*AA* 1146–1147), and cited from Harsdörffer's *FrauenzimmerGesprächsspiele* (1644–1649), served to hammer home how expressive are German proverbial expressions, for it is possible to construct entire letters out of them alone. Of course in practice, Schottelius pointed out, they should be used sparingly, like spices in food, or pearls and gold on a dress (*AA* 1111 §19).

- **The importance of thorough study and knowledge of German:** *daß leichtlich niemand sich einbilden dürfe in Teutscher Sprache sonderliche Kunst | es sey Schriftlich oder Mündlich | zuthun, wan er nicht der rechten Teutschen Redarten zugleich mit kündig* ('so that no one might flippantly imagine that he has particular skill in German, whether in writing or in speaking, if he does not at the same time have knowledge of the proper German idioms', *AA* 1112, § 19)

Schottelius recognized in the study of proverbs and idioms a tradition which reached back via Erasmus as far as Aristotle. In an implicit plea for recognition of his own achievement in compiling his collection, Schottelius remarked on the *Mühe | Nutz und ewige[r] Nachruhm* ('effort, usefulness and eternal fame') of Erasmus in collecting together his *Adagia*, which were thus portrayed as a model for Schottelius's collection. He also repeatedly emphasized the effort and serious study required to master German (cf. 5.4 for examples). Just as Erasmus's *Adagia* demonstrated the need to know Greek and Latin proverbs in order to master those languages, so proper education in German required education in German proverbs (*AA* 1110 §17). Otherwise—reverting to the notion of proverbs as the spice in language (*AA* 1111 §19)—one's German will seems like *ungesalzene Erbsbrühe*, like unsalted pea soup (*AA* 1112 §19), a point that is discussed more fully in the next (fourth) treatise on translating (cf. 4.3).

- **The special nature of the German language:** *lautere Teutschschmekkende Worte | die in anderer Sprache Saft und Kraft würden verliehren [...] der rechte schmak | rechte Kuhr und das eigene der Sprache* ('pure German-tasting words, which would lose their sap and force in another language [...] the proper flavour, proper character and the particularity of the language' *AA* 1111, § 19)

Schottelius argued that proverbs captured something unique to a language and culture (cf. his belief in a specifically German *SprachNatur*, 2.3.1). Several of the proverbs that he chose to discuss in more detail exemplify this cultural specificity. An example is *Penning ist Pfennings Bruder* (already found in Agricola, no. 71; *Penning* is simply the Low German form of *Pfennig*, 'penny'), which Schottelius explained as evidence of the sense of equality and fairness amongst the ancient Germans:

> Hieraus erweiset sichs / wie unsere alten Teutschen Collation / Wolleben und Freude gehalten haben / nemlich / daß ein jeder sein Essen hat mitbracht / und zum Getränk haben sie einen Pfennig neben den andern gelegt zu gleicher Zechen / und ist einer nicht höher beschweret worden dan der ander.

> This shows how our ancient Germans enjoyed eating together, a good life, and joy, namely that each brought his food, and for drinking they each laid a penny next to another in a row, and not one was burdened [financially] more than another.

(*AA* 1129)

Other proverbs also allowed Schottelius to highlight the ancient Germanic heritage, by referencing much older Germanic tales, as in the following four examples. *Ohn Stegreif in den Sattel springen* 'jump into the saddle without stirrups' (*AA* 1140) is interpreted as a reference to the old stories of the Germans where heroes such as Wolfdietrich leapt into their saddles without the help of stirrups, a sign of *eine[n] sonderliche[n] Männliche[n] Stärke und Muht[s]* ('a particular manly strength and courage'). A second example of this type is *Das weschet jhm der Rein nicht ab* ('Not even the River Rhine will wash that off him', *AA* 1113), presented as a reference to the tradition of the ancient Germans for which evidence is provided in a quotation from Caesar: the practice of testing the legitimacy of their children by throwing them in the Rhine. A full two columns of explanation, attributed to Franck are devoted to explaining the story behind *Du bist der Treue Eckhard* ('you are the loyal Eckhard'), meaning 'you warn everyone' (*AA* 1138). Here the Germanic hero Eckhard is dated, on Augustine's authority, to ca. 500 A.D., around the time of Dietrich von Bern (Theodoric the Great; *Bern* is the Middle High German form of Verona). The legend attached to Eckhard is then reported, according to which he warned people not to go into the Venusberg, the subterranean home of Venus, as Tannhäuser had done in legend, never to re-appear.

A fourth example illustrates how some proverbs listed required knowledge of the folk culture of Germany: *Er hat mit Sanct Gerdrut ein Wetlauf gethan* ('he raced against St. Gerdrut') (*AA* 1134) is a proverbial answer to the question of how someone grew improbably rich. It references a legend according to which the canny head of a hospital in Saxony prayed to an image of Saint Gertrude. He vowed that whichever of them—himself or the saint—got to the church-door first should keep the sack of money placed on the altar for the saint and the hospital. Naturally, the head of the hospital ran, the picture of the saint stayed where it was, and the head kept the money, whence his wealth.

There are only a handful of annotated proverbs which fall into this category of reflecting cultural specificity, but as the two columns that Schottelius devoted to the Eckhard saying show, he evidently viewed them as an opportunity to highlight both Germany's unique culture and the good qualities—the courage and nobility—of the ancient Germanic ancestors, from whom German had been passed down.[18]

- **Pansemioticism:** *Solche Sprichwörtliche Lehrsprüche und Redarten deuten ein anders und hohers an | als wohin die Worte lauten | begreiffen dennoch in sich eine [...] Warheit* ('Such proverbial sentences and idioms hint at something other and higher than that to which the words' meaning points, they nevertheless contain in themselves a [...] truth', *AA* 1110, § 16)

Finally, the proverbs had an important place in a pansemiotic world (cf. 3.7). Indeed, as already noted, the theoretical discussion of proverbs that preceded the list was a revised version of the preface to the emblem-book prepared by Schottelius for Franz Julius von dem Knesebeck (Knesebeck 1643; cf. 3.7), and provided a theoretical underpinning for the construction and interpretation of obscure, hidden meanings—not just in proverbs, but in symbols and emblems too. Like emblems, proverbs signified more than the face value of their literal meaning (*mehr verstanden | als geredt wird* 'more is understood than is said', *AA* 1110, §16). If Schottelius elsewhere valued the maximally clear relationship between the word and reality that he found in German, he judged proverbs by a different measure. Like emblems, proverbs depend on the ability of the recipient to interpret them, precisely because they are particular to the culture and traditions of their language. Therein lies their value: they can allude to a great deal of meaning (as some of the lengthy explanations testify) in a very concise phrase: they are the *Summa eines gantzen Handels* ('summary of a whole event') (*AA* 1110, §16). When Schottelius described a proverb as *dunkel* 'obscure' (as in the case of *Ein Weiser Mann der holdren abbruch machen kan*, 'A wise man can give up what is dearer to him' [if it is the right thing to do]), it was no criticism.

---

[18] It is interesting to note the parallels between Schottelius's use of proverbs as an expression of German culture and their instrumentalization in Nazi primary textbooks. See McLelland (*forthcoming*, b).

4.4.3 *The list of writers about Germany, and in or about German (AA 1148–1215)*

The treatise on German writers, which is at first glance a straightforward treatise with numbered paragraphs, is poorly structured compared to the rest of the *AA*, lacks a coherent argument, and appears to have been thrown together in haste. The broad chronological structure and comprehensive coverage of all eras, from the oldest classical accounts of Germans, right up to works published in 1662, provided the bones of what was surely intended to be the first history of the German language, but Schottelius himself conceded that he had in the event presented the authors *ohn Ordnung | und wie sie zur Hand kommen* ('not in order, and just as they come to hand'), and in the face of other competing duties (*nach zulassung der vielen Amtsgescheften AA* 1150 §1). However, Schottelius seems to have considered this section of the *AA* a debt that he owed the reader after indicating in the outline of contents in the first oration that Book V would include information on *d[ie] Teutschen Authoribus und* termini[s] *artium* (*AA* 1150 §1; cf. 6, 1: 15). The lack of order to this section, the unusual placing of the Latin summary at the end rather than at the beginning, and the fact that the list of technical terms (mentioned in the first oration in combination with the information on authors) in fact appeared separated from the list of authors, and likewise unordered, suggests that these elements were indeed the result of rushed work.

The 'treatise' is more aptly described as an annotated list (cf. Hundt 2000: 91): the Latin summary (*AA* 1215, § 7–11) accordingly sums up sixty of the sixty-four pages (corresponding to *AA* 1153–1213, i.e. all but four pages of introduction and conclusion) in an entirely uncommented list of names of writers. As Hundt notes, the contents of the treatise showed the range of text-types already represented in German (including chronicles, literary translations, theological works, legal texts, studies of German, grammars, and technical treatises on subjects from bird-trapping, to mining, to military fortification). Late humanist historians such as Aventinus (Johannes Turmair), and editors of older texts such as Melchior Goldast feature, but Schottelius was also at pains to ensure that his account of German was right up to date. Over thirty works published since the first edition of Schottelius's *Sprachkunst* (1641) are listed, including several published in the 1660s. Schottelius's own interests shine through in the number of legal texts he consulted, and in the prominence given to the works of the theologian Dilherr, who contributed one of the occasional poems in Schottelius's honour, and whose works are listed in detail *AA* 1210–12 (cf. Hundt 2000: 91, Moulin–Fankhänel 1997a). The emphasis on translations across many subject domains also furnishes practical models of the translation work called for in the dialogue on translating.

Listings often include details of place and date of publication, edition, and sometimes an assessment of the work's contribution to the study of German, provided either by Schottelius himself or by a citation from another scholar. Schottelius's description of the first rhetoric in German, by Johannes Meyfart (1634), may serve as an illustration (*AA* 1177):

> D. *Johannes Matthaeus Majfartus* ein bekanter berühmter *Theologus*, gebrauchet in seinen herausgegebenen Teutschen *Scriptis* einer sonderbahren auf die Wolredenheit gerichtete Schreibart / und erhellet gnugsam / wie er des Vermögens Teutscher Sprache kündig / und dieselbe hinwieder jhm oftmals mit Wollaut und Kraft zu dienst / auch willig und Wortmechtig gewesen; Es hat auch *Doctor Mejfartus* heraus gegeben eine Teutsche *Rhetoricam* oder Redekunst / darin / nach Laut des Tituls / <u>von aller Zugehör / Natur und Eigenschaft der Wolredenheit gehandelt / auch wie dieselbe in unsere Teutsche Muttersprache füglichen zubringen / und bey allerhand Geist-Weltlichen und Militarischen Verrichtungen / so wol in gebundener als ungebundener Rede zierlich zugebrauchen sey / nach Anleitung der berühmtesten Redner / in zweyen Büchern gezeiget wird.</u> Ist getrukt zu Koburg Anno 1634.

D. Johannes Matthaeus Meyfart, a well-known famous theologian, uses in his published German writings a manner of writing that is particularly aimed at eloquence, and illustrates sufficiently how knowledgeable he is of the capacity of the German language and how the same [language] has often served him well with its euphony and force, and been willing and word-mighty. Doctor Meyfart has also published a German Rhetoric or Art of Eloquence, in which, according to the title, <u>Everything pertaining to eloquence, its nature and characteristic is dealt with, and it is shown, in two books, how the same is to be applied suitably in our German mother-tongue and how it is to be used in a seemly way in church, worldly and military settings, both in prose and in verse, according to the guidance of the most famous speakers.</u> Printed in Coburg, 1634.

Here Schottelius provided the date, place, and full title (my underlining) of Meyfart's rhetoric. Such full titles alone account for much of the bulk of the treatise. Schottelius also, however, held Meyfart up as a model German writer: that is, as someone who was *properly knowledgeable* of German.

Other such assessments of some of the works listed in the treatise give us further indications of what Schottelius expected of good German writing across the ages. Discussing Sebastian Meichsner's 1576 edition of *Das alte Käyserliche und Königliche Land Lehnrecht*, a reworking of the *Sachsenspiegel* produced in the thirteenth century in Augsburg, Schottelius found that though the words were *klar und bekant* 'clear and familiar', the old German phrasing and style made the text *dunkel und schwer* 'obscure and hard'. However, he emphasized that the substance was of good quality, for just as fabrics like silk and velvet were good, even if the old fashions they were used for were outmoded, so the words remained *gut und vernemlich* 'good and easy to understand', merely the style of the time was now hard to follow (*AA* 1192–93). Gabriel Rollenhagen (1583–1619) is praised (*AA* 1191) for his translation of Lucian, done *mit fleiß [...] artig und wol nach der Teutschen doppelung* 'with diligence, skilfully and well in accordance with German compounding', thus demonstrating that German can render the content *ebenso kurtz und wol* 'just as concisely and well' as Greek. These judgements confirm what we already know of Schottelius's expectations of German writers writing in German: clarity, conciseness, diligence, and judicious use of the German capacity for compounding.

While most of Schottelius's prominent contemporaries from within the FG are mentioned approvingly in this list (cf. 6.3), as are key predecessors in German grammar (Albertus 1573 and Clajus 1578; *AA* 1183, 1204), his rival Gueintz is damned with faint praise. Schottelius noted him as the author of *Die Teutsche Rechtschreibung*, but with the phrase added, *ein Buchlein so genant* ('a book so titled'), a formulation which arguably already casts doubt on whether it merited the title. The existence of *[a]ndere Tractätlein* ('other little treatises') by Gueintz is noted, but Schottelius did not even mention his grammar by name.

Whatever Schottelius's original aspirations for this treatise, in reality the unordered list (though with recognizable loose groupings, and with some commentary) remains little more than a (far from exhaustive) documentation of works consulted, and sits rather oddly with the alphabetical but incomplete list of sources over five pages at the front of the *AA*.

4.4.4 *The list of rootwords (AA 1269–1450)*

> *Die Stammwörter sind das erste und letzte im Sprachwesen [...] Sie sind das Ziel und der Zwekk*

> 'The rootwords are the first and last in the essence of the language [...] They are the goal and the purpose.'

> (*AA* 1276, §11)'

The final list contained in Book V of the *AA* is an alphabetical list of rootwords, which, at over 180 pages (*AA* 1269–1450), would have been large enough to stand as a substantial book in its own right.[19] The excerpt in Figure 4.1 will give an impression of the list:

---

[19] The following overview is indebted to Neuhaus (1991), Barbarić (1981), and Hundt (2000: 92–95). For discussion of the theory of the rootword, cf. 2.4 and 3.8.2.

Leute *homines.* leutliebig / leutsälig / *urbanes, affibilis. In Otfrido & Willeramo saepe legitur* liut *homines, populus,* liutskar *multitudo populi.* Luitstam *homines.* Luitpaga (heimstrit) *seditio. v. Iun. in. W. p.61.*

Leu m. *Leo.* Lou / low.

Leych leychen *cohabitare,* sich zusammen halten. *vid.* laich.

Leyd n. *tristitia, luctus, fascherie,* leydtragen *lugere,* leidig *id est* betrübt *tristis. it. horridus,* da man Ekkel und Abscheu für hat.

Ley m. *Laicus* gemeiner Mann.

Leyme m. *lutum.* **leimen** *lutum conficere.*

Leyn leynen *inniti. vid.* lehnen.

Leyst (des Schusters) m. *forma sutoria.*

Leyst leisten *praestare, perficere, facere.*

Leyt / leyten *ducere, guider.* fuhren. **leyter** f. *scala.*

Licht / lichten *levare.* * **liddorn** n *gemursa.*

Lieb lieben *amare.* die liebe *amor.* liebchen *amica.*

Lieb charus. **liecht** n. *lumen, candela.* liechtscheu *lucifugus.*

Liecht *clarus,* hell / heiter / *resplendissant/* **Lied** n. *cantilena, chanson.*

Liederlich *(est vox derivata, hoc indicat terminatio* lich / *& inter primitiva non numeranda, sed de radice non adeo constat) significat dissolutum, levem, nullius pretij.*

Figure 4.1: An excerpt from Schottelius's list of rootwords beginning with L (*AA* 1357)

The word-list was, just like the orations, directly inspired by Stevin, who published the first such systematic listing of German(ic) (*Duytsch*) rootwords in 1586, and in expanded form in 1608. Schottelius intended his list to correct the false impression created by Stevin's pioneering but incomplete list of only 2170 words and to show that German is in fact far richer in rootwords (*AA* 61, 4: 33; *AA* 1276, §10). Schottelius's list therefore fulfilled a demonstrative function, once again supporting the assertion of German's *copia verborum*, here presented as the 'unique selling point' of German. As an evidence base, it was underpinned by approximately 400 references to sources and to cross-references to other parts of the *AA*.[20] More than three-quarters (316) are, however, merely cross-references to other sections of the *AA*. For example, 119—over a quarter of the total—simply indicate that the lemma is an

---

[20] Neuhaus (1991: 130) counted a total of 411 references; my own tally is 406, but some variance is inevitable, as one can treat more than one cross-reference for a single entry as one or more references.

irregular verb (*anomalum*) and refer the reader to the relevant listing in the grammar.[21]

Only 87 references are to external sources, and of these over a third are to Luther's Bible (Neuhaus 1990: 144).[22] Next to the Bible, the most important single source for Schottelius is Junius's edition and commentary of Williram von Ebersberg's eleventh-century German paraphrase of the Song of Solomon, referred to at least 19 times (Neuhaus 1990: 134). A small number of lemmata are given somewhat fuller discussion: two such are *Reim* 'rhyme' and *Ruhn ruhnen raunen* 'rune; to murmur' (*AA* 1384, 1389), both key entries for Schottelius's cultural-patriotic purpose of establishing the antiquity of the German literary and literate tradition.

Schottelius's rootword list contains 10,199 items by Neuhaus's count, nearly five times as many as Stevin's (Neuhaus 1991: 102). Neuhaus calculated that only about 1510 are pure stems, but this is less than the number of rootwords given by Stevin, so we can be sure that Schottelius would not have agreed with Neuhaus's reckoning, given his insistence that Stevin's list of 2170 rootwords for German was incomplete. Barbarić arrived at a far larger number of 4884 rootwords, which he admitted is a maximally generous total (Barbarić 1981: 1227ff., here *AA* 1242). Several factors contribute to the uncertainty over precise numbers:

i. The list of ostensible rootwords in fact includes some compounds, e.g. **Darum drum** *[…] ist ein* Compositum *von* **dar** *und* **um** ('*Darum, drum* [...] is a compound of *dar* and *um*', *AA* 1299).

ii. Some compounds or derivations, like *üppig* and *Vernunft*, are listed because Schottelius could not readily identify the rootword (as in Figure 4.1 above, where Schottelius comments that *liederlich* 'sloppy, slovenly' is clearly a derivation with *–lich*, but that its root is unclear). Schottelius commented *AA* 1274 §5: *Es ergibt sich je mehr und mehr | daß oft ein Wort | so man unstreitig für ein Stammwort halten solte | dennoch von einer anderen Teutschen Wurtzel herstamme* ('it is increasingly the case that often a word which one should uncontroversially consider a

---

[21] Similar cross-references are given for other aspects of grammar: prepositions (e.g. *für*), the auxiliary *haben*, the interjection *Potz*; there are also a few cross-references to the sections of the *AA* dealing with word-formation, e.g. for the compound *Demuht* 'humility', and for the two adjectives *ewig* and *ledig* ('eternal', 'single, unmarried'), which Schottelius points out are derivatives. In two cases, Schottelius emphasizes that he considers the lemma to be *ein Teutsch Wort* 'a German word': *Vasal* 'vassal' and *Zirkel* 'circle' (*AA* 1437, 1449). There are occasional references to the proverbs too, for example for *Schlump*, and two to his discussion of the term *Teutsch*, under the lemmas *Teut* and *Deutsch*.

[22] They are: *AA* 1277 *Achtz*; 1281 *Awe*; 1293 *Broch*, 1305 *Drum, zu drümmern gehen*; 1315 *Feser*; 1316 *Firn*; 1320 *Fron* ; 1327 *glüm* 1329 *grät* ; 1331 *Grütz*; 1342 *Kelter*, 1348 *Kobolt*; 1355 *Lech lechen*; 1366 *mumm*; 1377 *Polter*; 1379 *Prall* 1381 *raffelen*; 1382 *Raßel*; 1383 *Raun*; 1386 *Ringen*; 1391 *Sange*; 1404 *Schmieg*; 1409 *Schröt*; 1414 *Schwinge;* 1425 *Streif*; 1425 *Ströter;* 1429 *Tapp*; 1434 *Treuffel*; 1439 *Waat*; 1443 *Wiehl*; 1443 *Werst*; 1444 *Wispel*; 1446 *Zau*.

rootword nevertheless derives from another German root'), but adds
that to determine the root word would take more time.

iii. Alternative spellings may appear as separate entries, one cross-
referencing the other (e.g. *Ai* and *Ei*, 'egg').

iv. Variant stems (e.g. *lahm* vs. *lähmen*, the example given by Schottelius
AA 1275, §8) are also listed separately, as are dialectal variants.

v. Also listed, Schottelius noted, are words of foreign origin that have been
assimilated into German, for these have been grafted on (*eingepropft*,
AA 1273, §2) to the German language tree and must now be considered
part of it.

All these factors serve, conveniently, to increase the impressive length of the
word-list, but also explain the wide divergence in totals between Neuhaus
(1991) and Barbarić (1981).

The word-list did not just have demonstrative character. As Schottelius
made clear repeatedly in the *AA* (including here), he considered rootwords
the very essence of the language, and no reliable study of the language was
complete without an inventory of them:

> Die Stammwörter sind das erste und letzte im Sprachwesen [...] sind
> keine richtige Stammwörter in einer Sprache aufgezeignet / wakkelt
> dieselbe und endert sich immer fort
>
> 'The rootwords are the first and last in the essence of language [...] if
> no proper rootwords are recorded in a language, the language is
> unstable and keeps changing'
>
> (*AA* 1276, §11)

Recording the stock of rootwords was as essential to codifying the language
as a grammar. This list, then, the last element of the *AA* (besides the outline
of contents and the acclamation of peace), furnished the *Grund* of the
language, without which it was impossible either to use the language properly
(for the edifice would collapse), or to understand it as a foreigner.[23]

By this deft presentation of rootwords as the basis of the language,
Schottelius in effect made a virtue out of necessity. The list of rootwords
was presented as an asset, in the absence of the ideal, full dictionary of
German.[24]

---

[23] Schottelius explicitly considered the needs of foreign learners here, explaining that he had
glossed some words (irregular verbs in particular) in French as well as Latin, to aid French
learners of German (as in *Leyd* and *leyten* in Figure 4.1) (*AA* 1275).

[24] The attempts within the FG to work towards a dictionary, especially initiated by
Harsdörffer, are discussed by Hundt (2000: 307–316) and Neuhaus (1991: 76–95). See the
plans by Harsdörffer, with input from Schottelius, reprinted in Krause (1855 [1973]: 387–
392), and overlapping with those plans in content, Schottelius's own outline in the tenth
oration (first published 1651) (*AA* 159–166). On earlier lexicographical works, see Neuhaus
(1991: 54–59) and Schneider (1995). Stieler's *Sprachschatz* was the first dictionary to live up
to the demands of the FG (Stieler 1691). Cf. 7.5 on the lexicographical legacy of Schottelius.
See also Henne (2001a) and Ising (2001a).

Note that Schottelius interpreted the 'German language' in its widest scope, not just as contemporary High German (cf. 2.2). Neuhaus (1991) counted that 1500 of the entries included a dialectal variant (as for *Leu* in Figure 4.1), and according to Barbarić (1981), 260 rootwords (out of his larger total) are Low German, marked * by Schottelius, as for *licht .* *lichten* in Figure 4.1. For some 4%, Schottelius provided an attested usage, some dating as far back as Otfrid von Weißenburg in the ninth century (referred to eight times). The 'German' for which Schottelius listed the rootwords, then, was the idealized, ontologized German-language essence that remained unchanged over time and space (cf. 2.2, Gardt 1994, Hundt 2000).

4.5 THE POETICAL TREATISE (*AA* 791–997)

4.5.1 *Introduction to the poetics*

> 43. O daß ein Meister kem' / auch dieses Orts zuheben
>   Nach eingepflanzter Kunst / und Lehrsatzweis zugeben
>   Gewisse Zeit und Klang: denn die Grundrichtigkeit
>   Sich beut nach rechter Art hie überall bereit.

'Oh, that a master might come to raise up and to give in principles in this place, according to implanted art, certain measure and sound-quality; for the fundamental correctness [or perhaps here better: 'correct foundation' = *Grundrichtigkeit*, a term equated elsewhere with *analogia*; cf. 3.8.1] stands ready everywhere here according to the proper art.' (*Einleitung, AA* 1006)

> *Die Verse oder Reime auch künnen nach richtigen / durchgehenden / untrieglichen Gründen Teutscher Haubtsprache gemachet werden.*

'The verses or rhymes can also be made according to the proper, thorough, reliable grounds of the German language' (*AA* 801–02, Anm. 3)

The *Verskunst* of Book IV (*AA* 791–997), first published in 1645, answered the call made in Strophe 43 of the *Einleitung,* quoted above, for a poetics founded on *Grundrichtigkeit*, the fundamental regularity of the language. Table 4.2 gives an outline of the structure and contents of the *Verskunst*, which is sub-divided into three books: on metrical quantity and metrical feet, on metres, and on strophic forms. Each chapter consists of numbered rules, to which notes (*Anmerkungen*) are appended. It is a measure of how much Schottelius and his contemporaries were still bound up in the essentially Renaissance humanist, cultural-patriotic task of promoting

Table 4.2: Contents of the Verskunst *(AA 709–997)*

German as a worthy *literary* language that he considered a poetics
indispensable to a 'comprehensive' (*ausführlich*) work on the German
language, though being content to deal with aspects of rhetoric in
a scattered way throughout the *AA*. As suggested in 4.2, the authority
of Meyfart's (1634) *Teutsche Redekunst* may in part account for the lack of
perceived need for a separate rhetoric. But there was also a difference of
principle for Schottelius between rhetoric and poetics. Unlike rhetoric,

poetry relied on combining an additional set of basic elements to those needed in grammar. In grammar, those elements are the letters and words. The additional, fundamental elements of verse are the sounds of words, more particularly their quantity:

> Es ist also kein Wort in Teutscher Haubtsprache / welches nicht richtiger / grundmässiger / gewissester weise / eine / solcher ernanten Wortzeit oder Lautes in sich habe und also geschikt zu gebundener Rede sey / oder werden künne.

> 'So there is no word in German which does not properly, basically and most certainly have in it a so-called word-time [quantity] or sound and so is or can become suitable for verse'

> (*AA* 806)

These basic elements of poetry, then, needed to be described just like those of grammar. For rhetoric, there was no similar separate requirement. Again analogous to grammar, *Verskunst* was a learnable skill, with rules to master and then follow. Schottelius shared with his contemporaries this 'basically mechanical, combinatory approach' to poetry, inherited from Opitz (De Capua 1973: 42). They viewed poetry as a rule-governed science showing how to combine elements (*eine Wissenschafft recht und gewißmessiglich die Verse oder Reime zu machen*, 'a science of composing verses or rhymes correctly and according to correct metre', *AA* 799). Like grammar, poetics consisted for Schottelius of two parts: the study of the elements, and the study of their combination:

> Gleich wie die Sprachkunst richtiger weise muß abgetheilet und eingeschlossen seyn in die Wortforschung und die Wortfügung / ebener massen kan die Verskunst unterschieden werden / in die Maaßforschung und Reimfügung.

> 'Just as grammar must properly be divided into etymology [lit. word–study] and syntax [word-linking], in the same way the art of poetry can be separated into the study of quantity and the linking of rhymes.'

> (*AA* 802)

It followed that Schottelius excluded from consideration those aspects of poetics that did not fall under this rule–governed system. In any case, these other aspects—*inventio, dispositio* and *elocutio* (roughly: devising the arguments or the subject-matter, the arrangement of the material, and style)—were those that poetry shared with rhetoric. In explicitly excluding such matters as being part of *Dichtkunst* more generally, rather than of *Verskunst* (*AA* 801), Schottelius was not doing anything particularly unusual in his time. Opitz (1624) had likewise excluded them, for instance. In so doing, Schottelius reduced poetics to a specific case of the *ars combinatoria*, the art of combining signs to yield expressions according to fixed principles. It is in this light that we must read his deadpan explanation of how to find a rhyme-word. One should, he wrote, take a word and then run through the ABC to find a rhyming word. For *Acht*, for example, one would rapidly find *Bracht, Dacht, Facht, Fracht, Jacht, Kracht*, etc. (*AA* 860–61). This may seem today a laughably mechanistic technique for serious poetry, but it reflected the belief that the combinatorial method aided invention. As Leibniz commented, 'All our thinking is nothing but the connection or substitution of signs, whether these are words or marks or images' (as cited by Westerhoff 1999: 453).[25]

Schottelius did not doubt the importance of the rhetorical aspects of poetics, as his remarks in the oration on poetics (as well as *AA* 801) make clear:

> Bey uns Teutschen [...] machet das blosse Reimen und das Reimklappen gar keinen Vers / viel weniger einen Poeten.

> 'Amongst us Germans [...] the mere rhyming and metre-counting makes no verse, and much less a poet'

> (*AA* 116, 7: 32)

Indeed, Schottelius devoted the remaining paragraphs of the seventh oration to the matter of suitable topics (i.e., in essence, *inventio*: §32), style (§33–34), and a demonstration of the capacity for varying style by drawing on *copia verborum* with a list of synonyms for death, §35, noted earlier). In the poetics itself, Schottelius also raised the question of the *genera* available to a writer, noting that to treat the genres of German in full would require a *weitleuftige Ausführung / und völlige[n] Tractat* 'lengthy discussion and complete treatise' (*AA* 994). However, he reassured his readers that much on this subject could already be found in the (Latin) writings of Julius Scaliger and Antonio Possevino (1533/34–1611). We are also referred, in this updated edition of the *Verskunst*, to Harsdörffer's *Poetischer Trichter* (which had appeared 1648–53). Nor was *everything* about poetry merely learnable, as the seventh oration, on poetics, made clear:

> Diese verborgene Kunst wird nicht eben durch Fleiß und Arbeit / sonderen aus einer Göttlichen Erleuchtung zugleich erlernet

> 'This hidden art is not learnt just by diligence and labour, but also at the same time by divine inspiration.'

> (*AA* 105, 7: 6)

---

[25] Leibniz's Latin original is as follows: *Omnis Ratiocinatio nostra nihil aliud est quam characterum connexio et substitutio, sive ille characteres sint verba, sive notae, sive denique imagines* (Gerhardt 1875–1890, vol. III: 605).

But what remained—the elements of verse and their rule-governed combination—fell within Schottelius's remit here.

4.5.2 *The* Verskunst *in the context of its predecessors in the genre*

Cherubim (1996) considered Schottelius's *Verskunst* to have had little influence. On the other hand, Meid (1986: 21–22) saw in its first publication in 1645 an important systematization of the innovations in German verse that had taken place since Opitz's influential treatise of 1624. Opitz had insisted on respecting of German stress patterns in verse, but his means of achieving it was to combine only trochaic (long–short) and iambic (short–long) feet, which resulted in rather inflexible alternating rhythms of stressed and unstressed syllables (De Capua 1973: 71–72). According to Meid, Philip von Zesen's *Deutscher Helikon* (1640; revised and expanded editions 1641, 1649, 1656) allowed the use of the dactyl (‾ ˘) and anapest (˘ ‾), following the teachings of August Buchner, who influenced a whole generation of poets and theorists, even though his own *Kurzer Weg-Weiser zur Deutschen Tichtkunst* (1663) 'Short guide to German poetics' and *Anleitung zur Deutschen Poeterey* and 'Introduction to German poetics' (1665) did not appear until after his death. Zesen even went as far as permitting a mixture of different feet (iambs, dactyls and trochees) and thus allowed for the use of classical verse forms in German verse, which was the concern of Johann Peter Titz in his *Zwey Bücher Von Der Kunst Hochdeutsche Verse und Lieder zu machen* 'Two books on the art of making High German verses and songs' (1642).

It was Schottelius's poetics which brought this incremental discussion of metrical matters to a preliminary close, with its systematic presentation of feet and metres. Schottelius presented only a selection of the many different feet from classical poetics that could be used, dismissing others as unnecessary in German (*AA* 835–39). He then presented 57 metrical patterns: 16 purely iambic, 16 trochaic, eight dactylic and eight anapestic, varying only in the number of syllables per line, plus nine further metrical schemes where certain mixtures of feet were permitted. The point was thus made, *Das also weder Lateiner noch Grieche einigen Vorzug / sondern vielmehr das Nachtreten haben / in betracht der lieblichen Mannigfaltigkeit und Menge unserer Teutschen Reimarten* 'that neither Latin nor Greek have any advantage, bur rather fall behind in regard to the delightful multiplicity and quantity of our German verse-types' (*AA* 919–20). There is nothing particularly innovative here. On the contrary, Schottelius gave numerous examples from his contemporaries to illustrate each verse form presented.[26] Meid (1986) noted that Zesen's and Schottelius's

---

[26] The largest single source of examples is, however, Schottelius's own verse, indicated by *. See 6.3.

systematizations found their way as accepted views into later poetical treatises, such as Harsdörffer's *Poetischer Trichter* (1648–53), and that attention subsequently turned away from concerns with prosody towards questions of imagery. Schottelius's work in this area of metre was, then, if not innovative, an important step of systematization when first published in the 1640s.

4.5.3 *Founding poetics on* Grundrichtigkeit

> *Als ist ferner nach rechter kunstmeßiger Anweisung [...] die Reimkunst aus der Sprachkunst entstanden*

> 'Further, so has the art of poetry emerged from the art of grammar according to correct instruction in accordance with the rules of the art'

> (*AA* 995)

Besides the systematization of existing theory just discussed, Schottelius also attempted a significant break with tradition. In an innovation that Berns (1984: 417) called anti-classical, he attempted to *derive* poetics (or what remained of poetics once the rhetorical aspects of *inventio* and *dispositio* were excluded) from grammar, in accordance with the belief that it too must be subject to *Grundrichtigkeit* (cf. strophe 43 of the *Einleitung*, cited under 4.5.1). The first section of the book, on prosody, presented Schottelius's innovative system for deriving *Verskunst* from the *grundrichtig* principles of grammar (more particularly, from Schottelius's own account of German grammar, based on the notion of the rootword). Here Schottelius explained how to recognize quantity in German. The basic element of verse, *quantity* (whether a syllable is short, long or 'either') was, Schottelius argued, determined by how the basic elements of language combined in the morphological structure of the word. So far, so good. Once length had been determined by this purely morphological criterion, the metrical feet could be correctly measured out.

Schottelius encountered a fundamental problem, however, in that he confused 'length' with stress. Schottelius stated, for instance, that inseparable prefixes and inflectional endings are all short. So far, the system seems plausible: since such syllables are unstressed, they will indeed be 'short' (in fact: unstressed). The problem becomes clear once Schottelius moves on to whole words, however. For it is plain that besides the small number of prefixes and endings that are regularly unstressed, there are many rootwords that may or may not take stress (for Schottelius: be 'long') depending on their position in the sentence or in a compound. For example, Schottelius contrasted *Arm bin ich ja zu nennen* 'I am to be called poor', where *bin*, *ja* and *nenn* took the stress and so appeared to him long; with

Arm bin ich ja gar zu nennen (with the addition of the emphatic particle *gar*), where he allocated the stress (the 'length') to *Arm, ich, gar* and (again) *nenn* (*AA* 826). In fact, it was sentence stress that Schottelius described here, but he attempted to account for prosody starting not at sentence level, but at the other extreme, with the *elements* of language, the monosyllabic rootwords. To deal with cases such as the *Arm bin ich* example, where it appeared that many words might or might not be short or long (i.e. they might be stressed or not), Schottelius gave monosyllabic rootwords a category of their own, *mittlere Wortzeit* ('medium length', equated with the *anceps* of Greek metre), meaning in effect that they might be *either* short *or* long. Yet this is not possible, because length is phonologically distinctive in German. For example, *den* (long, 'the' m. acc. sg.) and *denn* (short, 'for, because') are distinguished by vowel length.[27] Compound words composed of two monosyllabic rootwords took the 'length' on the first rootword, e.g. *Vorwort* (*AA* 819), making *–wort* short, even though on its own a monosyllable like *Wort* could be long or short (*AA* 825). In sum, the confusion of length with stress, and the attempt to assign stress bottom-up, proceeding from the morphological elements of language, rather than top-down from sentence stress, was all patently unworkable (though it does make much better sense if one simply reads 'stressed' for 'long' and 'unstressed' for 'short'), and this aspect of Schottelius's poetics—the innovative aspect—did indeed have no real influence. His contemporaries' doubts were already obvious in the reactions of Rist and Prince Ludwig to the Latin outline of his poetics (submitted by Schottelius late in 1642), where they took issue with many of Schottelius's analyses of individual words, though without grasping the underlying problem (Krause 1855 [1973]: 281–305).

4.5.4 *Verse types and* ars combinatoria

The final book of Schottelius's poetics outlined 28 different types of verse, beginning with the well–established Alexandrine (the form adopted for the verse *Einleitung* in the treatise that immediately follows it) and other familiar forms, but including in the later chapters a number of more or less playful verse forms, including picture rhymes, acrostics, anagrams, and even rhymes where substituting numbers for letters yielded a particular, significant number. This rich array of rhyme types showed, first, the richness of German alongside other languages. Second, the inclusion of more playful forms had a popularizing function, disseminating the cultural-patriotic mission. Versifying was presented as a creative parlour game by

---

[27] This phonological distinction is nowadays marked in various ways in the orthography (including double consonants after short vowels, as in the *den/denn* example), but was much less obvious in the spelling of Schottelius's day.

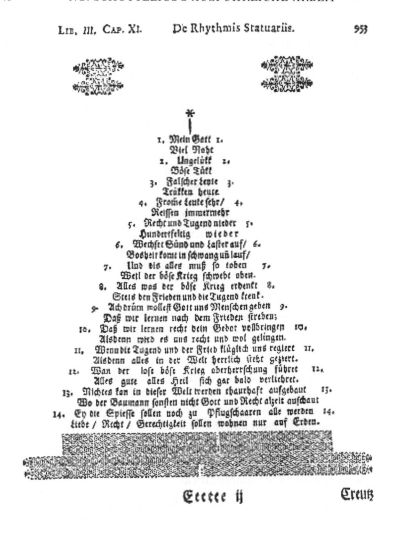

Figure 4.2: *Eine Piramide oder ThurnSeule von Lauter Trogaischen oder langkurtzen Versen | darin die vierzehn Arten der Trogaischen Reime begriffen seyn* ('A pyramid or obelisk of all trochaic or long–short verses, in which the fourteen types of trochaic rhymes are included' *AA* 953).

which the resources of the language could be explored, admired and even added to (most fully in Harsdörffer's *FrauenzimmerGesprächsspiele* (1644–1649) (see Hundt 2006). For readers today, these language games above all reflect the attraction for Baroque thinkers of the *ars combinatoria*, with seeking, combining and interpreting signs in novel ways. Three examples will suffice: that of the picture rhyme, the *Trittreim*, and the anagram.

Recall that the pyramid was Schottelius's personal coat-of-arms, symbolizing labour (for it was associated with the motto *Surgit labore bene ordinato*'; Berns 1984: 419), 'He/it rises through well-ordered labour' (cf. 1.4.3). The virtuosic picture-rhyme reproduced in Figure 4.2 uses all fourteen trochaic rhyme-types, and was thus both a demonstration of the fruits of labour applied to German (to a pious end), and—in the pyramid—a visual symbol of it.

The *Trittreim* (step–rhyme) required not just virtuosity from the poet, but also ingenuity on the part of the reader, who must step from one line to the next and back again to extract the meaning of the poem. Here is Schottelius's example of a 'two-step' rhyme:

> Die Faulheit / Völlerey / was gaile Leute schreiben /
> Die Augenlust / die Red' und der Geselschaft treiben /
> Wirf weg / vermeide stets / das lege von dir hin /
> Verblende / höre nicht / entfern von deinem Sinn.

(*AA* 957)

This poem, Schottelius explained, should be read not only in the order it appears, but also by associating each phrase from one line with the corresponding phrase two lines below (hence two-step rhyme). Thus, alongside the obvious linear reading, we should also read: *Die Faulheit wirf weg, Völlery vermeide stets, Was gaile Leute schreiben, das lege von dir hin, Die Augenlust verblende, die Red' höre nicht, und der Geselschaft treiben entfern von deinem Sinn* ('Throw off laziness, Always avoid gluttony, Cast off what crazed people write. Blind lustful eyes, don't listen to the talk and remove from your mind what society is up to.'). Unlike the picture rhyme, the underlying meaning was not immediately obvious, but had to be decoded by careful reading according to the rules of the game.

Our third example is that of the anagram. While the number rhyme yielded meaning by letter substitution, the anagram rested on the conceit of rearranging the letters to yield a new but related meaning (cf. Westerhoff 1999: 455–56). As Schottelius explained at the end of his Syntax:

> Man kann unter vielen Kunststükken und mancherley Füglichkeiten der Teutschen Wörter auch dieses beobachten / daß die Zustimmung / Gleichlautung / Letterwechslung / & c. fast angenehm der Natur des Dinges zustimmig [...] sein mag

> 'Amongst many artful features and several capacities of German words this too can be observed, that accord, homophony or switching of leters, etc. may be very pleasantly in accord with the nature of the thing'

(*AA* 784)

Schottelius gave numerous examples of such anagrams over pages *AA* 971–74 of his poetics. For example, *Sophie Elisabet Hertzogin zu Braunschweig und Lüneburch* becomes by anagram *Gantz voller Schöne | wie ein hübpsch reiches Abbilt zur Tugend* ('Quite full of beauty like a fair, rich image of virtue', *AA* 974), with some forcing of the spelling, particulaly noticeable in *hübpsch* 'pretty'. Such anagrams were, like Harsdörffer's *Denckring*, an aid to *inventio*, a way of furnishing a topic for an occasional poem, as a verse *Erklärung* must be devised to elucidate the anagram. However, they were also, for Schottelius at least, an exemplification of the unique property of German words, that they are in accord with the nature of their referent (cf. 2.3). Applied to onomatopoeia and to the sound-painting (*Klangmalerei*) that characterized the Nuremberg group of poets, this was not new:

> Denn es ist ein sonderliches Kunststükke in Teutschen Worten / daß sie gleichfalls / mit der innersten Natur eine Verwantschaft und einen solchen Thon / Kraft und ansehen haben / wie die Eigenschaft der Dinge / derer Andeutungen sie sind

> 'For it is a particular artful feature in German words that they have a most intimate relationship with nature, and have such a tone, force and dignity as the qualities of the things to which they refer'

> (*AA* 832)

It is more striking, though, to see this notion applied to the letters *regardless of their pronunciation* (though in the passage above, the meaning of *ansehen* may already suggest this, if it means 'appearance', rather than an abstract quality of dignity; it is ambiguous). Even when re-arranged in anagram, and, it seems, quite independent of their pronunciation, the letters from which words or names like that of the Duchess Sophie Elisabeth were composed could yield new meanings that enhance our understanding of the source words. Schottelius's poetics ends up, then, as a celebration of the special connection of German words with reality.

In sum, Schottelius's *Verskunst* built on the tradition inherited from his predecessors since Opitz. However, he also innovated, both at the level of theory and at the level of exemplification, to demonstrate again the *grundrichtig* qualities of German and its accord with nature. Specifically, in the poetics Schottelius demonstrated, to his own satisfaction at least, the following:

On the level of theory:

- that the science of poetry in German rests on knowledge of the science of language, i.e. grammar
- that the science of poetry is also analogous to the science of grammar, for it too consists of elements and rules on how to combine them

On the level of demonstration:

- that German is the equal of any other language in the range of metres and verse types at the poet's disposal
- that German poetry gives scope for new combinations of letters and words to yield new meanings, that may require the ingenuity of the reader as well as the poet
- that German words and their elements are in accord with their nature.

4.6 VERSE

Aside from the numerous, sometimes virtuosic demonstrations of the rhyme-forms in the poetics, the only verse element in the *AA* is the *Einleitung zur Teutschen Sprache* 'Introduction to the German language', presented as the first 'treatise' of Book V, and so immediately following the *Verskunst* (*AA* 1002–28, including the accompanying explanatory notes). It too has a hypotext: it is an abridged version of the 1643 publication. It was a practical illustration of the Alexandrine verse form or *Heldenart* (the 'heroic form'), as Schottelius called it in German (*AA* 922). It consisted of 136 four-line strophes, composed of couplets of thirteen and twelve syllables. Its re-publication in the *AA* served two purposes. First, in its compressed form, the poem rehearsed many of the same arguments expressed at greater length in the orations, using much of the same imagery (cf. Hundt 2000: 87–88), but aiming at a less scholarly audience. The subjects covered include criticism of *Alamode* borrowing from other cultures (cf. ninth oration), the worth of German and its place alongside other vernaculars, the range and breadth of the language (cf. eighth oration), reflected in its dialects (cf. tenth oration), the large number of rootwords (cf. fourth oration), the sound of German words in accord with nature (cf. fourth oration), the need for a German dictionary (cf. tenth oration), German as a language through which to access all knowledge of the world (cf. first oration), and the need to cultivate one's own culture (cf. tenth oration). The detailed endnotes allowed Schottelius to give the lay reader, their curiosity piqued by the assertions of the personified German language in the poem, more information about the topics covered.

Besides this aim of instructing the audience through its content, the poem is of course also a demonstration of the art of poetry in German, the concern of Book IV which immediately precedes it. Here is not the place to consider Schottelius's merits as a poet, although the consensus—even allowing for later generations' antipathy to the stylistic ideals of Baroque poets—is rather negative. Berns (1976: 18) called his poetry 'heavy and clumsy'; Koldewey (1899) was already dismissive; Padley (1988: 306) agreed with Jagemann (1893) that Schottelius's poems were 'among the worst products' of the period, and branded one, the *Lamentatio* of 1640 that was his first verse foray into print, 'impassioned doggerel'. Still, we should pause to consider how Schottelius sought to demonstrate the capacities of German poetry in his own verse. Adopting the ancient metaphorical equation of life with a journey by ship, as in many Baroque writings (Polenz 1994: 308), the personified German language of the *Einleitung* assures the reader that German has all the resources needed for us to 'board the ship' for a journey to take in all that God and nature have created:

> 85. So sind der Teutschen Kunst verliehen auch die griffe /
>   Daß ein geübter Geist in einem Teutschen Schiffe /
>   Den Grentzstrich wol ümfährt / und durch beschauet recht Was
>   Gott und die Natur ins Jrdisch' hat gelegt

'So German art is granted the techniques such that a practised spirit circumnavigates the girdle of the world in a German ship and sees properly what God and nature has put into the earthly domain.'

(*AA* 1010)

This capacity of the German language to encompass the world is demonstrated in poetic form over the following strophes. Peaceful moonlight, stormy seas and rocky shore, war and death, peace and joy, spring and love, as well as the limits of art and science, are all evoked over the next eight strophes, with many striking alliterative effects, which illustrate the meaning-bearing onomatopoeic quality claimed for German in the orations. Strophe 89 is an example; note the evocative repetition of *w*, *m*, and *l*, as well as the juxtaposed and contrasting auditory shapes of *sausen* and *fortweltzen*:

> 89. Ich wil zur wilden See / gantz furchtlos / doch mit grausen /
>   Wil mit den Wellen mich und mit der Winde sausen /
>   Fortweltzen in die Luft: will einen Wasserberg
>   Hinwerfen auf ein Schif / gerad und über zwerg.

'I want to go to the wild sea, quite fearless, yet with terror; want to experience the roar of the waves and the winds, and be spun up into the air; want to cast a mountain of water upon a ship, straight for it and over the top of it.'

(*AA* 1010)

The personified language herself boasts that the sound of German words reflects nature, and that German words contain the essential image of things (*der Wörter Schall [...] die Deutung der Natur [...] das Wesenbild der Dinge, AA* 1006, strophes 46–47). Many of the notes accompanying the poem demonstrate the creative potential of German vocabulary, which is a recurrent theme both of the *AA* as a whole and of the poem in particular.

For instance, compounds coined in the poem are explained, such as the splendid *Menglingsweis-gebrümme* (strophe 17, meaning approximately in literal terms 'mongrelwise din') to describe the unpleasant sound of words borrowed from other languages used in German (for rejection of foreign influence is one of the key themes of the poem). This coining is an example of the metaphorical compound, a combination of two or more elements that are often conceptually alien to each other. Such compounds were an important and innovative (by contrast with Opitz) feature of the poetry of Harsdörffer, Klaj, and others of the Nuremberg circle of poets (De Capua 1973: 75), and Schottelius provided the theoretical justification with his *Stammwort*-theory for such combinatorial techniques (Polenz 1994: 307). The poem as a whole also demonstrated the function of didactic poetry as an efficient means of political agitation, combining persuasion and emotion with rational arguments (cf. Berns 1984: 422).

4.7 CONCLUSION

The wide range of text-types in the *AA* had, first, an exemplary function. They demonstrated how the capacities of German could be applied in rhetoric, poetry and dialogue. Second, lists of words, names, phraseologisms, and (in the poetics) verse-forms provided the evidence for the richness of German on several levels. Third, in the orations in praise of the language, and in the lists of proverbs and of proper names—all established humanist genres—Schottelius presented himself as a learned heir to the patriotic humanism of sixteenth–century Europe. He even, implicitly, perhaps styled himself with a certain chutzpah as heir to the mantle of Martin Luther, as champion of the vernacular in a new linguistic epoch.

Every part of the *AA* examined in this chapter, however, is tied to the theoretical exposition of German grammar in Books II and III. To address those books within their own text-type tradition is the task of Chapter 5.

5

THE *SPRACHKUNST* OF THE *AUSFÜHRLICHE ARBEIT* AND ITS ARCHITEXTS—TRADITION, INNOVATION, *COPIA* AND RHETORIC

5.1 INTRODUCTION

This chapter considers how Schottelius's grammar—books II and III of the *AA*, though already published in 1641 and 1651—combined and extended the German and Latinate grammatographical traditions identified in Chapter 3, to replace Clajus's slim Latin volume (1578) as the default reference for German grammar for the next hundred years or so (cf. 7.6). Inevitably, therefore, we shall review at some length the already well-studied contribution of Schottelius to German grammatography, measuring the achievements of his grammar against its predecessors (5.5). Beyond that, we shall address themes that have thus far remained fairly peripheral to previous examinations of Schottelius's grammatical theory, but which nevertheless had an important impact on the final shape of the text and how it was received and read. First, Schottelius's rivalry with the very different grammar of Gueintz (1641) is important for understanding the context in which the grammar was produced, and is the starting-point for this chapter (5.2). We shall also consider the development of the grammar from the earlier editions to that of 1663, including the ultimate dislocation in 1663 between the German text (with its origins in 1641), and the Latin paragraphs, added *post hoc* for the 1663 edition (5.3); how Schottelius constructed his authority as *the* grammarian of his era (5.4); and how the emphasis on German *copia* helps determine the shape of the grammar (5.6). A final section considers Schottelius's role in establishing a German grammatical terminology (5.7). It will become clear that the grammar has a strong rhetorical flavour, both in its execution and in its orientation. We shall also see the importance accorded to the *demonstration* and *exemplification* of Schottelius's assertions about the grammar of German. Once again, the twin theoretical notions of the rootword and analogy permeate and underpin the grammar. As Chapter 7 will show, these notions became the legacy of Schottelius to his successors in linguistic studies, within Germany and beyond.

Figure 5.1: Dichotomous divisions in Gueintz's *Sprachlehre* (adapted from Hundt 2000: 142–49; the 'section numbers' are not Gueintz's)

5.2 Schottelius's grammar in competition with Gueintz (1641)

In 1641, two grammars of German appeared within months of each other. One was the first edition of Schottelius's *Sprachkunst*, published hastily, still missing the tenth of the orations in Book I, preceding the grammar of Books II and III. The other was Christian Gueintz's *Sprachlehre*, of which Schottelius had already seen a manuscript copy and which he had roundly criticized. His review is published in Krause (1855 [1973]: 246–52). Gueintz's grammar sank virtually without trace, while Schottelius's grammar was reprinted in expanded form in 1651, before it was finally incorporated, further expanded, into the *AA* of 1663, and went on to have considerable influence. Gueintz and Schottelius represent two competing approaches to German grammar in the early to mid-seventeenth century (cf. Takada 1981), and the difference between them is obvious at a glance. Schottelius's grammar belongs to the 'Latinizing' tradition of German grammars (Padley 1988: 267), whose authors took the grammatical categories and organizational structures of Latin grammars, especially as presented in Melanchthon (1526), and sought to apply them to the vernacular (Jellinek 1913: 66). The Latinizing stream prior to Schottelius is represented by the first three grammars of German, all published in the 1570s, by Albertus (1573), Ölinger (1573), and Clajus (1578), as well as by the later works of Ritter (1616) and Schöpf (1625).[1] All of these were aimed at foreign learners of German, particularly French learners in the case of Ölinger and Ritter. Gueintz, on the other hand, was the latest in a series of grammars of a Ramist bent, starting with Wolfgang Ratke (1619), for whom a grammar of German was a way of teaching German-speaking pupils the principles of a universal grammar. Ramists—followers of the

---

[1] For literature on all these grammarians, see the relevant entries in Moulin-Fankhänel (1994, 1997b), as well as the surveys by Moulin-Fankhänel (2000) and Rössing-Hager (2000).

French logician Petrus Ramus (1515–1572)—divided any subject to be taught into two distinct parts. In the case of grammar, Ratke (Anon. 1619) subdivided grammar into *Wesen* and *Eygenschafft*, 'essence' and 'accidence'. Each of these subdivisions was further divided and sub-divided, always (or nearly always) into two parts, until the subject was exhausted. The bipartite division employed was the practical application of the Ramist dialectic 'method,' which proceeded from the general to the particular.[2]

Padley (1988: 267) describes Gueintz's grammar of 1641 as 'to a large extent a plagiarism' of the Köthener *Sprachlehr* of Ratke's circle of 1619, and there are strong similarities. But there is one critical difference: Gueintz's grammar, unlike the 1619 work, was virtually impossible to understand.[3]

As Figure 5.1 shows (adapted from the painstaking analysis of Gueintz's text by Hundt 2000: 142–49), Gueintz introduced so many sub-branches to his subject that the majority of his text was concerned with material between his sixth and fifteenth levels of dichotomy, at a level where—in the absence of a table of contents or other overview—any reader had long since lost the sense of the hierarchical structure (cf. Hundt 2000: 407). Case was situated at the twelfth level, for instance. In the less rigidly dichotomous Ratke grammar, case was only the sixth level.

If Gueintz's *structure* was impenetrable, so too the unfamiliar and not immediately transparent *terminology* made the subject matter very difficult to grasp, especially at the higher levels of the hierarchical divisions. Below is the definition with which Gueintz's grammar opens, and which gives the flavour of the text (Gueintz 1641 [1978]: [1]). Roman numerals in square brackets (and added by me) indicate the five levels of dichotomizing that the reader must endure between the initial defintion and the next stage of discussion of the 'actual' subject, the nature of German words. Much of the grammar is in fact concerned with defining its own structure.[4]

> *Die Deutsche Sprachlehre* [i] *ist eine dienstfertigkeit der zusammensetzlichen Deutschen wörter recht rein Deutsch zu reden.*

---

[2]   Petrus Ramus's pedagogical reform aimed to simplify the analysis of subject matter and its presentation to pupils (*Dictionary of the History of Ideas*, s.v. Ramism). See also Caravolas (1994, Vol. I, 179–181).

[3]   To a modern reader, it is surprising that Schottelius's review of Gueintz's grammar (Krause 1855 [1973]: 246–53) did not even take issue with the fundamental difficulty of structure, criticizing instead the incompleteness of the grammar, the failure to recognize the centrality of *Stammwörter* in the rules, and numerous points of detail.

[4]   Jellinek (1913: 124–125) also gives a sample of Gueintz's text, which is also available in a reprint edition (Gueintz 1641 [1978]). The term *dienstfertigkeit* ('ancillary skill', but literally 'service-skill') followed Ratke, who viewed grammar as an ancillary skill in his overall programme of systematizing knowledge, in contrast to the *Hauptlehr* 'main instruction', in turn divided into the study of the divine and the study of humans, under which come law and medicine, for example; cf. Ratke's (1619) table of the disciplines in his *AllUnterweisung*, reproduced in Gardt (1994: 191).

Worbey in acht zu nemen | die Endbetrachtung und mittelhandelung [ii].

In der Endbetrachtung sind etzliche sachen wesendlich | etzliche zufällig [iii].

Die wesendliche sind Jnnerlich | oder eußerlich [iv].

Innerlich sind die beschreibung des wortes | oder des dinges [v].

Beschreibung des wortes: Die Deutschheit oder Deutsche Sprache wird genennet vom Tuiscon: welcher der erste einwohner und erbauer Deutsches Landes ist; Aventinus im erste Buch am anfange.

'German grammar [i] is an ancillary skill regarding the combinable German words, to speak German correctly and purely.

In which the final examination and the usage are to be considered [ii].

In the final examination some things are essential, some accidental [iii].

The essential things are intrinsic or extrinsic [iv].

Intrinsic are the description of the word or of the thing [v].

Description of the word: Germanness or German language is named from Tuisco, who was the first inhabitant and cultivator of German land; [according to] Aventinus in the first book, at the beginning.'

The failure of Gueintz's grammar marks the end of the Ratichian universalist approach to German pedagogical grammar, although other pedagogical precepts of Ratke—the preference for teaching in the mother tongue, and for didactic progression from the familiar to the unfamiliar—lived on in the circle of Pietist educationalists centred around the *Pädagogium* of August Hermann Francke (1663–1727) in Halle, in particular in combination with the ideas of Jan Amos Comenius (1592–1670). Gueintz's competitor Schottelius offered a rather different 'universalist' view of grammar in his *Sprachkunst*,[5] but he shared one thing with Gueintz and the Ratichian tradition in which he stood: the desire to 'begin at the beginning', to break the study of the language down into its basic elements. It is just that this meant something very different for Schottelius. For Schottelius, the starting-point was the rootwords, or, one step further down, the letters that combined to form those rootwords. This meant more than just *beginning* the grammar with the letters, then examining words, and

---

[5]   This holds true notwithstanding the 'distinctly Ratichian resonance' noted by Padley (1985: 225) in Schottelius's expression of the harmony between language and nature (1641: 105–06). Cf. 2.3.1, and the Ratichian structure of the grammar (5.5.2).

then their combination, as grammars had done since time immemorial. It also meant that the rootwords were the fundamental units of analysis at every point in the grammar.

The most detailed examination of the grammar is that of Barbarić (1981),[6] who rightly summarized that

> In contrast to Gueintz, who rarely goes beyond what he found in his sources, in the *Ausführliche Arbeit* Schottelius summarizes the inherited grammatical and linguistic knowledge, develops his own grammatical rules and establishes new principles. He thus outdoes all his predecessors and becomes the model for numerous later grammarians. (Barbarić 1981: 1456)

5.3 THE GRAMMAR OF 1663 AND ITS HYPOTEXTS OF 1641 AND 1651

Glück (2002: 440) noted that the question of the suitability of the *AA* grammar for foreign learners has not yet been seriously addressed. Was it a practical teaching grammar for learners, a theoretical grammar, both, or neither? This section answers that question.

In the first, 1641 edition of the grammar, much material was glossed in French (and this was still true of the list of irregular verbs in 1663). The amount of French glossing in 1641 suggests that Schottelius, while competing with Gueintz for the German school market, also anticipated a similar readership to his predecessors in the Latinate tradition, Albertus, Ölinger, and Ritter: young French learners of German and their tutors. We also know that the earlier edition of the *Sprachkunst* was indeed used in schools in Nuremberg (Padley 1985: 224; cf. Krause 1855 [1973]: 333). It seems to have been successful; Clajus's (1578) grammar was probably only reprinted in 1651 because Schottelius's work had sold out (Jellinek 1913: 141). In its first incarnation, then, Schottelius's grammar was intended as a multi-purpose grammar like its prececessors in the Latinizing tradition, aimed both at German schools and at foreign learners.

By 1663, Schottelius's aims had changed very substantially. The 1663 *AA* was patently too large for a school-book (prompting the publication in 1676 of an abridged version of the orthography and the *etymologia*, i.e. the section describing the parts of speech and their forms), explicitly for use in schools, *Kurtze und gründliche Anleitung Zu der RechtSchreibung Und zu der Wortforschung In der Teutschen Sprache. Für die Jugend in den Schulen | und sonst überall nützlich und dienlich* ('A short and thorough introduction to the spelling and etymology of the German language. Useful and helpful for

---

[6] At 1464 pages, Barbarić's study of the *AA* and Stieler (1691) is nearly as long as Schottelius's *AA* itself. Jellinek (1913–1914) and Padley (1988) also looked at Schottelius's place in the German tradition.

young people in schools, and everywhere else', 1676). There are indications that Schottelius no longer envisaged that his grammar would be used by foreign learners either. Rather, in 1663 he gave advice to his readers as possible *teachers* of such young foreign learners. For instance, on the matter of the word order of separable verbs,[7] Schottelius advised consulting his section on the syntax of auxiliary verbs, for this was a tricky feature of German, which *komt einem Knaben oftmals schwer und seltsam vor* 'often seems difficult and strange to a lad', for *Die anderen Sprachen haben hierin mit der Teutschen gar keine gleichheit* 'the other languages are not at all similar to German in this' (*AA* 747).

If much of the French glossing had disappeared by 1663, the grammar was instead now essentially bilingual in German and Latin. Each chapter began with a Latin paragraph-by-paragraph summary, and headings of paradigms and definitions were given in Latin as well as German, though the Latin typically appeared second, in brackets, and in smaller type, as here:

> Das Nennwort (*Nomen*) ist ein wandelbares Wort / ein Nahm oder Nennung eines Dinges / oder welches anzeiget ein Ding / ohn Zeit und Tuhn. (Nomen est vox variabilis, significans rem & non actionem, sed sine tempore.)

> 'The noun (nomen) is an inflecting word, a name or naming of a thing, or which indicates a thing without time or action.'

> (*AA* 231)

The softening in Schottelius's attitude to Latin reflects a significant shift in how heavily he weighed each of the different discourse traditions that helped shape the *AA*. In earlier editions, Schottelius wrote, he had avoided Latin in order to show that the subject could be dealt with in German (explicitly following Stevin), but *auch teihls der hochlöblichen Fruchtbringenden Gesellschafft halber* ('partly also for the sake of the most praiseworthy Fruitbearing Society', *AA* 2, 1: 2), in accord with the Society's expectation that members lead by example in using the vernacular in their fields of endeavour (cf. 3.5.5). For this reason, Schottelius asserted, all terms and rules had been given in the earlier editions *nur mit Teutschen Wörteren* ('only with Geman words'). In 1641, indeed, Schottelius had been very firm about this, standing squarely in the purist tradition of cultural-patriotic discourse, as the passage cited in 3.5 (Schottelius 1641: 15) showed, where Schottelius called it 'repulsive and a disgrace' to use Latin rather than German terminology. Schottelius did indeed use very little Latin at all in the 1641 grammar, except to gloss possibly unfamiliar German grammatical terminology or lexical

---

[7] 'Separable' verbs in German consist of a verb and prefix (or particle), e.g. *durchbrechen*, as in *Das Volk brach mit grosser Mühe und Verlierung fast vieler Menschen innerhalb vier Stunden den grossen Dam durch*, 'the people broke through the large defence within four hours, with great effort and with the loss of very many people' (*AA* 747).

items, or in the stock phrase, *exempla sunt ubique obvia* ('obvious examples are everywhere'). The exceptions, where Latin did occur, are sufficiently few that they can be listed: pp. 178–79, 218–19; a few lines on p. 243; pp. 245, 270–73; a few lines on pp. 302, 395, 443, 512–13, a little on p. 552, a few lines on p. 570 and p. 576. In 1663, however, Schottelius was so keen to attract readers outside Germany that he was willing to subordinate the patriotic principles of the FG (now less of a force since the death of Prince Ludwig in 1650) to the practical need to make his grammar more accessible to those 'unpractised' in German (the *Ungeübte*). So *alles [ist] zugleich Lateinisch erkläret* ('everything [is] explained at the same time in Latin', *AA* 5, 1: 13, with specific reference to Books II and III). Seiffert (1990a: 255) sums up that Schottelius's experience had by 1663 guided him 'towards the very good (and not just expedient) reasons there are both for trying to develop vernacular terms, yet also for seeing Latin as your guide and freely using both Latin and German in your text.' Accordingly, the *AA* also contained a list at the end of *etzliche Teutsche Kunstwörter oder* termini artificiales *welche in diesem* Opere *hin und wieder gebraucht worden* ('numerous German technical terms or *termini artificiales* which have been used from time to time in this work', *AA* 1462–1466). The list of 150 terms was not exhaustive, and ended with an observation in Latin that it did not include many others which might occur but which were always explained in context (*AA* 1466).

Such bilingual presentation of grammatical rules might look like a return to the practice in many humanist grammars of the fifteenth and sixteenth centuries, from the glossed Donatus grammars of the later middle ages onwards (cf. Puff 1995), to many of the first printed grammars, which were bilingual to at least some degree (cf. Ising 1966, Müller 1882 [1969]). At that time, though, the authors were still engaged in apologetics for the inclusion of *German* as a way of easing the learning of their young pupils in (Latin) grammar. The FG would have been pleased to note that Schottelius now made an apology for his inclusion of *Latin* explanations in his German grammar, something which had still been self-evident in the preceding century. Visually, too, the German still had primacy, for German was the language glossed, rather than vice versa.

Schottelius did not always bother to reconcile the two versions of his text, Latin and German; so it is not quite accurate to describe the Latin as a translation of the German. Sometimes the Latin is a convenient ready-made definition from another Latin grammar; sometimes it says something altogether different. There are four possible degrees of dislocation between the German and the Latin in the grammar. The first case is that of close equivalence, as in the case of the Latin and German definitions of the noun cited above. A second possibility is a slight but significant mismatch between the two versions of the text. The Latin and German definitions of grammar, with which any grammar traditionally began, provide an example of how two quite distinct discourses—one Latinate, one in German—could be at odds in the bilingual *AA*. In all three editions, Schottelius's German definition read:

> Die Sprachkunst ist eine Wissenschaft / oder kunstmessige Fertigkeit / recht und rein Teutsch zureden oder zuschreiben.[8]

> 'Grammar is a science or an artful/skilful competence to speak or write German correctly and purely'

> (*AA* 180)

Added in parentheses to the 1663 edition was the Latin definition *Grammatica est certa congruè loquendi & scribendi ratio & scientia in lingua Germanica* 'Grammar is the certain rational basis and science of congruent speaking and writing in the German language.' Despite the superficial similarities between the two definitions, two quite distinct discourses met here, but were not quite reconciled. The Latin definition was standard, and had grown incrementally out of the Latinizing tradition of German grammar. Indeed, if we compare Albertus 1573 A1[r]: *Grammaticam esse constat, certam quandam loquendi et scribendi rationem*; or Clajus's *Grammatica congrue loquendi & scribendi ratio & scientia* [...] (Clajus 1578 [1894]: 10); or Ritter's (1616:[1]), *Grammatica Germanica est ars bene loquendi Germanicè*, it is tempting to see Schottelius's definition as taking the best from three of his four predecessors in Latin (the fourth, Ölinger 1573, had not given a definition): *congrue loquendi & scribendi ratio & scientia* from Clajus, with the qualification of *certa* taken from Albertus, and perhaps even the specific mention of *Germanica* as in Ritter. Whether or not this is precisely what Schottelius did is neither here nor there. The fact that it appears possible shows just how neatly his Latin definition slotted into an established Latin discourse. Yet this discourse tradition was independent of the German definition given, which the Latin only loosely translated. For one of the key terms in German, *rein* ('purely'), has no equivalent in the Latin text. The German definition, unchanged from 1641, must, on the other hand, be understood as part of a discourse within the FG, for Schottelius's formulation *recht und rein* in 1641 was no coincidence in the light of the discussions of his rival Gueintz's definition of that same year. As we saw in 5.2, Gueintz wrote:

> Die Deutsche Sprachlehre ist eine dienstfertigkeit der zu-sammensetzlichen Deutschen wörter recht rein Deutsch zu reden

> 'German grammar is an ancillary skill regarding the combinable German words, to speak German correctly and purely'

> (Gueintz 1641: A1[r], my emphasis)

---

[8] In Schottelius (1641:180), *Sprachkunst* had already been glossed as *grammatica*; in Schottelius (1651:326), *Fertigkeit* had additionally been glossed as *habitus*.

In his review of Gueintz's manuscript, August Buchner, the Wittenberg professor of rhetoric and poetics and member of the FG, had commented on this definition:

> Rein Deütsch. Es kann zwar dieses wohl stehen bleiben, doch wollte ich lieber sehen Recht Deutsch etc. allß Rein etc. Dann die Reinligkeit der Sprache kann nicht durch und durch auß der Grammatica oder Sprachlehre erlernet werden.

> 'Pure German. This can probably stay as it is, but I would rather see Correct German etc. than Pure etc. For purity of language cannot be learnt entirely from grammar.'

> (Krause 1855 [1973]: 234–35)

Prince Ludwig himself noted, *Könte vielleicht beydes stehen Recht und rein Deutsch,* 'Both could perhaps stand, Correct and pure German.' Gueintz responded, *Ob recht oder rein beßer sey, kann darauß ermeßen werden, daß nichts recht sey, wo es nicht rein ist, in der Sprache* 'Whether correct or pure is better, can be determined from the fact that nothing is correct in the language if it is not pure' (Krause 1855 [1973]: 234–35). There were arguments on both sides (both Buchner and Gueintz argued their cases with examples), and so Schottelius—an ambitious young newcomer in 1641—pragmatically adopted Prince Ludwig's suggestion of pairing the two terms. This discussion is simply not reflected in the Latin definition that he added twenty years later.[9]

The third possible relationship between the Latin and German texts is a far fuller account in the original German than in the Latin added later. For instance, Schottelius's German definition of the participle (some 75 words or nine lines long) drew together elements from his predecessors, included an explanation of why it was called the *Mittelwort* (because it shares features both with the noun and with the verb, it is in the 'middle' of the two, *AA* 606), and examples. The sixteen-word Latin definition was far more cursory and was just a slight re-wording of Clajus's (1578) definition (Barbarić; 1981: 891): *Participium est Nomen verbale seu dictio variabilis, significans non tam tempus, quam actionem & passionem aliquam* ('the participle is a verbal noun or declinable word signifying not so much tense as some action, or undergoing some action', *AA* 606). There is a similar discrepancy between the Latin and German definitions of the verb (*AA* 547). It is a moot point, and a relevant one for considering the reception of the grammar outside Germany, to what extent a reader of the Latin encountered a different, perhaps less theoretically rigorously coherent account of German grammar.

---

[9]   A similar debate in the correspondence of the FG likewise explains the double formulation in Schottelius's German term for *poetica, Reim- oder Verskunst.* Cf. 3.5.5.

A fourth and final possibility is the reverse of the above: the later Latin text is far more expansive than the original German. For instance, on the letter <w>, the German text was prescriptive and practical, noting the difficulty of pronunciation for learners without <w> in their languages, which replaced <w> with <g>, as in equivalences like *Wilhelm* = *Guillaume*. The Latin of 1663, in contrast, was not pedagogical in intent, but rather aimed to participate in learned discussion of <w> and its equivalents in other languages. There was no guide to pronunciation (surely essential if the Latin really was intended for non-German learners who, after all, do not have this letter!); instead, Schottelius cited scholarly authorities who concentrate not on the <w> / <g> correspondence at all, but on that of <w> / <b>, with the speculation that *die Barden* 'the poets' might be derived from *die Werden* 'the worthy ones'.

We should not read too much into such dislocations between the two languages. As is evident from the sketchy nature of the treatise on German writers (cf. 4.4.3), Schottelius's revisions and final preparation of the texts for the 1663 *AA* were sometimes hurried and imperfect. Nevertheless, it is important to be aware of the differences. The last example shows, too, that the role of Latin was not *merely* to make basic German grammar accessible to non-Germans. Latin was also the prestige language of international learned discourse on the nature and origin of language, a discourse in which Schottelius was eager to participate more fully in 1663—even at the expense of the aims of the FG.

It is in that light that we must read two theoretical sections largely in Latin, added in 1663, with no equivalent in German, which discuss the purpose of grammar in quite different terms to the cultural-patriotic purposes that are most obvious in the rest of the *AA*. In these sections, as we have seen in Chapter 3, Schottelius allied himself with the Latin tradition of grammar, citing in particular Vossius's *De arte grammatica* (1635), which was a synthesis of humanist grammatical scholarship to date. Indeed, it is not far-fetched to imagine that Schottelius may have seen in his *AA*, his own 'comprehensive' study, a landmark for studies of the German vernacular equivalent to that of Vossius for the Latinate tradition.

In his discussion of the function of grammar Schottelius followed Vossius, for whom grammar consisted of three parts (*AA* 177) (cf. Figure 5.2):

  i. The methodical or heuristic aspect of grammar consists in studying the rules of the language, providing the basis and rationale for instruction.

  ii. The historical or exegetic function lies in the interpreting of authors, which is achieved by studying the meaning of words, both simple and 'conjoined' (*conjunctarum*).

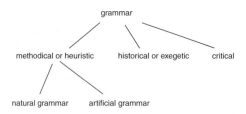

Figure 5.2: Vossius's view of the parts of grammar

iii. Critical (or 'mixed') grammar is a combination of the first two, applied to the task of textual criticism, by *emendatio* and *iudicium*.

Switching to German, Schottelius tells us that his grammar does all three (even though Vossius had dismissed the second as irrelevant to the rational description of language):

> In diesem *Opere* hat man in obacht gezogen / nicht allein was *ad Methodicam*, sondern auch *ad enarrativam*, auch ofters was *ad Criticam* gehörig seyn mag; Zumahl der Zwekk / welcher jst von [d]er Teutschen Sprache gründlich und außführlich nach aller sich anbietenden Gelegenheit zuhandlen / ein anders nicht hat erfodert.

> 'In this work one has paid attention not just to what might belong to methodical grammar, but also to exegetic grammar, and also quite often to critical grammar, especially as the purpose—which is to deal with the German language thoroughly and comprehensively as far as possible—required nothing else'.

(*AA* 177–78)

This all-embracing approach helped Schottelius justify the inclusion of other matters *so eigentlich zur Sprachkunst nicht gehörig seyn können* ('which do not properly belong to grammar', *AA* 178; cf. 3.6.1).

A second Latin addition, made in 1663 to the second chapter of the grammar, repeated another theoretical distinction made by Vossius: the division of *grammatica methodica* into natural and artificial grammar. Natural grammar dealt with those aspects of grammar common to all languages (the letters and their number, vowels, consonants, syllables and the parts of speech, subject–verb agreement, gender, number 'and the like', *AA* 180). It is this recognition of grammar common to all languages that prompted Padley (1985: 224–31) to see in Schottelius a universal grammarian of a sort. Artificial grammar, on the other hand, dealt with what was proper to each language: how words are inflected, what case they govern, and the like (*AA* 180–81). Crucially, analogy—the adherence to a regular pattern, of which the conjugation of regular verbs is an example—was a feature of natural grammar (cf. 2.6.2). Of course analogy will not be found in every word, but *Siquidem, non, quia analogia in quibusdam vocibus non est, icci[r]co*[10] *tollenda est; verum quia in caeteris est, ponenda est* ('because analogy is not found in certain words, that is no reason to do away with it; rather, because it is in others, it is to be added', *AA* 181). Finally, Schottelius briefly considered the sub-division of *grammatica methodica* (both artificial and natural) into sections.

Such theoretical speculations, largely in Latin (though with some codeswitching, *AA* 177–78), and all following Vossius (1635), have no equivalent in the German. Nor, added *post hoc*, did they genuinely underpin the structure and content of the grammar that followed. An exception is *analogia*, but even here, as we saw in Chapter 3, the explicit equation of *analogia* with *Grundrichtigkeit* was a later development, after the first edition of the grammar. These *post hoc* additions reflected Schottelius's desire to ally himself with the discourse of learned grammatical reflection in the Latin tradition, and so to portray himself as a theoretical grammarian with similar authority.

We can now return to the question posed at the outset, about the implied readers of the 1663 grammar, and of its 1641 and 1651 hypotexts. In 1641 Schottelius's *Sprachkunst* was a practical grammar to compete with Gueintz, and to be accessible to French learners. It was also a demonstration of what was possible in the vernacular, following Stevin and in accord with the expectations of the FG, of which Schottelius aspired to become a member. But by 1663 Schottelius had made his name in Germany, and his ambitions were greater. He intended this third edition of his grammar to be an expert's grammar, to be read by those already experienced in language study. They might use it to support their teaching, but it was not suitable for their pupils' use. Schottelius's primary concern now was to be read as a peer of other major figures in the European discourse about language, to become the Vossius of the vernacular grammatical tradition.

5.4 Rhetorical élan and constructing the authority of the grammarian

Schottelius's authority was further reinforced by his rhetorical verve, for his style within the grammar, as well as in the orations, is in places highly rhetorical. On the one hand, such rhetorical flair reflected Schottelius's desire to demonstrate the capacities of German for rhetoric, and his cultural-patriotic desire to win over his readers. On the other hand, it also had its precedents in the tradition of humanist grammar—Jensen (1990) noted how highly rhetorical are sections of Scaliger's theoretical grammar (1540), in particular where Scaliger advocated the analogist over the anomalist position, for instance.

[10] There is a misprint in the *AA*: *iccitco* for *iccirco*.

The very first chapter of Schottelius's grammar provides a demonstration of his rhetorical brio. It opens with a broad chronological sweep that likens Schottelius's task to that of the great Charlemagne himself, who, according to his biographer Einhard (ca. 770–840, in his *Life of Charlemagne*, Book III, chapter 29), began a German grammar, the crucial step that determined for Schottelius the first of the *Denkzeiten* or eras in the history of German in the third oration (cf. 2.2.4). In contrast to this praise for Charlemagne, the achievements of more recent German grammarians are rather unjustly belittled, described as *Bücher und Träctätlein* 'books and little treatises' (*AA* 173 §6), none of which merits the title of *ein völliges Werk*, 'a complete work'. The allusion to Charlemagne is a chance to remind the reader of the great German past: keywords are *tapffer*, *Macht* und *Majestät* ('valiant, might, majesty'). In one fell swoop, the greatness of German and the dignity of the grammarian's task are established (*AA* 171):

> Es ist bekant / und vorhin in etwas berühret / welcher Gestalt Käyser Carl der Grosse / nachdem er den Römischen Adler der Teutschen Hoheit einverleibt und den Teutschen tapfferen Namen zur Oberstelle in der Christenheit gebracht / er es seiner grossen Macht und Majestät wolanständlich und nötig ermessen / auch die algemeine Teutsche Landsprache mit hervor zusetzen / derobehuf er selbst angefangen [...] eine besondere *Grammaticam* über die Teutsche Sprache zumachen

> 'It is known, and something of it was said earlier, how Emperor Charlemagne—after he had brought the Roman eagle under German sovereignty and brought the valiant German name to the head of Christendom—considered it fitting and necessary to his great might and majesty to raise up the common German vernacular, to which end he himself began to write a grammar specifically about the German language'

Just as striking rhetorically, and more resonant throughout the work as a whole, are Schottelius's key conceptual metaphors of the language edifice and the language tree, which express the creative dimension of the grammarian's task, requiring both skill and diligence. Both the images—tending the tree rooted in the ground, and building on the right foundations—implied the need for a skilled human hand to carry out the necessary work. The role of the grammarian himself, and his authority, thus became (literally!) fundamental. Grammar was no longer conceptualized as the *ancilla*, the mere practical handmaiden to other branches of knowledge (cf. Gueintz's notion of *Sprachlehre* as a *Dienstfertigkeit* in 5.2), nor even as the first of the trivium, as the *ianua artium*, the door to the arts, from which learners soon passed on. The introductory chapter to the grammar (*Von der Nohtwendigkeit der Teutschen Sprachkunst*) makes this clear with characteristic rhetorical force (*AA* 173, §4):

Wie demnach ein fester ausgepfälter Grund ist der eintzige gewisse Aufenthalt eines Gebäues / also ist gleichfals die Grammatica die Seule und Grundfeste / worauf jeder Sprache Kunstgebäu beruhen / und richtigen sicheren Aufenthalt haben muß

'Just as a firm foundation is the only sure basis for a building, so in the same way is the grammar the pillar and firm foundation on which the artful edifice of every language must rest and have its proper sure hold'

The implied importance of the expert grammarian in these metaphors reinforced the authority vested in Schottelius through the paratextual material of the *AA*, where colleagues had likened him in their poems to Varro. It took great knowledge and application to explore the foundations of the language: from the first paragraph of the first oration, Schottelius repeatedly emphasized that the production of a grammar was a process of creative construction that required both diligence, *Fleiß* (*AA* 2, 1: 1 & 2; 10, 1: 31; 39, 3: 30; 122, 8: 35; 143, 9: 16), and skill, *Kündigkeit* (*AA* 2, 3: 3; 11, 2: 31; 67, 5: 1; 98, 6: 53; 143, 9: 16; 144, 9: 19). The grammarian needed *zureichenden fleiß und grundrichtige Kundigkeit* ('sufficient diligence and well-founded skill / knowledge', *AA* 148, 9: 31; cf. also the proverbs on *AA* 1122, discussed in 4.4.2, and Siegeraht's emphasis on the need for *Zeit / Fleiß und Arbeit* 'time, diligence and work', *AA* 1221).

Schottelius's rhetorical construction of his grammarian's authority in this way is one characteristic that really did distinguish him from earlier vernacular grammars. Vernacular grammar was a technical discipline, requiring expertise just like music (cf. 2.5.2). Schottelius, esteemed as a German Varro, and hoping to inaugurate a new epoch as had Charlemagne and Luther before him, left his readers in no doubt that he was the man for the job.

5.5 SCHOTTELIUS'S GRAMMAR AND ITS ARCHITEXTS: HIS PREDECESSORS IN THE DISCOURSE OF GERMAN GRAMMATOGRAPHY

5.5.1 *The existing grammatical tradition*

Despite Barbarić's (1981: 1456) assessment that Schottelius's grammar outdid all its predecessors, it remains equally true that 'Schottelius is not original as far as the individual rules are concerned'; 'in barely any point does he go beyond what one or other of the theoreticians of the seventeenth century had taught' (Jellinek 1913: 138–39). It is a plain fact that Schottelius was indebted to all his predecessors in the genre of 'grammars of German' (including his largely unacknowledged rival, Gueintz).

The chief of Schottelius's predecessors are listed in Table 5.1. They can be viewed in three groups (cf. Moulin-Fankhänel 2000): i. the Latinizing tradition, for educated foreign learners, but also for a local market; ii. the Ramist tradition, under the influence of Ratke, for German school-children; and iii. other primers for learners of German, where basic grammar was often combined with teaching reading. Schottelius's contribution to German grammar consisted in synthesizing what his predecessors had said, to give a more thorough account, adding more examples and details, and adopting a consistent terminology (some of it new, some already used by one or more predecessors), such that much of it became established with him. Beyond this, however, Schottelius was highly innovative, in the way that he made the twin notions of analogy and the rootword the arbiters of every decision over competing variants in the grammar. This lent the grammar—despite its basic adherence to the path laid down by its predecessors—an overall theoretical consistency which was new in the German grammatical tradition, and which helps explain its success. The following sections outline both Schottelius's practical contribution to describing the grammar of German within the existing tradition, and how that contribution was embedded in his novel linguistic theory.

5.5.2 *The structure of the grammar compared with its predecessors*

At first glance, Schottelius's two-part division of grammar into *Wort-forschung* (Book II, *etymologia*, also including orthography) and syntax (Book III) has more in common with the Ratichian line of grammars following Ramus, than with the traditional division made by the Latinizing German grammars into four sections: *orthographia, prosodia, etymologia,*

Table 5.1: Schottelius's predecessors in the grammatical tradition

	The Latinizing tradition for educated foreigners	The Ramist tradition for German schoolchildren	Other primers for learners of German
sixteenth century	Albertus (1573) Ölinger (1573) Clajus (1578)		Ickelsamer (1527, 1534) [and many others in the sixteenth century]
seventeenth century	Ritter (1616) Schöpf (1625) [Girbert (1653, already drawing on Schottelius, as well as on Gueintz]	Kromayer (1618), the first printed grammar *in* German Ratke (1619) Helwig (1619) Gueintz (1641)	Brücker (1620) (aimed at adult refugee learners? see McLelland 2005b) Olearius (1630)

Table 5.2: The grammar of 1663: outline of structure and contents

---

Book II *Wortforschung* 171–690
Ch.1 The necessity for a German grammar 171–78?
(need for a German grammar; on German dialects;
on the sections of the grammar)
Ch. II Orthography 179–223
Ch. III The article 224–30
Ch. IV Divisions of the noun 231–34
Ch V Inflection of the noun 235–45
Ch VI Comparison 245–60
Ch VII Gender of the noun 261–84
Ch IIX *[sic]* Number of the noun 285–97
Ch IX The case of the noun 298–300
Ch X The declension of the noun 300–16?(giving three
declensions by gender and a fourth for adjectives
acting as nouns)
Ch XI On the derivation of the noun 317–97 (lists of
examples for 23 derivational endings, as well as
principles of derivation)
Ch XII Noun compounds 398–533
Ch XIII The pronoun 533–46
Ch XIV The verb 546–605
Ch XV The participle 605–13
Ch XVI The preposition 613–55
Ch XVII The adverb 656–64
Ch XIIX *[sic]* The conjunction 665–66
Ch XIX The interjection 666–67
Ch XX Punctuation 668–79
Ch XXI Homonyms 679–90

Book III—Syntax 691–790
Ch I Syntax of the article 692–705
Ch II Syntax of the noun 706–29
Ch III Syntax of the pronoun 729–40
Ch IV Syntax of the verb 740–61
Ch V Syntax of the participle 761–63
Ch VI Syntax of the preposition 764–73
Ch VII Syntax of the adverb 773–85
Ch VIII Syntax of the Conjunctions 785–90

(There is no syntax of the interjections.)

and syntax (though Ritter 1616 had also adopted the bipartite structure). In practice, though, Schottelius remained traditional. As Table 5.2 shows, orthography preceded *etymologia* in the usual way, and the place and contents of prosody had already varied considerably in older grammars in any case (Barbarić; 1981: 353–55). Schottelius had no prosody at all in 1641, and when it was added in 1651, it appeared as an addition after the syntax. (In 1663, prosody was again removed from the grammar, and dealt with only in the poetics.)

In 1641, Schottelius had identified eight parts of speech, like Clajus, who had followed Greek, which unlike Latin had an article, but where the interjection was classed with the adverb. In 1651 and 1663, however, Schottelius treated the adverb and interjection separately, yielding nine parts of speech (as in Ratke's 1630 *Wortschickungslehr*). This was more than the 'model' of eight, but at least each part of speech was still sanctioned by its place in Latin or Greek grammar. The order in which the parts of speech were discussed was also largely in accord with Latin grammatical tradition, although the placing of the preposition after the participle was unusual. (It was more usual to deal with the adverb after the participle, as did Albertus, Ölinger, Clajus, Brücker, Gueintz, and Ratke's *Sprachlehr*). Schottelius then subdivided the parts of speech into those that inflected and those that did not (*wandelbar* and *unwandelbar*, the German terms already used by Ratke, Kromayer and Gueintz, and already by Schottelius in 1641).

In a significant change to the traditinal structure of 'Latinizing' German grammars, Schottelius removed *figura,* the traditional category where nouns and verbs were described as either *simplex* or *compositum* (simple or compound, e.g *machen* or *mitmachen*) from the accidences of the verb. Schottelius instead treated compound verbs under *Vorwörter*, the 'preposi-tions', which included for Schottelius the separable and inseparable prefixes that could form compound verbs, listed on *AA* 617–55, together with compounds of other categories whose first element is a *Vorwort*. Schottelius's *Vorwort* section itself was, as a result, much larger than in any of his predecessors' works.

A further detail in which Schottelius's grammar diverged structurally from tradition is idiosyncratic rather than systematic: the existence of a final chapter in Book II, *Von den zweydeutigen und gleichlautenden Wörteren* 'On homonyms and homophones'). The chapter is something of a rag-bag of afterthoughts that reflects additions made on points of detail over the three editions of the grammar, but the first part, dealing with homonyms, is another excellent illustration of how discussions within the FG could influence the content of the grammar. The case of the three potential homophones *wider*/*wieder*/*widder* is the very first example of its type given by Schottelius on p. 544 of the 1641 edition (cf. *AA* 681), and it is probable that the detailed recapitulation of the seventh spelling principle (see below) added here, at the end of the work, was Schottelius's reaction to a discussion between Gueintz and Schottelius of precisely these homophones (cf. the correspondence of the FG in Krause 1855 [1973]: 252, 257). Schottelius had criticized Gueintz's failure to distinguish *wider* ('against') and *wieder* ('again'), but Gueintz had retorted that Schottelius had overlooked *Wieder*, i.e. modern German *Widder* ('ram'). Schottelius responded by including all three in his addendum on homophones.

5.5.3 *Spelling*

Schottelius's account of spelling is a good illustration of how his grammar improved on its predecessors. Schottelius provided both a thorough synthesis of existing rules and controversies, and a re-statement of rules in terms of his crucial notion of analogy. His discussion of the individual letters provided the most systematic and thorough account in German grammar to date (Barbarić 1981: 227). The account of punctuation was also by far the most detailed to date, treating the virgula [/], the comma, colon and semi-colon, the hyphen, apostrophe, question mark, exclamation mark, and brackets, as well as the *Theilzeichen* (a double slash: //) (Barbarić 1981: 282ff.). Missing from the discussion were only the dash (which did get a mention in the poetics, *AA* 790), and inverted commas.[11]

Schottelius presented seven general principles of spelling (*AA* 188–98, § 12–18). They are summarized here to illustrate how the notions of analogy and the rootword really did underpin all the details of Schottelius's decisions:

> 1. Do not write 'unnecessary' letters, *diejenige Buchstabe | welche der Rede keine Hülfe tuhn, und also überflüssig seyn* ('those letters that do not help the pronunciation and so are superfluous') as in *Frauw, unndt*. (*AA* 188, § 12)

Applying this principle strictly led Schottelius to reject well-established spellings such as *diese*, where <ie> was traditionally prescribed as an

---

[11] Many grammars (as opposed to primers or *Formularbücher*) had not dealt with punctuation at all (Ölinger, Clajus, Ritter, and Olearius), or only very briefly (Kromayer had a single paragraph). Gueintz (1641: 118–21) had addressed it in greater detail than any of his grammar-writing predecessors, over four pages following his syntax. It is possible that Schottelius—who after all was claiming that his grammar was more complete than anything that had gone before it—added his own section on punctuation, likewise after syntax, at quite a late stage, having seen it in Gueintz's work (although Melanchthon's Latin grammar also separated punctuation from orthography and treated it after syntax: Barbarić 1981: 91). The possibility of an afterthought in response to Gueintz's work is lent weight by the fact that the introductory paragraph—which defines the role of punctuation with a reference to Harsdörffer's *Poetischer Trichter*, p. 131—was only added in 1651. The original introduction as it appeared in 1641 (Schottelius 1641: 524) had far more the character of an afterthought: *Nachdem in den vorhergehenden Capittelen verhoffentlich dasselbe | was zu völliger Untersuchung unserer Teutschen Wörter | und zwar | als ein Hauptstück mag nötig seyn | ist auff die Bahn gebracht | und gebührender massen bewiesen worden; Dabey aber durch und durch etzliche kleine Strichleine | Nebenzeichen und Punctleine gesehen | als wird diensam seyn | auch etwas richtiges von denselben herbey zufügen* 'After what may be necessary to a complete investigation of our German words has hopefully been set out in the preceding chapters, and indeed as the main part, and has been sufficiently proved, but various little lines, ancillary signs and little dots have been seen, it will be useful to add some correct information about them here too.' On the place of the punctuation in the grammar, cf. also 3.7.

indicator of length. Schottelius argued that there was no such indication of length in *mir, wir, dir*, etc., where the vowel was also long (*AA* 189–90).

Both the rootword and analogy underlie the second principle. The rootword is the unit of analysis, while analogy is the principle that governs its consistent spelling in all word-forms:

2. When in doubt about the final consonant of a rootword (e.g. *Pferd* or *Pfert* 'horse'?) [because of the neutralizing of the voicing distinction in syllable-final position, i.e. German *Auslautverhärtung*], consider the word when it carries an inflectional ending. Rootwords should be written in the same way, whether inflected or not, hence *Pferd* and *Pferde*, not *Pfert* and *Pferde* (*AA* 191–92, §13).

Like the second, the third principle relied on recognizing rootwords and applying to them the analogical principle:

3. Final consonants of rootwords are doubled in their base form if they are doubled in their inflected form. Because we write *Stimme, alle, volle, Männer* 'voice, all, full, men' we should write *Stimm, all, voll, Mann*, rather than *Stim, al, vol, Man* (*AA* 192, §14).[12]

Recognizing rootwords was central to the fourth principle too: rootwords must be spelled consistently, in accord with analogy, so that they are recognizable as such:

4. Words and syllables that essentially (*wesentlich*) belong together should be kept together. So when hyphenating, we should hyphenate according to rootwords, e.g. *Haus-es* 'house *gen. sg.*' (not *Hau-ses*, for instance) (*AA* 195, §15).

The fifth principle was not so much a genuine general principle as a special case of principle 1., avoiding unnecessary letters:

5. Write < *sl–* > etc. rather than < *schl–* > by analogy with < *st–, sp–* > (*AA* 196–97, §16).

It is characteristic of the primacy Schottelius gave to the written form of the language that he—uniquely amongst German grammarians up to this time—seriously entertained the notion of spelling < *sl–* > in words like *schlagen* and the like as *slagen* (and likewise < *sw– sm– sn–* > rather than

---

[12]   Cf. the statement of this rule in Schottelius's review of Gueintz's mansuscript in 1640, in Krause (1855 [1973]: 249–50). Schottelius did not apply this rule consistently, however. For example, he preferred *soll* but *solte* (in both cases simply following established usage); see 8.2 below.

<schw– schm– schn–>), because although it was out of step with current usage, he had seen such spellings in older German texts and therefore considered them to be closer to the true nature of the language.[13] (The underlying assumption was: antiquity = originality = natural essence; cf. 2.3.1). Here only the notion of analogy—and not the constancy of the rootword—was at stake, as the analogy with the very frequent *<st– sp–>* as in *stehen, spielen* (where the *<s>* already represented /ʃ/) appealed (*AA* 196–97). This fifth principle was the only one that Schottelius abandoned in favour of accepted usage. In the 1651 edition of the *Sprachkunst*, Schottelius had put the principle into practice in his own spellings, but only Bellin (1657) followed him (Takada 1998: 84–85). In 1663 Schottelius yielded to established usage: the principle still appeared as the fifth *algemeiner Lehrsatz* ('general principle'), but was undercut by an *Anmerkung* 'note', recognizing the *angenommener hochteutscher Gebrauch* 'accepted High German usage'.

6. The derivational endings *–lich* and *–ig* [where many speakers (and standard Geman today) pronounce the final consonants identically as [ç]] should be distinguished in spelling, because they are two distinct derivational suffixes, or *Hauptendungen*:[14] thus *fleißig* but *fürstlich*, not *fleißich* or *fürstlig*; cf. the oblique forms *fleißige, fürstliche* (*AA* 198, § 17).

The sixth principle, above, was a specific case of principle 2. ('spell in accord with oblique forms') and of principle 7., where the recognizability of rootwords (in writing) was again at stake. Primacy was given to the written form over any phonetic consideration:

7. Rootwords that are homophones should be distinguished in spelling, thus *das* (article or pronoun), *daß* (conjunction) (*AA* 198, § 18).

In sum, these seven spelling principles were the enactment of two higher-order, implicit principles:

1. Every rootword must be recognizable and distinct; and
2. Rootwords must be spelt consistently, in conformity with analogy.

Together with the unprecedented degree of attention that Schottelius paid to punctuation, these principles once again reflect the primacy that Schottelius gave to language in its written form (cf. 2.2.1)—it was the *written* language that must exhibit the analogical regularity proper to it.

---

[13]   In High German up to about 1350, these spellings reflected the pronunciation, in which the sibilant was not yet palatalized. Cf. König (1994: 151). The transition in spelling to *<sch–>* was still observable in sixteenth-century printed texts and chancery documents (cf. Ebert et al. 1993 § L 54 (4.3.3)).

[14]   In fact Schottelius overstated the distinction, viewing *–lich* as an adverbial suffix, and *–ig* as adjectival, although both are in fact adjectival (and all adjectives may be used adverbially).

5.5.4 Etymologia (*AA* 224–690): *inflection and word-formation*

The traditional title of *etymologia*, rendered by Schottelius as *Wortforschung*, subsumed (after orthography, in Schottelius's case) inflection and word-formation.

5.5.4.1. Inflection

Schottelius's treatment of the inflectional system illustrates how 'Latinizing' his grammar was, especially following the most successful grammar up to that time, Clajus (1578), and how it was essentially conservative. Nevertheless, it did represent progress in some areas.

While some grammarians had already reduced the number of cases to five (Ölinger) or even four (Ritter, Helwig) (Barbarić 1981: 631), Schottelius followed Clajus by listing all the six cases found in Latin, and therefore expected by many grammarians of the vernacular. (Recall that for Vossius, whom Schottelius followed, case was part of natural, universal grammar.) 'Ablative' and dative had identical forms (the 'ablative' was identified in what we call the dative after prepositions); the non-existent 'vocative' was also recognized in the traditional manner by an 'o', as in *O Gott* ('Oh God', *AA* 227). Schottelius did, though, reduce the number of genders from seven in Clajus (1578)[15] to four (where the fourth, 'general gender' allowed for adjectives and participles acting as nouns to be preceded by an article of any of the other three genders, *AA* 262). Schottelius was the first to devote a separate chapter to number in the noun, possibly inspired by the first full discussion of number by Gueintz (1641) (Barbarić 1981: 609ff.).

In the area of the verb, Schottelius noticed some irregular verbs that lacked an imperative and that retained their monosyllabic root in key indicative forms, but did not identify the modals as a separate group (*AA* 573–74, cf. Seiffert 1989). Schottelius's most obvious innovation was to list verbs not by their infinitive, but by the singular imperative form (e.g. for the auxiliary *sey oder biß*, 'be', *AA* 551), here and in the list of irregular verbs (*AA* 578–603). For Schottelius maintained—together with Harsdörffer, but otherwise in the face of massive criticism from members of the FG (see e.g. Krause 1855 [1973]: 368 and discussion in 3.8.2)—that this monosyllabic form of the verb constituted the rootword. Again, as in orthography, the notion of the rootword determined decisions of grammatical detail.

Schottelius built on Kromayer's innovation in giving the subjunctive forms in all tenses, an insight which became the norm after Schottelius.

---

[15] Clajus's seven genders are: masculine, feminine, neuter, common (as in *der* or *die Gevatter* 'godparent', which may be masculine or feminine depending on the referent), 'all' (for adjectives, because they can all be preceded by *der, die* or *das*), *epicaenum* (where a noun of one gender may refer to an animal of either biological sex, e.g. *die Katze* 'cat' f.), and 'doubtful' (for nouns with varying gender, e.g. *der/das Scepter* 'sceptre').

There were fewer confusions in the forms given than in his predecessors, too, though Schottelius still listed *wir seyn oder sind* in the present subjunctive (*sind* is actually indicative) (*AA* 552; cf. Barbarić 1981: 856, 818). Schottelius also followed Kromayer in abandoning the practice of giving imperatives in the first and third persons. His account of the past participle was the fullest to date (Barbarić 1981: 896), and was the first to discuss the future passive participle (*aufzulösend, dissolvendus* 'to be dissolved' *AA* 612). Schottelius divided the verbs into two groups, regular and irregular, a division he had noted was helpful to learners in his assessment of Gueintz's grammar (Krause 1855 [1973]: 252) and that was already found in Ritter (1616). To aid such learners, he listed 204 irregular verbs with their principal parts over the pages 578–603. Here again, Schottelius was more comprehensive than his predecessors: Clajus had listed 142, and Ritter 115 in alphabetical order (Barbarić 1981: 982–83).

5.5.4.2. Word-formation

Our impression so far of the *etymologia* must be of a grammar that was in many ways much like its predecessors, with incremental though significant improvements in the comprehensiveness of the account, and with more examples given. There was no attempt to break radically with established tradition. There is one massive exception, however: Schottelius's account of word-formation. Traditionally, matters of word-formation had been dealt with under accidence. Alongside inflection, *etymologia* also encompassed *figura* (which dealt with whether words were simple or compound) and the partially overlapping *species* (whether words were primitive or derivative). *Figura* and *species* were generally accepted as accidences for the noun, pronoun and verb; *figura* also applied to the participle, conjunction, adverb and sometimes preposition (Barbarić 1981: 1176). These sections of *etymologia* in German grammars ranged from collections of more or less interesting and/or useful curiosities (as in Albertus 1573 [1895]: 74, who emphasized the 'almost inexhaustible abundance' of compounds and derivations), or rumps reduced to little more than their definitions (as in Kromayer 1618). Schottelius's innovation was to transform these discussions, so that the rootwords and their combination appeared as the very essence of the language. Combining such words and endings was now described as a regular analogical process.

Albertus had used the term *radices* 'roots' in passing in 1573 (in Albertus 1573 [1895]: 74). Ritter (1616: 46) identified primitives (*prima*) with the Greek theme and the Hebrew root, and defined them as something 'not descended' from something else, e.g. *die Liebe* 'love'. Schottelius's monosyllabic rootword was a far more developed concept, however, dependent on Stevin and the tradition since Irencius's original pronouncement (1518, lib II cap 31 fo 38ᵛ). Stevin too offered the beginnings of analysis of internal word-structure: he recognized in a compound like *putwater* ('well-water') a *Grondt* word, *water*, and its *Ancleuing*, *put* ('well') (head word or base, and modifier; rendered by Schottelius as *Grund(wort)* and *Beyfügige* (e.g. sixth oration, *AA* 75, 6: 8).

What Schottelius added to Stevin can be summed up in the following three points (see also Barbarić 1981: 1176–1423).

First, he recognized and carefully defined three distinct types of 'word' as the elements of language: rootwords, inflectional endings (*zufällige Endungen*) and derivational endings (*Hauptendungen*). With the principled distinction between inflection and derivation, it becomes apparent that *etymologia* in fact consists of two fundamentally different processes: one generates a finite set of word-forms (inflection), the other is infinite, generating new lexemes (derivation and compounding).

Second, he set out rules governing the combination of these basic elements, going well beyond the basics of head-word and attribute outlined by Stevin. He identified the different combinations of rootwords that were possible in compounds, such as Noun + Noun, (e.g. *Schifholtz* 'ship-wood' *AA* 77, 6: 15) and Noun + Adjective (e.g. *kohlschwarz* 'coal-black' *AA* 83, 6: 24 I), *Vorwort* + Verb (e.g. *Auflösen*, dissolve, *AA* 90, 6: 34).[16] Schottelius also recognized the possibility of compounds that were more than binary in structure when he gave examples in the following format: *schuld, verschulden, wiederverschulden, unwiederverschuldet* ('debt, owe, owe back, not owed back' *AA* 90, 6: 34 I; cf. also *AA* 78, 6: 16 for other compounds of similarly complex structure). Such examples suggest that he was aware that derivation and compounding could be processes of successive steps (cf. also *AA* 195–96), but he did not give any theoretical account of the iterative process. He does not seem to have conceptualized a hierarchical constituent structure beyond that of the dependency of the modifier on the base in binary compounds (see also 7.7). His assumption that the meaning of compounds and derivates could regularly be derived from the sum of their parts was naïve (Hundsnurscher 1986; cf. 2.3.2); his primary interest lay not in the details of semantics, but in the possibilities of permutations.

Schottelius's attention to the finite set of rules to generate very large (if not infinite) numbers of combinations (*die Anzahl der abgeleiteten schetzet man billig unzahlbar / und jhren Nutz unschätzbar* 'one can fairly reckon that the number of derivations is infinite, and their usefulness priceless', *AA* 319) fitted very comfortably with the fascination with applying the *ars combinatoria* to language, already noted in Chapter 4.

---

[16]   To be exact, these rules were spelled out not in the grammar, but in the orations (cf. Table 4.1), to which the grammar gave cross-references (*AA* 400, 615). On Schottelius's concept of word-formation, see Faust (1981).

Third, as we have already seen, Schottelius expressed these insights in a strongly rhetorical, metaphorical discourse, in which the rootwords constitute (variously) the *Stamm*, the *Wurzel*, and the *Grund* of the language tree (the stem or trunk, the root, the ground or foundation) (cf. 2.4.1). It is this way of conceptualizing language makes reading Schottelius's grammar such a different experience to reading Wallis (1653) or Lancelot & Arnauld (1660), and certainly any of Schottelius's predecessors in the German tradition. Even at his most theoretical—indeed especially when at his most theoretical—Schottelius was an eloquent rhetorician.

Thus far, then, Schottelius's contribution to German grammar lies first in his more comprehensive treatment and exemplification of points of grammar that were already familiar from the inherited tradition. Next, the same thoroughness is also evident in the way he worked through his new principles of word-formation. Finally, he expressed his insights so vividly and so energetically that he managed to make German grammar appear both important and interesting, and so, ultimately, helped German studies become established as a serious academic subject.

5.5.5 *Syntax*

Schottelius's spelling rules illustrated how the application of the notion of the rootword determined the structure and details of the grammar. This section on syntax will show a second novelty, one less recognized in the history of grammatography. The syntax, or *Wortfügung*, is admittedly entirely typical for the period: it is largely a dependency grammar. That is, it is a syntax at the phrasal level, concentrating on what words govern what cases. Hence, syntax is divided into 'syntax of the noun', 'syntax of the verb', etc. (cf. Table 5.2). For instance, under adjectives, Schottelius and his contemporaries noted that certain adjectives may require a genitive, e.g. *des Diebstahls schuldig seyn* ('to be guilty of theft' *AA* 717). However, Schottelius's syntax was novel in its strong emphasis on language as a system of combinable and recombinable elements. A curious case is that of the *Widerwort* 'opposite-word, oxymoron', a compound whose meaning was yielded by combining elements of opposite meaning. Schottelius's favourite example, taken from Stevin (Dijksterhuis 1955: 83) was *Wasserfeuer* 'water-fire', i.e. water-borne fireworks, cited under the syntax of the noun (in Book III, *AA* 711) along with other *Widerwörter* such as *bittersüß* 'bitter-sweet'. Unlike most oxymoronic compounds, *Wasserfeuer* had the additional property that its elements—*Grund* 'head' and *Beyfügige* 'attribute'—could be reversed, yielding a new word: *Feuerwasser* 'fire-water'. Schottelius discussed both possibilities—oxymoronic and reversible compounds—in the sixth oration of Book I with other examples of his own

(*AA* 79–80, 6: 19–20).[17] Reversible compounds were also considered in his treatment of noun compounding (*AA* 401–408, §3). Such *Widerwörter* and reversible compounds were attractive to Schottelius for the same reason as anagrams were (cf. 4.5.4), and were altogether discussed three times in the *AA*. They involved rearranging rootwords to yield new, related meanings, but the game was here played with rootwords rather than letters.

As the area of grammar devoted to combining words appropriately to yield *eine gantze Meynung | und versamlete Teutsche Rede* ('a complete meaning and coherent German discourse', *AA* 181), syntax gave Schottelius plenty of further pretexts under which to emphasize the flexibility of German, and the almost infinite variety of its combinability. Schottelius was indebted to Clajus (1578) and to Ritter (1616) in particular for his syntax section (Jellinek 1913: 139), but he was original in the way he moulded the material to fit his own emphasis on combinability and variation. Often his discussion of variation concerned how these facilities could contribute to a good, varied style. To that extent, Schottelius's interest in syntax was that of a rhetorician; his syntax section actually concluded with a typical rhetorical exercise in variation, illustrating how words could be combined in German to form sentences which say the same thing in different ways, using the example of idioms for expressing thanks (*AA* 789–90). Just as Schottelius found evidence of the linguistic naturalness of German at the level of the letter and word (2.3.2), but not at the level of syntax and word order, a similar distinction applies here to his expectation of variation and uniformity. Regularity and lack of variation were essential expressions of the analogical principle in the rules for spelling, inflection, and word-formation. But at the level of syntax—the level of the phrase and above—Schottelius still judged variation by the precepts of rhetoric, and viewed it positively, as a guarantor of the richness of German.

Schottelius frequently pointed out alternative constructions for the syntactical rules he gave, emphasizing the varied ways in which elements of language could be combined in German to yield meaning. He discussed extended participial constructions as alternatives to a relative clause (*AA* 710); he noted *das* + adjective could serve as an alternative to a noun (*AA* 714), that genitive constructions might be replaced by one of a selection of prepositions (*durch, nach, mit, in, vermittelst, an* and *von* are all mentioned; *AA* 715–17), and that affixes with negative meaning offered alternatives to using the negative adverb (*un–, los–, ent–* etc., *AA* 776). In an addition to the traditional observation of the use of accusative case to express measurements (*einen Finger lang* 'one finger long' etc., *AA* 718), Schottelius also added that compounds could be used as an alternative way of

---

[17]   The very first grammar of German, Albertus (1573), had already drawn attention to compounds in German whose elements could be swapped over, such as *Spangrün* to *Grünspan* (in that case *without* a change of meaning, both meaning 'verdigris').

expressing the same thing: *Hand = breit, Finger = breit* 'hand-wide, finger-wide', etc., *AA* 721)—evidence both of richness and of *brevitas*.

Accordingly, many of Schottelius's paragraphs on syntax contain not prescriptions, but stylistic recommendations in the face of an explicitly valued degree of rich variation. That is the case with the recommendation to use participial phrases over relative clauses noted above (*AA* 710). Elsewhere the syntactic advice was explicitly for the sake of euphony, *Wollaut*. So Schottelius couched the principle that the infinitive part of a verb phrase should come last in a clause, separated from its auxiliary, not as a hard and fast rule, but rather as something which yielded *einen sonderlichen Wollaut* ('a particular euphony' *AA* 743; also 755, XXIII), but the rule is more baldly stated 745–46, and Schneider-Mizony (2010: 791–792) is right that evaluations like *lautet wol* and *ordentlich* ('sounds well', 'orderly, proper') amount to recognizing a norm here, even if it is inadequately described.

A further syntactical point was dealt with not under syntax, but as a matter of style in Book II, under the motion of the noun. Schottelius gave the rules that where *der, die* or *das* are followed by an adjective, the adjective always carries the 'feminine' ending (i.e. –e): *der gute Man |, die gute Frau | das gute Tiehr* 'the good man, woman, animal' (*AA* 236). However, for the sake of acoustic *Liebligkeit*, it was, Schottelius wrote, sometimes appropriate to give the adjective the same ending as a preceding masculine definite article: *der treflicher* [not –e] *Plutarchus* 'the excellent Plutarch' for this sounds good to *ein Teutsches Gehör* (*AA* 237).[18] Similarly, Schottelius warned his readers to avoid unintended rhymes of adjacent verbal forms, as in *Ich habe euren Bericht | welcher Gestalt jhr euch in Frankreich verhalten | erhalten* ('I have received the report of how you got on in France', *AA* 756), or excessive cumulations of monosyllables (*AA* 781). The last few pages of the syntax dealt with what might be better classified as rhetorical or poetic effects than as syntactical rules: the use of synonyms to avoid repetition, and the use of emphasis, repetition and rhyme for effect, pointing forward to the following Book IV, the poetics. This brings us to the next point to consider in assessing the grammar of the *AA*: the amount of space devoted to the partly cultural-patriotic, partly rhetorician's aim of inventorizing the richness of the language.

5.6. EXEMPLIFICATION OF *COPIA*

One of the advances Schottelius made over his predecessors was the number of examples he gave. His preference for real language, in the form of proverbial expressions or quotations from the writings of contemporary and earlier well-known writers, anticipated corpus-based grammars of our own era. But Schottelius exemplified some points of language at such length

---

[18]   On the relationship of this pronouncement to linguistic reality, see 8.5.

that, around the familiar grammatical skeleton of the Latinizing macro-structure, the body of the Schottelius grammar developed bulges in unexpected places. Any point of grammar could be taken as a pretext to demonstrate the 'copiousness' of the language (cf. 2.5.1), with particular reliance on the importance of the rootword and word-formation, both to contribute to cultural-patriotic discourse about the language, and, more concretely, to encourage the use of transparent native compounding instead of assimilating opaque loans.

Chapters 11 and 12 of the grammar dealt with word-formation, specifically derivation and compounding of the noun. The 23 derivational endings (*–bar, –schaft, –ung* etc.) were listed with copious examples over eighty pages; the chapter on compounding covers no less than 135 pages, with lists of the compounds that can be formed from 269 rootwords chosen as illustrations. Many other points of grammar likewise provided an opportunity for extensive lists of examples. In the orthography, the third 'general spelling principle', that of etymological spelling (e.g. that *Mann* is spelt with a double consonant at the end because the other forms of the word require it: *Männer, Mannes*, etc.; cf. 5.5.3), the mention of 'other forms' provided a springboard to list 41 possible inflectional endings (*zufällige Endungen*) (*AA* 193), as well as to demonstrate the ways in which new words could be formed through a process of combination: *Mann* yields *mannlich, mannbar, Mannschaft, mannlos* 'manly, marriageable, team, man-less/husband-less'. Similarly, the fourth principle, which dealt with rules for hyphenation, allowed Schottelius to showcase how words can be formed from combinations of rootwords and endings, such as *Un-auf-bring-lich* 'impossible to produce or achieve' (*AA* 195); it is *kein geringes Kunststükk unserer Muttersprache / welches ich abereins wiederhole / daß sie sich mit sothaner / fast unaussprechlich vieler Mannigfaltigkeit formen / und die Deutungen so wunderreich / durch einsilbige Wörtlein / änderen lesset* 'no small artful feature of our mother tongue which I repeat once again, that it allows itself to be formed with such completely ineffable multiplicity and its meanings to be changed so marvellously by monosyllabic little words' (*AA* 196).

Schottelius's treatment of comparison and superlative formation provides a similar instance. It is initially typical of the German grammatical tradition. Schottelius ran through the rules for formation, and like his predecessors, though oddly for readers today, barely mentioned the addition of the *–er* comparative ending, contrasting *ein Dummer* 'a stupid [person]' with *ein Dümmer* 'a more stupid [person]', and *ein Frischer* 'a fresh [one]' with *noch frischer* 'still fresher'. It was not the addition of *–er*, but rather Umlaut (*Kleinlaut* in Schottelius's terms) or the addition of a signal word such as *noch* which were the signs of the comparative, despite the fact that the examples do show that *–er–* is often the only marker, as in *Es ist nichts entfindlicheres noch schmertzhafteres* ('There is nothing more sensitive nor more painful', *AA* 247). Schottelius did not improve on traditional accounts, therefore (cf. McLelland 2001). Instead, after seven sides of admittedly more detailed, but otherwise traditional, explanation, he took the opportunity to tell the reader of a number of special words, *Ertz | uhr | hoch | höchst*, which, when prefixed to an adjective or participle, mean that *deroselben Deutung gleichsam ergrössert | erweitert | erhöhet | und von sonderlicher Wirkung wird* 'arch-, originally-, high-, highest-'; 'the meaning of the same becomes, as it were, increased, expanded, elevated, and of particular force' (*AA* 253). Examples of this followed over four sides.[19] Schottelius then used a list of kinship terms—a list of his own devising, without parallels elsewhere to my knowledge—to demonstrate that German could be far more specific than Latin by dint of compounding, for it had not just *Grosvater* (*avus* 'grandfather') and *Obergroselter Vater* (*atavus* 'great-grandfather') but supposedly also *Der Hochvorobergroselter Vater* (presumably 'great-great-great-grandfather'?).[20] The tenuous link to the grammatical topic at hand (comparison) appears to be that in this case Latin must rely on the less specific, *comparative* form *majores* (*AA* 258).

Schottelius's section on the number of the substantive and adjective was, as noted in 5.5.2, more detailed than those of his predecessors. But it was lengthened still more because Schottelius took the opportunity to remind us that rootwords with double consonants keep them in the plural too, hence *Mann, Männer*. The same rule applied, he noted, to all compounds of *Mann* too (*AA* 286), of which he then proceeded to list some 80 over four sides, utterly dwarfing the preceding grammatical explanation itself. Again, the traditional structure of the grammar provided a jumping-off point for Schottelius's rehearsal of the richness of the language, with the ultimate goal of proving modern German an intellectual instrument equal to expressing any and all concepts.

The chapter on the preposition gave Schottelius his next opportunity to showcase German word-formation. In keeping with a tradition since ancient Greek grammar, Schottelius included under prepositions not only what we today consider prepositions, but also prefixes such as *ge–* (as well as those identical to prepositions like *aus, vor, mit,* etc.). Of these 'prepositions' he gave 57 which were primitive rootwords, and listed numerous examples for almost all of these over the following 38 sides (*AA* 617–55). Finally, in the section dealing with punctuation, the use of the hyphen in compound words was illustrated over four sides (*AA* 671–75).

Adding up the pages devoted to listing examples of word-formation in Book II of the grammar yields a total of some 260 sides, or just over half of the 519 sides of the book. The grammar of 1663 was, then, as much about demonstrating the infinite combinability of German rootwords, as it was a

---

[19] Schottelius added another such intensifier, *blut*, as in *blutarm, blutsauer* ('very poor, very sour'), etc., in his discussion of the syntax of the noun, *AA* 728.

[20] On the history of kinship terms in German, see Jones (1990).

statement of grammatical rules. But these word-lists served not just to demonstrate *copia* through combinability. Many of the examples in the wordlists were taken from earlier German writers (especially Aventinus and Luther, and including Old High German words; cf. 4.4.4, 6.2) to emphasize the lasting, unchanging essence of German, whose rootwords were still recognizable across the centuries (cf. 2.3). Furthermore, the systematic listing of compounds must be seen in the context of contemporary poetic culture in which Schottelius was an eager participant (cf. 4.5, 4.6). Many compounds listed were drawn from contemporary writers, including Opitz, Harsdörffer, and Moscherosch. The use of nonce formations, often with metaphorical, or even looser, emblematic, association to their referent, was one of the most important means of *ornatus* in poetry, and a measure of the poet's learning and creativity (Polenz 1994: 303–08). One can see, then, why these word-lists are so extensive in the grammar, for they were useful and important evidence to Schottelius wearing all of his various hats: as a grammarian, a language historian, a cultural patriot and a poet.

5.7. Schottelius's grammatical terminology

> Wenn einer nicht hette so vielmal / und von jugend auf in den Schulen die gar bekanten Wörter *Etymologia, Participium, Conjugatio, Pronomen, Adverbium, Singulariter*, & c. gehöret / solten demselben wol solche und derogleichen Wörter nicht etwas frömd und unvernemlich zuerst vorkommen? [...] Wie oftmalige Wiederholung wird erfoder[t] / ehe man einem Knaben die *Terminos* einswatzen / und eine verständliche Fertigkeit in ihm bilden müge?

> 'If one had not heard the very familiar terms *Etymologia, Participium, Conjugatio, Pronomen, Adverbium, Singulariter*, & c. so many times and from one's youth onwards in schools, wouldn't such terms seem rather strange and incomprehensible? [...] How much repetition is required before one manages to drum these terms into a lad and inculcate in him an intelligent competence?'

> (*AA* 11–12, 1: 36)

As the passage cited above shows, although he was not unsympathetic to the problem of unfamiliar terminology, Schottelius was committed to establishing German grammatical terminology by consistent repetition, for without it, the German terms would never become familiar. One very clear aim of his grammar was to make the unfamiliar familiar, and so to demonstrate that

> Es ist [...] keine Unmöchligkeit / daß nicht allein in der Sprachkunst / sondern in anderen Künsten und Wissenschaften die Kunstwörter

Table 5.3: Examples of German grammatical terminology used in the AA (following Barbarić 1981, though references to Stevin are my own)

Schottelius's term	Translation	New coinage?	Previously used by?	Competing terms	Did it become established?
ableiten, Ableitung	derive, derivation	Yes		*Entspringliche* (Ratke) and others	Yes
Beyfügige	attribute	Yes	cf. Stevin *Ancleuing*		
einsilbig	monosyllabic	Yes		einlautend	Yes
Fügewort	conjunction		Ratke (*Fügwort*)		
Geschlechtswort	article		Gueintz		Yes
gleichfließend, ungleichfließend	regular, irregular		Becherer	cf. Dutch grammar in late seventeenth and eighteenth centuries: *gelijkvlooiend, ongelijkvlooiend*	
Grund(wort)	head word	Yes	cf. Stevin *grondt*		
Grundmässig(keit)	regularity	Yes			
Grundrichtig(keit)	analogy (approx.)		Ratke (in Helwig & Jungius 1614)		Yes into eighteenth century in some works
Hauchlaut	aspiration	Yes			
Hauptendung	derivational ending	Yes			Yes into eighteenth century
Hinterstrich	apostrophe	Yes			
Hülfwort	auxiliary verb		Olearius (*Hilfwort*)		
Mittelwort	participle		Ratke, Gueintz		Yes

Table 5.3: (*Continued*)

Schottelius's term	Translation	New coinage?	Previously used by?	Competing terms	Did it become established?
Nennwort	noun		coined by Helwig and Ratke?), used by Gueintz	*Nahm* (since Old High German) ; also used by Schottelius	Yes
Nennzeitwort	infinitive as noun	Yes			
Rechtschreibung	spelling		already in use	*Schreibkunst*	Yes
Rufwort	interjection	Yes			
Sprachkunst	grammar		already widely used	*Sprachlehre* (Ratke, Gueintz), arguably with more pedagogical connotations	Yes
Stamm	*thema*, root	Yes	Gueintz used *Stammwort* once, Helber *Wurtzel*, but cf. above all Stevin		Yes
Stammwort	*primitivum*, primitive element				Yes
verdoppeln, *Verdoppelung*	compound	Yes		*zusammensetzen*, *Zusammengesetzte* (Ratke, Helwig, Gueintz)	
Vorwort	preposition		Ratke, Gueintz		Yes
Wortforschung	*etymologia* (in the sense of word-formation and inflection)		coined by Ratke		Yes
Wurtzel	*Radix*, root		Helber		Yes
Zahlendung	inflectional ending (not just for number)	Yes	Yes		

Table 5.3: (Continued)

Schottelius's term	Translation	New coinage?	Previously used by?	Competing terms	Did it become established?
		Endung (Gueintz)			
Zeitnennwort	agentive verbal noun				
Zeitwort	verb	Yes	used once in fifteenth century, then Ratke and Gueintz		Yes
Zuwort	adverb		since the Middle Ages, alongside *Beiwort*		Yes
Zwischenwort	interjection	Yes			Yes into eighteenth century

Most of the terminology for moods was also coined by Schottelius (except *Weise*, *Gebietungsweise*, *Anzeigungsweise* 'mood', *imperative mood*, *indicative mood*').

recht deutlich Teutsch gegeben und aufgebracht werden künnen: Wie solches im Niederlande vielfältig gebräuchlich / auch sonderlich aus dem *Stevino* zusehen ist

'It is [...] not impossible to give and present the technical terms in proper clear German, not just in grammar but also in other arts and sciences, as is much the custom in the Netherlands, and which can be seen especially from Stevin'

(*AA* 13, 1: 42)

True to this aim, Schottelius was very consistent in his use of German terms, whether or not they were coined by him. Typically, Schottelius aided the reader by glossing his German terms with the usual Latin one at their first mention in the definition, but thereafter he used the German term consistently, and this did indeed help, as he foresaw, to establish many of them in the vernacular grammatical tradition, for instance the terms for the parts of speech: *Geschlechtswort, Nennwort, Mittelwort, Vorwort, Zeitwort, Zuwort, Zwischenwort* ('article, noun, participle, preposition, verb, adverb, interjection').[21] Particularly in the area of word-formation, Schottelius coined several workable terms himself, though his debt to Simon Stevin is obvious too. The coinings *ableiten* and *Ableitung* 'derive, derivation' in particular survive today as key terms in the field (*verdoppeln* on the other hand could not defeat the widely used and more generally applicable *zusammensetzen* 'to form a compound'). *Grund* ('head word) and *Beyfügig* ('attribute') are renderings of Stevin's Dutch terms *Grondt* and *Ancleuing* (cf. Stevin in Dijksterhuis 1955: 83). Table 5.3 provides an overview of Schottelius's use of key grammatical terminology against the background of the pre-existing German grammatical tradition.

Several of the terms that Schottelius coined were inseparable from the metaphorical frame of reference that gave rise to them, and so contributed to the rhetorical flair of the *AA*, even in the grammar (cf. 2.4, 5.4). Barbarić (1981: 934–39) made exactly this point about the term *gleichfließend* ('regular', of verbs): *fließen* had emphatically positive connotations, occurring elsewhere in the *AA* to describe the pleasant sound of the language (e.g. *AA* 26, 2: 42; 59, 4: 26; 88, 6: 33; 109, 7: 11; 112, 7: 18; 114, 7: 26; 832). Regular verbs were, then, not merely regular, but by implication pleasantly so, flowing in accord with the nature of the language. The connotations were even more inescapable in the terms *grundrichtig* and *Grundrichtigkeit*, where the recurrent imagery of the language edifice (the *Kunstgebäu*) throughout the *AA* keeps the metaphor alive. With evocative terms like this central to the grammar, Schottelius the grammarian never ceased to be Schottelius the rhetorician. This, as much as his innovations, made his grammar stand out both from its predecessors in Germany and from its contemporaries in Europe.

6

INTERTEXTUALITY, AUTHORITIES AND EVIDENCE IN THE *AUSFÜHRLICHE ARBEIT*

6.1 Hypotextuality and the *AA*

One of the most challenging aspects of the *AA* for modern readers is the complexity of the intertextual relationships with earlier works, something which sections 6.2–6.4 below are intended to clarify. One other intertextual relationship defined the *AA*, however: the *hypo*textual one, or the fact that the *AA* was largely a re–publishing and revision of earlier works. Schottelius made many more or less significant changes to his writings with each publication of them. The poetics was updated to some degree, for instance to take account of the completion of Harsdörffer's *Poetischer Trichter* (1648–1653) (*AA* 995), and from 1651 onwards some of the examples that Schottelius gave of language games and puzzles, though unchanged, were now given with reference to Harsdörffer's *GesprächsSpiele* (1644–49), which had appeared since the 1641 edition. I have already noted Schottelius's ongoing additions of references (3.6.3), his refinements to the concept of *Grundrichtigkeit* (3.8; cf. Takada 1985, 1998), and changes in the orientation of the grammar, from a practical text in 1641 to a scholarly work for an international readership in 1663 (5.3).

The orations of Book I also underwent constant revision. There are many minor changes to wording which amount to a discernable tendency to tone down the language of 1641 by 1663 to more cautious phrasings, as just a few examples in Table 6.1 illustrate. One systematic change between 1641 and 1663 is the elimination of a handful of double negatives (see 8.6 on the significance of this for Schottelius's language awareness). Other changes reflected Schottelius's changing views of analogy in spelling (cf. 5.5.3): Schottelius's expectation that the plural be marked regularly meant that he consistently gave the plural –e to plurals of the diminutive suffix –*lein* in 1641, but he abandoned this practice in 1651. The 1651 spelling of < sl– >, < sw– > for < schl– >, < schw– > was, however, in accord with his own rule (by analogy with < st–, sp– >; cf. *AA* 196–197 §16), but was reversed in 1663. The 1663 version tended more than in 1641 to spell with the lowered vowels, as in *möchte, könne*, rather than *müchte, künne*.

Table 6.1 Schottelius's toning down of his rhetoric between 1641 and 1663 (selected examples from the first three Lobreden)

	1641	1651	1663
AA 17, 2:5	*die Hebräische Sprache unfehlbar die Alleralteste* 'the Hebrew language infallibly the oldest of all'	as 1641	*die Hebräische Sprache die allerällteste* 'the Hebrew language the oldest of all'
AA 10, 1: 30	*darüber er sein Urtheil ausblase* 'about which he blows/ trumpets forth his judgement'	as 1641	*darüber er sein Urtheil ausspreche* 'about which he states his judgement'
AA 19, 2: 17	*samentlich geirret* 'erred wholly'	*nicht wenig geirret* 'erred not a little'	as 1651
AA 23, 2: 27	*halb göttliche Helden* 'half-divine heroes'	as 1641	*so vieler grosser Helden* 'so many great heroes' (more accurate translation of Opitz's Latin *ingentium heroum*)
AA 30, 3:6	*haben einen gnugsamen kräfftigen Schein.* 'have a sufficiently strong [i.e. convincing] appearance'	as 1641	*scheinen vielen nicht ungültig* 'seem to many not invalid'

Schottelius also continued to expand the orations. Table 6.2 notes the most significant additions made between 1641 and 1663, by paragraph. Only the fifth oration underwent no expansion between editions; the second and eighth saw the addition of six and four paragraphs respectively in 1651, and another two each in 1663. In 1651 the fourth, sixth, seventh and ninth orations were considerably expanded, and the tenth (probably written much earlier; cf. 6.4) was printed for the first time. In 1663, the first and tenth orations were further substantially expanded. Paragraphs were added to the first oration to serve as an introduction to the *AA* as a whole, while the tenth included material on German dialects for the first time (discussed in 7.3.2). The numbering of the paragraphs was itself an innovation of 1663, commented on in the final paragraph of the tenth oration (*AA* 169, 10: 23). Some additional material from Stevin was incorporated in 1651, and other additional references were added, such as those to Adriaan van Schrieck in the third oration (at paragraphs 7, 9, 10, 12, 15, 30), or those to Duret and Aventinus, added in 1651, but then cut again in 1663 (second oration, paragraphs 16 and 20). Such changes did not alter Schottelius's fundamental line of argument, but are evidence of his ongoing efforts to make that argument as convincing as possible.

Table 6.2: Paragraphs added to the orations between 1641 and 1663

Oration	Paragraphs added in 1651	Paragraphs added in 1663
1	28	1–19 (new outline of the work as a whole)
2	25, 31, 36, 38, 40, 43	28, 33
3	8, 18, 20, 27, 31, 37–59 (i.e. second half)	
4	5, 17–20, 24, 27–29, 37, 40–42	22
5		
6	25 (from Sichtender to end), 26, 39–53, 55–61	29, 54
7	12, 14–17, 21–23, 25–35	24 (replacing a passage which concluded the oration in 1641)
8	7 (though with longer citation from Duret than in 1663), 11–12, 14	8, 15
9	5–6, 9, 20–29, 31	11, 14, 16, 30
10	whole new oration added 1651	5–15 (new discussion of German dialects), 23

6.2 INTERTEXTS

Schottelius was a trained lawyer, and he placed heavy reliance in the *AA* on evidence, on persuading by reasoned argument, and on weighing authority against authority (cf. 3.2).[1] His text is therefore full of references to other texts, especially in the orations of Book I (which drew on some three hundred sources alone) and in the treatise on writers about Germany and in German in Book V (with well over two hundred authors listed).[2] It is worth noting that Schottelius specified for only one title listed in that treatise that he did not have access to a copy (Samuel Sturm's *Der verstörte Parnaß* [...] (Bremen: Vessel, 1660). We must assume, therefore, that he at least inspected all other titles that he referenced there. It may seem odd to characterize a work of the second half of the seventeenth century as 'late humanist' (as does Polenz 1994: 111), but the label is apt enough, for Schottelius relied particularly heavily on the works of the generations of scholars of a century and a half or so before him. Still, no source was too old or too new to be considered, whether as an authority *about* the German language and its history, or as an attestation *of* language: his earliest sources are from antiquity, and his latest references date from as late as 1662. So Augustine and Adriaan van Schrieck, separated by twelve centuries, could both 'participate' in Schottelius's discussion of the oldest language (cf. 3.6.3). Schottelius's dependence on his authorities makes him

---

[1] Harsdörffer—another trained jurist—argued by weighing authorities in a very similar way (Hundt 2000: 417–18).
[2] There is considerable overlap between these two groups of sources.

a man of his time,[3] for a century after him enlightenment thinkers would have freed themselves from these centuries of accumulated authorities. To take a well-known example, the prize-winning essay on the origin of language of Johann Gottfried von Herder (1744–1803) was certainly not burdened with references in the same way (Herder 1772; cf. Neis 2003).

Schottelius's reliance on certain types of sources has already been noted in some detail in the earlier chapters: his debt to Dutch scholars (cf. 3.4) and to the pre-existing grammatical tradition (cf. 5.5) in particular. We can now take stock of the full range of sources and authorities to which Schottelius made reference, in order to give an insight into the breadth of his evidence base. Names of authors appear in their standard form, often not identical with the form in which Schottelius gave them; only brief descriptions or abbreviated titles of works are noted. For full bibliographical details, the reader is referred to the Appendix, an alphabetical list (by author) of authors and sources referenced. The Appendix contains some 480 entries, but Schottelius often cited more than one work by the same author; he also referred to works variously by the original author or title, by their translator, or by their editor. More than one text might be contained in a single volume (especially editions of older texts, including legal codes). Over 60 entries in the appendix merely clarify such cross-references (or cross-reference between variants of names). The true number of works consulted is, therefore, difficult to calculate accurately, and depends too on one's definitions of 'source'—are the 120 or so works that are listed only in Treatise IV to be considered sources? What about those contained in the 'list of sources' (pp. c2, c3, De) and in the fourth treatise, but apparently not drawn on explicitly anywhere else in the *AA*? Rössing-Hager's (1985: 1582) estimate of about two hundred sources, cited by Moulin-Fankhänel (1997b: 306, fn. 22) is at any rate definitely too low, and the number is surely between three and four hundred, depending on one's definition.

Schottelius's often dense referencing and citing (especially in the orations) is both familiar to the 21st-century reader, and potentially alienating. Familiar, because referencing 'correctly' and exhaustively is a requirement of our academic discipline. Alienating, because despite the number of sources Schottelius references, his style of referencing—abbreviated, inconsistent, and elliptical—is bewildering to anyone not already familiar with the body of scholarship on which he drew in Wolfenbüttel, the largest European library of the day. To complicate matters further, many sources drawn on in the *AA* are not listed in the list of sources at the front of the work; and some listed there are apparently not otherwise referred to (e.g. the ninth-century monk Hucbaldus, listed c3ʳ, or the Dutch writer on military fortifications Gerard

---

[3] Polenz (1994: 195) noted the characteristic 'intertextuality' of German language cultivation 'in the sense of the collective work of generations, a joint and cumulative contribution to language cultivation, improving step-by-step'.

Melder, fl. 1658, noted c2ᵛ; cf. Jones 1999: 101). It will therefore be useful here to give an overview of the range of texts Schottelius referred to (6.2.1), and to note specifically his legal sources (6.2.2); texts in German on technical subjects (6.2.3); prescriptive works about German (6.2.4); chronicles and other historical works (6.2.5); philological studies (6.2.6); and sources dealing with languages beyond Europe (6.2.7). Section 6.3 notes contemporary literary figures referenced in the *AA*, concluding with the special case of Harsdörffer (6.4). For clarity, life-dates of all figures are given here, even for those introduced earlier in the book. While there is some duplication between the tables presented in this chapter and the Appendix, it is hoped that the thematic groupings of sources here and the comprehensive alphabetical listing in the Appendix will be of value in their different ways.

6.2.1 *The range of sources and authorities in the* AA

Schottelius's sources fall into three overlapping categories:

1. Attestations of German words cited by Schottelius, particularly in his discussions of German rootwords, derivation, and compounding (including older legal texts and other technical works, cf. 6.2.2 and 6.2.3), or attestations of German verse forms (rhyme and metre) in Book IV, the poetics (cf. 6.3).
2. Authorities for information about the history of German and Germany, as well as the history of other languages and nations for comparison. These are chiefly cited in the orations of Book I and in Treatise IV of Book V. They are mainly historical works and humanist studies exploring the origin of language and comparing languages (6.2.5 and 6.2.6).
3. Contemporary writers discussed in the fourth treatise of Book V, especially those whose works had appeared since the 1641 edition of the grammar, providing evidence of the quality and breadth of literary activity in German (6.3).

The works that Schottelius referenced to fulfil these three functions give us an insight into what German cultural patriots and scholars were reading (or at least referring to) in the mid-seventeenth century.[4] It is revealing, though not at all surprising, that amongst the 400 or so individuals listed, there is just one woman, Catharina Regina von Greiffenberg (1633–1694), an Austrian poet encouraged by male acquaintances who were members of the FG, and whose verse translation of French poetry of Guillaume de Salluste du Bartas (1544–1590) Schottelius praised as *treflich* 'excellent' on *AA* 863

---

[4] Though beyond the scope of the present study, it would be instructive to compare Schottelius's range of sources with those painstakingly identified by Colombat & Peters (2009) in their edition of Gessner's encyclopaedic study of languages, *Mithridates* (1555), published a century earlier.

of his poetics.[5] Outside the realm of verse, there was no scope at all for women to achieve in scholarship.

It is also typical of the era that Schottelius worked with several accumulated chronological 'layers' of authorities. He referenced sixty or so ancient authorities, going back as far as Greek works such as the Cratylos dialogue of Plato (429/8–347 B.C.) and the poetics of Plato's pupil Aristotle (384–322 B.C.). Examples include Greek and Roman linguistic scholars and critics like Varro (116–27 B.C.), Cicero (106–43 B.C.), Pomponius Marcellus (30 B.C.–30 A.D.), Quintilian (35–95 A.D.), and Lactantius (ca. 240–320), writers like the dramatist and epic poet Livius Andronicus (fl. 272–250 B.C.), the comic poet Plautus (ca. 254–184 B.C.), and the tragic poet Marcus Pacuvius (220–130 B.C.), historians like the Greek Polybius (203–120 B.C.), Julius Caesar (100–44 B.C.), Tacitus (ca. 55–116 A.D.), and Josephus (37–ca. 100 A.D.), the Spanish geographer Pomponius Mela (fl. ca. 43/44 A.D.), and the natural history of Pliny the Elder (23–79 A.D.). Such works were no more than the common European cultural inheritance, by authors that Schottelius would have encountered in his schooling, and/or used in his role as tutor to the Duke's children at Wolfenbüttel. Mid-seventeenth–century Schottelius might be, but he was thoroughly humanist in his reliance on these sources.

Schottelius owed a particular debt to those humanists who translated these ancient sources. In particular, he drew on five German translations of Greek and Latin sources for attestations of some of the rootwords in the third treatise of Book V (Neuhaus 1991: 150–54): the writings of the Greek geographer and historian Strabo (63/64 B.C.–26 A.D.); the influential pharmacopoeia by the Greek physician Pedanios Dioscurides (first century A.D.), of which three editions had been printed in the sixteenth century (cf. Neuhaus 1991: 151; Worstbrock 1976: 68); the *Epitome*, a history compiled by Florus (70–117 A.D.), largely based on Livy: Schottelius used a 1571 German translation by Zacharias Müntzer (1530/35–1586); Tacitus's *Germania*, of which Schottelius used a 1612 German edition; and Vitruvius (ca. 80–15 B.C.), the Roman architect whose work had been printed in 1548 in a translation by Walther Hermann Ryff (1500–1548).

In addition to such classical sources (and their later translations), other works that figure are the Bible (cf. 6.3.1), the authorities of the Church Fathers including Clement of Rome (fl. 96), Clement of Alexandria (ca. 150–215), Tertullian (160–220 A.D.), Jerome (ca. 347–420), and Augustine of Hippo (354–430), and other prominent teachers and writers from within the early medieval church: St. Isidore of Seville (ca. 560–636) and his *Etymologia* (a very influential compendium of knowledge throughout the

---

[5] Schottelius also mentions the Ancient Greek female poet Sappho in a list of other Greek poets, *AA* 145.

medieval era and beyond), the *Ecclesiastical History* of Bede (673–735), and the *History of the Franks* of Gregory of Tours (538–594).

The next chronological layer of sources covers the ninth to fourteenth centuries, especially medieval writers mediated for Schottelius by German humanist editions of their works. The oldest of these is Otfrid von Weißenburg (800–after 870), to whose Old High German *Evangelienbuch* (a rhymed life of Christ) Schottelius had access in a 1571 edition by Matthias Flacius Illyricus (1520–1575) (Moulin-Fankhänel 1997a: 306, Neuhaus 1991: 131). Schottelius cited Otfrid eight times in his list of rootwords to attest words in older (Old High) German. Next oldest is Williram von Ebersberg's (1010–1085) German paraphrase of the Song of Solomon. Schottelius used a 1598 edition by Paulus Merula (1558–1607) (Moulin-Fankhänel 1997a: 307), but also a commentary on it by Franciscus Junius (1591–1677), which was printed in 1655 (cf. Van de Velde 1966: 131–44). There are 27 references to the Williram text in the list of rootwords in the sixth treatise of Book V, 19 of them explicitly to Junius's edition (Neuhaus 1991: 132–40).

In order to present an unbroken written record of the German empire, Schottelius also relied on medieval chronicles, noted in the fourth treatise on 'Germany's and German writers'. The chronicles mentioned include those of Hermann of Reichenau (1013–1054), continued after his death by Bartoldus (ca. 1030–1088) and Radevicus (d. 1170–1177), that of Otto von Freising (ca.1114–1158), Helmoldus's (1120–1177) Slavic chronicle, the Saxon Chronicle (after 1225) attributed to Eike von Repgow (ca. 1170–after 1233), and Konrad von Lichtenau's (d. 1240) chronicle from the Flood to 1230. All of these chronicles had been printed in the sixteenth century. The *Sachsenspiegel* of Eike von Repgow, a Middle Low German law book (ca. 1225) was cited in the list of rootwords in the sixth treatise, using the 1569 edition by Christoph Zobel (1499–1560), and sections of it are also referred to separately elsewhere as *Lehnrecht* and *Weichbild* (Neuhaus 1991: 140–42). Schottelius also cited the Danish chronicler, Saxo Grammaticus (1150–1220) (Neuhaus 1991: 142–43), whose history was likewise printed in Germany during the sixteenth century.

The work of such sixteenth-century humanists, publishing classical sources in translation and producing editions of older German sources, was important to Schottelius, both as the source of attestations of the language, and as a source for information *about* Germany and German. Indeed, works published in the sixteenth century make up the largest single group of works to which Schottelius referred: over one hundred. Amongst them, the following furnished Schottelius with attestations in the list of rootwords (Neuhaus 1991: 154–166): the German historian Heinrich Meibom (1555–1625); Wolfgang Lazius (1514–1565), a doctor and historian whose work on the great migrations (*De gentium aliquot migrationibus*) was widely known; the German jurist Christoph Besoldus (1577–1638); the Swede Olaus Magnus (1490–1557), cited alongside Saxo Grammaticus as a reference on the topic of ancient 'Celtic rhyme' (*AA* 1384), and the Anglo–Dutch antiquary Richard Rowlands Verstegan (ca. 1565–1620), cited three times in the list of rootwords. Schottelius also drew on the incomplete German dictionary of Georg Henisch (1549–1618; cf. Kämper 2001). A key figure was the Swiss writer Melchior Goldast von Haiminsfeld (1576–1635), an industrious collector of documents on German medieval history and constitution (cf. Hertenstein 1975: 115–99; Baade 1993), who edited a number of Old High German texts, the *Interpretatio Keronis in Regulam Sancti Benedicti* 'Kero's interpretation of the rule of St Benedict' and the so-called *St Galler Schularbeit* 'St Gall school exercise' amongst others (Moulin-Fankhänel 1997a: 303, 307–08; Hertenstein 1975: 185, 194–95). Schottelius referred frequently to Goldast's *Alemannicarum Rerum Scriptores* 'Writers on Alemannic matters' (1606), especially the second volume, rich in Old High German material (Moulin-Fankhänel 1997a: 307), e.g. *AA* 183, 427, as well as to Part I of his *Paraenetica* 'Exhortations' (1604), which contained editions of the Middle High German works *König Tirol von Schotten* and the didactic poem *Der Winsbecke* (ca. 1201–1220). Schottelius (*AA* 1197–98) quoted from Goldast's preface to this edition. Goldast himself drew on the editions of Otfrid and Williram noted above, as well as on Justus Lipsius's 1602 letter to Henricus Schottius (cf. Table 6.8), so Schottelius may also have found his references to these in Goldast. Finally, Schottelius referenced Goldast's *Politische Reichshändel* (1614), an account of the regalia of the Holy Roman Empire from 1350, and his *Reichssatzung Deß Heiligen Römischen Reichs* in two parts (1609, 1613), which contain (later copies of) documents from the time of Charlemagne onwards.

Goldast also published the historical, political, philological and epistolary works of the Nuremberg humanist Willibald Pirckheimer (1475–1530) in 1610, to which Schottelius referred; he cited Pirckheimer at length in the treatise on translating, *AA* 1251–55, regarding the subject of proper names and their translation. Another Swiss influence was the naturalist and collector Conrad Gessner (1516–1565). His *Mithridates* (1555) provided Schottelius with Notker's (ca. 950–1022) version of the Lord's Prayer in Old High German, which he placed alongside versions in other Germanic languages (cf. 6.2.6). Schottelius also referred to a 1560 edition of the *Heldenbuch* (Frankfurt: Weigand Han for Sigmund Feyerabend), a collection of thirteenth-century epic poetry, chiefly around the figure of the Goth Dietrich von Bern (Theodoric).

Finally, Schottelius also cited many contemporaries. One example is Johann Lükteschwager Micraelius (1597–1658), whose history of Pomerania (1640) Schottelius drew on just once in his treatise of rootwords (*AA* 1287), though there is a detailed listing of the contents of its six books in the fourth treatise (*AA* 1185). Another contemporary is the Dane Ole Worm (Olaus Wormius, 1588–1655) who published in 1636 a study of runes and ancient Danish literature, and *Danicorum Monumentorum libri sex* (1643), noted in the fourth treatise, *AA* 1162–63, and who is referenced eight times in the list of rootwords (Neuhaus 1991: 164–166). Many other contemporaries of Schottelius, including members of the FG, are cited as evidence of the rich literary and translation activity in German, and are discussed in Section 6.4 below.

6.2.2 *Legal sources*

The influence of Schottelius's legal training (3.2) on his grammatical work is evident in the fact that he referenced over thirty juridical texts (Table 6.3; fuller details are given in the Appendix).[6] In addition to individual sources named, Schottelius also noted in the list of authors (*AA* c3ʳ) the abbreviation *J.C.* (*jureconsultus*) for terms used by jurists in *allerhand Acta und Ordnungen / so allemahl nicht kunten allegiret werden* 'all sorts of acts and ordinances that could not be listed' and for which he did not provide a specific attestation. When Schottelius cited a 1570 legal work, *Wasser Recht* [...], by Meurer, on the laws of the waterways (*AA* 1200), it was as evidence of a good translation of a technical subject into German, and in many cases works are cited as attestations of particular rootwords or compounds. But Schottelius also cited legal texts because it was lawyers who were particularly interested in older legal texts, and these, once printed, became important resources for philological study (Moulin-Fankhänel 1997a: 302). Zobel's 1569 edition of the *Sachsenspiegel* and the sets of laws contained in the *Codex legum antiquarum* (1613) compiled by Friedrich Lindenbrog (1573–1648) are cases in point. In the treatise on translating, Schottelius also cited extensively from an 'old' *Kolbenrecht* (source unknown, but also contained in Schottelius's own legal treatise of 1671)—i.e. the law on deciding conflicts by single combat—as an illustration of older German words and idioms (*AA* 1234–1242; cf. 4.3).

6.2.3 *Evidence of German used in technical domains*

Apart from the legal texts like Meurer's that furnished evidence of technical German, Schottelius also gleaned German words from many other technical language domains, as evidence of how suitable German was for discussing technical subjects, and to show how appropriate new terms could readily be coined by derivation and compounding. This, after all, was the achievement of the Dutch-Flemish mathematician Simon Stevin whom Schottelius emulated (cf. 3.4): to have written elegantly about his subject in his vernacular. The list of technical works in German to whom Schottelius referred in the fourth treatise of Book V covers a broad range of topics,

---

[6] The number would be larger still if one counted the works produced by jurists on topics and in genres outside the legal domain. In two further cases (Schneidewin and Spekhan), the identification with a jurist is not certain; see the corresponding entries in the Appendix.[7]

Table 6.3: Authors of legal texts referred to by Schottelius, listed alphabetically by author's surname

---

Berlich, Matthias (1586–1638): his *Conclusiones practicabiles* (1615–19, 5 vols.) are noted *AA* 393.

Bocer, Heinrich (1561–1630): *AA* 622 refers to his treatise *De Diffidationibus* [...] 'On feuds' (1625).

Burkhard, Franciscus (pseudonym of Andreas Erstenberger, 1520–1584): *AA* 488 refers to his *De autonomia. Das ist, von Freystellung mehrerley Religion und Glauben* ('On autonomy. That is, on allowing several religions and faiths') (1602).

Carpzovius, Benedictus (1595–1666): author of *Jurisprudentia Forensis* (1650), the source of many compounds cited by Schottelius, *AA* 78, 6: 16, and noted c2^r.

Draco, Johann Jakob (1595–1648): author of *De Origine Et Iure Patriciorum, Libri Tres* (1627), on Roman, Greek and Germanic politics, law and origins.

Faust, Maximilian (?–?): author of *Consilia Pro Ærario Civili, Ecclesiastico Et Militari, publico atque priuato* (1641), used by Schottelius in the grammar to attest various words (*AA* 329; 330; 367; 396; 429; 469).

Gail, Andreas (1526–1587): his *Practicarum Observationum, tam ad Processum Judiciarium, præsertim Imperialis Cameræ, quam causarum Decisiones pertinentium, Libri duo* 'Two books of practical observations' on legal procedure (1578) are noted *AA* c2^v.

Grotius, Hugo (1583–1645): his influential *De Ivre Belli ac Pacis* 'On the law of war and peace' (1626) set natural law above customary law (cf. 3.4).

Gryphiander, Johann (1580–1652): his study of Saxon law based on extracts from the *Sachsenspiegel* is cited *AA* 129.

Herden, Eitel Friedrich von = Rudolf von Heiden (1627–1661): three references are presumably to his *Grundfeste Des Heil. Römischen Reichs Teutscher Nation* 'The Foundations of the Holy Roman Empire of the German nation' (1660).

Hunnius, Helfrich Ulrich (1583–1636): Schottelius referred to his *Tractatus de authoritate et interpretatione juris, tam canonici, quam civilis* 'Treatise on the authority and interpretation of civil and canon law' (1630).

Keller, Adam (fl. 1618?): Schottelius referred to Keller's treatise on the law of inheritance *De Jure Succedendi Ab Intestato: Das ist, Von Erbfalls Recht. Tractatus Brevis* (1618).

Klammer, Balthasar (1504–1578): c3^r referred to Klammer's legal compendium, *Compendium Iuris, Das ist: Kurtzer Außzug, vieler und vornehmer Rechtsbücher* (1616).

Kniche[n] *or* von Knichen, Andreas (1560–1621): Schottelius referred to his *De Sublimi Et Regio Territorii Iure, Synoptica Tractatio* 'on the sovereign and royal law of territory' (1603) (*AA* 129).

König, Kilian (Chilianus) (1470–1526): Schottelius cited his *Practica [...]* (1550), a work on Saxon and imperial law.

Lerch von Dürmstein, Caspar (1575–1642): noted c2^r, his treatise on the order of knights, *Ordo equestris Germanicus Caesareus bellopoliticus* (1625/26, 1631/32) is cited several times.

Limnaeus, Johannes (1592–1663): Schottelius cited his study of German and imperial law, *Tomus [...] Ivris Pvblici Imperii Romano-Germanici* (1629–) and his *Capitulationes* (1651) (*AA* 1194).

Lindenbrog, Friedrich (1573–1648): Schottelius referred to several sets of Germanic laws in Lindebrog's collection of ancient laws, the *Codex legum antiquarum* (1613). Many of the sources contained in the codex are listed separately under L (for *Lex*) on *AA* c3^r.

Mascardus, Josephus = Giuseppe Mascardi (d.1588): his work on legal proofs *Conclusiones probationum omnium [...]* (1584) is noted *AA* c3^r.

Table 6.3: (Continued)

Menochio, Giacomo (1532–1607): Schottelius cited his 1576 *De Arbitrariis Iudicum [Judicum] Quaestionibus et Causis [...]*, a study on Roman and canon law, *AA* 8, 1: 23 & 26.

Meurer, Noë (1525/28–1583): his German-language work on the laws of the waterways (*AA* 1200), *Wasser Recht [...]* (1570) is cited *AA* 1200.

Paurmeister, Tobias (?–?): *AA* 426 refers to his *De Iurisdictione Imperii Romani Libri II* ('Two volumes on the laws of the Roman Empire') (1608).

Perneder, Andreas (1500–1543): noted as the translator of legal works into German (*AA* 1166).

Reinkingk, Theodor von (1590–1664): Schottelius referenced both a 1654 edition of his work on ecclesiastic and secular law, *Tractatus De Regimine Seculari Et Ecclesiastico* (1619 and later editions), and *Biblische Policey [...]* (1654) (*AA* c3^v, 1193).

Schard[ius], Simon (1535–1573): Schottelius cited his legal dictionary (*AA* c3^v): *Lexicon Iuridicum* (1582).

Schrader, Ludolph (1531–1589): his *Tractatus feudalis* (1594) is listed *AA* c3^v.

Seckendorf, Veit Ludwig von (1626–1692): his handbook of German public law, *Teutscher Furstenstaat* (1660, a revision of the 1656 edition) is noted *AA* 1193.

Speidel, Johannes Jacobus (1600– after 1666): his *Notabilia [...]* (1634) is listed *AA* c3^v, 1169, as well as his *Thesaurus Practicus* (1629) and his *Speculum [...]* (1659).

Spelman, Henry (1564–1641): Schottelius cited his glossary of Anglo-Saxon and Latin law terms, *Archaeologus in modum glossarii* (1626).

Sprenger, Johann Theodor (d. 1668): *AA* 498 probably refers to his *Lucerna moderni status S. Rom Imperii [...]* (1567).

Stephani, Mathaeus (1576–1646): Schottelius referred to his treatise *De Iurisdictione [...]* (1610).

Wehnerus, Paulus Matthias (1583–1612): his *Practicarum [...] liber singularis* on imperial law (noted *AA* 1184) is a frequent source of attestations of words.

Wolf, Johannes (1537–1600): Wolf's *Lectiones Memorabiles et reconditae* (1608) are cited *AA* 357 for the use of the word *Altfränkisch*.

---

including hunting, mathematics, architecture, medicine, agriculture, geography, and logic (Table 6.4; for full details see the Appendix).

Amongst these technical writers is the mathematician Simon Stevin. We have already seen how extensively Schottelius drew on Stevin, to the extent of citing almost half of his *Uytspraeck* in the orations. For completeness, Table 6.5 lists the sections of the orations of Book I where Schottelius drew on Stevin (cf. also Kiedrón 1985a).

6.2.4 *Didactic and prescriptive works on German language and style*

We have had ample occasion already to see how Schottelius interacted with the German grammatographical tradition (Clajus, Ratke and Gueintz in particular). For completeness, Table 6.6 notes in chronological order the works in the area of grammar, spelling and good style in German which Schottelius included in his treatise on writers—both contemporaries and older writers. In addition to these, Schottelius also

Table 6.4: A selection of Schottelius's evidence base for German technical language in the fourth treatise, listed alphabetically by author's surname

Aitinger, Johann Conrad (1577–1637): a 1653 edition of his *Kurtzer und einfältiger Bericht vom Vogelstellen*, a work on trapping birds (*AA* 1205).

Anon., *Uhrsprung und Ordnungen der Bergwerge* [*sic*] [*...*], published 1616 (*AA* 1189).

Bapst (von Rochlitz), Michael (1540–1603): a medical compendium, *Wunderbarliches Leib und Wund Artzneybuch* (1596–1597) (*AA* 1187).

Bock (or Tragus), Hieronymus (1498–1554): a 1546 German *Kreuterbuch* 'herbal', to which Schottelius had access in a 1565 edition (*AA* 1188).

Böckler, Georg Andreas (attested 1644–1698): an architectural manual of 1659 and a work on arithmetic for military purposes (1661) (*AA* 1207).

Bohemus [= Behm], Martinus (1557–1622): a church calendar, *Kirchen Calender: Das ist, christliche Erklerung, des Jahres u. der zwölff Monaten*, to which Schottelius had access in a 1608 edition (*AA* 1196).

Brunfels, Otto (1489/90–1534): a pharmaceutical work, *Reformation der Apotecken* (1536, in the same volume as Eles, below) (*AA* 1187).

Coler, Johann (1566–1639): a 1645 edition of Coler's *Oeconomia Ruralis Et Domestica*, containing information on agricultural and household work (*AA* 1189).

Dögen, Matthias (1605/6–1672): a work on military fortification in a 1648 translation by Philipp von Zesen, *Heutiges tages übliche Kriges Bau-kunst* (*AA* 1207).

Dürer, Albrecht (1471–1528): theoretical treatises in German on measurement and human proportions (*AA* 1164).

Eichholz, Petrus (d. 1655): *Geistliches Bergwerk* (1655), a Christian allegory of mining, apparently containing many useful German technical terms (*AA* 1203).

Eles, Hans (?–?): *Wie man Sirupen, Latwergen und Konfekt machen soll* (a recipe book for syrups and confectionary, printed 1536, together with Brunfels; see above) (*AA* 1187, with *Klas* in error for *Eles*).

Helvetius, Johann Friedrich = Johann Friedrich Schweitzer (1625–1709): a work on 'medical physiognomy' of 1660 (*AA* 1188).

Hulsius, Levin(us) (ca. 1546–1606): *Tractat der mechanischen Instrumenten* (1604), on the construction of geometrical instruments (noted *AA* 147).

Lonicerus [= Lonitzer], Adam (1528–1586): a *Kreuterbuch* 'herbal' published in 1587 (*AA* 1187).

Mathesius, Johann (1504–15685): a treatise in German on mining, *Sarepta* [*...*], published in 1562 (*AA* 1165).

May or Maius [von Sangershausen], Theodorus (fl. 1605–1619): German translations of works on agriculture, *Agricultur, oder Ackerbaw der beyden hocherfahrnen und weitberühmbten Römer, L. Columellae & Palladii* [*...*] (1612) (*AA* 1182).

Münster, Sebastian (1489–1552): a German *Cosmographia* (1537) (*AA* 1168). Schottelius also cited his definition of *Gau* in the list of rootwords (Neuhaus 1991: 149–50).

Ryff, Walther Hermann (1500–1548): in Ryff's *Ejn wolgegründt nutzlich vnd [und] heylsam Handtbüchlin gemeyner Practick der gantzen leibartzney* (1541) many medical terms are translated *nach altem Teutschen und in gutem Verstande* 'according to old German and in good sense' (*AA* 1187). A 1614 edition of Ryff's 1548 translation of Vitruvius's work on architecture is noted *AA* 1181.

Starck, Andreas (1580–1608): a medical work, *Krancken Spiegel* (1598) is noted *AA* 1187.

Table 6.4: (Continued)

Stevin, Simon (1548–1620): Flemish mathematician, referred to *AA* De^r as a *hochgelahrter Mann* 'highly learned man' who wrote on mathematical topics. Schottelius used Stevin's *Vytspraeck vande Weerdicheyt der deytsche tael* (1586) (*AA* 1167 and passim in the orations). Cf. discussion in 3.4 and below.

Wasserleider, Goswin (fl. 1584?): a 1590 German translation of Wasserleider's Ramist work on logic, *Logica Ad P. Rami Dialecticam Conformata* (1584) (*AA* 1209).

Wittich, Johannes (1537–1598): a *Vade Mecum*, or medical manual, of 1597 (*AA* 1187).

---

mentioned Enoch Hannman (1621–1680) for his activities in the area of grammar and poetics in the first oration of Book I (*AA* 4, 1: 9). Significantly, Schottelius did not mention his rival Gueintz's grammar (1641) at all, though he did not note his treatise on spelling and other 'little treatises' (*AA* 1202).

6.2.5 *Chronicles and other historical works*

Schottelius listed many historical sources, especially chronicles, in the fourth treatise of Book V, to show the long and unbroken tradition of writing about German achievements, and many snippets of information (or speculation) gleaned from them on the history and origins of German and Germany are scattered through the orations of Book I. It is evident from a glance at Table 6.7 (ordered chronologically) how reliant Schottelius was on the achievements of the humanists of the sixteenth century, as figures like Simon Schard (whose legal dictionary Schottelius also used) had made accessible medieval chronicles and sources. Johann Niddanus Pistorius (1546–1608) is also noted for his collection of medieval German historical sources (*AA* c3^r). Others published their own historical accounts of their country or region.

6.2.6 *Philological study and speculation*

Schottelius did more than note the existence of works on German history. He also mined them and other works for clues about the older German language and people, and about their origins (see Table 6.8). He referred to Cuspinianus and Rhenanus, for instance, for the notion of the monosyllabic rootword (cf. 3.8.2). But he was also in the happy position of following a number of scholars from about 1550 onwards who had devoted themselves to specifically linguistic matters. Symptomatic of the growing interest in language history in the sixteenth century (always related to the cultural patriotic history of the peoples; cf. 2.1 and Sonderegger 1998, 1999) was the growth of interest in Gothic (cf. Brough 1985). Bonaventura Vulcanius (1538–1614), one of a group of

Table 6.5: Schottelius's debt to Stevin in the orations of Book I

	Stevin (references are to Dijksterhuis 1955)	Topic	Schottelius (page, oration: paragraph)	Cited, translated, paraphrased?
1.	384–87, 390–91,	suitability of *Duytsch* for technical terms	12, 1:37 (added in 1651)	cited in Dutch
2.	86–87	suitability of *Duytsch* for technical terms	13–14, 1:42	abridged and translated
3.	390–91, continued from passage cited at 12, 1:37 (see 1. above)	encouragement to take pride in *Duytsch*, even if others run it down	14, 1:44 (added in 1651)	cited in Dutch, slightly abridged
4.	58	lamenting disregard for *Duytsch* amongst its speakers	20, 2:19 (partly repeated at 9:25)	translated
5.	p. 60	dialects of High and Low German (incl. *Dat Wat vs. Das Was* 'that, what')	41–42, 3: 37 (added in 1651)	cited and translated
6.		requirements that rootwords must fulfil	50–51, 4:2	similar criteria in Stevin (1586)
7.	p. 80	monosyllabic names of letters in *Duytsch*	51, 4:3 (added in 1651; also mentioned 57, 4: 18)	cited in Dutch and paraphrased
8.	p. 80	any art must begin with the most basic elements—in the case of the language, with monosyllables	51–52, 4:5–6 (added in 1651)	cited in Dutch, followed by close paraphrase
9.	p. 80	examples to argue by analogy that German *Lied* 'limb' is the origin of Latin *littera* 'letter'	53, 4:7	examples taken from Stevin
10.	p. 90, also draws loosely on 58–62	achievements in cultivating language in accord with Nature while yet barbarians	55, 4:14	paraphrased

Table 6.5: (Continued)

11.	80–81	monosyllabic rootwords are indicative of the highest perfection; how many in *Duytsch*	61, 4: 31, cf. also 4:33	referenced only
12.	according to Kiedrón (1985: 347), the paragraph is an amalgam of Becanus and various fragments from Stevin	monosyllables are first used by children	61, 4: 32	
13.	88–89	the sound of French	64, 4: 39	cited in Dutch, paraphrase
14.	86–87	the *beweeglicheyt* of *Duytsch* words, i.e. their emotional appeal; an anecdote about Heinrich Glarean as evidence	64–65, 4: 41–42 (§42 added in 1651);	translated; §42 is a paraphrase and abridgement
15.	84–85	structure of compounds:	75, 6: 8	the division of compounds into *Grundwort* and *Beyfügig* follows Stevin
16.	82–83	compounds where component rootwords can be reversed	79–80, 6: 19–20	paraphrased, and examples selected from Stevin
17.	108–09	definition of *Sichtender Horizon*	85, 6:25 (added in 1651)	cited in Dutch (a longer passage was cited in 1651)
18.	90–91	Nature does not go against Nature	93, 6: 38	translated
19.	90–91	on the natural rhythm of words	104, 7	referenced
20.	62–63	kinship between French, Spanish and *Duytsch* on the basis of – correspondences	128, 8: 9 (added in 1663)	referenced
21.	82–83	compounding of words	Book II (*AA* 409, §5, on noun compounds)	cited at length in Dutch

Table 6.6: Authorities on German spelling, grammar and style noted by Schottelius, in chronological order

14th century [1626]	Tauler, Johannes (1300–1361): Schottelius referred to 1621 and 1656 prints of this medieval mystic theologian's devotional work *Nachfolgung deß armen Lebens Christi* 'Pursuing the life of Christ', and praised his *fromme Teutsche Worte* 'pious German words', *AA* 1198.
1528	Huge, Alexander (1455–1529): his *Rhetorica und Formularium Deutsch* (1528), is noted without naming its author, *AA* 1192.
1531	Frangk, Fabian (ca. 1490–after 1538): his *Orthographia Deutsch* (1531) is noted *AA* 18 and 157.
1534	Ickelsamer, Valentin (ca. 1500–1541): his *Teutsche Grammatica* (1534) is referred to in the orations, e.g. *AA* 59 (4:25), 60 (4:30). Schottelius described him *AA* c3[r] as a *vetus Author, scripsit libellum, quem nominat Grammaticam Germanicam*, 'an old author, [who] wrote a little book, which he calls German grammar.'
1573	Albertus, Laurentius [Ostrofrank] (1540?–after 1583). Schottelius considered Albertus's grammar of 1573 (the first German grammar) inadequate and incomplete; *AA* c3[v], 1183.
1574	Ölinger, Albertus (fl. 1574–1587): author of the second German grammar (1574). Schottelius listed Ölinger as a figure whom he had *not* discussed in the treatise in his final paragraph, on *AA* 1214.
1578 [1625]	Clajus, Johann(es) (1535–1592): author of the most widely used grammar before Schottelius (Clajus 1578). Schottelius acknowledged his debt to Clajus, whose observations he said he included in his own grammar (*AA* 1204). He used the seventh (1625) edition.
1611	Sattler, Johann Rudolph (1577–1628): Schottelius referred *AA* 1166 to a 1611 folio edition of Sattler's *Notariat* and *Formularbuch*, manuals respectively for preparing legal documents and contracts, and for writing letters.
1614 [1647]	Volckmann, Adam (fl. 1614): Schottelius referred to Volckmann's four-volume *Notariat-Kunst*, to which he had access in a 1647 edition, *AA* 1166.
1634	Meyfart, Johann Matthaeus (1590–1642): Schottelius mentioned *AA* c3[r] his *Teutsche Redekunst* (1634); he is praised too in the list of German writers, *AA* 1177.
1645	Gueintz, Christian (1592–1650): his treatise on spelling, *Die Deutsche Rechtschreibung* (1645), is noted *AA* 1202, but not his grammar of 1641; see also Table 6.10.
1658	Tscherning, Andreas (1611–1659): Schottelius mentioned Tscherning's 1658 work on abuses in the German language, *AA* 1200: *Unvorgreiffliches Bedencken über etliche Miszbräuche in der deutschen Schreib- und Sprach-Kunst, insonderheit der edlen Poeterey [...]*, and cited Tscherning's poetry several times in the poetics (e.g. *AA* 859).
1648, 1659	Butschky von Rutinsfeld, Samuel (1612–1678): Schottelius noted Butschky's *Hochdeutsche Kantzeley* (1659) as well as his *Der hóchdeutsche Schlüszel zur Schreibrichtigkeit oder Rechtschreibung* (1648), but he was critical of the poor organization of the material in the latter (*AA* 1204).
1657, 1661	Bellin, Johannes (1618–1660): Schottelius noted *AA* 1202 Bellin's *Hochdeudsche Rechtschreibung* of 1657 and his 1661 work on the syntax of German prepositions, *Syntaxis Praepositionum [...]*.

Table 6.7: Authors of historical works to which Schottelius referred, in chronological order. (The left column indicates date of publication, or, in the case of older works, date of composition, with date of printing in brackets.)

fl.. 530 A.D.	Jornandes, Gothus: a sixth-century Gothic historian. Schottelius called him the first historian of Germanic blood, *AA* 1154, and cited his use of the word *gothiscanzia*, *AA* 46, for a Gothic military defence.
8th century [1475]	Bede (the Venerable / Beda Presbyter) (673–735): a Benedictine monk whose ecclesiastical history *Historia ecclesiastica gentis Anglorum* first appeared in print in Strasbourg (1475), referred to *AA* 57, 131.
8th century [1566]	Turpinus, Johannes (d. 794): his *Life* of Charlemagne and Roland was published in 1566 by Simon Schard (*AA* 1154).
9th century	Egenhard (or Einhard) (ca. 770–840): secretary to Charlemagne whose *Life* of Charlemagne Schottelius noted *AA* 1154 and c2ᵛ.
10th century [1566]	Regino abbas Prumiensis, i.e. abbot of Prüm (d. 915): author of a world chronicle printed by Simon Schard in 1566 (*AA* 1154).
10th century [1532]	Widukind of Corvey (925–after 973): his Saxon chronicle was printed in Basle in 1532 (*AA* 1154).
10th–11th century [1556]	Ditmar, Bishop of Merseburg (975–1018): his chronicle was published by Reiner Reineck in 1580 (see separate entry below). Schottelius noted a 1606 printing of Ernst Brotuff's German translation of 1556 (*AA* 1155, 1182).
11th century [1556]	Cedrenus, Georg: his account of the lives of Roman and German emperors was printed in 1566 (*AA* 30, 2:30).
11th century [1529]	Hermann Contractus (of Reichenau) (1013–1054): author of a chronicle up to his own day, printed in Basle in 1529 (*AA* 1155).
11th–12th century [1566]	Sigebert of Gembloux (ca. 1035–1112): his *Chronicon sive Chronographia* was published by Simon Schard in 1566 (*AA* 1155).
12th century [1515]	Otto von Freising (1114–1158): German bishop and chronicler, whose chronicle was printed in 1515 (*AA* c3ᵛ).
13th century [1537]	Konrad von Lichtenau (d. 1240): German abbot whose chronicle up to the year 1230 was printed in 1537 (*AA* 1156).
14th century [1553]	Albertus Argentinensis (Albrecht von Strassburg) (d. 1378): fragments of his chronicle up to the year 1349 were printed in the sixteenth century, including in 1553 with Cuspinianus's *Austria* (q.v.) (*AA* 1156).
15th century [1560]	Nauclerus, Johannes (d. 1510): a German translation by Heinrich Panthaleon (1522–1595) of his chronicle, which reached 1500, appeared in 1560 (*AA* 1158).
1499	Polydorus Virgilius (ca. 1470–1555) (also known as P.V. Castellensis): English historian of Italian extraction. His *De Inventoribus Rerum* (1499) is referred to *AA* 167.
1518	Irenicus, Franciscus (Franz Friedlieb) (1495–1559): his description of Germany in twelve books (noted c2ᵛ) appeared in 1518.
1520–	Krantzius / Crantzius, Albertus (1448–1517): German historian. Schottelius cited his work on the Saxons, *Saxonia* (1520), and referred to a German translation by Basilius Faber of the *Saxonia* (1563) (*AA* c3ʳ, 1158).
1527–1528	Cuspinianus, Johannes (1473–1529): his *Austria* (1527–1528, unfinished), an important historical–geographical regional survey up to the year 1494, was cited by Schottelius as an authority for monosyllabic rootwords (*AA* 40, 3:31).

Table 6.7: (Continued)

1531	Franck, Sebastian (1499–1539 or 1542/43): author of various works, including a chronicle printed in 1531 (*AA* c3^v; 45, 3: 44). (Schottelius also used his 1548 collection of proverbs).
1532	Carion, Johannes (1499–1537): Carion's chronicle (1532) was continued by Philipp Melanchthon and Caspar Peucer (1525–1602). Schottelius cited the Frenchman Jean Bodin's (1530?–1596) praise of it (*AA* 1191).
1546 ff.	Lazius, Wolfgang (1514–1565): particularly known for his history of Vienna (*Vienna Austriae*, 1546) and his book on the great migrations (*De gentium aliquot migrationibus*, 1557), and as a cartographer. He wrote a two-volume work of *Commemorationum Historicorum Rerum Graecorum Libri Duo* and a twelve-volume work of *Commentariorum reipublicae Romanae [...] libri duodecim* (*AA* 1159). Cited frequently, including in the list of proper names.
1548	Stumpf, Johannes (1500–1577/78): author of a Swiss chronicle (1548) (*AA* 129, 8: 9).
1549	Kolding (Coldingensis), Jon Jensen (d. 1609): a historian whose *Descriptio Daniae* (1594) Schottelius noted *AA* c3^r, 130, 8: 10.
1550	Jovius, Paulus = Paolo Giovio (1483–1552), Italian historian, whose *Historiarum sui temporis libri XLV* gives a detailed account of European history for the period 1494 to 1544. His work was printed in Italy from 1550; an edition appeared in Basle in 1560, noted *AA* 1157.
1554	Magnus, Johannes = Johan Månsson (1488–1544): Swedish scholar; Schottelius referred to his history of the Swedes and Goths (1554) (*AA* c3^r).
1555	Sleidan(us), Johannes (1506–1556): his history of the Reformation appeared 1555 (*AA* c3^r).
1555–	Meibom(ius), Heinrich (1555–1625): Schottelius referred to 17 historical works by Meibomius (listed by Neuhaus 1991: 155–157) (*AA* 1209).
1556	Aventinus, Joannes = Johannes Turmair (1477–1534): his *Bayrische Chronik*—his own German rendering of his original Bavarian chronicle in Latin—was published after his death, in 1556. Schottelius referred to the German version (*AA* c2^r and passim in the orations).
1576	Reineccius, Reinerus = Reineck, Reiner (1541–1595): professor of history at Helmstedt and author of a history of the nobility of Meißen (1576) (*AA* c3^v, 1184).
1576	Saxo Grammaticus (ca. 1150–1220): Danish author whose history of Denmark, first printed in Germany in 1576, Schottelius noted (*AA* 1156).
1584 [1630]	Bünting, Heinrich (1545–1606): Schottelius noted his German chronicle of Braunschweig and Lüneburg (*AA* 1190).
1585–1586	Hund, Wiguleus (1514–1588): Hund's genealogy of the Bavarian nobility, *Bayrisch StammenBuch [...]* (1585, 1586), is noted *AA* 497; 503; 504.
1586, 1615, 1627	Camden, William (1551–1623): English historian, cited *AA* 127 (8: 9), who wrote *Britannia* (1586), a survey in Latin of the British islands (translated into English in 1610), and *Annales rerum Anglicarum [...]*, a history of the reign of Queen Elizabeth in two parts (1615, 1625).
1594	Welser, Marcus (1558–1614): Schottelius referred to his history of Augsburg (1594), *AA* 138.

Table 6.7: (Continued)

1595	Huitfeldius, Haraldus = Arild (Arvid) Huitfeldt (1546–1609): author of the first major history of Denmark, in Danish, published (1595–1603) in eight volumes (*AA* 56, 4: 17).
1596	Letzner, Johann (1531–1613): author of a chronicle of Dassel and Einbeck (Schottelius's home town), *AA* 1171.
16th–17th century	Meteranus = Van Meteran, Emanuel (1535–1612): his chronicle of Low Countries history up to 1598 (*AA* 1195) had several continuators after his death.
1610	Erich, Adolar (ca. 1530–1634): his chronicle of the Lower Rhine, *Gülichische Chronic* (1611), is noted *AA* 1184.
1612	Lehmann, Christoph (1570?–1638): the 'German Livy', author of the *Speyerische Chronik* (1612), a chronicle of Speyer (*AA* 61, 4:31, 1186).
1615	Sachs, Michael (1542–1618): Schottelius noted his chronicle in German from Julius Caesar to Emperor Matthias (1615), to which he had access in a 1644 edition, *AA* 1191. He also noted a devotional work by Sachs, *AA* 1196.
1619, 1629	Besoldus, Christophorus (1577–1638): Schottelius cited two of his many works as sources for the history, language, and antiquity of German (*AA* 33, 3: 12, 1170).
1621	Londorpius, Michael Caspar (pseudonym Nicolaus Bellus) (1580–1629): published a (rather uncritical) collection of documents on contemporary history, noted *AA* C3^r.
1659–1662	Meyer, Martin (= Philimerus Irenicus Elisius) (1630–1670): Schottelius referred *AA* 1200 to his account of events in Europe 1657–1659, *Kurtze Beschreibung denkwürdigster Sachen [...]*.

scholars that Van de Velde (1966: 66) calls the 'Leiden philological school', had published an edition of fragments of Ulphilas's Gothic Bible from the Codex Argenteus, as he called it, in 1597, in his *De literis et lingua Getarum*,[7] and the Swede Johannes Magnus (1488–1544) had written *Historia Gothorum libris XXIV* (1554) (or *Chronicon von den Schweden und Gothen*), edited and published by his brother. In the eighth oration, Schottelius cited Georg Henisch's preface to his incomplete dictionary (1616) and quoted from Ogier de Busbecq's (1520–1591) fourth Turkish letter as sources for words of Crimean Gothic. He also added a reference to Gessner (1555: 43) on the subject of Gothic in 1663. In the fourth oration, he also cited Duret on the subject of the Gothic alphabet, along with fellow Frenchman Guillaume Postel (1510–1581), Becanus, Lazius, Ole Worm, and Johannes Trithemius (1462–1516) (*AA* 54, 4: 11).

---

[7] Goropius Becanus had printed fragments (the Lord's Prayer and a few other sentences from the Gospel of St Mark, transliterated into the Roman alphabet) in his *Origines Antwerpianae* (Becanus 1569: 740–751). The first to print fragments in Gothic script was Arnold Mercator (ca. 1573). See Van de Velde (1966: 26–27, 36).

Table 6.8: Schottelius's authorities for the origin and history of German and other Germanic languages (chronologically by date of publication). Page references to the AA are illustrative rather than comprehensive. See appendix for further details.

?	Torrentius, Laevinus (1520–1595): According to Schottelius, Torrentius wrote a defence of the ancient 'Teutsch or Celtic language', in reply to Joseph Scaliger (*AA* 20, 2:18, 1168).
1531	Rhenanus, Beatus (1485–1547): German humanist, whose 1531 *Rerum Germanicarum libri tres* ('Three books on Germanic matters') was the first major treatment of the origins and cultural achievements of the Germanic peoples.
1548	Bibliander, Theodor (1504–1564): Swiss theologian, linguist, and university teacher. Schottelius cited his *De Ratione communi omnium linguarum et literarum commentarius* (1548) (*AA* 131, 8: 11; 150, 10: 4; 168, 10: 22).
1554	Magnus, Johannes (1488–1544): Schottelius listed this Swedish archbishop's history of the northern peoples, i.e his *Historia Gothorum libris XXIV* (1554) (*AA* c3ʳ) (Neuhaus 1991: 156–57).
1555	Gessner, Conrad (1516–1565): author of *Mithridates de differentiis linguarum* (1555); Schottelius cited Notker's Old High German Lord's Prayer from it, and referenced his entry on Crimean Gothic (Moulin-Fankhänel 1997a: 308; Metcalf 1963a, b).
1569, 1572	Goropius Becanus, Joannis (1519–1572): Schottelius cited his *Originum Gentium libri IX [...]* 'on the origin of the peoples, 9 books', (1569), and his *Origines Antwerpianæ* 'the origins of Antwerp' (1572). Cited e.g. *AA* 18, 2: 14. See 3.4.
1593	Jónsson, Arngrímur (1569–1648): Schottelius referred to his *Brevis commentarius de Islandia* (Hafnia, 1593) (*AA* c2ʳ, 56, 4: 17) as *de primordiis Gentis Islandiae* 'of the beginnings of the people of Iceland'.
1597	Vulcanius, Bonaventura (1538–1614): published excerpts from the Gothic Bible in his study *De literis & lingua Getarum siue Gothorum [...]* (Leiden: Plantijn, 1597), to which he had access in the so-called Codex Argenteus, in Gothic letters with a transliteration in Roman alphabet (*AA* 56, 4: 17).
1602	Lipsius, Justus (1547–1606): Schottelius cited Lipsius's letter to Henricus Schottius (*AA* 47–48, 133), containing his glosses of psalms, and comparisons between German and Persian.
1610	Grotius, Hugo (1583–1645): besides his 1625 work on natural law (cf. Table 6.3), Schottelius used Grotius's *De antiquitate reipublicae Batavicae* ('On the antiquity of the Batavian Republic') (1610) and a 1655 edition of his *Historia Gothorum, Vandalorum & Longobardorum Historia*, as well as other works listed *AA* 1167–68.
1612	Mylius, Abraham (1563–1637): Schottelius cited Mylius's view in his *Lingua Belgica* (1612) that Flemish was primordial (*AA* 32, 3: 9; 113, 7: 21) (Metcalf 1953b).
1613	Duret, Claude (1565–1611): Duret's *Thresor de L'Histoire des langves de cest vnivers* (1613) is one of a very small number of French sources to which Schottelius made reference.[8] Schottelius cited him numerous times, sometimes on comparisons of German with French, as well as on Gothic, and where Duret criticized Goropius Becanus.
1613	Vaget, Joachim (1585–1613): Vaget's geographical and historical survey of the world, *Praecidanea De Orbe Habitabili, Sive Geographistoriae Locorum, Rerum, Hominum toto orbe memorabilium Theorian compendio exhibentis Apospasma I. [...]* (1613), is referred to *AA* 356–57.

---

[8] Others are the chronicler and linguist Charles de Bovelles (1470–1533), Jean Bodin (1530–1596), and Guillaume Postel (1510–1581). See Appendix.

Table 6.8: (Continued)

1615, 1620	Schrieck, Adriaan van (1560–1621): Schrieck wrote two works on the origins of Belgian in an ancient 'Scythian' language, *Monitorum secundorum libri V* (1615), and *adversariorum libri IIII*. *His argumentis: Linguam Hebraicam esse divinam et primogeniam* (1620) (*AA passim* in third oration; *AA* 1161).
1616	Cluverius, Philipp (1580–1623): a German geographer and historian, praised by Schottelius (*AA* 32, 3: 9 and *passim* in the third oration, *AA* 56, 4: 15; 1160) as the person who had written in most detail and most thoroughly about 'old Germany'. His *Germaniae antiquae libri tres* appeared in 1616.
1616	Cruciger, Georg (ca. 1575–1637): his *Harmonia Linguarum* (1616) presented the four 'cardinal' languages of Greek, Hebrew, Latin and German alongside each other, aiming to show that Hebrew contained the roots from which German, Greek and Latin words were derived (*AA* 71, 5: 11; 1185).
1620	Helwig, Andreas (1572–1643): his *Etymologiae, sive origines dictionum Germanicorum [...]* (Frankfurt: Hummius, 1611), a dictionary of the origins of German words, is noted by Schottelius (*AA* c2^v; *AA* 142, 9: 14).
1636, 1643	Worm, Ole (Wormius, Olaus, 1588–1655): Schottelius referred to this Danish scholar's 1636 work on runes, *Runir seu Danica literatura antiquissima* and his *Danicorum Monumentorum libri sex* (1643). Cited in the rootwords s.v. *Kampf, Mare, Monat, Reim, Ruhn, Tag, Ting, Uhr* (Neuhaus 1991: 164–65), and *AA* 54, 4: 11; 1162.
1639	Hayne, Thomas (1582–1645): Hayne's *Linguarum Cognatio, seu: de linguis in genere, et de variarum linguarum harmonia dissertatio* (1639) is cited *AA* 62, 4: 37; 143, 9: 15.

6.2.7 *Looking beyond Europe*

Despite Schottelius's obvious primary interest in German, its ancestors and its close relatives, his generation was beginning to look beyond Europe, and he drew comparisons with languages beyond Europe where he could; sources that refer to languages further afield are listed in Table 6.9.

6.3 CONTEMPORARY LITERARY FIGURES REFERENCED IN THE *AA*

One of Schottelius's purposes in the latter part of the fourth treatise of Book V was to provide a 'round-up' of the literary activity of his contemporaries whose works were not otherwise featured in the *AA* but whom he considered worthy of mention. Prominent amongst these are members of the FG. Schottelius cited the works of twenty members of the FG (not including himself) in the fourth treatise of his *AA* (Table 6.10), though he also referred to his patron Duke August (under the pseudonym of Selenus) in the orations of Book I. In eleven of these twenty cases, he explicitly noted their efforts in undertaking translations into German—an indication of how significant Schottelius (and the FG as a whole) considered translation for modelling good literary language and for enriching German culture.

Table 6.9: Sources for knowledge of the world beyond Europe, in chronological order

1534	Grynäus, Simon (1493–1541): German scholar and theologian. Schottelius referred *AA* 1195 to his 1534 account of the New World, *Die New Welt, der landschafften unnd Insulen*.
1583	Turnheuserus, Leonhardt (1530–1596): Schottelius cited this German physician and traveller's collection of exotic words and phrases (*Kai hermeneia [...]*, 1583) (*AA* 57, 4: 17).
1589	Busbecq, Ogier de (1522–1592): known for his letters as imperial ambassador to the Turkish sultan Süleiman the Great in Constantinople, *Legationis Turcicæ Epistolæ IV* (1589). Schottelius quoted from one letter containing evidence of Crimean Gothic, *AA* 132.
1596	Acosta, José de (1539–1600): Spanish Jesuit. Schottelius repeated Johannes de Laet's (see below) extract from Acosta's writings, presumably *De natura novi orbis libri duo [...]* (1596) on American Indian communication by knots in rope, *AA* 58, 4: 22.
1613	Purchas, Samuel (?1575–1626): English travel writer. His *Purchas, his Pilgrimage; or, Relations of the World and the Religions observed in all Ages* appeared in (1613), but Schottelius appears to have had access to a Latin translation, referred to *AA* 57.
1616	Hepburn, James (1573–1620): Schottelius cited this Scotsman's account of 72 different alphabets in his study of foreign languages, the *Virga Aurea* (or *The Heavenly Golden Rod [...]*) (1616).
1625	de Laet, Johannes (1593–1649): Schottelius listed *AA* c3ʳ his history of the New World, first published in Dutch in 1625 as *Nieuwe Wereldt ofte Beschrijvinghe van West-Indien [...]*. A Latin version appeared in 1633.
1631	Gottfried, Johann Ludwig (1584–1633): Schottelius referred *AA* c3ʳ to his *Historia Antipodum oder Newe Welt* (1631), a heavily-illustrated collection of material relating to the antipodes.
1654	Olearius (Ölschläger), Adam (1599–1671): geographer who travelled to the east. Schottelius noted a number of Olearius's works based on his travels, *AA* 1195–1196, and his translation of the medieval Persian poet, Schich Schaadi (1184–1283/1291?), *Persianischer Rosenthal* (1654), *AA* 1206.

Several of the FG members mentioned in the fourth treatise were noted as poets, and Schottelius cited Zesen, Buchner, Rist, Harsdörffer, Hübner, von Birken, von dem Werder and Opitz in his poetics, alongside Johann Klaj (1616–1656), Andreas Tscherning (1611–1659), Johann Vogel (1589–1663), and others (Table 6.11). Schottelius was familiar too with the theoretical treatises in the nascent field of German poetics that had been produced since Opitz's genre–founding *Buch der deutschen Poeterey* (1624), as well as with the wider tradition going back to the poetics of Aristotle and Horace, via J.C. Scaliger (whom Schottelius called a *Held* 'hero' in his poetics, *AA* 994), and represented in Dutch and in French by the likes of Heinsius and Ronsard. Buchner, Opitz, Harsdörffer, Tscherning, and Klaj represent a line of theorists who are all referenced for their contributions to German poetical theory in the

Table 6.10: Members of the FG whose works are referred to in the fourth treatise, in alphabetical order

Name, life-dates, FG name and membership number, and page reference to fourth treatise	Explicit reference to translation activity?
[August, Duke of Braunschweig and Lüneburg, under the pseudonym Gustav Selenus (1579–1666), *der Befreiende*, no. 227: cited in the *AA*, but not in the fourth treatise.]	
Abele, Matthias (von Lilienberg) (1616 or 1618–1677), *der Entscheidende*, no. 585: *AA* 1203.	Yes
Birken, Sigmund von = Sigismundus Betulius (1626–1681), *der Erwachsene*, no. 681: *AA* 1176, also in the poetics; cf. Table 6.11.	
Buchner[us], August[us] (1591–1661), *der Genossene*, no. 362: *AA* 1205; also cited several times in the poetics; cf. Table 6.11.	
Glasenapp, Joachim von (ca. 1600–1667), *der Erwachsende*, no. 451: *AA* 1173.	
Gueintz, Christian (1592–1650), *der Ordnende*, no. 361: already noted in Table 6.6.	
Harsdörffer, Georg Philipp (1607–1656), *der Spielende*, no. 368: see Table 6.11 and cf. section 6.4 below.	Yes
Hille, Carl Gustav von (1590–1647), *der Unverdrossene*, no. 302: *AA* 1176.	
Hortleder, Friderich (1579–1640), *der Einrichtende*, no. 343: *AA* 1160.	Yes
Hübner, Tobias (1578–1636), *der Nutzbare*, no. 25: *AA* 1183; cf. Table 6.11.	Yes
Kalchum / Calchum, Wilhelm von (Lohausen) (1584–1640), *der Feste*, no. 172: *AA* 1174, 1182.	Yes
Kunowitz, Hans Dietrich von (1624–1700), *der Vollziehende*, no. 660: *AA* 1182.	Yes
Ludwig von Anhalt-Köthen, Prince (1579–1650), *der Nährende*, no. 2: *AA* 1183, 1204–05.	Yes
Moscherosch, Johann Michael (1601–1669), *der Träumende*, no. 436: *AA* 1177.	
Neumark, Georg (1621–1681), *der Sprossende*, no. 605: *AA* 1203.	
Opitz, Martin (1597–1639), *der Gekrönte*, no. 200: *AA* 1179, 1206; also cited frequently in the poetics; cf. Table 6.11.	Yes
Rist, Johann(es) (1607–1667), *der Rüstige*, no. 467: *AA* 1176; see Table 6.11.	
Stubenberg, Johann Wilhelm von (1619–1663), *der Unglückselige*, no. 500: *AA* 1173.	Yes
Vintzelberg, Joachim von (d. 1680), *der Vierblättrige*, no. 299: *AA* 1202; cf. Table 6.13.	
Werder, Diederich von dem (1584–1657), *der Vielgekrönte*, no. 31: *AA* 1174, 1192; cf. Table 6.11.	Yes
Werder, Paris von dem (1623, 1674, son of Diederich), *der Friedfertige*, no. 339: *AA* 1174.	
Zesen, Philipp von (1619–1689), *der Wohlsetzende*, no. 521: *AA* 1201 and frequently in the poetics; cf. Table 6.11.	Yes

fourth treatise of Book V too. The poet whom Schottelius cited most frequently in the poetics was himself, modestly identified by an asterisk (*).[9] As already noted, the FG and other language societies explicitly recognized the importance of translation, especially literary translation, as a first step towards producing independent literary work in German (Polenz 1994: 119, Otto 1972: 64ff.) A few dozen members of the various societies are known to have been active in translating, and Schottelius noted eleven such members of the FG too (cf. Table 6.11). Translation was necessary not just as an exercise in literary style, but non-literary translation too was important as a means of establishing appropriate new terms in German. This is reflected in Schottelius's assiduous listing of earlier, sixteenth-century translations of histories and works on technical subjects in his fifth treatise. Some of those translators (where not already noted elsewhere in this chapter) are listed in Table 6.12 (with references to Worstbrock 1976 where appropriate). As can be seen, Schottelius appears to have considered translation of the classics and of more recent literature to be equally worthy of mention. The list of translations would be extended by including poetic translations by members of the FG, such as Diederich von dem Werder's *Rasender Roland* (cf. Table 6.10 and 6.11).

6.3.1 *Christianity and* Spracharbeit

As the acclamation for peace and his many explicitly devotional writings remind us, Schottelius's oeuvre was an expression of his pious Protestantism. So the plot of *Amadis de Gaula*, translated into German anonymously, was considered by Schottelius to contain too much *Zauberey* 'sorcery' at odds with Christian teachings. His own poems—his most important source

---

[9] In the earlier editions of the poetics, the use of the asterisk to mark Schottelius's own poetry was explained in the address to the reader (*Erudito Lectori Salutem* of the 1656 edition, which is available online: navigate from http://www.zeno.org/Literatur/W/Inhaltsverzeichnis)

> Weil aber diese neue Form der Verskunst / und so viel bißhero unbekante neue Reimarten / des Authoris Erklärung und behülfliche Hand oftmahls erfodert haben / als sind die *exempla*, so der Author aus den seinigen hinbey gefüget / alle mahl mit diesem * unterzeichnet. Welches zu dienlicher Nachricht zuerinneren / gefellig gewesen; Der Leser wolle dasselbige / weil es nötig unvermeidlich war / übeler ausdeutung befreien / und mit sauberem Verstande eines oder anderes vergleichen und beurtheilen.

> 'But because this new form of poetry and so many new, hitherto unknown rhyme-schemes have required the explanation and helping hand of the author, so the examples which the author has added from his own [verses] are all indicated with this *, which was a helpful reminder. May the reader refrain from attaching any bad interpretation to it, for it was necessary, and may he judge and compare one or the other with unsullied reason.'?

The explanation is not given in the 1663 edition, since it does not contain the address to the reader.

Table 6.11: Poets and authors of poetical treatises featured in the poetics, listed alphabetically

---

Bergmann, Michael (fl. 1662): Schottelius mentioned his collection of poetical expressions only in the fourth treatise of Book V, for it had only been published in 1662, *Deutsches aerarium poeticum, oder, Poetische Schatzkammer [...]* (1662) (*AA* 1201).

Birken, Sigmund von (1626–1681): member of the FG. German poet, writer and playwright, as noted in Table 6.10.

Buchner, August (1591–1661): member of the FG, poet and classical philologist who taught rhetoric and poetics at Wittenberg university. Schottelius cited Buchner's verse a number of times in the poetics, and his views on poetics, e.g. *AA* 861, and also referenced him *AA* 1205.

Greiffenberg, Catharina Regina von (1633–1694): noted as the author of the *Teutsche Uranie*, a translation of a work by Guillaume de Salluste du Bartas, in the poetics *AA* 865.

Harsdörffer, Georg Philipp (1607–1658): member of the FG. *AA* 1175–76 gives a list of his works; *AA* 1206 noted him as translator of a Spanish work, *Diana*. Schottelius's poetical treatise noted his *Gesprächsspiele* and *Poetischer Trichter*, and is prefaced by a recommendation by Harsdörffer himself (*AA* 794–98). See section 6.4.

Hübner, Tobias (1578–1636): jurist, member of the FG, and author of a verse translation of the works of Guillaume de Saluste du Bartas, which appeared in 1622. Schottelius praised the skill of the translator, but noted that the metre does not always accord with what is now proper for German verse (*AA* 1183). Nevertheless his verse is cited a few times in the poetics (identified as *Bartas*).

Klaj (Claius), Johann (1616–1656): German poet. Schottelius noted his *Teutsche Poemata AA* c3^r, and his *Lobrede der Teutschen Poeterey* (1645) (*AA* 1203), and his verse is cited in the poetics (under the name *Clajus*, but not to be confused with the sixteenth-century grammarian).

Opitz, Martin (1597–1639): member of the FG, poet, translator and purist. Schottelius cited his poetry several times for exemplification in the poetics. Schottelius also noted his *Aristarchus* (1617), and a number of his literary translations (*AA* c3^v, 1179, 1206).

Rist, Johann(es) (1607–1667): member of the FG, poet and purist from north-west Germany. *AA* c3^v states that Rist *hat unterschiedliche und sonderlich Geistliche / fast liebliche und nützliche Sachen in Teutscher Sprache geschrieben* 'has written various and especially religious, very charming and useful things in German'. His verse is cited several times for exemplification in Schottelius's poetics.

Tscherning, Andreas (1611–1659): poet, translator, and professor of poetics. Schottelius mentioned his 1658 work on abuses in the German language: *Unvorgreiffliches Bedencken über etliche Miszbräuche in der deutschen Schreib- und Sprach-Kunst, insonderheit der edlen Poeterey*. He also cited Tscherning's poetry several times in his poetics, as well as his views on poetics (*AA* 859).

Vogel, Johann (1589–1663): Schottelius referenced his translation of the psalms, *Verteutschte Psalmen: Die Psalmen Davids [...]* (1638) (*AA* 1179).[10]

Werder, Diederich von dem (1584–1657): member of the FG. His translation of Tasso was published under the auspices of the FG: *Torquato Tasso, Gottfried von Bulljon oder das erlösete Jerusalem* (1626). Schottelius also referred to his translation of Ariosto's *Orlando Furioso* (1632–36), but identified the translator only as a member of the FG (*AA* 1179, 1192).

Zesen, Philipp von (1619–1689): member of the FG, poet, novelist, and champion of the purification of the German language. His works include *Deutscher Helikon* 'German Helicon' (1640) and a phonetic orthography. Schottelius granted that Zesen has some poetical ability, but was critical (*AA* 1201) of his sometimes *Unteutsches Teutsch* 'un-German German', presumably a criticism of his perceived overzealous coining of neologisms. Schottelius cited his verse and views on poetics several times in his own poetics (e.g. *AA* 863, 1176).

---

[10] Schottelius also listed other translators of the psalms: Paul Schede Melissus (1539–1602), Cornelius Becker (1561–1604), Andreas Heinrich Bucholz (1607–1671), and Opitz.

Table 6.12: Selected translations mentioned by Schottelius, in chronological order of the translation

Original	Translator and comments	Date of translation, where known
Book of the Knight of the Tower (French) (1371–72)	Marquart von Stein (fl. 1493), *AA* 1190.	1423
Giovannis Boccaccio's *De mulieribus claris* 'On famous women' (1361–62)	Heinrich Steinhöwel (ca. 1412–1478), Swabian humanist author and translator, noted *AA* 1182.	1473
Cicero	Johann von Schwarzenberg (1463–1528) (cf. Worstbrock 1976: 50–51).	1531
Justinus, early Christian apologist and Church Father (100–165)	Translated by Hieronymus Boner (d. 1522) in 1532 (cf. Worstbrock 1976: 93), but Schottelius believed that a better translation was that of Johann Friedrich Schweser (?–?; see also below) (1656), *AA* 1181.	1532, 1656
Thucydides (460–390 B.C.) Greek historian and author of the History of the Peloponnesian War	Schottelius referred on *AA* 1181 to a 1533 translation by Hieronymus Boner (d. 1552) (cf. Worstbrock 1976: 152).	1533
Plutarch, Lucius Mestrius (46–120)	Hieronymus Boner (d. 1552), *AA* 1182, translated Plutarch's 'Lives' of eminent men in 1534 (Worstbrock 1976: 117).	1534
Dictys Cretensis Ephemeridos: 4th century Latin chronicle of the Trojan war, purporting to be a translation of the legendary Dictys' Greek text	Printed in German translation by Marcus Tatius (Alpinus) (1509–1562) in 1536 (cf. Worstbrock 1976: 67).	1536
Ditmar of Merseburg's medieval chronicle (975–1018)	Ernst Brotuff (1497–1565).	1556
Petrarca, Francesco (1304–1374)	Two German translations are noted *AA* 1206.	1559, 1637
Manlius, Johannes (fl. 1562) (=? Jakob Mennel 1460–1526), a book of commonplaces	Johann Huldrich Ragor (1534–1604), *AA* 1191.	1566
Florus, Publius Annius (70–117 A.D.)	Zacharias Müntzer (1530/35–1586), noted *AA* 1207.	1571

Table 6.12: (Continued)

Amadis de Gaula, a prose chivalric Romance in Castilian Spanish, translated into French. (The earliest printed Spanish version is by Garci Rodríguez de Montalvo, 1508.)	Anon. Schottelius praised an anonymous 1583 German translation from a French version, *AA* 1193. On the identity of the German translators, one of whom was Johann Fischart (1546/47–ca. 1590), see Weddige (1975: 59–95).	1583
Herodotus (ca. 485– 425 B.C.), Greek historian	Georg Schwarzkopf (?–?). Schottelius referred *AA* 1180 to German translations by Georg Schwarzkopf of Braunschweig (1593) and Duke Heinrich Julius of Braunschweig and Lüneburg (no date given).	1593
Sleidan, Johannes (1506–1565), and others	Georg Lauterbeck (d. 1578) translated Sleidan's Latin translation of Plato, and other translations, from Latin and French, as well as on courtly life, *AA* 1191.	16th century
Pedemontanus, Alexius (Alessio Piemontese, pseudonym of Girolamo Ruscelli, 1500–1556), *The Secrets of Alexis Piedmont* (1555)	Johann Jakob Wecker (1528–1586). Translation under title of *Kunstbuch Des Wolerfarnen Herren Alexij Pedemontani vo[n] mancherley nutzlichen vnnd [und] bewerten Secreten oder Künsten*, *AA* 1188.	1613
Bartas, Guillaume de Salluste du (1544–1590), author of epic religious poems epic poems *La Sepmaine; ou, Creation du monde* (1578) and the unfinished *La Seconde Sepmaine* (1584)	Tobias Hübner (1578–1636). See Table 6.11 for details.	1622
Barclay, John (1582–1621), *Argenis*, a political romance, and *Iconum animorum*	Martin Opitz (1579–1639). Schottelius (*AA* 1206, 1222) noted a 1626 translation or *Argenis* by Martin Opitz, and a translation of his *Iconum animorum* by Johann Winckelmann (1551–1626), date unknown.	1626, ?
Ariosto, Ludovico (1474–1533) and Tasso, Torquato (1544–1595)	Diederich von dem Werder (1584–1657). See Table 6.11 for details.	1626, 1634

Table 6.12: (Continued)

Prudentius Aurelius Clemens (348–after 405), Roman Christian poet	Michael Schneider (1612–1639). His translation titled *Lobgesang deß, den Weisen aus Morgenland durch den Wunder Stern geoffenbarten newen Königes* is noted *AA* 1204.	1636
François de Rosset (?–?), *Histoires des amans volages de ce temps*.	Johann Friedrich Schweser (?–?). His translation is noted *AA* 1209, *Histoires des amans volages de ce temps. Das ist Geschichte von den wanckelmühtigen Liebhabern zu dieser zeit* (1638).	1638
Sallust, Gaius Crispus (86–34 B.C.), Roman historian	Wilhelm von Kalchum (1584–1640).	before 1640
Pona, Francesco (1530–1615)	Johann Helwig (1609–1674), *Lieb–und Helden–Gedicht*, *AA* 1183.	1648
Sallust, Gaius Crispus (86–34B.C.), Roman historian	Balthasar Kindermann (1636–1706), *AA* 1182, 1193.	1662

of examples in the poetics—were rather pious verse, and amongst the list of authors in the fourth treatise, he took the trouble to name several contemporary hymnists and edifying writers (Table 6.13). He also made frequent reference to Luther's translation of the Bible: Neuhaus (1991: 146–47) has documented his references to the Bible in the list of rootwords (see 4.4.4, note 19); there are others in the grammar, too (e.g. *AA* 237, 272, 274, 282). Schottelius also cited Luther's letter on translation (*AA* 1229, cf. 5.3), Luther's views on the unparalleled expressiveness of German (*AA* 60, cf. 2.3.1), and a treatise on proper names attributed to Luther (cf. 4.4.1), leaving no doubt as to his Protestant allegiance.

6.4 A SPECIAL RELATIONSHIP: SCHOTTELIUS AND GEORG-PHILIPP HARSDÖRFFER

Schottelius's interaction with Georg Philipp Harsdörffer was a model of the symbiotic, mutually beneficial co-operation to which the FG aspired and which it made possible: the collaboration of individuals with complementary talents towards the common goal of *Spracharbeit*. Both Schottelius and Harsdörffer published philological works; both published poetry and poetical treatises. But while Schottelius theorized, Harsdörffer was chiefly a practitioner and popularizer, on the one hand relying on Schottelius's theory, on the other hand making it accessible to a wider audience (just as

Table 6.13: Contemporary Christian writings noted by Schottelius in the fourth treatise, listed by date of publication

1653	Grundmann, Martin (1619–1696): Schottelius referred *AA* 1208 to his *Deliciae Historiae* (1653), anecdotes and legends for Christian edification.
1654	Vintzelberg, Joachim von (d. 1680): FG member, priest and hymnist, whose collection of German hymns (1654) Schottelius mentioned *AA* 1202.
1661	Röser, Jacob Nicolaus (fl. 1661): Schottelius mentioned Röser's *Epistolographia emblematica: Das ist Abhandlung der sonntäglichen und Fest-Episteln durchs gantze Jahr* (1661), *AA* 1204.
1662	Wider, Philipp Ehrenreich (= Philippus Ericus Widerus) (fl. 1662): Schottelius cited Wider's *Evangelische Sinn-Bilder* or 'Evangelical emblems' [...] (1662), *AA* 1196.
mid-17th century	Lassenius, Johannes (1636–1692): Schottelius mentioned a number of books by this German devotional poet and writer, *AA* 1204.
mid-17th century	Gesenius, Justus (1601–1673): German theologian and hymn-writer noted *AA* 1179.

he did for the mathematician Daniel Schwenter (1585–1636) in his *Mathematische und Physische Erquickstunden* (1651; cf. Hundt 2000). The mutualism between Schottelius and Harsdörffer has been noted by Zeller (1974: 163, n. 345), Moulin-Fankhänel (1997a: 316), and Hundt (2000: 43, n. 53), but the precise details of the reciprocal influences have not been studied. There is no scope for comprehensive discussion here either, but Harsdörffer gave references to Schottelius's grammar in many of the language games of his *FrauenzimmerGesprächsspiele* (Harsdörffer 1644–1649, henceforth *FZG*; Zeller 1974: 163)—his language games could pique the interest of readers in a feature of German, and they could then follow up their interest in Schottelius's work. Harsdörffer was also responsible for encouraging the use of the grammar in schools in Nuremberg (cf. 5.3). Meanwhile Harsdörffer often appears to be the inspiration behind the linguistic playfulness in Schottelius's work (Hundt 2006), and the frequent references to *disq.* in Schottelius's grammar point to the individual *disquisitiones* of Harsdörffer's own 1646 *Specimen Philologiae Germanicae*.[11]

The reciprocity of their relationship is most apparent in Schottelius's poetics. For instance, Schottelius drew on Harsdörffer's *Poetischer Trichter* (published in three parts, 1648–1653) for his account of the 'paragram' or number rhyme (*AA* 990), and an example composed by Harsdörffer in honour of Schottelius also appeared at the front of the *AA* (cf. 1.5.2). After giving an example of a paragram, Schottelius referred the reader to Harsdörffer's 167th *Spiel* in the *FZG* for more detail. Furthermore, Schottelius's careful

---

[11] Schottelius's grammatical war also included plentiful references to that of Harsdörffer (Fonsén 2006, 2007).

distinction between two types of riddle—the *Rätselreim* and the *Wortgriflein* (a more narrowly linguistic riddle)—picked up on the text-type of the *Wortgriflein* demonstrated by Harsdörffer in his *FZG* (III 326; cf. Zeller 1974: 22), and the echo rhyme described by Schottelius (*AA* 946–48) was in turn the subject of one of Harsdörffer's games (*FZG*, nr. 55; cf. Zeller 1974: 10). Schottelius likewise illustrated the *doppelgängige* rhyme ('double rhyme', with the rhyme scheme AAB) using a poem composed by himself to Harsdörffer (*AA* 958, where the first line begins *Mein Freund* 'my friend'). Both he and Harsdörffer explored anagrams as a way of revealing a hidden meaning of a name (*AA* 971; for examples in the *FZG* cf. Zeller 1974: 12–14). Schottelius praised Harsdörffer's *Poetischer Trichter* and recommended the third part of it to readers who wanted an account of *Dichtkunst* (i.e the rhetorical side of poetry, the *inventio* and *dispositio* of one's subject) in addition to *Verskunst*, the technical side of poetry, to which Schottelius had deliberately restricted himself in his own poetics (*AA* 995). Schottelius's poetics was in turn prefaced by a recommendation by Harsdörffer (*AA* 794–98).

Schottelius and Harsdörffer also evidently shared ideas about the need for a dictionary of German. Harsdörffer's plan of work (presented to the FG in 1648; cf. 7.5) was submitted before Schottelius had published his own outline of how a dictionary should be structured, in the tenth oration added in 1651. However, it is likely that Schottelius's outline was nearly complete as early as 1641, for at the end of the ninth oration, Schottelius had written that the tenth, which was to deal amongst other things *de modo & methodo conficiendi Lexicon in lingua Patria* ('about a manner and method of constructing a lexicon in the mother-tongue', Schottelius 1641: 172), could not be included there because of its length. Harsdörffer's plan—though dealing more with the practicalities—clearly drew on that of Schottelius (or on conversations or correspondence with Schottelius about it, something about which the ongoing FG correspondence project may be able to tell us in due course: Conermann 1992–2006). The shared origin is superficially obvious, for instance, in the fact that both outlines include sample entries for the rootword *brech–* (compare *AA* 161 and Krause 1895 [1973]: 390–92).

In addition to his many popularizing efforts in the German language, Harsdörffer also produced a *Specimen Philologiae Germanicae* 'Specimen of German Philology' (1646). Hundt (2000: 56–57) follows Blume (1972) in believing that Harsdörffer deliberately tacked the *Specimen* on to a long poem in honour of Duke August of Braunschweig (the *Porticus virtutis*), to ensure that it would receive the necessary approval for printing from the head of the FG, Prince Ludwig. Indeed, the *Specimen*, which was in Latin, and which adopted the Schottelian, analogist viewpoint about language, was otherwise likely to meet with strong criticism from Prince Ludwig and Gueintz. (It did in any case, in particular the section on spelling: cf. Krause 1855 [1973]: 356–72). The *Specimen* consisted of twelve 'disquisitions' (referred to in the following by I–XII) and, though not slavishly following

Schottelius's orations,[12] it covered much of the same ground. For example, Harsdörffer discussed the origin of the term *Teutsch* and the language's descent from Hebrew, brought to Europe by Ascenas (II), the antiquity of German, with Old High German examples (III), the wide reach of *Teutsch* across Europe (IV), the origin of German letters (VI), and German poetics (IX). Schottelius added references to the *Specimen* when his own *Sprachkunst* was reprinted in 1651 (cf. Moulin-Fankhänel 1997a: 316), but Harsdörffer's more profound debt to the Schottelian concept of language is most evident in his seventh and tenth disquisitions. In the seventh, on the capacity for word-formation (seen as parallel to that in Hebrew), Harsdörffer explicitly agreed with Schottelius on the centrality of the monosyllabic rootword, identical with the second person singular imperative of the verb. In the tenth, he presented the two principles on which orthography could rest: *ratio* and authority, siding ultimately with Schottelius in preferring *ratio*, i.e. analogy.

With his *Specimen*, Harsdörffer managed to get these theoretical reflections on German to an international audience. In Denmark at least, the grammarian Peder Syv first encountered Schottelius's ideas as mediated by Harsdörffer. The reception of Schottelius's work by Syv and others in Germany and beyond is the subject of the next chapter.

---

[12] For example, Harsdörffer took the view that Hebrew was the oldest language, and spent much time therefore trying to establish the relationships between Hebrew and German, to which Schottelius paid little attention.

THE LEGACY OF THE *AUSFÜHRLICHE ARBEIT* IN GERMANY AND IN EUROPE

7.1. Introduction

'One of the fathers of German studies' (Berns 1976: 9)

'The impact of Schottelius remained slight' (Fricke 1933: 122)

'an indispensable grammatatical compendium for over 80 years' (Cherubim 1996: 840)

Assessments of Schottelius's impact on the course of linguistic studies in Europe vary greatly. Berns (1976: 9), perhaps the scholar most familiar with the whole of Schottelius's oeuvre, called him one of the fathers of German studies, and, as noted at the start of this book, the Wolfenbüttel tourist authority calls him *the* father of German grammar. Yet Padley (1985: 307) considered that such claims 'can be readily dismissed', and Fricke (1933: 122) had already called Schottelius's influence 'slight' (*gering*). There are good reasons for these rather contrasting assessments. Fricke and Padley both emphasized that Schottelius marked the end of an era, rather than the start of a new one.[1] He was one of the very last European scholars dealing with questions of language origin and history who remained hamstrung by the need to integrate any explanation with the accounts arrived at by biblical exegesis. By the time Schottelius published his *AA* in 1663, new philosophical currents were emerging elsewhere in Europe that were already influencing studies of language and which would come to dominate the eighteenth century: the rationalim of Descartes, the empiricism and sensual realism of Francis Bacon (1561–1626) and Thomas Hobbes (1588–1679) (Padley 1976: 132–45). In England, Wallis's grammar (1653) already reflected the new stream of empiricism in the importance Wallis attributed to the real sounds of language. In France, meanwhile, the Port-Royal *Grammaire générale et raisonnée* (1660) of Lancelot & Arnauld was avowedly rationalist, viewing language as the expression of a mental reality.

---

[1] Fricke (1933: 122) wrote, 'The rapidly developing current of rationalism did away with the medieval language myth just as thoroughly as with the baroque treatment of language'. Despite the comment by Padley cited here, it should be noted that Padley gave more credit to Schottelius elsewhere, calling him 'epoch-making', and ushering in a new sense of the language (Padley 1985: 259, 1988: 315)—see section 7.4.2 and 7.6 below.

Schottelius too held a 'rationalist' view of language, in one sense, for he stood in the same tradition of Latinate rationalism that also influenced the Port-Royal grammarians. But while the latter assumed that a universal *ratio* underlay the way the human mind formulated and expressed propositions in language, Schottelius conceived of *ratio* as common to all languages in their own right. In practice, however, Schottelius's concern was really only with German and with how to cultivate it such that the inherent *ratio*—expressed in *analogia*—could best be restored. In the history of linguistic thought, it was the truly universalist current that won out. Beginning in Germany with Gottfried Leibniz (1646–1715), although the philosopher was also clearly influenced by Schottelius (cf. 7.3.5 below), it came to dominate the latter seventeenth and the eighteenth centuries. Linguistic chauvinists like Schottelius had nothing to contribute to such discussions, even though their linguistic purism continued strongly into the eighteenth century in Germany—albeit with changing motivations— alongside these new currents, and their purist endeavours served as the model for purists elsewhere in Europe (Thomas 1991: 197).

In another seventeenth-century development, empiricist approaches began to cast doubt on the reliability of mere words for ascertaining metaphysical truth. Projects for artificial universal languages replaced attempts to restore an original, natural language, for the imperfections of natural languages (such as homonymy or synonymy) now seemed obvious. Exponents in the German-speaking world of artificial language schemes were already publishing their efforts even as Schottelius was completing his *AA*: Johann Joachim Becher and Athanasius Kircher published their schemes in 1661 and 1663 (Strasser 1988: 155–95; see pp. 192–94 on the probably mutual influences between these two), and the most elaborate universal language scheme, the *Essay Towards a Real Character* of Bishop John Wilkins (1614–1672), appeared just five years later, in 1668 (cf. Lewis 2007). Schottelius shared with such projects the typically seventeenth-century belief in the importance of a perfect correspondence between reality and words, a correspondence without which words are hopelessly unreliable as a means to discern truth. But Schottelius merely used this requirement to argue for the superiority of German over other natural languages. German, with its infinite capacity for creating transparent compounds, with which to label the world, came closest to the ideal correspondence (cf. 2.3).

As observed at the outset of this book, Schottelius's *AA* appears in this narrative as a mere branchline in the history of (universalist) linguistic reflection in Europe. Yet Schottelius did take important steps forward in grammatical theory, which were long-lived and which spread around Europe, especially the Germanic-speaking parts. Following on from Vossius (1635), Schottelius was at the cutting edge of linguistic theory in his reflections on analogy and anomaly and in applying them rigorously to a vernacular language. His development of the notion of the rootword and the analysis of processes of word-formation that it made possible were new not just in German linguistic theory, but in European linguistic theory as a whole. If this has not been fully acknowledged to date, it is because Schottelius took the further, highly significant step of making not Latin, but his vernacular the language for which a linguistic theory must by default account. He has therefore been considered first and foremost in the German grammatical tradition. But that does not make his view of language relevant only to German, as later grammarians around Europe realized. Grammarians of Danish, Dutch, Swedish and Russian all incorporated Schottelian insights (analogy *vs* anomaly; the rootword; word-formation) into their studies of their vernaculars. To that extent, even without regard to Schottelius's incremental contribution to the development of home-grown German grammatical studies, Schottelius's impact was important and lasting. It has just been rather hidden in the studies of the separate vernacular traditions.

Thanks to a number of studies produced over the last twenty years years or so, however, we are now far better placed to assess the impact of Schottelius on linguistic ideas and linguistic practice internationally and at home (Schaars 1988, Subirats-Rüggeberg 1994, Schneider 1995, Takada 1998, Hundt 2000, Huterer 2001, Haapamäki 2002). This chapter assesses the reception and influence of Schottelius's ideas from the following perspectives:

> 7.2 Cultural patriotism: the popularization of interest and pride in German
> 7.3 Language history
> 7.4 Conceptualizing language (7.4.5 Excursus: Leibniz and Schottelius)
> 7.5 Lexicography
> 7.6 Subsequent grammars of German
> 7.7 Pedagogical grammars for foreign learners
> 7.8 Grammatography in other languages[2]

Schottelius's influence on language use, and his contribution to the standardization of the German language, will be assessed in Chapter 8.

7.2 Cultural patriotism: the popularization of interest in and pride in German

After the publication of his *AA* in 1663, Schottelius produced two further works on language which aimed to reach a wider lay audience in Germany than could be expected of the scholarly *AA*. His 1676 *Kurtze und gründliche Anleitung Zu der RechtSchreibung Und zu der Wortforschung In der*

---

[2] Parts of 7.3 and 7.8 appeared in McLelland (2010).

Teutschen Sprache. Für die Jugend in den Schulen [...] was an abridged
version of the *AA* for use in schools, as the title indicated. His *Horrendum
bellum grammaticale* (1673) was an application of the genre of the
grammatical war to German. The grammatical war had developed initially
as a genre for school-children, to help them learn irregularities in Latin.
Harsdörffer evidently considered the genre suitable for adults too: he
included his own short 'grammatical war' (the first version of the genre in
German) in his conversation books (Harsdörffer 1644–1649; cf. 2.4 above),
and when Schottelius followed Harsdörffer's example, his *Schrecklicher
Sprachkrieg* included plentiful cross-references to his *AA* (Fonsén 2006,
2007). However, the effects of Schottelius's own efforts to disseminate his
ideas amongst a wider lay audience were outstripped by those of Harsdörffer.
Although Harsdörffer had died in 1658, before the *AA* itself was even
published, his efforts to disseminate Schottelius's ideas from the first
publication of his grammar (1641) onwards were very important, as Hundt
(2000) has demonstrated in detail (cf. also 6.4). It was Harsdörffer too who
saw to the introduction of the grammar in schools in his area (cf. the letter
from Harsdörffer in Krause (1855 [1973]: 333). Still within FG circles, Georg
Neumark's (1621–1681) *Neu-Sprossender Teutscher Palmbaum* (1668), a
detailed description of the FG, cited Schottelius prominently in the opening
pages of its introduction (he corresponded with Schottelius; Berns 1978: 96),
and served to popularize his ideas for current and later generations too. We
know that the writer Jean Paul (1763–1825) made notes on Neumark's work
in 1803; his notes include a reference he found in Neumark to Stevin's tally of
rootwords, information of clearly Schottelian provenance (Martin 2000: 47).
In 1817 the Berlin German Language Association (*Berliner Gesellschaft für
deutsche Sprache*) made producing an updated version of Schottelius's *AA*
the subject of a prize, and the *AA* remained esteemed in the nineteenth
century as part of the nationalistic philological movement (cf. Raumer 1870:
72ff.). A century later, Hugo von Hofmannsthal (1874–1929) significantly
began his anthology of older texts about the German language, *Wert und
Ehre deutscher Sprache* (1927: 15–34), with a set of extracts from Schottelius
(including *AA* 99, 6: 55–56 on the richness of the language thanks to its
rootwords). As one of the leading voices of cultural patriotism, then,
Schottelius's contribution was still giving pause for thought more than 250
years after his *AA* was published.

7.3. LANGUAGE HISTORY

7.3.1 *The origin of German and the origin of language*

Before Schottelius, speculations on the origin and history of German and
of other languages could be found scattered throughout works published

across a wide range of disciplines (history, law, editions of older texts), as well as in more narrowly language-focused works such as those by Bibliander (1548) and Gessner (1555) (cf. Rössing-Hager 1985; Jones 2001). But Schottelius's discussion of the history of German was the most thorough and coherent treatment of the question to date, and he referred to all the leading late humanist writers on the subject, as well as to many contemporaries. As already outlined in earlier parts of this book, he dealt with the age and origin of German and its relationship to other languages, and reproduced Gessner's samples of Germanic languages, in the shape of excerpts from the Lord's Prayer to show their obvious similarity to German (*AA* 130–31, 8: 10). He rehearsed the commonplace explanations of the time for language change: the passage of time, the mixing of peoples, and neglect by the language's speakers (*AA* 166, 10: 20; cf. 2.2.4). He compared Old High German words with contemporary forms to highlight the continuity in the language despite changes, and he presented the first periodization of German language history into five eras. Fifty years later that periodization was largely adopted by Reimmann (1709) (Jones 2001: 1110; cf. also Sonderegger 1998: 430), while Johann Georg von Eckhart (Eccardus, 1664–1730) drew on many of the sources brought together by Schottelius, for his history of the etymological study of German (Eckhart 1711). However, Schottelius's potential to influence later scholars of language history was limited by the fact that he—amongst the very last generation of scholars to do so—still attempted to answer the big questions about language origin within the framework of the explanations provided by biblical exegesis. As a contemporary of the Dublin bishop and scholar James Ussher (1581–1656), whose famous reckoning of the age of the earth since creation was published in 1650, Schottelius still considered it reasonable to count, as the German humanist historian Aventinus had done, how many years separated the foundation of the 'German kingdom' from the beginning of the world (*AA* 136–37, 9: 2), and to expect to be able to trace the history of German from its presumed origins in the confusion of tongues at the Tower of Babel, whence it was brought to Europe by Noah's descendants. Despite the apparent mass of data assembled from various sources in the orations, his argumentation was still logic-based rather than data-driven, trying to use rational arguments to decide between competing explanations (Rössing-Hager 1985: 1582). In this regard, Schottelius stood at the very end of a late-humanist tradition, soon to become irrelevant.

If discussion about the origin of language came to be framed quite differently after Schottelius, one of his crucial tenets did survive into this new discussion: the notion of original monosyllabic words. Although the idea had not begun with Schottelius, it seems most probable that it was his influential grammar (rather than Goropius Becanus, Stevin or the earlier humanist sources for the idea discussed in 3.8.2) that was responsible for the longevity of this idea in the thinking of German scholars on the origin of language. According to Rousseau (1984: 303), Leibniz followed Schottelius in his assumption that the imperative singular of the verb was the original root form, even once the question of language origin was viewed as arising through social need rather than divine gift.[3] Both Leibniz and Johann Christoph Adelung (1732–1806) in turn inspired continued reflections on original monosyllabic roots by other writers. Adelung (1781/1782; here 1782: 227) used the terms inherited from Schottelius, but refined the concepts. Schottelius had written of *Wurtzelen oder Stammwörter* as synonyms (e.g. *AA* 5, 1: 11), but Adelung now distinguished carefully between primitive *Wurzelwörter* (the first monosyllabic words, of interest for the origins of language), and *Stammwörter* (monosyllabic words from which others are derived (*abstammen*), of relevance when looking at word-formation). As we have seen, Schottelius had argued that monosyllabic rootwords were in natural accord with our rapid thoughts (2.3.2), and had found in the monosyllables with which children begin to speak further support for the idea that natural, original words (Adelung's *Wurzelwörter*) are monosyllabic (*AA* 61, 4: 32). Adelung (1781/1782, specifically 1782: 193–194, 200) advanced a distinctly similar argument, which Samuel Friedrich Günther Wahl (1760–1834) in turn adopted in his Arabic grammar (Wahl 1789: 128), following Adelung's wording. Like Adelung, Wahl took the view that *jedes nackte Wurzelwort war ursprünglich einsilbig*, consisting of *zwei oder drei Hauptlauten mit einem Hülfslaut*, because *in dem Naturmensch seine ganze Vorstellung mit Einer Oeffnung des Mundes hervordrängte* ('each rootword was originally monosyllabic', consisting of 'two or three main sounds [i.e. consonants] with an auxiliary sound [i.e. vowel], because 'in the natural human, his whole conception pressed forth in one opening of the mouth'). The arguments in Adelung, adopted by Wahl, relied on the same assumption as that made by Schottelius: that individuals gaining language (for Adelung and Wahl now the primordial

---

[3] Schulenburg (1973: 40–48) discussed Leibniz's concept of the root, but I have not been able to ascertain where (and whether) Leibniz made an explicit claim about original monosyllabic rootwords, although something like that is implicit in his remark quoted by Schulenburg (1973: 6, n. 24) from Hannover MS IV, 470 (a folder of loose papers on language), *Je crois effectivement que les particules et particulierement les interjections, c'est a dire les sons articules et rudes, que les hommes ont commence a pousser a la vue, ou a l'occasion de certains objects sont les elemens de langues* 'I believe in effect that the particles and especially the interjections, that is to say the articulate and crude sounds that men began to produce, either at the sight of or on the occasion of certain objects, are the elements of language'. On the other hand, MS IV, 470, lists on folio 2 both *Anglo saxonica Monosyllaba ex Graecis detruncata* and *Cimbrica monosyllaba ex Olai Wormii lexico Runico & alij* [illegible]. Leibniz is clearly interested in monosyllables, but the mention of Anglo-Saxon monosyllables *detruncata* 'shortened' from Greek suggests that he did not view them as necessarily original. I am grateful to John Considine for supplying me with these references.

Naturmensch, rather than children as for Schottelius) make simple sounds, and that these are the natural basis of language.[4] In the nineteenth century, Wilhelm von Humboldt (1767–1835) drew on recent European scholarship of the Sanskrit and Semitic languages, but likewise still took the view that monosyllables were the original forms of words (Humboldt 1836 in Humboldt 1903–36, vol. VII: 260–62). For Humboldt, the typically disyllabic roots of the Semitic languages must have emerged from an earlier monosyllabic stage; only in a second stage of linguistic development, he believed, did the recognition of a need for grammatical specification lead to the addition of a second syllable for the purposes of inflection (cf. Rousseau 1984: 300, 320).[5] All this suggests that the idea of the original monosyllabic rootword was a widespread assumption. It is all the more striking, then, that Herder (1772), arguing against Johann Peter Süßmilch (1707–1787), had already daringly rejected the idea of the monosyllabic root, instead arguing that *bi*syllabic roots are closer to the original babbling of the human race in its infancy. (See McLelland 2010: 14–15).

7.3.2 *Historical linguistic methodology*

Despite his soon to be outdated beliefs, Schottelius made a modest lasting contribution to the *methodology* of studying language history in Europe. Following Metcalf (1974; see also Metcalf 1953a), we can say that Schottelius—together with other contemporaries like Mylius (1563–1637), Schrieckius, De Laet, Stiernhielm and Jäger—belonged to a group of scholars who, between them, contributed three key tenets which would ultimately contribute to the comparative method in philology. These insights were:

1. An acceptance of the idea of a parent language which yielded the major languages of Europe. For Schottelius, this was the language he called *Die alte Celtische od[er] alte Teutsche Sprache*, the 'ancient Celtic or Geman language' (*AA* 154, 10: table) (cf. Figure 2.1 in 2.2.). The teleological labelling made German appear the natural successor to and continuation of the parent language, but Schottelius considered this language to be the parent not just of Germanic but also, possibly at least, of Latin (*AA* 40, 3: 34) and of those languages derived from Latin.
2. The application to German(ic) of the recognition that languages could divide into dialects which could in turn become distinct languages.

---

[4] Adelung (1806), however, reverted to a post-diluvian account of language origin—a very late throw back to this view.
[5] Wahl and Humboldt—though speculating here on the origin of language—did so in the context of examining the nature of the root in the Semitic languages. The importance of Schottelius's insistence on the monosyllabic root for developments in the study of the Semitic languages is discussed below, 7.8.5.

Schottelius divided the parent 'ancient Celtic or Geman language' into the *abstimmige* ('deviating')—the English, Scottish, Swedish, and Dutch languages, for instance—and *Zustimmige* ('conforming'), under which were grouped High and Low German and their respective dialects.

3. Some minimum standards for determining the status and direction of borrowings. Metcalf (1974: 246) emphasized the significance of Schottelius's recognition of the typically German(ic) word-structure of a stem (rootword) with derivational and inflectional endings. Schottelius (*AA* 43, 3: 43) believed (like Mylius) that the endings were so varied as to be useless in etymologizing. Nineteenth-century philologists would admittedly come to a quite different conclusion,[6] but at least Schottelius's emphasis on the root as a basis for comparison furnished an etymological principle. It was following this principle that Schottelius rejected the possibility that *Königen* could be derived from the superficially similar κυνηγεῖν ('to hunt') for the bare root form of the word (in this case *König*, 'king', rather than the inflected *Königen*) should form the basis of comparison (*AA* 54, 4: 9). Schottelius also called for caution in deducing kinship from superficial similarities in words, since some similarities were bound to arise by coincidence (*AA* 142–43, 9: 13–17).

7.3.3 *Understanding linguistic change in German*

As for Schottelius's contribution to knowledge of linguistic change in German, we noted in 7.3.1 how he compared words from Old High German texts with their modern equivalents to show how they have changed (without recognizing any systematic processes at work) (cf. 2.2.4). It is also worth recalling his recognition of the division of German into High and Low German dialects, not new in itself, and his correct assertion that in the correspondence of Low German *t* with High German *s*, the *t* is the original form (*AA* 157, 690; Watts 2001; Francis 2003).

Of greater consequence, Schottelius's analysis of word-formation and its application to German word-histories laid useful groundwork for successors studying German etymologies (Jones 2001). In producing his inventory of German rootwords, he conjectured for instance that the word *Vernunft* ('reason') was composed of the recognizable *Vorwort* 'prefix' *ver–* and a postulated rootword *–nunft*. Such reflections as these on word formation and their implications for etymology are all carefully noted by

---

[6] For August Schlegel (1767–1845) and those who followed him, isolated word-stems were not enough: rather, comparative grammar, which examined the internal structure of languages, would provide insights into the kinships among languages. For discussion of this within the wider question of the organic metaphors used to describe language, see Haas (1956–57).

Johannes Clauberg (1622–1665) in his *Ars etymologica Teutonum e Philosophiae fontibus derivata*, published in 1663 (but drawing already on Schottelius 1641, 1651), where Clauberg discussed the specific case of *Vernunft* too. Clauberg even went beyond Schottelius, using analogical patterns recognizable in whole series of words to justify many of his individual etymologies (even if there is no shortage of wild conjecture in Clauberg too). The successor to Clauberg's *Ars etymologica* was Vorst's *Observationum in linguam vernaculam specimen,* many of whose etymologies are still considered valid today (Vorst 1669 [or 1668; cf. Jellinek 1913: 195 n.1]). A quarter of a century later, Johann Augustin Egenolff's *Historie der Teutschen Sprache* (1716–20) was the first single work devoted to the history of the German language and where etymology was recognized as a branch of study requiring its own methods. In it, Egenolff adopted Schottelius's atomistic view of the language, according to which the elements, rootwords, were combined together to produce new units. Egenolff went a step further, to regard the meaning of such compounds strictly as the sum of the meanings of their components (Rössing-Hager 1985: 1595). Egenolff also inherited the Schottelian view that monosyllabic rootwords are closer to the origin of language than are more complex units, as well as adopting his reasons for language change and his criteria for determining the age of a language (particularly the assumption that a language with more monosyllabic rootwords will be older than others with fewer such words). But already in Egenolff (1716) the biblically based explanations of language origin found in Schottelius were superseded, as Egenolff appealed now to Descartes for the underpinning of his (essentially still Schottelian) view of language as composed of small parts.

7.4 Conceptualizing language

7.4.1 *Linguistic rationalism*

As we have seen, Padley (1985: 224–31) placed Schottelius at the 'beginnings of the universalist approach' because of his distinction, following Vossius (1635), between natural grammar—common to all languages—and artificial grammar, peculiar to individual idioms (cf. 5.3). However, we must not overstate Schottelius's apparent adherence to universal grammar, nor confuse his 'rationalism'—that of Sanctius, Scaliger and Vossius—with the new mentalist, Cartesian rationalist universalism of the Port-Royal grammar, nor with other programmatically universal grammars of the seventeenth and eighteenth centuries (including Ratke 1619 and Helwig 1619 in Germany; see Ising 1959, Kaltz 1978). Schottelius's observation on the distinction between natural and artificial grammar was an addition made only in 1663 (perhaps, one might even speculate, in dim awareness of developments in France, though I have no evidence for this), and it stood isolated in his work. It is, therefore, rather a daring stretch to place him at the start of universalist language reflections of the later seventeenth and eighteenth centuries, as Padley implied. (One might equally place him at the end of universalist leanings with roots in medieval speculative grammar).

Rössing-Hager (1985: 1583) highlighted the close relationship that Schottelius saw between language and thought, and the fact that he saw the primary function of language in the communication of thought. Schottelius did indeed remark, *Dieses ist eine recht künstliche Eigenschaft der Sprache | daß sie den Inhalt des Gedächtnisses austrükke* ('This is a right artful feature of language, that it expresses the content of the memory [which Rössing-Hager perhaps takes in a wider sense: 'mind']', *AA* 61, 4: 32), and in his discussion of proverbs, he called speech (*Rede*) the *höchstkünstliche Erklärerin der Vernunft,* the *Dolmetscher* of *die Menschliche Vernunft,* and *eine Abbildung unser selbst* ('the most artful explainer of reason', 'the interpreter of human reason', and 'a representation of ourselves' *AA* 1103). Language as an expression of human reason differentiates us from the animals, then, but Schottelius did not develop this connection between speech and reason in the mentalist way of the Port-Royal grammar. The latter was concerned with language as the statement of mental propositions. Schottelius's belief that language expressed thought, on the other hand, was limited to the concern with *individual words*; and German monosyllabic rootwords were particularly well-suited to their task as vehicles of thought (*AA* 61, 4: 32). This feature, far from being common to all (or even to many) languages, marked German out as particularly excellent in comparison to others. We cannot, therefore, trace a line of continuity here between Schottelius's limited remarks on language as the expression of thought, and the views of his successor at Wolfenbüttel, Leibniz. Leibniz certainly drew on Schottelius in other ways, though, including in the importance he attributed to words as the essence of language, as we shall see in 7.4.5.

7.4.2 *Hypostasization of the language and the 'spirit' of the language*

More lasting in its reach was the aspect of Schottelius's language conception that was, in a way, the very reverse of universalism: his idealized and 'hypostasized' view of 'the' German language as having substance, a *unique* essence, unchanging across time and space (Padley 1985: 228; Gardt 1994; cf. 2.2). That view is evident for instance in Schottelius's table of related languages in the tenth oration (*AA* 154; Figure 2.1), where the Germanic languages deviating from the *alte Teutsche Sprache* are still viewed as *Teutsch* in *Ankunft, Grund und Wesen* ('origin, foundation and essence'). Schottelius was not the very first to talk in such terms about German, but the hypostasization of the language's 'essence' found in his *AA* its first and most emphatic expression in the German vernacular, and Gardt (1994) rightly treats this as a key feature of Schottelius's patriotic language conception.[7] (Schottelius repeatedly emphasized the peculiar essence or spirit of German as compared with that of other languages (further evidence that he was at heart far from a language universalist). He conceived of a *Sprachgeist* (without yet using that compound term), of the *in jeder Sprache sich findende[n] Geist* (*AA* 94, 6: 39 'the spirit found in every language'), bringing to life the language *durch dessen eigenen Odem* ('with its own breath'). A few paragraphs later (*AA* 100, 6: 57), Schottelius drew attention to the 'great difference' between the *Geist[e] Eigenschaft und Vermögen der Teutschen Sprache* ('the spirit, characteristic and capacity of the German language') and those of French, Latin and other languages in their capacity to use compounding to express ideas succinctly. The spirit of the language is also adduced *AA* 167, 10: 21, as well as in the Latin summary of the first oration, *AA* 2, 1: 32, where Schottelius refers to the *linguae [...] geniu[s]*). Schlaps (2000), tracing the notion of a German 'language spirit' in its various and changing guises from the time of Schottelius, via the likes of Johann Andreas Fabricius (1696–1769), Humboldt (whose view is already evident in the title give to his 1822 fragment *Ueber den Nationalcharakter der Sprachen* 'on the national character of languages'), to Jacob Grimm (1785–1863), has demonstrated that just what content filled the concept of *Sprachgeist* varied from writer to writer and over time (whether the spirit of the language be viewed in grammatical, stylistic, semantic, organological or nationalist terms). It would not, therefore, be helpful to suggest that Schottelius directly 'influenced' later writers, simply because they used similar terms to talk about German and other languages. It is, however, fair to say that Schottelius was an early, emphatic, and widely known exponent of this particular discourse style for talking about language and languages, and their relationship to peoples, nations and identity.

7.4.3 *Correct language* (Sprachrichtigkeit)

One aspect of Schottelius's view of language had a directly observable influence on the normative discourse about a standard German language in the eighteenth century (on which still see Josten 1976). Schottelius clearly laid out the claims of competing criteria—language-internal analogy *vs* established usage—for determining correct language. The question of what counted as established usage Schottelius settled to his satisfaction as being that of the written authorities, of *vieler gelahrten Männer* 'of many learned men' (*AA* 16, 2: 2), rejecting the customary pronunciation of any one area

---

[7]   Likewise already Padley (1988: 315).

in Germany as a guide. But the same question was raised again and again over the succeeding decades. Fabricius (in Christian Friedrich Weichmann's (1698–1770) *Poesie der Nieder-Sachsen* II (1723), cited in Jellinek 1913: 214) asserted that what counted as usage must be: 1. that of a. learned and b. unlearned people of every level (*Stand*) of society; 2. frequent; and 3. used in writing and in speech. Schottelius would have accepted 1.a, but for the rest he would have been spinning in his grave. Johann Friedrich Christ (1700–1756) reiterated instead in 1746 the Schottelian view that correct language was that found in good books and used by learned men, wherever in Germany they lived (see Jellinek 1913: 224). This last detail—'wherever in Germany'—is significant, for with it Christ rejected the claim made for East Central German, more specifically for *Meißnisch*, to serve as the model of correct usage. Johann Christoph Gottsched (1700–1766) tried to reconcile both positions. A *Sprachkunst* was according to Gottsched a guide to speaking and writing *nach der besten Mundart* 'according to the best dialect/ variety' (§1 of the introduction, Gottsched 1748, cited Jellinek 1913: 235). In his syntax Gottsched cited the *angenehm[e] Mundart* 'pleasant dialect/ variety' spoken in Dresden, especially at court, but he also hedged his bets by commenting *Es ist keine Landschaft, die recht rein hochdeutsch redet: die Uebereinstimmung der Gelehrten aus den besten Landschaften, und die Beobachtungen der Sprachforscher müssen auch in Betrachtung gezogen werden* 'there is no region that speaks pure correct High German; the agreement of learned men from the best regions and the observations of language researchers must also be taken into account' (note cited by Jellinek 1913: 235). Adelung (1774–1776), on the other hand, was unbending in his adherence to *Meißnisch* as the model, and so gave greater credence to usage than to analogy, in effect now reversing the weighting of the two criteria arrived at by Schottelius. For our purposes here it is sufficient to note that although different writers came to different conclusions, they all, in effect, merely shuffled the criteria Schottelius had developed, prioritizing them differently (Kilian 2000: 843). It was Schottelius who set out the foundation on which the normative debate of the eighteenth century could be carried out.

7.4.4 *Discourse strategies for talking about language: metaphor*

Looking at the shadow cast by the hypostasization of the German language and by the notion of a language's *spirit* in Schottelius and others of his era (7.4.2) highlights the importance of cognitive metaphors, of images that are not mere rhetorical adornment, but the very tools that we rely on for conceptualizing an idea. Schottelius deployed a wide range of cognitive metaphors to talk about language that were then—and many of which still remain today—commonplaces in cultural-patriotic and/or more narrowly puristic discourse (cf. 3.5.2). The most important of his metaphors is the language tree, a prime example of a cognitive metaphor, for it truly underpins Schottelius's entire theoretical conception of the German language. We can see this in the passage (already cited 2.4.1, but reproduced here for convenience), where the inflectional and derivational endings are introduced as the aerial shoots alongside the main roots in the language, conceived of as a banyan or Indian fig-tree:

> Gleich wie aber unsere Teutsche Letteren und die Teutsche Stammwörter einsilbig / festes Grundes / reines Ursprunges / und eines lieblichen Geläutes sind: Also sind gleicher weise an diesem Sprachbaume die ausgewachsene Rieser und NebensPröslein / die durch und durch in dem gantzen Baume von oben bis unten nebenwachsen / nebenstehen / und durch solchen jhren Neben = oder Beystand / eine absonderliche schöne Gestalt und Wirkung / dem / dabey sie stehen / geben / einsilbig oder einlautend. Solche Neben = Spröslein oder Neben = wörter sind entweder in Teutscher Sprache die zufälligen Endungen / als: e / em / en / es / et / er / ern / est / ete / etest / etet / ere / erer / erest / erster / erstes / erstem / ersten / este / ester / estes / estem / esten / [...]

> [§]7. Oder aber es sind die Hauptendungen der abgeleiteten: daheraus in der Teutschen Sprache entstehet die Ableitung. An der Zahl sind solcher Haubtendungen drey und zwanzig / als: Bar / e / ey / el / er / en / haft / heit / icht / ig / inn / isch / keit / lich / ling / lein / niß / sal / sam / schaft / tuhm / ung

'Just as our German letters and the German rootwords are monosyllabic, of a firm foundation, of pure origin and of a charming sound, so in the same way on this language tree are the grown twigs and sideshoots, which grow alongside in the whole tree, through and through, from above to below, standing alongside, and which, by this their standing or support alongside, give a particular, beautiful form and effect to that which they support, monosyllabic. Such off-shoots or affix-words are in German either the inflectional endings, namely e / em / en / es / et / er / ern / est / ete / etest / etet / ere / erer / erest / erster / erstes / erstem / ersten / este / ester / estes / estem / esten /. [...]

[§]7. Or they are the main endings of the derived [words]: out of these derivation arises in German. Such main endings are twenty-three in number, as Bar / e / ey / el / er / en / haft / heit / icht / ig / inn / isch / keit / lich / ling / lein / niß / sal / sam / schaft / tuhm / ung.'

(*AA* 68–69, 5: 6–7)

This analogy and its underlying metaphor were very deliberately adopted by some of Schottelius's successors. Stieler (1691) made the image of the language tree even more explicit to the reader than had Schottelius, in the engraving on the title page of his dictionary (see Figure 2.3), and Becher (1668) also employed the evidently familiar and influential image of the language tree in his German grammar. The parallels are so close that the influence from Schottelius is beyond doubt, but Becher nevertheless adapted the image to express his own rather different theoretical framework, a 'three-connection' model of the grammar of words:

> [...] gleich wie ein Baum vnden nur einfach ist/ oben sich in etliche stärckere Aest außtheilet/ welche sich zu End in vnzehlig viel Reyser/ Zweig und Blätter außbreiten/ welche doch alle von den Haupt-Aesten vnd dise ins gesambt/ von dem Baum ernehrt werden/ [...] also ist es auch mit den Wörtern beschaffen/ die sich in der primâ connexione derivationis wie der Baum/ in der secundâ connexione significationis gleich den grösseren Aesten/ nun aber in diser tertia connexione praedicationis gleich den Blättern/ Zweigen vnd übrigen Aestlein verhalten/ aber doch alle von dem Stamm/ nemblich à primâ connexione primitivorum & derivatorum jhre Vnderhaltung haben/

> 'Just as a tree is only simple [unitary] at its base, but above splits up into several strongish boughs, which at their end spread out into countless twigs, branches and leaves, but which are all fed from the main boughs, and these in turn are all fed from the tree, [...] so it is too with words. In the first connection, that of derivation, they are like the tree. In the second connection, that of meaning, they are like the larger boughs, and in the third connection, that of predication, like the leaves, branches and remaining small boughs.'

(Becher 1668:104–105, cited in Subirats-Rüggeberg 1994:320).

For Becher, the tree stood not for the language as a whole, but for the grammar of words. The trunk stood for the derivatives and compounds linked to their roots by the 'first connection' of derivation. The larger boughs stood for the multiple paradigmatic, semantic relations between words, while the still more numerous twigs and leaves stood for the infinite, ever-renewable ways in which words could be combined in syntagms to make statements about the world. Arguably Becher's use of the image is a little forced. The progression from less to more numerous types of connections—from trunk to leaves and twigs—makes sense, but it is less clear why each of the three connections should depend on its previous one, as do the leaves, boughs, trunk and roots.

If the tree was the most characteristically Schottelian image, other metaphors abound in his *AA*, many of them commonplaces in German puristic discourse of the period.[8] One such familiar cultural-patriotic metaphor for language used by Schottelius was that of language as currency (cf. Jones 1999: 98–99), an image with a pedigree stretching back to Quintilian and Horace at least: *Daher* Horatius *spricht / daß die Wörter einer Landgültigen Müntze gleich weren / darin nicht so sehr ihr Schrot und Korn / als ob sie gäng und gebe weren / zubeobachten* 'And so Horace says that the words are like a coin of currency, whose value lies not so much in its weight and alloy, but in whether it is in common use' (*AA* 8, 1: 23). This last image in particular took on a new lease of life in eighteenth-century philosophy (Gray 1996). Indeed, one of that next generation of scholars who made the image his own was Schottelius's successor in Wolfenbüttel,[9] Leibniz, in his *Unvorgreiffliche Gedanken betreffend die Ausübung und Verbesserung der Teutschen Sprache* (written around 1697 and published in 1717). It has often been noted that Leibniz's *Unvorgreiffliche Gedanken* shared many assumptions and concerns with Schottelius, and the work was once held to be by Schottelius himself (cf. Schulenburg 1973: 124–25). Yet the misattribution by Schmarsow (1877) is still surprising, for there are also immediately striking differences in both style and substance between Schottelius and this work of Leibniz.[10] The similarities illustrate Schottelius's legacy to the eighteenth-century linguistic reflection in Germany. The differences, meanwhile—the ways in which recognizably Schottelian preoccupations are passed over by Leibniz, or are re-shaped in the light of new influences—illustrate the limits of his legacy. For these reasons, it is worth dwelling on this essay by Leibniz for a moment.

7.4.5 *Excursus: Schottelius and Leibniz*

Leibniz's *Unvorgreiffliche Gedanken betreffend die Ausübung und Verbesserung der Teutschen Sprache* is one of the quarter or so of his works that Leibniz wrote in German. (The remainder were written in Latin and French). It is not possible here to offer a thorough interpretation of the *Unvorgreiffliche*

---

[8] As we saw in 3.5.2, examples include the notion of the foreign yoke under which German is enslaved (*AA* 110, 7: 13; 167, 10: 21), purity *vs* contamination or pollution (e.g. *AA* 21, 2: 23), impoverishment (e.g. *AA* 166, 10: 21), language anthropomorphized as a vulnerable female (queen, pure maiden, whore, *AA* 137–38, 9: 6), and foreign borrowings as bastard offspring (*AA* 5, 1: 11) or ragged clothing (*AA* 49, 3: 59). For discussions of such imagery in seventeenth- and eighteenth-century purist and cultural–patriotic discourse, see Jones (1999: 59–84) and Stukenbrock (2005: 80–106, 171–201). Jones (1995) is an anthology of such texts.

[9] Leibniz arrived to join the employ of the Duke in late 1676, shortly after Schottelius's death in the October of that year.

[10] Schmarsow was misled by the fact that the manuscript copy with which he was working bore the name *Dr. Schottel* on its cover (Schulenburg 1973: 124.)

Gedanken, and certainly not an overview of Leibniz's philosophy of language.[11] My purpose is rather to show the extent to which Leibniz both drew on and moved away theoretically from Schottelius, and so to exemplify both the overlap and transition from the end of Schottelius's era of linguistic reflection to the start of a new one.[12] Leibniz's cultural-patriotic concern for the cultivation of the German language, his moderate purism, and the terms in which he couched these, are very reminiscent of Schottelius, as the selected examples in the Table 7.1 below show. (It would be easy to multiply them, though it should be noted that they could also be found in numerous other cultural-patriotic writings of the period).

Leibniz also echoed Schottelius's organic imagery of language as a tree, with rootwords and their off-shoots,[13] as in his outline of how to organize an etymological dictionary, both alphabetically and by its roots:

Table 7.1: Characteristic descriptions of the German language in Schottelius and Leibniz

	Schottelius	Leibniz
Glanz, Reichtum (splendour and richness)	*die Sprache [...] durch den Glantz jhrer Schönheit / und durch die Macht jhres Reichtuhms der Teutschen eiferige Liebe auch auf sich gernest wenden wolte AA* 110, 7: 13	*der Teutschen Sprache Reichtum, Reinigkeit und Glantz* (§56) *herrliche[r] Glantz* (§29)
uhralte Hauptsprache (ancient cardinal-language)	*passim*, including: *AA* 32, 3: 9 *diese uhralte Hauptsprache der Teutschen AA* 110, 7: 13: *in dieser uhralten Hauptsprache AA* 40–41, 3: 35 *diese so mächtige und vollkommene Hauptsprache AA* 145, 9: 20	*Teutsch[e] uhralt[e] Sprache* (§46) *unser ansehnliche Haupt-Sprache* (§11) *unsere Haupt- und Helden-Sprache* (§21)
rein (pure)	*unsere angeborne / vollkommene / reine / wortreichste Muttersprache AA* 167, 10: 21	*die reine Teutsche Sprache* (§11)

[11] Leibniz wrote about twenty items relating directly or indirectly to language (Schulenburg 1973: 309–11); cf. Waterman (1974), Mueller (1985). For recent discussion of Leibniz's language conception see Leweling (2005: 45–82).

[12] Citations from Leibniz are according to the digital version of his *Unvorgreiffliche Gedanken* prepared by Thomas Gloning (http://www.uni–giessen.de/gloning/tx/lbnz–ug.htm), which in turn follows the standard edition by Pietsch (1908). See also Kürschner (1986) for a comparison of Schottelius and Leibniz.

[13] Leibniz knew too of Stieler's dictionary with its title page featuring the banyan tree (1691), writing on 6/16 August 1694 to Hiob Ludolf that *Stileri dictionarium quaedam habet non contemnenda* 'Stieler's dictionary has certain things that are not to be despised' (Leibniz, *Sämtliche Schriften und Werke*, 1970ff., I, 10, 502). I am grateful to Bill Jones for this reference.

Und solte ich dafür halten, es würde zwar das Glossarium Etymologicum, oder der Sprach-Qvell nach den Buchstaben zu ordnen
seyn, es könte aber auch solches auf zweyerley Weise geschehen:
nach der ietzigen Aussprache, und nach dem Ursprung, wenn man
nemlich nach seinen Grund-Wurtzeln gehen, und ieder Wurtzel,
oder iedem Stamm seine Sprossen anfügen wolte

'And I would argue that the etymological glossary or language–
spring should be ordered by letter, but the ordering could also be
done in two ways: according to the current pronunciation, and
according to the origin, if one wanted to go by its basic–roots, and
add to each root or stem its offshoots.'

(Leibniz 1717: §78; Pietsch 1908: 348–49)

The image is also found, though with a slight shift in the metaphor, in §32,
where idioms are the fruits that grow on the *Grund und Boden*, the words of
the language (Pietsch 1908: 336):

Der Grund und Boden einer Sprache, so zu reden, sind die Worte,
darauff die Redens–Arten gleichsam als Früchte herfür wachsen

'The foundation and ground of a language, so to speak, are the
words, on which the idioms grow forth like fruits'

Leibniz also used some of the same examples that Schottelius had drawn
on to demonstrate the richness of the language. Like Schottelius, Leibniz
commented on the particular richness of German in the specialist
languages of mining, hunting, shipping and the like (§9; Pietsch 1908:
330; cf. Schottelius *AA* 46, 3: 50; 100, 6: 58; 160, 10: 18), as well on the
legal decrees (*Reichsabschiede*) of the sixteenth century as instances of
good practice in the use of German (Leibniz 1717 §24; Pietsch 1908: 333;
cf. Schottelius *AA* 46, 3: 49, and 97, 6: 53). Leibniz's moderate purism,
warning against becoming a language puritan who avoids foreign words
like mortal sins (§16), is in sympathy with that of Schottelius (with
similarities in the imagery too, such as that of the foreign yoke (Leibniz
1717 §21; Pietsch 1908: 333; cf. *AA* 110, 7: 13, and *AA* 166, 10: 21).

Leibniz's three-stage model for borrowing words from other languages
would also have found favour with Schottelius. According to Leibniz,
words from *Sprachen Teutschen Ursprungs* 'languages of German origin'
(§69; Pietsch 1908: 347) would be most readily adopted, especially Dutch,
being the closest in language and culture to German. Leibniz's second
preference was for words from English and Nordic, these being *etwas
mehr von uns entfernet* ('somewhat more distant from us', §70; Pietsch
1908: 347) than Dutch. Third and finally, words might be borrowed from
Latin, French, Italian, and Spanish, but here caution needs to be

exercised about *ob und wie weit* 'whether and to what extent' such borrowings are advisable, to avoid a foreign *Mischmasch* (§73; Pietsch 1908: 347).

New in Leibniz by contrast with Schottelius, though, and indicative of the growing preoccupation with language as a suitable vehicle for constructing thought, is Leibniz's concern that because many do not understand the full import of the foreign words they use (*die Krafft der fremden Worte eine lange Zeit über nicht recht fassen*, §22; Pietsch 1908: 333), they will end up thinking badly (*übel dencken*). *Übel dencken* is to be understood here not in a moral sense (the kind of concern that Schottelius did express, e.g. *AA* 146–47, 9: 26). Leibniz the philosopher worried rather that words poorly used could lead to confused thinking, and so away from metaphysical truth. Like Schottelius, Leibniz saw words as the very basis (*Grund und Boden*) of language, but Schottelius had every confidence that original German words, at least, accorded with the reality of things. Leibniz, in contrast, shared the key rationalist insight that linguistic signs stand not for things, but for the mental concepts of things (*Gedanken*).

This difference is evident in Leibniz's development of the currency metaphor that Schottelius had cited from Horace (*Ars Poetica*, 70–72; *AA* 8, 1: 23), according to which words were like coins whose value lay not in themselves, but in whether or not they were recognized as currency. The influence of the Port-Royal grammar on Leibniz is clear here. He adopted the same currency metaphor, but applied it to the function of language to represent thoughts. Token money does not physically hold, but merely *represents* its actual value. In the same way, Leibniz tells us, we rely on words as *Rechen-Pfennige* ('counting-coins', Pietsch 1908: 329, §7), as second-order signs of things that save us the effort of having to conceptualize each thing every time it occurs. We can content ourselves both *in äußerlichen Reden* and *in den Gedancken und innerlichen Selbst-Gespräch* 'in external speech' and 'in the thoughts and internal conversation with oneself' with 'replacing the thing with the word' (§5; Pietsch 1908: 238; cf. Gray 1996). Leibniz's preoccupation with words and with good writing and speaking appears similar to that of Schottelius, but his ultimate goal is in fact quite different, that of determining metaphysical truth through thinking with language.

Another aspect of Leibniz's interest in words did clearly follow in Schottelius's footsteps: his interest in the lexicography of German, common to many at the turn of the eighteenth century (cf. 7.5 below). But again we can discern in Leibniz's treatment of the topic significant developments away from his Wolfenbüttel predecessor. Leibniz called not merely for one dictionary of German (Stieler's had in fact already appeared in 1691), but for three, based on the model he had encountered in France (§33; Pietsch 1908: 337). The first dictionary, a *Lexicon* or *Sprachbrauch* ('language usage'), should contain only everyday words (cf. the views of Kramer, discussed in 7.5); the second, a *Sprach-Schatz* ('language treasury'), should list technical terms; but the third, a *Glossarium* or *Sprachquell* ('language spring') should include archaic and regional words that are of use 'for investigating the origin' of the language. The origin of the language, then, was no longer to be investigated by means of weighing up arguments, built up over centuries and still painstakingly rehearsed by Schottelius and his generation, about whether Hebrew or German was logically the oldest or the original language (though Leibniz did still believe German to be closer to the beginning than many others (§50; Pietsch 1908: 341). *Ursprung* did not mean to Leibniz finding an original or post-Babel biblical language, but merely—without further elucidation—the *Ursprung der Europäischen Völcker und Sprachen* (§46; Pietsch 1908: 340), the *Ursprung und Brunquell des Europäischen Wesens* (§48; Pietsch 1908: 341) ('the origin of the European peoples and languages', 'the origin and well-spring of the European essence'). Leibniz thus broke completely with the humanist inheritance that Schottelius had waded through—or rather, for Leibniz, it is simply as if it had never been. We can rightly talk here of a paradigm shift.[14] Leibniz did not dispute, however, that many of the other European languages contained many words whose origin was *guten Theils* 'to a large extent' German (§42; Pietsch 1908: 339). Hence his assertion that the origin sought is that of the *European* peoples and languages (or European 'essence'). The means of determining these origins was by etymologizing, as Clauberg did (praised by Leibniz, §50; Pietsch 1908: 341), and of which Leibniz gave an example in his *Unvorgreiffliche Gedanken* (§49; Pietsch 1908: 341). The purpose of the search was now also quite different. It was no longer patriotic, but metaphysical, to show that *Die Wort nicht eben so willkührlich oder von ohngefehr herfürkommen*, that the origin of words is not as random as some would think, for everything in the world has sufficient cause, if we can only discover it—a fundamental Leibnizian principle.

In sum, Leibniz shared many of Schottelius's phrasings and metaphors, and employed them to praise German and to exhort his readers to its careful cultivation. But both the task of language itself—to express thoughts clearly—and the aim of investigators of language—to identify a sufficient cause and origin of European language and culture—were now those of a new intellectual generation.

---

[14] Robins (1998: 202) observed that Lebiniz was cautious about publicly shaking 'established religious positions'. Here, though, in refraining from rehearsing or even alluding to any of the arguments about language origin that were still so relevant to Schottelius, Leibniz's essay betrays the change in perspective.

7.5 LEXICOGRAPHY

Schottelius never produced a dictionary, but he was a lexicographer in intent at least, laying down plans for a dictionary organized by rootwords. His lists of rootwords in the *AA* were intended as a model (cf. 4.4.4), and the tenth oration offered sample entries for *brech–* and *lauff–* ('break' and 'run') (*AA* 161–65, 10: 18).[15] Ratke had already proposed that in a lexicon the *vrsprungliche[n] word* ('original words') should be listed alphabetically, and under each *alle seine entsprungene* 'all its derivatives' should follow, and then the *zusamen gesetzten* 'compounds' (Ratke, after 1630 [Ising 1959]: 308). Schottelius's principles according to which a German dictionary should be structured (set out in his tenth oration, first printed in the 1651 edition; *AA* 159–61, 10: 18) elaborated on the general idea laid out by Ratke:

1. All rootwords should be listed, with an explanation in Latin, French, and Greek.

2. The gender, genitive case and plural of each [noun] rootword should be given.

3. For each rootword, the derivations formed from it should be listed and explained.

4. Compounds should be listed under their *Grund*-word (i.e. according to their head-morpheme).

5. Point 4 should particularly be borne in mind when dealing with the *Vorwörter*—which encompassed for Schottelius prepositions, prefixes, even some adverbs (*hinaus*) and adjectives (e.g. *voll*)—for these yield a great many more words than in Greek or Latin.

6. For every verb rootword, it should be noted whether the verb is regular or irregular, and the forms should be given for the first and second person present, the imperfect and the past participle.

7. In order that the meaning of the words be correctly explained *aus dem Grund* 'from its foundation', German authors' works should be read, as evidence of correct usage.

8. Specialist vocabulary (mining, trades, milling, shipping, fisheries, hunting, printing, botany, philosophy, the arts, the sciences 'and other faculties') should be included, and be explained appropriately. So too should sayings and proverbs be included as demonstrations of how each word can be used with *allerhand Blumen der Redekunst* ('all the flowers of rhetoric') (*AA* 160, 10: 18).

---

[15] Cf. also Harsdörffer's sample entry for *brech–* in Krause 1855 [1973]: 390–91; see 6.4.

As noted in 3.4, Harsdörffer had submitted a similar outline to the FG in 1648, but Schottelius's plan, though not printed till 1651, probably predates it. Harsdörffer had also included a concrete plan for actually getting the dictionary done, proposing that members of the FG could each be responsible for the rootwords for one letter of the alphabet. The plan came to nothing, but a decade or so after Schottelius's death, Kaspar Stieler produced what Schottelius had been aiming for: a combined grammar and dictionary of German (1691). The dictionary contained some 60000 entries, six times more than Schottelius's list (cf. Schneider 1995: 111–16). A member of the FG, Stieler was probably in close personal contact with Schottelius before the latter's death (cf. Ising 1968: IX). Stieler wrote in the dedication of his completed dictionary that he had above all to thank [the library at] Wolfenbüttel and *dem wackern Suchenden* 'the valiant seeker', i.e. Schottelius, for his achievement, and the tree of his frontispiece is clearly the Indian fig-tree or banyan tree that Schottelius used in his *AA* to describe German. In Stieler's dictionary, the *Stammwörter* were listed alphabetically, and for each *Stammwort*, the associated compounds and derivates (the *Fortwachs* or 'further growth' of the programmatic title) were also listed, as Stieler's entry for *Baum* ('tree'), substantially abridged in Figure 7.1, shows (Stieler 1691: col.113–17):

Baum / der / pl. die Beume / *arbor, arbos*. Baum *etiam quod dicitur quodvis lignum aedificationi aptum.* […] Beume pflanzen / *arbustare, arbores serere* […] Der Baum trägt ein Jahr ums ander / *arbor alternat fructus.*

Fachbaum […]

Obstbeume […]

Wilde Beume […]

Beumlein / das. *dim. arbuscula* […]

Beumen […]

Faulbaumen […]

Kürbaumen […]

Baumlechtig [*sic*, NMcL] & beumechtig […]

Baumelen […]

Baumelung […]

Figure 7.1: Sample entry for *Baum*, abridged from Stieler (1691: col. 113–117)

As can be seen, Stieler gave the gender and plural of nouns, but seldom the genitive, despite Schottelius's stipulation in the *AA*. For irregular verbs, the principal parts were given; for adjectives the comparative and superlative were also often given. Examples of usage in phrases and sayings were listed too. Stieler also took the injunction to list derivates and compounds seriously, so much so that some of those he listed were rare, or indeed were not attested anywhere else at all but were *potentielle Wortbildungen* 'potential word-formations' (Wiegand 1998: 655). Matthias Kramer criticized the inclusion of such 'potential' words in the preface to his Italian–German dictionary of 1700 (Kramer 1700–02; cited by Ising 1968: XI; see also below),[16] but Stieler apparently accepted with Schottelius that the principles of compounding and derivation in the language permitted one to form by analogy words that were in accord with the *Grund* of the language, even where usage had yet to discover them.

Stieler was Schottelius's lexicographical successor within the FG, but he was nevertheless not the first to produce a German dictionary arranged by rootword.[17] Becher's *Methodi Becherianae Didacticae Praxis, Ejusdemque Liber*, (1669) contained two Latin–German glossaries: one alphabetical, the other grouped by rootword. But it was the polyglot language teacher Matthias Kramer (1640–1729) who first implemented the idea of a full rootword dictionary, in *Das neue Dictionarum oder Wort-Buch, in Italiänisch-Teutscher und Teutsch-Italiänischer Sprach* (1676–1678; cf. Jones 2000: 459–62). The entries in Kramer's earlier German–Italian dictionary of 1672 (known as the *Allgemeiner Schau-Platz*) had been organized by part of speech; within the nouns section, there were further thematic sub-groupings (see Jones 2000: 458–59; and Jones 1991 for comparison of Kramer and Stieler). His second attempt at a dictionary for this language pair was instead arranged as Schottelius advocated: alphabetically by rootword, including basic grammatical information and examples of phrases and idioms. Symbols to mark specialized humorous, vulgar or poetic usages were Kramer's innovation, for as a practical and lively language teacher he was critical in his preface of those who had included in their dictionaries archaic or rare words, or words that nobody would use. Derivatives and compounds were grouped under the roots to which they were related. Not only was Kramer the first to produce a

---

[16] Kramer wrote in the preface to his 1700 dictionary that *ein anderer sonst trefflicher Lexikographus* 'an otherwise excellent lexicographer'—i.e. Stieler—had included derivates and compounds *die sich zwar nach den Gesetzen der teutschen Derivir- und Compinir-Kunst von einem Stammwort abstammen lassen, aber doch nie nirgend in gangbare Übung kommen seynd* 'that could be formed from a rootword according the rules of the German art of derivation and compounding, but that had never come into any circulation'. Kramer explicitly differentiated such unattested words from those *Poetische[n], Romantzische[n] hochfliegende[n] Derivatis und Compositis* 'poetic, literary high-flying derivates and compounds' that a writer could, of course, coin for poetic use. On the difficulty of judging today which words were indeed only *potentiell*, see Wiegand (1998: 655).

[17] For the following, see Schneider (1995), Subirats-Rüggeberg (1994), Stammerjohann (1996: 529–30); Wiegand (1998), Jones (2000: 458–472); Glück (2002: 441–447), Watts (2003). See also Ising (1956) on Stieler and Kramer.

dictionary along Schottelian lines for German, he also applied the same rootword principle to lexicography in other languages: Italian (in Kramer (1676–78; cf. also Kramer 1700–02), but also French and Dutch in his French–German and Dutch–German dictionaries (Kramer 1712, 1719).[18]

The ordering of derived and compound words by their rootword rather than strictly alphabetically soon proved unwieldy for the user. The *Teutsch–Lateinisches Wörterbuch* (1741) of Johann Leonhard Frisch (1666–1743; cf. Powitz 1959) had already started to combine the alphabetical order by rootword with a strict alphabetical listing (where the link to the supposed root was not obvious, or was doubtful). Nevertheless, the lasting influence of the rootword approach to lexicography is evident in the Middle High German dictionary published in the mid–nineteenth century by Wilhelm Müller (1812–1890) and Friedrich Zarncke (1825–1891) on the basis of preparatory work by Georg Frierich Benecke (1762–1844) (Benecke et al. 1854–1866). That dictionary was organized by rootword, so that under *singen*, we find *wolsingen, sincschule, besinge*, etc. It was used by generations of students and scholars and is only now being superseded by a project running since 1994 in Trier and Göttingen (cf. Gärtner & Grubmüller 2000). The disadvantages of the rootword lemmatization were still felt, though, and it was soon accompanied by an alphabetical index (Lexer 1872–1878).

7.6 Subsequent grammars of German

'All future developments in German grammatical theory take their starting part from him.' (Padley 1985: 231)

Das vollständigste Werck das in der Teutschen Sprache und Tich-tereykunst hervorgekommen / ist des Herrn Schottels seines / we[l]ches billig allen andern vorzuziehen / dann er sich beflissen / alle Stücke der Teutschen Sprachkunst vollenkömlich außzuführen / und da ers nicht gethan / solchen Entwurff vorzustellen / wornach es weiter ausgeübt werden könne

'The most complete work on the German language and poetics that has been produced is that of Mr Schottel, which is easily to be

---

[18] Kramer's dictionary did not follow Schottelius in one important respect, of course. Kramer preferred good usage to analogy, as his later objection to Stieler's unattested words would indicate, and Bill Jones (p.c.) points out that the title page of Kramer's 1678 (German–Italian) volume of his bilingual Italian–German dictionary stated that its contents were drawn *besonderlich [...] aus dem bewehrten Gebrauch vornehmer Leute / und wolgegründeter Ubung* 'especially from the well–tested usage of fine people and from well–founded practice'.

preferred to all others, for he has been diligent to detail all parts of German grammar in full and, where he has not done so, to present an outline according to which it can further be put into practice.'

(Morhof 1682: 457)

The reception of Schottelius in the grammatical tradition of Germany can be read in Jellinek (1913–14: 184–244), who gives a still useful chronological overview of grammarians 'from Schottelius to Gottsched' (thus his running header for that section of his book). More recent overviews can be found in Polenz (1994: 135–80) and Moulin-Fankhänel (2000). Already Jellinek's running header gives an indication of Schottelius's place in the grammatical tradition. His grammar of German was a milestone, and though not suitable for school use itself, it became a resource drawn on for about a century, until Gottsched (1748). Prasch (1687) called Schottelius's *AA* a *güldenes Buch* 'a golden book', but feared that most would not be able to understand it. The *AA* left room, therefore, for successors to produce grammars for use in German schools, now that formal instruction in German was well-established.

Pudor (1672) had already paid homage to Schottelius's guiding principle in his title (*Der Teutschen Sprache Grundrichtigkeit/ Und Zierlichkeit*; my emphasis). After Schottelius's death, the grammars of Morhof (1682), Bödiker (1690) and Stieler (1691) all stood very firmly in Schottelius's shadow, not only in the details of grammar but also in their broad principles, even if all also made various alterations of their own. Morhof devoted considerable space to the importance of monosyllabic rootwords, and referred the reader to Schottelius for detailed accounts of word-formation, syntax and rhyme-types, for example (Morhof 1682: 416, 474, 579). Both Bödiker and Stieler shared Schottelius's view that a grammar was an incomplete account of the language without—and indeed merely laid the foundation for—a dictionary. Stieler's grammar was published together with his dictionary (discussed above); Bödiker published sample entries for his planned dictionary in 1694. Stieler, Morhof and Bödiker's works in turn helped disseminate Schottelius's ideas, including abroad, as we shall see in 7.8. A grammar like Langjahr's (1697), which Jellinek (1913: 203) called *ganz unselbständig und unbedeutend* ('wholly derivative and insignificant') and which can rightly be considered a mere abridged version of Schottelius (cf. Kärna 2007), is evidence of the extent to which Schottelius represented the key reference for the mainstream in German grammar of the late seventeenth and early eighteenth centuries. Well into the eighteenth century, the *AA* was praised in detail in an anonymous contribution (Anon. 1734) to the *Beiträge Zur Critischen Historie der Deutschen Sprache, Poesie und Beredsamkeit*, a journal for German studies founded by Gottsched. The author of another anonymous essay of 1742 explicitly stated that the division of words into rootwords, derivates and compounds was so familiar that it would be otiose to go into it (Kaltz 2004: 33), and Gottsched (1748: 182–83), Aichinger (1754: 137, 157) and Adelung (1783: 36–37) all adopted it in their own grammars (Kaltz 2004: 33–35). An important step was taken when Adelung finally dropped the Graeco–Latin framework for describing word-formation altogether, *figura* and *species* (within which Schottelius had still nominally operated), relying now entirely on the Schottelian approach (Kaltz 2004: 34). The term *Wortbildung* 'word-formation' (as opposed to *Bildung der Wörter*) for this now autonomous aspect of grammar was coined by Fulda (1778: 28; cf. Kaltz 2004: 36.)

While Schottelius's innovative principles of word-formation entered the mainstream, succeeding generations of grammarians were meanwhile making incremental improvements in all areas of grammar. In the area of syntax, Stieler (1691) was the first grammarian to devote a chapter to word order, and the treatment of syntax in Steinbach (1724) became dominant until Aichinger (1754). In the area of word-formation, Bödiker (1690) recognized the need to allow for non-syllabic derivational elements, and also noted the possibility of derivation without addition (i.e. conversion, or derivation by a change to the stem vowel only). Longolius (1715) further improved on Schottelius's treatment of compounding, adding the possibility of noun + verb stem compounds (although these had been noted much earlier in the tradition of German grammars for foreign learners, by Kramer 1694; see 7.7). Longolius's quite different view of derivation—allowing for monosyllables to be derived from polysyllables (his criterion for derivation being semantic rather than morphological)—also challenged the centrality of the mono-syllabic rootword to the analysis of word-formation. Frisch's (1723) re-working of Bödiker (1690) likewise reduced the importance of the rootword. Where Bödiker had stated, true to Schottelius's view, in rule 48 of his etymology *In den Verbis ist der Imperativus das Stamm-Wort* 'in the verbs, the imperative is the rootword', Frisch now loosened this dogma in two ways, when he re-worded: *In den Verbis kan das Praesens oder der Imperativus als das Stammwort seyn, oder zur Formation dienen* 'In the verbs the present or the imperative can be the rootword, or serve for formation' (cited Jellinek 1913: 206). That is, for Frisch, the first-person present *or* the second person singular imperative could be viewed as the rootword (abandoning Schottelius's controversial insistence on the imperative as the root), and, furthermore, the rootword was reduced to the starting point for conjugation. The *Stammwort* was thus now a helpful pedagogical notion, but not a theoretical foundation to the grammar. Again, though, this is a development already anticipated in the German grammatical tradition for foreign learners, by Aedler (1680) (see 7.7 below).

Schottelius's system of declension and (especially) verb conjugation were also gradually superseded by better accounts, and Freyer (1722), a spelling book written for use by the Pietist educationalists based in Halle, was a model of clarity which surpassed Schottelius's principled approach to orthography by reducing his rules to four orthographical principles: *Pronuntiation, Derivation, Analogie* ('pronunciation, derivation, analogy') and *Usus scribendi* ('custom in writing'). Of these, Schottelius's analogy was the one least used by Freyer himself (Heinle 1982: 142–43).

By the third decade of the eighteenth century, then, Schottelius's grammar seems to have been out of date in spelling, declension and conjugation, syntax and word-formation. True, his *AA* was reprinted in 1737, but only, Jellinek plausibly suggested (1913: 228, n.1), because there was no other large grammar available, a gap which Gottsched then sought to fill with his 1748 *Grundlegung der deutschen Sprachkunst*. That Gottsched's own grammar was itself far from perfect does not change the fact that—as Jellinek's heading indicates—it marked the end of the reign of Schottelius as the mainstream German grammatical reference point.

Nevertheless, even if Schottelius's grammar itself fell out of use, we have already seen that certain linguistic terms that he used became established after him, including *Sprachkunst, Mundart, Lautwort, Rechtschreibung, Geschlechtwort, Zahlwort* ('grammar, dialect, onomatopoeia, spelling, article, numeral').[19] In content too, much of his contribution to prescriptive German grammar persisted into the nineteenth century, as can be seen by taking the fifth edition of Johann Friedrich Heynatz's (1744–1809) grammar as a point of comparison (Heynatz 1803). The first version of the grammar had appeared in 1770, so Heynatz's work must have been in use for over thirty years, and its author was an experienced teacher himself. The work is thus a good example of a late eighteenth-century grammar in practical use (Ewald 2006: LXXXIII). It should also be noted that Heynatz is known for his allegiance to established usage, and that he gave only scant and belated recognition to the power of analogy as an arbiter of correct language (Ewald 2006: XIII, XXVI). It is telling indeed, then, that Schottelius's legacy is still very recognizable in Heynatz's work, both at the level of detail and on matters of principle. Although Heynatz divided punctuation marks into three groups (signs of division, differentiation, and omission), which Schottelius had not done, the list of marks is overall ordered very similarly to the list in Schottelius, which, it should be recalled, was by the far most detailed to date. The German terminology is also similar, and in several cases identical (cf. Table 7.2). As for matters of grammatical theory, Schottelius's legacy likewise survived into the nineteenth century intact. Heynatz's section on *Wortforschung oder Etymologie* began with a statement of the nature of German word-formation which still used both the terminology and the fundamental insights of Schottelius:

[19] See 5.7. Jagemann (1893) also credits Schottelius with coining *Nachdruck* (emphasis) and *zweideutig* ('ambiguous'), and suggests that the Dutch word *woordenboek* 'dictionary', which Jagemann could not find in the title of any dictionary before 1641, may also be owed to Schottelius (as a calque on *Wort-Buch*).

Table 7.2: Punctuation marks discussed in Schottelius (1663) and Heynatz (1803), in the order listed in those works

Schottelius (*AA* 667–668)	Heynatz (1803: 92–93)
/ Beystrichlein (Comma) ; Strichpünctlein (Semicolon); : Doppelpunct (Colon). . Punkt (Punctum)	**Abtheilungszeichen:** , / der Beistrich oder das Komma : die zwei Punkte oder das Kolon ; der Strichpunkt oder das Semikolon . der Punct oder das Punctum § das Zeichen des Absatzes oder Paragraphen
- *or* = Mittelstrichlein ' Hinderstrich (apostrophe)	**Unterscheidungszeichen** „ " das Anführungszeichen = or – das Zertheilungszeichen der Sylben = das Bindezeichen
? Fragzeichen (signum interrogationis) ! Verwunderungszeichen (signum admirationis) ( ) Einschluß (parenthesis)	( ) der Einschluß (Parenthesi) ? das Fragezeichen
= Theilzeichen (signum vocis divisae seu separatae)	! das Ausrufungszeichen **Auslassungszeichen** ' der Apostroph, der von einigen der Oberstrich, von anderen der Hinderstrich genannt wird das Zeichen einer abgebrochenen Rede

Ein jedes Deutsches Wort hat entweder von keinem andern Worte dieser Sprache seinen Ursprung, und heißt ein Stammwort (Primitivum); oder es kömmt von einem einzelnen andern Deutschen Worte her, und heißt ein Abgeleitetes (Deriuatum); oder endlich es ist dadurch entstanden, daß man zwei oder mehrere Wörter an einander gesetzt hat, und heißt ein Zusammengesetztes (Compositum).

'Every German word either has its origin from no other German word, and is called a *Stammwort* (*Primitivum*); or it comes from a single other German word, and is called an *Abgeleitetes* (*Deriuatum*); or finally it has come into being by putting two or more words next to one another, and is called a *Zusammengesetztes* (*Compositum*).'

(Heynatz 1803: 97)

Refinements had been made: Heynatz noted the possibility of compounds that were more than binary, calling them *Doppelzusammengesetztes* (*Decompositum*), for instance (Heynatz 1803: 97). Nevertheless, Schottelius's continued legacy is obvious.

In fact, as any student of German linguistics knows, Schottelius's account of word-formation remains current in 21st-century introductions to German morphology. Naumann (2000b: 42) makes the distinction in essentially the same terms as Schottelius and Heynatz:

> Für die Bildung deutscher Wörter [...] hat die Wortbildungs-forschung vor allem zwei Grundtypen erarbeitet, den Typ der Komposition oder Zusammensetzung ursprünglich voneinander abhängiger Wörter zu einem neuen Wort aus mindestens zwei Teilen und den Typ der Derivation oder Ableitung, d.h. Wortbildung mittels Affixen, also Präfixen, Infixen und Suffixen.

> 'For the formation of German words [...] word-formation research has primarily established two basic types, the type of compounding or *Zusammensetzung* of words originally independent of each other to form a new word made up of at least two parts, and the type of derivation or *Ableitung*, i.e. word-formation by means of affixes: prefixes, infixes and suffixes.'

Naumann goes on to distinguish a head (*Grundwort*) and modifier (*Bestimmungswort*) in determinative compounds. Despite the addition of new concepts (such as word-formation by conversion) and terminology (such as infixes), Schottelius's insight still forms the basis of modern German morphological theory.

7.7 Pedagogical grammars for foreign learners

Preceding sections have already noted that some of the changes made by later grammarians to Schottelius's tenets are evident earlier in the parallel tradition of foreign language grammars. It is to that tradition that we now turn, beginning with the works of Matthias Kramer. It was not just in his lexicographical work (cf. 7.5) that Kramer followed Schottelius. He also adopted and made important refinements to Schottelius's word-structure theory in his *I veri Fondamenti della Lingua Tedesca* (1694), a German grammar for Italians (Subirats-Rüggeberg 1994). Schottelius had provided a descriptive account of the German lexicon. For example, he described *–lich* as a derivational suffix found on adjectives and meaning *Eigenschaft/ Zugehör/ Besitzung/ Stand usw.* 'characteristics, attribute, property, state, etc.' (*AA* 364). Even where he talked the reader through an example of successive derivation, his focus remained on the semantics, rather than on generalizing the rules of the morphological process, as in the following:

> **Ungehorsamkeit** / alhie ist die Wurtzel oder das Stammwort / **hör**; **ge** / ist ein Vorwörtlein / daraus wird **gehör**: **sam** / aber die Haubten-dung verändert nicht den wesentlichen Verstand des Wortes **gehör** / sondern gibt jhm eine zufällige Eigenschaft **gehorsam** / welcher gerne

Gehör gibt / das ist / gehorsamet: **keit** / die andere Haubtendung in
Gehorsamkeit / enderet gleichfals durch jhren Hinterstand die we-
sentliche Deutung nicht / sondern veruhrsachet den Verstand eines
anderen Zufalles / nemlich der **Gehorsamkeit: un** / aber ist ein ver-
neinendes Vorwort / und also wird aus diesen fünf Wörteren / **Un
ge = hor = sam = keit.**

'*Ungehorsamkeit* [*Disobedience*] Here the root or trunk-word is *hör*
['hear']; *ge* is a little preposition [here: prefix]. Out of that *gehör* is
made. Now, the derivative ending *sam* does not change the essential
meaning of the word *gehör*, but gives it the contingent characteristic
gehorsam, 'who gladly hearkens', that is *gehorsamet* [obeys]. The
second derivative ending *keit*, placed at the end, also does not
change the essential sense, but causes the meaning to have another
contingency, namely *Gehorsamkeit* [obedience]. Now, *un* is a
negating prefix, and so out of these five words we get *Un–ge–hor–
sam–keit* [disobedience].'

(*AA* 91, 6: 35)[20]

In contrast, Kramer (1694: 246–47) did not just indicate the meaning of a
suffix such as *–lich*; he also specified syntactical constraints: that it could be
added to a substantive, adjective or verb, to yield an adjective or verb; and
he noted that a change must be made to the stem: *mà l' –a–| –o– ò –u– di
esso, si cangia in –ä–| –ö–| –ü–* 'but the *–a–| –o–* or *–u–* of this changes to–
ä–| –ö–| –ü–,' as in *Bruder* 'brother' > *brüderlich* 'brotherly'. That is,
Kramer spelled out the regularities of and constraints on the morphological
processes in far greater detail.

As for compounding, Subirats–Rüggeberg (1994) overstated somewhat
the difference between Kramer's typology and that of Schottelius. Out of
the eight groupings given by Kramer (1694: 277), only two do not
correspond to Schottelius's classification of the sixth oration of the *AA*.
Still, Kramer did add two important compound types not recognized by
Schottelius: 1. adding a verbal imperative (i.e. the verbal root, for
Schottelius) before a noun or adjective base, as in *Fecht–boden* 'fighting-
ground', and 2. the possibility of verbal (infinitival) nouns serving as base
words, to which a substantive is added as the first element, e.g. *Fisch–fangen*

---

[20] Note that Schottelius does not distinguish clearly between words and elements that cannot
stand alone in this account. Other examples that implicitly recognize the possibility of
successive derivation are:
   Treib / = ab = treiben / wieder = ab = treiben / un wieder = ab treiblich.
   Treffen / hintreffen / überhintreffen / dar über hin = treffen.
   Setzen / ersetzen / wiederersetzen / un = wieder er = setzlich.
   Denken / gedenken / eingedenk / wiedereingedenk / un = wieder = ein = gedenk
   (*AA* 90, 6: 34; and cf. 5.5.4).

'fish-catching' (Subirats-Rüggeberg 1994: 307). This possibility was not recognized within the German–for–native–speakers tradition until twenty years later, by Longolius (1715). Within the particles (Schottelius's *Vorwörter*, such as *aus, an, ur, er*), Kramer also distinguished those combining with a noun or adjective from those combining with a verb, something Schottelius and Stieler did not do.

Kramer also clarified a fuzzy point in Schottelius's theory, the relationship between derivation and compounding. Generally, Schottelius treated these as distinct, but at the same time, derivation was presented as a subcategory of *Verdoppelung* (*AA* 90–91, 6: 35), and words such as *Willigkeit* and *Mannschaft* 'willingness, team', clearly composed of a rootword with *derivational* suffixes, were treated under compounding (cf. 2.4.1). Kramer (1694: 239–42) more accurately described such words as double derivations: *Will + ig > Will–ig*, then *Will–ig + keit > Willigkeit*. Again, Kramer's innovation was to recognize explicitly the productive process by which such words were derived, in two steps. Kramer furthermore clarified the structure of compounds consisting of more than two roots, such as *Landfriedbruch* ('breach of the peace'; three roots) or *Erbmannstammgut* ('ancestral property'; four roots) (cf. Schottelius *AA* 399). Schottelius did not discuss their internal hierarchical structure, describing them simply as a succession of rootwords, but Kramer instead recognized them as binary compounds, of which one or both elements was already a compound, represented graphically by Kramer as follows (see Subirats-Rüggeberg 1994: 313).

Über-zug ⎱ Bett-über-zug
Bett   ⎰

Feuer-werck ⎱ Feuer-werck-zeug-meister
Zeug-meister⎰

Here too, then, while Schottelius analysed the make-up of compounds and derivatives, Kramer captured the morphological *process* and the hierarchical structure of compounding, and he was then able to apply his insights to the study of rootwords in other languages too. Despite Glück's assessment (2002: 441) that Kramer was not a particularly original grammarian, then, Kramer introduced important refinements to the theory inherited from Schottelius, and he applied them in practice to new languages. It is worth noting that Kramer's *Veri Fondamenti* was also published in Latin by the Jesuit Andreas Freyberger in 1733, and so Kramer's insights ultimately found their way back into the native German grammatical tradition, specifically into Catholic circles (cf. Jahreiß 1990).

Martin Aedler's practical grammar of German for English learners, the *High Dutch Minerva* (1680),[21] developed the notion of the rootword in a different way. Aedler, whom Van der Lubbe (2007: 185) calls a 'veritable *Stammwort*-enthusiast', used the terms *Radix* and *primitive* in English, and used the notion of the rootword (like Schottelius) as a guiding principle in his orthography. He also drew on it to explain intonation and the German rule of first–syllable stress on native words:

> Every true both High- and Low-dutch Radix has its tonick accent, (and that either soft when the syllable is long, or sharp when the syllable is short), in the first syllable, where it still remains both in derivativs [sic] and compounds' (Aedler 1680: 30, cf. also 34)

It was Aedler's innovation to use the twin notions of root and affix as a device permitting systematic comparison of German and English (Aedler 1680: 131–62). However, for all that he may have been a '*Stammwort*-enthusiast', Aedler was not a *Stammwort*–purist as Schottelius was. Against Schottelius's view that the root was the second-person imperative, Aedler preferred to present the root as the verb 'in the first person' (without specifying singular or plural, and without allowing for their endings –*e* or –*en*). In practice, Aedler described derivation from verbs as proceeding by removing –*en* from the infinitive, so that he was not actually operating even with his own definition of the root (Van der Lubbe 2007: 186).

Aedler categorized suffixes by the formal criterion of whether they are added to the noun, adjective or verb (as Kramer would do later). Of the 23 *Hauptendungen* (derivational endings) listed by Schottelius, Aedler did not include –*ei*, and he added several of his own that would not have qualified for Schottelius as endings, either because in Schottelius's view they were rootwords in their own right (–*los*, –*voll*, –*arm*, –*rei[c]h* '–less, –ful, –poor, –rich' (Van der Lubbe 2007: 186)[22] so that they should properly be treated under compounding, or because (even worse, to Schottelius) they were not monosyllabic, but were themselves already derived, and consisted of rootwords with a derivational ending added (–*haftig*, –*sühtig*, –*girig* 'containing __, seeking __, desiring __'). Aedler was not interested in the niceties of theoretical, principled distinction between rootwords and derivational endings, nor in the Schottelian dogma that such basic elements of the language must be monosyllabic. Aedler instead treated the rootword and affix as 'a teaching strategy', emphasizing the 'close relationship

---

[21] See Van der Lubbe (2007) for a full study, including Aedler's biographical details.

[22] *Los, –voll, –arm, –rei[c]h* would be considered by many linguists today to be suffixoids because of their productivity. Aedler also opted to treat comparative and superlative formation as derivation rather than inflection (as in Schottelius). In both cases, the difference between the two grammarians concerns an area of the language where linguists today still recognize an ambiguity. The spelling –*reih* is consistent with Aedler's spelling throughout, hence also *ih* for *ich* 'I', etc.

between German and English, which will allow the learner to apply principles of English word–building to German' (Van der Lubbe 2007: 188). He was concerned simply with presenting learners with productive affixes.

Aedler and Kramer both provide clear evidence of Schottelius's impact on the pedagogical grammars of German for foreign learners at the time. Aedler illustrates a watering down of Schottelius's theoretical tenets to pedagogical ends. Kramer, in contrast, represents a refinement of the theory.

7.8 Grammatography in other languages

Sprachverwante Nordenleute / rahmt den Kunstweg recht mit ein:

('Language-related Northern people, join us on the path of art.'; from the *Erklärung des Kupertitels;* cf. 1.5.3).

Schottelius certainly hoped for international recognition, so he would have been gratified to know that the influence of his grammatical theory is palpable in the early stages of the grammatical traditions of (at least) Danish, Swedish, Dutch and Russian: in the works of the Dane Peder Syv (1663, 1685), in Nils Tiällmann's *Grammatica Suecana* (1696), in the *Nederduitsche Spraekkunst* of Alfred Moonen (1706), and in the *Anweisung zur Erlernung der Slavonisch-Rußischen Sprache* (1705–1729) of Johann Werner Paus. Indirectly, he also had an influence on European descriptions of the Semitic languages.

7.8.1 *Danish grammar*

Peder Syv (Petrus Septimius, 1631–1702) is best known for his collection of Danish proverbs (Syv 1682, 1688), but he published his first philological work, *Nogle Betænkninger om det cimbriske Sprog* ('Some remarks on the Cimbrian language', 1663), in the same year as Schottelius's *Ausführliche Arbeit*, and also produced the first grammar of Danish written *in* Danish (*Den danske Sprogkunst eller Grammatica*, Syv 1685). He was awarded the title of 'Royal Philologist of the Danish Language' (*Philologus regius linguæ Danicæ*) in 1682.

In his 1663 work on 'Cimbrian' (i.e. the ancestral language of Danish and other Germanic languages), Syv did not yet cite Schottelius (though the latter's grammar would have been available in the earlier editions of 1641 and 1651), but he was already aware of the activities of the FG (Syv 1663 [1979]: 82, 124), and he referenced Harsdörffer's Latin *Specimen Philologiae Germanicae* (1646) directly (Syv 1663 [1979]: 88, 92, 106, 150).[23] In fact,

---

[23]   In the absence of a modern edition of Harsdörffer's *Specimen*, see Hundt (2000: 71–83) for a detailed description. Cf. also Blume (1972), Forster (1991).

Syv's work covered many of the same concerns as Harsdörffer's *Specimen Philologiae Germanicae* and so, indirectly, the concerns of Schottelius, for Harsdörffer in turn expressed many of the views first mooted in FG circles by Schottelius in his 1641 grammar: views on the relationship of languages amongst each other, the age of the ancestral language and its status alongside other languages, etc. (cf. 6.4). Because Syv also referenced Harsdörffer's source Becanus directly, it is difficult to be sure to what extent Syv's 1663 work was indebted to Harsdörffer and, through him, to Schottelius, but it is striking that Syv addressed the two key planks in Schottelius's language theory: the conflict between custom and regular analogy (Syv 1663 [1979]: 83, 107, 128), and the identification of monosyllabic rootwords with the second person singular imperative of the verb (Syv 1663 [1979]: 90, 92, 132–33). In both cases, Syv took a Schottelian view. Custom against reason was not acceptable (Syv 1663 [1979]: 83).[24] Rootwords were monosyllabic and, in the case of verbs, were identical with the second person imperative of the verb (Syv 1663 [1979]: 132).

In his grammar of 1685, Syv now mentioned Schottelius by name (Syv 1685 [1979]: 227, 235), in one case on the subject of a 'new' way of hyphenating which sought to respect the integrity of the rootword (Syv's example is *bliv–e* rather than the 'old' division of *bli–ve* 'to become'). Analogy (*lighed*) was also a guiding principle to Syv in his grammar. For example, borrowings from Latin should be spelt by analogy to native words: *Regel* like *Segel* 'rule, sail' (and not *Regul*) (Syv 1685 [1979]: 163–164). Similarly Syv dismissed spellings of genitives with *–is* rather that *–es*. 'Here analogy [*Lig-rigtighed*] applies, for many words end in *–e* in singular and plural [...], so the other words follow them in taking S or *–es*' (Syv 1685 [1979]: 235, my translation). Although, his grammar, which stands alongside Erik Pontoppidan's work (1616–1678) at the very beginning of the normative grammatical tradition in Denmark, was still very Latinizing in structure and content, Syv showed an awareness of some of the ideas of Schottelius in points of detail.

7.8.2 *Swedish grammar*

As the first grammarian of the vernacular in Danish, Peder Syv in turn served as a model for the grammar of the Swede Nils Tiällmann (1696), but Tiällmann had direct knowledge of Schottelius too. Haapamäki (2002: 54) calls Schottelius one of Tiällmann's 'foremost models' (*främsta förebilder*), even though Tiällmann only mentioned the 1641 edition of Schottelius's *Sprachkunst*, his 1643 *Der Teutschen Sprach Einleitung*, and his 1676

---

[24] Hovdhaugen (2000: 888) identifies Syv with 'a moderate application of Julius Scaliger's rule that one should write as one speaks'.

abridged version of the *AA* for use in schools, and so appears not to have had access to his 1663 work. (Tiällmann also made reference to other German grammars, such as Morhof's *Unterricht Von der Teutschen Sprache und Poesie* (1682), where he would also have encountered Schottelius's grammatical precepts). Tiällmann's preface discusses the question of usage vs. *ratio*, but he appears to rely largely on the Dutch scholar Perizonius, alias Jakob Voorbroek (1651–1715), who edited Sanctius's *Minerva* (1587), and through whom Tiällmann was exposed to the ideas of Sanctius, but also Scaliger and Vossius.[25] This is the same Latinate tradition as that which Schottelius drew on, but Tiällmann does not discuss Schottelius's views. However, Schottelius certainly contributed to his views on correct usage in the grammar proper. His statement of how to decide on the spelling of Swedish (Tiällmann 1696: 17) is a paraphrase of Schottelius, to whom he refers here: one should write *efter fornuften rigtighed og den rette brug* ('according to correct dictates of reason and correct usage', which one finds *i de gamle eller ny skrifter* ('in old and new writings'). Tiällmann also referred the reader to Schottelius (as well as to Georg Stiernhielm) on the subject of language change (Tiällmann 1696: 35), and admired the efforts of the FG in promoting their language, about which it seems he had read either in Peder Syv's work or in the *Historia orbis terrarum Geographica & Civilis* (1673) of Johann Christoph Becman (1641–1717).

Tiällmann also adopted the notion of the monosyllabic rootword. Haapamäki (2002: 55) suggests that the notion of the rootword was already a 'given' for Swedish language scholars of the Baroque. Georg Stiernhielm apparently encountered it in Becanus, and it is telling that Tiällmann also cited the relevant passage from Becanus (from his *Hermathena*, 1580), rather than taking Schottelius as his authority. However, Tiällmann listed irregular verbs by their root (Tiällmann 1696: 212–13), which he took like Syv to be the imperative. In this, the very point that was so controversial among Schottelius's German contemporaries, both Tiällmann and Syv's notion of the rootword seems to be specifically Schottelian. Another example of the influence of Schottelius is Tiällmann's criticism of spelling with 'unnecessary' letters (something of which Tiällmann considered German spelling to be particularly guilty: Haapamäki 2002: 54). Tiällmann also cited Schottelius in defence of hyphenation that kept the letters of the rootword distinct from the inflectional endings (cf. 5.5.3 and *AA* 195): *literae radicalae (monosyllaborum) böra åtskillias ifrån accidentalibus* ('the root-letters (of monosyllables) should be distinguished from the inflections', Tiällmann 1696: 191; again, cf. Syv), as in *vakt–a, agt–a* ('to keep watch, to be careful'). Finally, it is worth

---

[25] Rademaker (1992: 119) counted 179 references to Vossius in Perizonius's commentary of Sanctius's *Minerva*. Perizonius's commentary itself makes up about half of the pages of his edition of the *Minerva*.

noting that although Tiällmann elected to leave much of his grammatical terminology in Latin, some at least of the Swedish terms (*till–ord, medel–ord, tid–ord*) appear to be calqued on the German terms (*Zuwort, Mittelwort, Zeitwort* for 'adverb, participle, verb') which Schottelius did not himself coin but certainly helped to become established (cf. 5.7).

7.8.3 *Dutch grammar*

For Tiällmann, Schottelius was a clear influence, but not the dominant one. In contrast, Schottelius's *AA* provided the basis for much of a grammar by the Dutchman Arnold Moonen (1644–1711), the *Nederduitsche Spraek-kunst* (1706), which became one of the leading Dutch grammars for ninety-nine years (Schaars 1988: 369).[26] As Schaars has shown, there are frequent word-for-word translations of Schottelius in Moonen's grammatical definitions and explanations, as well as structural characteristics copied from Schottelius. So too some of Moonen's examples were merely translated from the German. For example, (near) word-for-word translations can be found in the explanation of the bi-partite division into *Woortgronding* and *Woortvoeging* 'etymology, syntax', itself a structural borrowing from Schottelius; in the division of letters into consonants and vowels, the division of long and short vowels, and the description of the consonants; in much of the discussion of the noun, including definition of case; in explanations of derivation and compounding; in discussion of the inflection of the verb; and in the definition of the conjunction. Just as Schottelius had borrowed wholesale from the Leiden scholar Stevin for his rootword theory, merely paraphrasing or translating Stevin's Dutch in German (cf. 6.2.3), now the Dutchman Moonen returned the compliment in his grammar.

If Schottelius aimed to produce a comprehensive theoretical grammar to rival that of Vossius's *De arte grammatica* (1635), then he would have been gratified that he and Vossius between them provided the theoretical underpinning for much of Moonen's work. For instance, the overall structure of Moonen's section on number followed Vossius, but it incorporated insights from Schottelius, as well as from the Trivium-grammars of Dutch (the *Twe–spraack* of 1584, Van Heule 1625 and 1633, Kók 1649 and Leupenius 1653). Similarly, the treatment of Dutch syntax combined the approach of Vossius with the structure of material following Schottelius. Moonen's close adherence to Schottelius also meant that he introduced some grammatical points to the Dutch grammatical tradition for the very first time. The circumlocution of the comparative and

---

[26] For the following, see Schaars (1988); Klijnsmit (1993) draws on Schaars for his discussion of Moonen and Schottelius.

superlative with *meer* and *meest* and the first thorough discussion of the article are two examples.

Although Moonen did not care to list rootwords exhaustively in the way that Schottelius had done, he nevertheless accepted their centrality to the grammatical analysis of the language. For instance, just like Tiällmann (1696), Moonen's starting-point for the inflection of the verb was the rootword, which he also took like Schottelius to be the second person imperative (e.g. *hoor!* 'listen!'). The rootword was also central to Moonen's discussion of spelling, and this is perhaps the most interesting part of the grammar to compare with Schottelius. For Moonen adopted Schottelius's principles, but came in part to different conclusions for Dutch from those that Schottelius had arrived at for German. Schaars (1988) identified the following two principles invoked by Moonen to adjudicate between competing spelling variants:

1. the *oirsprongkelykheit* [sic] principle, or the 'originality principle', which relates to keeping the original rootword intact: *Stam- of Wortelwoorden, die nootwendigh altyt geheel en ongbrooken blyven* ('stem- or rootwords, which necessarily always remain whole and unbroken', Moonen 1706: 42, cited by Schaars 1988: 85).
2. the phonetic principle, according to which one should not write superfluous letters that do not contribute to the pronunciation of the words (*Weshalve Letters, die den Woorden in de Uitspraeke geene hulp toebrengen, als overtolligh, uitgelaeten en niet geschreeven moeten worden*, Moonen 1706: 3, 34, cited by Schaars 1988: 90, 91)

Both these principles are taken from Schottelius (*AA* 195 and 188). Moonen invoked them in his discussion of the problematic area of consonant alternation at the ends of words in Dutch. In German, Schottelius (*AA* 191–92) adjudged that we should write *Pferd* because of the inflected form *Pferde*, even though the *–d* in *Pferd* sounds like a *–t* because of final devoicing (or final fortition) (cf. 5.5.3). The rootword principle, as a special instance of the more general analogical principle, dictated here that the rootword should remain the same throughout all word-forms. Moonen held with Schottelius that the rootwords should remain the 'same', but he accepted that this 'sameness' could include consonant alternations that reflected actual pronunciation. He was thus the first of a series of eighteenth-century Dutch grammarians to take issue with the forms that strict analogy would require, such as *wijv–wijven* ('woman, women', see Schaars 1988: 92), preferring instead to mark the difference in pronunciation. So Moonen accepted alternations of voiceless and voiced consonants in word-forms like *geef–geeven* ('give', first person sg., and infinitive or pl.). Wilhelm Séwel (1708) would follow Moonen, and the defeat of the analogical principle by the phonetic became established. The result is still evident in the contrast between standard Dutch and standard German

Table 7.3: Consonant alternations in Dutch spelling, compared to German

Dutch	German	(English)
huis, huizen	*Haus, Häuser*	'house'
geef, geven	*gib!, geben*	'give'

spelling, where Dutch alternates consonants, and German does not (Schaars 1988: 94) (Table 7.3).[27]

However, while Moonen was prepared to make a concession on the consonants of the rootwords, he insisted on preserving the same spelling of the *vowels* in rootwords. He therefore advocated forms like *geef–geeven* (not *geven*, as in modern Dutch), similarly *draeg, draegen* (not *dragen*). In the rootwords *geef, draeg*, etc., the double vowel (or *ae* for long a) was needed to indicate vowel length in a closed syllable. In *geeven, draegen*, Moonen accepted the syllabification of *gee–ven, draeg–en* still practised today (even though he would have preferred *geev–en*, in accordance with the requirement to keep the letters of the rootword together). Such syllabification made *gee–* an open syllable, and so the vowel would by default be pronounced long, and the double vowel was superfluous, as Moonen recognized. But in this instance, Moonen did decide to invoke the rootword principle above the phonetic principle, keeping the vowels constant across all word-forms of the root word. (In this, however, modern Dutch spelling has not followed him).

Moonen, then, is an important instance of the reception and adaptation of Schottelius's grammatical work outside the German-language grammatical tradition. In the *Nederduitsche Spraekkunst*, Schottelius's precepts were adopted, and many of them were cited verbatim, merely translated into Dutch. But Moonen was not just a slavish imitator. He combined Schottelius's theoretical insights with those of Vossius and with the practical insights of his Dutch predecessors, and so made an important contribution to Dutch grammatography whose influence is still felt today, most obviously in the case of spelling.[28]

7.8.4 *Russian grammar*

Thus far this chapter has examined the reception of Schottelius's work in other Germanic-speaking countries, where grammarians were answering

---

[27] Compare English *wife–wives, hoof–hooves*.

[28] Rutten (2004) observes that Moonen's more famous successor, Lambert ten Kate (1674–1731) (*Aenleiding tot de kennisse van het verhevene deel der Nederduitsche sprake*, 1723) also shows some parallels with Schottelius, particularly in his interest in roots as a means of tracing the origin and history of the language, and in the importance attributed to analogy. However, there is no suggestion of direct influence

Schottelius's call to the *Sprachverwante Nordenleute* to follow his example. It may come as a surprise that Schottelius also had a significant impact on at least one grammar of Russian. Since the end of the sixteenth century, German schools had become established in Russia, and by the later eighteenth century large numbers of Germans were contributing to the development of the Russian education system (and to much else, including administration, trade, and industry) during and in the aftermath of the reforms of Peter the Great, who reigned 1682–1725. Indeed, by the 1780s, some 8% of the Petersburg population were German.[29] While many German teachers were engaged in teaching German to Russians, Germans also made a significant contribution to the grammatical study of Russian. The first substantial grammar of Russian was the *Grammatica Russica* of the German Pietist Heinrich Wilhelm Ludolf (written with foreign learners in mind and printed in Oxford in 1696 [1959]).[30] The first normative grammar of Russian was that of Michail Lomonosov (1711–1765) (*Rossiskaja grammatika* 1755/1757; see Koch 2002: 46), with which the native Russian grammatical tradition begins. Between these two landmarks of 1696 and 1755 stands the grammar of Johann Werner Paus (1670–1735) that concerns us here: the *Anweisung zur Erlernung der Slavonisch-Rußischen Sprache* (1705–1729).[31] Paus, who was engaged as a translator at the Petersburg Academy of Sciences, submitted a manuscript fair copy of his grammar to the tsar in 1720, but it mysteriously disappeared. He submitted a second fair copy in 1729, but it was rejected for publication, apparently because of some kind of clash of personalities. However, although it was never printed, Paus's second fair copy was kept in the academy, where it was regularly consulted by later researchers. It may, therefore, have had a significant impact, despite its failure to make it to press. Typically Pietist in its adherence to Ratichian educational principles (cf. 5.2), Paus's grammar represents what might have happened had Gueintz, the Ratichian pedagogue, and Schottelius, the analogist and word-formation theorist, not been bitter rivals but collaborators. Paus's

---

[29] For this background, I rely on the excellent study of Koch (2002) (the population statistic is given by Koch 2002: 44–45) and on Glück (2002, section 6.4). Incidentally, one of the many Germans living there was Dietrich Wilhelm Soltau (1745–1811), who spent 32 years there as a merchant—also collecting additional German words (mainly relating to seafaring) to be added to Adelungs's German dictionary (Flood 1996: 288–289).

[30] Pietism was a branch of German Lutheranism which emerged in response to the political and moral devastation of the Thirty Years' War. It emphasized personal piety, expressed in the belief in the personal experience of faith, in the view of the church as a practising community, in the possibility of individual transformation and improvement, and in a concrete eschatology. See Brecht's introduction, in Brecht (1993: 1), and Heinle (1982: 52). Pietists founded the University of Halle in 1694, and Halle went on to supply large numbers of German Pietists to be preachers and tutors in Russian noble houses, as well as to establish and teach in German-language schools in Russia.

[31] For the following, see Huterer (2001).

definition of grammar and the discussion of the means required to study it, cited below, illustrates the marriage of these two schools of thought well.

> Welches sind denn die *instrumenta*|Mittel, dadurch die teutsche Zunge zum *Rußi*schen und *Slavoni*schen gelöset wird?

> [...] das 1. und Haubt instrument [wird] seyn die *Grammatic*, (darunter auch das *Azbúki* das ist *Abc* Buch gehört, welches das erste instrument ist, damit die Zunge zur rechten Aussprach kann gelöset werden) und 2. *Vocabularium*, das Wörter Buch gehöret, darum man anfangs nur die alltäglichen und brauchbarsten Wörter lernt, so daß man aus diesen beyden Büchern erstlich Simplicia und hernach Composita [...] sich bekandt zu machen [...] hat.

> 'Which, then, are the *instrumenta*| means by which the German tongue is released to the Russian and Slavonic?

> The 1. and main instrument will be the grammar (to which belongs the *Azbúki,* that is the ABC, which is the first instrument, so that the tongue can be released to the right pronunciation), and 2. *Vocabularium*, the dictionary, for one at first learns only the everyday and most common words, so that out of these two books one must make oneself acquainted with first *Simplicia* and then *Composita* [...]'

(*Anweisung*, Einleitung p. 7ʳ)

The question-and-answer format here is Ratichian; so too is the characteristic use of the term *Instrument* / *Mittel* (e.g. compare Ratke (ca. 1629), *Von der Schreibungslehr*; Ising 1959: 61) and the didacticized structuring of the material, beginning by 'learning only everyday and most frequent words', and by learning simplex words before compounds. On the other hand, the insistence that a grammar and dictionary together[32] are necessary to study a language in full sounds more Schottelian (but also recalls Kramer), and the definition of grammar itself follows very much in Schottelius's footsteps:

> Die SlavonischRußische Grammatic ist [...] eine kunstmäßige Fertigkeit [...] recht und rein Slavonisch und Rußisch aus dem Fundament und Analogie der Sprache zu reden, zu lesen und zuschreiben.

> 'The Slavonic–Russian grammar is [...] an artful skill to speak, read and write Slavonic and Russian correctly and purely in accordance with the foundation of and with the analogy of the language.'

---

[32] Paus produced a substantial *Lexicon Slavono Russicum cum Germano et Latino idiomate* which has not survived; cf. Huterer (2001: 22).

(*Anweisung*, Etymologia, p. 10ʳ; compare Schottelius *AA* 180: *Die Sprachkunst ist eine Wissenschaft | oder kunstmessige Fertigkeit | recht und rein Teutsch zureden oder zuschreiben*. 'Grammar is a science or an artful skill to speak or write German correctly and purely', *AA* 180; cf. 5.3.)

Paus did not merely adopt Schottelius's definition, but even added the dual emphases—implicit everywhere in Schottelius's work, but not explicit in his grammar definition—on seeking the true foundation (*Fundament*) of the language and on analogy. It is interesting to note too that Paus added reading to writing and speaking in the definition, a reflection of his own concern with reading and translating texts.

While Paus's didactic approach had clear Ratichian and Pietist influences, the underlying grammatical theory was that of Schottelius. Like Moonen, Paus followed Schottelius in dividing the grammar into two parts. Paus also followed Schottelius in devoting considerable space to word-formation, for his two chapters on nominal derivation and compounding take up fifty pages. Like Schottelius with his belief in 'the' *Teutsche HauptSprache*, Paus hypostasized 'the' language too, and even more audaciously. 'The' Slavo-Russian language did not yet exist, but would, Paus believed, come into existence in his synthesis of Church Slavonic and Russian grammar and lexis. Of this *slavonisch-russische Sprache*, Paus commented:

> Durch Beybehaltung beyder *dialectorum* wird beyde Sprach einerley und geht keiner etwas ab, sonder beyde werden *combini*rt, aus ieder etwas genommen, daß eine verbeßerte *Grammatic* herauskomme

> (p. 3ʳ, cited Huterer 2001: 27–29)

> 'By keeping both dialects, both languages become one and neither loses anything, but rather both are combined, something is taken out of each, so that an improved grammar comes out of it.'

Paus's belief that by considering both dialects, the best of both could be combined to create a better grammar for 'the' language, is really a statement of what Schottelius did to will a unified German *Hauptsprache* into existence by writing a grammar of it, particularly when he included *Low* German rootwords as nevertheless important and real parts of the object language (cf. 2.2, 3.8.2).

Paus also adopted Schottelius's imagery, perhaps mediated by Bödiker (1690) and Stieler (1691), but still with explicit reference to Schottelius, to describe the basic elements of the language as a source out of which new words can grow or flow, particularly the notion of the language tree and of the language spring. (The latter is less prominent in Schottelius, but still present, e.g. *AA* 98, 6: 53 *Wort– und Springquellen*; Huterer (2001) also points out the parallel with Bödiker 1698: 126):

> Die 1. Frage. Was ist die Ableitung?
>
> vid. an cum Schottelio
>
> Die Ableitung, (lat. *Derivatio*), ist eine Anweisung, auf was Art und Weise die Wörter von ein ander, als die Bächlein von dem Brunn-quell, oder als die Pflantzen und PfropffReiser von ihrem Saamen und Wurzel entspringen, for wachsen und richtig hergeleitet werden.

> 'The 1. question. What is derivation?
>
> Cf. Schottelius[33]
>
> Derivation, (lat. *Derivatio*), is an instruction in the ways in which the words originate in, grow forth from and are correctly derived from each other, like the brooks from the spring-source, or the plants and grafting twigs from their seed and root.'

> (p. 65^r, cited Huterer 2001: 72)

In the details of Russian grammar, Paus applied the twin notions of analogy and of the rootword, but like Moonen, Kramer and Aedler he made his own adjustments. Like Aedler and Tiällmann, Paus seems to have been aware of a broader notion of the rootword than that propounded by Schottelius. He used the Schottelian term *StammWort*, but also gave the Latin terms *vox primogenia* or *primitivum* (from which he coined the Russian calque первообразное, lit. 'of original form'). He explained the terms to mean that such words were the original words from which others were derived, or, historically speaking, the first words (in the sense that Becanus and Stiernhielm were interested in rootwords). Just as Aedler tacitly allowed for roots that were not monosyllabic, using the term loosely to allow him to identify productive derivative suffixes for the learner (such as *–haftig*), so too Paus accepted polysyllabic roots. However, he went much further, explicitly *praising* polysyllabic roots as a characteristic of Russian that made it *desto öffter nachdrüklicher* and *desto ansehnlicher* (Paus 1732: 3^v, 'often all the more emphatic and more attractive'). Just like Schottelius, Paus equated analogy with the true nature of the language, and he stipulated in his introduction that grammatical rules must be derived *aus der Natur der Sprache selbst, welche sonst Analogia Aenligkeit genenet wird* (*Anweisung*, Einleitung, p. 6^v, cited Huterer 2001: 32, 'out of the nature of the language itself, which is otherwise called Analogia, *similarity*'). He also

---

[33] Comparison with other usages of the abbreviation *vid. an cum* (lit. 'see whether with') suggests it equates to *cf.*, as translated here.

considered the relationship between analogy and usage, but came to a conclusion that would have horrified Schottelius and that was more akin to Fabricius's (1723) views on the subject (in Weichmann 1723), in accepting current usage as a basis for grammatical description, even that of ordinary people (cf. 7.4.3):

> der Gebrauch entweder guter bewehrter Autoren und Ausleger ja auch der gemeinen Leuthe ist selber eine Regul und der beste SprachMeister

> 'the usage of well-proven authors and printers, and even also of ordinary people, is itself a rule and the best language teacher'

(pp. 36ᵛ–37ʳ, cited Huterer 2001: 34)

Kramer, it may be recalled, criticized the fact that Schottelius's and Stieler's analogical drive led them to list compounds that were regularly produced by analogy, but that were rare or indeed unattested. Despite Paus's readiness to consult everyday usage (and his sources cover a wide range of texts that he would have encountered in his professional life as a translator: texts on law, mathematics, philosophy, theology, history, etc.; Huterer 2001: 52), he could have been accused by Kramer of the same error. He sometimes systematically applied rules of derivation to yield forms that contradicted current usage and that in fact revealed his imperfect knowledge of the language. For example, some of his diminutives were incorrect (as in the form *мышица* rather than the more usual *мышца* or *мышка* 'muscle'), or overlooked regular consonant alternations (as in the case of **розокъ* instead of *рожокъ* 'little horn'), or the need for palatalization of a vowel after a soft consonant (as in the diminutive form **огонокъ* 'little fire, little light', produced by adding the hard suffix *–ок* rather than the soft *–ек*). All of these errors resulted from the too-diligent application of a rule (Huterer 2001: 136–37; 147 discusses the same difficulty in Paus's treatment of patronymics.)

Paus followed Schottelius closely—and cited him repeatedly—in his treatment of compounding, but showed more independence in the area of derivation, in which Russian is very rich. While Kramer went in the direction of characterizing derivation by more strictly morphological criteria than Schottelius had, Paus went in the opposite direction, focusing rather on semantic categories, in which he recognized that Russian was particularly rich (for instance in its fondness for the semantic category of diminutives).

Like Moonen, Paus faced the practical difficulty that his object-language did not conform readily to the expectation that rootwords should be preserved in all word-forms. Russian has plentiful regular consonant alternations in inflected and derived word-forms (e.g. *рука* > *ручка* 'hand, little hand', *человек* > *человечески* 'person (n.), human (adj.)'). Moonen had accommodated the necessary consonant alternations in Dutch by giving precedence to the phonetic principle over the *oirsprongkelykheit* 'originality' principle. Paus chose instead to treat the consonant alternations that are part of Russian derivational processes such as forming diminutives under the heading of analogy. Diminutives *werden nach der* Analogie *in großer Anzahl* formi*rt von ihren* primitivis *[...], daher die formation leicht ist* 'are formed in large numbers from their primitives by analogy [...], so the formation is easy', pp. 70^v–71^r, Huterer 2001: 132). Paus emphasized the regularity of such alternations, reminding the reader that similar alternations are found in German too, as in *schreiben-Schrifft* (p. 1 of the fragment of Paus's fair copy, cited by Huterer 2001: 100–01).[34]

This passage was cited almost word for word in the so-called Schwanwitz grammar of 1731 (*Compendium Grammaticae russicae* [...]; cf. Huterer 2001: 101, 301), and so is evidence that Paus's Schottelius-influenced grammar of Russian was indeed taken note of by subsequent grammarians. Indeed, Martin Schwanwitz (d. 1740) was an influential pedagogue: his German grammar of 1730 was one of the most popular Russian grammars of German throughout the eighteenth century, and also had an important influence on later Russian grammars (Koch 2002: 224–26, 324–26).

7.8.5 *The rootword in Semitic and Sanskrit languages*

Schottelius did not take the concept of the rootword from Hebrew grammar, though that has often been assumed (cf. 3.8.2, n. 52). The reality is more complicated. Schottelius may well have borrowed the idea of root-letters from that tradition, where Postel (1539) had made the distinction between radical and servile letters (Rousseau 1984: 287), but that is not where the equation of the root with the second person imperative originated. There was evidently a belief circulating that in Hebrew the imperative functioned as the root (cf. Peder Syv's assertion to that effect in Syv 1663: 132), but this is erroneous. The third person perfect was (and is) the usual citation form. Furthermore, while Schottelius took the root to be monosyllabic, it was axiomatic to Arabic grammarians until the seventeenth century—whether in the native tradition or in European scholarship—that the root was *bi*syllabic, as in Arabic *KiTaB* 'book'.[35] Similarly, in Hebrew studies, most seventeenth-century Christian Hebraists considered

---

[34] It is ironic that both Moonen and Paus, in loosening the notion of the rootword, accepted variability in the consonants more readily than in the vowels. In contrast, in its Hebrew origins, the rootword is of course consonantal, and Schottelius also passed over vowel-changes caused by derivation or comparison without comment.

[35] Gueintz made exactly this point in his commentary on Harsdörffer's *Specimen Philologiae Germanicae* (cf. Hundt 2000: 71–83), published in Krause (1973 [1855]: 363–72, here 368).

the Hebrew root to be triliteral (and bisyllabic, therefore), following the medieval model of David Kimhi (ca. 1160–1235?), which had been further clarified by Elias Levita (1469–1549) in the sixteenth century.[36] Only in the late seventeenth century (beginning with works like Neumann 1696) did western—specifically, German—scholars of Arabic start to want to reconcile the bisyllabic root with a belief in original monosyllabicity, which they did by finding ways to reduce three-consonant roots to two-consonant roots.

In fact, the discussion of monosyllabicity in the Semitic languages, emerging in Germany after Schottelius's work had been published, owed a debt to Schottelius's ideas, rather than the other way round. The very terminology used by these grammarians of Semitic languages already suggests an indirect debt to Schottelius, for they used terms like *Grund- oder Stammwort* (Michaelis 1771: 41), *Stammwort* (Wahl 1789) and *Stamm Wörter* (Vater 1802) to translate the indigenous terms for Arabic or Hebrew roots. Furthermore, in the case of at least two German grammarians of Arabic, a direct line of influence can be traced. The 1787–89 grammar of Ignaz Aurelius Fessler (1756–1839), of which the second part is devoted to Arabic, referenced Leibniz for the view that the verbal root was the imperative, and we can be confident that Leibniz had this feature of the rootword from Schottelius (Rousseau 1984: 303). (Such a view was novel in Arabic studies, where Europeans had held since Martellotus (1620) that the verbal root form was the third person preterite; no such view held at all in the indigenous Arabic tradition). Second, Wahl (1789) constructed a system for Arabic very close to that outlined for German by Adelung (1781/ 1782), who was in turn, of course, still very clearly indebted to Schottelius (cf. 7.3.1 and 7.6). According to Wahl, the three-consonant 'roots' of Arabic were not original roots at all, but were themselves derived from original two-consonant (and hence monosyllabic) roots (cf. Rousseau 1984: 298–310). As we have seen, Humboldt agreed, arguing that the original monosyllables had only been given a second syllable later, when the need for grammatical specification had been recognized (cf. Rousseau 1984: 300, 320).

Franz Bopp (1820) extended the debate about monosyllabicity to Sanskrit in comparison with the Semitic languages, seeking to demonstrate that Sanskrit roots were monosyllabic; that they 'may contain as few letters as are requisite to constitute a monosyllable' (Bopp 1820: 8, cited Rousseau 1984: 309, 311). Rousseau (1984) has argued that it was out of this systematic, synchronic comparison of Semitic and Sanskrit roots by Bopp and others that the idea of the root as an abstraction, removed from etymological speculations, gradually emerged, which ultimately made 'thinkable' the idea of the morpheme (Rousseau 1984: 294). If Rousseau

---

[36] I am grateful to Stephen G. Burnett (p.c.) for clarifying this for me. Cf. also Burnett (1996).

is right, then we must note Schottelius's role, at several removes, in developing the abstract notion of the morpheme. Even if, as Rousseau argues, the monosyllabicity discussion itself was ultimately rather a cul-de-sac, we must at the very least credit Schottelius with a significant impact on the European study of Semitic languages.

7.9 CONCLUSION

Schottelius had a predictable influence on succeeding native German grammars and dictionaries. This much is not new. But it is now evident that Schottelius had an important influence too on grammars of Danish, Dutch, Swedish, and Russian, all grammars that were in turn influential works in the early years of their own vernacular grammatical traditions. Schottelius's influence was also felt in works that were read by English, French, Dutch and Italian language learners. Beyond his importance in German grammatography, he was the most influential theoretical grammarian of his century in some parts of Europe, and, to that extent, a successor to Vossius. It was Schottelius's theoretical tenets, more so than those of the nearly contemporaneous Port-Royal grammar (which was, however, undeniably a milestone for quite different reasons that have more to do with the philosophy of language), that influenced the grammatical descriptions of a number of European vernaculars for the next hundred years.

8

PRESCRIPTION AND PRACTICE: SCHOTTELIUS AND THE DEVELOPMENT OF A STANDARD LANGUAGE

8.1 INTRODUCTION: HOW CAN WE ASSESS SCHOTTELIUS'S INFLUENCE ON LANGUAGE USAGE?

'The [grammatical] theoreticians who emerge from the second quarter of the sixteenth century onwards [as the last of whom Moser lists Schottelius] had near enough no influence on the development of the written language in the Early New High German era.' (Moser 1929: 3, my translation)

From the question of Schottelius's importance for subsequent grammatical study, this chapter turns to the mundane but difficult question of whether Schottelius's grammar—whose claim to authority was matched by its high price[1]—had any impact on the everyday use of the German language. Historical sociolinguists have over the past couple of decades started to investigate the extent to which European grammarians' stipulations about language were adopted in practice, or whether, in fact, they did little more than codify existing practice after the event (Tieken-Boon van Ostade 1982 and ongoing work in her Leiden project *The Codifiers and the English Language*, Azad 1989, Sairio 2008, all with respect to English; Langer 2001 for German; Auer 2009, looking at German and English; Caron & Ayres-Bennett, *forthcoming*, for French; Rutten, Vosters & Vandenbussche, *forthcoming*, for Dutch). That question is in turn part of a wider one: to what extent does language change occur 'from above', at the level of conscious adoption of new forms (whether or not prescribed by grammarians), and to what extent from below the level of consciousness? Surprisingly little work has been done on the question as it relates to German since Moser's pessimistic pronouncement of 1929, cited above, but an important first assessment for Schottelius's era is the study by Takada (1998), who investigated two corpora over the years 1630 to 1710 to determine the extent of seventeenth-century grammarians' influence on orthography, word formation, inflection, and syntax, using as evidence the

---

[1] As noted in 1.5.2, the *AA* was expensive. Though I have not been able to establish its price in 1663, in 1674 it cost two *Taler* and four *Groschen* unbound, plus eight *Groschen* for the binding (Jones 2000: 620). In the mid-eighteenth century, the *AA* still cost two *Taler*. Other grammars appear to have been far cheaper, costing between three and ten *Groschen*.

corrections made to texts when they were reprinted.[2] Takada examined editions of the Luther Bible printed between 1630 and 1710 in Wittenberg by Wust, in Lüneburg by Endter, and in Nuremberg by Stern, as well as a second corpus of texts selected to represent a range of genres and geographical distribution (though chiefly in the Protestant areas) over the same time period (see Takada 1998: 17–19, 304–319). This was Takada's solution to the practical difficulty in assessing the influence of the grammarians on practice: the lack—then as now, even a decade after Takada's study was published—of suitable electronic corpora for the crucial period.[3] Overall, Takada found that the relationship between codification and practice covered the full range, from aspects of the language where grammarians' codifications run parallel with practice (e.g. in preferring the full rather than the reduced inflectional forms, as in *des Tages, dem Tage* rather than *des Tags, dem Tag*, Takada 1998: 218) to those where they ride roughshod over it, as in advocating redundant strong endings like *der guter Mann* rather than *der gute Mann*. In some instances at least, however, the prescriptions of Schottelius do appear to have had some effect on orthographical practice. For example, both Schottelius's printer Zilliger (in Braunschweig) and Stern (the Nuremberg printer of the Luther bible) had by 1690 broadly adopted the spelling principles advocated by Schottelius, especially the morphological-etymological principle, i.e. that a rootword should be identifiable in all its forms, and that distinct rootwords that were potential homophones should be clearly distinguished. The recognition of the need for such distinctions was not new, but it was Schottelius who formulated as a principle what earlier orthographers such as Werner (1629) had required without generalizing the rule (see Moulin 2004: 56–58, Werner 1629 [2007]: XIX). The distinction between the suffixes *–lich* and *–ig* was also made consistently by the end of the seventeenth century, as Schottelius and his successors had demanded.

There is, then, clear evidence in Takada's study that spelling practice evolved significantly between the 1640s and the 1690s, and that in some cases the evolution followed new prescriptions systematized in Schottelius and adopted by later grammarians. Takada concludes that it is therefore no longer tenable to suggest that grammarians only followed established practice, codifying *post hoc*. Overall, Takada's evidence suggests that

---

[2] Also valuable for the relationship between prescription and practice in the area of grammar for Early New High German is Langer (2001, already noted), whose study examines the stigmatization of *tun* in auxiliary verb functions, as well as the stigmatization of double negation and of the double perfect. Auer (2009; reviewed by Pickl 2010) investigates the relationship between practice and prescription for the German and English subjunctive in the eighteenth century.

[3] The texts in the Bonn Early New High German corpus (http://www.gldv.org/fnhd/) are selected from the *second* half of each century, which means that while we can compare texts from before 1600 with those after 1650, we crucially cannot compare those from the earlier seventeenth century with those of the latter part of the seventeenth century.

Schottelius certainly contributed along with his contemporaries to the gradual standardization of the (printed) language, even if his contribution was, like that of others, modest and incremental. However, the positive findings noted above must be balanced by others. Schottelius called for restraint in signalling compounds by hyphenation, yet Takada (1998: 164) found that this became very common in the Nuremberg and Lüneburg prints of his corpus between 1680 and 1700 (cf. also Erben 2007).

My assessment in this chapter of Schottelius's influence on subsequent linguistic practice draws both on Takada's work and on my own corpus investigations within the limitations of the materials currently available. It seeks both to differentiate between different groups of writers, and to systematize the types of influence (or non-influence) that grammarians may have on linguistic practice. The following three corpora have been used:

i. The 'Bonn' corpus consists of extracts of ca. 2000 words from selected texts from the Bonn corpus of Early New High German (http://www.gldv.org/Fnhd/). Extracts of ca. 2000 words were used in order to ensure that practice in each text was equally represented in the corpus. Ten extracts, each from a different author, were taken for the period 1550–1600 (approx. 20,000 words), and nine for 1650–1700 (also approx. 20,000 words; one text printed in Zürich in the corpus was not sampled for the purposes of this study).

ii. The GerManC Early New High German newspaper corpus (http://www.llc.manchester.ac.uk/research/projects/germanc/) consists of extracts from 1650–1800, covering five regions and three periods: (1650–1700, 1701–1750 and 1751–1800), together totalling about 100,000 words. This corpus of texts written for rapid distribution, and often containing war reports which appear to have been printed verbatim from first-hand accounts, offers a sample of everyday 'journeyman' writing. As Polenz observes of German newspapers— which were consumed in this period by readers from across the social classes, including those who could *not* read, but who would have been read to—'in the interests of news value, the newspaper had to appear as soon as possible after the arrival of the post-rider or carriage, and this meant that clear textual coherence, careful word choice and stylistic revision had to go by the board' (Polenz 1994: 371, my translation).

iii. The *Sprachhelden* corpus. In part to address the dearth of texts, in both corpora above, from the crucial years in the early and middle decades of the seventeenth century, a small corpus of texts of varying length (ca. 43,000 words in total) was selected from Jones (1995 *Sprachhelden und Sprachverderber*), an anthology of texts by writers interested in the cultivation of the language, from the period 1600–1700.[4] In many cases, several shorter extracts from a single author were combined to provide a longer text sample for that author; in other cases the extracts are much shorter than the target of 2000 words. Texts by Schottelius himself were not included. The selected texts were divided into four groups: 1600–1639 (before the publication of the first edition of Schottelius's grammar; ca. 8,300 words), 1640–1643 (the years surrounding pre-publication discussion of both Gueintz's and Schottelius's grammars in the FG, and their publication in 1641, ca. 14,700 words); 1664–1675 (the decade following the publication of Schottelius's definitive *AA* in 1663; ca. 12,200 words); and 1680–1700 (ca. 7,700 words).

The *Sprachhelden* corpus is small, and could at best be described as serendipitous, at worst haphazard, but it is—albeit imperfectly— representative of writers who were active in the *Spracharbeit* discourse of the seventeenth century. Its inclusion therefore allows some tentative comparison between the usage of this group of writers and that of the contemporary functional writing found in the the GerManC newspaper corpus, as well as with the Bonn corpus and with Takada's findings.

The corpus composition has many methodological imperfections, but has been used *faute de mieux* (although the next stage of the GerManC project, and a project by Wegera and colleagues in Germany, which includes digitizing texts for the period 1600–1650,[5] will greatly improve the situation).

When we consider the relationship between a given prescription and linguistic practice, the following scenarios are theoretically possible. First, as far as the relationship between prescription and current or previous practice is concerned, the following scenarios are possible:

1. The prescription codifies what is already widespread or even dominant practice.

2. The prescription codifies practice that is found, but which is still more or less marginal compared with other forms, spellings or structures that dominate.

3. The prescription stigmatizes a form, spelling or structure that is found in contemporary usage.

4. The prescription advocates spellings, forms or structures that are not found at all in the practice of the time.

---

[4] I am extremely grateful to Bill Jones for generously making available to me the electronic files that he used in producing his volume (Jones 2005).
[5] Klaus-Peter Wegera, p.c.

5. The prescription is silent with regard to a spelling, form or structure which is nevertheless attested and whose frequency subsequently changes.

Within these scenarios, the following permutations are possible, when we consider the relationship between prescription and *subsequent* practice.

1. Where prescription codifies what is already widespread or even dominant practice,

    a. subsequent practice may continue to follow established practice as confirmed by prescription,

    OR

    b. other variants may become dominant, irrespective both of established dominant practice and of prescription or stigmatization.

2. Where prescription codifies practice that is found, but which is more or less marginal compared with other forms, spellings or structures that dominate,

    a. subsequent practice may continue to follow the established dominant practice,

    OR

    b. the minority or marginal variant favoured by the prescription may increase in frequency in subsequent practice, but temporarily only, or locally only. This may result in a period of increased variation and uncertainty, but no ultimate change,

    OR

    c. the minority or marginal variant favoured by the prescription may become established and widespread, ultimately ousting the previously dominant variant(s).

3. Where the prescription stigmatizes a form, spelling or structure that is found in contemporary usage,

    a. the variant may nevertheless continue to be used and may ultimately become established,

    OR

    b. the variant may disappear from usage, as a disfavoured variant.

4. Where the prescription advocates spellings, forms or structures that are not found at all in the practice of the time,

a. Subsequent practice may continue to follow established practice, irrespective of the prescription,

OR

b. the advocated variant may gain in ground either for a time, or in certain areas only, or in the longer term. In such cases, prescription guides practice.

5. Where the prescriptive authority is silent with regard to a form, spelling or structure that is nevertheless attested,

a. the variant may increase in frequency, regardless of the lack of backing from authorities,

OR

b. the variant may decrease in frequency, regardless of the lack of explicit stigmatization from authorities.

It is under the headings of these various scenarios that this chapter investigates to what extent Schottelius's grammar—which dominated German grammatical thinking for nigh on a century, as we have seen—also influenced actual language usage. In practice, it is easiest to compare Schottelius's pronouncements with linguistic practice in the areas of orthography and inflection, since these are the areas where grammarians made clear stipulations. It must be borne in mind, however, that orthography was often not in the hands of the individual author, but of the printer or individual typesetter. To take a highly relevant example, Metcalf (1978), who compared the copyright patent (*Privilegium*) printed by Zilliger in Schottelius's *AA* with the original, found that alterations made did not accord with Schottelius's own orthographical stipulations. Grammatical inflection too frequently boils down in print to a decision to typeset a letter or not (*-e* or *-er*, for example), and so might be beyond the author's control for the same reasons as spelling. Syntactical structures are less subject to the whim of the publishing house, but syntactical structures about which Schottelius made clear pronouncements tend to be already so universally established as to be uninteresting (for example, that the adjective precedes the noun in German, *AA* 707–708; cf. Takada 1998: 221), or they tend to be non-obligatory structures, and are furthermore difficult to 'trawl' for in electronic corpora, such as the extended participial attribute of the form *Die hohe vor Augen schwebende Not*, 'the great danger that looms' lit. 'the great before-our-eyes-hovering danger' (*AA* 710; cf. Takada 1998: 222). Frequently, too, Schottelius's comments on syntax are not prescriptive at all, but highlight alternative ways to say the same thing (cf. 5.5.5), as in:

Das Beyständige kan erwehnter massen bey das Selbständige ge-
setzet/ oder auch wol in sein Selbständiges geendet *[sic, but read
geendert]* / und das Wörtlein / von / vorn gesetzet werden/ als:

Ein güldner Becher / *vel* ein Becher von Gold / *vel* von Gold ein
Becher

'The adjective can, as has been mentioned, be placed next to the
noun, or can also well be changed into its noun and the word *von* 'of'
placed in front, as in:

A golden cup / *or* a cup of gold / *or* of gold a cup.'

(*AA* 708–709)

Schottelius's presentation of German syntax as a wide variety of
combinable and recombinable elements accords with his intention to
highlight the suitability of German as a rich language, capable of expressing
any and all ideas well (cf. 5.6)—but it makes it difficult to investigate
whether his account of syntax had any influence on language use.
Regularities recognized tend to be stated as frequent rather than obligatory,
as in the case of the omission of the auxiliary in compound tenses
(*gemeiniglich, zum oftern* 'commonly, often', *AA* 743, 744; cf. Schneider-
Mizony 2010: 794). For this reason my investigation below is almost
entirely limited to matters of orthography and inflection (including verb
conjugation).[6] Unless otherwise indicated, it should not be assumed that
variants in any given text are to be ascribed to the will of the author himself,
rather than to the printer or typesetter.

The example of Schottelius's pronouncement on structures like *Ein
Becher von Gold* raises one final matter: the concept of 'prescriptivism' in
grammars. Although the oversimplified view of grammars as categorically
either descriptive *or* prescriptive is on the wane (cf. discussion in Hodson
2006), it is worth emphasizing that Schottelius is by turns descriptive *and*
prescriptive. In some cases Schottelius describes variants, before clearly
prescribing a preferred form; in many other cases—especially in the syntax,
but not only—he describes variants, without valuing one over another.
With regard to the linguistic features chosen for discussion below, however,
Schottelius *does* prescribe—either explicitly, or implicitly (e.g. by the
inclusion of one or more variants in a verb paradigm, and the omission of
others). Indeed, Schottelius evidently went further than the eighteenth-
century English grammarians who have inspired much of the recent
discussion about prescriptivism.[7] According to Azad (1989: 3, cited Hodson

---

[6] See, however, 8.3 for discussion of one example concerning syntax: the formation of the
passive.
[7] See Donhauser (1989) for description *vs* prescription in the context of Early Modern
German grammars.

2006: 68), eighteenth-century English grammarians 'never advocated a modern view of authoritative language usage only to ignore it and "prescribe" instead. To prescribe correctness was to describe usage.' This is simply not true of Schottelius: in a number of instances, discussed below, his analogical approach to language led him to advocate forms that had little or no foundation in current usage, 'authoritative' or otherwise.

8.2 SCENARIO 1: PRESCRIPTION OF PRACTICE THAT IS ALREADY WIDESPREAD

In many cases, Schottelius advocated what was already widely established practice. Not surprisingly, the forms he advocated—which had already attained critical mass in the language—grew in strength and became established as the only dominant forms. Schottelius's spelling of *sol/soll* 'should' is a case in point. Schottelius's listing (*AA* 597) of the first and third person singular present *soll* (rather than *sol*) maintains the integrity of the root *soll–* (cf. infinitive *sollen* 'should'), and so appears to fall into the same category as his principled preference for *Mann* over *Man* by spelling principle 3 (*AA* 192, cf. 5.5.3). This may be so, but in fact Schottelius's choice of *soll* merely reflects dominant practice (see Table 8.1): the Bonn 1550–1600 sub-corpus already shows a preference for *soll* over *sol* in over

Table 8.1: sol *and* soll *in the corpora*

Bonn corpus

	1550–1600	%	1650–1700	%
soll	110	77.5	17	94.4
sol	32	22.5	1	5.6
TOTAL	142		18	

Sprachhelden corpus (% are not given for individual time periods, since the raw figures are so low)

	1600–1639	1640–43	1664–1675	1680–1700	Total 1600–1700
Soll	4	5	9	4	22 (56.4%)
Sol	2	6	9	0	17 (43.6%)
TOTAL	6	11	18	4	39

GerManC newspaper corpus

	1650–1700	%	1701–1750	%	1751–1800	%
soll	30	81.1	19	95.0	30	100.0
sol	7	18.9	1	5.0	0	0.0
TOTAL	37		20		30	87

three-quarters ($110/142$ = 77.7%) of the possible contexts, a figure which rises to 94% ($17/18$) a century later, in the 1650–1700 Bonn corpus. While the GerManC newspaper corpus shows a significantly lower figure of 81% ($30/37$ contexts) for the same period, there too the frequency rises (and significantly so) through each of the next two periods.[8] There is a complication, however. The *Sprachhelden* corpus reveals much stiffer competition between *soll* and *sol: soll* does not account for more than half of the instances until 1680–1700, where it appears in four out of four possible contexts. One might speculate that the *Sprachhelden* texts give a higher priority to a competing requirement, that of avoiding superfluous letters (Schottelius's first spelling principle), causing a more equal competition between forms amongst this group of writers than in the other corpora.[9] Perhaps, then, Schottelius's preference for *soll was* important for this group of writers participating in language cultivation, affirming the late sixteenth-century practice in the face of doubts amongst his own social group.

It is important to be aware that Schottelius's preference for the integrity of the rootword is imperfectly applied: he gives for the preterite of *sollen* not *sollte* (analogous to *soll*) but *solte* (*AA* 597). Though the rootword logic would dictate *sollte*, that form is not attested in any of the corpora until 1673, where there is one lone instance in the GerManC corpus 1650–1700 (see Table 8.2). It emerges there as a competing variant only in the first half of the eighteenth century ($5/17$ contexts, or just under 30% of a small sample), and does not become the dominant variant until the second half of the eighteenth century.[10] One would therefore be inclined to conclude that Schottelius was following usage as much as principle in his spelling of these verb forms. Sometimes the spelling accorded with the rootword principle; sometimes it did not.[11]

Another salient feature of orthography is the spelling of word-final *ei/ey*. Schottelius (1641) was in line with a number of other grammarians in his view that a German word should not end in *–i* (Takada 1998: 77–78). Schottelius (*AA* 614, 625) accordingly listed the preposition *bei* as *bey*, despite his general assertion that *–ej* should be used for such contexts (*AA* 214, as in *frej, sej*). Here too, the *bey* spelling that Schottelius chose was the

---

[8] $\chi^2_{(DF)}$ = $7.649_{(2)}$, p = 0.022. The difference between time periods in the Bonn corpus is not significant: $\chi^2_{(DF)}$ = $2.813_{(2)}$, p = 0.245. Nor are there significant differences between the different periods of the *Sprachhelden* corpus: $\chi^2_{(DF)}$ = $2.837_{(2)}$, p = 0.242. The difference among the corpora for the period 1650–1700 is significant, however ($\chi^2_{(DF)}$ = $7.606_{(2)}$, p = 0.022). I am most grateful to Dr Tom Reader for his assistance with the statistical analysis in this chapter.

[9] Takada (1998: 101) observes that one of Schottelius's works from 1668 used the form *sol*, but that he switched to *soll* in 1674.

[10] The differences among the three time periods are significant: $\chi^2_{(DF)}$ = $28.156_{(2)}$, p < 0.001.

[11] My finding here is, however, at odds with Takada's (1998: 131) finding that *sollte* was already in use at the time Schottelius was writing.

Table 8.2: solte *and* sollte *in the corpora*

Bonn corpus

	1550–1600	%	1650–1700	%
sollte	0	0	0	100
solte	32	100	9	0
TOTAL	32		9	

Sprachhelden corpus (% are not given for individual time periods, since the raw figures are so low)

	1600–1639	1640–43	1664–1675	1680–1700	Total 1600–1700
sollte	0	0	0	0	0
solte	5	9	14	9	37
TOTAL	5	9	14	9	37

GerManC newspaper corpus

	1650–1700	%	1701–1750	%	1751–1800	%	Total 1650–1800	%
sollte	1	7.7	5	29.4	16	100	22	47.8
solte	12	92.3	12	70.6	0	0	24	52.2
TOTAL	13		17		16		46	

established one (already at 89% in the Bonn 1550–1599 sub-corpus), and despite the fact that its frequency drops significantly in the 1650–1700 Bonn corpus, *bey* averages around 90% in the *Sprachhelden* and GerManC corpus in the eighteenth century (see Table 8.3). Only in the second half of the eighteenth century did the *bei* variant at last emerge as a competitor, after *bey* would appear to have won out (reaching 100% of 135 tokens in the 1701–1750 corpus),[12] and long, long after at least some grammarians had been advocating it (Olearius 1630, Bellin 1657, and Stieler 1691 already all preferred *–ei*).

Another similar case, in the area of inflection, is Schottelius's choice of *gewesen* for the past participle of *sein* 'to be', which accounts for 75% (127/ 169) of tokens in the Bonn 1550–1600 sub-corpus, against one token of *gesyn*, and 24% (41/169) *gewest*, which is itself thereafter found only occasionally in the later corpora (and not at all in the *Sprachhelden* corpus) (see Table 8.4).[13]

---

[12] The difference between the time periods is significant ($\chi^2_{(DF)} = 8.499_{(1)}$, p = 0.014); so too is that among periods in the GerManC corpus ($\chi^2_{(DF)} > 30_{(2)}$, p < 0.001), but not that among periods in the *Sprachhelden* corpus ($\chi^2_{(DF)} = 1.20_{(6)}$, p = 0.273).

[13] The differences among time periods for each of the GerManC and Bonn corpora are not significant ($\chi^2_{(DF)} = 0.895_{(2)}$, p = 0.639, and $\chi^2_{(DF)} = 0.123_{(3)}$, p = 0.936 respectively).

Table 8.3: bey, bei *and* bej *in the corpora*

Bonn corpus

	1550–1600	%	1650–1700	%
bej	0	0	0	0
bei	29	10.8	12	26.7
bey	239	89.2	33	73.3
TOTAL	268		45	

Sprachhelden corpus

	1600–1639	%	1640–43	%	1644–1675	%	1680–1700	%	Summed 1600–1700	%
bej	0	0.0	0	0.0	1	1.8	0	0.0	1	0.7
bei	1	3.0	0	0.0	12	21.4	0	0.0	13	7.8
bey	33	97.0	39	100.0	43	76.8	36	100.0	151	90.10
TOTAL	34		39		56		36		165	

GerManC newspaper corpus

	1650–1700	%	1701–1750	%	1751–1800	%
bej	0	0.0	0	0.0	0	0
bei	12	8.8	0	0.0	96	50.3
bey	124	91.2	135	100.0	95	49.7
TOTAL	136		135		191	

All of these examples (*soll, solte, bey* and *gewesen*) fall under the heading of Scenario 1a: Schottelius's prescription appears to do no more than back the variant(s) that are already the winners (notwithstanding the much later change in the case of *bey/bei*). There is, however, one noteworthy instance of Scenario 1b, where a usage grows in frequency independent of Schottelius's prescription in that area of language. One of Schottelius's innovations as a grammarian was the attention he paid to punctuation, and in his discussion of the hyphen, he devoted most of his attention specifically to explaining its 'correct' use in constructions involving *und* 'and' or *oder* 'or', as in *ihre aigne angeborne teutsche Tauff- und Zunamen* ('their own native German baptism and second names', from Grimmelshausen 1673) (principles I–IV on *AA* 672–73; see also *AA* 102, 6: 62–63). Yet the use of the hyphen in such structures only first emerges, and at low frequencies, in the *Sprachhelden* corpus (gradually increasing through the seventeenth century), occurs too in the 1650–1700 Bonn corpus (15/156 uses of the hyphen, 9.6%), but does not occur at all in the GerManC newspaper corpus (see Table 8.5). This distribution pattern suggests that it might have been a usage that caught on chiefly among elite writers (and indeed it arguably

Table 8.4: The distribution of the past participle of the verb 'to be' in the corpora 1550–1800

Bonn corpus

	1550–1600	%	1650–1700	%	1664–1675	%
gewesen	127	75.1	12	85.7	8	100.0
gewest	41	24.3	2	14.3	0	0.0
gesyn	1	0.6	0	0.0	0	0.0
total past participle of 'to be'	169		14		8	

Sprachhelden corpus

	1600–1639	%	1640–1643	%	1680–1700	%	1640–1700 pooled	%
gewesen	7	100.0	14	100.0	5	100.0	27	100.0
gewest	0		0	0.0	0	0.0	0	0.0
gesyn	0		0	0.0	0	0.0	0	0.0
total past participle of 'to be'	7		14		5		27	

GerManC newspaper corpus

	1650–1700	%	1701–1750	%	1751–1800	%
gewesen	46	95.8	46	97.9	16	100.0
gewest	2	4.2	1	2.1	0	0.0
gesyn	0	0.0	0	0.0	0	0.0
total past participle of 'to be'	48		47			

Table 8.5: Hyphenation in the three corpora

Bonn corpus

	1550–1600	1650–1700
No. of tokens of hyphenation in compounds, e.g. *Lehr-satz*	1	141
Frequency of hyphenation in compounds per 1000 words	0.05	6.93
No. of tokens of the type *Tauff- und Zunamen* (with *und* or *oder* and a following compound element)	0	15
No. of *Tauff- und Zunamen* type compounds per 1000 words	0	0.74
Total uses of hyphen	1	156

Sprachhelden corpus

	1600–1639	1640–43	1664–1675	1680–1700	All periods combined
No. of tokens of hyphenation in compounds, e.g. *Lehr-satz*	14	95	111	93	313
Frequency of hyphenation in compounds per 1000 words	1.67	6.42	9.10	12.00	7.26
No. of tokens of the type *Tauff- und Zunamen* (with *und* or *oder* and a following compound element)	3	8	5	15	31
No. of *Tauff- und Zunamen* type compounds per 1000 words	0.36	0.54	0.41	1.94	0.72
Total uses of hyphen	17	103	116	108	344

GerManC newspaper corpus

	1650–1700	1701–1750	1751–1800	All three time periods combined
No. of tokens of hyphenation in compounds, e.g. *Lehr-satz*	376	711	140	1227
Frequency of hyphenation in compounds per 1000 words	11.19	21.28	4.27	12.29
No. of tokens of the type *Tauff- und Zunamen* (with *und* or *oder* and a following compound element)	0	0	0	0
No. of *Tauff- und Zunamen* type compounds per 1000 words	0	0	0	0
Total uses of hyphen	376	711	140	1227

remains restricted to formal or technical language today too).[14] However, the case of the hyphen is more complex than that, for the use of the hyphen within compounds (e.g. Zesen's *Lehr-satz*, translating *Regula* 'rule', Jones 1995: 225) constitutes evidence both for the emergence of a variant to which the grammarian paid scant attention, and for the subsequent and not very effective stigmatization of a variant.

Schottelius did not even mention the use of the hyphen in compounds as in *Lehr-satz* 'rule' until the fifth principle in relation to the hyphen (*AA* 674), where he viewed it as optional (VII, *AA* 675), though elsewhere he called for restraint in its use in such contexts (*AA* 102, 6: 62). After him, other grammarians increasingly stigmatized this usage in compounds. According to Takada (1998: 149–150), Bellin (1642: 61) noted the hyphen without judgement, but rejected it in 1657 (Bellin 1657: 149), and towards the end of the seventeenth century Bödiker (1690: 33) considered it acceptable under limited conditions only, while Stieler (1691: 35) observed that it was used by *ungelerte leute* 'uneducated people'. The growing stigmatization of the hyphen in compounds over this fifty-year period appears to be a reaction to the growth in the frequency with which it was used. From a frequency of only 0.05 instances per 1000 words in the 1550–1600 Bonn corpus, the *Sprachhelden* corpus suggests a steady increase in frequency, up to a peak of 12.00 per 1000 words in the *Sprachhelden* corpus of 1680–1700, a comparable 11.19 in the GerManC corpus of 1650–1700, and ultimately 21.28 in the GerManC corpus for the first half of the eighteenth century.[15] Takada (1998: 164) also reports that such hyphenated compounds became very common in the Nuremberg and Lüneburg prints of his corpus between 1680 and 1700 (cf. also Erben 2007). Here, then, we find a steady increase in one use of the hyphen, to which Schottelius had paid only scant attention, but which would, at the peak of its popularity in the seventeenth century, also become most clearly stigmatized.[16]

Meanwhile, the capitalization of the second element within compounds (as in Buchner's *Frauen-Zimmer* 'ladies' in Jones (1995: 458) also increased steadily over time,[17] in both the *Sprachhelden* and the GerManC corpora (see Table 8.6). Even when the second half of the eighteenth century finally shows a steep decline in the overall frequency of such hyphenated

---

[14] The increase in frequency across time periods for both the Bonn and *Sprachhelden* corpora are significant: $x^2_{(DF)}$ 14.285$_{(1)}$, $p < 0.001$ and $x^2_{(DF)} > 30_{(3)}$, $p < 0.001$ respectively.

[15] The differences among time periods for each of the three corpora are significant: *Sprachhelden* ($\chi^2_{(DF)} > 30_{(3)}$, $p < 0.001$; Bonn $\chi^2_{(DF)} > 30_{(1)}$, $p < 0.001$; GerManC $\chi^2_{(DF)} > 30_{(3)}$, $p < 0.001$.

[16] In contrast, the pedagogue Matthias Kramer made a point of using the hyphen to clarify German word-structure for learners (Glück 2002: 444).

[17] The increase in capitalisation over time is statistically significant (linear regression: $F_{(DF)} = 71.55_{(1,2)}$, $p = 0.014$). Note that there are also significant differences among the three corpora ($\chi^2_{(DF)} > 30_{(2)}$, $p < 0.001$). Although not separately investigated here, capitalization is also very frequent in non-hyphenated compounds as well as in those with hyphens, e.g. *HaubtSprache* (in Schottelius's own usage).

Table 8.6: Frequency of compounds with capitalization of the element after the hyphen in the corpora examined

Bonn corpus		Sprachhelden corpus				GerManC newspaper corpus		
1550–1599	1650–1700	1600–1639	1640–1643	1664–1675	1680–1700	1650–1700	1700–1750	1751–1800
n/A	111/144 = 77.08%	6/11 = 54.5%	56/95 = 58.9%	77/111 = 69.4%	72/93 = 77.4%	374/376 = 99.5%	711/711 = 100%	140/140 = 100%

compounds compared to the first half, they are still *all* capitalized internally. Stieler's (1691: 30) stigmatization of such capitalization, noted by Takada, as *gar nicht fein* 'not at all good style' thus again seems to be a case of a grammarian attempting to shut the door after the horse has bolted. Overall, when these established practices, hyphenation inside compounds and capitalization of the second element, were stigmatized (gently by Schottelius, more forcefully by others after him), the stigmatization had no discernible effect.

8.3 SCENARIO 2: THE PRESCRIPTION CODIFIES PRACTICE THAT IS FOUND, BUT WHICH IS STILL MORE OR LESS MARGINAL COMPARED WITH OTHER FORMS, SPELLINGS AND STRUCTURES

Did Schottelius's prescription have any effect in supporting variants that were not dominant (either not yet, or no longer) in contemporary language use? In the following, a number of spellings (*dis* vs *dies* for 'this', *–b* in words like *um* or *umb* for 'around', initital vocalic *i–* or *j–*, and *u–* or *v–*) are considered, as well as one instance of inflection (the third person plural of the verb 'to be'). To begin, however, it is worth noting the case of a structure that Takada (1998) presents as an instance of my Scenario 2. Takada suggested that structures of the form *ist ge____ worden* for the perfect passive were not very common at the time Schottelius was writing (Takada 1998: 252–3), and so he views Schottelius's listing of the form (e.g. Schottelius 1663: 548 *ich bin geschlagen worden*) as an instance of him running ahead (*vorauseilen*) of common usage (my Scenario 2). However, my corpus evidence does not support this claim. The Bonn 1550–1600 corpus already has 176 tokens of *ge____ worden*, even if many of these suppress the auxiliary *sein*. Although it is difficult to quantify how many instances of this construction for the perfect passive would warrant the label 'frequent', it is certainly not infrequent. For comparison, the same corpus contains 122 tokens of the word *mir* 'me' [dative].[18]

To turn now to spelling, the limited data for the early decades of the seventeenth century suggest that Schottelius's preference for *dis–* over *dies–* for the demonstrative 'this' (*AA* 1663: 189–90; cf. Takada 1998: 82) was already going against the trend. Although *dis–* accounts for 56.1% of tokens in the 1550–1600 Bonn corpus, that figure drops to 6.8% for the second half of the seventeenth century (where all ten tokens are accounted

---

[18] On the other hand, the form *worden* is not yet reserved for the passive only: 34 instances of *worden* out of 205 (16.6%) are in the full sense of *werden*, 'to become'. The use of *geworden* rather than *worden* for 'become' first emerges in the corpus with about 7% in the *Sprachhelden* corpus for the period 1640–1700; 4 out of 11 contexts for 'become' in the 1650–1700 GerManC corpus, 3/6 for the period 1701–1750, and finally 3/3 in the second half of the eighteenth century.

for by a single text, by Marcus Eschenloher, *Augsburgischer Arzt*, Augsburg 1678) (see Table 8.7).[19] In the *Sprachhelden* corpus, *dis-* is already marginal in 1600–1639, with *dies-* in over 90% of contexts.[20] In contrast, in the more everyday writing of the GerManC newspaper corpus, *dis-* still accounts for nearly a third of contexts in 1650–1700, and still a good 15% in the period 1701–1750, though there is a significant decline over the three time periods.[21] Schottelius's preference for *dis-* (in an ideal world—it was not reflected even in his own practice) therefore seems to be a case where he chose not only the dispreferred form, but arguably also the lower prestige form, to judge by the difference in distribution between the *Sprachhelden* corpus and the newspaper corpus over the second half of the seventeenth century.[22] In this case, as the data from both the Bonn and the GerManC corpora show, Schottelius's prescription of *dis-* did nothing to stop the decline in frequency of this once widespread, indeed dominant, form (see Table 8.7).

Another area of variation in spelling was that of the historical *-b* in *um* or *umb* 'around' (cf. Middle High German *umbe*). Gueintz (1641) still considered *umb* an acceptable spelling, but all others after him rejected it (cf. Takada 1998: 84); Schottelius did so where he discussed his first spelling principle, dealing with superfluous letters (*AA* 188; also *AA* 648, cross-referring there to *AA* 204 on the letter *b*). In preferring *um*, Schottelius and his fellow-grammarians advocated a variant which—to judge by all three corpora—had not yet gained the upper hand, and was still in relatively even competition with *umb* (see Table 8.8). Not until the eighteenth century did the form *um* clearly gain the upper hand, and it ousted *umb* in the second half of the eighteenth century in the GerManC corpus.[23] This is even later than the shift observed by Takada (1998: 126) in the Lüneburg and Nuremberg printings of the Luther Bible after 1680. My scanty data

---

[19] Within the Bonn corpus, *dis-* is significantly less common in the later time period (chi-squared test: $\chi^2_{(DF)} > 30_{(1)}$, $p < 0.001$). *Dis-* is also significantly less common in the earliest samples from the *Sprachhelden* corpus than in the 1550–1600 samples from the Bonn corpus (chi-squared test: $\chi^2_{(DF)} > 30_{(1)}$, $p < 0.001$).

[20] Within the *Sprachhelden* corpus, the relative frequencies of *dies-* and *dis-* are not significantly different among time periods (chi-squared test: $\chi^2_{(DF)} = 2.943_{(3)}$, $p = 0.230$).

[21] Within the GerManC newspaper corpus, there are significant differences among time periods (chi-squared test: $x^2_{(DF)} > 30_{(2)}$, $p < 0.001$).

[22] The differences among the three corpora for samples in the period 1650–1700 are significant (chi-squared test: $x^2_{(DF)} > 30_{(2)}$, $p < 0.001$). We shall see below that in his preference for *-ere* as the marked plural of nouns ending in *-er* and for polyflection, Schottelius also advocated forms that were less prestigious. In these cases—and in preferring the temporarily more successful *-kk* rather than *-ck*—the forms Schottelius chose are closer both to Dutch, whose authors were such a strong influence on Schottelius, and to Low German, Schottelius's native dialect, which he considered closer to the 'true' language. Cf. 2.2.

[23] Pooling data from the three corpora reveals significant differences among time periods in the relative frequencies of *um* and *umb* (chi-squared test: $x^2_{(DF)} > 30_{(3)}$, $p < 0.001$), driven by the change post-1700 (while small differences among earlier time periods are not significant).

Table 8.7: The relative frequency of dies– and dis– in the three corpora

Bonn corpus

	1550–1600	%	1650–1700	%
dies–	242	43.9	137	93.2
dis–	309	56.1	10 all *Augsburgischer Arzt*	6.8
TOTAL	551		147	

Sprachhelden corpus

	1600–1639	%	1640–1643	%	1664–1675	%	1680–1700	%
dies–	37	94.9	64	100	72	93.5	31	96.9
dis–	2	5.15	0	0	5	6.5	1	3.1
TOTAL	39		64		77		32	

GerManC newspaper corpus

	1650–1700	%	1701–1750	%	1751–1800	%	1680–1700	%
Dies–	159	67.9	190	84.4	258	100	31	96.9
Dis–	75	32.1	35	15.6	0	0	1	3.1
TOTAL	234		225		258		32	

Table 8.8: The distribution of um *and* umb *in the corpora (including the variants* vm(b) *where found)*

Bonn corpus

	1550–1600	%	1650–1700	%
um	19	44.2	11	52.4
umb	24	55.8	10	47.6
TOTAL	43		21	

Sprachhelden corpus

	1600–1639	%	1640–43	%	1664–1675	%	1680–1700	%	All 1600–1680	%
um	8	53.3	0	0	2	40.0	4	100	14	47
umb	7	46.7	6	100	3	60.0	0	0	16	53
TOTAL	15		6		5		4		30	

GerManC newspaper corpus

	1650–1700	%	1701–1750	%	1751–1800	%	1680–1700	%	All 1600–1680	%
um	30	47.6	61	62.9	96	100.0	4	100	14	47
umb	33	52.4	36	37.1	0	0.0	0	0	16	53
TOTAL	63		97		96		4		30	

likewise show a change after 1680, where the *umb* variant disappears from the *Sprachhelden* corpus; and in the newspaper corpus, the shift appears to occur later still. One could interpret these data as possible evidence for the influence of prescription on practice, but with a delay of at least some decades. Furthermore, it is worth noting that both my (very limited) data from the *Sprachhelden* corpus and Takada's data show the shift occurring after 1680, while it does not appear to reach the GerManC corpus until the eighteenth century.[24] Significantly, this might constitute evidence for a shift first in more elite writing, only later reaching the more journeyman-like writing of the newspaper texts. However, this is a speculation that needs further investigation.

The spelling of words with initial *i–* for the vowel *i* is another area where Schottelius advocated a spelling that was not yet dominant, though present. From 1641 onwards (the date of the first edition of Schottelius's *Sprachkunst*), all grammarians called for a principled distinction between *i–/j–* and *u–/v–* (e.g. *und, ihn* instead of *vnd, jhn*). Schottelius (1641; cf. *AA* 213–214) had agreed with Gueintz (1641) and Bellin (1642) on this point, and 13 out of the 14 grammars after 1641 (up to Stieler 1691) examined by Takada (1998: 94–95) adopted this stipulation. Both the Bonn corpus and the earlier data from the *Sprachhelden* corpus indicate that before 1650, initial *j–* dominates over *i–* in the spelling of *ihn* and *ihnen* ('him *acc.*', 'them *dat. pl.*', investigated here as relatively high-frequency contexts for *i–/j–*), but the evidence suggests that the total elimination of *j–* in such contexts occurred quite rapidly from the late 1640s onwards, coinciding with, or coming hard on the heels of, the grammarians' advocacy of *i–* in these contexts. The Bonn corpus already shows 75% *i–* tokens for the 1650–1700 corpus;[25] the *Sprachhelden* corpus shows 100% for the post-1650 texts (a significant difference compared to the sixteenth-century Bonn corpus data),[26] and the newspaper corpus has no tokens of *j–* after 1700 (See Table 8.9).[27] Takada (1998: 121) likewise noted changes in new printings after 1650 in his corpora. Here, then, a swift change around the middle of the seventeenth century seems to coincide with the unified view of grammarians from 1641 onwards. We can also say that the change became established first, and most strongly, in the *Sprachhelden* corpus. Furthermore, within

---

[24] It should be noted that for the period 1650–1700, there is no significant difference in the relative frequencies of *um* and *umb* among the three corpora (chi-squared test: $x^2_{(DF)}$ = $0.229_{(2)}$, p = 0.892), but the concurrence of my own *Sprachhelden* data with the findings of Takada (both indicating a change post-1680) is still noteworthy.

[25] The difference in the relative frequencies of *ihn(en)* and *jhn(en)* between periods in the Bonn corpus is significant (chi-squared test: $\chi^2_{(DF)} > 30_{(1)}$, p < 0.001).

[26] For the period 1650–1700, there is a significant difference in the relative frequencies of *ihn(en)* and *jhn(en)* among the three corpora (chi-squared test: $\chi^2_{(DF)}$ = $11.645_{(2)}$, p = 0.003), driven by the fact that *jhn(en)* is less common in the *Sprachhelden* corpus.

[27] Within the GerManC newspaper corpus, there are significant differences among periods, with *ihn(en)* again being more common in the later periods (chi-squared test: $\chi^2_{(DF)}$ = $25.427_{(2)}$, p < 0.001).

Table 8.9: *i–* and *j–* in ihn *and* ihnen *in the corpora*

Bonn corpus

	1550–1600	%	1650–1700	%
total *ihm(en)*	11	7.0	27	75
total *jhn(en)*	158	93.5	9	25
TOTAL *i/jhn(en)*	169		36	

Sprachhelden corpus

	1600–1639	%	1640–43	%	TOTAL 1600–1643	%	1664–1675	%	1680–1700	%
total *ihm(en)*	2	18.2	8	36.4	10	30.3	40	100.0	14	100.0
total *jhn(en)*	9	81.8	14	63.6	23	69.7	0	0.0	0	0.0
TOTAL *i/jhn(en)*	11		22		33		40		14	

GerManC newspaper corpus

	1650–1700	%	1700–1750	%	1751–1800	%
total *ihm(en)*	32	82.1	60	100.0	76	100.0
total *jhn(en)*	7	17.9	0	0.0	0	0.0
TOTAL *i/jhn(en)*	39		60		76	

that corpus, there is a significant difference between the data before 1650 and those for 1664 onwards.[28] This is perhaps as close as it is possible to come to showing that a swift change in usage began in concert with a unified decision in the grammarians' prescription. As in the case of *um/umb* above, then, we might interpret these data as suggesting that the *Sprachhelden* authors, those closest to debates about spelling, implemented the change first, and that it spread thereafter to wider circles. It seems probable, then, that it may be adoption first by a prestige group that secures a subsequent change in the community at large (model i. in Figure 8.1 below), rather than the direct effect of prescription on the wider community (model ii.).

Model i.
Prescription > adoption by those language users socially close to the authorities > adoption by the wider community
Model ii.
Prescription by authorities > adoption by the wider community

Figure 8.1: Two possible models of how prescription influences wider language usage

The similar case of differentiating initial vocalic *u–* from consonantal *v–*, here examined by investigating spellings in the high-frequency word *und* 'and', may give us a clue as to how to interpret the relationship between prescription and practice for *i–/j–* and *um/umb*. The prescription landscape is identical to that of *i–* vs. *j–*. From 1641 onwards all grammarians, including Schottelius, distinguished consonantal *v–* from vocalic *u–* (cf. Schottelius 1663: 213; cf. Takada 1998: 94–95). Now, in the sixteenth-century Bonn corpus, *v–* still clearly dominated, but in the second half of the seventeenth century it was facing stiff competition from *u–*.[29] The *Sprachhelden* corpus shows a steep increase in *und* from the first to the second half of the seventeenth century. Yet while the *Sprachhelden* data for the second half of the century suggest a virtually total shift to *u–* in *und*, both the Bonn corpus and the newspaper corpus lag behind for the same period (a statistically significant difference),[30] and the newspaper corpus does not reach 100% acceptance till the second half of the eighteenth century, i.e. a full century later than the *Sprachhelden* writers (see Table 8.10). Once again, then, and more clearly than in the case of

---

[28] Within the *Sprachhelden* corpus, the frequency of *ihn(en)* is significantly higher after 1650 (chi-squared test: $\chi^2_{(DF)} > 30_{(1)}$, p < 0.001). There are no significant differences among periods before 1650 (chi-squared test: $\chi^2_{(DF)} = 1.148_{(2)}$, p = 0.563).

[29] The difference between the two time periods within this corpus is significant (chi-squared test: $\chi^2_{(DF)} > 30_{(1)}$, p < 0.001).

[30] For the period 1650–1700, there is a significant difference in the relative frequencies of *und* and *vnd* among the three corpora (chi-squared test: $\chi^2_{(DF)} > 30_{(2)}$, p < 0.001). Within the *Sprachhelden* corpus, there are significant differences among periods in the relative frequencies of the two variants (chi-squared test: $\chi^2_{(DF)} > 30_{(3)}$, p < 0.001), with *und* clearly becoming more common over time. The same pattern is seen within the GerManC newspaper corpus (chi-squared test: $\chi^2_{(DF)} > 30_{(2)}$, p < 0.001).

Table 8.10: Distribution of und *and* vnd *in the corpora (including* undt, unndt, *etc.)*

Bonn corpus

	1550–1599	%	1650–1700	%
und	371	10.3	295	48.7
vnd	3588	90.6	311	51.3
TOTAL	3959		606	

Sprachhelden corpus

	1600–1639	%	1640–1643	%	1664–1675	%	1680–1700	%	total 1664–1700	%
und	73	19.3	144	31.2	333	99.7	264	100.0	597	99.9
vnd	306	80.7	318	68.8	1	0.3	0	0	1	0.1
TOTAL	379		462		334		264		598	

GerManC newspaper corpus

	1650–1700	%	1700–1750	%	1751–1800	%
und	926	78.6	987	93.0	1178	100.0
vnd	252	21.4	74	7.0	0	0
TOTAL	1178		1061		1178	

i– considered above, we have evidence of a change which was first adopted by elite writers—those closest to grammarians—and which took rather longer to gain the same level of acceptance more widely. On this basis, we have fairly clear evidence for model i. in Figure 8.1—in which the practice of an influential group of writers close to the discussions is later adopted by writers more widely—and one might reasonably expect a similar process to have taken place in the case of *i–/j–* and *um/umb.*

The examples considered so far under Scenario 2 are orthographical, so it is useful to examine at least one instance of variation in inflection. Grammarians in the seventeenth century give three alternatives for the third person plural of the verb sein 'to be': *sind, seyn* and *seind* (and their orthographical variants).[31] Schottelius (*AA* 563) gives *sind/ oder seyn* (he gives only *sind* in the auxiliary to form the perfect tense of *sein,* but lists *sie seyn geworden* for the equivalent of *werden, AA* 555). Stieler (1691: 127) gives the third variant, however: *wir seyn/ sind und seind.* The Bonn corpus for the sixteenth century indicates a fairly even split between these three forms, so the exclusion by Schottelius of the form *seind* is striking, especially as the Bonn corpus data for 1650–1700 suggest that the *seind* form had perhaps even *gained* ground by this time, where it accounts for 50% of the available contexts (Table 8.11), though of only a small number of tokens (17/34—the apparent difference in distribution compared to the earlier period is not significant).[32] However, although the *Sprachhelden* corpus contains only a small number of contexts for this verb form (88 across the whole corpus), and again, the apparent differences are not significant,[33] the data hint at a preference for *sind,* with a possible slight decline in the use of *seind* variants, which are in any case much more sparsely represented here than in the Bonn corpus for the same century. Turning to the newspaper corpus, we find that the *seyn/sein* variant is marginal from the second half of the seventeenth century onwards—presumably dispreferred because of its identity with the infinitive?—but that *seind* variants account for almost half of the tokens.[34] In short, Stieler's listing of *seind* appears to reflect linguistic reality. Only in the second half of the eighteenth century does the *sind* variant win out. Here, then, Schottelius might, under the most generous of interpretations, be said to have selected the form that ultimately won out, *sind*—but alongside the form (*sein*)

---

[31] The three variants (each having various orthographical realizations) are: monophthong with alveolar plosive at the end (*sind,* etc.); diphthong with no alveolar plosive (*seyn,* etc.); and diphthong with alveolar plosive at the end (*seind,* etc.).

[32] Within the Bonn corpus there is no significant difference between periods in the relative frequencies of these variants (chi-squared test: $\chi^2_{(DF)} = 2.976_{(2)}$, p = 0.226).

[33] Within the *Sprachhelden* corpus there are no significant differences among periods in the relative frequencies of the three variants (chi-squared test: $\chi^2_{(DF)} = 4.387_{(4)}$, p = 0.112).

[34] The difference among periods in the relative frequencies of these variants in the GerManC corpus is significant (chi-squared test: $\chi^2_{(DF)} > 30_{(2)}$, p < 0.001).

Table 8.11: The relative frequency of variants for the third person plural of the verb 'to be' in the corpora

Bonn corpus

	1550–1600	%	1650–1700	%
sei/yn	143*	32.9	6	17.6
Sind	154	35.5	11	32.4
sey/ind(t)	137	31.2	17	50.0
TOTAL	434		34	

Sprachhelden corpus

	1600–1639	%	1640–43	%	1664–1675	%	1680–1700	%	TOTAL 1600–1700	%
sei/yn	1	12.5	5	14.3	1	3.8	4	21.1	11	12.5
Sind	4	50	27	77.1	18	69.2	14	73.7	63	71.6
sey/ind(t)	3	37.5	3	8.6	7	26.9	1	5.3	14	15.9
TOTAL	8		35		26		19		88	

GerManC newspaper corpus

	1650–1700	%	1700–1750	%	1751–1800	%
se/yn	4	4.2	4	4.2	0	0
Sind	45	47.4	55	57.3	127	100
sey/ind(t)	46	48.4	37	38.5	0	0
TOTAL	95		96		127	

* There were 617 hits for *seyn/sein*: a random selection of 160 was sampled, of which 37 were the third person plural of the verb; extrapolating the figures for the total of 617 yields a notional total of 142.7.

that rapidly declined, and ignoring altogether another form, *seind*, that was well-represented until the end of the seventeenth century and beyond.

To summarize Scenario 2: Schottelius's preference for the already less frequent *dis–* over *dies–* had no effect whatsoever. In the case of *um/umb*, there is evidence of a possible delayed response to the grammarians' prescriptions (including Schottelius's) after 1680. As for the rule governing initial vocalic *i–* and *u–*, here the grammarians do seem to have had an effect on wider language use, with the development being spearheaded first by the *Sprachhelden*. In the case of the third person plural of 'to be', Schottelius recognized the form that did ultimately win out, *sind*—but gave equal status to the form that was on its way out, *sein*.

8.4 Scenario 3: A variant is stigmatized

We have seen already that Schottelius's call for caution in the use of the hyphen and in capitalization within compounds, discussed above under Scenario 1, was succeeded later by firmer stigmatization, an instance of Scenario 3a. As for Scenario 3b, where stigmatized forms disappear from usage, this may often happen as a corollary of Scenarios 1 or 2: where prescribed forms remain or become established, competing forms are dispreferred. This is more likely to be the case for orthography and inflection, where standardization means pressure to select between competing variants; it is less likely to apply to syntactic structures for which it is difficult to define obligatory contexts. A case in point is the gradual stigmatization of auxiliary *tun* (e.g. *ich tue schreiben* 'I do write' rather than *ich schreibe* 'I write') in Early New High German. The process has been examined by Langer (2001), but grammarians like Schottelius do not comment on the form before 1680—rather, it was stigmatized by his contemporaries 'in poetics, epistolographies and rhetorics' as poor style (e.g. as a lazy way of manoeuvring the infinitive into final position for easy rhymes) and only later attracted the attention of grammarians (Langer 2001: 189–195, cited here p. 189).

8.5 Scenario 4: Schottelius advocates spellings, forms or structures that are not found at all in earlier practice

In some instances, Schottelius advocated out of personal conviction variants—especially certain spellings—that were at best rare in contemporary language use. Such instances are potentially of particular interest to us in assessing Schottelius's individual contribution to language practice. They are also of interest because, if successful, they would constitute unequivocal examples of 'change from above', where language users *consciously* notice and adopt variants.[35] Did any of Schottelius's recommendations catch on?

Schottelius's least successful such attempt is without doubt the advocacy in his fifth spelling principle of the spelling < *sl*– > in words like *schlagen* 'to hit' (and < *sw*– *sm*– *sn*– > rather than < *schw*– *schm*– *schn*–>) (*AA* 196–97), which he preferred because, although at odds with contemporary usage, it was common in older German texts which better retained the true nature of the language (see 5.5.3). Here none of the corpus evidence suggests that these forms ever found favour, with the single exception of Schottelius's own grammar of 1651 (cf. 5.5.3).

A second seemingly idiosyncratic stipulation in orthography was also ultimately unsuccessful, but does seem to have had some limited influence in the short term: Schottelius's preference for –*kk*– over –*ck*– by analogy with the general tendency for double consonants in such contexts (cf. modern German *we<u>ck</u>en* 'to wake' but *we<u>ll</u>en* 'to wave, be wavy'. The medial or final *kk* spelling had somewhat broader support amongst grammarians and orthographers than did the *sl*– spelling. Schottelius advocated the *kk* spelling in 1651 (cf. 1663: 206) following Zesen (1643), though in fact citing Harsdörffer (*loco ck hodierni Critici ponunt kk* 'in place of ck today's critics write kk', *AA* 206). Bellin (1657) followed suit. It seems that a certain circle of linguistically aware writers accepted it too. Takada found that works by Zesen, but also Rist, Carl Gustav von Hille, and Sigmund von Birken all used the spelling *kk*, and the *Sprachhelden* corpus for the years 1664–75 yields a total of 44 occurrences in works by five of the eight authors in that corpus, accounting for just over 30% of the 142 available contexts for *ck/kk*: Christian Weise (1642–1708), Christian Franz Paullini (1643–1712), Joachim Rachel (1618–1669), Georg Neumark (1619/21–1681), and Karl Christoph von Marchalk-Meerheim (fl. 1642–1676) (as well as one in a Philipp von Zesen text for the period 1640–43). Weise, Paullini and Marschalk-Meerheim could all be viewed as belonging to the next generation after Schottelius, so that there was a chance that this innovation might have become established among younger writers. Takada also found *kk* in over half (103.169 or 61%) of the printings he examined from the period 1640–1700 from 32 different cities (Table 4

---

[35] For clarity, note that 'change from above' refers to 'change from above the level of consciousness', rather than specifically a top-down change in terms of social class, percolating down from a prestige group (Labov 1972, 1994; cf. McMahon 244).

in Takada 1998: 104–119), including Zilliger, Schottelius's own printer in Braunschweig.[36] Yet *kk* did not become established in the long term. Out of a total of 101 possible contexts, no *kk* instances are found in the *Sprachhelden* 1680–1700 corpus; the Bonn sub-corpus for 1650–1700 yields instances of *kk* in only one text, Georg Goetze's (1633–1699) *Leich–Abdanckungen* (Jena, 1664); and there are no tokens at all in the GerManC newspaper corpus across the whole period from 1650 to 1800. Here, then, we have relatively clear evidence of a grammarian-induced development which had some success for a period of 50 years or so in some circles close to the prescriptivists but which did not become more widely established. Again, if one accepts that the *Sprachhelden* authors represent the elite, and the newspaper texts the product of journeyman writers, one might suggest that this was a 'top-down' attempt to introduce a change which, however—unlike the *u–/v–* and *i–/j–* cases, and despite some support from leading writers—did not succeed.

Schottelius's prescriptions also went against the grain in certain areas of inflection. Throughout all three editions of his grammar, Schottelius maintained that nouns ending in *–er, –el* should have a distinct plural form, by the addition of *–e*, thus *Bürgere, Himmele*, etc. (*AA* 305; see Takada 1998: 191–4), but he was flying in the face of established usage. Despite attestations of such forms in Luther (Solms & Wegera 1991: 173), the Bonn sub-corpus for 1550–1600 yields no tokens at all. Although two grammarians (Girbert 1653 and Bödiker 1691) followed Schottelius, the remainder were highly critical (starting already with Gueintz in 1640 in reaction to Schottelius's report on *his* grammar), and Moscherosch appears to be the only writer in Schottelius's network of acquaintances whose texts used the forms with some frequency: the Bonn sub-corpus for 1650–1700 yields one token from a 1650 text by Moscherosch, and Moscherosch's use

---

[36] Locally too, there is some apparent influence of Schottelius's on printing. Takada reports that the first work printed at Wolfenbüttel, where Schottelius lived and worked, to use the spellings advocated by Schottelius (1641) was a spiritual tract written by Schottelius's patron Duke August in 1644. A set of school regulations (a *Schulordnung*) printed in 1651 also reflected partial implementation of Schottelius's precepts. In the excerpt below (cited by Takada 1998: 97), the spellings *dy, Glük–* and *Zweks* all reflect Schottelius's first principle that superfluous letters that do not contribute to the pronunciation (as in *die, Glück, Zweck*) should be omitted (though Schottelius suggested *dj* rather than the *dy* we find here, and the *–kk* that he advocates is also not found where we might expect it in *Gluck, Zweck*) (*AA* 188–89).

> Nun dictiret dy Vernunft selbst/ daß zu Erhaltung solches hochnüzlichen Zweks/ aller Menschen zeitlicher und ewiger Glükseligkeit/ zweyerley Haupt = Mittel verordnet/ Erstlich/ daß dy Jugend fleissig/ mit grosser Behütsamkeit/ und zimlicher Strenge erzogen/ [...]

> 'Now reason itself dictates that to attain such a highly useful purpose, the worldly and eternal happiness of all people, two main means [be] instituted. First, that the youth [be] brought up diligently, with great care and fitting strictness'

of the *–ere* plural is also noted by Wegera (1987: 190–91), along with one token from Sigmund von Birken and another from Johann Justus Winkelmann (1620–1699). In the newspaper corpus (1650–1800) there is a lone instance from 1701 (Hanau, West Central German). The marginal usage by Moscherosch, Birken and Winkelmann thus constitutes the only possible evidence to date of a deliberate adoption of this 'new' form in response to the grammarian's prescription (although *–ere* endings were apparently common in West Upper German *Amtssprache*, and still persist in some dialect areas; Takada 1998: 194).

A third area of inflection where Schottelius's prescription stood out from the prevailing norm is so-called polyflection, or the double marking of case/gender on adjectives following an article which already marks it (e.g. *der guter Mann* rather than *der gute Mann*). This type of marking was perhaps attractive to grammarians because it followed the pattern of Latin, where all modifiers of the noun would mark case, gender and number equally explicitly (e.g. *hic vir bonus* 'this good man') and because it avoided the appearance of a 'feminine' *–e* in a masculine noun phrase, but it was at odds with the distinction between strong and weak adjective inflection in German. Grammarians agreed that both polyflection and monoflection were possible, but differed as to which they preferred as more pleasing to the ear. Schottelius (*AA* 1663: 235–236) appears to give preference to the *der ADJ-er* forms as sounding better (*mit besserem Wollaute*).

The linguistic reality appears to be that polyflection occurs marginally from 1550 right up to 1800. The Bonn sub-corpus for 1550–1600 yields eleven instances of polyflection in a masculine *der ADJ-er* structure (10%) out of a possible 107 contexts, though all eleven are accounted for by a single text, by Johann Gropper (Cologne 1556); the GerManC newspaper corpus furnishes a small percentage for each of the three periods, apparently declining over the period, though the data are too scanty to be of any statistical significance (see Table 8.12).[37] There are no instances of polyflection in a masculine noun phrase at all in the *Sprachhelden* corpus. A sole instance in a feminine dative noun phrase (*der Helden-sprachmässiger Wohlsäzzenheit*) is surely intended to be a parody, in line with the

Table 8.12: Frequency of polyflection in masculine noun phrases introduced by der *in the GerManC newspaper corpus*

1650–1700	%	1700–1750	%	1751–1800	%
44	91.7	56	96.6	43	97.8
4	8.3	2	3.4	1	2.2
48		58		44	

[37] Chi-squared test: $\chi^2_{(DF)} = 2.211_{(2)}$, p = 0.331.

overblown style and bizarre spelling of the satirical text by Christian Weise where it occurs, *Die drey ärgsten Ertz-Narren in der gantzen Welt* 'The three worst arch-fools in the whole world' of 1672 (see Jones 1995: 496):

> Und da müste Zizero saelbst ferstummen / ja dem Firgilius und Horazius ingleichen dem Ofidius würde es an gleichmässigen Glükkwünschungs-Wohrten fermangelbahren. Bei so angelaassenen Sachchen / solte ich schweugen / um meine in der Helden-sprach-mässiger Wohlsäzzenheit gahr wänig ausgekünstelt habende / und nicht allzu woortsälig erscheunende Schreibrichtigkeit [...]

> 'And Cicero himself would have to fall silent, and adequate words of congratulation would fail Virgil and Horace and Ovid too. That being so, I should say nothing about the correctness of my writing, which has undergone very little elaboration in the well-composed-ness of its heroic language, and which does not seem over-blessed with words.'[38]

In this case, the evidence—including the parody just cited—suggests that polyflection, always marginal, was also well on the way to being stigmatized in the second half of the seventeenth century. Amongst the many voices criticizing it (including Gueintz, Zesen, and Bellin) both Tscherning (1659) and Pölmann (1671) criticized the structure explicitly as a (hypercorrect?) Low German form (Takada 1998: 185). Schottelius was here out of step with the majority of his linguistically aware colleagues—perhaps indeed because of his Low German origins, to which Takada (1998: 194) also attributes his adherence to the *–ere* forms.

Under Scenario 4, then, where Schottelius went out on a limb, his prescriptions had no effect except in the case of *kk*, where there is very interesting evidence of an artificially induced change, albeit a temporary one—perhaps one of the earliest instances of language planning that imposed a change not already based in usage.[39]

8.6 SCENARIO 5: SCHOTTELIUS IS SILENT WITH REGARD TO A FORM WHICH NEVERTHELESS CHANGES IN FREQUENCY IN SUBSEQUENT USAGE

To conclude, and to give a rounder picture of the influence of grammarians like Schottelius on established usage, it is worth noting here two linguistic changes which escaped Schottelius's attention altogether. The first change in question is from *ward(e)* to *wurd(e)* for the third person singular

---

[38] I am grateful to Bill Jones for his assistance in rendering the deliberately overblown German of this passage in something approaching natural English.

[39] A more recent instance of such orthographical changes being imposed by authorities on a speech community is the German spelling reform (introduced over the years 1998–2008), a change that did not go smoothly. See Johnson (2005) and Johnson & Stenschke (2005).

preterite of the verb *werden* ('to become', also used as an auxiliary for the formation of the passive). This was a vowel change resulting from verb levelling, in line with the preterite plural *wurden*. Where he gave the conjugation of *werden* in full, Schottelius himself gave the preterite forms of *werden* as *ich war, du warest, er war, wir waren, ihr waret, sie waren* (*AA* 551); that is, he in fact gave the preterite of the verb 'to be'. However, in the formation of the passive of regular verbs, Schottelius gave (only) the older form in *er ward gehöret* 'he was heard' (*AA* 560). Yet the Bonn corpus data suggest quite a dramatic change taking place by the second half of the seventeenth century,[40] as the form *wurde*—not noted by Schottelius at all, though Stieler (1691: 129) gives it alongside *ward*—already accounted for one third of contexts for the verb in the sixteenth century, and became the dominant one (averaging two-thirds) for the seventeenth century.[41] However, caution is needed here: there are also significant differences among the corpora for the period 1650–1700 (see Table 8.13).[42]

Finally, there is also modest evidence that Schottelius himself was sensitive in his own practice to linguistic changes that he did not mention or codify at all. One systematic change in style (or grammar) that he made between 1641 and 1663 is his elimination of a handful of double negatives (like *keiner [...] nicht* 'no one [...] not', documented in Table 8.14). This constitutes the earliest evidence of a grammarian's sensitivity to poly-negation in German. Schottelius himself still listed double negatives of the form *mit nichten nicht* as an acceptable emphatic form of negation in the grammar of 1663 (*AA* 777), and it would be almost a century before Adelung (1754) issued the first explicit warning against it (Langer 2001: 167; but cf. also Davies & Langer 2006: 241–259). That is, Schottelius appears to have done away with his own double negatives systematically, but without commenting himself, and almost a century before their first stigmatization by a grammarian. It is likely that he did so in reaction to their potential ambiguity, since evidence from Hamburg commercial records suggests that two negatives were already being used with a positive reading in the seventeenth century, rather than as an emphatic negative (Lange 2008: 286). At any rate, in this case a new linguistic practice was emerging which Schottelius appears to have been dimly aware of on some level, but which he did not comment on explicitly, and which indeed did not excite *any* grammarian's comment for another 89 years.

---

[40] The difference is significant: $\chi^2_{(DF)} = 13.297_{(1)}$, p = 0.001. The differences between the time periods in the GerManC corpus are not significant ($\chi^2_{(DF)} = 3.863_{(1)}$, p = 0.145).

[41] Note that these % figures do not allow for *war* in place of *ward* or *wurde*, but express only the relative distribution of *ward(e)* and *wurd(e)*. There is an apparent resurgence of *ward* in the second half of the eighteenth century. Whether this is more than an artefact of the corpus selection is a question that must wait for the completion of the GerManC corpus project.

[42] Chi-squared test: $\chi^2_{(DF)} = 6.210_{(2)}$, p = 0.045.

Table 8.13: *Distribution of the forms* wurd(e) *and* ward(e) *in the corpus data, 1550–1800 (raw figures, with % in bold)*

	16th century	17th century				18th century	
	Bonn 1550–1600	Bonn 1650–1700	Spracheheldan 1640–1700	GerManC newspapers 1650–1700	TOTAL 17th century	GerManC Newspapers 1701–1750	GerManC Newspapers 1751–1800
ward (*warde*)	144 (of which 2 *warde*) **66.7%**	6 **27.3%**	9 **60%**	3 **20%**	18 **34.6%**	6 **28.6%**	20 **45.5%**
wurde (*wurd*)	72 **33.3%**	16 (of which 1 *wurd*) **72.7**	6 **40%**	12 **80%**	34 **65.4%**	15 **71.4%**	24 **55.5%**
Total	216	22	15	15	52	21	44

Table 8.14 Double negatives eliminated between 1641 and 1663

	1641	1651	1663
AA 10, 1: 31	*und wird mit nichten nicht*	as in 1641	*und wird nicht*
AA 10, 1: 31	*Es sol und kan keiner nicht*	*Es sol und kan keiner*	as in 1651
AA 20, 2: 17	*gar nichts nicht*	as in 1641	passage deleted
AA 123, 8: 2	*mit nichten nicht*	as in 1641	*mit nichten*

8.7 CONCLUSION

It would be impossible to give a complete assessment of the influence of Schottelius's grammar on subsequent practice here, for that would require another book. However, investigating the various possible scenarios here has revealed—as Takada's study already suggested—the full gamut of influence, from variants that Schottelius advocated that were never adopted, to variants where Schottelius (and others) may well have played a part in cementing them as standard, to the case of the double negative, which Schottelius himself avoided in his use, but whose stigmatization came only much later. The investigation has also shown that Schottelius was in some individual cases more guided by usage than principle, perhaps more than he realized, as he gave *soll* but not *sollte*, which, though it would have been analogically 'correct', is not attested in my corpora at the time he was writing. The investigation has also shown how the scenarios outlined at the outset can succeed one another: Schottelius's silent replacement of double negatives was to yield over the following century to active stigmatization; so too views hardened after him on hyphenated compounds and on compounds with internal capitalization, apparently in reaction to their increasing frequency. Particularly interesting is the evidence of the *i–/j–* and *u–/v–*, as it shows how certain variants, already in use, became firmly established in the circle of the *Sprachhelden*, the social group closest to the grammarians, before spreading to the language community more widely. Finally, the *kk* spelling is a strikingly early instance where a language variant with no historical basis in the language could be artificially imposed by authorities on language users, albeit with only temporary and limited success.

9
CONCLUSION

Schottelius's *Ausführliche Arbeit* is portrayed in the paratextual material as a work to further the refinement of the German language in accord with its nature, in order to promote a prosperous, peaceful, Christian realm and to set an example to other Germanic nations. Taking the work on those terms, this book has presented for the first time a coherent interpretation of the multifaceted 'Comprehensive work on the German language', and has considered its legacy in Germany and abroad. Looking at the architexts of the word-lists, orations, dialogue, verse, and poetics has illuminated Schottelius's selection of text-types. We have also seen how the confluence of distinct discourse traditions—from the local cultural patriotism of the *Fruchtbringende Gesellschaft* to international scholarly theorizing about language—shaped Schottelius's conception of language, his evidence base, and his argumentational and rhetorical strategies.

Schottelius's training in law had exposed him to legal texts edited by the earlier generations of humanists, which helped him grasp how German had changed but was still recognizably 'the same'. That legal background also helped determine Schottelius's manner of discussing the pressing questions of his era about the nature, origin and kinship of German, a manner that combined a requirement for evidence and careful weighing of testimonies with persuasive rhetoric. As a grammarian, Schottelius followed the basic structure of the 'Latinizing' German grammars that had been appearing since the 1570s, but he made refinements in description and terminology, and added more details and examples which were in turn taken over by his successors. For the first time in German—and, in the first edition of 1641, very possibly for the first time in any European vernacular—he combined the practical grammatical genre with a unified theory of the nature of language. That theory combined Vossius's (1635) principle of analogy, from the 'cutting edge' in Latin grammar with Grotius's view of natural law, and with a cultural-patriotic faith in Germanic monosyllabic rootwords as the basic units of analysis. Schottelius was steeped in the linguistic scholarship of the preceding century or so, and following in the footsteps of earlier generations of German and Low Countries scholars in particular, he saw the rootword as guarantor of German antiquity, purity, flexibility and richness. His account of derivation and compounding, the first of its type in any European language, was founded on his belief in the unique qualities of the German(ic) rootword, conceptualized in the image of the ever-spreading banyan tree.

Just as the twin notions of *analogy* and the *rootword* in Schottelius grew out of the intersection of intellectual traditions that crossed national and discourse boundaries, so their legacy similarly crossed national boundaries. As Chapter 7 showed, Schottelius's combination of the analogical principle with a rootword-based linguistic analysis was to leave a lasting impression on the grammatographical traditions of Dutch especially, but also of Swedish and Russian; it was also adapted to teaching German as a foreign language in England and elsewhere; and it influenced discussions of the origin and nature of language at least until Humboldt. Through Schottelius, the notion of the monosyllabic rootword ultimately reached as far as studies of Russian, Semitic and even Sanskrit. Within Germany, Schottelius's grammar, though reprinted in 1737, was superseded by others by the later eighteenth century, but those grammars themselves still bore the clear traces of Schottelius's legacy, at least as far as Heynatz (1803). Schottelius's account of word-formation laid the basis for mainstream German morphological studies and, minus its imagery, it still forms the basis of modern word-formation theory. As for the vexed question of whether any grammar has an effect on language usage, it remains extremely difficult to assess to what extent Schottelius's work can be credited with directly helping to shape the emerging standard German language. In one instance, a temporary and limited change in spelling (*kk*) does seem directly attributable to Schottelius's influence, but overall the answer to the question of his influence on practice appears to be 'perhaps some, along with others, but not that much' (Chapter 8). As a contributor to German cultural patriotism, however, Schottelius's legacy lasted at least until the 1920s, when Hugo von Hofmannsthal (1927) cited him.

In sum, Schottelius was not just a 'German Varro', as he was styled in the paratextual material of the *AA* (Chapter 1), but arguably also a 'vernacular Vossius', who showed how recent grammatical theory could be applied to the vernacular (Chapters 2 and 5), and so enabled others to follow his example for their vernaculars too (Chapter 7). As a cultural patriot, Schottelius strove to inaugurate a new epoch in the German language, as he believed that Charlemagne and Luther had done in centuries past, supplying genres in the vernacular that demonstrated the cultural specificity and the cultural prestige of German (Chapter 4). As a grammarian of German, he left a legacy that lasted at least 150 years. Finally, as an energetic rhetorician who saw language through the typically pansemiotic lens of his era, Schottelius championed the task of studying German with such verve and vividness that he showed once and for all that studying the German language is important, relevant, challenging, and fascinating.

APPENDIX

AUTHORITIES AND SOURCES REFERENCED IN THE *AUSFÜHRLICHE ARBEIT*

Schottelius's inclusion of a name in the ostensible list of sources on pages c2–De at the front of the *AA* does not appear to correlate either with its prominence in the *AA* as a whole, or with its prominence in the list of good writers (Treatise IV of Book V). Hucbaldus, for instance, is listed on c3^r, but does not appear to be referenced anywhere else in the *AA*, likewise Mattheus Paris (c3^v). This appendix lists authors and works referenced by Schottelius anywhere in the *AA*, whether in the list on pages c2, c3 and De, in the orations of Book I, the grammar (Books II and III), or the poetics (Book IV), or in the treatises of Book V. I have also drawn on Neuhaus (1991) and Moulin-Fankhänel (1994, 1997a, 1997b). Use has also been made of the two online catalogues of German sixteenth- and seventeenth-century imprints: the *Verzeichnis der im deutschen Sprachbereich erschienenen Drucke des 16. Jahrhunderts* (http://www.bsbmuenchen.de/16-Jahrhundert-VD16.180.0.html) and the *Verzeichnis der im deutschen Sprachraum erschienenen Drucke des 17. Jahrhunderts* (http://www.vd17.de/). References to entries in these catalogues generally begin *VD16* or *VD17*; such references are not given throughout, but are supplied in cases where the work is less widely known, or to specify a particular edition.

It is almost inevitable that in a work the size and density of the *AA*, some sources referenced will have been overlooked, and I would be grateful to be advised of any such omissions, as well as of any errors.

The following principles have been followed in compiling this list:

1. Entries are arranged alphabetically by author, but Schottelius's own abbreviations are also included in cases where it would not be obvious to what or to whom they refer, with a cross-reference to the main entry as appropriate. Where authors are known by both Latin and German names (e.g. Aventinus / Turmair), both names are listed.

2. Page references to the *AA* are not necessarily exhaustive, but are intended to be indicative of the parts of the *AA* where the source is cited. Listed first are any page references to the list of authors and their abbreviations on pages c2–De, and to the fourth treatise of Book V (on German writers, *AA* 1148–1215), which also serves in part as a list of sources. Thereafter page references are in numerical order. References to the orations of Book I are given in the form

page, oration: paragraph; for example, *9, 1: 27* refers to page 9, first oration, paragraph 27. References to the grammar give paragraph number where appropriate, in the form *page.paragraph*, e.g. 174.9 refers to paragraph 9 on page 174.

3. Authorities only mentioned or cited within citations from other authorities, and not referred to by Schottelius directly, are not generally included, except where listed in the fourth treatise of Book V.

4. I have not attempted to verify systematically whether in some cases Schottelius accessed sources indirectly, as seems to be the case with Dresser, for example.

5. Life-dates have been taken from readily available online sources, including library catalogues but also online encyclopaedias. They are given as a guide, though they have been verified where possible against the *Allgemeine Deutsche Biographie*, its successor the *Neue Deutsche Biographie,* and Koerner (2008).

6. In many cases it was not possible to determine which edition of a named work Schottelius had access to. In these cases I have cited either the earliest edition I have been able to identify, or an edition that it is possible Schottelius might have had access to because it is held at the Herzog August Library in Wolfenbüttel.

REFERENCES TO THE BIBLE

Besides the references listed below, there are frequent biblical references in the *AA*. These are discussed briefly in Chapter 6, but because Schottelius referred to the books of the bible by their Latin abbreviations, the following list gives those Latin abbreviations used by Schottelius that would not be immediately recognizable to the modern reader.

Abbreviation	Book
Eccles.	Ecclesiastes
Esai.	Isaiah
Ier. /Jer.	Jeremiah
Iob	Job
Matth.	Matthew's Gospel
Num.	Numbers
Par., Paral. (= *Paralipomena*)	Chronicles (I or II)
Reg.	Kings (I or II)
Thren. (= *Threnodes*)	Lamentations

ALPHABETICAL LIST OF SOURCES REFERRED TO BY SCHOTTELIUS IN THE *AUSFÜHRLICHE ARBEIT*

passim in the poetics and in Treatise VI of book V. In the poetics, examples from Schottelius's own poetry are marked with a *, as explained in the preface to the reader of the 1656 edition of the poetics, but not in the 1663 edition itself, where the preface to the reader does not appear. Schottelius used his own examples over 150 times, which makes him his own most important 'source' of examples in the poetics. In the the sixth treatise of Book V, the list of rootwords, * indicates words of Low German origin (cf. *AA* 1274: 7).

A.R.. 84, 6: 25. Reference given for the compound *Mordbrenner*. Perhaps *Alfreds Reg.* (see under *L. L.* below) or similar, for which see Lindenbrog, and see 6.2.2.

Abbas Spanheimensis. 176. See Trithemius.

Abele, Matthias (von Lilienberg) (1616 or 1618–1677). 1203. Member of the FG. Schottelius noted his *Metamorphosis. Telæ Judiciariæ: Das ist: Seltzame Gerichtshändel* (Nuremberg: Endter, 1654; VD17 23:679729B).

Acosta, Josephus = José de Acosta (1539–1600). 58, 4: 22. Spanish Jesuit. Schottelius repeated de Laet's extract from Acosta's writings, presumably from *De natura novi orbis libri duo* (Cologne: Mylius, Birckmann, 1596; VD16 A 119) on American Indian communication by knots in rope.

act. = *Acta und Ordnungen.* c2ʳ; 365. Page C2ʳ glosses the abbreviation as *allerhand Acta und Ordnungen / so allemahl nicht kunten allegiret werden* 'all sorts of acts and ordinances that could not all be listed'.

Adalarius Erichius (ca. 1530–1634). 1184. See Erich, Adolar.

Agathias Scholasticus (536–582/594). 1154. Greek (Byzantine) historian and poet.

Agobard, Bishop of Lyon (779–840). 517. The bishop's works were re-discovered in Lyon and published in 1605 by Papirius Masson (1544–1611). The Wolfenbüttel library holds a copy published in Paris by Duvallius (1605).

Agricola, Johannes (1494–1566). Schottelius drew on an expanded, posthumous edition of the theologian Agricola's proverb collection (VD16 A 969): *Siebenhundert vnd funfftzig Deutscher Sprüchwörter[…]* (Wittenberg: Gedruckt bey M.Johan.Krafft, 1592).

Aimoin (c. 960–c. 1010). 450. French chronicler, from whose *Historia Francorum* a letter by Hincmar, Archbishop of Reims (806–882), is cited (perhaps indirectly from Lindenbrog, q.v.).

Aitinger, Johann Conrad (1577–1637). 1205. Schottelius referred to Aitinger's 1653 work in German on hunting birds, *Kurtzer und einfältiger Bericht vom Vogelstellen* (Cassel; VD17 23:232417M).

Albertus Argentinensis = Albrecht von Strassburg (d. 1378). 1156. German historian whose work covered the period from Emperor Rudolph I to Charles IV, i.e. up to 1349. Fragments of his chronicle were printed in 1569 with Cuspinianus's (q.v.) *Austria* (Basle: Oporinus, 1553; BV011382638).

Albertus, Laurentius (Ostrofrank / Osterfrank) (1540?– after 1583). c3ᵛ; 1183. Schottelius noted Albertus's grammar of 1573 (the first German grammar), but called it inadequate and incomplete. Cf. Moulin-Fankhänel (1994: 39–43).

Albinus, Petrus (Peter von Weiße) (1543–1598). c3ᵛ; 1184. Author of historical works on Saxony and Meißen. He contributed to Wolfgang Krauß's *Stam vnd Ankunfft|| DEs Hochlöblichen Hauses zu Sachsen [...]* (Magdeburg: bey Johann Francken, 1587; VD16 K 2307); his *Meißnische Land– und Bergchronik* in two volumes appeared 1589–90 (Dresden: Bergen, Gimel d.Ä.; VD16 W 1678), and includes some remarks on the German language.

Alexandrinus, Clemens (ca. 150–215). 34, 3: [13]. See Clement of Alexandria.

Alpinus. See Tatius, Marcus.

Althamer(us), Andreas (ca. 1500–1539). 41, 3: 30; 1020. Reformer and humanist, author of numerous theological writings.

Amadis de Gaula. 1193. Prose chivalric Romance in Castilian Spanish of which the earliest printed Spanish version known is that of Garci Rodríguez de Montalvo in 1508. Schottelius praised the anonymous German translation in an edition of 1583 (believing the French to be the original), but was critical of some of the prominence of sorcery (*Zauberey*) in the plot. The 1583 Frankfurt edition was in fact a compendium of the multi-volume octavo edition that preceded it, 1569–75. On the identity of the German translators, one of whom was Johann Fischart (1546/47–ca. 1590), see Weddige (1975: 59–95).

Andlo, Petrus de = Peter von Andlaw (1425–1480). c3ᵛ; 291. See Freher, Marquard.

Annius of Viterbo (1432?–1502). 1202; 31, 3: 7; 134, 9: 15. Schottelius referenced Annius's well-known *Antiquitatum Variarum* in 17 vols. (Venice, 1499, and many later editions), in which Annius, a member of the Dominican order, published supposed writings and fragments of various pre-Christian Greek and Latin authors (including Berosus) which he claimed to have discovered in Mantua, but which are not authentic. A sixteenth-century edition is: Antwerpen: Steelsius, 1552. Schottelius took the reference to him as Vetulonius Annius from Duret (1613: 822), where Duret noted *Vn certain Annius Vetulonius au parauant le susdict Beconaus avoit tenu la mesme opinion contre lequel Lylius Giralldus a amplement discouru en son histoire des poetes dialogue 1* 'a certain Annius Vetulonius before the aforementioned Becanus held the same opinion, against which Lylius Giralldus discoursed amply in his history of the poets dialogue 1'. (*Vetulonia* was identified with modern Viterbo by Annius himself.)

Anon. Chronicle. 1171. See Bartolomeo Platina.

Anon. Saxon chronicle [in old Saxon]. 1171. A Saxon chronicle (after 1225) attributed to Eike von Repgow (ca. 1170–after 1233), q.v., where Schottelius found many Saxon words 'not known in High German'.

Anon., *Uhrsprung und Ordnungen der Bergwerge* (1616). 1189. Schottelius noted this work on mining: *Ursprung und Ordnungen der Bergwerge inn Königreich Böheim, Churfürstenthum Sachsen, Ertzhertzogthum Osterreich, Fürstenthumb Braunschweig und Lüneburgk, Graffschafft Hohenstein: darin eins theils biß an hero noch nie in Druck ausgangen; Alles mit vleis zusammen getragen, und, was in iedem gehandelt, auff nachfolgendem Blat zu befindenn* (Leiptzigk: Gross, 1616; VD17 3:003835W).

Appian of Alexandria (1st century A.D.). 1150; [mentioned] 37, 3: 26. Greek historian, who wrote a history of Rome.

Apuleius = Lucius Apuleius Platonicus (120–155 A.D.). 1181. Author of a Latin picaresque novel, translated by Johann Sieder.

Arc. 365. See Sidney, Philip.

Aretinus, Leonhardus Brunus = Bruni (Aretino), Leonardo (1369–1444). 1182. Florentine humanist, historian and translator of Greek authors. Schottelius noted Tatius's (q.v.) translation of Bruni's first published work of history, *De primo bello punico* (1422), based largely on Polybius.

Ariosto, Ludovico (1474–1533). 1191. See Werder, Diederich von dem, for his translation of Ariosto's *Orlando Furioso* (1532).

Aristotle (of Stageria) (384–322 B.C.). 16, 2: 2; 51, 4: 5; 112, 7: 18. Philosopher (Stammerjohann 1996, 2009, s.v. Aristotle.).

Arndt, Johann (1555–1621). 1179. Lutheran theologian and author of influential devotional works.

Augustinus = St. Augustine (Aurelius) of Hippo (354–430). 31, 3: 8; 35, 3: 18; 40, 3: 32. One of the great 'Church Fathers'. Born in Northern Africa, he became Bishop of Hippo. Schottelius cited his *On The City of God* (*De Civitate Dei*) (413–426), which attempted to interpret the history of the Roman Empire (particularly the sack of Rome in 410) as the action of God in the world.

Aventin(us), Joannes = Johannes Turmair (1466 or 1477–1534). 1156; 17, 2: 5; 35, 3: 16; 171: 1; 176: 12; 213, 32.3; 371 and *passim* in the grammar; 1016; 1018; 1031; 1032; 1036; 1037; 1039; 1047; 1049; 1051; 1052; 1053; 1060; 1084; 1097; 1389 *Ruhn*; 1408 *Schranner*. Johannes Turmair, who called himself Aventinus in Latin after his home town of Abensberg, was commissioned by the Dukes Wilhelm and Ludwig to write a history of Bavaria, the *Annales ducum Baioariae,* completed in 1521, and then translated the work into German in 1522, as the *Bayrische Chronik,* in the process of which he also made various changes. The works were not printed until after his death 1554 in Ingolstadt (the Latin version) and 1556 in Frankfurt (the German version). His history followed the humanist ideals of critical use of sources (rather than simply compiling from earlier authorities). According to Neuhaus (1991:148), Schottelius used the 1566 edition (Frankfurt: Feyerabendt; VD16 T 2320) of 848 pages plus numerous tables and illustrations. See also Jones (1995: 18–20).

Bacon, Francis (Baron of Verulam, Viscount of St. Albans) (1561–1626). 148, 9: 30. Leading figure in natural philosophy and scientific methodology. Schottelius referred to his *De Dignitate Et Augmentis Scientiarum. Ad Regem Suum. Libri IX.* (1624; German edition e.g. Argentorati: Bockenhoferus, 1654; VD17 3:312494M).

Bapst (von Rochlitz), Michael (1540–1603). 1187. Pastor and writer of popular medical works. Schottelius noted his medical compendium, *Wunderbarliches Leib und Wund Artzneybuch* in three vols. (Eißleben: Grosse, 1596–1597).

Barclaius = Barclay, John (1582–1621). 1206; 6, 1: 15; 24, 2: 32; 259; 1222. Writer of Scottish origin, though born in France, famous for the elegance of his wit. Wrote Latin works in prose and verse, including a *[Euphormionis Lusinini] Satyricon* in four parts. In his *Icon Animorum,* the third part of the *Satyricon* (London, 1614), he described the character and manners of the European nations. The Wolfenbüttel library holds a 1620 edition (Frankfurt: Aubrii), and Schottelius (*AA* 1206) noted a 1626 translation by Opitz (q.v.) of Barclay's best-known work, the *Argenis,* a political romance, as well as a translation of his *Iconum animorum* by Winckelmann (q.v.).

Bartas, Herr von = du Bartas, Guillaume de Salluste (1544–1590). c2^r; 85, 6: 26; 115–16, 7: 30. French Huguenot soldier and poet, known chiefly for his epic poems *La Sepmaine; ou, Creation du monde* (1578) and the unfinished *La Seconde Sepmaine* (1584), which retell the main events of the bible from a Protestant viewpoint. His verse was translated into German by Tobias Hübner, q.v. Schottelius gave examples of his French compounds *AA* 85, 6: 26.

Barthius = Caspar von Barth (1587–1658). c2^r; 186. German philologist and writer. Schottelius referred to his *Adversariorum commentariolum* in 60 books (Frankfurt: Aburii, 1624; VD17 3:311505M), some 3000 pages of miscellaneous material.

Bartoldus (Berthold of Reichenau) (ca.1030–1088). 1155. Continuator of the chronicle of Hermann Contractus, q.v.

Bartolomeo Platina (1421–1481). 1194 (unnamed). Schottelius referred to Bartolomeo Platina's chronicle of popes up to Pope Sixtus IV, printed

1494. (Schottelius's reference to Sixtus V—who died in 1590—must be a typographical error). The reference is presumably to Bartolomeo Platina's *Vitae pontificum* ('Lives of the Popes', 1479), early editions of which were sometimes anonymous and undated. I have not identified a 1494 edition, but a wrong dating (e.g. on the basis of an early dated ownership inscription) is possible.

Baurm. De jurisd. 426. See Paurmeister, Tobias.

Becanus, Joannes Goropius. See Goropius Becanus, Joannes.

Becmann, Christian (1580–1648). 21, 2: 21; 142, 9: 15. Evangelical theologian and pedagogue. Schottelius referred to his *Manuductio ad latinam linguam* (Wittenberg: Helwig, 1608), and to his *De originibus linguae latinae* (Wittenberg: Helwig, 1609).

Becker, Cornelius (1561–1604). 1179. Noted as a translator of the psalms; see Vogel, Johann.

Beda Presbyter = Bede the Venerable (673–735). 57, 4: 17. Benedictine who wrote a *Historia ecclesiastica gentis Anglorum*, an Anglo-Saxon ecclesiastical history much quoted by later British historians, and which first appeared in print in Strasbourg, 1475. It gives an account of Christianity in England from its beginnings to Bede's own days, also citing earlier sources.

Belinus = Bellin, Johannes (1618–1660). 1202; noted 4, 1: 8; 681. Schottelius noted Bellin's *Hochdeudsche Rechtschreibung* of 1657 and his 1661 work on the syntax of German prepositions, *Syntaxis Praepositionum Teutonum oder Deudscher Forwörter Kunstmäßige Fügung* (both Lübeck: Volk). Noted *AA* 681 for his collection of homophones. See Moulin-Fankhänel (1997b: 37–43), Jones (1995: 446–447).

Bergmann, Michael (fl. 1662). 1201; 117, 7: 34. Schottelius referenced Bergmann's collection of poetical expressions published in 1662, *Deutsches aerarium poeticum, oder, Poetische Schatzkammer: das ist, Poetische Nahmen, Redens-Arthen und Beschreibungen, so wol geist- als weltlicher Sachen, Gedicht und Handlungen ... Theils aus Hn. Martini Opitzens, Paul Fleminges ... theils aus dem Lateinischen der Jugend bekanten ... / reimstimmig übersetzet und ausgefertiget durch M. Michael Bergmann [...]* (Jena, Stettin: Mamphras, 1662).

Berlich, Matthias (1586–1638). 393. Jurist, author of *Conclusiones practicabiles* (Leipzig, 1615–19. 5 vols; revised third edition 1628, and several other editions).

Besold(us), Christoph(orus) (1577–1638). 1170; 4, 1: 9; 33, 3: 13; 125–26, 8: 4–6; 257; 272; 288; 307; 321; 337; 624 and *passim*; 1033; 1037; 1049; 1053; 1077; 1408 *Schorn*. German jurist and publicist. Cited in the list of rootwords (Neuhaus 1991: 160–61), as well as in the orations. Amongst his 50 books are *De natura populorum eiusque pro loci positu, temporisque decursu variatione: Ac insimul etiam, De linguarum ortu et immutatione*. Schottelius consulted the 1632 edition (Tübingen: Philibertus Brunnius) held in Wolfenbüttel (as opposed to the earlier 1619 edition, Tübingen: Johan-Alexandri Cellii). He also cited his *Thesaurus practicus continens explicationem terminorum atque Clausularum, in Aulis & Dicasteriis usitatarum* (Tübingen: apud Philibertum Brunnium, 1629). This work was also contributed to by Speidel (q.v.), whom Schottelius names elsewhere as an author of it.

Betulius. See Birken, Sigmund von.

Bibliander, Theodorus (Georg Buchmann) (1504–1564). 57, 4; 21; 60, 4: 30; 74, 6: 3; 97, 6: 53; 176: 12; 1044. Swiss theologian and teacher. Bibliander called himself *homo grammaticus*; he was versed in the Semitic dialects and was master of several modern languages. Most of his writings were never published, but are preserved in manuscript in Zürich. Schottelius referred to his *De Ratione communi omnium linguarum et literarum commentarius ... : cui adnexa est compendiaria explicatio doctrinae recte beateque vivendi, et religionis omnium gentium atque populorum, quam argumentum hoc postulare videbatur* (Tiguri: Froschauer, 1548) (cf. Metcalf 1980).

Birken, Sigmund von = Sigismundus Betulius (1626–1681). c3ᵛ; 1176; 201; 625 and *passim*; 863. Member of the FG. German poet, writer and playwright. Cited in the grammar (once) and in the poetics; contributed a dedicatory poem. See Jones (1995: 379–393).

Birkhemerus, Bilibaldus = Willibald Pirckheimer. 1159. See Pirckheimer, Willibald.

Bocatius = Boccaccio, Giovanni (1313–1375). 1182. See Steinhöwel, Heinrich.

Boccalini, Traiano (1556–1613). 1205. Schottelius referred to a 1644 edition of a German translation of Boccalini's work: *Relation aus Parnasso [...] das ist, Allerhand lustige anmüthige so wol politische historische als moralische Discurs* (Franckfurt: Beyer; VD17 23:291655Y).

Bocer, Heinrich (1561–1630). 622. Jurist and Tübingen professor who published many legal treatises. *AA* 622 referred to his treatise *De Diffidationibus [...]* 'on feuds' (Tübingen: Wildius, 1625; VD17 23:316147C).

Bock (or Tragus), Hieronymus (1498–1554). 1188. Schottelius noted Bock's 1546 German *New Kreütter Buch* or 'herbal', to which he had access in a 1565 edition (Strasbourg: Rihel). Schottelius cited a lengthy passage from the preface in which Bock noted German ignorance about plants, which his book aimed to remedy, and Schottelius considered he did the German language *guten Dienst* 'good service'.

Böckler, Georg Andreas (*= Bokl.; Bolckl.* at the bottom of p. 531 is presumably an error) (attested 1644–1698). 1207. 418, 448; 531. Schottelius referred to Böckler's architectural manual *Manuale architecturae militaris, oder Handbüchlein uber die Fortification und Vestungs Bawkunst* (Frankfurt: Götze, 1659) and his work on arithmetic for military purposes (Nuremberg: Endter, 1661).

Bodinus = Jean Bodin (1530?–1596). 1191. 23–24, 2: 30–33, 140, 9: 10. Bodin, who was from Angers, France, wrote *Methodus ad facilem historiarum cognitionem* (Paris: Martin Juvenis, 1566), a treatise on historiography. Schottelius noted, *AA* 1191, that it was rare for Bodin to praise Germans, but that he did praise the *Chronicon Carionis* with additions by Melanchthon and Peucer.

Bohemus [=Behm], Martinus (1557–1622). 1196. Schottelius referred to Behm's *Kirchen Calender: Das ist, christliche Erklerung, des Jahres u. der zwölff Monaten* (Wittenberg: Berger, 1608).

Bonaventura Hepburnus, Iacobus (1573–1620). 56, 4: 17. See Hepburn, James Bonaventura.

Boner, Hieronymus (d. 1556). 1181–82. Noted as translator of Justinus, Thucydides, Plutarch (q.v.), as well as of Herodianus (cf. Worstbrock 1976: 75).

Bovillus, Carolus = Charles de Bovelles (1470–1553). 124, 9: 4. A very productive writer from Vermandois, France. Schottelius cited his *De differentia vulgarium linguarum et gallici sermonis varietate* (Paris: Stephanus, 1533) dealing with etymology.

Brant, Sebastian (1458–1521). 1170. German satirical poet most famous for his *Narrenschiff* ('Ship of Fools'), printed in 1494 (Basle: Johann Bergmann von Olpe), noted by Schottelius *AA* 1170.

Brotuvius, Ernestus = Brotuff, Ernst (1497–1565). 1182. Schottelius noted a 1606 printing of Brotuff's 1556 German translation of Ditmar of Merseburg's chronicle (q.v.).

Brun(fels), Otto: Brun in error for Brunfels (1489/90–1534). 1187. Schottelius referred to Brunfels's *Reformation der Apotecken* (Strasbourg: Riel, 1536; VD16 B 8567). See also Eles.

Bruni (Aretino), Leonardo. See Aretinus, Leonhardus.

Bucelin, Gabriel (1599–168). 1190. Benedictine humanist historian and cartographer. Schottelius noted without comment his *Germaniae topo-chrono-stemmatographia sacra et profana* (Augustae Vindelicorum: Praetorius, 1655), which deals with the genealogy of distinguished members of the German clergy and nobility.

Buch(h)oltz, Andreas Heinrich (1607–1671). c2^r; 1179; 1185; 676–77; 774. Schottelius noted that Buch(h)oltz translated Horace (*Odenbuch des Horatius, deutsch* and *Verteutschte Poetereikunst des Horatius*, both 1639), Lucian (*Lucians satirische Geschichte, deutsch*, 1659), and the psalms. He also wrote religious poetry: *Christliche Weihnachtsfreude* (1639), *Advents-gesang* (1640), and *Herzlicher Friedenswunsch* (1643). C2^r refers to his *Geistliche Teutsche Poemata* (Braunschweig: Zilliger, 1651). The front matter of the *AA* includes a dedicatory poem by him.

Buchner(us), August(us) (1591–1661). 1205. 117, 7: 33, and several times in the poetics, e.g. 861. Member of the FG, German poet and classical philologist who taught rhetoric and poetics at Wittenberg university. For his works, see *Werke: Lateineische Dichtungen, Reden u. gelehrte Prosawerke; Ausgg. v. Horaz, Plautus, Plinius u. zahlr. Komm.—Epistolae Buchneri*, Dresden 1679 (2nd ed. 1720). Schottelius cited Buchner's verse a number of times in the poetics, and his views on poetics, e.g. *AA* 861. See Jones (1995: 455–462).

Bünting, Heinrich (1545–1606). 1190. Theologian and chronicler. Schottelius noted his *Braünschweigische vnd Lunebürgische Chronica* (Magdeburg: Kirchner, 1584/85, 4 vols.), to which he had access in a 1630 edition.

Burkhard, Franciscus (pseudonym of Andreas Erstenberger) (1520–1584). 488. Privy secretary to the German imperial court. Schottelius cited his *De autonomia. Das ist, von Freystellung mehrerley Religion und Glauben* ('On autonomy. That is, on allowing several religions and faiths'), of which the VD17 contains a 1602 edition (Munich: Berg, 1602; VD17 12:110054A).

Busbequius, Augerius Gislenius = Busbecq, Ogier de (1522–1592). 133, 8: 13. From Boesbeke, South Flanders, Busbecq wrote four letters as imperial ambassador to the Turkish sultan Süleiman the Great in Constantinople, published as *Legationis Turcicæ Epistolæ IV* (Paris, 1589), in which he reported his experiences. Schottelius cited his fourth Turkish letter on the Crimean Goths.

Butschky von Rutinfeld, Samuel (1612–1678). 1204. Schottelius noted Butschky's *Hochdeutsche Kantzeley* (1659) and his *Der hóchdeutsche Schlüszel zur Schreibrichtigkeit oder Rechtschreibung* (1648), but was critical of the poor organization of the material in the latter. See Jones (1995: 393), Moulin-Fankhänel (1997b: 56–65).

Caelius Rodiginus, Ludovicus = Ludovico Ricchieri (1450–1520). 58, 4: 21. Schottelius cited the posthumous second and expanded edition of Ricchieri's work (Basel: Froben, 1542); the first edition consisted of 16 books (Venice 1516).

Caesar, (Gaius) Julius (100–44 B.C.). c2[r]; 339; 525. 70, 5: 6. See Julius Caesar.

Caesius, Philippus = Philipp von Zesen (1619–1689). See Philipp von Zesen.

Camden, William (1551–1623). 127, 8: 9. English antiquary and historian who wrote *Britannia* (1586), a survey in Latin of the British islands (translated into English in 1610), and *Annales rerum Anglicarum* [...], a history of the reign of Queen Elizabeth in two parts (1615, 1625).

Camer. lib. 2 medit. hist. 175: 9. A reference either to the German botanist Joachim Camerarius the Younger (1534–1598), e.g. his *Symbola et emblemata*, a natural history of the bible (Nuremberg, 1590–1604); or to a work of his father, the theologian Joachim Camerarius the Elder (1500–1574).

***Capit. C., Capit. Caesar.*, etc.** See Limnaeus, Johannes.

Carion, Johann (1499–1537). 1191. Carion's *Chronika* (1532) was continued by Melanchthon and Peucer (q.v.). Schottelius cited the Frenchman Jean Bodin's (q.v.) praise of it.

Carp./ Ca. = Carpzovius, Benedictus (1595–1666). c2^r. 323; 307; 522 460; 505; 522; 647 and *passim*; numerous references incl. 78, 6: 16. According to c2^r, *Ca.* followed by three figures refers to Benedictus Carpzovius's *Jurisprudentia Forensis* (Frankfurt: Press, 1650), where the first number indicates the part of book, the second the *constitutio*, and the third the decision.

Cassiodorus = Flavius Magnus Aurelius Cassiodorus Senator (ca. 490–ca. 583). c2^r. 173: 4; 547. Roman writer and statesman. Schottelius noted his assertion in the *Institutiones divinarum et sæcularium litterarum*, written between 543 and 555, that grammar is the foundation of the liberal arts (*AA* 173).

Cato the Younger, Marcus Porcius Cato Uticensis (95–46 B.C.). 176:10. 107, 7: 10; 167, 10: 21; also mentioned at 134, 8:15. Roman politician and statesman famed for his tenacity and integrity. No works mentioned by name.

Cedrenus, Georg (11th century). 30, 2: 30. Cedrenus's account of the lives of Roman and German emperors was printed in the sixteenth century. An edition held at Wolfenbüttel is *Georgii Cedreni annales, [...]* (Basileae: Oporinus et Episcopius, 1566).

Cicero, Marcus Tullius (106–43 B.C.). c2^r. 1184; 1207. 172: 3; 176: 10; 237: 4. 9, 1:27; 11, 1: 34; 13, 1: 41; 16, 2: 2; 36, 3: 22; 40, 3: 32; 57, 4: 21; 144, 9: 19; 1025; 1028. Schottelius referred *AA* 1207 to a 1550 German translation of Cicero's *Officia*, but also cited his *Academica* 'Academic Questions' and his *Brutus; sive, De claris oratoribus liber* 'Brutus or History of Famous Orators' in the orations. See also Johann von Schwarzenberg. In the grammar, on polyflection, *AA* 237: 4, Schottelius cited Cicero's advice, 'let your ears be the judge'.

Clai(us), Johann = Johann Klaj (1616–1656). c3^r. 1203. 436; 779–80 and several times in the poetics. German poet. See Klaj, Johann.

Clajus, Johann(es) (1535–1592). 1204. Author of a German grammar, 1578, the most widely used before Schottelius. Schottelius acknowledged his debt to Clajus, whose observations he said he included in his own grammar. He used the seventh edition (Lipsiae: Gross, 1625). Cf. Moulin-Fankhänel (1994: 51–61).

Clapmarius, Arnold (1574–1604). c2^r. 18, 2: 10. German jurist and publicist best known for his *De Arcanis Rerumpublicarum: Libri Sex*, first published after his death by his brother (Bremae: Wessel, 1605), cited by Schottelius.

Clement of Alexandria (ca. 150–215). 34, 3:[13]. A Church Father and Greek theologian who applied Greek philosophical ideas to Christian doctrine, believing that Greek philosophy was a divine gift to humanity.

Clement of Rome (Pope Clement I, St. Clement of Rome) (fl. 96 A.D.). 51, 4: 4. Early Bishop of Rome.

Cluver(ius), Philipp (also Klüwer, Cluwer, or Cluvier) (1580–1623). 1160. 250: 9; 253: 12; 284; 287; 292; 337; 451; 483; 520; 585; 687. 1272. 32, 3: 9

and *passim* in the third oration, 56, 4: 15; 1017; 1018; 1033; 1034; 1037; 1071; 1250; 1255. German geographer and historian, praised by Schottelius (*AA* 32, 3: 9) and cited *passim* in the third oration, and elsewhere, as the person who had written in most detail and most thoroughly about 'old Germany', with much information about the older German language and old German words. His *Germaniae antiquae libri tres* appeared in 1616 (Leiden: Elzevier).

C.O. = *CammerGerichtsOrdnung.* c2^v. 391, 392, 626, 640, 649. Lit. 'rules for the supreme court'. Not further identified but perhaps contained in Goldast's collection of statutes? See Goldast.

Coldingensis, Jonas = **Jon Jensen Kolding** (d. 1609). c3^r. 130, 8: 10. Danish historian who wrote *Descriptio Daniae*, cited by Schottelius. Wolfenbüttel holds an edition published Frankfurt: Feyerabendt, 1594.

Coler, Johann (1566–1639). 1189. 650. Schottelius had access to a German 1645 edition (Mäyntz: Heyll) of Coler's *Oeconomia Ruralis Et Domestica* (Wittenberg: Helwich, 1593), containing information on argricultural and household work.

Conradus Abbas Urspergensis = **Konrad von Lichtenau** (d. 1240). 1156. German abbot and chronicler, whose chronicle covered the period from the Flood to 1230. His chronicle was printed in 1537 (Argentoratis: Mylius).

Conring, Hermann (1606–1681). 1160. 3, 1: 8. Leading German jurist and intellectual, adviser to the Wolfenbüttel library that Schottelius used, and professor at Helmstedt. Conring contributed a poem at the front of the *AA*. Schottelius in turn cited Conring's guide to good writing in his first oration. Conring's assessment of Cluverius (q.v.). is cited by Schottelius, *AA* 1160.

Corv. = **Corvinus, Andreas** (1589–1648). c2^v. 329; 355; 620 and *passim* in the grammar; 1352 *Kummet*. Rhetorician and jurist; Schottelius referred to his *Fons Latinitatis* (Leipzig 1623; later editions include Frankfurt: Goetzius, 1653).

Crantzius, Albert(us) 1158. See Krantzius, Albert(us).

Cruciger, Georg(ius) (*alias* **Kreutzger**) (ca. 1575–1637). 1185. 207: 28. 71, 5: 11. In his *Harmonia Linguarum* (1616), which presented the four 'cardinal' languages of Greek, Hebrew, Latin and German alongside each other, Cruciger aimed to show that Hebrew contained the roots from which German, Greek and Latin words were derived: *Harmonia Linguarum Quatuor Cardinalium; HEBRAICAE GRAECAE LATINAE & GERMAN-ICAE* (Frankfurt: Tampachius, 1616).

Curtius = **Quintus Curtius Rufus** (?) (fl. 41–54 A.D.). 29, 2: 2. Cited as 'Curtius', Quintus Curtius Rufus was a Roman historian and author of the life of Alexander the Great.

Cuspinianus, Johannes (**Johann Spießhaymer**) (1473–1529). c2^v. 1157. 40, 3: 31; 1033. Author of *Austria* (1527–1528, unfinished), a historical-geographical regional survey up to the year 1494, cited by Schottelius as an authority for monosyllabic rootwords. A seventeenth-century edition is Cuspinianus (1601) (VD17 1:000114V).

D. Hard. Disq. = **Harsdörffer.** See Harsdörffer.

Damhuderus, Jodocus = **Joost de Damhouder** (1507–1581). 1166. 390. Damhouder's legal work *Practica criminalis & civilis* was translated into German by Johannes Vetter (Frankfurt: Basseus, 1581).

Decret. Tas. c3^r. *Decretum Tassilionis Ducis*; cf. Lindenbrog.

Demosthenes (384–322 B.C.). 145, 9: 21. [mentioned]. The greatest of the Athenian orators, cited by Schottelius as an instance of oratory in Greek.

Desmarets de Saint-Sorlin, Jean (1596–1676). 1205. Schottelius noted that a German translation of Desmarets' *L'Ariane* (1632) was published in Holland in 1659 (not identified).

Desselius Taxander, Valerius Andreas (1588–1655). De^r. Schottelius consulted Desselius's *Bibliotheca Belgica* (Louvain, 1643; rpt. Nieuwkoop: de Graaf, 1973).

Dictys Cretensis = **Dictys of Crete** [legendary]. 1182. A fourth-century Latin chronicle of the Trojan war, *Dictys Cretensis Ephemeridos belli Trojani*, purporting to be a translation of Dictys' Greek text, was printed in German translation by Marcus Tatius [Alpinus], q.v., in 1536 (Augsburg: Heinrich Steiner, 1536) (Worstbrock 1976: 67).

Die New Welt, der landschafften unnd Insulen [...] (1534). 1195. See Grynäus, Simon.

Dilherr, Johann Michael (1604–1669). c2^v; 1210–1212. 276; 460; 485; 516; 530; 611; 617; 635; 683; 767; 786 and *passim*; 1276. German Protestant theologian and philologist. He contributed a dedicatory poem to the *AA*. Schottelius listed 41 books by him in German, *AA* 1210–12. Also mentioned by title in the grammar of the *AA* are: *Libri 3 Electorum. In quibus rituum, tam sacrorum, quam secularium, farrago continetur* (Nuremberg: Endter, 1644) (*AA* 276) and *Conc. 1 die Nativ.* (*AA* 460, not identified).

Diodorus Siculus ('of Sicily') (ca. 90–20 B.C.). c2^v; 26, 2: 41. Historian from Sicily who travelled widely in Asia and Europe to collect material for his *Bibliothecae Historica*, a universal history from earliest mythical ages down to Caesar's Gallic wars, in 40 books, of which 15 survive, plus some fragments. Schottelius referred to book 5.

Dioscurides, Pedanios (first century A.D.). 1389 *Ruhn*. Greek physician, whose work had been printed in three editions in the sixteenth century (cf. Neuhaus 1991: 151; Worstbrock 1976: 68).

Ditmar(us) of Merseburg (975–1018). c2^v; 1155; 1182; 126, 8:5; 1031. Bishop of Merseburg. His chronicle was published by Reiner Reineck (q.v.) (*Chronicon*, Frankfurt: Wechel, 1580), whose preface is referred to *AA* 126, 8: 5. See also Brotuvius, Ernestus.

Dog. = **Dögen, Matthias** (1605/6–1672). 307; 484; 1207. Schottelius referred to the Dutchman Dögen's work on military fortification in a translation by Philipp von Zesen, *Heutiges tages übliche Kriges Bau-kunst* (Amsterdam: Elzevier, 1648). See Jones (1999: 100–101).

Draco, Johann Jakob (1595–1648). c2^v; 259; 431. Author of *De Origine Et Iure Patriciorum, Libri Tres* (Basel: Genath, 1627), on Roman, Greek and Germanic politics, law and origins. Schottelius listed the work c2^v. In the orations, it is cited only indirectly, in a citation from Spedelius, q.v.

Dresser(us), Mattäus (1536–1607). c2^v; 17, 2: 8. The reference may be to , (Frankfurt: Tröster, 1578). It is likely Schottelius did not consult the work directly, but via Goldast, whom he cited immediately preceding the single reference to Dresser.

Dürer, Albrecht (1471–1528). 1164. Schottelius praised Dürer first for his work as an artist, then for his theoretical treatises written in German on measurement and human proportions.

Duret, Claude (1565–1611). 21, 2: 22; 24, 2; 34; 31, 3: 7; 3, 35: 20; 54–55, 4: 11 and elsewhere in the same oration; 111, 7: 17; 127, 8: 7; 141, 9: 12; 173; 174. Duret's *Thresor de L'Histoire des langves de cest vnivers* (Cologny: Societé Caldoriene, 1613) is one of a very small number of French sources to which Schottelius made reference. Schottelius cited him numerous times, sometimes on comparisons of German with French, as well as on Gothic, and where he is critical of Becanus.

Edict. Theod. c3^r. *Edictum Theodirici Regis*; cf. Lindenbrog.

Egenhard = Einhard (ca. 770–840). c2^v; 1154. Mentioned 55, 4: 12 in a passage cited from Aventinus. Secretary to Charlemagne whose *Life* of Charlemagne Schottelius noted *AA* 1154 and c2^v.

Eichholz, Petrus (d. 1655). 1203. Schottelius noted Eichholz's *Geistliches Bergwerk* (1655), a Christian allegory of mining, containing many 'useful' German technical terms, following on from Mathesius (q.v.).

Eike von Repgow (ca. 1170–after 1233). See *Sachsenspiegel* and Anon., Saxon Chronicle.

Eles, Hans (?–?). 1187, with Klas in error for Eles. Schottelius noted Eles's *Wie man Sirupen, Latwergen und Konfekt machen soll* (Strasbourg: Rihel, Wendelin d.Ä., 1536; VD16 E 992) alongside Otto Brunfels (q.v.), *Von edlen Steinen, wie die zu kennen und wa zu sie nütz seien* (VD16 B 8577), with which it was printed under the title *Reformation der Apotecken* (Strasburg: Riel, 1536; VD16 B 8567).

Epiphanius (ca. 310–403). 34, 3: [13]. Bishop of Salamis, considered a Church father, and mentioned as sharing with the other Church fathers Jerome, Augustine and Clement of Alexandria the view that 72 languages emerged at Babel.

Erich, Adolar (ca. 1530–1634). 1184. Author of a chronicle about the Lower Rhein, the *Gülichische Chronic* (Leipzig: Apel und Schürer, 1611).

Estienne, Henri. See Stephanus, Henricus.

Eusebius of Caesarea (263–339). 1166; 37, 3: 28. Early church historian, often referred to as the Father of Church History. Schottelius referred to his *Praeparatio evangelica* ('Preparation for the Gospel'), which attempted to prove the superiority of Christianity over other religions and philosophies, and noted the translation by Caspar Hedion (1492–1552) of Eusebius's ecclasiastical history, *AA* 1166 (Basle: Herwagen, Strasbourg: Köphlin, 1545).

Eutropius (4th century A.D.). 512. Roman historian, whose history of Rome, known as the *Brevarium*, Schottelius referred to for his mention of a monument in Mainz.

Eyering, Eucharius (1520–1597). 1172. Eyering published a collection of German proverbs. Schottelius referred to editions from 1601 and 1603 (Eißleben: Gross).

Fabius l.9. Instit. Theoret. c2[v]; 39, 3: 30; 178:13. See Quintilian.

Faust, Maximilian (?–?). c2[v]; 329; 330; 367; 396; 429; 469. Schottelius referred to Faust's legal work, *Consilia Pro Ærario Civili, Ecclesiastico Et Militari, publico atque priuato* (Frankfurt: the author, 1641).

Ficino, Marsilio (1433–1499). c2[v]; 58, 4: 24. Humanist philosopher whose Florentine Academy sought to recreate Plato's Academy; the first translator of Plato's complete extant works into Latin.

Flacius Illyricus, Matthias (1520–1575). c2[v]; 42, 3: 37; 52, 4: 11. Schottelius used Flacius Illyricus's 1571 edition of the Old High German *Evangelienbuch* (a rhymed life of Christ) of Otfrid von Weißenburg (800–870, q.v.), referred to eight times (Moulin-Fankhänel 1997a: 306, Neuhaus 1991: 131).

Flemming = Fleming, Paul (1609–1640). 1177; 63–64, 4: 38; 621; 675. German poet, whose verse is cited *AA* 63–64. Schottelius noted the posthumous edition of his German poems *Teütsche Poemata* (Lübeck: Jauch, 1646).

Florus, Publius Annius (70–117 A.D.). 1207; 1287. Roman historian who compiled, chiefly from Livy, a brief sketch of the history of Rome from the foundation of the city to 25 B.C., *Epitome of the Histories of Titus Livy*, cited s.v. *Bier* in the list of rootwords. Schottelius noted a 1571 translation by Zacharias Müntzer, q.v.

***Fr. V. H.*.** 346; 347. See Herden, Eitel Friedrich von.

Franck, Sebastian (1499–1539 or 1542/43). c3[v] (under S); 1195; 44, 3: 44; 451. Humanist and radical reformer. Schottelius referred c3[v] to a version of Franck's *Sprichwoerter* printed after his death (Frankfurt: Egenolff, 1548, based on his 1541 collection), but also referred (*AA* 44, 3: 44 and 1195) to his *historia*, i.e. his *Weltbuch* or *Chronica, Zeitbuch und Geschichtsbibel*, largely a compilation on the basis of the Nuremberg Chronicle (1493). Schottelius specified a 1534 edition, which I have not identified, but the Wolfenbüttel library holds a 1531 edition (Strasbourg: Beck, 1531). See also Jones (1995: 21–22).

Frangk, Fabian (ca. 1490—after 1538). 18, 2: 12; 157, 10: 13. Author of *Orthographia Deutsch* (Cologne, 1531) and other works (Moulin-

Fankhänel 1994: 65–75). Cited for his call for a grammar, and for his remarks on German dialects.

Freher, Marquard (1565–1614). c2^v; c3^v (under *Petrus de Andlo*); 23, 2: 30; 25, 2: 38; 213; 273; 288; 462; 480; 494; 499; 514; 567;. 1054. German historian and jurist. Schottelius made reference to his *Origines Palatinae* (Heidelberg: Voegelinus, 1599, and later editions). The abbreviation in the orations, *Notae ad Petrum de Andlo,* refers to Freher's edition of a work by Peter von Andlaw (1425–1480), *Petri De Andlo ... De Imperio Romano, Regis Et Avgvsti Creatione, Inavgvratione, administratione; officio & potestate Electo* (Argentorati: Rihelius, Rietschius, 1603); *not. ad Fœd. Lud. Germ. & Carl. Gall. Reg.* refers to *Foederis Lvdovici Germaniae, Et Karoli Galliae Regvm* (Heidelberg: Vögelin, 1611). The reference (c3^v, second column) to a *Glossarium Freheri* is not clear, but Freher owned a partial MS of the Glossary of Aelfric (Considine 2008: 257), so the reference may be to this or to another MS glossary in his possession—or perhaps to a glossary or *index verborum* in one of his editions, such as the *Rerum Bohemicarum scriptores*?

Freinsh. = **Johannes Caspar Freimshem(ius)** (1608–1660). c2^v; 1212; 62–63, 4: 38; 380; 416; 427; 663; 762; 787. German historian and classical scholar. C2^v specifies *Johannis Freimshemii opus, de novo Germanorum Hercule,* i.e. *Teutscher Tugentspiegel oder Gesang von dem Stammen und Thaten deß Alten und Newen Teutschen* (Strasbourg: Hercules, 1639). Schottelius cited verse by Freinsheim (*AA* 62, 4: 38).

Frey, Johann Thomas (1543–1583). 492. Pedagogical reformer with links to Ramus; Schottelius referred to Frey's *Neüwe Practica Iuris und Formulen oder Concepten allerley, in zwen theil abgetheilet* (Basle: Henricpetri, 1574).

Frischlin, Philipp Nikodemus (1547–1590). 1021. German philologist, poet, and commentator on Virgil.

Frisingensus, Otto = **Otto von Freising** (ca. 1112–1158). c3^v; 1155. German bishop and chronicler whose chronicle was printed in 1515.

Furttenbach, Joseph (1591–1667). c2^v; 468; 481; 513. German architect and mathematician. Schottelius listed several of his works on civil, naval and military architecture published over the years 1630–49, as well as a work on gun-making, *Halinitro-Pyrobolia: Beschreibu[n]g Einer newen Büchsenmeisterey* (Ulm: Saur, 1627), on c2^v.

G.B. = **Güldene Bulle**. c2^v; 367; 519. The Golden Bull of Emperor Charles IV (1356), which set out the procedure for the election of the German emperor / king by the *Kurfürsten*, contained in Goldast's *Reichssatzungen* (1613), q.v.

Gail, Andreas (1526–1587). c2^v; 9, 1: 25; 238: 4; 332; 402. Listed on c2^v as J.C., i.e. lawyer. German jurist. Author of a legal treatise, *Practicarum Observationum, tam ad Processum Judiciarium, præsertim Imperialis Cameræ, quam causarum Decisiones pertinentium, Libri duo* (Coloniæ Agrippinae: Gymnicus, 1578), noted *AA* c2^v.

Gebhardus, Hermannus (1625–1651). 1202. Priest whose collection of sayings from the Church Fathers, rendered into German, Schottelius noted (Goslar: 1651; edition not identified).

Gellius, Aulus (ca. 123–165 A.D.). c2^v; 54, 4: 9; 58, 4: 24, 59, 4: 26; 63, 4: 40; 77, 6: 15; 82, 6: 24; 98, 6: 54; 237:4; 1025. Latin grammarian. Schottelius did not specify a work, but reference is presumably to Gellius's *Noctes Atticae* 'Attic nights', a work with numerous extracts from Greek and Roman writers, so-called because Gellius wrote it in long winter nights near Athens. There were many editions; the earliest held in Wolfenbüttel is (Argentinae: Knobloch, 1517).

Gellus, Johan Baptista = Gelli, Giovanni Battista (1498–1563). 1183. Schottelius did not name the translator of this Florentine humanist's philosophical dialogues known as *La Circe* (1548), which appeared in German translation in 1620, but it is Ludwig von Anhalt-Köthen, q.v.

Gesenius, Justus (1601–1673). 1179. Noted by Schottelius as a German theologian and hymn-writer.

Ges(s)ner(us), Conrad von (1516–1565). 1180; 126, 8: 6; 128, 8: 9; 131, 8: 10; 132, 8: 12–13; 150–51, 10: 5,7; 157, 10: 12; 271; 339; 778–79; 1017; 1037. Swiss naturalist, author of *Historiae animalium* in four volumes (1551–1558), and of *Mithridates de differentiis linguarum* (Tiguri: Froschauer, 1555; ed. Colombat & Peters, 2009), an account of about 130 known languages, with the Lord's Prayer in twenty-two languages. Schottelius cited Notker's Old High German Lord's Prayer from the *Mithridates*, though with some orthographical adjustments and errors (Moulin-Fankhänel 1997a: 308; Metcalf 1963). Schottelius also referenced his entry on Crimean Gothic (1555: 43) and used Gessner's *Bibliotheca Universalis* (1545), a universal catalogue of books previously printed.

Giucciardini, Ludovico (1521–1589). 1152. Italian writer who lived in Antwerp, known for his *Descrittione di Lodovico Guicciardini patritio fiorentino di tutti i Paesi Bassi altrimenti detti Germania inferiore*. Wolfenbüttel holds a Latin translation, *Totius Belgii Descriptio* (Amstelodami: Jansonius, 1652).

Glarean(us), Henricus / Heinrich (1488–1563). 64–65, 4: 42; 124, 8: 4. Swiss humanist. Schottelius's reference to Glarean's speech in Freiburg *AA* 64–65 is taken from Stevin (cf. Table 6.5).

Glasenapp, Joachim von (ca. 1600–1667). 1173. Religious poet and member of the FG. Schottelius noted his *Vinetum Evangelicum, Evangelischer Weinberg/ Welchen zu fruchtbringendem Waxtuhm der Gottseligkeit sezzet/* (Wolfenbüttel: Bißmark, 1647).

Goldast von Haiminsfeld, Melchior (1576–1635). c2^v; 1159; 1196–1198; 17, 2: 8; 18, 2; 12; 48, 3: 52, 57; 52, 4: 6; 87, 6: 29; 97, 6: 53; 110–11, 7: 15; 140, 9: 10; 155, 10: 12; 173; 207: 27.5; 263; 264; 288; 334; 337; 465; 473; 492; 500; 527; 690 and *passim*; 1036; 1044; 1047; 1338 *Hube*; 1446. Swiss writer and industrious collector of documents on German medieval history and constitution (cf. Baade 1993) who edited a number of Old High German texts, including the *Interpretatio Keronis in Regulam Sancti Benedicti* and the so-called *St Galler Schularbeit* amongst others (Moulin-Fankhänel 1997a: 303, 307–08; Herstenstein 1975). The latter are both contained in Goldast's *Alemannicarum Rerum Scriptores*, which Schottelius drew on frequently (1606; cf. Moulin-Fankhänel 1997a and Hertenstein 1975). Schottelius also referred to Part I of his *Paraenetica* (1604), which contained editions of the Middle High German works *König Tirol von Schotten* and the didactic poem *Der Winsbecke* (ca. 1201–1220); and *AA* 1197–98 cited at some length from Goldast's preface to this edition. Schottelius also referenced Goldast's *Politische Reichshändel* (1614), an account of the regalia of the Holy Roman Empire from 1350, and the *Reichssatzung Deß Heiligen Römischen Reichs* in two parts (1609, 1613). Reference to Rotweil laws and to *Schwabenspiegel* (q.v.) are to sections of this work. See also Hortleder, Dresser, and Pirckheimer, whose works Schottelius accessed via Goldast. Cited twice in the list of rootwords, s.v. *Hube* and *Zabel* (Neuhaus 1991: 161–62).

Goropius, Joannes Becanus (1519–1572). 4, 1: 9; 18, 2: 14; 30, 3: 5; 32, 3: 9; 54, 4: 9; 174. 9; 222: 48; 400; 1037; 1276–77. Flemish physician and linguist. Though much mocked by some, Becanus was esteemed by Schottelius and others for his studies of the origins of languages, and for his belief in original monosyllabic words. Schottelius referred to his *Origines Antwerpianæ* 'the origins of Antwerp' (1569), also referred to as *Originum Gentium libri IX* [...] 'on the origin of the peoples, 9 books', and his *Hermathena* (1580, published posthumously, ed. Laevinus Torrentius, q.v.).

Gottfried, Johann Ludwig (1584–1633). c3^r; 1179; 130, 8: 10. Page c3^r lists *De historia antipodum = Historia Antipodum oder Newe Welt [...]* (Frankfurt, Matthias Merian, 1631), a heavily–illustrated collection of material relating to the 'antipodes'. While some material deals with South America and the oceans of the southern hemisphere, there is much on North America and the West Indies.

Gregory (St. Gregory, Gregory the Great), Bishop of Tours (538–594). 1154; 517. Schottelius referred to Gregory's *History of the Franks AA* 1154.

Greiffenberg, Catharina Regina von (1633–1694). 863. Noted as the author of the *Teutsche Uranie*, i.e. a translation of a work by du Bartas (q.v.).

Grevelinger, Georg = Greflinger, Georg (1620–1677). 1204. Writer and poet. Schottelius referred to his German *Epigrammata* (Danzig, 1645; edition not identified).

Grotius, Hugo (Huig de Groot) (1583–1645). c2^v; 1167; 16, 3: 2; 18, 2: 13; 29, 3: 3; 45, 3: 44; 166, 10: 21; 204.26; 219: 43; 333; 376; 402; 453; 480; 531; 562; 636; 1035–1037; 1041; 1042; 1048; 1057; 1059; 1065; 1070; 1072; 1075; 1078; 1080; 1082; 1085–86; 1089; 1090; 1096. Page c2^v refers to Grotius's *De jure belli ac pacis libri tres* ('On the Law of War and Peace: Three books'; Paris: Buon, 1625). Besides this, Schottelius used his *De Republica Hollandiae. De antiquitate reipublicae Batavicae* ('On the Antiquity of the Batavian Republic') (Leiden: Plantijn, 1610) and a 1655 edition of his *Historia Gothorum, Vandalorum & Longobardorum* (Amstelodami: Elzevier, 1655), as well as other works listed *AA* 1167–68. See also Jones (1995: 35–36).

Grundman = Grundmann, Martin (1619–1696). 1208. Schottelius referred to Grundmann's *Deliciae Historiae* (Görlitz: M. Hermann, 1653), anecdotes and legends for Christian edification.

Grynäus, Simon (1493–1541). 1195. German scholar and theologian of the Reformation. Schottelius referred to a folio edition of his account of the New World *Die New Welt, der landschafften unnd Insulen* (Strasbourg: Ulrich, 1534).

Gryphiander, Johannes (1580–1652). c2^v; 4, 1: 9; 129, 8: 9; 168, 10: 22; 174: 7 ; 175: 9; 253:12; 288; 336; 402 and *passim*; 1071; 1228. Jena law professor; c2^v refers to his *De Weichbildis Saxonicis sive Colossis Rulandinis urbium quarundam Saxonicarum* (Frankfurt: Emmelius, 1625), i.e. his study of part of Saxon Law (cf. *Sachsenspiegel*).

Gueintz, Christian (1592–1650). 1202. Member of the FG and Schottelius's rival as German grammarian. Schottelius noted Gueintz's *Rechtschreibung* (1645) and other 'little treatises' (*AA* 1202), but did not mention his grammar of 1641, of which he had written a scathing review. Cf. 5.2. See Jones (1995: 195–198), Moulin-Fankhänel (1997b: 79–91).

Hannman, Enoch (1621–1680). 4, 1: 9. Mentioned by Schottelius amongst others who began work on a poetics or grammar. He published an annotated version of Opitz's poetics (1645), which also contained sections on grammar (cf. Jones 1999: 173, 225; Jones 1995: 394–398; Moulin-Fankhänel 1997b: 104–109).

Harsdörffer, Georg Philipp (1607–1656). c2^v; 1175; 1206; 117, 7: 34; 138, 9: 6; 141, 9: 10; 147, 9: 30; 174.7; 183.5; 187.1; 189.12; 191.12; 205.27.4; 207: 27.5; 221.47; 222.48; 329; 403; 409; 549 and *passim*; several times in the poetics. Member of the FG and friend of Schottelius until his death. References to *disq.* (frequent in the grammar) are to *Disquisitiones* in his 1646 *Specimen Philologiae Germanicae. AA* 1175–76 gives a list of his works; *AA* 1206 noted him as the translator of the Spanish work, *Diana*,by Jorge de Montemayor; see also Kuefstein, Hans Ludwig von. The reference to an *Ars Emblematica AA* 446 is to a collection of emblems that appeared in Dilherr's (q.v.) *Heilige Sonn- und Festtags-arbeit* (Nuremberg: Endter, 1660; VD17 23:322362Z), and which was not published separately until ca. 1669 (*Drei-ständige Sonn- und Festtag-Emblemata, oder Sinnebilder*; VD17 14:083360B); Schottelius's poetical treatise noted Harsdörffer's *Gesprächsspiele* (1644–49; c2^v explains that references like *204. 3* give the number of the *Gesprächsspiel*, followed by the number of the paragraph; see bibliography) and *Poetischer Trichter* (Nuremberg: Endter,

1648–1653 in three parts; VD17 14:019688V) (also referred to in the grammar, *AA* 205). The poetics is prefaced by a recommendation by Harsdörffer himself (*AA* 794–98). Cf. Section 6.4. See also Hundt (2000, 2006); Jones (1995: 243–269), Moulin-Fankhänel (1997b: 104–109).

Hayne, Thomas (1582–1645). De^r (under *Thomas*); 62, 4: 37; 143, 9: 15. Schottelius referred to Hayne's *Linguarum Cognatio, seu: de linguis in genere, et de variarum linguarum harmonia dissertatio* (London: Kirton & Warren, 1639).

Heinsius, Daniel (1580–1655). c2^v. 1169. 22, 2: 24; 84, 6: 25; 86, 6: 26; 91, 6: 35; 106, 7: 6; 113, 7: 23. Daniel Heinsius (or Heins) was a professor and then librarian at the University of Leiden. In 1601 he published, under the pseudonym of Theocritus à Ganda ('Theocritus from Ghent'), *Quaeris quid sit Amor?* ('Do you ask what love is?') (Amsterdam: Buck, 1601), the first emblem-book in Dutch. Heinsius also wrote Dutch poetry after classical models. His efforts were collected by his friend Petrus Scriverius (q.v.) and published as *Nederduytsche poemata* ('Dutch poems'; Amsterdam: Janßen, 1616; facsimile Bern: Lang, 1983). They were greatly admired by Martin Opitz, who, in translating the poetry of Heinsius, introduced the German public to the use of the rhyming alexandrine. Schottelius cited Valerius Andreas's (1588–1665) *Bibliotheca Belgica* (1643) in praise of Heinsius, *AA* 1169.

Heldenbuch. 1194. A collection of thirteenth-century epic poetry, chiefly around the figure of the Goth Dietrich von Bern (Theodoric). Schottelius referred to a 1560 edition printed in Frankfurt by Weigand Han for Sigmund Feyerabend.

Helmoldus (1120–1177). 1156; 129, 8: 9. German monk known for his Slavic Chronicle, edited by Reiner Reineck (q.v.) (Frankfurt: Wechel, 1581).

Helvetius, Johann Friedrich = Johann Friedrich Schweitzer (1625–1709). 1188. Physician and alchemist. Schottelius cited his work on 'medical physiognomy', *Amphitheatrum Physiognomiæ Medicum: Runder Schauplatz/ der Artzeneyschen Gesicht-Kunst* (Heidelberg: Broun, 1660), praising the fact that plant names in particular are given *in gut Teutsch* 'in good German'.

Helvigius = **Helwig, Andreas** (1572–1643). c2^v; 130, 8: 9; 142, 9: 14; 143, 9: 16. According to *AA* c2^v, Helwig *edidit origines dictionum Germanicarum* 'the origins of German[ic] words', i.e. *Etymologiae, sive origines dictionum Germanicorum, ex tribus illlis nobilibus antiquitatis eruditae linguis, Latina, Graeca, Hebraea derivatarum* (Frankfurt: Hummius, 1611).

Helwig, Johann (1609–1674). 1183. Author of *Ormund Das ist: Lieb-und Helden-Gedicht* (Frankfurt: Zunner, 1648), a translation of a work by Francesco Pona.

Henischius, D. Georgius = Georg Henisch (von Bartfeld) (1549–1618). c3^r; 1172; 21, 2: 23; 61, 4: 31; 132, 8: 13; 159, 10: 17; 427; 688; 1016; 1291 *Bös*. Schottelius referred to Henisch's *Thesaurus Linguae & Sapientiae*

Germanicae (Augsburg: Francus, 1616) (cf. Considine 2008). This dictionary only reached as far as the letter G, but according to Neuhaus (1991) it was seen in the FG, especially by Prince Ludwig, as a source and model for a complete dictionary. In addition to the references in the orations and once in the list of rootwords (s.v. *Bös*), Schottelius also cited him without naming him, for example in the entry for *Bak*, which Neuhaus states he 'repeats almost word for word' from Henisch, likewise *ferm, fermen, firmen*. Schottelius praised Henisch's work *AA* 1172 but emphasized that it was not a 'proper' dictionary, and referred the reader to his own plan for a dictionary *AA* 159–60 in the tenth oration.

Hepburn, James. See Bonaventura Hepburnus.

Herc. = *Hercinia Opitii:* cf. **Opitz.** 453; 711. A pastoral poem on the nymph Hercynia (1630). See Opitz.

Herden, Eitel Friedrich von = **Rudolf von Heiden** (1627–1661). 346; 347; 530. Reference is presumably to this jurist's *Grundfeste Des Heil. Römischen Reichs Teutscher Nation* (Frankfurt: Götz,1660), of which the Herzog August library in Wolfenbüttel holds a copy.

Hermannus Contractus = **Hermann of Reichenau** (1013–1054). c3^r; 1155; 128, 8: 9. Hermann's eleventh–century chronicle from the birth of Christ to his own present day was printed in the sixteenth century (*Chronicon* [...], Basle: Petrus, 1529). It compiled for the first time the events of the first millennium A.D., scattered in various chronicles, in a single work and ordered them after the reckoning of the Christian era.

Herodotus (ca. 485–425 B.C.). c3^r; 1180; 51, 4:4; 1033. Greek historian, and 'father of history' whose history in nine books aimed to give an account of the struggles between the Greeks and Persians up to 478 B.C. Schottelius referred *AA* 1180 to the German translation by Georg Schwarzkopf (1593), q.v.

Hesiodus (fl. ca. 735 B.C.). 87, 6: 28; 98, 6: 53. One of the earliest Greek poets who lived about a century later than Homer, and who was famous for his periodization of history.

Heuter Delfius (i.e. of Delft), Pontus de (1535–1602). 452. A Dutch historian, known for his *Rerum Burgundicarum libri sex, in quibus describuntur res gestae regum, ducum, comitumque utriusque Burgundiae* (Antwerp: n.p., 1583) which covered Burgundian history until ca. 1480, and to which the abbreviation *rer. Belgica* appears to refer.

Hieronymus = **St. Jerome.** See *Jerome, St.*

Hildebr. 487. Presumably *Hildebrand*. Not identified, but a likely candidate is Joachim Hildebrand (1623–1691), who became professor of theology in Helmstedt in 1648 and who published a number of theological works there.

Hille, Carl Gustav von (1590–1647). 1176. Mystic, writer and poet, member of the FG. Author of *Der Teutsche Palmbaum* (Nuremberg: Endter, 1647), a work in praise of and documenting the FG. See Jones (1995: 403–417).

Homer (8th C. B.C.). 87, 6: 28. Greek poet; mentioned a few times as a poet, and the *Iliad* is cited 87, 6: 28.

Horace (Horatius, Flaccus Quintus) (65–8 B.C.). c3^r; 7–8, 1: 19, 23; 12–13, 1: 39; 42, 3: 40; 106, 7: 7; 110, 7: 13; 113, 7: 23; 167, 10: 21; 1025; 1243. Roman poet, whose *Ars poetica* and other verse Schottelius cited several times.

Hornschuch, Hieronymus (1573–1616). c3^v; 190: 12. *Orthotypographia. Hoc est: Instructio pro operas typographicas correcturis,* one of the first technical manuals for printers (Leipzig: Lantzenberger, 1608).

Hortleder, Friderich (1579–1640). 1160. Schottelius referred to Goldast's (q.v.) 1645 edition of the statesman Hortleder's collection of documents on the War of the League of Schmalkalden and its aftermath (1546–1559). Hortleder became a member of the FG in 1639.

Hübner, Tobias (= der Nutzbare) (1578–1636). 1183. Jurist, member of the FG, and author of a verse translation of the works of Guillaume de Saluste du Bartas, q.v., *La Seconde Sepmaine* (Cöthen: Anhalt, 1622). Schottelius praised the skill of the translator, but noted that the metre did not always accord with what was now proper for German verse. Nevertheless his verse is cited a few times in the poetics (identified as 'Bartas'). See Jones (1995: 80–81).

Hucbaldus (840 or 850–930). c3^r. Benedictine monk, music theorist, composer, teacher, writer, and hagiographer. Not cited outside the list on c3^r?

Huge, Alexander (1455–1529). 1192. *Stadtschreiber* from southern Germany, i.e. a scribe in a town chancellery. Schottelius noted the *Rhetorica und Formularium Deutsch* (Tübingen: Morhart, 1528), without naming its author.

Hugh de Clers. 288. A treatise attributed to Hugh/ Hugues de Clers, *De Seneschallia Franciae,* appeared in volume 4 of the *Historiae Francorum scriptores* (5 vols. 1636–1649), a work intended as a compendium of sources of medieval French history, and planned to extend to 24 volumes. Two volumes were published by André Duchesne (1584–1640), and three more by his son.

Huitfeldius, Haraldus = Arild (Arvid) Huitfeldt (1546–1609). 56, 4: 17. Author of the first major history of Denmark, in Danish, published 1595–1603 in eight volumes, *Danmarks Riges Krønike* ('The Chronicle of the Realm of Denmark'. Wolfenbüttel holds an edition (Copenhagen: Moltke, 1652–55).

Hulsius, Levin(us) (van Hulsen) (ca. 1546–1606). 147, 10: 29. Born in Belgium but working in Germany, Hulsius was a publisher and printer, linguist and lexicographer, who also wrote extensively on the construction of geometrical instruments. The reference *AA* 147 is to the preface of his *Tractat der mechanischen Instrumenten* (Frankfurt am Main: published by the author, 1604). See Moulin-Fankhänel (1994: 96–105).

Hunger(us), Wolfgangus (1507–1555). De[r] (under W); 4, 1: 9; 123–24, 8: 3–4; 132, 8: 12; 139, 9: 7; 140, 9: 10. Schottelius referred to Hungerus's *Linguae Germanicae vindicatio contra exoticas quasdam* (Argentorati: Jobin, 1586).

Hund, Wiguleus (1514–1588). 497; 503; 504. Schottelius cited Hund's genealogy of the Bavarian nobility (Ingolstadt: Sartorius, 1585; VD 16 H 5927) (with a second volume printed in 1586).

Hunn. = Hunnius, Helfrich Ulrich (1583–1636). 8, 1: 21. Schottelius referred to Hunnius's legal work, *Tractatus de authoritate et interpretatione juris, tam canonici, quam civilis* (Marburg: Hampelius, 1630).

Husanus, Johann Friedrich (1566–1592). 508. Schottelius referred to the *Tractatus de servis vel famulis et hominibus tam liberis quam propriis* of the Italian lawyer Ippolito Bonacossa (1541–1591), to which Husanus, also a lawyer, added summaries and an index (Cologne: Gymnich, 1590; VD16 B 9793; reprinted 1620).

Hutten, Ulrich von (1488–1523). De[r] (listed under V); 475. Humanist and writer, an outspoken adherent of the Lutheran Reformation. De[r] refers to *Equitis Germani Arminius*, a dialogue of which Wolfenbüttel holds a 1630 edition. Cited *AA* 475 s.v. *Haubtstraffe*.

Hutter, Elias (1553–1605/09). 16, 2: 4; 17, 2: 7; 18, 2: 10. Schottelius referred to Hutter's *Offentlich Außschreiben, An allgemeine Christliche Obrigkeit* [...] (Nuremberg: n.p., 1602).

Hutterus, Wolfgang (fl. 1572). 1170. According to Schottelius, Hutterus published in 1572 a *Linguae Germanicae Vindicatio* [...] in which he argued that French grammarians failed to realize the German origins of many French words.

Ickelsamer, Valentin (ca. 1500–1541). c3[r]; 59, 4: 25; 60, 4: 30; 380. Author of *Teutsche Grammatica* (1534), referred to in the orations. Schottelius described him *AA* c3[r] as a *vetus Author, scripsit libellum, quem nominat Grammaticam Germanicam*, 'an old author, [who] wrote a little book, which he calls German grammar.' Cf. Moulin-Fankhänel (1994: 106–15).

Irenicus, Franciscus (Franz Friedlieb) (1495–1559). c3[v]; 140, 9: 10; 219: 43. German reformist humanist and historian who described Germany in twelve books: *Germaniæ exegeseos volumina duodecim a Francisco Irenico Ettelingiacensis exarata* (Nuremberg: Koberger, 1518). The earliest writer to formulate the notion of a Germanic monosyllabic rootword.

Isidore of Seville (Isidorus Hispalensis) (ca. 560—636). c3[r]; 40, 3: 32; 168, 10: 22. Isidore's *Etymologiae* was one of the most influential compendia of knowledge of the medieval period and was still cited by Schottelius.

Islandus, Arngrimus Ionas = Arngrímur Jónsson (1569–1648). See Jónsson, Arngrímur.

Isocrates (436–338 B.C.). 87, 6: 28. Greek rhetorician. Schottelius cited a Greek compound attested in Isocrates.

Jäger, Balthasar. See Venator, Balthasar.

J.C., also I.C., *Jcti* **= Termini apud Jureconsultos usitati.** c3^r ; 454. *passim.* Used to indicate a lawyer, or a term commonly used by lawyers.

Jerome (St.) (= Eusebius Hieronymus Sophronius) (ca. 347–420). 31–32, 3: 8–9; 34, 3: [13]. Christian apologist and Church Father best known for his Latin translation of the Bible (the Vulgate version), but his letters are cited in the orations.

Jónsson, Arngrímur (1569–1648). c3^r; 56–57, 4: 17, 20; 1219. Schottelius referred to Jónsson's *Brevis commentarius de Islandia* (Hafnia: n.p., 1593) (*AA* c2^r, 56, 4: 17) as *de primordiis Gentis Islandiae,* 'of the beginnings of the people of Iceland'.

Jornandes (or Jordanes), Gothus (fl. 530 A.D.). c3^r; 1154; 45–46, 3: 44. Sixth-century Gothic historian. Schottelius (*AA* 1154) called him the first historian of Germanic blood and cited his use of the word *gothiscanzia,* *AA* 45–46, for a Gothic military defence.

Josephus, Flavius (37–ca.100 A.D.). 35, 3: 16; 51, 4: 4. Jewish historian whose *Jewish Antiquities* Schottelius cited, an account in 20 books of Jewish history from the creation of the world to the Jewish revolt ca. 66 A.D.

Jovius, Paulus = Paolo Giovio (1483–1552). 1157. Italian historian, whose *Historiarum sui temporis libri XLV* gives a detailed account of European history for the period 1494 to 1544. His work was printed in Italy from 1550; an edition appeared in Basle in 1560. Schottelius referrred to a 1552 edition, not identified.

Julius Caesar, (Gaius) (100–44 B.C.). c2^r; 70, 5: 6; 339; 525. Roman emperor and military commander. Schottelius cited his *Commentarii,* which relate the history of the Gallic Wars in seven books, and Civil war in three books.

Junius, Franciscus (The Younger) (1591–1677). 162, 10: 18; 1035; 1037; 1058; 1069; 1094; 1095; 1285; 1286 *Bider*; 1290 *Bokk*; 1306 *dualm*; 1320 *fried*; 1348 *Knoul*; 1357 *Leumd*; *Leute*; 1358 *List*; *Lokk* ; 1370 *Niud*; 1375 *Pflantz*; 1388 *Ruach*; 1408 *Schorn*; 1410 *Schuh*; 1423 *Stof*; 1429 *Taug*; 1439 *Wahn.* French philologist born in Heidelberg who lived principally in Holland and England, a pioneer in the study of Gothic and Anglo-Saxon. Schottelius referenced his *Observationes in Willerami Abbatis francicam paraphrasin cantici canticorum* (Amsterdam: n.p., 1655), a commentary on the German paraphrase of the Song of Solomon of Williram von Ebersberg (1010–1085, q.v.). There are 19 explicit references to it in the list of rootwords in the sixth treatise of Book V (Neuhaus 1991: 132–40; Van de Velde (1966: 130–65). There are also several references in the list of proper names.

Justinus = Justin Martyr (100–165). 1181. Early Christian apologist and Church Father. Translated by Hieronymus Boner (d. 1552, q.v.) in 1532 (cf. Worstbrock 1976: 93), but, according to Schottelius (*AA* 1181), a better translation is that of Johann Friedrich Schweser (q.v.) (1656).

Kalchum / Calchum / Calcheim, Wilhelm von (= Colonel Lohausen) (1584–1640). 1174; 1182; 226.5; 273; 384. Member of the FG, noted by Schottelius as a translator of Italian and Latin literature into German, including Sallust.

Keckermann(us), Bartholomaeus (1571–1609). 139, 9: 7. German writer, Calvinist theologian and philosopher. Schottelius cited his etymology of *Schöpfen*, but it is not clear which work is referred to.

Keller, Adam (variously abbreviated as *Kell.*, *Kel.*, *Keller.*, and [erroneously] *Kellerm.*) (fl. 1618?). c3^r; 372, 378; 504; 625; 644. Schottelius referred to Keller's treatise on the law of inheritance *De Jure Succedendi Ab Intestato: Das ist, Von Erbfalls Recht. Tractatus Brevis* (Frankfurt: Emmelius, 1618).

Kil. See König, Kilian.

Kill./ Killing. = **Kyllinger, Jakob Werner** (1598–1620). 418; 515; 525. Schottelius cited Kyllinger's work on fortification: *De ganerbiis castrorum sive de arcium pluribus communium condominis: Von den Ganerben und Burgmäunern gemeiner Schlösser, Vösten oder Burgen* (Tübingen: Typis Iohan-Alexandri Cellii, 1620).

Kindermann, Balthasar (1636–1706). 1182; 1193. Kindermann wrote both a German rhetoric (1660) and a poetics (1664). Schottelius referred to his *Kurandors Unglückseliges Nisette* (Frankfurt an der Oder: Klosemann, Becman, 1660), as well as his German translation of Sallust (Wittenberg: Fincelius, 1662). See Moulin-Fankhänel (1997b: 153–165).

Kirchner, Hermann (1562–1620). 517. Professor of history, poetics and rhetoric at Marburg. Schottelius referred to his *Disputatio Iuridico-Politica Nobiliores Aliquot Ex Ipsis Ictorum Et Politicorum fontibus assertiones exhibens* (Marburg: Hutwelcker, 1610; VD17 3:679944N).

Klaj, Johann (1616–1656). c3^r; 1203; 436, 779–80. Page c3^r notes Klaj's *Teutsche Poemata* (Lipsiae: Gross, n.d.). *AA* 1203 also notes his *Lobrede der Teutschen Poeterey* (1645), and his verse is cited (attributed to *Clajus*, but not to be confused with the sixteenth-century grammarian of that name, q.v.) in the poetics. See Jones (1995: 398–401).

Klammer, Balthasar (1504–1578). c3^r; 643. Page c3^r refers to Klammer's legal compendium, *Compendium Iuris, Das ist: Kurtzer Außzug, vieler und vornehmer Rechtsbücher* (Leipzig: Börner, 1616).

Klas, Hans. 1187. A misprint for Eles, Hans, q.v.

Klock, Caspar (1583–1655). c3^r; 482; 491; 496; 502; 618; 619; 621; 631; 648. Schottelius noted two works by this expert on finance and taxation on c3^v: his collected works (under the title *Consilia*, Frankfurt: Endter, 1649–60) and his work on currency, *Tractatus juridico-politico-polemico-historicus de ærario* (Nuremberg: Endter, 1651). *AA* 502 *de aerar.* refers to the *Tractatus nomico-politicus de contributionibus in Romano-Germanico-Imperio et aliis regnis ut plurimum usitatis* (Bremen: Typis Villerianis, 1634).

Knefsteiner, Johann Ludwig. Typographical error for von Kuefstein, Johann Ludwig, q.v.

Knich. = Kniche[n] *or* **von Knichen, Andreas** (1560–1621). 129, 8: 9; 487; 499. German jurist. The text referred to by Schottelius is *De Sublimi Et Regio Territorii Iure, Synoptica Tractatio: In Qua Principum Germaniae Regalia Territorio Subnixa, Vulgo Landes Obrigkeit indigitata, nuspiam antehac digesta, luculenter explicantur* (Francofurti: In Officina Literaria Palthe-niani Collegii, 1603).

Kolbenrecht.1234–1242. Schottelius cited the 63-article *Kolbenrecht* (source unknown, but it is also contained in Schottelius's legal treatise, Schottelius 1671)—i.e. the law on deciding conflicts by single combat—as an illustration of older German words and idioms (*AA* 1234–1242).

König, Chilianus (Kilian) (1470–1526). c3^r; 1166; 360; 521; 545; 552; 636; 638; 647; 734 and *passim*; 1026. Schottelius referred *AA* 1166 to König's legal treatise in German on Saxon law, *Practica oder Proces der Gerichtsläuffe/ nach dem brauch Sechsischer Landart/ aus den gemeinen Bepstlichen/ Keyserlichen vnd Sechsischen Rechten*. I have not established the date of the first edition; the earliest copy in VD16 is 1541.

Krantz(ius) / Crantzius, Albert(us) (1448–1517). c3^r; 41, 3: 36; 136, 9: 2; 175: 9; 1158. German church historian and theologian. Schottelius cited his work on the Saxons, *Saxonia* (Cologne: Soter, 1520), and referred *AA* 1158 to a German translation by Basilius Faber of the *Saxonia* (Leipzig: Vögelin, 1563).

Kuefstein, Johann (Hans) Ludwig von (1582/3–1656/7). Translator of the Spanish work *Diana* by Jorge de Montemayor (1520?–1561) (Linz: Blanck, 1624). A later version, in which Harsdörffer appears to have collaborated, was printed in 1646 (Nuremberg: Endter; VD17 23:286741L).

Kunowitz, Johann Dietrich von ('der Vollziehende') (1624–1700). 1182. Member of the FG. Schottelius noted von Kunowitz's translation of Cornelius Nepos or Aemilius's work on the life of heroes *Cornelius Nepos Oder Aemilius Probus/ Von dem Leben und Thaten vortrefflicher Helden* (Cassel: Schütze, 1661).

L. Alem or *leg. alem.* c3^r; 272; 277; 443. *Leges Alamannorum*; cf. Lindenbrog (Alemannic legal code).

L. L. Alfreds Reg. 46, 3: 44. Not further identified. A legal code of King Alfred, perhaps part of *Lex Anglorum*, in Lindenbrog's codex (cf. c3^r).

L. Angl. 446. *Lex Anglorum*; cf. Lindenbrog (English legal code).

L. L. Canuti Reg. 517. See Lindenbrog. Not identified, but presumably a reference either to the 'first' and 'second' law codes of Cnut (Canute), the last surviving codes issued in the name of an Anglo–Saxon king, or the compilation known now as the *Pseudo–leges Canuti*.

L. Rip. c3^r; 277; 289. *Lex Ripuarium*; cf. Lindenbrog (Ripuarian legal code).

L. Sax. c3^r. *Lex Saxonum*; cf. Lindenbrog (Saxon legal code).

L. Wisig. c3^r. *Leges Wisigothorum,* cf. Lindenbrog (Visigoth legal code).

L.R. = **LehnRecht or Lubecks Recht.** c3^r; 1201; 263; 272; 325; 352; 419. The same abbreviation occurs twice on c3^r, for these two legal sources. *Lehnrecht* is further described *AA* 1201. Schottelius had access to the *Lehnrecht* (Neuhaus 1991:140) as part of *Sechsisch Weychbild vnd Lehenrecht/ Jtzt auffs naw ... restituirt/ sampt eim nawen Register oder Remissorio ... vber diese zwey bücher/ vn[d] den Sachsenspiegel gemacht/ Darzu bey dem Weychbild vnd Lehenrecht vill nützlicher addiciones ... Auch etliche Vrteil ... zunutz allen denen/ so sich Sechsischs rechtens gebrauchen müssen,* published by Christoph Zobel (1499–1560, q.v.), and to which Schottelius had access in a 1559 edition.

L.Sal. c3^r; 517. *Lex Salicae;* cf. Lindenbrog (Salic legal code).

Lactantius (ca. 240–320). 35, 3: 19. Lactantius, a Latin-speaking native of North Africa, was a pupil of Arnobius and taught rhetoric in various cities of the Eastern Roman Empire, ending in Constantinople.

Laertius, Diogenes (3rd century). c3^r; 172.2; 293. Biographer of the Greek philosophers.

Laet, Johannes de (1593–1649). c3^r; 58, 4: 22. Director of the Dutch West India Company. Schottelius listed *AA* c3^r his history of the New World, first published in Dutch in 1625 as *Nieuwe Wereldt ofte Beschrijvinghe van West-Indien* [...]. Wolfenbüttel holds both a 1630 (second) edition of (Leiden: Elzevier, 1630) and a copy of the first Latin edition (Leiden: Elzevier, 1633).

Lambert of Hersfeld, also known as 'of Aschaffenburg' (ca. 1024– ca. 1088). 1154; 157, 10: 13. Schottelius described Lambert *AA* 1154 as a monk who wrote a history of German emperors up to the year 1077, published by Schard (q.v.), and about whom Schottelius had learnt from Gessner's (q.v.) *Bibliotheca Universalis.* Lambert's *Annales* were first published in 1525. The Schard edition was in the 1566 *Germanicarum rerum quatuor celebriores vetustioresque chronographi ... Quorum nomina sunt: Iohannes Turpinus De vita Caroli Magni et Rolandi. Rhegino Abbas Prumiensis diocesis Treviren. Sigebertus Gemblacensis eiusque continuator Robertus de Monte. Lambertus Schaffnaburgensis, alias Hirsfeldensis dictus.* Cf. Turpinus, Johannes.

Lansius, Thomas (1577–1657). c3^r; 1204; 23–25, 2: 31, 33, 38. Professor of rhetoric and politics. Schottelius referred to Lansius's *Orationes pro & contra Germaniam.* Paragraphs 31 and 33 of Schottelius's second oration are based on the oration *Contra Galliam.* Cf. *Orationes aliquot* (Tübingen: Typis Theodorici Werlini, 1616).

Lassenius, Johannes (1636–1692). 1204. German devotional poet and writer. Schottelius mentioned a number of works by him *AA* 1204.

Laudismann(us), Caspar (fl. 1614–1623). c3^r; 4, 1: 9; 25, 2: 37. Laudismann wrote *Consiliis de Addiscendis linguis exoticis Gallia et Italia* (Leipzig:

Tobias Beyer, 1614), i.e. advice on teaching foreign languages in France and Italy.

Lauterbeck, Georg (d. 1578). 1191. Schottelius listed five publications by Lauterbeck, a German humanist: on government in war and peace, a German translation of Sleidanus's (q.v.) Latin translation of Plato, and other translations, from Latin and French, as well as on courtly life.

Laymann, Paul (1574–1635). 491. Schottelius referenced the Jesuit Laymann's *Theologia Moralis: Jn Qvinqve Libros Partita* (Monachii: Formis Nicolai Henrici, 1625).

Lazius, Wolfgang (1514–1565). c3^r; 1159; 26, 2: 41; 43, 3: 42; 55, 4: 13; 56, 4: 17; 124, 8: 4; 126, 8: 4; 129, 8: 9; 132, 8: 12; 140, 9: 10; 151, 10: 9; 155, 10: 13; 166, 10: 21; 219: 43; 290; 374; 412; 490; 505; 523; 568; 632; 689; 1031; 1033; 1035–37; 1050; 1064; 1068; 1078; 1086; 1090; 1255; 1295 *Buttel*. Particularly known for his history of Vienna (*Vienna Austriae*, Basle: Oporinus, 1546), for his book on the great migrations (*De gentium aliquot migrationibus*, Basle: Oporinus, 1557), and as a cartographer. Lazius wrote a two-volume work of *Commemorationum Historicorum Rerum Graecorum Libri Duo* (of which Schottelius used a 1605 edition, Hanoviae: Marnius & Aubrius) and a twelve-volume work of *Commentariorum reipublicae Romanae [...] libri duodecim* (of which Schottelius used a 1598 edition, Frankfurt: Marnius & Aubrius) (*AA* 1159). Cited in the list of rootwords s.v. *Buttel* (Neuhaus 1991:154–55), and *passim* in the list of proper names.

Leg. Boj. c3^r; 439; 484. *Lex Bojorum, Bajuvariorum*; cf. Lindenbrog (Bavarian legal code).

Leg. Burg. c3^r; 288, 289; 336. *Lex Burgundionum*; cf. Lindenbrog (Burgundian legal code).

Leg. Fris; L. Fris. c3^r; 275. *Lex Frisionum*; cf. Lindenbrog (Frisian legal code).

Leg. Lomb; L. Long. c3^r; 338. *Lex Longobardorum*; cf. Lindenbrog (Langobard legal code).

Legib. torneam. 517. Apparently a reference to the laws of tournaments; the most likely candidate is a work by Limnaeus, q.v.

Lehmann(us), Christoph(orus) (1570?–1638). c3^r; 1186; 61, 4: 31; 97, 6: 53; 166, 10: 21; 257; 338; 518 and *passim*; 1034; 1037. Historian known as the German Livy, author of the *Speyerische Chronik* (1612), a chronicle of the city of Speyer, in which he praised German for its expressiveness, so that there was no need to borrow words, and praised the ancient Germans for being concerned about the purity of their language, just like the Romans (cf. Jones 1995: 32–33). Schottelius also referenced his *Politischer Blumengarte* on c3^r, i.e. *Florilegium politicum: politischer Blumengarten; darinn außerlesene Politische Sententz, Lehren, Reguln und Sprüchwörter auß Theologis Jurisconsultis, Politicis* (n. pl.: published by the author, 1630).

Lerch, Caspar à = **Caspar Lerch von Dürmstein** (1575–1642). c2^r; 343; 380; 403; 462; 464; 527. A member of the lower nobility and a competent administrator, who also published several works on legal matters. *AA* 462 *de ord. Germ* refers to his treatise on the order of knights, *Ordo equestris Germanicus Caesareus bellopoliticus* in four parts (Mainz: Möres 1625/26, 1631/32; cf. VD17 12:658310U); the citation at *AA* 343, on knighthood, is presumably from the same work.

Lez. = **Letzner, Johannes** (1531–1613). c3^r; 1171. Letzner published in 1596 a chronicle of Dassel and Einbeck (Schottelius's home–town) (Erfurt: Beck, 1596).

Ligurinus (12th century). 1156; 107, 7: 10. Conrad Peutinger (1465–1547) published a poem in 1507, written by Gunther of Paris, known as the *Ligurinus* or the *Ligurinus sive de gestis Frederici I libri X* (twelfth century), a description of the battles which Frederick Barbarossa fought with the Milan people whom he calls Ligures. This poem had been discovered in a monastery by Conrad Celtis (1459–1508), who gave it to Peutinger. In 1531 an edition by Jacob Spiegel appeared in Strasbourg, referred to *AA* 107, 7: 10, *Ligurinus, seu opus de rebus gestis Imp. Caesaris Friderici, I. Aug.* (Argentorati: Schott, 1531).

Limnaeus, Johannes (1592–1663). 1194; 289; 335; 442; 474; 495; 515; 618; 767. Jurist whose study of Roman and German imperial law Schottelius cited *AA* 1194: (Argentorati: Ledertz, 1629–). *AA* 517 refers to *legib. torneam.*, likely to be a reference to Book IV of this work, whose contents include *De torneamentis* 'about tournaments'. Schottelius also referred to his *Capitulationes imperatorum et regum Romanogermanorum, Caroli V. Ferdinandi I. Maximiliani II* (Argentorati: Spoor, 1651) in the grammar, using the abbreviation *Capit.*

Lindeberg, Peter (1562–1596). 56, 4: 17. Poet from Rostock. Schottelius referred *AA* 56 to him *in suo rerum memorabilium commentario* 'in his commentary on memorable matters'. It is not clear which work this is.

Lindenbrog, Friedrich (1573–1648). c3^r; 1213; 52, 4: 7; 98, 6: 54; 272; 337; 341; 450 and *passim*; 1046. Lindenbrog published a collection of laws called *Codex legum antiquarum* (Frankfurt: Marnius, 1613). Its fuller title lists the laws covered: *Codex legum antiquarum, in quo continentur: Leges Wisigothorum. Edictum Theodorici regis. Lex Burgundionum. Lex Salica. Lex Alamannorum. Lex Baiuvariorum. Decretum Tassilonis ducis. Lex Ripuariorum. Lex Saxonum. Angliorum et Werinorum. Frisionum. Longobardorum. Constitutiones siculæ sive neapolitanæ. Capitulare Karoli M. et Hludowici impp. & c. Quibus accedunt Formulæ solennes priscæ publicorum privatorumque negotiorum, nunc primum editae: et glossarium* […]. Schottelius referred to several sets of Germanic laws in Lindenbrog's collection, especially for word attestations (Moulin-Fankhänel 1997a: 307). Many of the sources contained in the codex are listed separately under *L* (for *Lex* 'law') on *AA* c3^r. See in this appendix entries under *L*. and *Leg*., and *Decretum Tassilionis Ducis*.

Lipsius, Justus = Joest Lips (1547–1606). c3^r; 47–48, 3: 52; 133, 8: 14; 341. Dutch humanist and classical scholar. Schottelius cited Lipsius's letter to Henricus Schottius (*AA* 47–48, 133), letter no. 44 in a printed edition (the first printed edition was 1602), containing Lipsius's glosses of psalms, and including comparisons between German and Persian (cf. Moulin-Fankhänel 1997a: 307, n. 26; Quak 1981: 39–50 for a facsimile edition).

Livius Andronicus, Lucius (fl. 272–250 B.C.). 107, 7: 10. Roman dramatist and epic poet, cited once in the oration on poetics.

Livius, Titus = Livy (59 B.C.–17 A.D.). c3^r; 26, 2: 41; 36, 3: 21; 523; 1032; 1150; 1207; 1287 *Bier*; 1325 *Ges*. Roman historian, born at Padua, but lived most of his life in Rome, author of a history of Rome in 142 books, from its foundation to 9 B.C. 35 of these books survive, but also 'Epitomes' of nearly all the rest. A 1571 translation by Zacharias Müntzer (1530/35–1586), q.v., is noted *AA* 1207, and Livy is also mentioned in the list of rootwords, s.v. *Ges* and *Bier* (Neuhaus 1991: 153–54).

Lohausen. See Kalchum, Wilhelm von.

Löhneysen = Löhneyss, Georg Engelhardt von (1552–1622?). 1189. Printer of numerous works listed by Schottelius, and known for their luxurious finish. His press was at Remlingen, near Wolfenbüttel.

Londorpius, Michael Caspar (pseudonym Nicolaus Bellus) (1580–1629). c3^r; 238.4; 256; 323 and *passim*. Londorpius published a (rather uncritical) collection of documents on contemporary history, noted *AA* c3^r. Schottelius referred to these *Acta Publica* [...] (Moeno-Francfurti: Weißius, 1621).

Lonicerus [= Lonitzer], Adam (1528–1586). 1187. German botanist. Schottelius referred to his *Kreuterbuch* or herbal (Frankfurt/Main: Egenolff, Christian d. Ä. (Erben), 1587).

Lucanus, M. Annaeus (= Lucan) (39–65 A.D.). c3^r; 36, 3: 21; 115, 7: 29; 145, 9: 21. Roman poet, born in Spain but who moved to Spain at an early age, mentioned in the orations as a poet, but also as an attestation for a Gaulish God called *Teut*.

Ludwig von Anhalt–Köthen [Prince] (1579–1650). 1183; 1204–5. Head of the FG. Schottelius referred to his poetical treatise of 1640 (without naming its author) as well as his *Der Fruchtbringenden Geselschaft Nahmen, Vorhaben, Gemählde und Wörter: Nach jedes Einnahme ordentlich in Kupfer gestochen u. in achtzeilige Reimgesetze verfasset* (1646). Also the unnamed translator of Gelli's *La Circe* (q.v.).

Luitprandus (ca. 922–972). 1154. Lombard historian and author whose history in six volumes was printed in 1514 in Paris.

Luther, Martin (1483–1546). c3^r; 1173; 46, 3: 48; 60, 4: 26; 110, 7: 13; 145, 9: 22; 146, 9: 26; 147, 9: 30; 166, 10: 21; 236.4; 237.4; 238.4; 296; 334; 567; 610; 687 and *passim*; 1016; 1035; 1037; 1049; 1052; 1065; 1068; 1071; 1074;

1079; 1082; 1090; 1228–29; 1258; 1291 *Bomm*; 1372 *Pad.* Founder of the Protestant Reformation. Page c3^r lists *H[err] Lutherus in seinen Teutschen Thomis.* Neuhaus (1991:143–47) examined references to Luther in the list of rootwords: there are two direct references to Luther (s.v. *Bomm* and *Pad*) plus 35 biblical quotations from the 1535 Luther bible. References are not always accurate or exact, according to Neuhaus. There are also numerous biblical references in the grammar. Schottelius also cited Luther's letter on translating. References in the treatise on proper names are to a work attributed to Luther at the time: *Aliquot Nomina Propria Germanorum ad Priscam Etymologiam restituta* (published anonymously in Wittenberg in 1537 but attributed in editions from 1559 onwards to Luther; cf. Fiedler 1942; Sonderegger 1998: 425).

Machiavelli, Niccolò (1469–1527). c3^r; 29, 3: 3. Italian diplomat and political philosopher, best known for his *Principe* ('The Prince') (1513). Schottelius cited *Disputationes de republica, quas discursus nuncupavit* (e.g. Mompelgarti: Folietus, 1588).

Magnus, Johannes = Johan Månsson (1488–1544). c3^r (under I); 54, 4: 10; 110, 7: 14; 175.9. Schottelius listed this Swedish archbishop's history of the northern peoples, i.e his *Historia Gothorum libris XXIV* (or *Chronicon von den Schweden und Gothen*) (1554), edited and published by his brother Olaus Magnus (see below) (Neuhaus 1991:156–57).

Magnus, Olaus (1490–1557). c3^r under Iohannes Magnus, and c3^v under O; 53, 4: 8; 54, 4: 10; 1019; 1384 *Reim.* Swedish historian and geographer. Olaus Magnus compiled *Historia de gentibus septentrionalibus,* an important work dealing with history, geography, and natural history, mentioned c3^r (Rome, 1555; Antwerp, 1558; Basle, 1567; Frankfort, 1618). German translation: Strasbourg and Basle, 1567; English: London, 1658; Dutch (Amsterdam, 1665). Cited in the list of rootwords s.v. *Reim* (Neuhaus 1991: 157–58).

Maifartus, Johann Matthäus (1590–1642). See Meyfart, Johann Matthäus.

Manlius, Johannes (= Mennel, Jakob?) (Mennel 1460–1526). 1191. Author of a book of commonplaces, translated by Ragor, q.v.

Marcellinus, Ammianus (325/330–after 391). c2^r (under Ammianus); 1153; 142, 9: 13; 111, 7: 15; 1019; 1053. Roman historian who wrote the last surviving major account of the late Roman empire, *Res Gestae Libri XXXI.*

Marquart vom Stein (fl. 1493). 1190. Schottelius noted Marquart's 1493 translation of the French *Book of the Knight of the Tower* (1371–72), a courtesy text consisting of exempla, although the German title Schottelius cited is rather mangled (*Einsamkeit* instead of *Erbarkeit*). Edition not identified.

Martinius, Matthias (1572–1630). c3^r; 53, 4: 8; 58, 4: 22; 126, 8: 6. Theologian and philologist, author of *Lexicon philologicum, praecipuè etymologicum, in quo Latinae et a Latinis auctoribus usurpatae tum purae tum barbarae voces ex originibus declarantus* [...] (Bremae: Villerius, 1623).

Mascardus, Josephus = Giuseppe Mascardi (d. 1588). c3^r; 9, 1: 27. Mascardi published a work on legal proofs (noted *AA* c3^r), *Conclusiones probationum omnium* [...] (Venetiis: Zenarius, 1584).

Mathesius, Johann M. (1504–1565). 1165. Lutheran theologian who published a treatise in German on mining, *Sarepta* [...] (Nuremberg: Vom Berb & Newber, 1562).

May *or* **Maius (von Sangershausen), Theodorus** (fl. 1605–1619). 1182. Schottelius referred to May's German translation of works on agriculture, *Agricultur, oder Ackerbaw der beyden hocherfahrnen und weitberühmbten Römer, L. Columellae & Palladii* [...] (Magdeburg: Francke, 1612).

Meibom(ius), Henricus / Heinrich (1555–1625). 1209; 4, 1: 9; 125, 8: 4; 213:32; 218–9: 43; 383; 499; 1034; 1070; 1071; 1354 *Lager*. German historian and writer. Schottelius referred to 17 historical works by Meibomius (listed by Neuhaus 1991: 155–157) (*AA* 1209), and referenced him in the list of rootwords s.v. *Lager* and in the list of proper names.

Meichsner, Sebastian (fl. 1576). 1192; 1323. Schottelius referred to Meichsner's 1576 edition of *Das alte Käserliche und Königliche Land-Lehnrecht*, a reworking of the *Sachsenspiegel* (q.v.) produced in the thirteenth century in Augsburg. The first version of this re = working was printed in 1505. See Duntze (2007: 122–23). Schottelius conceded that the style of its German was now outmoded (drawing a comparision with fashions in clothing), but that the words themselves were *gut und vernemlich* (*AA* 1193). Cited in the list of rootwords once, s.v. *Gau* (Neuhaus 1991: 149–50).

Melanchthon, Philipp (1497–1560). 1191. German reformer, theologian and scholar, noted by Schottelius *AA* 1191 as a continuator of Carion's chronicle (q.v.).

Melder, Gerard (fl. 1658). c2^v. Master of fortifications in Utrecht. Schottelius referred c2^v to a German translation of Melder's work on military fortification, *Kurtze jedoch Grundmässige Unterweisung Der Regular und Irregular Fortification Mit deren Aussenwercken, Von Praxi Offensivè et Defensivè* (Osnabruck: Schwänder, 1661), translated from the Dutch, *Korte en klare instructie der regulaire en inregulare fortificatien met haere buytenwerken enz. met eene korte wederlegging der sustenu van den heer Henric Ruse, over de hedendaagsche fortificatie* (1658). Schottelius referred to Melder as Gebhard Melder(es). See Jones (1999: 101).

Melissus = Paulus Melissus Francus = Paul Schede Melissus (1539–1602). c3^v; 1179. Writer and humanist, noted as translator of the psalms, cf. (Heidelberg, 1572).

Menoch. = Menochio, Giacomo (1532–1607). 8, 1: 23 & 26. Jurist and professor at university of Padua. Schottelius cited his 1576 *De Arbitrariis Iudicum [Judicum] Quaestionibus et Causis* [...], a study of Roman and canon law (Lugduni: Tinghi, 1576).

Merian, Matthäus (The Elder) (1593–1650). De^r under *Th. Eur.*; 1186; 78, 6: 16; 128, 8: 9; 353; 369; 500; 517; 529; 622; 745 and *passim*. Schottelius cited Merian's Swiss topography, *Topographia Helvetiae, Rhaetiae, et Valesiae* (Amsterdam: n.p., 1644; rpt. 1960) in the orations. His *Theatrum Europaeum*, continued by his son of the same name (1621–1687) (Frankfurt: Merian, 1633–) appeared in six volumes. References to *Th. Eur.* provide attestations for compounds, *AA* 78, 6: 16.

Merula, Paulus (1558–1607). Schottelius used Merula's edition of Williram von Ebersberg's Old High German paraphrase of the Song of Solomon (*Canticum canticorum paraphrasis*, Leiden: Raphelengius, 1598). See Williram von Ebersberg.

Meteranus = van Meteren, Emanuel (1535–1612). c3^v; 1195; 79, 6: 19; 344; 506; 732 and *passim*. Dutch chronicler whose chronicle of Low Countries history (continued after his death) was translated into High Geman, and reprinted several times. Wolfenbüttel holds a German translation, (Arnheim: Jansen, n.d.).

Meurer, Noë (1525/8–1583). c3^v listed under N; 336; 518; 639; 1200. Author of a German-language work on the laws of the waterways (*AA* 1200), *Wasser Recht* [...] (Frankfurt: Feyerabend, 1570).

Mevius, David (1609–1670). c3^v; 238:4; 241: 6; 333; 505; 514; 577. Jurist whose works included the *Commentarius in Ius Lubecense* (1642–1643) referred to by Schottelius.

Meyer, Martin (= Philimerus Irenicus Elisius) (1630–1670). 1200. Schottelius referred to Meyer's account of events in Europe 1659–1662: *Philemeri Irenici Elisii Diarium Europæum.* [...] (Frankfurt: Ammon 1659–1683, specifically parts 3–8).

Meyfart, Johann Matthaeus (1590–1642). c3^r; 1177; 22, 2: 24; 412. Page c3^r mentions Meyfart's *Teutsche Redekunst* (1634); a fuller praise is accorded to the same work in the list of German writers, *AA* 1177. See Jones (1995: 81–83).

Micellus = Jakob Moltzer (Micyllus) (1503–1558). His German translation of Tacitus's *Germania* (q.v.) was published in 1535 (Mainz: Schöffer, Ivo; VD16 T 20).

Micrellius = Johann Lükteschwager Micraelius (1597–1658). c3^v; 1185; 131, 8: 11; 157–58, 10: 13; 278; 335; 497; 1037; 1287 *Bier*. Pomeranian historian whose history of Pomerania, *Altes PommerLand* [...] (Alten Stettin: Rhete, 1640) Schottelius drew on once in his treatise of rootwords (*AA* 1287). There is a detailed listing of the contents of its six books in the fourth treatise (*AA* 1185). Cited s.v. *Bier* in the list of rootwords (Neuhaus 1991: 162–63).

Mindanus, Petrus Friderus (d. 1616). c3^v; 367; 441. German jurist, author of various works. No work specified.

Möller, Alhard (fl. 1651–1662). 1192. Schottelius referred to the second (Magdeburg: Gerlach, 1660) edition of Möller's *Viridarium Epistolicum:*

Das ist: Ein Lust-Garte/ Vieler/ mit anmuhtiger Wort-Zierligkeit/ und edlen Red= Arte[n]/ jetztbeliebtem Styli nach/ eingekleidten Send-Schreiben, which he considered contained some 'good expressions'.

More, Thomas (1478–1535). 1268. English lawyer, social philosopher and statesman, whose *Utopia* (1516) Schottelius cited *AA* 1268.

Moscherosch, Johan Michael (1601–1669). c3^r; 1177; 329; 335; 346; 639; 713 and *passim*. Member of the FG, German satirist and moralist. Schottelius mentioned various 'useful' books by Moscherosch. See Jones (1995: 269–281).

Müntzer, Zacharias (1530/35–1586). 1207. Protestant cleric, historian and translator; author of a German translation of Livy and Florus (q.v.), *Von Ankunft und Ursprung des Römischen Reichs* (Frankfurt: Rabe; Han, 1571).

Münster(us), Sebastian (1489–1552). c3^v; 1168; 4, 1: 9; 131, 8: 10; 487; 499; 1322 *Gau*. Munsterus's German *Cosmographia oder Beschreibung aller Lender* (Basle: durch Heinrich Petri, 1544) was well known and popular in the sixteenth and seventeenth centuries (Neuhaus 1991:149–50).

Mylius, Abraham = Myl(e), Abraham van der (1563–1637). 32, 3: 9; 113, 7: 21. Schottelius cited Mylius's *Lingua Belgica* (Lugduni Batavorum: n.p., 1612), in which he maintained that Flemish had suffered no change over time, and was therefore primordial. Other languages were more or less corrupted dialects of Flemish (*AA* 32, 3: 9, 113 7: 21) (Metcalf 1953b).

Myns. = Mynsinger von Frundeck, Joachim (1514–1588). 9, 1: 27; 611. Jurist and humanist active in Wolfenbüttel. Schottelius cited his *Responsorum Iuris: Sive Consiliorum Centuria* [...] (Prostant In Officina Paltheniana Francofurtensi […], 1601).

Nauclerus, Johannes (d. 1510). 1158. Historian whose chronicle reached 1500. It was translated and printed by Heinrich Panthaleon (1522–1595) in Basle in 1560.

Neumark, Georg (1621–1681). 1203. Composer, poet and secretary to Duke Wilhelm II of Sachsen-Weimar when president of the FG, from 1651 onwards. Schottelius noted his poetical works. See Moulin-Fankhänel (1997b: 207–210).

Noricus, Elias (fl. 1593). 1202. Schottelius praised the content of Noricus's edificatory work *Das Newe Jahr* (1593) but noted that the rhymes are according to *damaliger Art* 'the style of the time'.

Nottnagel, Christopher (1607–1666). c3^v; 1207. Schottelius listed Nottnagel's (Wittenberg: Fincelius, 1659). See Jones (1999: 101).

Nov.; also *Judex. Nov. aug = Novellae Augusti*. c3^v; 78, 6: 16; 84, 6: 25; 90, 6: 33; 92, 6: 37; 288; 353; 386; 389. Schottelius referred to the four parts of the new *Verordnung* of August, Elector of Saxony, as sources of compounds listed in the sixth oration.

Olearius (= Öhlschläger), Adam (1599–1671). 1195–1196; 1206. Geographer who as secretary to the ambassador sent by Frederick III, Duke of

Holstein-Gottorp, to the Shah of Persia, travelled to the east. Schottelius noted a number of Olearius's works based on his travels, and his translation of the Persian poet, Schich Schaadi, *Persianischer Rosenthal* (1654).

Ölinger, Albert (fl. 1574–1587). c3^v; 1214. Author of the second German grammar (Ölinger 1574). Schottelius listed Ölinger as a figure whom he had *not* discussed in the treatise in his final paragraph, on *AA* 1214. Cf. Moulin-Fankhänel (1994: 146–51).

Opitz, Martin (1597–1639). c3^v; 1179; 1206; 202.23; 203.24; 209.29; 228.6.III; 236.4; 240.5; 209.29; 242.7; 244.9.I; 266; 417; 491; 539 and *passim*; several times in the poetics; 1222–25. Member of the FG, German poet, translator and purist (Jones 1995: 37–58). Schottelius cited his poetry several times for exemplification in the poetics. His *Aristarchus* (1617) is noted c3^v, his German translation of the psalms is noted *AA* 1179, and he is cited many times in the grammar for, amongst other things, his views on on epenthetic *e*, e.g *genädig* for *gnädig* (*AA* 209.29). See also his pastoral poem *Hercinia* (*Herc.*).

Oppian of Apamea (or Pella) (fl. after 211). 1256. Poet from Apamea (or Pella) in Syria, whose extant poem on hunting (*Cynegetica*) is dated to after 211. See Virgil.

Ortelius, Abraham (1527–1598). 142, 9: 13. Flemish cartographer and geographer. Schottelius referred to his *Thesaurus geographicus*, first published in 1587 (Antwerp: Plantijn).

Ostrofrank. See Albertus, Laurentius.

Otfrid von Weißenburg (800–after 870). c3^v; 1194; 52, 4: 6; 197.16; 210.29; 443; 1018; 1286; 1287 *bider, Bild*; 1349 *Jos*; 1355 *lauter*; 1357 *Leute*; 1370 *Niud*; 1388 *Ruach*; 1445 *Wunne*; 1349; 1355; 1357; 1370; 1388; 1445. Schottelius had access to Otfrid's Old High German *Evangelienbuch* (a rhymed life of Christ) in a 1571 edition by Matthias Flacius Illyricus (1520–1575, q.v.) (Moulin-Fankhänel 1997a: 306; Neuhaus 1991: 131). Schottelius cited Otfrid eight times in his list of rootwords to attest words in Old High German. *AA* 1194 Schottelius cited Otfrid's reference to writing in *theodisca* as early evidence of the awakening distinction between *theodisca[m], the = hoch = ditsche (die Hochteutsche)* and *Teutisca* or *Teutonica*.

Otto von Freising (ca. 1114–1158). c3^v; 1155. German bishop and chronicler, whose chronicle was printed in 1515 (Strasbourg: Schürer, 1515; VD16 O 1434).

Ovid (Ovidius, Naso P.) (43 B.C.– 18 A.D.). 1090; mentioned elsewhere. Roman poet whose works include *Ars Amatoria, Metamorphoses, Fasti* (kind of poetical Roman calendar), *Tristia* and *Epistles ex Ponto*.

Pacuvius, Marcus (220 B.C.–130 A.D.). 93: 6, 38. Roman tragic poet who based his works on the great Greek writers, but who allowed himself more scope in his adaptations, not mere translations.

Paris, Mattheus (1200–1259). c3^v. Benedictine monk and English chronicler. *AA* c3^v notes the *Historia Anglorum*, a history of England.

Pastorius, Melchior Adam (1624–1702). 1195. Jurist and writer who served in Windsheim as counsellor, elder burgomaster, judge, and councillor to the Prince of Brandenburg. He published a number of works: Schottelius referred to Pastorius's history of emperors and electors, *Römischer Adler* [...] of 1657.

Paulus Diaconus = Paul the Deacon (720–799). c3^v; 57, 4: 18; 175.9. Lombard historian. Schottelius referred to 'book 12' without specifying a work, but perhaps he had access to an edition such as *Historia miscellae* [...] *Libri XXIV* (Ingolstadt: Angamarius, 1603).

Paurmeister, Tobias (?–?). 426. Schottelius referred to Paurmeister's *De Iurisdictione Imperii Romani Libri II* ('Two volumes on the laws of the Roman Empire') (Hanoviae: Kopffius, 1608; VD17 75:701327K).

Pedemontanus, Alexius = Alessio Piemontese, pseudonym of **Girolamo Ruscelli** (1500–1556). 1188. Italian humanist physician and alchemist. See Wecker, Johann Jakob.

P.H.O = Peinliche Halsgerichts Ordnung. c3^v; 335; 356; 360. This abbreviation presumably refers to the *Peinliche Halsgerichts Ordnung* of Emperor Charles V, dating from 1532, and available in the seventeenth century, for example in *Aller des Heiligen Römischen Reichs gehaltener Reichstage Ordnung* (Mainz: Johan Albin, 1607). There is also a Bamberg *Peinliche Halsgerichts Ordnung* dating from 1507.

Perneder, Andreas (ca. 1500–1543). 1166. Perneder translated the *Insitutiones Iuris* (principles of law) and 'other imperial laws' and legal works. Schottelius referred to Wolfgang Hunger's (q.v.) support for printing various of Perneder's works in a 1581 edition.

Petrarch [Petrarca], Franceso (1304–1374). 1206. Italian scholar, poet, and 'father of humanism'. Schottelius noted German translations of his works *AA* 1206.

Petronius arbiter (ca. 27–66). 93, 6: 38. Roman writer to whom the *Satyricon* is attributed. Schottelius cited a Latin compound from his work.

Peucer, Caspar (1525–1602). 1191. German humanist, mentioned by Schottelius as a continuator of Carion's chronicle (q.v.).

Philimerus Irenicus Elisius = pseudonym of Martin Meyer. See Meyer, Martin.

Pirckheimer, Willibald (1475–1530). 1159; 1250–55. Nuremberg humanist. Schottelius referred to the collection of his historical, political, philological and epistolary works published by Goldast (q.v.) (Frankfurt, 1610), and cited him in the treatise on translating, *AA* 1251–55, on the subject of proper names and their translation. Cf. Harlfinger (1989: Nr. 148).

Pistorius, Johann (The Younger) Niddanus [from Nidda in Hessen] (1546–1608). c3^r; 4, 1:9; 132, 8: 12; 404. Page c3^r notes Pistorius's *Illustratium veterum scriptorum de rebus Germanicis editi tomi, i.e. Rerum*

Germanicarum veteres jam primum publicati scriptores aliquot insignes medii ævi ad Carolum V (Frankfurt, 1583–1607), a collection of medieval German historical sources.

Plato (429/8—347 B.C.). c3^v; 30, 3: 6; 35, 3: 19; 38, 3: 29; 58, 4: 24; 60, 4: 27; 63, 4: 39–40; 141, 9: 11; 151, 10: 8; 1273. Greek philosopher. Schottelius cited his *Symposium, Phaedo,* and *Cratylos.*

Plautus, M. (= Plautus T. Maccius) (ca. 254–184 B.C.). 93, 6: 38; 1033. Roman comic poet.

Pliny the Elder (23–79 A.D.). 1151; 45, 3: 44; 150, 10: 6; 151, 10: 9; 172.2; 281; 688; 1151. Pliny the Elder wrote much but only his *Historia Naturalis* 'Natural history' has survived.

Plutarch, Lucius Mestrius 'of Chaeronea' (45–120 A.D.). 1182. Roman historian of Greek descent whose 'Lives' of eminent men were translated by Hieronymus Boner (q.v.), published as *Plutarch Teutsch* (Augsburg: Steiner, 1534) (Worstbrock 1976: 117).

Polyaenus (fl. 153 A.D.). 25, 2: 41. Greek author of *Strategems of war*, eight books of 900 anecdotes, of which 833 survive. Schottelius's reference to him in regard to the Germans' beastlike voice is to Book 8.

Polybius (203–120 B.C.). c3^v; 39, 3: 30; 1150; 1181. Greek historian. *AA* 1181 makes reference to the German translation by Wilhelm Xylander (1532–1576) (Basel: Henricpetri, 1574).

Polydorus Virgilius (ca. 1470–1555). c3^v. 36, 3: 22; 168, 10: 22. English historian of Italian extraction. Schottelius referred to his *De Inventoribus Rerum* (Venetiis: De Pensis, 31.VIII.1499).

Pomponius Marcellus, Marcus (30 B.C.–30 A.D.). 97, 6: 53 [mentioned]. Pomponius Marcellus, a severe critic of Latin, was reputed to have said that not even Caesar could govern the words used by his subjects. The passage was a seventeenth-century commonplace, after Martin Opitz used it in his *Aristarchus* (cf. Jones 1995: 37–38).

Pomponius Mela (fl. ca. 43/44 A.D.). c3^v; 24, 2: 36. Native of Spain, the earliest Roman geographer, whose *de Situ Orbis Libri III* was published in Latin in 1471.

Pona, Francesco (1530–1615). 1183. Italian writer, translated by Johann Helwig, q.v.

Possevinus, Antonius = Possevino, Antonio (1533/34–1611). 994. Italian Jesuit theologian and papal envoy. In the poetics, *AA* 994, Schottelius referred to the judgement of J. C. Scaliger (q.v.) in his *Bibliotheca Selecta* (Rome, 1593), on the method of study, teaching, and practical use of various sciences; the second part of the work contains a critical bibliography of various sciences.

Postellus, Wilhelmus = Guillaume Postel (1510–1581). c3^v; 54, 4: 10. French linguist, diplomat and religious universalist. Schottelius c3^v cited *De originibus seu de varia et potissimum orbi Latino ad hanc diem incognita aut inconsyderata historia* (Basle: Oporinus, 1553).

Procopius of Caesarea (ca. 500–565). 1053. Scholar and historian of the ancient world, author of the *Wars of Justinian*, the *Buildings of Justinian* and the *Secret History*.

Purchassius Anglus, Samuel = Purchas, Samuel (1575?–1626). 57, 4: 17. English travel writer whose *Purchas, his Pilgrimage; or, Relations of the World and the Religions observed in all Ages* appeared in 1613, but Schottelius appears to have had access to a Latin translation.

Quintilian, Marcus Fabius (ca. 35–95 A.D.). c2^v as 'Fabius'; also c3^v; 8, 1: 22; 93, 6: 38; 107, 7: 10; 144, 9: 19; 167, 10: 22. Roman rhetorician, author of *de Institutione Oratoria Libri XII*.

R.A., Reichsabschiede. c3^v; 1200; 76: 6: 10; 84, 6: 25; 294, 296. Imperial decrees in German, viewed as models of good language (cf. Josten 1976: 148 ff.). The compounds *Reichstadt, Legstadt, Grentzstadt, Bergstadt, Haubtstadt, Erbstadt* (*AA* 76, 6: 10) are taken from the *Reichsabschiede*, according to an annotation in Schottelius's 1641 *Sprachkunst*; likewise *Landverderber*, *AA* 94: 6: 25.

Radevicus = Rahewin (d. 1170–77). c3^v; 1155. German chronicler from Freising and continuator of Otto von Freising's history, q.v.

Ragor, Johann Huldrich (1534–1604). 1191. Schottelius noted Ragor's translation of Johannes Manlius's (q.v.) book of commonplaces (Frankfurt: Feyerabend, 1574).

Regino abbas Prumiensis (Abbot of Prüm) (d. 915). 1154. Author of a chronicle of world history from the life of Christ to 910, printed in 1566 by Simon Schard, q.v.

Reimarus, Albert (fl. 1662–1668). 1184. Published a translation from an Italian work, titled *Abgebildetes Altes Rom*, i.e. an illustrated acccount of ancient Rome (Arnheim: Haagen,1662; BV001477331).

Reineccius, Reinerus = Reiner Reineck (1541–1595). c3^v; 1184; 126, 8: 5; 489; 1031; 1067; 1089. Professor of history at Helmstedt. *AA* c3^v specifies a work on the history of the nobility and of Meißen (Leipzig: Steinmann, 1576): *Von der Meissner anfenglichem herkommen, geschichten, thaten, verenderung der Sitzen, mancherley Herrschafften, und wie sie endlich in Deudschland kommen, kurtzer bericht* [...] See also Ditmar and Helmoldus, whose chronicles Reineck published in 1580 and 1581.

Reineke Voss (anon.). 1200; 1259–62. Low German fable of Reynard the Fox. Schottelius noted it *AA* 1200 and criticized an unspecified High German translation of it in the treatise on translating, *AA* 1261–62. The only High German translation by then had first been printed in 1544 (Frankfurt am Main: Cyriacus Jakob), tentatively attributed by Menke (1992:317) to Michael Beuther (1522–1587) (cf. Flood 1996).

Reinking, Dietrich = Reinkingk, Theodor von (1590–1664). c3^v; 431; 495; 1193. Jurist and statesman, author of *Tractatus De Regimine Seculari Et Ecclesiastico* (Giessae Hessorum: Hampelius, 1619 and later editions), and

Biblische Policey [...] (1654); Wolfenbüttel holds a 1653 edition (Franckfurt am Mäyn: Kämmpfer, 1653).

Rhenanus, Beatus (1485–1547). 1158; 4, 1: 9; 27, 2: 45; 37, 3: 25; 61, 4: 31; 126, 8: 6; 137, 9: 3; 157, 10: 13; 373; 483; 499; 620; 1033; 1036; 1037; 1042; 1158; 1090; 1250. German humanist, religious reformer, and classical scholar. His work of 1531 was the first major treatment of the origins and the cultural achievements of the Germanic peoples: *Rerum Germanicarum libri tres* 'Three books on Germanic matters' (Basle: Froben, 1531; cf. edition ed. Mundt, 2008).

Rhetorica oder Formularium Teutsch. 1192. See Huge, Alexander.

Rhodius, Andronicus (fl. ca. 70 B.C.). 16, 2: 3. Peripatetic scholar who arranged and wrote commentaries on the works of Aristotle and Theophrastus. Schottelius cited him in German translation (not identified).

Rif, Gualtherus H. = Ryff, Walther Hermann (1500–1548). 1181; 1187. See Ryff, Walther Hermann.

Rist, Johann(es) (1607–1667). c3^v; 1176; 63, 4: 38; 106, 7: 5; 113, 7: 21; 237: 4; 412; 424; 523; 619; 700; several times in the poetics. Member of the FG, German poet and purist from north-west Germany. *AA* c3^v states that *Rist hat unterschiedliche und sonderlich Geistliche / fast liebliche und nützliche Sachen in Teutscher Sprache geschrieben* 'Rist wrote various and especially spiritual, very delightful and useful things in German'. Rist's verse is cited several times for exemplification in Schottelius's poetics; he also contributed a dedicatory letter which appears in the front matter of the *AA*. See Jones (1995: 88–130).

Rol. f. c3^v; 288; 622; 631; 640; 653; 700 and *passim*. See Werder, Diederich von dem.

Rollenhagen, Gabriel (1583– ca. 1619). 1191. Schottelius cited Rollenhagen's *Vier Bücher Wunderbarlicher biß daher unerhörter/ und ungleublicher Indianischer reysen/ durch die Lufft/ Wasser/ Landt/ Helle/ Paradiß/ und den Himmel* (Magdeburg: Kirchner, 1603; rpt. of 1605 ed. Stuttgart: Hiersemann, 1995), which he recognized consisted of translations from a number of Latin and Greek sources. He cited Rollenhagen's successful translation of Lucian's Greek compounds as proof that German compounding can work *eben so kurz und wol* 'just as concisely and well' as Greek.

Ronsard, Pierre de (1524–1588). c3^v; 93, 6: 38; 217.39 on his attempt to replace <q> with <k> 708. French Renaissance poet praised by Opitz, and cited in Schottelius's sixth oration, as evidence of French language's capacity for compounding. Schottelius acknowledged Ronsard's skill grudgingly, but would not extend the praise to French as a whole.

Rosern = Jacob Nicolaus Röser (fl. 1661?). 1204. Schottelius mentioned Röser's *Epistolographia emblematica: Das ist Abhandlung der sonntäglichen und Fest-Episteln durchs gantze Jahr* [...]. (Leipzig: Kirchner, 1661).

Ryff, Walther Hermann (1500–1548). 1181; 1187. Schottelius considered that in Ryff's *Ejn wolgegründt nutzlich vnd [und] heylsam Handtbüchlin gemeyner Practick der gantzen leibartzney* (Strasbourg: Beck, 1541), many medical terms were translated *nach altem Teutschen und in gutem Verstande* 'according to old German and in good sense' (*AA* 1187). A 1614 edition of Ryff's 1548 translation of Vitruvius's (q.v.) work on architecture is also noted, *AA* 1181: *Vitruvius, Des aller namhafftigisten unnd hocherfahrnesten/ Römischen Architecti/ unnd kunstreichen Werck oder Bawmeisters/ Marci Vitruvij Pollionis/ Zehen Bücher von der Architectur und künstlichem Bawen* (first ed. Nuremberg: Truckts Johan Petreius, 1548; Basel: Henricpetri, 1614) (cf. Neuhaus 1991: 152–3; cf. Worstbrock 1976: 159 for the 1548 edition).

Sachs, Michael (1542–1618). 1190; 1196. German pastor. *AA* 1191 notes his chronicle in German from Julius Caesar to Emperor Matthias (1615), to which Schottelius had access in a 1644 edition. *AA* 1196 Schottelius cited Sachs's *Christlicher Zeitvertreiber oder geistliches Rätzelbuch*, to which he had access in a 1601 edition.

Sachsenrecht (= **S.R.**). De^r; 64, 3: 46; 78–79, 6: 17; 92, 6: 37; 137, 9: 3; 276; 280; 297; 325; 512. See *L. Sax.* above; or perhaps a reference to König's publication (q.v.).

Sachsenspiegel (after 1224–before 1235). 1201; 517; 1351 *Krüppel*. In the list of rootwords, the legal code *Sachsenspiegel* 'mirror of the Saxons' of Eike von Repgow (q.v.) glossed by Burchhard von Mangelfeld, in the 1569 edition by Christoph Zobel (q.v.) is cited once, *AA* 1351 s.v. *Krüppel*. The *Sachsenspiegel* includes the *Lehnrecht* and *Weichbild*, the latter also published separately glossed by Burchhard von Mangelfeld (cf. Neuhaus 1991: 140). See also *Sachsenrecht* above.

Sachsische Landrecht. 139, 9: 7; 342; 343; 1227; 1228. See *L. Sax.* above.

Sächsische Weltchronik (after 1225). 1384. Attributed to Eike von Repgow. According to Neuhaus (1991:142), Schottelius referred it once in the list of rootwords, *AA* 1384 s.v. *Reim*.

Sallust(us), Gaius Crispus (86–34 B.C.). 1182. Roman historian. Schottelius noted translations by von Kalchum (= Lohausen) (1663) and Kindermann (1662), q.v.

Sattler, Johann Rudolph (1577–1628). 1166. Schottelius referred *AA* 1166 to a 1611 folio edition of Sattler's *Notariat* and *Formularbuch*, manuals for preparing legal documents and contracts and for writing letters. Cf. Moulin-Fankhänel (1997b: 264–73).

Saxo Danicus (Grammaticus) (ca. 1150–1220). 1156; 111, 7: 15; 1019; 1056; 1384 *Reim*. Danish author of a history of Denmark whose chronicle, *Danica Historia Libris XVI*, was first printed in Germany in 1576 (Frankfurt: Wechel). There is one reference to him in the list of rootwords, s.v. *Reim* (Neuhaus 1991: 142–3).

Scaffnaburgensis / Schafneburgensis [*error for* **Aschaffenburg**], **Lambertus**. 1154; 157, 10: 13. See Lambert of Hersfeld.

Scaliger, Joseph Justus (1540–1609). 31, 3: 7; 60, 4: 27; 109, 7: 12. French scholar and son of Julius Caesar Scaliger; critical of Becanus.

Scaliger, Julius Caesar (1484–1558). c3^v; 9, 1: 26; 64, 4: 39; 105, 7: 3; 106, 7: 6; 112, 7: 18; 113, 7: 23; 115, 7: 29; 142, 9: 15; 168, 10: 22; 299; 455; 687; 994; 1090; 1243. Author of *De causis linguae latinae* (Lyon 1540; see Chapter 3), and of a poetics, *Poetices libri septem* (Lyon 1561), cited e.g. *AA* 106, 7: 6; Schottelius also cited him as an authority on poetics (calling him a *Held* 'hero') in Book IV, *AA* 994. His commentary on Jerome Cardan's (1501–1586) *De subtilitate,* with the title *Exortericarum exercitationum liber quintus decimus de subtilitate* (Lutetiae: Vascosanus, 1557), was cited by Schottelius *AA* 455.

Scard. = Schard[ius], Simon (1535–1573). c3^v; 56, 4: 15; 140, 9: 10. Humanist publisher and writer who published a legal dictionary, *Lexicon Iuridicum* (Basle: Episcopius, 1582), as well as a history, *Historicvm Opvs*, in four parts (Basle: Henricpetri, 1574). He also published medieval histories of Sigebert, Regino Abbas Prumiensis and Lambert of Hersfeld (q.v.) in his 1566 *Germanicarum rerum quatuor celebriores vetustioresque chronographi* [...] *Quorum nomina sunt: Iohannes Turpinus De vita Caroli Magni et Rolandi. Rhegino Abbas Prumiensis diocesis Treviren. Sigebertus Gemblacensis eiusque continuator Robertus de Monte. Lambertus Schaffnaburgensis, alias Hirsfeldensis dictus* (Frankfurt: Rab, Feyerabend, Han).

Scer. 255; 340. Not identified. Listed as an attestation for the words *Schwerzüngler* and *Ertzstand*.

Scheraeus, Bartholomeus (fl. 1605–1624). c3^v; 4, 1: 9; 53, 3: 8; 337; 342. Schottelius referred to Scheraeus's *Sprach-Schule*, i.e. *Symmikta ierarchika Miscellanea hierarchica. Geistliche, weltliche, und häusliche Sprachen-Schule*: [...] (Wittenberg: Selfisch 1619), which satirized gallomania.

Schich Schaadi = Sheikh Saadi (1184–1283/1291?). 1206. Major Persian poet, whose works Adam Olearius (q.v) translated into German.

Schneider, Michael (1612–1639). 1204; 493; 503. Schottelius noted Schneider's *Lobgesang deß, den Weisen aus Morgenland durch den Wunder Stern geoffenbarten newen Königes*, a translation of a work by Aurelius Prudentius, to which he had access in a 1636 edition.

Schneidwinnus. c3^v. Perhaps the jurist Johannes Schneidewin (1519–1568), whose commentary on Justinian's *Institutes* was printed many times in the sixteenth and seventeenth centuries.

Schrader, Ludolph (1531–1589). c3^v; 8, 1: 21. Jurist and author of *Tractatus feudalis* (Frankfurt: Ex Officina Paltheniana, published posthumously in 1594).

Sc(h)rieckius / Skriekkius, Rodornus Finnius, Adrianus = Adriaan van Schrieck (1560–1621). c3^v; 1161; 292; 523. *passim* in the third oration; 105, 7: 6; 109, 7: 12; 123, 8: 2; 126, 8: 6; 128, 8: 9; 130, 8:10; 143–44, 9: 17; 1090.

Van Schrieck wrote two works on the origins of 'Belgian' in the ancient Scythian language, *Monitorum secundorum libri V* (Ypris Flandorum: Bellettus, 1615), and *Adversariorum libri IIII. His argumentis: Linguam Hebraicam esse divinam et primogeniam* (Ipres: 'Bellettus', 1620). See Swiggers (1984), Kiedrón (1985b: 346). Schottelius was very inconsistent in his spelling of the name.

Schupp(ius), Johann Balthasar (1610–1661). 1199. German satirist and poet, and professor of rhetoric in Marburg. Schottelius cited his defence of using German rather than Latin as the language of instruction in schools. See Jones (1995: 192–195).

Schwarzenberg, Johann von (1463–1528). 1184. Statesman and humanist who produced a German Cicero; Schottelius used the edition from 1535 (Augsburg: Heinrich Steiner) (cf. Worstbrock 1976: 50–51).

Schwarzkopf, Georg (?–?). Schottelius referred *AA* 1180 to German translations by Georg Schwarzkopf of Braunschweig (1593) and Duke Heinrich Julius of Braunschweig and Lüneburg (no date given). Not further identified.

Schweitzer, Johann Freidrich (1625–1709). See Helvetius, Johann Friedrich.

Schweser, Johann Friedrich (?–?). 1209. Schweser translated the Frenchman François de Rosset's *Histoires des amans volages de ce temps. Das ist Geschichte von den wanckelmühtigen Liebhabern zu dieser zeit* (Hamburg: n.p., 1638), as well as Justinus (q.v.).

Scriverius, Petrus = Peter Schrijver *or* Schryver (1576–1660). c3ᵛ; 22, 2: 26. Dutch writer and scholar, born in Amsterdam, and educated at the University of Leiden, where he was close to Daniel Heinsius. He published notes on Martial, Ausonius, the *Pervigilium Veneris*, editions of the poems of Joseph Justus Scaliger (Leiden: Plantijn, 1615), and historical works including *Batavia Illustrata* (Leiden: Elzevier, 1609) and *Inferioris Germaniae* [...] *historia* (Leiden: Elzevier, 1611). Scriverius's verse cited in the second oration is an extract from his poem prefaced to Daniel Heinsius's (q.v.) *Nederduytsche Poemata* (1616: 11–12).

Seckendorf, Veit Ludwig von (1626–1692). 1193. Statesman and scholar who wrote a handbook of German public law, *Teutscher Furstenstaat* (Franckfurt: Götze, 1660, a revision of the 1656 edition).

Selenus, Gustavus = *pseudonym of* Duke August of Braunschweig and Lüneburg (1579–1666). c2ᵛ (under Gustavus); 60, 4: 30; 80, 6: 20; 92, 6: 37; 105, 7: 4; 139, 9: 8; 385; 387; 447. Schottelius's patron and a member of the FG. In 1624, he published a *Cryptographia* under the name Gustavus Selenus.

Seneca, Lucius Annaeus (5 B.C.–65 A.D.). c3ᵛ; 8, 1: 21; 16, 2: 2. Roman philosopher, born in Spain.

Sidney, Philip (Sir) (1554–1586). c2ʳ; 115, 7: 30 [mentioned]; 365; 1220. English Elizabethan poet; *AA* c2ʳ refers to a German translation of his *Arcadia* (1580, published 1590), translated by Valentinus Theocritus von

Hirschberg (pseudonym of Daniel Mögling, 1596–1635). Editions of the German translations date from 1629 and 1638.

Sigebertus, Gemblacensis Caenobii Monachus = Sigebert of Gembloux (ca. 1035–1112). c3^v; 1155. Sigebert's world chronicle, *Chronicon sive Chronographia*, was printed in Frankfurt in 1566 by Simon Schard, q.v.

Sigismundus Betulius = Birken, Sigmund von. See Birken, Sigmund von.

Silvius (Ambianus, 'of Amiens') = Dubois, Jacques (1478–1555). 124, 9: 4. Author of a French grammar, *In linguam Gallicam isagoge* (Paris: Ex Officina Roberti Stephani, 1531).

Simler(us), Johann Wilhelm (1605–1672). 1206. Swiss poet, who adopted Opitz's prescriptions for poetry.

Sleidan(us), Johannes (1506–1556). c3^r; 64, 4: 41. German historian. Wrote a history of the Reformation, *Commentariorum de statu religionis et republicae, Carolo V. Caesare, libri XXVI* (Argentorati: Rihelius, 1555). Cf. also Lauterbeck.

Spec. Sax. 517. *Speculum Saxonum* is Latin for *Sachsenspiegel*, q.v.

Spe[i]d., Spe[i]delius = Speidel, Johannes Jacobus (1600– after 1666). c3^v; 1169; 4, 1: 9; 24, 2: 35; 85, 6: 25; 100, 6: 57; 139, 9: 7; 203: 24; 243:7; 259; 271; 289; 307; 334; 337 and *passim*; 1037; 1071; 1092 . Jurist. C3^v specifies his *Notabilia*, i.e. his *Notabilia Juridico-Historico-Politica, Selecta Ex Legum Sanctionibus, Juris-Fevdalis Consvetvdinibvs, Cameræ Imperialis Et Aliorum Summorum Tribunalium rebus judicatis* (Argentorati: Sumptibus Lazari Zetzneri, 1634). Reference is made in the orations to a *Thesaurus practicus* (Tübingen: apud Philibertum Brunnium, 1629; cf. also Besoldus), and in the treatise on proper names to his *Speculum iuridico-politico-philologico-historicarum observationum et notabilium* (Nuremberg: Endter, 1657).

Spekhan, Ebert [Wilhelm?] (?–?). 498. *AA 498 Ebert Spekhan cent 2. quaest. 35 clas. 4. Num. 15* is perhaps a reference to Wilhelm Spekhan's contribution to the legal work *Disputatio Iuridica, Continens selectarum utiliorumq[ue] Iuris Quaestionum Decadem De Testamentis* (Bremae: Villiers, 1651; VD17 7:646995E), where he is listed as one of several contributors.

Spelman, Henry (1564–1641). 1056. English antiquarian who compiled a glossary of Anglo–Saxon and Latin law terms used in early charters and records. The first volume, *Archaeologus in modum glossarii*, was published at his own expense in 1626. (A second volume, *Glossarium archaiologicum*, appeared posthumously, 1664.).

Spiegel, Jakob (1483–1547). Jurist and humanist. See Ligurinus.

Sprachposaun (1650). De^r; 137, 9: 5. A linguistic–patriotic text (1650). Anonymous, but possibly with the involvement of Christoph Schorer (1618–1671), even if he took over the project from someone else. Cf. Jones (1995: 287–288).

Sprenger, Johann Theodor (d. 1668). 496. German jurist. Schottelius's abbreviation *de lineat. Stat. imp.* is likely to refer to *Lucerna moderni status S. Rom Imperii* [...] (Antehac Francofurti impressa, 1567) held at Wolfenbüttel.

Sprenk. 369; 390; 432; 526. Not identified. Possibly an abbreviation of Sprenger, above?

Springfeld de Apanagio, Georgius Henricus = **Georg Heinrich Springsfeld** (1602–1646). De^r. Springsfeld's treatise *De apanagio* was published at Erfurt in 1641.

Starck, Andreas (1580–1608). 1187. Schottelius noted the physician Starck's *Krancken Spiegel* (Mülhausen: Hantzsch, 1598).

Steinhöwel, Heinrich (ca. 1412–1478). 1182. Swabian author, humanist and translator. In 1473 he published a translated version of Boccaccio's *De mulieribus claris* printed by Johann Zainer in Ulm, noted *AA* 1182.

Stephani, Mathaeus (1576–1646). 255 s.v. *Uhr*; 287; 421; 489; 496. Schottelius referred in the grammar to the legal treatise *De Iurisdictione* [...] (Frankfurt: Kopffius, 1610).

Stephanus, Henricus = **Estienne, Henri** (1528–1598). 124, 8:4. Paris printer. Schottelius cited his book on Graecisms, *De abusu linguae Graecae, in quibusdam vocibus quas Latina usurpat* (Genf: Stephanus, 1563).

Stevin, Simon (1548–1620). De^r; 1167; *passim* in the orations; 409; 1275–76 (see Table 6.5). Dutch mathematician. Referred to *AA* De^r as a *hochgelahrter Mann* 'highly learned man' who wrote on mathematical topics in *Teutsch* and showed the *Vermögen der Teutschen Sprache* 'capacity of the German language'. Schottelius used Stevin's *Vytspraeck vande Weerdicheyt der deytsche tael* (1586).

Stolterphotius, Jacobus = **Stolterfoth, Jacob** (1600–1668). De^r; 361; 435. Translator of Seneca's *De Providentia*: *Schönes Büchlein von der göttlichen Providentz, Vorsehung und Regierung* (Lübeck: Brehm, Meyer, 1642), noted De^r.

Stormius, Johannes (?–?). 1158. Stormius's opinion of Beatus Rhenanus (q.v) is cited *AA* 1158. Not identified.

Strabo (63/64 B.C.–24. A.D.). 48, 3: 56; 291 on the etymology of *Germanen*; 1389 *Ruhn*. Greek geographer and historian mentioned in the third oration; a German translation of his work served as a source for the list of rootwords, s.v. *Ruhn* (Neuhaus 1991: 150).

Stubenberg, Johann Wilhelm von (1619–1663). 1173. Translator and member of the FG, mentioned as the translator of various French and Latin works into German, and as a *Liebhaber* 'lover' of the German language.

Stumpfius = **Stumpf, Johannes** (1500–1577/78). 129, 8: 9; 203.24; 260; 351; 483. Author of a Swiss chronicle (Zurich: Froschauer, 1548; VD16 S 9864), first published under the title that Schottelius used, *Schweytzer Chronick* (*AA* 129, 8: 9), in 1606 (Zurich: Wolff).

Sturm, Samuel (fl. 1667). 1202. Sturm's *Der verstörte Parnaß* [...] (Bremen: Wessel, 1660) is noted by Schottelius, but he did not have access to a copy. The work is listed by Flood (2006: 2043–46) as one of a number of works, all published at Bremen or Emden between 1660 and 1664, that seem to be the work of Samuel Sturm, a lawyer from Leipzig. Flood distinguishes three individuals of this name. The other two were a poet and physician.

Suetonius = Gaius Suetonius Tranquillus (ca. 69/75–after 130). De^r; 172: 3. Historian in the Roman Empire, best known for his biographies of twelve Roman rulers, from Julius Caesar to Domitian (*De Vita Caesarum*), but Schottelius referred in the grammar to his *De claris grammaticis* 'Lives of the grammarians'.

Sw. S= Schwabenspiegel (ca. 1275). De^r. This legal code, whose title means 'mirror of the Swabians', was written about 1275 in Augsburg, drawing on the *Sachsenspiegel* (q.v.). It is contained as pp. 31–116 in Goldast's collection of legal codes, *Reichssatzung* [...] (part I, 1609). See Goldast, Melchior.

Swenterus, M. Daniel = Schwenter, Daniel (1585–1636). De^r; 1208. Schwenter's popularizing work on mathematics was adapted by Harsdörffer (q.v.): *Mathematische und Physische Erquickstunden* (1651; cf. Hundt 2000).

Tacitus, Cornelius (ca. 55–116 A.D.). De^r ; 26, 2: 41; 27, 2: 43; 29, 3: 1; 126, 8: 6; 150, 10: 4; 292; 1019–20; 1047; 1058; 1061; 1062; 1068; 1077; 1086; 1090; 1151; 1181; 1287 *Bier*; 1389 *Ruhn*. Tacitus's *Germania* (*De Situ, Moribus et Populis Germaniae*) was probably written in A.D. 98; cf. Neuhaus (1991: 152) for references in the list of rootwords s.v. *Ruhn* and *Bier*. *AA* 1181 refers to the 1612 edition of *Germania* with a German version by Jakob Micellus, q.v.

Tasso, Torquato (1544–1595). 1174. A translation of Tasso by Diederich von dem Werder (1584–1657, q.v.) was published under the auspices of the FG.

Tatius (Alpinus), Marcus (1509–1562). 1182. Swiss-German humanist, translator and Neo-Latin poet. He translated works attributed to Dictys Cretensis and Dares Phrygius in 1540. Schottelius also noted his translation of Aretinus, q.v.

Tauler(us), Johannes (1300–1361). De^r; 1198; 344; 629; 634; 650; 734 and *passim*. Schottelius had access to 1621 and 1656 prints (not identified) of this medieval mystic theologian's devotional work *Nachfolgung deß armen Lebens Christi*, and praised his *fromme Teutsche Worte* 'pious German words', *AA* 1198. On Tauler see Weithase (1961: 33–40).

Tertullian, Quintus Septimius Florens (ca. 160–ca. 220 A.D.). 172: 2. Schottelius referred to the *De corona militis* ('On the military garland') of this early Christian theologian, perhaps citing him indirectly from Vossius.

Th. Eur.= Theatrum Europaeum. 353; 369; 517; 529; 622; 745 and *passim*. See Merian, Matthäus.

Thucydides (460–390 B.C.). 1181. Greek historian and author of a history of the Peloponnesian War. Schottelius referred *AA* 1181 to a 1533 translation by Hieronymus Boner (d. 1552), q.v. (cf. Worstbrock 1976: 152).

Top. Zel. De^r. See Zeiller, Martin.

Topog. = *Topographia Meriani.* De^r. See Merian, Matthäus.

Torrentius, Laevinus (1520–1595). c3^r (listed under *Levinus*); 1168. 20, 2: 18. According to Schottelius, who followed Lipsius in this (q.v.), the poet Torrentius (Bishop of Antwerp) wrote a defence of the ancient 'Teutsch or Celtic language', in reply to Joseph Scaliger. Torrentius published some of Becanus's writings after his death (Goropius Becanus 1580).

Trithemius (Abbot) Johannes (von Trittenheim) (Abbot of Spanheim) (1462–1516). De^r; 111, 7: 15; 131, 8: 11; 169, 10: 22; 176–177.12. German Benedictine abbot, whose writings include *Polygraphiae libri sex* ('Six Books on Cryptography') (Basle: Haselberg, 1518), to which Schottelius referred in the orations and grammar.

Tscherning, Andreas (1611–1659). 1200; 4, 1: 9; several times in the poetics, e.g. 859. German poet, translator, and professor of poetics. Schottelius mentioned his 1658 work on abuses in the German language, *Unvorgreif-fliches Bedencken über etliche Miszbräuche in der deutschen Schreib-und Sprach-Kunst, insonderheit der edlen Poeterey* (Lübeck: Volck, 1659). Schottelius also cited Tscherning's poetry several times in his poetics, as well as his views of poetics (*AA* 859). See Jones (1995: 83–88), Moulin-Fankhänel (1997b: 328–332).

Turnheuserus = Thurneysser Zum Thurn, Leonhardt (1530–1596). 57, 4: 17. German physician who travelled in the east and in northern Africa. Schottelius cited his collection of exotic words and phrases (*Kai hermeneia* [...], Berlin: durch Nicolaum Voltzen, 1583).

Turpinus, Johannes (d. 794). 1154. The *Historia de vita Caroli Magni et Rolandi* attributed to Turpin (Bishop of Reims) was published in 1566 by Schard (q.v.) (Francoforti ad Moenvm: Coruinus, Feyrabend, Gallus, 1566).

Vaget(ius), Joachim (1585–1613). 356–67. Schottelius referred to Vaget's geographical and historical survey of the world: *Praecidanea De Orbe Habitabili, Sive Geographistoriae Locorum, Rerum, Hominum toto orbe memorabilium Theorian compendio exhibentis Apospasma I.* [...] (Frankfurt: Hummius, 1613; VD17 23:270995E).

Varro, Marcus Terentius (116–27 B.C.). 10, 1: 28; 38, 3: 29; 181.2. Prolific Roman writer. Schottelius referred to his *De Lingua Latina*; cf. discussion in Chapter 3.

Varro, Publius Terentius (ca. 82–36 B.C.). De^r; 40, 3: 32–33. Latin poet, seemingly conflated with M. Terentius Varro on *AA* 40.

Vegetius = Publius Flavius Vegetius Renatus (4th C. A.D.). 1019. Roman author of military works. Schottelius referred to his *Epitoma rei militaris* (or *De Re Militari*) *AA* 1019.

Venator (= Jäger), **Balthasar** (1594–1664). c2^r; 409. Schottelius cited Venator's *Panegyricus Iano Grutero scriptus* (Geneva: Aubertus, 1631), his panegyric to his former professor in Heidelberg, the historian Jan Gruter (1560–1627).

Verstegan / Versteeghan, Richard Rowlands (ca. 1565–1620). 1163; 1279 *Allmanach*; 1365 *Monat*; 1437 *Uhr*. Anglo-Dutch antiquary cited three times in the rootword list (Neuhaus 1991: 158–59), including regarding the names of months. His works include *A Dialogue on Dying Well* (1603), a translation from the Italian; *Restitution of Decayed Intelligence in Antiquities concerning the English Nation*, dedicated to King James I (1605); *Neder Dvytsche Epigrammen* (1617); *Sundry Successive Regal Governments in England* (1620); *Spiegel der Nederlandsche Elenden* (1621).

Verulamius = Bacon, Francis. See Bacon, Francis.

Vetolonius, Annius. See Annius of Viterbo.

Victor Episcopus Uticensis = Victor de Vita, or Victor Vitensis (ca. 440–after 484). 158, 10: 13. Bishop of Byzacène. Schottelius referred to Victor de Vita's *Libri III de persecutione Vandalica* (printed in the sixteenth century, e.g. Basileae: Froben & Episcopius, 1544).

Vintzelberg, Joachim von (d. 1680). 1202. Member of the FG, priest and hymnist, whose collection of German hymns (Hildesheim, 1654) Schottelius mentioned: *Lehr- Buß- Trost- Bitt- und Dank-Lieder: Welche meisten Theils/ so wol auff bekante [...] Weisen/ Als auch Auff neue [...] Melodeien können gesungen und gespielet werden* (Hildesheim: Geißmar, 1654) (VD17 23:670660Q).

Virgil = Publius Vergilius Maro (70 B.C.–19 A.D.). 1256. Classical Roman poet. Schottelius referred to his Latin translation of Oppian's poem on hunting (*Cynegetica*).

Viterbiensis, Annius (= Giovanni Nanni, Annius of Viterbo). See Annius of Viterbo.

Vitruvius Pollo, Marcus (ca. 80–15 B.C.). De^r; 1181; 525; 640; 1284. Roman writer and architect referenced in translation in the list of rootwords (Neuhaus 1991:152–3). Schottelius cited the use of *Bauchung* as a technical term in Ryff's (q.v.) translation.

Vogelius, Johannis = Johann Vogel (1589–1663). De^r; 1179; 1208; 433; 492; 637; 644; 890. Schottelius noted Vogel's *Verteutschte Psalmen: Die Psalmen Davids [...]* (Nuremberg: Dümler, 1638). On AA *1179* Schottelius also listed other translators of the psalms: Paul Schede Melissus, Cornelius Becker, Bucholz, and Opitz, q.v.

Volckmann, Adam (fl. 1614). 1166. Schottelius referred to Volckmann's four volume *Notariat-Kunst* (Leipzig: Großen, 1621), to which he had access in an edition published in Leipzig (In Verlegung Henning Grossens des Jüngern [1642–]/1647), as *Informatio notariorum*.

Vollziehende, der. 1182. See Kunowitz, Johann Dietrich von.

Vossius, Gerhard (1577–1649). 1153; 172.2; 173.3; 177.13; 181.2; 186.10; 207.27.5. Dutch scholar, humanist and theologian. Cf. discussion in Chapters 2, 3 and 5 for the influence of his *De arte grammatica* (1635) on Schottelius's grammatical theory.

Vulcanius, Bonaventura of Bruges (*alias* de Smet) (1538–1614). 56, 4: 17. Humanist who taught Heinsius and Grotius; a member of the Leiden school of philologists (Van de Velde 1966: 66), he published excerpts from the Gothic Bible in his study *De literis & lingua Getarum siue Gothorum* [...] (Leiden: Plantijn, 1597), in Gothic letters with a transliteration in Roman alphabet (*AA* 56, 4: 17).

W.B. = *Weichbild*. 326; 342 and *passim*; 1421 *Steig*. See *Weichbild*.

Wasserleider, Goswin (fl. 1584?). 1209. Schottelius had access to a 1590 German translation of Wasserleider's Ramist work on logic, *Logica Ad P. Rami Dialecticam Conformata* (Frankfurt: Wechel, 1584). Schottelius was critical of the Ramist approach and of some of the German terms coined there.

Weber, Georg (fl. 1645–49?). 1202. German musician, whose pious works *Kampf und Sieg oder gantzer Lebens-Lauff eines recht Christlichen Kreutzträgers* (Hamburg: Autor, 1645), and *Lebensfrüchte* (Danzig: Andree, 1649) Schottelius noted.

Wecker, Johann Jakob (1528–1586). 1188. German translator of Alexius Pedemontanus's book (q.v.), *De' secreti del reuerendo donno Alessio Piemontese* 'The Secrets of Alexis of Piedmont' (Venice: per Sigismondo Bordogna, 1555), under the title of *Kunstbuch Des Wolerfarnen Herren Alexij Pedemontani vo[n] mancherley nutzlichen vnnd [und] bewerten Secreten oder Künsten* (Basle: Waldkirch, 1605), to which Schottelius had access in a 1613 edition (VD17 1:000049Q).

Wehnerus, Paulus Matthias (1583–1612). De[r]; 1184; 84, 6: 25; 98, 6: 54; 255 s.v. *Uhr*; 283; 287; 336; 568; 637 and *passim*; 1037. Jurist. Schottelius consulted his *Practicarum iuris obseruationum augustissimae Camerae Imperialis liber singularis* (Frankfurt: Wolfgang Richter for Johann Theobald Schönwetter, 1608; VD17 1:059558H) as containing useful explanations of German terms and sayings.

Weichbild, das Sachsiche (1180/1190–after 1233). 1201; 326; 342 and *passim*; 1421 *Steig*. Extracts from the *Sachsenspiegel* glossed by Burchhard von Mangelfeld (Neuhaus 1991:140). Cf. also Gryphiander and *Sachsenspiegel*.

Weidner, Johann Leonhard (1588–1655). 1172. Weidner issued additonal parts of the *Teutsche Apophthegmata* by Zinkgref (q.v.) (*Teutscher Nation Apophthegmatum* Parts III–V, Amsterdam: Elzevier, 1653, 1655).

Welser (Velserus), Marcus (1558–1614). 138, 9: 7. A magistrate of Augsburg, well-known humanist and scholar. Schottelius referred to his history of Augsburg: *Rerum Augustanarum Vindelicarum Commentarii,*

Nominis Et Populi Eius Originem; Urbis Augustae situm; Insignium Eiusdem Explicationem [...] (Frankfurt: Egenolff, 1594).

Werder, Diederich von dem = **'der Herr von Werder'** (1584–1657). 1174, 1191; 863. Statesman, poet, and member of the FG, whose translation of Tasso was published under the auspices of the FG: *Torquato Tasso, Gottfried von Bulljon oder das erlösete Jerusalem* (Frankfurt: Aubrius, 1626; VD17 3:005078L; rpt. Tübingen: Niemeyer, 1974). Schottelius also referred to his translation of Ariosto's *Orlando Furioso* (1632–36) as *Rol. f.* (q.v.), but identified the translator only as a member of the FG.

Werder, Paris von dem (1623–1674). 1174. Member of the FG, noted as the author of a 'very fine' *FriedensRede* (Hamburg: Gundermann, 1639); son of Diederich von dem Werder, q.v.

Wesenb. = **Wesenbeck, Matthaeus** (1531–1586). 8, 1: 23; 375. Belgian Protestant jurist who taught at Jena and Wittenberg. Schottelius's reference to him in the first oration is to *ad ff. de leg. N. ult.* Wesenbeck published a number of works on law; it is not clear which one is referred to here.

Wider, Philipp Ehrenreich (= **Philippus Ericus Widerus**) (fl. 1662?). 1196. Schottelius cited Wider's *Evangelische Sinn-Bilder* [...] (Nuremberg, Tauber: 1662), a Christian emblem-book.

Widukind of Corvey (925–after 973). 1154. German (Saxon) monk and chronicler whose *Res gestae saxonicae sive annalium libri tres* is an important chronicle of tenth-century Germany, first printed Basle, 1532.

Wilhem von Saluste = **Du Bartas, Guillaume de Salluste** (1544–1590). 1183. French poet. See du Bartas, and see also Hübner, Tobias.

Williram von Ebersberg (Abbot) (1000/10–1085). De^r; 1170; 197.16; 1018; 1280; 1286; 1287; 1290; 1327; 1306; 1319; 1348; 1355; 1357; 1358; 1360; 1361; 1370; 1375; 1384; 1388; 1408; 1410; 1429; 1437; 1439; 1443. According to Neuhaus (1991: 132–40) and Moulin-Fankhänel (1997a: 307) Schottelius used Paulus Merula's (q.v.) 1598 edition of Williram's Old High German paraphrase of the Song of Solomon, but also the commentary of it by Franciscus Junius (q.v.), which was printed in 1655. There are 27 references to Williram (19 explicitly to the Junius edition) in the list of rootwords, discussed in detail by Neuhaus (1991: 132–40).

Winckelmann, Johannes Just (1551–1626). 1202. Schottelius praised Winckelmann's translation of Barclay's *Iconum animorum* (q.v.). under the title *Spiegel Menschlicher Gemühtsneigungen* (or, in full, *Joh. Barclai Spiegel Menschlicher GemüthsNeigungen |Auß dem Latinische[n] ins HochTeutsche versetzt*, Frankfurt and Bremen: Berger, 1660; VD17 23:280371G).

Wittich, Johannes (1537–1598). 1187. Schottelius noted Wittich's *Vade Mecum*, or medical manual (Leipzig: Schnelboltz, 1597).

Wittikindus. 1154. See Widukind of Corvey.

Wolf, Johannes (1537–1600). 357. German jurist, whose *Lectiones Memorabiles et reconditae* [...] 'memorable and recondite lessons' (Lauingae: Winter, 1608; VD17 1:651450V) Schottelius cited for his use of the term *Altfränkisch*.

Wormius, Olaus = Worm, Ole (1588–1655). c3ᵛ (under O); 4, 1: 9; 54, 4: 11; 1017; 1018; 1037; 1049; 1056; 1162; 1219; 1276; 1342 *Kampf*; 1361 *Mare*; 1365 *Monat*; 1384 *Reim*; 1389 *Ruhn*; 1428 *Tag*; 1431 *Ting*; 1437 *Uhr*. Danish physician and collector of early Scandinavian literature and language. He published a work on runes, and Schottelius referred to his 1636 work *Runir seu Danica literatura antiquissima* (but referring to a 1653 edition, not identified). *AA* 1162 also lists *Danicorum Monumentorum libri sex* (Hafniæ: Apud Ioachimum Moltkenium Bibliopolam ibidem primar., 1643). Cited in the rootwords s.v. *Kampf, Mare, Monat, Reim, Ruhn, Tag, Ting, Uhr* (Neuhaus 1991: 164–65).

Xylander, Wilhelm (1532–1576). See Polybius.

Zeiller, Martin (1589–1661). Deʳ; 1178; 1092. German travel writer and topographer. Schottelius noted his *M. Z. Itinerarii Germaniae novantiquae compendium, das ist, Teutschlandes neuverkürztes Räisebuch*, a compendium published posthumously (Ulm: Wildeisen 1662), and listed the works of the author that are given in the preface. Deʳ makes mention of his *Topographiae* 'topographies' (of which there were several, covering Scandinavia, Germany, France, Bohemia, etc.). See Jones (1995: 346–355).

Zesen, Philipp von (1619–1689). 1176; 1201; several times in the poetics, incl. 863. Member of the FG, German poet and novelist. Zesen was a major champion of the purification of the German language (Jones 1995: 198–343). His works include *Deutscher Helikon* 'German Helicon' (1640) and a phonetic orthography (1643); cf. Moulin-Fankhänel (1997b: 346–353). Schottelius granted that Zesen had some poetical ability, but was critical (*AA* 1201) of his sometimes *Unteutsches Teutsch* 'un-German German', presumably a criticism of overzealous coining of neologisms. Schottelius cited his verse and views several times in his poetics.

Zinkgref, Julius Wilhelm (1591–1635). 1172. Zincgref published *Teutsche Apophthegmata* (or aphorisms), to which additional parts were added by Johann Leonhard Weidner (q.v.). Schottelius noted the edition *Teutsche Apophthegmata das ist, Der Teutschen Scharfsinnige kluge Sprüche* (Amsterdam: Elzevier, 1653–55). See Jones (1995: 72–77).

Zobel, Christoph (1499–1560). 502; 507. There are references in the grammar to the jurist Zobel without further explanation, but see also L.R. = *Lehnrecht* for Zobel's edition of that text.

BIBLIOGRAPHY – PRIMARY SOURCES

Note that this bibliography does *not* include works that are listed as sources in Chapter 6 or the Appendix unless they are otherwise referred to in this book.

ADELUNG, JOHANN CHRISTOPH. 1774–1786. *Versuch eines vollständigen grammatisch-kritischen Wörterbuches der Hochdeutschen Mundart.* Leipzig: Breitkopf.

ADELUNG, JOHANN CHRISTOPH. 1781a. [1970] *Ueber den Ursprung der Sprache und den Bau der Wörter, besonders der Deutschen. Ein Versuch,* republished Berlin 1782 as part of *Umständliches Lehrgebäude der Deutschen Sprache zur Erläuterung der Deutschen Sprachlehre für Schulen.* 2 vols. Rpt. Hildesheim: Olms, 1970.

ADELUNG, JOHANN CHRISTOPH. 1781b. *Johann Christoph Adelungs Deutsche Sprachlehre. Zum Gebrauche der Schulen in den Königl. Preuß. Landen.* Berlin: Bey Christian Friedrich Voß und Sohn. [Reprinted in other editions 1792, 1795, 1800, 1806, 1816].

ADELUNG, J. C. 1783. 'Von neuen Wörtern durch die Ableitung'. *Magazin für die deutsche Sprache* (Leipzig: Breitkopf) 1(4): 36–78.

ADELUNG, J. C. 1806–1817. *Mithridates oder allgemeine Sprachenkunde: mit dem Vater Unser als Sprachprobe in bey nahe fünfhundert Sprachen und Mundarten / von Johann Christoph Adelung, Churfürstl. Sächsischem Hofrath und Ober-Bibliothekar* [Author named in Part II with the addition: *grossentheils aus dessen Papieren fortgesetzt und bearbeitet von Johann Severin Vater.* Part III: *Mit Benützung einiger Papiere desselben fortgesetzt, und aus zum Theil ganz neuen oder wenig bekannten Hülfsmitteln bearbeitet von Johann Severin Vater.* Part IV: *Mit wichtigen Beyträgen zweyer grossen Sprachforscher fortgesetzt von Johann Severin Vater*]. Berlin: Vossische Buchhandlung.

AEDLER, MARTIN [anon.]. 1680 [1972]. *The Hig* [sic] *Dutch Minerva // a-la-mode// or // A Perfect Grammar // never extant before // whereby // The English // may both // easily and exactly / | learne // the Neatest Dialect of the German // Mother-Language // used throughout all Europe.* London: Printed for the author. Facsimile rpt. Menston, England: Scolar Press, 1972.

AGRICOLA, JOHANNES. 1592. *Siebenhundert vnd funfftzig Deutscher Sprüchwörter/ ernewert/ vnd gebessert/ Durch Johan. Agricola. Mit vielen schönen lustigen vnd nützlichen Historien vnd Exempeln erkleret vnd ausgelegt.* Wittenberg: Gedruckt bey M.Johan.Krafft.

AICHINGER, KARL FRIEDRICH. 1753/54 [1972]. *Versuch einer teutschen Sprachlehre*. Frankfurt am Main, Leipzig 1753, Wien 1754. Rpt. ed. Monika Rössing-Hager, Hildesheim: Olms, 1972.

ALBERTUS, LAURENTIUS (Ostrofrancus). 1573 [1895]. *Teutsch Grammatick oder Sprach-Kunst. Certissima ratio discendae, augendae, ornandae, propagandae, conservandaeque linguae Alemannorum sive Germanorum, Grammaticis Regulis et exemplis comprehensa & conscripta*. Augsburg: Michaël Manger. Rpt. ed. Carl Müller-Fraureuth. Strasbourg: Trübner.

ANON. [Ratke, Wolfgang]. 1619. *Allegemeine Sprachlehr: Nach der Lehrart Ratichii*. Köthen: n.p.

ANON. 1734. 'D. Just. Schottels Ausführliche Arbeit von der deutschen Hauptsprache'. *Beiträge Zur Critischen Historie Der Deutschen Sprache, Poesie und Beredsamkeit* 7: 365–412.

ANON. [Schwanwitz, Martin?]. 1745. *Teutsche // Grammatica // Aus unterschiedenen Auctoribus // ehmahls // zusammen getragen // nunmehro aber von neuem übersehen // und // viel verbessert // Zum Gebrauch // des // St. Peterburgischen // Gymnasii //herausgegeben*. St Petersburg: Kayserl. Academie der Wissenschaften.

ARNAULD, ANTOINE, AND CLAUDE LANCELOT. 1660 [1966]. *Grammaire générale et raisonnée ou La Grammaire de Port-Royal*. Edition critique présentée par H. E. Brekle. Stuttgart-Bad Canstatt: Frommann-Holzboog.

BECANUS, JOANNES GOROPIUS: See GOROPIUS BECANUS, JOANNES.

BECHER, JOHANN JOACHIM. 1668. *Methodvs Didactica*. Munich: Maria Magdalena Schellin/ Wittib.

BECHER, JOHANN JOACHIM. 1669. *Methodi Becherianae Didacticae Praxis Ejusdemque Liber seu annus primus, primam vocabvlorum connexionem continens qvae in affinitate 'Primitivorum' cum 'Derivatis'*. Frankfurt am Main: Johann David Zunner.

BECHERER, JOHANN. 1596. *Synopsis grammaticæ tam germanicae qvam latinae et graecæ, in usum jubentatis scholasticae conscripta à Johanne Becherero*. Jena: Typis Tobiae Steinmanni.

BECMAN, JOHANN CHRISTOPH. 1673. *Historia orbis terrarum Geographica & Civilis*. Frankfurt an der Oder: Sumptibus Heredum Jobi Wilhelmi Fincelii, Prelo Becmaniano.

BELLIN, JOHANN. 1642. *Teutsche Orthographie*. Place and publisher not given. See Moulin (1997b: 37) for locations.

BELLIN, JOHANN. 1657 [1973]. *Hochdeutsche Rechtschreibung*. Lübeck: Volk. Rpt. Hildesheim: Olms, 1973.

BIBLIANDER, THEODOR. 1548. *De Ratione communi omnium linguarum et literarum commentarius: cui adnexa est compendiaria explicatio doctrinae recte beateque vivendi, et religionis omnium gentium atque populorum, quam argumentum hoc postulare videbatur*. Tiguri: Froschauer.

BÖDIKER, JOHANN 1690 [1723]. *Grund-Sätze der Deutschen Sprachen.* Cölln an der Spree: Ulrich Liebpert. 1723 edition *verbessert und vermehrt* 'improved and enlarged' by Johann Leonhard Frisch, Berlin: Nicolai.

BOPP, FRANZ 1820 [1974]. 'Analytical Comparison of the Sanskrit, Greek, Latin and Teutonic Languages, Shewing the Original Identity of Their Grammatical Structure'. *Annals of Oriental Literature* 1: 1–64. Rpt. ed. E.F.K. Koerner, Benjamins: Amsterdam, 1974.

BRÜCKER, JACOB. 1620. *Teutsche Grammatic/ das ist / Kurzter Unterricht/ wie eyner etlicher massen recht reden und schreiben lehrnen solle. Allenn denn jenigenn / so etwa nichts studiert / oder noch forthin bei dem studiern erzogen werden/ oder bleiben können / und doch gerne eynen geringen Anfang recht zu reden und zu schreiben hättenn/ zum besten auff die Teutsche Spraach gerichtet/.* Frankfurt am Main: Luca Jennis.

BUCHNER, AUGUST. 1663 [1977]. *Kurzer Weg-Weiser zur Deutschen Tichtkunst.* Jena: Sengenwald. Rpt. Leipzig: Zentralantiquariat der Deutschen Demokratischen Republik, 1977.

BUCHNER, AUGUST. 1665 [1966]. *Anleitung zur Deutschen* Poeterey. Wittenberg: Wenden. Rpt.Tübingen: Niemeyer, 1966.

CARON, WILHELM J. H., ed. 1953. *Christiaen van Heule, De Nederduytsche grammatica ofte spraec-konst (I) and De Nederduytsche spraec-konst ofte tael-beschrijvinghe (II).* Groningen & Djakarta: J.B. Wolters [Rpt. Groningen 1971].

CLAJUS, JOHANNES. 1578 [1894]. *Grammatica Germanicae Linguae M. Iohannis Claij Hirtzenbergensis: Ex Bibliis Lutheri Germanicis et aliis eius libris collectis.* Leipzig: Johannes Rhamba. Rpt. with an introduction by Friedrich Weidling, Strasbourg: Trübner, 1894.

CLAUBERG, JOHANNES. 1663. *Ars etymologica Teutonum e Philosophiae fontibus derivata.* Duisburgi ad Rhenum: Asendorp.

CLÜVER, PHILIPP. 1616. *Philippi Clüveri Germaniae antiquae libri tres: Opus post omnium curas elaboratissimum, tabulis geographicis et imaginibus, priscum Germanorum cultum moresque referentibus exornatum; Adjectae sunt Vindelicia et Noricum, ejusdem auctoris.* Lugduni Batavorum: Elzevir.

CUSPINIANUS, JOHANNES. 1601 [1994]. *Austria [...].* Francofvrti: Marnius & Aubrius. Microfiche edition Munich: Saur, 1994.

DIBBETS, GEERT R.W. ed. 1985. *Twe-Spraack vande Nederduitsche letterkunst (1584),* edited with an introduction and commentary by Geert R.W. Dibbets. Assen-Maastricht: Van Gorcum.

DIJKSTERHUIS, E.J. ed. 1955. *The Principal Works of Simon Stevin.* Vol. I. Amsterdam: C.V. Swets & Zeitlinger.

DU BELLAY, JOACHIM. 1549. *Défense et illustration de la langue française (1549).* Text available online at http://www.tlfq.ulaval.ca/axl/

francophonie/Du_Bellay.htm, following edition of Paris: Nelson, 1936 [complété par l'édition Louis Humbert chez Garnier].

DUPLEIX, SCIPION. 1651. *Liberté de la langue françoise dans sa pureté*. Paris: D. Becnet.

DURET, CLAUDE. 1613 (2nd ed. 1619). [1972] *Thrésor de l'histoire des langues de cest univers; Contenue les origines, beautés, perfections, décadences, mutations, changemens, conversions, et ruines des langues. / Claude Duret. Pyramus de Candole* [ed.]. Cologny: Societé Caldoriene [Printer] Berjon. Rpt. Geneva: Slatkine Reprints, 1972.

ECKHART (ECCARDUS), JOHAN GEORG VON. 1711. *J. G. Eccardi ... Historia studii etymologici linguæ Germanicæ hactenus impensi ... accedunt et quædam de lingua Venedorum in Germania habitantium, tandemque proprium de lexico linguæ Germanicæ etymologico componendo consilium aperitur*. Hanover: Foersterus.

EGENOLFF, JOHANN AUGUSTIN. 1716–20 [1978]. *Historie der Teutschen Sprache*. Leipzig. Rpt. Leipzig: Zentralantiquariat der Deutschen Demokratischen Republik.

ERASMUS, DESIDERIUS. 1500. *Collecteana Adagiorum*. Paris: J. Philippi.

FABRICIUS, JOHANN ANDREAS. 1723. See WEICHMANN, CHRISTIAN FRIEDRICH (1723).

FESSLER, IGNAZ AURELIUS. 1787. *Institutiones linguarum orientalium. Hebraicae, Chaldaicae, Syriacae et Arabicae, cum Chrestomathia Arabica J. G. Eichornii*. Pars prior. Vratislaviae. Pars posterior: Institutiones linguae Chaldaicae et Arabicae complectens. Leopoli.

FREYBERGER, ANDREAS. 1733. *Fundamenta linguae Germanicae*. Prague: Matthias Adam Höger. (See also Kramer 1694.)

FREYER, HIERONYMUS. 1722 [1999]. *Anweisung zur Teutschen Orthographie*. Rpt. of the Halle/Saale 1722 edition Hildesheim: Olms, 1999.

FRISCH, JOHANN LEONHARD. 1723. See BÖDIKER.

FULDA, FRIEDRICH CARL. 1778. *Grundregeln der Teutschen Sprache*. Stuttgart: Johann Benedict Mezler.

GERHARDT, CARL IMMANUEL, ed. 1875–1890. *Die philosophischen Schriften von Gottfried Wilhelm Leibniz*. Berlin: Weidmann.

GESSNER, CONRAD. 1555 [2009]. *Mithridates. De differentiis linguarum tum veterum, tum quae hodie apud diversas nationes in tote orbe terrarum in usu sunt*. Tiguri: Froschauer. Critical edition and translation: *Mithridates (1555). Conrad Gessner. Introduction, texte latin, traduction française, annotation et index par Bernard Colombat et Manfred Peters*. Geneva: Droz, 2009.

GIRBERT, JOHANN. 1653. *Die Deutsche Grammatica oder Sprachkunst: auß Denen bey dieser Zeit gedruckten Grammaticis, vornemlichen Johannis Claii ... Vinariensis zum newen ... Christ Gueintzii ... Justi Georg. Schottelii ... zusammen getragen/ in kurtze Tabellen eingeschrenckt/ und Dem öffentlichen Liecht ... ubergeben*. Mülhausen in Düringen: Hüterus.

GOLDAST, MELCHIOR. 1609, 1613. *Reichssatzung des Heiligen Römischen Reiches*. Hanaw: Halbey and Frankfurt am Main: Kopff, 1609; Frankfurt am Main: Hoffmann, 1613.

GOROPIUS BECANUS, JOANNES (JOHANN VON GORP). 1569. *Origines Antwerpianiae sive Cimmeriorum Becceselana novem libros complexa*. Antwerp: Ex officina Christopheri Plantini.

GOROPIUS BECANUS, JOANNES (JOHANN VON GORP). 1580. *Opera hactenus non edita, nempe Hermathena, Vertumnus, Gallica, Francica, Hispanica* [ed. Laevinus Torrentius]. Antverpiae: Excudebat C. Plantinus.

GOTTSCHED, JOHANN CHRISTOPH. 1748. *Grundlegung der deutschen Sprachkunst, Nach den Mustern der besten Schriftsteller des vorigen und jetzigen Jahrhunderts abgefasst von Johann Christoph Gottscheden*. Leipzig: Verlegts Bernh. Christoph Breitkopf. 2nd ed. 1749. 3rd ed. 1752. From 4th ed. (1757) onwards with the title *Vollständigere und Neuerläuterte Deutsche Sprachkunst, Nach den Mustern* [etc. etc.].

GROTIUS, HUGO. 1626 [1950]. *De Ivre Belli ac Pacis*. Moeno-Francofvrti: Wechelius. Ed. Walter Schätzel, Tübingen: Mohr, 1950.

GRYPHIUS, ANDREAS. 1663 [1991]. *Horribilicribrifax Teutsch: Scherzspiel*. Rpt. ed. Gerhard Dünnhaupt, Stuttgart: Reclam, 1991.

GUEINTZ, CHRISTIAN. 1641 [1978]. *Deutscher Sprachlehre Entwurf*. Köthen: n.p. Rpt. Hildesheim: Olms, 1978.

HAGER, CHRISTOPH ACHATIUS. 1634. *Orthographia oder Teutscher Sprache Wegweiser. Das ist: Naturgemäßer und wolbegründter Unterricht: Wie die Hochlöb= und liebliche Teütsche Sprache / recht zu läsen und zu schreiben / Der Jugendt / oder den Ohnerfahrnen / mit leichter Mühe und weniger Zeit / sol vorgetragen werden: Dergleichen noch niemals im Druck kommen. Liß: verstähe: urteihle*. Hamburg: Andreas Venus.

HARSDÖRFFER, GEORG PHILIPP. 1644–1649 [1968–1969]. *Frauenzimmer Gesprächsspiele*. Nuremberg: Endter. Rpt. ed. Irmgard Böttcher. Tübingen: Niemeyer, 1968–69.

HARSDÖRFFER, GEORG PHILIPP. 1646. *Specimen Philologiae Germanicae*. Nuremberg: Endter.

HARSDÖRFFER, GEORG PHILIPP. 1648–1653 [1971]. *Poetischer Trichter*, Teile I–III. Nuremberg: Endter. Rpt. Hildesheim: Olms, 1971.

HEINSIUS, DANIEL. 1601 *Quid sit amor* […]. Amsterdam: Buck.

HELBER, SEBASTIAN. 1593 [1882]. *Teutsches Syllabierbüchlein*. Freiburg im Uechtland: Abraham Gemperle. Rpt. ed. Gustav Roethe, Freiburg im Bresgau: Akademie-Verlag-Buchh. von Mohr, 1882.

HELWIG, CHRISTOPH, & JOACHIM JUNGIUS. 1614. *Kurtzer Bericht von der Didactica oder LehrKunst Wolfgangi Ratichii*. Jena: Rauchmaul.

HELWIG, CHRISTOPH. 1619. *Sprachkünste*. Gießen: Caspar Chemlin.

HENISCH, GEORG. 1616 [1973]. *Teütsche Sprach und Weißheit: Thesaurus linguae et sapientiae Germanicae, A-G*. Augsburg: Francus. Rpt. Hildesheim: Olms, 1973.

HERDER, JOHANN GOTTFRIED VON. *Abhandlung über den Ursprung der Sprache, welcher den von der Königl. Akademie der Wissenschaften für das Jahr 1770 gesetzten Preis erhalten hat.* In: *Johann Gottfried Herder, Frühe Schriften 1764–1772.* Ed. Ulrich Gaier, Frankfurt am Main: Deutscher Klassiker Verlag, 695–810.

HEULE, CHRISTIAEN VAN. 1625. See CARON, WILHELM J. H.

HEYNATZ, JOHANN FRIEDRICH. 1803 [2006]. *Deutsche Sprachlehre zum Gebrauch der Schulen. Fünfte vermehrte und verbesserte Auflage (1803). Die Lehre von der Interpunktion. Zweite, durchgängig verbesserte Auflage (1782),* ed. Petra Ewald. Hildesheim: Olms.

HOFMANNSTHAL, HUGO VON. 1927. *Wert und Ehre deutscher Sprache, in Zeugnissen.* Munich: Bremer Presse. (Hofmannsthal's preface to this anthology, 'Wert und Ehre deutscher Sprache', first appeared in *Münchner Neueste Nachrichten,* 26.12.1927, and is reprinted in *Hugo von Hofmannsthal: Gesammelte Werke in zehn Einzelbänden. Reden und Aufsätze.* 3 vols. Vol. 1, 128–133, Frankfurt am Main: Fischer, 1979).

HUMBOLDT, WILHELM VON. 1836. *Über die Verschiedenheit des menschlichen Sprachbaues und ihren Einfluß auf die geistige Entwickelung des Menschengeschlechts.* In: *Gesammelte Schriften,* ed. Albert Leitzmann et al. 17 vols. Berlin: Akademie der Wissenschaften. Rpt. Berlin: de Gruyter, 1968, vol. 7. (Rpt. of *Über die Verschiedenheit* also Cambridge: CUP, 2009).

ICKELSAMER, VALENTIN. 1527 [1971]. *Die rechte weis aufs kürtzist lesen zu lernen.* Ed. Karl Pohl, Stuttgart: Klett, 1971.

ICKELSAMER, VALENTIN. 1534. *Teütsche Grammatica.* See Pohl 1971, and Müller 1882 [1969]. These reproduce two slightly different editions.

IRENICUS, FRANCISCUS. 1518. *Germaniae exegeseos volumina duodecim | a Francisco Irenico Ettelingiacensi exarata. Eiusdem oratio protreptica in amorem Germaniae ... urbis Norimbergae descriptio, Conrado Celte enarratore.* Hagenoae: typis Thomae Anshelmi ...: sumptibus Ioannis Kobergii ... .

ISING, ERIKA. 1959. *Wolfgang Ratkes Schriften zur deutschen Grammatik (1612–1630).* Teil I: *Abhandlung.* Teil II: *Textausgabe.* Berlin: Akademie Verlag.

KATE, LAMBERT TEN. 1723. *Anleiding tot de Kennisse van het Verhevene Deel der Nederduitsche Sprake, waer in Hare Grondslag, edelste Kragt, nuttelijkste Onderscheiding, en geregeldste Afleiding overwogen en naegesporrt, en tegen het Allervornaemste der Verouderde en Nog-levende Taelverwanten, als 't Oude MOESO-GOTTHISCH, FRANK-DUITSCH, EN ANGEL-SAXISCH, beneffens het Hedendaegsche HOOG-DUITSCH en YSLANDISCH, vergeleken wordt.* Amsterdam: Rudolph and Gerard Wetstein.

KIRCHER, ATHANASIUS. 1669. *Ars magna Sciendi, sive Combinatoria : in XII libros digesta.* Amsterdam: Weijerstraet.

KLAJ, JOHANN. 1644, 1645 [1965]. *Redeoratorien und 'Lobrede der Teutschen Poeterey'*, ed. Conrad Wiedemann. Tübingen: Niemeyer.

KNESEBECK, JULIUS VON DEM. 1643. *Dreiständige Sinnbilder.* Braunschweig: Buno.

KÓK, ALHARDT LODEWIJK. 1649 [1981]. *Ont-werp der Neder-duitsche letter-konst.* Amsterdam, Johannes Troost. Rpt. ed. Geert R.W. Dibbets, Assen: Van Gorcum: 1981.

KRAMER, MATTHIAS. 1672. *Allgemeiner Schau-Platz/ auf welchem vermittelst einer kurtzen Frag-Ordnung vorgestellet wird die Teutsche und Italiänische Benennung aller Haupt-Dinge der Welt / gantz neu gestellt ...* . Nuremberg: Endter.

KRAMER, MATTHIAS. 1676–1678. *Das neue Dictionarum oder Wort-Buch, in Italiänisch-Teutscher und Teutsch-Italiänischer Sprach.* 2 vols. Nuremberg: Endter.

KRAMER, MATTHIAS. 1680. *Neues hoch-nützliches Tractätlein von der Derivatione & Compositione, Das ist: Herleit- und Doppel-Kunst der Italiänischen Primitivorum oder Stamm-Wörteren.* Nuremberg: Wolfgang Moritz Endters/ und Johann Andreä Endters Sel. Söhnen.

KRAMER, MATTHIAS. 1689. 2nd ED. *Von d. Autore selbsten übersehen. verb. u. verm. Vollständige italiänische Grammatica: Das ist: Toscanisch-romanische Sprach-Lehre, nunmehr aus ihren untersten Fundamentis und Füglichkeit bis zu der höchsten Perfection und Zierlichkeit, Der Deutschen Nation zum besten Aufs klärlichst-ordentlichst- und fleissigst ausgeführt und vorgetragen.* Nuremberg: Endter.

KRAMER, MATTHIAS. 1694. *I veri Fondamenti della Lingua Tedesca ò Germanica, Hormai aperti alla Natione Italiana.* Nuremberg: Johann Andreae Endters Seel. Söhne. (Latin transl. by Andreas Freyberger, *Fundamenta Linguae Germanicae.* 2 vols. Prague: Matthias Adam Höger, 1733).

KRAMER, MATTHIAS. 1700–1702 [1982]. *Das herrlich Grosse Teutsch-Italiänische Dictionarium, oder Wort- und Red-Arten-Schatz Der unvergleichlichen Hoch-teutschen Grund-und Haupt-Sprache.* 2 vols. Nuremberg: Johann Andreä Endters Sel. Söhne. Rpt. with introduction by Gerhard Ising, Hildesheim: Olms, 1982.

KRAMER, MATTHIAS. 1712. *Das recht vollkommen- Königliche Dictionarium Radicale, Etymologicum, Synonymicum, Phraseologicum & Syntacticum Frantzösisch-Teutsch nach Ordnung der Frantzösischen Stamm-/ und Quasi-Stamm-Wörtern.* Nuremberg: Johann Andreä Endters Sel. Söhne.

KRAMER, MATTHIAS. 1719. *Das Königliche Nider-Hoch-Teutsch/ und Hoch-Nider-Teutsch Dictionarium, oder/ beider Haupt-/ und Grund-Sprachen Wörter-Buch.* Nuremberg: bei dem Autore, oder dessen Erben.

KRAUSE, GOTTLIEB, ed. 1855 [1973]. *Der Fruchtbringenden Gesellschaft ältester Ertzschrein. Briefe, Devisen und anderweitige Schriftstücke. Herausgegeben nach den Originalien der Herzogl. Bibliothek zu Cöthen.*

Leipzig: Verlag der Dyk'schen Buchhandlung. Rpt. Hildesheim: Olms, 1973.

KROMAYER, JOHANNES. 1618 [1986]. *Deutsche Grammatica zum newen Methodo der Jugend zum besten zugerichtet.* Rpt. Hildesheim: Olms, 1986.

LANCELOT, CLAUDE, AND ANTOINE ARNAULD. 1660 [1967]. *Grammaire générale et raisonnée.* Facsimile rpt. Menston: The Scolar Press Limited.

LANGJAHR, JOHANN JAKOB. 1697. *Kurtzgefaßte Doch Gründliche Anleitung zu Leichter Erlernung der Teutschen Sprache.* Eisleben: Liebe.

LANSIUS, THOMAS. 1616. *Orationes aliquot.* Tübingen: Typis Theodorici Werlini.

LEUPENIUS, PETRUS. 1653 [1958]. *Aanmerkingen op de Neederduitsche taale.* Amsterdam: Hendryk Donker. Rpt. ed. Wilhelm J. H. Caron, Groningen: J.P. Wolters, 1958.

LEXER, MATTHIAS. 1872–78 [1979]. *Mittelhochdeutsches Handwörterbuch: zugleich als Supplement und alphabetischer Index zum Mittelhochdeutschen Wörterbuch von Benecke-Müller-Zarncke.* Rpt. of the Leipzig edition 1872–78. Stuttgart: Hirzel, 1979.

LEIBNIZ, GOTTFRIED. 1970ff. *Sämtliche Schriften und Briefe,* ed. Deutsche Akademie der Wissenschaften. Berlin: Akademie-Verlag. See also PIETSCH, PAUL.

LOMONOSOV, MICHAEL. 1755–57. *Rossiskaja grammatika.* St Petersburg: Izdatel'stvo Akademii nauk.

LONGOLIUS, JOHANN DANIEL. 1715. *Einleitung zur gründtlicher Erkäntniß einer ieden, insonderheit aber der Teutschen Sprache.* Budissin: Richter.

LUDOLF, HEINRICH WILHELM. 1696 [1959]. *Grammatica Russica.* Oxford: e Theatro Sheldoniana, 1959. Facsimile rpt. ed. Boris Unbegaun, Oxford: OUP, 1959.

LUTHER, MARTIN. 1530. *Ein Sendbrieff vom Dolmetzschen.* Wittenberg: Rhaw.

LUTHER, MARTIN. 1537. *Aliquot Nomina Propria Germanorum ad Priscam Etymologiam restituta. Per quendam antiquitatis Studiosum.* Wittenberg: Impressum Witembergs per Nicolaum Schirlentz.

MAALER, JOSUA. 1551. *Die Teütsch spraach. Alle wörter | namen | und arten zu reden in Hochteütsche spraach | dem ABC nach ordenlich gestellt | und mit gutem Latein ganz fleissig unnd eigentlich veroltmetscht | dergleychen bishär nie gesähen | durch Josua Maaler burger zu Zürich.* Tiguri: Froschauer. Rpt. Hildesheim: Olms, 1971.

MELANCHTHON, PHILIPP. 1526. *Grammatica Latina.* Hagenau. Later edition, *... Ab autore nuper aucta et recognita,* Coloniae: Iohannes Soter, 1527.

MEYFART, JOHANN MATTHÄUS. 1634 [1977]. *Teutsche Rhetorica oder Redekunst.* Coburg: Friderich Gruner. Rpt. Tübingen: Niemeyer 1977.

MOONEN, ARNOLD. 1706. *Nederduitsche Spraekkunst.* Amsterdam: François Halma.

MORHOF, DANIEL GEORG. 1682. *Unterricht von der Teutschen Sprache und Poesie.* Kiel: Reumann.

MÜLLER, JOHANNES. 1882 [1969]. *Quellenschriften und Geschichte des deutschsprachlichen Unterrichts bis zur Mitte des 16. Jahrhunderts.* Rpt. with an introduction by Monika Rössing-Hager, Hildesheim: Olms, 1969.

MÜNSTER, SEBASTIAN. 1543. *Cosmographia oder Beschreibung aller Lender.* Basle: durch Heinrich Petri.

MYLIUS, ABRAHAM (ABRAHAM VAN DER MYLE). 1612. *Lingua Belgica.* Lugduni Batavorum: n.p.

NEUMANN, CASPAR. 1696. *Genesis linguae sanctae V. T.....* . Nuremberg: n.p..

NEUMARK, GEORG. 1653 [1970]. *Neu-Sprossender Teutscher Palmbaum.* Nuremberg. Rpt. in *Die Fruchtbringende Gesellschaft. Quellen und Dokumente,* ed. Martin Bircher, vol. 3, Munich: Kösel, 1970.

OFFELEN, HEINRICH. 1687. *A Double Grammar for Germans to Learn English and for English-men to learn the German Tongue [...] Zwey-fache gründliche Sprach-Lehr, für Hochteutsche, englisch, und für Engelländer hochteutsch zu lernen [...].* London: Old Spring Garden by Charing Cross.

OLEARIUS, TILMANN. 1630. *Deutsche Sprachkunst. Aus den allergewissesten / der Vernunfft und gemeinen brauch Deutsch zu reden gemässen / gründen genommen. Sampt angehengten newen methodo, die Lateinische Sprache geschwinde und mit lust zu lernen.* Halle: Melchior Oelschlegel.

ÖLINGER, ALBERTUS. 1573 [1975]. *Underricht der HochTeutschen Spraach: Seu Institutio Verae Germanicae Linguae, in qua Etymologia, Syntaxis & reliquae partes omnes suo ordine breviter tractantur. In usum iuventutis maximè Gallicae, ante annos aliquot conscripta, nunc autem quorundam instinctu in lucem edita, plaerisque vicimis nationibus, non minus utilis quàm necessaria.* Strasbourg: Nicolaus Vuyriot. Rpt. Hildesheim: Olms, 1975.

OPITZ, MARTIN. 1617 [1968]. 'Aristarchus sive de contemptu linguae Teutonicae'. In *Martin Opitz. Gesammelte Werke. Kritische Ausgabe,* ed. G. Schulz-Behrend, 51–75. Stuttgart: Hiersemann, 1968.

OPITZ, MARTIN. 1624 [1963] *Buch von der Deutschen Poeterey.* Breßlaw; Brieg: David Müller; [printer:] Gründer. Edition by Richard Alewyn: *Martin Opitz. Buch von der Deutschen Poeterey (1624). Nach der Edition von Wilhelm Braune neu herausgegeben von Richard Alewyn.* Tübingen: Niemeyer, 1963.

PAUS, JOHANN WERNER. 1705–1729. *Anweisung zur Erlernung der Slavo-nisch-Rußischen Sprache.* Unpublished manuscript, Biblioteka Rossijskoj Akademii nauk [Library of the Russian Academy of Sciences], Otd. ruk., Sobr. inostr. ruk., Q 192/I, St Petersburg.

PAUS, JOHANN WERNER. 1732. *Observationes, inventiones et experimenta circa Literaturam et Historiam Russicam in camera obscura et optica ad Academiam Scientiarum instituta.* Unpublished manuscript, Archive of the Russian Academy of Sciences, St. Petersburg section, R. III, op. 1, No. 168a.

PERIZONIUS, JACOBUS. See SANCTIUS, FRANCISCUS.

PIETSCH, PAUL, ed. 1908. 'Leibniz und die deutsche Sprache (III)'. In: *Wissenschaftliche Beihefte zur Zeitschrift des Allgemeinen Deutschen Sprachvereins, Vierte Reihe*, Heft 30 (1908): 313–356 and 360–371.

POHL, KARL, ed. 1971. *Ickelsamer, Valentin. Die rechte weis aufs kürtzist lesen zu lernen. Ain Teütsche Grammatica.* Stuttgart: Klett.

PÖLMANN, ISAAC. 1671. *Neuer hoochdeutscher Donat, zum Grund gelegt der neuen hoochdeutschen Grammatik ...* Berolini: Pölmann; Berolini: Runge.

PONTOPPIDAN, ERIK ERIKSEN. 1668. *Grammatica Danica.* Hauniæ: Typis Christiani Veringii Acad. Typogr.

POSTEL, GUILLAUME. 1539, 1543. *Grammatica Arabica.* Paris: Gromorsus.

PRASCH, JOHANN LUDWIG. 1687. *Neue, kurtz-und deutliche Sprachkunst.* Regensburg: Johann Georg Hofmann.

PUDOR, CHRISTIAN. 1672 [1975]. *Der Teutschen Sprache Grundrichtigkeit/ Und Zierlichkeit. Oder Kurtze Tabellen/ Darinnen gewiesen wird/ wie man nicht allein grundrichtig Teutsch reden/ und schreiben; Sondern auch/ wie man eine einfältige Teutsche Rede* [...] *ausschmücken kan.* Köln an der Spree: In Verlegung des Autoris. Rpt. Hildesheim: Olms, 1975.

RATKE. See under ANON. and under ISING, ERIKA.

RAUMER, RUDOLF VON. 1870. *Geschichte der germanischen Philologie vorzugsweise in Deutschland.* Munich: Oldenbourg.

REIMMANN, JAKOB. 1709. *Versuch einer Einleitung in die Historiam Literarum Antediluvianam.* Halle: Renger.

RHENANUS, BEATUS. 1531 [2008]. *Rerum Germanicarum libri tres.* Basle: Froben, Johann (Erben). Modern edition ed. Felix Mundt, *Beatus Rhenanus. Rerum Germanicarium Libri Tres (1531): Ausgabe, Übersetzung, Studien.* Tübingen: Niemeyer, 2008.

RITTER, STEPHAN. 1616. *Grammatica Germanica Nova usui omnium aliarum nationum hanc linguam affectantium inserviens, praecipue vero ad Linguam Gallicam accommodata: ex cujus methodicis praeceptionibus, ductu regularem & exceptionum plenarium, facili negotio Linguae istius cognitio comparari poterit.* Marburg: Hutwelcker.

RIVES, JAMES B., ed. 1999. *Tacitus' Germania.* Oxford: Clarendon Press.

SANCTIUS, FRANCISCUS (FRANCISCO SÁNCHEZ DE LAS BROZAS). 1587. *Minerva. De causis linguae Latinae.* Salamanca: Renaut. Edition with a commentary by Jacobus Perizonius Amsterdam: apud Viduam et Filium Salomonis Schouten, 1687.

SATTLER, JOHANN RUDOLPH. 1604. *Teutsche Rhetorik, Titular und Epistelbüchlein.* Basle: Ludwig König.

SCALIGER, JULIUS CAESAR. 1540. *De causis linguae latinae.* Lugduni / Lyons.

SCHÖPF, HEINRICH. 1625. *Institutiones in linguam Germanicam sive Alemannicam. Ex quibusvis probatissimis authoribus excerptae, ac in gratiam studiosae, imprimisque Lotharingicae, iuventutis conscriptae.* Mainz: Typis Hermanni Meresii.

SCHOTTELIUS, JUSTUS GEORG. 1640. *Lamentatio Germaniae exspirantis. Der numehr hinsterbenden Nymphen Germaniae elendste Todesklage.* Braunschweig: Balthasar Gruber.

SCHOTTELIUS, JUSTUS GEORG. 1641. *Teutsche Sprachkunst / Darinn die Allerwortreichste/ jhren Gründen erhoben/ dero Eigenschafften und Kunststücke völliglich entdeckt/ und also in eine richtige Form der Kunst zum ersten mahle gebracht worden. Abgetheilet in Drey Bücher.* Braunschweig: Gruber.

SCHOTTELIUS, JUSTUS GEORG. 1643. *Der Teutschen Sprach Einleitung Zu richtiger gewisheit und grundmeßigem vermügen der Teutschen Haubtsprache / samt beygefügten Eklrärungen.* Lübeck: Johan Meyer.

SCHOTTELIUS, JUSTUS GEORG. 1645. *Teutsche Vers- oder Reimkunst darin Vnsere Teutsche MutterSprache in eine richtige Form der Kunst zum ersten mahle gebracht worden.* Wolfenbüttel: in Verlegung des Authoris.

SCHOTTELIUS, JUSTUS GEORG. 1647 [1967]. *Fruchtbringender Lustgarte.* Wolfenbüttel: Johann Bissmarck. Rpt. with a *Nachwort* by Max Wehrli. Munich: Kösel, 1967.

SCHOTTELIUS, JUSTUS GEORG. 1648 [1900]. *FriedensSieg. Ein Freudenspiel.* Wolfenbüttel: Buno. Ed. Friedrich Ernst Koldewey. Halle: Niemeyer.

SCHOTTELIUS, JUSTUS GEORG. 1651. *Justi-Georgii Schottelii Teutsche Sprach Kunst: vielfaltig vermehret und verbessert, darin von allen Eigenschaften der so wortreichen und prächtigen Teutschen Haubtsprache ausführlich und gründlich gehandelt wird.* Braunschweig: Zilliger.

SCHOTTELIUS, JUSTUS GEORG. 1656 [1976]. *Teutsche Vers- oder Reimkunst. Nachdruck der Ausgabe 1656 Lüneburg.* Hildesheim: Olms.

SCHOTTELIUS, JUSTUS GEORG. 1663 [1967]. *Ausführliche Arbeit von der teutschen Haubtsprache,* Braunschweig: Zilliger. (Second ed., anonymous, and with an altered title, Hildesheim: n.p., 1737.) Facsimile ed. Wolfgang Hecht, Tübingen: Niemeyer, 1967.

SCHOTTELIUS, JUSTUS GEORG. 1666. *Jesu Christi Nahmens-Ehr: worin alles auf den süssen Nahmen Gottes und dessen Wort eingerichtet, mit vielen Kupferstükken gezieret und in gebundener und ungebundener Rede verfasset ist.* Wolfenbüttel: Buno.

SCHOTTELIUS, JUSTUS GEORG. 1668. *Eigentliche und sonderbare Vorstellung des Jüngsten Tages: und darin künfftig verhandenen grossen und letzten Wunder-Gerichts Gottes ... nachdenklich in teutscher Sprache beschrieben mit nöthigen Erklärungen und schönen Kupfer-Stükken.* Braunschweig: Zilliger.

SCHOTTELIUS, JUSTUS GEORG. 1669 [1980]. *Ethica. Die Sittenkunst oder Wollebenskunst.* Wolfenbüttel: Weiß. Rpt. with an afterword by Jörg Jochen Berns Bern: Francke, 1980.

SCHOTTELIUS, JUSTUS GEORG. 1671. *De singularibus quibusdam & antiquis In Germania Juribus & Observatis. Kurtzer Tractat Von Unterschiedlichen*

Rechten in Teutschland. Reprinted 1686 and ca. 1725. Frankfurt am Main, Leipzig: Gottlieb Heinrich Grentz.

SCHOTTELIUS, J. G. 1673a. *Sonderbare Vorstellung von der ewigen Seeligkeit: in teutscher Sprache nachdenklich beschrieben ... an stat des andren Theils ist beigefügt eine Sterbekunst, oder sonderliche Erinnerung gern, recht bald und frölig zusterben.* Braunschweig: Zilliger.

SCHOTTELIUS, JUSTUS GEORG. 1673b [1991]. *Horrendum Bellum Grammaticale (Der schreckliche Sprachkrieg).* Ed. by Friedrich Kittler and Stefan Rieger, Leipzig: Reclam, 1991.

SCHOTTELIUS, JUSTUS GEORG. 1675. *Concordia seu harmonia quatuor Evangelistarum: Auf sonderliche Art vernehmlich u. mit ungezwungenen deutlichen Reimen oder Versen in teutscher Sprache ausgefertiget.* Braunschweig: Zilliger.

SCHOTTELIUS, JUSTUS GEORG. 1676a. *Grausame Beschreibung und Vorstellung Der Hölle Und der höllischen Qwal, Oder des andern und ewigen Todes: in Teutscher Sprache nachdenklich, und also vor die Augen geleget ... ; Mit etzlichen Schrekkniß-vollen Kupfferstükken zugleich vorgebildet.* Wolfenbüttel: Buno.

SCHOTTELIUS, JUSTUS GEORG. 1676b. *Grund-Lehre des Heyligthums von der Väterlichen Fürsorge und Regierung Gottes ... Hrn. Justi Georgii Schottelii ... : aber gewichenen 1676.* Wolffenbüttel: Weisz.

SCHOTTELIUS, JUSTUS GEORG. 1676c. *Brevis & fundamentalis Manuductio ad Orthographiam & Etymologiam in Lingua Germanica. Kurtze und gründliche Anleitung Zu der RechtSchreibung Und zu der Wortforschung In der Teutschen Sprache. Für die Jugend in den Schulen / und sonst überall nützlich und dienlich.* Braunschweig: Zilliger.

SCHOTTELIUS, JUSTUS GEORG. 1674. *Sonderbare Vorstellung, wie es mit Leib und Seel des Menschen werde kurtz vor dem Tode, in dem Tode, und nach dem Tode bewandt seyn.* Braunschweig: Zilliger.

SCHRIECKIUS, ADRIANUS RODORNIUS (ADRIAAN VAN SCHRIECK). 1615. *Adriani Schriecki Rodorni monitorum secundorum libri V.: Quibus Originium rerumq[ue] Celticarum & Belgicarum opus suum nuper ed., altiùs & auctiùs è fontibus Hebraicis, impsâque rerum origine deducit, probat, firmatque. de vera et falsa origine monimentum, sive Europa rediviva.* Ypris Flandrorum: Bellettus.

SCHRIECKIUS, ADRIANUS RODORNUS (ADRIAAN VAN SCHRIECK). 1620. *Adversariorum libri IIII. His argumentis: Linguam Hebraicam esse divinam & primogeniam.* Ypres: Franciscus Bellettus.

SÉWEL, WILLEM. 1708. *Nederduytsche Spraakkonst.* Amsterdam: Assuerus Lansvelt.

SPERONI, SPERONE. 1542 [1975]. *Dialogo delle Lingue. Herausgegeben, übersetzt und eingeleitet von Helene Harth.* Munich: Fink, 1975.

STEINBACH, CHRISTOPH ERNST. 1724. *Kürtze und gründliche Anweisung zur Deutschen Sprache. Vel succincta et perfecta Grammatica LINGVAE*

GERMANICAE Nova methodo tradita. Rostochii et Parchimi: Apud Georg Ludw. Fritsch.

STEVIN, SIMON. 1586. *De weeghdaet* (contains: *Vtspraeck vande weerdicheyt der dvytsche tael*). Leiden: Plantijn. A later edition, from 1605, bears the title *Vande weeghconst* (Leiden: Bowensz, 1605). See also DIJKSTERHUIS 1955.

STEVIN, SIMON. 1608. *VANDE VERNIEVWING DES Wysentijts,* contained in *vant Eertclootschrift,* in turn published as part of *Tweede deel des Weereltschrifts.* Leyden: Ian Bowenszon. See also DIJKSTERHUIS 1955.

STIELER, KASPAR. 1968 [1691]. *Der Teutschen Sprache Stammbaum und Fortwachs [...].* Nürnberg: Johann Hoffman. Rpt. with an afterword by Stefan Sonderegger. Munich: Kösel.

STIERNHIELM, GEORG. 1671. *De linguarum origine Praefatio,* published as a preface to the edition of Wulfila's Gospels: *D.N. Jesu Christi SS. Evangelia | ab Ulfila. Ex graeco gothice' translata, nunc cum parallelis versionibus, Sveo-Gothicâ, Norraenâ, seu Islandicâ, & vulgatâ latinâ edita.* Stockholmiae: N. Wankie.

SYV, PEDER. 1663 [1979]. *Nogle Betænkninger om det cimbriske Sprog.* Rpt. in *Danske Grammatikere fra Midten af det syttende til Midten af det attende Aarhundrede,* ed. Henrik Bertelsen. Copenhagen: Det Dankse Sprog- og Litteraturselskab, C.A. Reitzels Boghandel. Reprint series first published 1917–1929. (6 volumes), Vol. I, 75–272.

SYV, PEDER. 1682,1688. *Almindelige Danske Ordsprog og korte Lærdomme,* Bd. I. 1682, Bd. II. 1688. Copenhagen: Christian Geertzen.

SYV, PEDER. 1685 [1979]. *Den danske Sprogkunst eller Grammatica.* Copenhagen: Joh. Phil. Bockenhoffer. Rpt. in *Danske Grammatikere fra Midten af det syttende til Midten af det attende Aarhundrede,* ed. Henrik Bertelsen. Copenhagen: Det Dankse Sprog- og Litteraturselskab, C.A. Reitzels Boghandel. Reprint series first published 1917–1929. (6 volumes), Vol. III, 147–250.

TIÄLLMANN, NILS. 1696. *Grammatica Suecana, Äller En Svensk Språk= Ock Skrif=Konst | Välment sammansrkifen| ock i liuset gifen | mäd egen bekostnad.* Stockholm: Keiser.

TITZ, JOHANN PETER. 1642. *Zwey Bücher Von Der Kunst Hochdeutsche Verse und Lieder zu machen.* Danzig: Hünefeld.

TSCHERNING, ANDREAS. 1659. *Unvorgreiffliches Bedencken über etliche Miszbräuche in der deutschen Schreib- und Sprach-Kunst, insonderheit der edlen Poeterey: wie auch Kurtzer Entwurff oder Abriesz einer deutschen Schatzkammer, von schönen und zierlichen poetischen Redens-Arten, Umbschreibungen, und denen Dingen, so einem getichte sonderbaren Glantz und Anmuht geben können.* Lübeck: Volk.

VALLA, LAURENTIUS. 1471. *De linguae Latinae elegantia libri sex.* Rome: Philip de Lignamine.

VATER, JOHANN SEVERIN. 1802. *Handbuch der Hebräischen, Syrischen, Chaldäischen und Arabischen Grammatik: Für den Anfang der Erlernung dieser Sprachen bearbeitet.* Leipzig: Crusius.

VAUGELAS, CLAUDE FAVRE DE. 1647. *Remarques sur la langue françoise utiles à ceux qui veulent bien parler & bien escrire.* Paris: J. Camusat & P. le Petit.

VORST, JOHANN. 1669 (or 1668). *Observationum in linguam vernaculam specimen.* Coloniae Brandenburg: In Verlag Georg Schulzens.

VOSSIUS, GERARDUS JOANNES. 1635. *De arte grammatica.* Amsterdam: Willem Janszoon Blaeu.

WAHL, SAMUEL FRIEDRICH GÜNTHER. 1789. *Elementarbuch für die arabische Sprache und Litteratur.* Halle: bei Johann Jacob Gebauer.

WALLIS, JOHANNIS. 1653 [1972]. *Grammatica linguae Anglicanae. Cui præfigitur, De loquela sive sonorum formatione tractatus grammatico-physicus.* Oxoniae: Robinson. Ed. Alan J. Kemp: *John Wallis's Grammar of the English Language.* London: Longman, 1972.

WEICHMANN, CHRISTIAN FRIEDRICH. 1721, 1723. *Weichmanns Poesie der Nieder-Sachsen.* Hamburg, Bey Johann Christoph Kißner.

WERNER, JOHANN. 1629 [2007]. *Manuductio Orthographica.* Altenburgi: published by the author; Meuschken. Rpt. ed. Claudine Moulin, Hildesheim: Olms, 2007.

WILKINS, JOHN. 1668 [1968]. *An Essay Towards a Real Character and a Philosophical Language.* Facsimile rpt. Menston: Scolar Press, 1968.

ZESEN, PHILIPP VON. 1640 [1971]. *Deutscher Helicon.* Text of 1641 ed. In: *Philipp von Zesen. Sämtliche Werke,* ed. Ferdinand van Ingen. Berlin: de Gruyter, vol. 9.

BIBLIOGRAPHY – SECONDARY LITERATURE

ALLAN, KEITH. 2007. *The Western Classical Tradition in Linguistics.* London: Equinox.

ALLEN, GRAHAM. 2000. *Intertextuality.* London: Routledge.

AUER, ANITA. 2009. *The Subjunctive in the Age of Prescriptivism. English and German developments during the eighteenth century.* London: Palgrave Macmillan.

AUROUX, SYLVAIN, KONRAD KOERNER, HANS-JOSEF NIEDEREHE & KEES VERSTEEGH, eds. 2000, 2001, 2006. *History of the Language Sciences. An International Handbook on the Evolution of the Study of Language from the Beginnings to the Present.* 3 vols. (HSK 18:1–3). Berlin: de Gruyter.

AZAD, YUSEF. 1989. *The government of tongues: common usage and the 'prescriptive' tradition 1650–1800.* Unpublished doctoral dissertation, Oxford University.

BAADE, ANNE A. 1993. *Melchior Goldast von Haiminsfeld. Collector, Commentator and Editor* (Studies in Old Germanic Languages and Literatures, 2). Bern: Lang.

BARBARIĆ, STEPJAN. 1981. *Zur grammatischen Terminologie von Justus Georg Schottelius und Kaspar Stieler: mit Ausblick auf die Ergebnisse bei ihren Vorgängern.* Bern: Lang.

BARNER, WILFRIED. 1970. *Barockrhetorik. Untersuchungen zu ihren geschichtlichen Grundlagen.* Tübingen: Niemeyer.

BENTZINGER, RUDOLF. 2003. 'Textkomposition und Rhetorik-Tradition bei Reformationsdialogen 1520–25'. In *'Vir ingenio mirandus'. Studies presented to John L. Flood*, eds. William J. Jones, William A. Kelly & Frank Shaw. Göppingen: Kümmerle, 263–278.

BERNS, JÖRG JOCHEN. 1974. 'Der weite Weg des J.G. Schottelius von Einbeck nach Wolfenbüttel'. *Einbecker Jahrbuch* 30: 5–20.

BERNS, JÖRG JOCHEN. 1976. *Justus Georg Schottelius 1612–1676. Ein Teutscher Gelehrter am Wolfenbütteler Hof.* Braunschweig: Waisenhaus-Buchdruckerei. (Ausstellungskataloge der Herzog August Bibliothek 18).

BERNS, JÖRG JOCHEN. 1978. 'Probleme der Erschließung und Edition des Schottelius-Briefwechsels'. In *Briefe deutscher Barockautoren. Probleme ihrer Erfassung und Erschließung*, ed. Hans-Henrik Krummacher. Hamburg: Hauswedell, 95–106.

BERNS, JÖRG JOCHEN. 1980. 'Nachwort'. In: Schottelius 1669 [1980], ed. Berns. Bern: Francke, 3–68.

BERNS, JÖRG JOCHEN. 1981. 'Trionfo-Theater am Hof von Braunschweig-Wolfenbüttel'. *Daphnis* 10: 663–710.

BERNS, JÖRG JOCHEN. 1984. 'Justus Georg Schottelius'. In *Deutsche Dichter des 17. Jahrhunderts. Ihr Leben und Werk*, ed. Harald Steinhagen & Benno von Wiese. Berlin: Schmidt, 415–434.

BESCH, WERNER, OSKAR REICHMANN, & STEFAN SONDEREGGER, eds. 1984–1985. *Sprachgeschichte. Ein Handbuch zur Geschichte der deutschen Sprache und ihrer Erforschung* (HSK 2), Berlin: de Gruyter. 2 vols.

BESCH, WERNER, ANNE BETTEN, OSKAR REICHMANN, & STEFAN SONDEREGGER, eds. 1998–2004. *Sprachgeschichte. Ein Handbuch zur Geschichte der deutschen Sprache und ihrer Erforschung* (HSK 2.1–2.4). Second edition. Berlin: de Gruyter. 4 vols.

BIRCHER, MARTIN, ed. 1991. *Briefe der Fruchtbringenden Gesellschaft. Die Zeit Herzog Augusts von Sachsen-Weißenfels 1667–1680*. Tübingen: Niemeyer.

BIRCHER, MARTIN, ed. 1992. *Im Garten der Palme: Kleinodien aus dem unbekannten Barock; Die Fruchtbringende Gesellschaft und ihre Zeit* (Ausstellungskataloge der Herzog August Bibliothek, 68). Wiesbaden: Harrassowitz.

BLACKALL, ERIC A. 1959. *The Emergence of German as a Literary Language 1700–1775*. Cambridge: CUP. Second edition Ithaca & London: Cornell University Press, 1978.

BLUME, HERBERT. 1972. 'Harsdörffers "Porticus" für Herzog August d.J. (Zu bisher unbekannten bzw. unbeachteten Briefen Harsdörffers)'. *Wolfenbüttler Beiträge* 1: 88–101.

BLUME, HERBERT. 1978. 'Sprachtheorie und Sprachlegimitation im 17. Jahrhundert in Schweden und in Kontinentaleuropa'. *Arkiv för nordisk filologi* 93: 205–218.

BLUME, HERBERT. 1983. 'Rudbecks Atlantica und Schottelius' Hauptsprache. Beobachtungen zum Sprachstil gelehrter Prosa des 17. Jh. in Schweden und Deutschland'. In *Studien zur europäischen Rezeption deutscher Barockliteratur*, ed. Leonard Forster. Wiesbaden: Harrassowitz, 181–197.

BOLTE, JOHANNES. 1908. *Andreas Guarnas 'Bellum Grammaticale' und seine Nachahmungen*. Berlin: Hofmann.

BONFANTE, GIULIANO. 1953. 'Ideas on the kinship of the European languages from 1200 to 1800'. *Cahiers d'histoire mondiale* 1: 679–699.

BORNEMANN, ULRICH. 1976. *Anlehnung und Abgrenzung. Untersuchungen zur Rezeption der niederländischen Literatur in der deutschen Dichtungsreform des 17. Jahrhunderts*. Assen/Amsterdam: Van Gorcum.

BORST, ARNO. 1960 [1995]. *Der Turmbau von Babel. Geschichte der Meinungen über Ursprung und Vielfalt der Sprachen und Völker*. Stuttgart: Hiersemann. Reprint Munich: DTV, 1995.

BRECHT, MARTIN, & KLAUS DEPPERMANN, eds. 1993, 1995. *Geschichte des Pietismus*. Vol. 1 ed. Brecht alone, *Der Pietismus vom siebzehnten bis zum frühen achtzehnten Jahrhundert*. Vol. 2 ed. Brecht & Deppermann, *Der*

Pietismus im achtzehnten Jahrhundert. Göttingen: Vandenhoeck & Ruprecht.

BROUGH, SONIA 1985. *The Goths and the concept of Gothic in Germany from 1500 to 1750. Culture, language and architecture.* Frankfurt: Lang.

BURKE, PETER. 1989. 'The Renaissance Dialogue'. *Renaissance Studies* 3: 1–12.

BURKE, PETER. 2004. *Languages and Communities in Early Modern Europe.* Cambridge: CUP.

BURNETT, STEPHEN G. 1996. *From Christian Hebraism to Jewish Studies. Johannes Buxtorf (1564–1629) and Hebrew learning in the 17th century.* Leiden: Brill.

CAMPBELL, FIONA. 2003. 'Dialog und Dialogizität in den Flugschriften der frühen Reformation'. In *Dialoge. Sprachliche Kommunikation in und zwischen Texten im deutschen Mittelalter*, ed. Nikolaus Henkel et al. Tübingen: Niemeyer, 337–348.

CARAVOLAS, JEAN. 2000. 'Les origines de la didactique des langues en tant que discipline'. In AUROUX ET AL. 2000, VOL. 1, 1009–1022.

CARAVOLAS, JEAN-ANTOINE. 1994. *La didactique des langues. Précis d'histoire I. 1450–1700. Anthologie I. A L'ombre de Quintilien.* Tübingen: Gunter Narr.

CARON, PHILIPPE, & WENDY AYRES-BENNETT. Forthcoming. 'La prescription linguistique en France de 1647 à 1720: l'exemple des remarqueurs'. To appear in *Prescriptions en langue (histoire, succès, limites), Actes du Colloque international (HTL), Paris, 15–16 novembre 2007*, ed. Danielle Candel & Douglas Kibbee.

CARON, WILHELM J. H. ed. 1958. *Petrus Leupenius, Aanmerkingen op de Neederduitsche taale.* Groningen: J.P. Wolters.

CHERUBIM, DIETER. 1995. 'Varro-Teutonicus. The reception of classical Latin linguistics in the early modern age. Schottelius' *Ausführliche Arbeit von der Teutschen Haubtsprache* and Varro *De latina lingua. Zeitschrift für germanistische Linguistik* 23:125–152.

CHERUBIM, DIETER. 1996, 2009². s.v. Schottel(ius), Justus Georg(ius). In *Lexicon Grammaticorum. Who's Who in the History of World Linguistics*, ed. Harro Stammerjohann. Tübingen: Niemeyer.

CHERUBIM, DIETER. 2001. 'Schottelius and European traditions of grammar'. In *Indigenous Grammar Across Cultures*, ed. Hannes Kniffka. Frankfurt: Lang, 559–574.

CHERUBIM, DIETER, & ARIANE WALSDORF. 2004. *Sprachkritik als Aufklärung. Die Deutsche Gesellschaft in Göttingen im 18. Jahrhundert*, Ausstellungskatalog der Niedersächsischen Staats- und Universitätsbibliothek.

CHRISTMANN, HANS HELMUT. 1980. 'Zum Begriff der Analogie in der Sprachbetrachtung des 16. bis 19. Jahrhunderts'. In *Stimmen der Romania. Festschrift W.T. Ewert*, ed. G. Schmidt. Wiesbaden: Heymann, 519–535.

CONERMANN, KLAUS, ed. 1992, 1998, 2003, 2006. *Briefe der Fruchtbringenden Gesellschaft und Beilagen: Die Zeit Fürst Ludwigs von Anhalt-Köthen 1617–1650*. Bd. 1 1617–1626 (1992), Bd. 2 1627–1629 (1998), Bd. 3 1630–1636 (2003), Bd. 4 1637–1638 (2006). Tübingen: Niemeyer.

CONSIDINE, JOHN. 2008. *Dictionaries in Early Modern Europe. Lexicography and the Making of Heritage*. Cambridge: CUP.

CONSIDINE, JOHN. 2010. 'Why was Claude de Saumaise interested in the Scythian hypothesis?' *Language and History* 53(2): 81–96.

CONSIDINE, JOHN. & TOON VAN HAL. 2010. 'Introduction: classifying and comparing languages in post-Renaissance Europe (1600–1800)'. *Language and History* 53(2): 63–69.

CORDES, GÜNTER. 1966. *Die Quellen der Exegesis Germaniae des Franciscus Irenicus und sein Germanenbegriff*. Tübingen: Georg Nolte.

COTTONE, MARGHERITA. 2000. 'Die Bedeutung des Gartens in der Barockzeit: Gartenkunst und Gartenmetaphorik bei J.G. Schottelius'. In *Künste und Natur in den Diskursen der frühen Neuzeit*, ed. Hartmut Laufhütte et al. Wiesbaden: Harrassowitz, 986–998.

CRAM, DAVID, & MAAT, JAAP. 2000. 'Universal language schemes in the seventeenth century'. In AUROUX ET AL., 2000, vol. 1, 1030–1043.

CZAPLA, RALF GEORG. 1988. 'Wie man recht verteutschen sol. Der Traktat des Justus Georg Schottelius als Paradigma einer Übersetzungstheorie in der frühen Neuzeit. Mit einem Exkurs zur Vergil-Übersetzung im 16. bis 19. Jahrhundert'. *Morgen Glantz* 8: 197–226.

CZUCKA, ECKEHARD. 1997. 'Das universelle Babylon. Justus Georg Schottels *Horrendum Bellum Grammaticale*'. In *Fremdsprachen und Fremdsprachenerwerb*, ed. Kristian Bosselmann-Cyran. Berlin: Akademie-Verlag, 67–82.

DAVIES, WINIFRED, & NILS LANGER. 2006. *The making of bad language. Lay linguistic stigmatisations in German: past and present*. Frankfurt am Main: Lang.

DE CAPUA, ANGELO GEORGE. 1973. *German Baroque Poetry. Interpretative Readings*. Albany: State University of New York Press.

DEUMERT, ANA, & WIM VANDENBUSSCHE, eds. 2003. *Germanic Standardizations. Past to Present*. Amsterdam: Benjamins.

DIBBETS, GEERT R.W. 1985. 'De Twe-spraack en haar duitse tijdgenoten'. In *Handelingen van het acht en dertigste Nederlands Filologencongres*. Amsterdam: Apa-Holland Universiteits Pers, 245–252.

DIBBETS, GEERT R.W. 1992. 'Dutch philology in the 16th and 17th century'. In *The history of linguistics in the Low Countries*, eds. Jan Noordegraaf, Kees Versteegh & Konrad Koerner. Amsterdam: Benjamins, 39–62.

DIBBETS, GEERT R.W. 2000. 'Frühe Grammatische Beschreibungen des Niederländischen (ca.1550–ca.1650)'. In Auroux et al., vol. 1, 784–792.

DONHAUSER, KARIN. 1989. 'Das Deskriptionsproblem und seine präskriptive Lösung. Zur grammatalogischen Bedeutung der Vorreden in den Grammatiken des 16. bis 18. Jahrhunderts'. *Sprachwissenschaft* 14: 29–57.

DROIXHE, DANIEL. 2000. 'Ideas on the Origin of Language and Languages from the 16th to the 19th centuries'. In AUROUX ET AL., 2000, vol. 1, 1057–1071.

DRUX, RUDOLF. 1984. 'Lateinisch/Deutsch'. In BESCH ET AL., 1984–1985, vol. 1, 854–861.

DÜNNHAUPT, GERHARD. 1990–93. *Personalbibliographien zu den Drucken des Barock. Zweite, verbesserte und wesentlich vermehrte Auflage des Bibliographischen Handbuchs der Barockliteratur.* Bd. I (1990), Bd. 2 (1990), Bd. 3 (1991), Bd. 4 (1991), Bd. 5 (1991), Bd. 6 (1993). Stuttgart: Hiersemann.

DUNTZE, OLIVER. 2007. *Ein Verleger sucht sein Publikum: Die Strassburger Offizin des Matthias Hupfuff (1497/98–1520).* Berlin: de Gruyter.

DYCK, JOACHIM. 1969. *Ticht-Kunst. Deutsche Barockpoetik und rhetorische Tradition.* 2nd edition. Bad Homberg, Berlin & Zürich: Gehlen.

EBERT, ROBERT P., OSKAR REICHMANN, HANS-JOACHIM SOLMS & KLAUS-PETER WEGERA. 1993. *Frühneuhochdeutsche Grammatik.* (Sammlung kurzer Grammatiken germanischer Dialekte. Hauptreihe). Tübingen: Niemeyer.

ECO, UMBERTO. 1995. *The search for the perfect language.* Oxford: Blackwell.

EIKELMANN, MANFRED. 1995. 'Sprichwörtersammlungen (deutsche)'. In *Die deutsche Literatur des Mittelalters. Verfasserlexikon,* 2nd ed. Berlin: de Gruyter, vol. 9, cols. 162–179.

ENTNER, HEINZ. 1972. 'Zum Dichtungsbegriff des deutschen Humanismus'. In *Grundpositionen der deutschen Literatur im 16. Jahrhundert,* ed. Ingeborg Spriewald et al. Berlin: Aufbau-Verlag, 330–499.

ENTNER, HEINZ. 1984. 'Der Weg vom *Buch von der deutschen Poeterey.* Humanistische Tradition und poetologische Voraussetzungen deutscher Dichtung im 17. Jahrhundert'. In *Studien zur deutschen Literatur im 17. Jahrhundert,* ed. Werner Lenk et al. Berlin: Weimar, 11–144.

ERBEN, JOHANNES. 2007. 'Die Tendenz zum Aufbau mehrgliedriger Wörter im Deutschen und Versuche, die wortinterne Gliederung lautlich oder graphisch zu verdeutlichen'. *Zeitschrift für deutsche Philologie* 126: 111–118.

EWALD, PETRA. 2006. 'Johann Friedrich Heynatz als Orthograph — sein Beitrag zur Deskription und Kodifikation der deutschen Rechtschreibung'. In Johann Friedrich Heynatz, 1803 [2006]. *Deutsche Sprachlehre zum Gebrauch der Schulen. Fünfte vermehrte und verbesserte Auflage (1803). Die Lehre von der Interpunktion. Zweite, durchgängig verbesserte Auflage (1782),* ed. Petra Ewald. Hildesheim: Olms, [V]–XCII.

FAIRCLOUGH, NORMAN. 1992. *Discourse and social change*. Cambridge: Polity Press.

FAUST, MANFRED. 1981. 'Schottelius' concept of word-formation'. In *Logos semantikos. Studia linguistica in honorem Eugenio Coseriu*, ed. Horst Geckeler et al. Berlin: de Gruyter, 359–370.

FIEDLER, H.G. 1942. 'The Oldest Study of Germanic Proper Names'. *The Modern Language Review* 37: 185–192.

FLOOD, JOHN L. 1993. 'Nationalistic currents in early German typography'. *The Library*, 6th series, vol. 15, 2: 125–41.

FLOOD, JOHN L. 1996. 'Dietrich Wilhelm von Soltau und seine Übersetzungen des *Reynke de Vos*. Ein Beitrag zur Erforschung der deutsch-englischen Literaturbeziehungen um 1800'. *Archiv für Geschichte des Buchwesens* 45: 283–336.

FLOOD, JOHN L. 2006. *Poets Laureate in the Holy Roman Empire. A Bio-bibliographical Handbook*. Berlin: de Gruyter.

FONSÉN, TUOMO. 2006. *Künstlöbliche Sprachverfassung unter den Teutschen. Studien zum Horrendum Bellum Grammaticale des Justus Georg Schottelius (1673)*. Frankfurt am Main: Lang.

FONSÉN, TUOMO. 2007. 'Zur Vorgeschichte der deutschen Philologie. Justus Georg Schottelius's *Horrendum Bellum Grammaticale*'. *Neuphilologische Mitteilungen* 108: 423–431.

FORSTER, LEONARD. 'Zu Harsdörffers *Specimen Philologiae germanicae*'. In *Georg Philipp Harsdörffer. Ein deutscher Dichter und europäischer Gelehrter*, ed. Italo Machele Battafarano. Bern: Lang, 9–22.

FOUCAULT, MICHEL. 1977. *L'ordre du discours*. Paris: Gallimard.

FRANCIS, TIMOTHY. 2003. 'Perceptions of Low German to Schottelius: A chronological overview and review'. In *'Vir ingenio mirandus'. Studies presented to John L. Flood*, eds. William J. Jones, William A. Kelly & Frank Shaw, 817–834. Göppingen: Kümmerle.

FREDERICKX, EDDY. 1971–72. 'Ioannes Goropius Becanus, arts, linguist, graecus'. *Hermeneus* 43: 129–136.

FREDERICKX, EDDY. 1973. *Ioannes Goropius Becanus 1519–73. Leven en werk*. Leuven.

GABRIELSSON, ARTUR. 1983. 'Die Verdrängung der mittelniederdeutschen durch die neuhochdeutsche Schriftspache'. In *Handbuch zur niederdeutschen Sprach- und Literaturwissenschaft*, ed. Gerhard Cordes & Dieter Möhn. Berlin: Erich Schmidt, 119–153.

GARDT, ANDREAS. 1994. *Sprachreflexion in Barock und Frühaufklärung. Entwürfe von Böhme bis Leibniz*. Berlin: de Gruyter.

GARDT, ANDREAS. 1995. 'Das Konzept der Eigentlichkeit im Zentrum barocker Sprachtheorie'. In *Sprachgeschichte des Neuhochdeutschen*, eds. Andreas Gardt, Klaus J. Mattheier & Oskar Reichmann. Tübingen: Niemeyer, 145–167.

GARDT, ANDREAS. 2008. 'Natürlichkeit: eine strukturelle und pragmatische Kategorie der Sprachnormierung in Texten der Frühen Neuzeit'. *German Life and Letters* 61: 404–419.

GARDT, ANDREAS. 1999. *Geschichte der Sprachwissenschaft in Deutschland vom Mittelalter bis ins 20. Jahrhundert.* Berlin: de Gruyter.

GARDT, ANDREAS, ed. 2000. *Nation und Sprache. Die Diskussion ihres Verhältnisses in Geschichte und Gegenwart.* Berlin: de Gruyter.

GÄRTNER, KURT, & KLAUS GRUBMÜLLER, eds. 2000. *Ein neues Mittelhochdeutsches Wörterbuch: Prinzipien, Probeartikel, Diskussion.* Göttingen: Vandenhoeck & Ruprecht.

GENETTE, GÉRARD. 1982. *Palimsestes. La littérature au second degré.* Paris: Seuil.

GEORGI, THEOPHILUS. 1742. *Allgemeines Europäisches Bücher-Lexikon.* Leipzig: Georgi.

GILMAN, SANDER. 1977. 'Johann Agricola of Eisleben's Proverb Collection (1529): The Polemicizing of a literary form and the reaction'. *Sixteenth-century journal* 8: 77–84.

GILMAN, SANDER, ed. 1971. *Johannes Agricola von Eisleben. Die Sprichwörter-Sammlungen.* Berlin: de Gruyter.

GLÜCK, HELMUT. 2002. *Deutsch als Fremdsprache in Europa vom Mittelalter bis zur Barockzeit.* Berlin: de Gruyter.

GRAVELLE, SARAH STEVER. 1988. 'The Latin-vernacular question and humanist theory of language and culture'. *Journal of the history of ideas* 49: 367–386.

GRAY, RICHARD T. 1996. 'Buying into Signs: Money and Semiosis in Eighteenth-Century German Language Theory'. *The German Quarterly*, 69: 1–14.

GUNDOLF, FRIEDRICH. 1930. 'Justus Georg Schottel'. In *Deutschkundliches. Friedrich Panzer zum 60. Geburtstag von Heidelberger Fachgenossen*, ed. Hans Teske. Heidelberg: Carl Winter, 70–86.

GÜTZLAFF, KATHRIN. 1988. 'Simon Stevin und J.G. Schottelius — Spuren der deutsch-niederländischen Beziehungen im 17. Jahrhundert'. In *Sprache in Vergangenheit und Gegenwart. Beiträge aus dem Institut für Germanistische Wissenschaft der Philipps-Universität Marburg*, ed. Wolfgang Brandt, with Rudolf Freudenberg. Marburg: Hitzeroth, 91–107.

GÜTZLAFF, KATHRIN. 1989a. *Von der Fügung teutscher Stammwörter. The Word-Formation in J.G. Schottelius' 'Ausführliche Arbeit von der Teutschen Hauptsprache'.* Hildesheim: Olms.

GÜTZLAFF, KATHRIN. 1989b. 'Der Weg zum >Stammwort<. Der Beitrag von J.G. Schottelius zur Entwicklung einer Wortbildungslehre des Deutschen'. *Sprachwissenschaft* 14: 58–77.

HAAPAMÄKI, SAARA. 2002. *Studier i svensk grammatikhistoria.* Åbo: Åbo Akademis Förlag.

HAAPAMÄKI, SAARA. 2007. 'Schwedische Sprachlehren und Sprachpflege – Kontinuität oder Diskontinuität?' [abstract of paper presented at Henry Sweet Society colloquium, July 2007, Helsinki]. *Henry Sweet Society Bulletin* 49: 65.

HAAS, ALOIS. 1997. *Der Kampf um den Heiligen Geist: Luther und die Schwärmer*. Berlin: de Gruyter.

HAAS, ELKE. 1980. *Rhetorik und Hochsprache. Über die Wirksamkeit der Rhetorik bei der Entstehung der deutschen Hochsprache im 17. und 18. Jahrhundert*. Frankfurt am Main: Lang.

HAAS, W. 1956–57. 'Of living things'. *German Life and Letters*, 10: 62–70, 85–96, 251–257.

HANKAMER, PAUL 1927 [1976]. *Die Sprache. Ihr Begriff und ihre Deutung im sechzehnten und siebzehten Jahrhundert. Ein Beitrag zur Frage der literarhistorischen Gliederung des Zeitraums*. Bonn: Friedrich Cohen. Rpt. Hildesheim: Olms, 1976.

HANKAMER, PAUL 1960 (2nd edition). *Jakob Böhme. Gestalt und Gestaltung*. Hildesheim: Olms.

HARLFINGER, DIETER, ed. 1989. *Graecogermanica. Griechischstudien deutscher Humanisten. Katalog Wolfenbüttel*. Weinheim: VCH, Acta Humaniora (Ausstellungskatalog der Herzog August Bibliothek, 59).

HECHT, WOLFGANG 1967. *Nachwort*, in SCHOTTELIUS 1663 [1967], ed. HECHT, 3*–19*.

HEINLE, EVA–MARIA. 1982. *Hieronymus Freyers Anweisung zur Teutschen Orthographie. Ein Beitrag zur Sprachgeschichte des 18. Jahrhunderts*. Heidelberg: Winter.

HEITSCH, DOROTHEA, & JEAN-FRANÇOIS VALLÉE. 2004. *Printed Voices. The Renaissance Culture of Dialogue*. Toronto: University of Toronto Press.

HENNE, HELMUT. 2001a. 'Deutsche Lexikographie und Sprachnorm im 17. und 18. Jahrhundert'. In *Deutsche Wörterbücher des 17. und 18. Jahrhunderts. Einführung und Bibliographie*, ed. Helmut Henne. Hildesheim: Olms.

HENNE, HELMUT, ed. 2001b. *Deutsche Wörterbücher des 17. und 18. Jahrhunderts. Einführung und Bibliographie. 2., erweiterte Auflage*. Hildesheim: Olms.

HERTENSTEIN, BERHARD. 1975. *Joachim von Watt (Vadianus), Bartholomäus Schobinger. Melchior Goldast. Die Beschäftigung mit dem Althochdeutschen von St. Gallen in Humanismus und Frühbarock*. Berlin: de Gruyter.

HERZOG, URS. 1979. *Deutsche Barocklyrik*. Munich: Beck.

HESS, PETER. 2000. '"Nachäffin der Natur" oder "aller Völker Sprachen"? Zur Rolle visueller Bildlichkeit in Poetik und Rhetorik der Barockzeit'. In *Künste und Natur in den Diskursen der frühen Neuzeit*, ed. Hartmut Laufhütte et al. Wiesbaden: Harrassowitz, 1047–1062.

HODSON, JANE. 2006. 'The problem of Joseph Priestley's (1733–1804) descriptivism'. *Historiographia Linguistica* 33(1/2): 57–84.

HÖPEL, INGRID. 2000. 'Beziehungen zwischen Sprichwort und Emblem. Justus Georg Schottelius und die *Dreiständigen Sinnbilder* (1643)'. In *Künste und Natur in den Diskursen der frühen Neuzeit*, ed. Hartmut Laufhütte et al. Wiesbaden: Harrassowitz, 999–1017.

HÖPEL, INGRID. 2002. 'Elster, Kanone und Fledermaus. Zum Verhältnis von Sprache und Moral in den *Dreiständigen Sinnbildern* von 1643'. In *Polyvalenz und Multifunktionalität der Emblematik*, eds. Wolfgang Harms & Dietmar Peil. Frankfurt am Main: Lang, 635–655.

HOVDHAUGEN, EVEN. 2000. 'Normative studies in the Scandinavian countries'. In AUROUX ET AL., vol. 1, 888–893.

HUBER, CHRISTOPH. 1984. *Kulturpatriotismus und Sprachbewußtsein. Studien zur deutschen Philologie des 17. Jahrhunderts*. Frankfurt am Main: Lang.

HÜLLEN, WERNER. 1996. 'Johann Joachim Becher (1635–1682) and his theory of language teaching'. *Historiographia Linguistica* 23: 73–88.

HÜLLEN, WERNER. 1999. *English dictionaries 800–1700. The topical tradition*. Oxford: Clarendon.

HÜLLEN, WERNER. 2002. *Collected Papers on the History of Linguistic Ideas*: The Henry Sweet Society for the History of Linguistics 8. Münster: Nodus.

HUNDSNURSCHER, FRANZ. 1986. 'Das Problem der Bedeutung bei Justus Georg Schottelius'. In *Sprache und Recht. Beiträge zur Kulturgeschichte des Mittelalters. Festschrift für Ruth Schmidt-Wiegand*, ed. Karl Hauck et al. Berlin: de Gruyter, 305–320.

HUNDT, MARKUS. 2000. *'Spracharbeit' im 17. Jahrhundert. Studien zu Georg Philipp Harsdörffer, Justus Georg Schottelius und Christian Gueintz*. Berlin: de Gruyter.

HUNDT, MARKUS. 2002. '"Wortforschung" im Sprachpatriotismus des 17. Jahrhundert'. In *Historische Wortbildung des Deutschen*, ed. Mechthild Habermann. Tübingen: Niemeyer, 289–313.

HUNDT, MARKUS. 2006. 'Sprachtheorie und Sprachspielpraxis im 17. Jahrhundert'. In *Harsdörffer-Studien. Mit einer Bibliografie der Forschungsliteratur von 1847 bis 2005*, eds. Hans-Joachim Jakob & Hermann Korte. Frankfurt am Main: Lang, 97–133.

HUNDT, MARKUS. 2007. 'Schottelius, Justus Georg'. *Neue Deutsche Biographie*. Berlin: Duncker & Humblot, Vol. 23: 498–500.

HUTERER, ANDREA. 2001. *Die Wortbildungslehr in der Anweisung zur Erlernung der Slavonisch-Rußischen Sprache (1705–1729) von Johann Werner Paus*. Munich: Verlag Otto Sagner.

INGEN, FERDINAND VAN. 1986. 'Die Sprachgesellschaften des 17. Jahrhunderts. Zwischen Kulturpatriotismus und Kulturvermittlung'. *Muttersprache* 96: 137–146.

INGEN, FERDINAND VAN. 1990. 'Dichterverständnis, Heldensprache, Städtisches Leben. Johann von Klaj's *Lobrede der Teutschen Poeterey*. In *Opitz und seine Welt. Festschrift*, eds. George Schulz-Behrend & Barbara Becker-Cantarino. Amsterdam: Rodopi, 251–266.

ISING, ERIKA. 1959. *Wolfgang Ratkes Schriften zur deutschen Grammatik (1612–1630). Teil I: Abhandlung. Teil II: Textausgabe.* Berlin: Akademie Verlag.

ISING, ERIKA. 1966. *Die Anfänge der volkssprachlichen Grammatik in Deutschland und Böhmen. Dargestellt am Einfluss der Schrift des Aelius Donatus. De octo partibus orationis ars minor. Teil I: Quellen.* Berlin: Deutsche Akademie der Wissenschaften zu Berlin.

ISING, ERIKA. 1970. *Die Herausbildung der Grammatik der Volkssprachen in Mittel- und Osteuropa. Studien über den Einfluß der lateinischen Elementargrammatik des Aelius Donatus. De octo partibus orationis ars minor.* Berlin (Ost): Veröffentlichungen des Instituts für deutsche Sprache und Literatur 47, Reihe A Beiträge zur Sprachwissenschaft.

ISING, GERHARD. 1956. *Die Erfassung der deutschen Sprache des ausgehenden 17. Jahrhunderts in den Wörterbüchern Matthias Kramers und Kaspar Stielers.* Berlin: Akademie-Verlag.

ISING, GERHARD. 1968. *Einführung.* In STIELER 1691 [1968].

ISING, GERHARD. 2001a. 'Einführung und Bibliographie zu Kaspar Stieler, Der Teutschen Sprache Stammbaum und Fortwachs oder Teutscher Sprachschatz (1691)'. In *Deutsche Wörterbücher des 17. und 18. Jahrhunderts. Einführung und Bibliographie*, ed. Helmut Henne, 75–94. Hildesheim: Olms.

ISING, GERHARD. 2001b. 'Einführung und Bibliographie zu Matthias Kramer, Das herrlich grosse Teutsch-Italiänische Dictionarium (1700–02)'. In *Deutsche Wörterbücher des 17. und 18. Jahrhunderts. Einführung und Bibliographie*, ed. Helmut Henne. Hildesheim: Olms, 95–106.

JAGEMANN, H.C. 1893. 'Notes on the Language of J.G. Schottel'. *Proceedings of the Modern Language Association, N.S.* 8: 408–431.

JAHREIß, ASTRID. 1990. *Grammatiken und Orthographielehren aus dem Jesuitenorden. Eine Untersuchung zur Normierung der deutschen Schriftsprache in Unterrichtswerken des 18. Jahrhunderts.* Heidelberg: Winter.

JELLINEK, MAX. 1898 [1985]. 'Ein Kapitel aus der Geschichte der deutschen Grammatik'. *Abhandlungen zur germanischen Philologie* ed. Richard Heinzel & Ferdinand Detter. Halle/S.: Max Niemeyer, 31–111. Rpt. Hildesheim: Olms, 1985.

JELLINEK, MAX. 1913–1914. *Geschichte der neuhochdeutschen Grammatik von den Anfängen bis auf Adelung.* Heidelberg: Carl Winter.

JENSEN, KRISTIAN. 1990. *Rhetorical philosophy and philosophical grammar. Julius Caesar Scaliger's theory of language.* Munich: Fink.

JOHNSON, SALLY. 2005. *Spelling trouble? Language, ideology and the reform of German orthography.* Clevedon: Multilingual Matters.

JOHNSON, SALLY, & OLIVER STENSCHKE, eds. 2005. *After 2005: Re-visiting German Orthography*. Special issue of *German Life and Letters. 58/4*. With contributions from Theodor Ickler, Horst Sitta and Jens Sparschuh.

JONES, WILLIAM J. 1990. *German Kinship Terms (750–1500)*. Berlin: de Gruyter.

JONES, WILLIAM J. 1991. 'Lingua Teutonum Victrix. Landmarks in German lexicography (1500–1700)'. *Histoire, Épistémologie, Langage* 13: 131–152.

JONES, WILLIAM J. 1995. *Sprachhelden und Sprachverderber (1478–1750)*. Berlin: de Gruyter.

JONES, WILLIAM J. 1999. *Images of Language. German attitudes to European languages from 1500 to 1800*. Amsterdam: Benjamins.

JONES, WILLIAM J. 2000. *German lexicography in the European context: a descriptive bibliography of printed dictionaries and word lists containing German language (1600–1700)*. Studia Linguistica Germanica 58. Berlin: de Gruyter.

JONES, WILLIAM J. 2001. 'Early dialectology, etymology and language history in German-speaking countries'. In AUROUX ET AL., vol. 2, 1105–1115.

JONES, WILLIAM J. 2003. 'From *aalbraun* to *zypressengrün*. German colour nomenclature during the early modern period'. In *'Vir ingenio mirandus'. Studies presented to John L. Flood*, eds. William J. Jones, William A. Kelly & Frank Shaw. Göppingen: Kümmerle, 877–895.

JONES, WILLIAM J. 2009. 'Review: John Considine, Dictionaries in Early Modern Europe'. *Historiographia Linguistica* 37: 214–220.

JONGENEELEN, GERRIT H. 1992. 'Lambert ten Kate and the origin of 19th-century historical linguistics'. In *The history of linguistics in the Low Countries*, ed. Jan Noordegraaf, Kees Versteegh & E.F. Konrad Koerner. Amsterdam, Benjamins, 201–219.

JOSEPH, JOHN. E. 2000. *Limiting the Arbitrary. Linguistic naturalism and its opposites in Plato's 'Cratylus' and modern theories of language*. Amsterdam: Benjamins.

JOSTEN, DIRK. 1976. *Sprachvorbild und Sprachnorm im Urteil des 16. und 17. Jahrhunderts. Sprachlandschaftliche Prioritäten. Sprachauthoritäten. Sprachimmanente Argumentationen*. Frankfurt am Main: Lang.

JUNGEN, OLIVER, & HORST LOHNSTEIN. 2007. *Geschichte der Grammatiktheorie. Von Dionysius Thrax bis Noam Chomsky*. Munich: Fink.

KALTZ, BARBARA. 1978. 'Christoph Helwig, ein vergessener Vertreter der allgemeinen Grammatik in Deutschland'. *Historiographia Linguistica* 3: 227–235.

KALTZ, BARBARA. 2004. 'Zur Herausbildung der Wortbildungstheorie in der deutschen Grammatikographie (1600–1800)'. *Beiträge zur Geschichte der Sprachwissenschaft* 14: 23–40.

KALTZ, BARBARA. 2005. 'Zur Herausbildung der Wortbildungslehre in der deutschen Grammatikographie von den Anfängen bis zum Ende des 19.

Jahrhunderts'. *Geschichte der Sprachtheorie. 6/1 Sprachtheorien der Neuzeit*, vol. *III/1*, ed. Peter Schmitter. Tübingen: Narr, 105–161.

KÄMPER, HEIDRUN. 2001. 'Einführung und Bibliographie zu Georg Henisch, *Teütsche Sprach vnd Weißheit. Thesavrus lingvae et sapientiae Germanicae* (1616)'. In *Deutsche Wörterbücher des 17. und 18. Jahrhunderts. Einführung und Bibliographie*, ed. Helmut Henne. Hildesheim: Olms, 39–74.

KÄRNA, AINO. 2007. 'Adverbien in lateinischen und deutschen Grammatiken der frühen Neuzeit'. *Beiträge zur Geschichte der Sprachwissenschaft* 17: 159–200.

KÄRNA, AINO, & MATTHAIOS, STEPHANOS. 2007. 'Dem Adverb auf der Spur. Zur Einleitung'. *Beiträge zur Geschichte der Grammatikographie* 17: 3–12.

KIEDRÓN, STEFAN. 1985a. 'Taalkundige Opvattingen van Simon Stevin en hun weerspiegeling in de *Ausführliche Arbeit von der Teutschen Hauptsprache* von Justus Georg Schottel'. *Neerlandica Wratislaviensia* 2: 241–271.

KIEDRÓN, STEFAN. 1985b. 'Niederländische Einflüsse auf die Stammworttheorie von Justus Georg Schottelius'. *Leuvenser Bijdragen* 74: 345–356.

KIEDRÓN, STEFAN. 1987. 'Deutsch und Niederländisch in den Auffassungen von Justus Georg Schottel'. *Neerlandica Wratislaviensia* 3: 133–144.

KIEDRÓN, STEFAN. 1989. '"Sittenkunst" und "Zedekunst". Schottelius und Coornhert'. *Neerlandica Wratislaviensia* 4: 247–267.

KIEDRÓN, STEFAN. 1991. *Niederländische Einflüsse auf die Sprachtheorie von Justus Georg Schottelius*. Wrocław: Wydawnictwo Uniwersytetu Wrocławskiego.

KILIAN, JÖRG. 2000. 'Entwicklungen in Deutschland im 17. und 18. Jahrhundert außerhalb der Sprachgesellschaften'. In AUROUX ET AL., 2000, vol. 1, 841–851.

KLIJNSMIT, ANTHONY J. 1993. 'Schottel and the Dutch – The Dutch and Schottel'. In *Das unsichtbare Band der Sprache. Studies in German Language and Linguistic History in Memory of Leslie Seiffert*, eds. John L. Flood, Paul Salmon, Olive Sayce & Christopher Wells. Stuttgart: Verlag Hans-Dieter Heinz, 215–235.

KNAPE, JOACHIM. 1984. 'Das Deutsch der Humanisten'. In BESCH ET AL. 1984–1985, vol. 1 1408–1415.

KOCH, KRISTINE. 2002. *Deutsch als Fremdsprache im Rußland des 18. Jahrhunderts*. Berlin: de Gruyter.

KOLDEWEY, FRIEDRICH ERNST. 1899. 'Justus Georg Schottelius und seine Verdienste um die deutsche Sprache'. *Zeitschrift für den deutschen Unterricht* 13: 81–106.

KÖNIG, WERNER. 1994 (revised edition). *dtv-atlas zur deutschen Sprache*. Munich: dtv.

KOPPITZ, HANS-JOACHIM. 2008. *Die kaiserlichen Druckprivilegien im Haus-, Hof- und Staatsarchiv Wien. Verzeichnis der Akten vom Anfang des 16.*

Jahrhunderts bis zume Ende des Deutschen Reichs (1806). Wiesbaden: Harrassowitz.

KREBS, CHRISTOPH. 2010. 'A dangerous book: the reception of Tacitus' Germania'. In *The Cambridge Companion to Tacitus*, ed. A. J. WOODMAN. Cambridge: CUP, 280–299.

KÜRSCHNER, WILFRIED. 1986. 'Zur Geschichte der Sprachkultur in Deutschland. Notizen zu Schottelius und Leibniz'. In *Pragmantax: Akten des 20. Linguistischen Kolloquiums Braunschweig 1985*, ed. ARMIN BURKHARDT. Tübingen: Niemeyer, 335–345.

KÜRSCHNER, WILFRIED. 1988. 'Anfänge grammatischer Terminologiebildung im Deutschen'. In *CHLOE. Beihefte zum Daphnis. Bd. 8 Zwischen Renaissance und Aufklärung*, 73–92.

KUSOVA, R. I. 1986. *Justus Georg Schottelius i nemeckoe jazykoznanie*. Ordzonikidze: Severo-Osetinskij gosudarstvennyj universitet. [In Russian.]

LABOV, W. 1972. *Sociolinguistic Patterns*. Philadelphia: University of Pennsylvania Press.

LABOV, W. 1994. *Principles of linguistic change. Internal factors*. London: Blackwell.

LAKOFF, GEORGE, & MARK JOHNSON. 1980. *Metaphors we live by*. Chicago: University of Chicago Press.

LANGE, MARIA B. 2005. 'Bad language in Germany's past – the birth of linguistic norms in the seventeenth century?' In *The making of bad language. Lay linguistic stigmatisations in German: past and present*, eds. NILS LANGER & WINIFRED DAVIES. Frankfurt am Main: Lang, 62–85.

LANGE, MARIA B. 2008. *Sprachnormen im Spannungsfeld schriftsprachlicher Theorie und Praxis. Die Protokolle der Commerzdeputation Hamburg im 17. Jahrhundert*. Berlin: de Gruyter.

LANGER, NILS, & WINIFRED DAVIES, eds. 2005. *Linguistic Purism in the Germanic Languages*. Berlin: de Gruyter.

LANGER, NILS. 2000. 'Zur Verbreitung der Tun-Periphrase im Frühneuhochdeutschen'. *Zeitschrift für Dialektologie und Linguistik* 67: 287–316.

LANGER, NILS. 2001. *Linguistic Purism in Action. How Auxiliary Tun was Stigmatized in Early New High German*. Studia Linguistica Germanica 60. Berlin: de Gruyter.

LAUSBERG, HEINRICH. 1998 [1960]. *Handbook of Literary Rhetoric. A foundation for literary study*[= *Handbuch der literarischen Rhetorik. Eine Grundlegung der Literaturwissenschaft*], transl. Matthew T. Bliss, Annemiek Jansen & David E. Orton, and edited by David E. Orton & R. Dean Anderson. Leiden: Brill.

LAW, VIVIEN. 2003. *The History of Linguistics in Europe from Plato to 1600*. Cambridge: CUP.

LEIRA, HALVARD. 2007. 'At the Crossroads: Justus Lipsius and the Early Modern Development of International Law'. *Leiden Journal of International Law* 20: 65–88.

LEPSCHY, GIULIO, ed. 1998. *History of Linguistics*. Volume III. *Renaissance and Early Modern Linguistics*. London: Longman.

LESER, ERNST. 1912. *Geschichte der grammatischen Terminologie im 17. Jahrhundert*. Lahr in Baden: Schauenberg.

LESER, ERNST. 1914. 'Fachwörter zur deutschen Grammatik von Schottel bis Gottsched. 1641–1749'. *Zeitschrift für deutsche Wortforschung* 15: 1–98.

LEWELING, BEATE. 2005. *Reichtum, Reinligkeit und Glanz – Sprachkritische Konzeptionen in der Sprachreflexion des 18. Jahrhunderts*. Frankfurt am Main: Lang.

LEWIS, RHODRI. 2007. *Language, Mind and Nature: Artificial languages in England from Bacon to Locke*. Cambridge: CUP.

LINN, ANDREW R. 1998. 'Ivar Aasen and V.U. Hammershaimb: Towards a Stylistics of Standardization'. *Ivar Aasen-Studiar* 1: 93–118.

LINN, ANDREW R. 2008. 'The birth of applied linguistics. The Anglo-Scandinavian School as discourse community'. *Historiographia Linguistica* 35: 342–84.

LINN, ANDREW R., & LEIGH OAKES. 2007. 'Language policies for a global era: the changing face of language politics in Scandinavia'. In *Standard, Variation und Sprachwandel in germanischen Sprachen*, eds. Christian Fandrych & Reinier Salverda. Tübingen: Gunter Narr, 59–90.

MACFARLANE, ALAN. 1997. *The Savage Wars of Peace: England, Japan and the Malthusian Trap*. Oxford: Blackwell.

MACHÉ, ULRICH. 1991. 'Author and Patron: On the function of dedications in seventeenth century German literature'. In *Literary Culture in the Holy Roman Empire, 1555–1720*, ed. James A. Parente. Chapel Hill: University of North Carolina Press, 195–205.

MARRAS, CRISTINA. 1999. 'Analogische und metaphorische Verfahren bei Gottfried Wilhelm Leibniz (1646–1716)'. In *Sprachdiskussion und Beschreibung von Sprachen im 17. und 18. Jahrhundert*, eds. Gerda Haßler & Peter Schmitter. Münster: Nodus, 69–83.

MARTIN, DIETER. 2000. *Barock um 1800. Bearbeitung und Aneignung*. Frankfurt am Main: Vittorio Klostermann.

MAST, THOMAS. 2001. 'Patriotism and the Promotion of German Language and Culture: Johann Rist's *Rettung der Edlen Teutschen Hauptsprache* (1642) and the Language Movement of the Seventeenth Century'. *Daphnis* 30: 71–96.

MATTHEWS, PETER. 1994. 'Greek and Latin linguistics'. In *History of Linguistics. Volume II. Classical and Medieval Linguistics*, ed. Giulio Lepschy. London: Longman, 1–133.

MCLELLAND, NICOLA. 2001. 'Albertus (1573) and Ölinger (1574). Creating the first grammars of German'. *Historiographia Linguistica* 28: 7–38.

McLELLAND, NICOLA. 2002. 'Schottelius, Language, Nature and Art. Buildings and Banyans'. *Beiträge zur Geschichte der Sprachwissenschaft* 12: 65–92.

McLELLAND, NICOLA. 2003. 'Schottelius, the notion of *Teutsch* and sleight of hand'. In *'Vir ingenio mirandus'. Studies presented to John L. Flood*, eds. William J. Jones, William A. Kelly & Frank Shaw. Göppingen: Kümmerle, 835–854.

McLELLAND, NICOLA. 2004a. 'Dialogue & German language learning in the Renaissance'. In *Printed Voices. The Renaissance Culture of Dialogue*, eds. Dorothea Heitsch & Jean-François Vallée. Toronto: University of Toronto Press, 206–225.

McLELLAND, NICOLA. 2004b. 'A historical study of code-switching: German and Latin in Schottelius' *Ausführliche Arbeit von der Teutschen Hauptsprache* (1663)'. *International Journal of Bilingualism* 8: 499–523.

McLELLAND, NICOLA. 2005a. 'Authority and audience in seventeenth-century German grammatical texts'. *Modern Language Review* 100: 1025–1042.

McLELLAND, NICOLA. 2005b. 'German as a second language for adults in the seventeenth century? Jacob Brücker's *Deutsche Grammatic* (1620). *Flores Grammaticae'. Essays in Memory of Vivien Law*, ed. Nicola McLelland & Andrew R. Linn. Münster: Nodus, 171–185.

McLELLAND, NICOLA. 2006a. 'Emblems in Everyday Life in Early Modern Europe. Review of Strasser & Wade (2004)'. *H-Net: www.h-net.org/reviews/showpdf.phpid?id=11873*. Accessed June 1, 2011.

McLELLAND, NICOLA. 2006b. 'Letters, sounds and shapes in early modern German linguistic awareness'. *Transactions of the Philological Society* 104: 1–30.

McLELLAND, NICOLA. 2008. 'Approaches to the semantics and syntax of the adverb in German foreign language grammars'. *Beiträge zur Geschichte der Sprachwissenschaft* 18.1 (Themenheft: *Das Adverb in der Grammatographie* – Teil II, ed. Aino Kärna & Stephanos Matthaios), 37–58.

McLELLAND, NICOLA. 2009. 'Linguistic Purism, Protectionism, and Nationalism in the Germanic Languages Today'. *Journal of Germanic Linguistics* 21: 93–112.

McLELLAND, NICOLA. 2010. 'Justus Georgius Schottelius (1612–1676) and European linguistic thought'. *Historiographia Linguistica* 37.1: 1–30.

McLELLAND, NICOLA. 2011. 'Lessons from literary theory: applying the notion of transtextuality (Genette, 1982) to early modern German grammars'. *ICHOLS XI (2008)*, ed. GERDA HASSLER. Amsterdam: Benjamins, 187–200.

McLELLAND, NICOLA. *forthcoming* a. 'From humanist history to linguistic theory: the case of the Germanic rootword'. In *Language and History — Linguistics and Historiography*, ed. Nils Langer, Steffen Davies, & Wim Vandenbussche. Frankfurt am Main: Lang.

McLELLAND, NICOLA. *forthcoming* b. 'Germanic virtues in linguistic discourse in Germany (1500–1945)'. In *Germania Remembered*, eds. Christina Lee & Nicola McLelland. Tempe, Arizona: Arizona Mediaeval and Renaissance Texts.

McMAHON, APRIL. 1994. *Understanding Language Change*. Cambridge: CUP.

MEID, VOLKER. 1986. *Barocklyrik*. Stuttgart: Metzler.

MENKE, HUBERTUS. 1992. *Bibliotheca Reinardiana I*. Stuttgart: Hauswedell.

MERTENS, DIETER. 2004. 'Die Instrumentalisierung der „Germania" des Tacitus durch die deutschen Humanisten. Take-off Phase der deutschen Tacitus-Rezeption und der Umbau der Geschichtsbilder'. In *Zur Geschichte der Gleichsetzung germanisch—deutsch. Sprache und Namen, Geschichte und Institutionen*, eds. Heinrich Beck, Dieter Geuenich, Heiko Steuer & Dietrich Hakelberg. Berlin: de Gruyter, 37–101.

MERVELDT, NIKOLA VON. 2007. 'Galahot als Grenzgänger. (Trans)Texte rund um eine ambivalente Figur'. In *Lancelot. Der Mittelhochdeutsche Roman im europäischen Kontext*, eds. Klaus Ridder & Christoph Huber. Tübingen: Niemeyer, 173–192.

METCALF, GEORGE J. 1953a. 'Schottel and Historical Linguistics'. *Germanic Review* 28: 113–125.

METCALF, GEORGE J. 1953b. 'Abraham Mylius on Historical Linguistics'. *Publications of the Modern Language Association of America* 68: 535–554.

METCALF, GEORGE J. 1963a. 'Konrad Gesner's Views on the Germanic Languages'. *Monatshefte für deutschen Unterricht, deutsche Sprache und Literatur* 55: 149–156.

METCALF, GEORGE J. 1963b. 'The views of Conrad Gesner on Language'. In *Studies in Germanic languages and literatures*, eds. E. Hofacker & L. Dieckmann. St Louis: Washington University Press, 15–26.

METCALF, GEORGE J. 1974. 'The Indo-European hypothesis in the sixteenth and seventeenth centuries'. In *Studies in the History of Linguistics: traditions and paradigms*, ed. Dell Hymes. London: Bloomington.

METCALF, GEORGE J. 1978. 'The copyright patent in Schottelius' *Ausführliche Arbeit* (1663): the blue pencil helps shape the Haubtsprache'. In *Wege der Worte. Festschrift für Wolfgang Fleischhauer*, ed. Donald C. Riechel. Cologne: Böhlau, 11–26.

METCALF, GEORGE J. 1980. 'Theodor Bibliander and the languages of Japhet's progeny'. *Historiographia Linguistica* 7: 323–333.

MIEDER, WOLFGANG. 1982. 'Die Eintselluing der Grammatiker Schottelius und Gottsched zum Sprichwort'. *Sprachspiegel* 38: 70–75.

MIEDER, WOLFGANG. 2003. 'Grundzüge einer Geschichte des Sprichwortes und der Redensart'. In BESCH ET AL., 1998–2004, vol. 3, 2559–2569.

MOHR, WILLIAM. 1966. *J.G. Schottelius' spelling rules compared with the practices of some of his printers*. Dissertation, University of Chicago.

MOSER, VIRGIL. 1929. *Frühneuhochdeutsche Grammatik*. Heidelberg: Carl Winter.

MOULIN, CLAUDINE. 1992. 'Aber wo ist die Richtschnur? wo ist die Regel?' Zur Suche nach den Prinzipien der Regeln im 17. Jahrhundert'. In *Studien zur Geschichte der deutschen Orthographie*, eds. Dieter Nerius & Jürgen Scharnhorst. Hildesheim: Olms, 23–60.

MOULIN, CLAUDINE. 2004. 'Das morphematische Prinzip bei den Grammatikern des 16. und 17. Jahrhunderts'. *Sprachwissenschaft* 29: 33–73.

MOULIN-FANKHÄNEL, CLAUDINE. 1994. *Bibliographie der deutschen Grammatiken und Orthographielehren. I. Von den Anfängen der Überlieferung bis zum Ende des 16. Jahrhunderts*. Heidelberg: Carl Winter.

MOULIN-FANKHÄNEL, CLAUDINE. 1997a. 'Althochdeutsch in der älteren Grammatiktheorie des Deutschen'. In *Grammatica ianua artium. Festschrift für Rolf Bergmann zum 60. Geburtstag*, eds. Elvira Glaser & Michael Schlaefer. Heidelberg: Carl Winter, 310–327.

MOULIN-FANKHÄNEL, CLAUDINE. 1997b. *Bibliographie der deutschen Grammatiken und Orthographielehren. II. Das 17. Jahrhundert*. Heidelberg: Carl Winter.

MOULIN-FANKHÄNEL, CLAUDINE. 2000. 'Deutsche Grammtikschreibung vom 16. bis. 18. Jahrhundert (Artikel 132)'. In BESCH ET AL., 1998–2004, vol. 2, 1903–1911.

MUELLER, HUGO JOHANNES. 1985. 'Leibniz as a linguist'. In *Scientific and Humanistics Dimensions of Language*, ed. Kurt Jankowsky. Amsterdam: Benjamins, 375–386.

MÜLLER, KARIN. 1990. *'Schreib, wie du sprichst!' Eine Maxime im Spannungsfeld von Mündlichkeit und Schriftlichkeit. Eine historische und systematische Untersuchung*. Frankfurt am Main: Lang.

NATE, RICHARD. 1995. 'Jacob Böhme's linguistic ideas and their reception in England'. *Beiträge zur Geschichte der Sprachwissenschaft* 5: 185–202.

NAUMANN, BERND. 1986. *Grammatik der deutschen Sprache zwischen 1781 und 1856. Die Kategorien der deutschen Grammatik in der Tradition von Johann Werner Meiner und Johann Christoph Adelung*. Berlin: Schmidt.

NAUMANN, BERND. 2000a. 'Die 'allgemeine Sprachwissenschaft' um die Wende zum 19. Jahrhundert'. In AUROUX ET AL. 2000, vol. 1, 1044–1056.

NAUMANN, BERND. 2000b. *Einführung in die Wortbildungslehre des Deutschen*. Tübingen: Niemeyer.

NEIS, CORDULA. 2003. *Anthropologie im Sprachdenken des 18. Jahrhunderts: Die Berliner Preisfrage nach dem Ursprung der Sprache (1771)*. Berlin: Walter de Gruyter.

NEUHAUS, GISELA M. 1991. *Justus Georg Schottelius: Die Stammwörter der Teutschen Sprache Samt dererselben Erklärung/und andere die Stammwörter betreffende Anmerkungen. Eine Untersuchung zur frühneuhochdeutschen Lexikologie*. Göppingen: Kümmerle.

NOORDEGRAAF, JAN. 2001. 'Historical Linguistics in the Low Countries: Lambertus ten Kate'. In AUROUX ET AL., vol. 2, 1115–1124.

NYSTRAND, MARTIN. 1982. *What Writers Know: The Language, Process, and Structure of Written Discourse.* New York: Academic.

OGDEN, CHARLES KAY & IVOR ARMSTRONG RICHARDS. 1923. *The Meaning of Meaning: A Study of the Influence of Language upon Thought and of the Science of Symbolism.* London: K. Paul, Trench, Trubner.

OTTO, KARL F. 1972. *Die Sprachgesellschaften des 17. Jahrhunderts.* Stuttgart: Metzler.

PADLEY, GEORGE ARTHUR. 1976. *Grammatical Theory in Western Europe 1500–1700. The Latin tradition.* Cambridge: CUP.

PADLEY, GEORGE ARTHUR. 1985, 1988. *Grammatical Theory in Western Europe 1500–1700: trends in vernacular grammar.* 2 vols. Cambridge: CUP.

PARKER, GEOFFREY, SIMON ADAM, & GERHARD BENECKE. 1997. *The Thirty Years' War.* London: Routledge.

PERCIVAL, W. KEITH. 1975. 'The grammatical tradition and the rise of the vernaculars'. In *Current Trends in Linguistics. vol. 13 Historiography of linguistics,* ed. Thomas A. Sebeok, 231–275. The Hague, Paris: Mouton.

PICKL, SIMON. 2010. 'Review: Anita Auer. *The Subjunctive in the Age of Prescriptivism. English and German developments during the eighteenth century* (London: Palgrave Macmillan, 2009)'. *Historiographia Linguistica* 37: 263–266.

PLATTNER, JOSEF. 1967. *Zum Sprachbegriff von J.G. Schottel, aufgrund der Ausfürhlichen Arbeit von der Teutschen HaubtSprache von 1663.* Diss. Zürich. Thusis: Werner Roth.

POLENZ, PETER VON. 1994. *Deutsche Sprachgeschichte vom Spätmittelalter bis zur Gegenwart.* Vol. II. *17. und 18. Jahrhundert.* Berlin: de Gruyter.

POLENZ, PETER VON. 2000. 'Die Sprachgesellschaften und die Entstehung eines literarischen Standards in Deutschland'. In AUROUX ET AL., 2000, vol. 1, 827–840.

POWITZ, GERHARDT. 1959. *Das Deutsche Wörterbuch Johann Leonhard Frischs.* Berlin: Akademie-Verlag.

PUFF, HELMUT. 1995. *'Von dem schlüssel aller Künsten | nemblich der Grammatica.' Deutsch im lateinischen Grammatikunterricht 1480–1560.* Tübingen: Francke Verlag.

QUAK, AREND, ed. 1981. *Die altmittel- und altniederfränkischen Psalmen und Glossen.* Amsterdam: Rodopi.

RADEMAKER, CORNELIS S.M. 1992. 'Gerardus Joannes Vossius (1577–1649) and the study of Latin grammar'. In *The history of linguistics in the Low Countries,* eds. Jan Noordegraaf, Kees Versteegh & Konrad Koerner, 109–128. Amsterdam: Benjamins.

RADTKE, EDGAR. 1996. 'Kramer (Krämer), Matthias'. In *Lexicon Grammaticorum. Who's Who in the History of World Linguistics,* ed. Hanno Stammerjohann. Tübingen: Niemeyer, 529–530.

ROBINS, R. H. 1998. *Texts and Contexts. Selected papers on the history of linguistics.* Münster: Nodus.

ROBINS, R.H. 1997⁴. *A Short History of Linguistics.* London: Longman.

ROBINSON, DOUGLAS. 2002. *Western Translation Theory. From Herodotus to Nietzsche.* Manchester: St Jerome Publishing.

RÖLCKE, THORSTEN. 2000. 'Der Patriotimus der barocken Sprachgesellschaften'. In *Nation und Sprache. Die Diskussion ihres Verhältnisses in Geschichte und Gegenwart*, ed. Andreas Gardt. Berlin: de Gruyter, 139–168.

RÖMER, RUTH. 1986. 'Schottels Lobreden'. *Muttersprache* 96: 132–136.

RÖSSING-HAGER, MONIKA. 1984. 'Konzeption und Ausführung der ersten deutschen Grammatik. Valentin Ickelsamer: >Ein Teütsche Grammatica<'. In *Literatur und Laienbildung im Spätmittelalter und in der Reformationszeit. Symposium Wolfenbüttel 1981*, eds. Ludger Grenzmanm & Karl Stackmann. Stuttgart: Metzler, 534–536.

RÖSSING-HAGER, MONIKA. 1985. 'Ansätze zu einer deutschen Sprachgeschichtsschreibung vom Humanismus bis ins 18. Jahrhundert'. In BESCH ET AL., 1985, vol. 2, 1564–1614.

RÖSSING-HAGER, MONIKA. 2000. 'Frühe grammatische Beschreibungen des Deutschen'. In AUROUX ET AL., 2000, vol. 1, 777–784.

ROUSSEAU, JEAN. 1984. 'La racine arabe et son traitement par les grammairiens européens (1505–1831)'. *Bulletin de la Societé de Linguistique de Paris* 79:285–321.

RUTTEN, GISBERT. 2004. 'Lambert ten Kate and Justus-Georg Schottelius: theoretical similarities between Dutch and German early modern linguistics'. *Historiographia Linguistica* 31: 277–296.

RUTTEN, GIJSBERT, RIK VOSTERS & WIM VANDENBUSSCHE. *forthcoming.* 'As many norms as there were scribes? Language history, norms and usage in 19th-century Flanders'. In *Language and history—linguistics and historiography*, ed. Nils Langer, Steffan Davies & Wim Vandenbussche. Frankfurt de Main: Lang.

SAIRIO, ANNI. 'Bluestocking letters and the influence of eighteenth-century grammars'. *Studies in Late Modern English Correspondence: Methodology and Data*, ed. Marina Dossena & Ingrid Tieken-Boon van Ostade. Bern: Lang, 137–162.

SALMON, VIVIAN. 1972. *The works of Francis Lodwick. A study of his writings in the intellectual context of the seventeenth century.* London: Longman.

SALVERDA, REINIER. 2001. 'Newtonian Linguistics. The contribution of Lambert ten Kate (1674–1731) to the study of language'. In *Proper words in proper places. Studies in lexicology and lexicography in honour of William Jervis Jones*, ed. Máire C. Davies, John L. Flood, & David N. Yeandle. Stuttgart: Akademischer Verlag, 115–132.

SCHAARS, FRANS. 1988. *De Nederduitsche Spraekkunst (1706) van Arnold Moonen (1644–1711).* Wijhe: Quarto.

SCHADE, RICHARD ERICH. 1991. 'Poets portrayed: iconographic representations and allusions to the empire'. In *Literary Culture in the Holy Roman Empire 1555–1720*, ed. James A. Parente. Chapel Hill: University of North Carolina Press, 179–194.

SCHAEFFER, PETER. 1983. 'Baroque philology: the position of German in the European family of language'. In *German Baroque Literature. The European Perspective*, ed. G. Hoffmeister. New York: Ungar Publishing Co., 72–84.

SCHAFFERUS, ELLA. 1932. 'Die Sprichwörtersammlung bei Schottelius'. *Korrespondenzblätter des Vereins für niederdeutsche Sprachforschung* 45: 53–57.

SCHLAPS, CHRISTIANE. 2000. 'Das Konzept eines deutschen Sprachgeistes'. In *Nation und Sprache. Die Diskussion ihres Verhältnisses in Geschichte und Gegenwart*, ed. Andreas Gardt. Berlin: de Gruyter, 303–347.

SCHLAPS, CHRISTIANE. 2004. 'The "genius of language"'. Transformations of a concept in the history of linguistics'. *Historiographia Linguistica* 31: 367–388.

SCHMARSOW, AUGUST. 1877. *Leibniz und Schottelius. Die unvorgreiflichen Gedanken*. Strasbourg: Trübner.

SCHNEIDER, ROLF. 1995. *Der Einfluß von Justus Georg Schottelius auf die deutschsprachige Lexikographie des 17./ 18. Jahrhunderts*. Frankfurt am Main: Lang.

SCHNEIDER-MIZONY, ODILE. 2010. 'Syntaktische Präferenzen als Kommunikationsmaximem in der Grammatikographie 1500–1700'. In *Historische Textgrammatik und Historische Syntax des Deutschen*, ed. Arne Ziegler. Berlin: de Gruyter, Vol. II, 781–798.

SCHULENBERG, SIGRID VON. 1973. *Leibniz als Sprachforscher*. Frankfurt am Main: Klostermann.

SCHUSTER, BRITT-MARIE. 2001. *Die Verständlichkeit von frühreformatorischen Flugschriften. Eine Studie zu kommunikationswirksamen Faktoren der Textgestaltung*. Hildesheim: Olms.

SCHWITALLA, JOHANNES. 1983. *Deutsche Flugschriften 1460–1525*. Tübingen: Niemeyer.

SEIFFERT, LESLIE. 1988. 'Justus Georg Schottel on the praises of the German language and of its words'. *Newsletter of the Henry Sweet Society for the History of Linguistic Ideas* 11: 8–11.

SEIFFERT, LESLIE. 1989. 'Three stages in the long discovery of the German modals: Ratke, Schottel, Grimm'. In *Speculum historiographiae linguisticae. Kurzbeiträge der IV. Internationalen Konferenz zur Geschichte der Sprachwissenschaften*, ed. Klaus D. Dutz. Münster: Nodus, 277–296.

SEIFFERT, LESLIE. 1990a. 'The vernacularist and Latinist Justus-Georgius Schottelius and the traditions of German linguistic purism'. In *Understanding the historiography of linguistics. Problems and Projects*, ed. Werner Hüllen. Münster: Nodus, 241–261.

SEIFFERT, LESLIE. 1990b. 'Von Fremd- und Lehnwörtern und von Kunst- und anderen auserlesenen Deutungs-reichen Wörtern, oder: Darf man noch zu einer elften Lobrede ansetzen?' In *Deutsche Gegenwartssprache. Tendenzen und Perspektiven*, ed. Gerhard Stickel. Berlin: de Gruyter, 302–331.

SEUREN, PIETER. 1998. *Western linguistics. An historical introduction.* Oxford: Blackwell

SIEBS, THEODOR. 1898. *Deutche Bühnenaussprache.* Berlin, Köln & Leipzig: Albert Ahn.

SMART, SARAH. 1989. 'Justus Georg Schottelius and the Patriotic Movement'. *Modern Language Review* 84: 83–98.

SOLMS, HANS-JOACHIM, & KLAUS-PETER WEGERA. 1991. *Grammatik des Frühneuhochdeutschen. Beiträge zur Laut- und Formenlehre. Vol. 6 Flexion der Adjektive.* Heidelberg: Carl Winter.

SONDEREGGER, STEFAN. 1998. 'Ansätze zu einer deutschen Geschichtsschreibung bis zum Ende des 18. Jahrhunderts'. In BESCH ET AL., 1998–2004, vol. 1, 417–442.

SONDEREGGER, STEFAN. 1999. 'Die Vielschichtigkeit des Sprachbewusstseins in frühneuhochdeutscher Zeit'. In *Das Frünneuhochdeutsche als sprachgeschichtliche Epoche. Festschrift Werner Besch*, ed. Walter Hoffmann et al., 175–208. Frankfurt am Main: Lang.

SONDEREGGER, STEFAN. 2002. 'Tschudis Stellung im Rahmen der humanistischen Philologie des 16. Jahrhunderts'. In *Aegidius Tschudi und seine Zeit*, eds. Katharina Koller-Weiss & Christian Sieber. Basle: Krebs, 193–207.

STAMMERJOHANN, HARRO, ED. 1996, ²2009. *Lexicon Grammaticorum. Who's Who in the History of World Linguistics.* Tübingen: Niemeyer.

STOLT, BIRGIT. 1964. *Die Sprachmischung in Luthers Tischreden. Studien zum Problem der Zweisprachigkeit.* Stockholm: Almqvist & Wiksell.

STRASSER, GERHARD F., & MARA R. WADE, eds. 2004. *Die Domänen des Emblems.* Wiesbaden: Harrassowitz.

STRASSER, GERHARD. 1988. *Lingua Universalis. Kryptographie und Theorie der Universalsprachen im 16. und 17. Jahrhundert.* Wiesbaden: Harrassowitz.

STUKENBROCK, ANJA. 2005. *Sprachnationalismus. Sprachreflexion als Medium kollektiver Identitätsstiftung in Deutschland (1617–1945).* Berlin: de Gruyter.

SUBBIONDO, JOSEPH L., ed. 1992. *John Wilkins and 17th-Century British Linguistics.* Amsterdam: Benjamins.

SUBIRATS-RÜGGEBERG, CARLOS. 1994. 'Grammar and lexicon in traditional grammar. The work of Matthias Kramer and Johann Joachim Becher'. *Historiographia Linguistica* 21: 297–350.

SWALES, JOHN. M. 1990. *Genre Analysis: English in academic and research settings.* Cambridge: CUP.

SWIGGERS, PIERRE. 1984. 'Adrianus Schrieckius: De la langue des Scythes à l'Europe'. *Histoire, Epistémologie, Langage* 6: 17–35.

TAKADA, HIROYUKI. 1981. 'Eine vergleichende Untersuchung der beiden barocken Grammatiken von Ch. Gueintz und J.G. Schottel' [in Japanese with German summary]. *Doitsu-Bungaku-ronkô. Forschungsberichte zur Germanistik* 23: 41–60.

TAKADA, HIROYUKI. 1985. 'J.G. Schottelius, die Analogie und der Sprachgebrauch. Versuch einer Periodisierung eines Sprachtheoretikers'. *Zeitschrift für germanistische Linguistik* 13: 129–153.

TAKADA, HIROYUKI. 1998. *Grammatik und Sprachwirklichkeit von 1640– 1700. Zur Rolle deutscher Grammatiker im schriftsprachlichen Ausgleichsprozeß.* Reihe Germanistische Linguistik 203. Tübingen: Niemeyer.

TAVONI, MIRKO. 'Renaissance Linguistics'. In *History of Linguistics*, vol. III. *Renaissance and Early Modern Linguistics.* G. Lepschy. London: Longman, 1–122.

THOMAS, GEORGE. 1991. *Linguistic Purism.* London: Longman.

TIEKEN-BOON VAN OSTADE, INGRID. 1982. 'Double negation and eighteenth-century English grammars'. *Neuphilologus* 66: 278–285.

VAN DE VELDE, ROGER G. 1966. *De studie van het Gotisch in de Nederlanden.* Ghent: Secretariat van de Koninklijke Vlaamse Academie voor Taal- en Letterkunde

VAN DER LUBBE, FREDERICKA. 2007. *Martin Aedler and the High Dutch Minerva. The First German Grammar for the English.* Duisburger Arbeiten zur Sprach- und Kulturwissenschaft. Duisburg Papers on Research in Language and Culture 68. Frankfurt am Main: Lang.

VISWANATHAN, SHEKAR. 1968. 'Milton and Purchas' Linschoten. An additional source for Milton's Indian Figtree'. *Milton Quarterly* 2: 43–45.

WALDBERG, MAX VON. 1891. 'Schottelius'. In *Allgemeine Deutsche Biographie*, ed. Karl von Schmidt & G. E. Schulze. Leipzig: Duncker & Humblot. Vol. 32: 407–12.

WATERMAN, JOHN T. 1974. 'Leibniz on Language Learning'. *The Modern Language Journal* 58: 87–90.

WATTS, RICHARD J. 2008. 'Grammar writers in eighteenth-century Britain: A community of practice or a discourse community?' In *Grammars, Grammarians and Grammar-Writing in Eighteenth-Century England*, ed. Ingrid Tieken-Boon van Ostade. Berlin: Mouton de Gruyter, 37–56.

WATTS, SHEILA. 2001. '"Wer kan wider eines gantzen Landes Gewohnheit?" Justus Georg Schottelius as a dialectologist'. In *Proper Words in Proper Places — Studies in Lexicology and Lexicography in Honour of William Jervis Jones*, eds. Máire C. Davies, John L. Flood & David Yeandle. Stuttgart: Heinz, 101–114.

WATTS, SHEILA. 2003. 'Caspar Stieler's false friends'. In *Vir ingenio mirandus'. Studies presented to John Flood*, eds. William J. Jones, William A. Kelly & Frank Shaw. Göppingen: Kümmerle, vol. 2, 855–876.

WEDDIGE, HILKERT. 1975. *Die 'Historien von Amadis aus Frankreich'. Dokumentarische Grundlegung zur Entstehung und zur Rezeption.* (Beiträge zur Geschichte des XV. bis XVIII. Jahrhunderts, 2). Wiesbaden: Steiner

WEICKERT, RAINER. 1997. *Die Behandlung von Phraseologismen in ausgewählten Sprachlehren von Ickelsamer bis ins 19. Jahrhundert. Ein Beitrag zur historischen Phraseologie.* Hamburg: Verlag Dr. Kovac.

WEINRICH, HARALD. 1960. 'Vaugelas und die Lehre vom guten Sprachgebrauch'. *Zeitschrift für romanische Philologie* 76: 1–33.

WEINRICH, HARALD. 1989. 'Vaugelas et la théorie du bon usage dans le classicisme français'. In *Conscience linguistique et lectures littéraires*. Paris: Editions de la Maison des sciences de l'homme, 189–217. (Originally published in *Wege der Sprachkultur*, Stuttgart: DVA, 104–135.)

WEITHASE, IRMGARD. 1961. *Zur Geschichte der gesprochenen deutschen Sprache.* Tübingen: Niemeyer. 2 vols.

WESTERHOFF, JAN C. 1998. 'Poësis Combinatoria. Relations between the Project of the Characteristica Universalis and German Baroque Poetry'. *Beiträge zur Geschichte der Sprachwissenschaft* 8: 209–244.

WESTERHOFF, JAN C. 2000. 'Polyhistor and Poeta Doctus. Notes on the Baroque Conception of Signs and Signification'. *Beiträge zur Geschichte der Sprachwissenschaft* 10: 91–130.

WESTERHOFF, JAN C. 2001. 'A world of signs: Baroque pansemioticism, the *Polyhistor* and the Early Modern *Wunderkammer'. Journal of the History of Ideas* 62: 633–650.

WESTERHOFF, JAN C. 1999. 'Poeta Calculans: Harsdörffer, Leibniz, and the mathesis universalis'. *Journal of the history of ideas* 60: 449–467.

WIEGAND, HERBERT ERNST. 1998. 'Historische Lexikographie'. In BESCH ET AL., 1998, 2000, vol. 1, 643–715.

WORSTBROCK, FRANZ JOSEF. 1976. *Deutsche Antikenrezeption 1450–1550, Teil I: Verzeichnis der deutschen Übersetzungen antiker Autoren. Mit einer Bibliographie der Übersetzer.* Veröffentlichungen zur Humanismusforschung 1. Boppard am Rhein: Boldt.

WORTH, VALERIE. 1988. *Practising Translation in Renaissance France: The Example of Etienne Dolet.* Oxford: Clarendon.

ZELLER, ROSMARIE. 1974. *Spiel und Konversation im Barock.* Berlin: de Gruyter.

INDEX OF WORDS AND MORPHEMES (GERMAN, DANISH, DUTCH, GOTHIC, SWEDISH, RUSSIAN) CITED OR DISCUSSED IN THIS BOOK

Russian words are found at the end of this list.
Some Latin technical terms are listed in the main index.

INDEX OF SUBJECTS AND NAMES